CONUNDRUM

CONUNDRUM
SUBHAS BOSE'S LIFE AFTER DEATH

CHANDRACHUR GHOSE & ANUJ DHAR

Vitasta
LET KNOWLEDGE SPREAD

Published by
Renu Kaul Verma
Vitasta Publishing Pvt Ltd
2/15, Ansari Road, Daryaganj
New Delhi-110 002
info@vitastapublishing.com

ISBN 978-93-86473-57-8
© Chandrachur Ghose & Anuj Dhar
First Edition 2019
3rd Reprint 2019
MRP ₹995

Cover by Koushik Banerjee. Picture on the right is a digitally modified version of the original on the left. Created for representional purpose by Biplab Chatterjee at the request of authors.

Layout by Somesh Kumar Mishra

Printed by Replika Press Pvt Ltd

CONTENT

Acknowledgement   *vii*

Introduction   *ix*

ONE   A sleepy town shoots into fame   1

TWO   A holy man appears   23

THREE   A sadhu here and a sadhu there   61

FOUR   All the Netaji's men   79

FIVE   The road to Faizabad   133

SIX   Forensic fraud   149

SEVEN   The man who wasn't there   188

EIGHT   Hide-and-seek   196

NINE   All in the family   232

TEN   Interregnum   288

ELEVEN A Phantom's Homeland   344

TWELVE Der Übermensch   373

THIRTEEN More things in heaven and earth   460

FOURTEEN Mendicus   496

FIFTEEN So'ham   533

SIXTEEN Metamorphosis   622

Appendix A   *745*

Appendix B   *761*

Appendix C   *771*

ACKNOWLEDGEMENT

This book was conceptualised on the spur of a moment and even before the structure was detailed out, our publisher Renu Kaul Verma gave us the go ahead without any hesitation. We cannot express our gratitude enough for her unstinting support, especially at times when we were compelled to stretch the deadlines several times. Equally enthusiastic has been the involvement of Veena Batra who very painstakingly and professionally edited the book. She also played the role of a critique. Somesh Kumar Mishra worked beyond his brief to complete the layout and design of the book in order to meet the final non-negotiable deadline.

We are grateful to Faiza Yameen, director (production), for ensuring the timeliness and quality under several constraints.

Sreejith Panickar, one of Mission Netaji's founding members, has been the first reader of the manuscript as it was written. We depended greatly on his eagle eyes which are trained to catch even the smallest of mistakes.

Three more people are responsible for providing us with the fundamental inputs without which this book would have remained just another hypothetical scenario-building exercise like the few books on Netaji mystery that have been published in the last couple of years. Indian Americans Deepak Nijhawan and Abhishek Bose ran the process of identifying the best possible expert and then having the handwriting comparison done. Quality comes with a high price tag, which was borne by Nijhawan and Bose. Closer home, Ranendra Mohan Roy, second son of the legendary Pabitra Mohan Roy, opened up the treasure chest of hundreds of letters that Bhagwanji wrote to his father.

Although we were not allowed full access to the material in the custody of Bhagwanji's followers Surajit Dasgupta (who is sadly no more with us) and Bijoy Nag, they shared a good deal of material with us, without which this book would have remained incomplete.

Our friend Koushik Banerjee exceeded all our expectations in designing the book cover.

INTRODUCTION

This volume was conceived at a time when circumstances were quite different from the shape they acquired as we came closer to finishing it. In that sense, this book has become what we did not intend it to be. Towards the middle of 2016, we were keenly optimistic as a Commission of Inquiry set up by the Uttar Pradesh government, three years after being asked by the Allahabad High Court, set out to establish the identity of 'India's most famous unknown man',[1] who was given the moniker 'Gumnami Baba' by the local people and the vernacular press. We were optimistic that the inquiry headed by retired Justice Vishnu Sahai would bring a closure to the most intriguing aspect of India's most enduring political controversy—the fate of Subhas Chandra Bose. An unseen holy man lived in several parts of UP for nearly three decades and was claimed by most of his followers, and later by investigative journalists, to have been Bose in disguise. The commission was to verify these claims—to state whether these were true or not. Our aim, consequently, was to aid the inquiry as conscientious citizens,

---

1   Sandeep Unnithan, 'Man of Mystery,' *India Today*, 18 April 2016, p 26.

as we had by dint of our single-minded pursuit of a decade and half amassed information relevant to this inquiry.

Today, however, we are constrained to characterise this book as the result of an inquiry which Sahai Commission could not, rather would not, undertake despite a clear mandate. In the course of our own investigation, we, two private persons with modest means, were able to dig deeper and retrieve far more than the commission of inquiry having statutory powers and public funds at its disposal. But then, the virtual non-working of the Sahai Commission must be seen in the context of a long tale of apathy characterising the approach of the establishments in India since 1947. Even the courts could not persuade them to get their act together and piece together this gargantuan jigsaw puzzle. Why they did not want to do that will become clear in the subsequent chapters detailing what we have been able put together.

It would be in order to lay the context before dwelling deeper into the matter. Before anything else, we are perfectly aware of the fact that the subject matter of this book isn't going to give us an ideal head start. To most, the very idea that Subhas Chandra Bose could somehow be linked to some nondescript holy man would be outrageous—or even part of some sinister design to denigrate a national icon. On 21 February 2019, members of the Bose family called a press conference in Kolkata and slandered us for 'betraying the nation' accusing that we have been running a 'sinister campaign' to taint Netaji's image. It was painful for us to see these kin, who came into national prominence because of our efforts in the first place, launch such a tirade. Claiming that it was a 'criminal offence' to link Baba to Bose, they went to the extent of issuing a public threat to national-award winning filmmaker Srijit Mukherji, who is making a movie on Gumnami Baba based on this book that he 'might have to leave India'. The kin, underlining their political clout and with bouncers in tow, brazenly called upon Home Minister Rajnath Singh to let loose the Intelligence Bureau after us, so as to prevent us from making public our findings.

With that sort of backdrop weighing down on us, and our reputation, and probably safety, on the line, let us begin by admitting that years ago when we hadn't had the opportunity to scrutinise the incredible legend of the so-called Gumnami Baba, we thought as much. Our thinking patterns were fashioned by what we had absorbed growing up as regular people of India. To even think that Netaji, dead since the days of our grandparents, was living till the 1980s, of all the places in Faizabad, was as patently absurd a proposition for us as all those farcical Elvis Presley spotting and alien abduction claims.

It was only much later that we realised—to borrow a dialogue from the spy movie *Tinker Tailor Soldier Spy* based on the John le Carré classic—that 'things aren't always what they seem!' It is an odd co-relation to make, but there are details in the Gumnami Baba tale which compel one to think along this line. These details would fascinate anyone interested in politics, mystery, history, intelligence, intrigue, skullduggery, occult, etc.—not just those who are keen to know more about the disappearance of Subhas Bose.

We are laying out before you these details in all earnestness. This volume, a digest made from reams of material, has been written especially to flag a particular aspect which we think holds the key to unravelling modern India's longest running mystery. Our main aim in doing so is to enable the people of India to take an informed stand. We do so in deference to a court order, and would present ourselves for any inquiry by the court (or even the Intelligence Bureau should it wish to launch one to the view of the Bose family members).

So what exactly is this controversy about Netaji's 'disappearance'? Wasn't he killed in an air crash? How can one place this enigmatic holy man tale in it? How do we, the authors, figure in all this? Are we trained historians? Where are we coming from? Who are we affiliated with? Do we have any ulterior motive in pushing this particular line?

The good thing is that the last few years have cleared much of the cobwebs. This utterly complex plot has been cleared up to an extent that now we find three clear options on the table as to what really happened to Subhas Bose. One, the official version has it that he was reportedly killed following an air crash in Taiwan in August 1945, and his remains later deposited at Renkoji temple in Tokyo. Two, it has been alleged, that he was in USSR after 1945 and was subsequently liquidated as a result of a conspiracy involving Soviet dictator Joseph Stalin and Prime Minister Jawaharlal Nehru. God forbid this should be true, but this is how this hideous theory goes. Three, Netaji secretly returned to India and lived in the disguise of a holy man who came to be known as Gumnami Baba in various parts of UP till 1985, when he would have been 88 years old. Many of those who oppose this theory claim that after Netaji was killed in Soviet Russia, an imposter was set up by the Intelligence Bureau (IB) to misguide the people of

India. In private talks, some members of Netaji's family, with past connection to the Left, are further suggesting that the Rashtriya Swayamsevak Sangh (RSS) had something to do with the planting of this baba, an impostor.

The air crash theory was based entirely on the 'eyewitness' accounts, mainly that of Bose's fiercely loyal ADC Col Habibur Rahman. While they appear genuine on the face of it, these accounts turned out to be sketchy—marred as they were by numerous contradictions and loopholes which shouldn't have been there if indeed Bose's death was witnessed by some people as claimed. That's the reason the Central government set up the Justice Mukherjee Commission of Inquiry in 1999, as directed by the Calcutta High Court. In 1998, the court was informed by the Central government itself that 'the information that Netaji died in the plane crash on August 18, 1945, is full of loopholes, contradictions and, therefore, is inconclusive'. The court order came as a result of a PIL filed by Gumnami Baba's followers in Kolkata—a little detail that's often missed.

Unable to find any direct evidence of Bose's reported death, MK Mukherjee, a former Supreme Court judge, rejected the air crash theory 'on the basis of robust circumstantial evidence' showing that the fake news of Bose's death was planted to ensure his passage towards Soviet Russia. What happened thereafter the judge couldn't tell as he did not get access to some vital security and intelligence related archives in Russia. The commission looked into the UP holy man theory and concluded that the evidence for it was not 'clinching'—which is to say that there was evidence, but it was not clinching.

A twist in the tale came in 2010 when an independent filmmaker inadvertently recorded Justice Mukherjee's off-the-record comment about Gumnami Baba. The judge stated that he was '100 per cent' sure that Gumnami Baba was Subhas Bose. He rued that he could not prove that in his report due to non-cooperative attitude of the Government and some members of the Bose family. If he had been successful in proving that Bose was alive and in India in his report, Mukerjee would have discarded the seemingly far more plausible Russia killing and the air crash theories of Bose's death that remain in currency among most people in the country today. For if he was alive in India till 1985, Netaji couldn't have died either in Taiwan or Siberia as claimed or alleged.

In 2013, the Allahabad High Court gave a verdict on PILs filed in 1986 by Subhas Chandra Bose's niece Lalita Bose (who died before she could depose before the Mukherjee Commission) and another one by Shakti Singh of Faizabad, in whose house Gumnami Baba had lived last from 1983 to 1985. The court surveyed the entire matter and agreed that 'there appears to be no room for doubt that there was substantial oral and documentary evidence which prima facie makes out a case for scientific investigation with regard to the identity of late Gumnami Baba'. Stating that the 'materials and belongings of Gumnami Baba are national assets and must be protected for future generations', the court directed that they be moved to a local museum. The court also suggested that an inquiry headed by a retired judge be carried out to ascertain the identity of Gumnami Baba, 'treated as Netaji by a substantial section of public'. In other words, the High Court saw some merit in the claims that the holy man could have been Netaji.

For one reason or the other, the state government couldn't make up its mind till 13 February 2016 when a group of Subhas Bose admirers and his family members, including the authors, met then UP Chief Minister Akhilesh Singh Yadav to press for an inquiry in national interest. Making good on his promise to us, Yadav cleared the formation of the commission, and on 29 June 2016, an official announcement was made to set up a judicial commission under the chairmanship of Justice Vishnu Sahai, a former acting Chief Justice of Allahabad High Court.

This brings us to the question of who 'we' are and why should our stand and opinion be taken seriously. The reason is quite simple. Our actions make for our credentials. The unprecedented surge in interest in Netaji that India has witnessed in the recent years is largely owing to our activities.

In 2005, the controversy surrounding the death of Bose was heading towards an imminent burial at the hands of a hostile government, and no one in the academic or historical circles was concerned about it. Rather, many of them were plainly hostile. They were parroting the Central government's narrative, which in turn was inspired by political/personal considerations with roots going back to the circumstances in which colonial British transferred power in 1947. At a time when the heretical report of the Justice Mukherjee Commission of Inquiry ruling out the death of Bose in Taiwan was in the process of being dismissed, a few ordinary people decided to do something extraordinary. Sayantan Dasgupta, Sreejith Panickar, Vishal Sharma and the authors got together on an internet chat room and decided to do something to clear the cobwebs. We formed what would evolve into a pressure group Sreejith had christened as 'Mission Netaji'. Since then, the number of people extending their support from across India and the world has gone on increasing. Saibal Majumdar, Diptasya Jash, Koushik Banerjee, Jayanta Dutta Majumdar, Amlan Chakraborty, Abhishek Singh, Sayak Sen, Sourav Ghosh, Ashoke Bhattacharya, Sanjay Sen, Suvadeep Sen, Sudipta Ghosh (in Kolkata), Akhilesh Singh, Adheer Som, Gaurav Prakash and Arvind Sharma (in Lucknow), Anindya Ghosh, Sujoy Banerjee (Australia), Deepak Nijhawan, Abhishek Bose, Kanchan Banerjee, Hari Kishan Charora, Ananda Sankar Bandyopadhyay, Abhijit Dutt, Nagamohan Metta, Anjan Roy, Shridhar Damle, Sudiep Mukhopadhyay, Sourav Das, Dev K Jha, Sarvesh Gowda, Subroto Mitro, Jayendran Muthushankar, Somanjana Chatterjee, Bhanu Gouda, Judhajit Senmazumdar, Debabrata Dey, Paul Upadhyay (United States); Anirban Mukhopadhyay, Parijat Bhattacharjee, Arijit Ghosh Dastidar, Mrinal Choudhury, Suhas Khale, Suranjan Som (United Kingdom) and Prasenjit Basu and Goutam Majumdar (Singapore) to name a few.[2]

Aware that the issue was too old to make the general public feel connected to it, we wondered how to reinvent it to draw public attention. Chandrachur Ghose came up with the idea of using the Right to Information Act to obtain documents kept under lock and key so far so that people could form an informed opinion. And so we decided to shift the focus of the case from

---

2   We'd like to make it clear that all our friends and well-wishers supported us only for the cause of finding out the truth about Netaji. Our views, then and now, are not necessarily their views. All of them acted in good faith, with a view to aid our efforts over a matter that has intrigued Indians through generations.

mystery to transparency. The mission began in June 2006 with the filing of the first request under the newly enacted Right to Information Act, seeking certain documents—'exhibits' that were used by the Shah Nawaz Committee of 1956 and the GD Khosla Commission of 1970-74 set up to probe Bose's reported death. The Special Officer on Duty in the Ministry of Home Affairs (MHA), the nodal ministry in the matter, who handled our RTI request wasted no time in telling us that it could not be 'acceded to' for reasons covered by section 8(1) of the RTI Act. This was the section empowering the Government not to part with security classified information. After receiving this point-blank refusal, we complained to the Central Information Commission (CIC). Information Commissioner AN Tiwari, a former Secretary to the Government, was the adjudicator. In the first hearing, the Ministry officials asserted that they did not know of any such exhibits. Official documents now available thanks to declassification prove that they were lying.

Back then, round one went to the MHA officials. Noting that 'the matter was quite old and the institutional memory was quite blurred', Tiwari directed us to seek specific documents. It was a tough task, considering that no details of the exhibits were available anywhere in any archive or library. But before the next hearing we were able to give the ministry a memory booster. A copy of a classified record listing out 202 documents used as exhibits by the Khosla Commission (1970) was furnished along with a revised application seeking release of all these documents.

'Where did you get this list from?' the shocked MHA official asked Anuj Dhar, then a journalist, at the start of the next hearing.

It was of no use; the tables had been turned on them. Tiwari directed the ministry to release the 202 records specified by us. He wondered why the Government was keeping Subhas Bose related records secret in the first place. 'Why don't you send them to the National Archives?' he asked. He got the answer by the year end.

A 'Secret' letter from the Home Secretary, a friend of his stated that the 'matter had been considered carefully at the highest level in the ministry'. Some records related to Bose were determined to be 'sensitive in nature'. The disclosure of some of them, in the Home Secretary's estimate, was most likely to 'lead to a serious law and order problem in the country, especially in West Bengal'. This was too much for Tiwari to bear. He transferred the matter to be heard by the full Bench of the commission in an extraordinary session. On 5 June 2007, the full Bench of the CIC comprising Chief Information Commissioner Wajahat Habibullah and Information Commissioners Dr OP Kejariwal, Padma Balasubramanian, and Prof MM Ansari and AN Tiwari (who succeeded Habibullah as the chief) hammered home that the matter was of 'wide public concern and therefore of national importance'.

The Ministry officials had to agree because there was no running away from it. They admitted to the utter shock of the Information Commissioners that apart from the records sought by us, the ministry had in its possession Bose related records 'running into 70,000 pages'. The officials repeated that some of these documents were 'top secret in nature and may lead to chaos in the country if disclosed'.

There were heated exchanges before the Commission tilted to our side. In its decision favouring us, it directed the MHA to release 202 records to us and even recommended that those 70,000 pages should be sent to the National Archives. 'By doing so, the MHA would not only be discharging its legal duties and rendering an essential service to a public cause, it may finally help resolve an unsolved mystery of independent India,' the Commission's landmark decision read.

As conceded by the MHA officials before the Commission that 'the decision concerning disclosure has to be taken at the highest level', in late September-November 2007, Home Minister Shivraj Patil took the issue of the 202 records to the Cabinet Committee on Political Affairs. The CCPA decided in favour of release because it was felt, as reported in *Hindustan Times*, 'the worst that the Congress-led coalition government may have to face was a controversy that would die a natural death'. But despite this highest-level decision, out of 202 only 91 exhibits were eventually released by the MHA to us. One paper—a note by Prime Minister Jawaharlal Nehru, which has since then been released by the Modi government—remained classified. There was no word about the rest 110—including Home, Foreign ministry records/files; letters from Home Minister, High Commissioner, Taiwan government and Intelligence Bureau Director; a report on the INA treasure said to have been lost along with Bose and a memo from Director of Military Intelligence about Mahatma Gandhi's views on the matter.

The matter was further pursued rather vigorously by way of another RTI request from Chandrachur Ghose. Eventually, after years of a tug of war, the ministry was compelled to declassify a big chunk from their 70,000 page cache. In 2012, 1,030 files/items were sent to the National Archives. In November 2014, these records were opened to the researchers. As Anuj Dhar rummaged through these records, he spotted among them the photocopies of two West Bengal Intelligence Branch files on Subhas Bose's nephews Amiya Nath Bose and Sisir Bose, who had been put under surveillance for no logical reason. It was evident that these copies had reached the archive due to an oversight as the original files remained locked up in a secret locker in Kolkata. The contents of the files read like the details from Watergate scandal era in the United States. Without wasting much time, Dhar wrote about it in his online column in *Swarajya* magazine and then on the *Daily O*, which belongs to the *India Today* group. This was how the top editors at the magazine came to know about the files. The magazine went on to do a detailed, insightful cover story. This *India Today* story on snooping on the Bose family imploded the Netaji issue on the national scene like never before in history. Declassification of the Netaji files by the Bengal and the Central governments followed.

Prime Minister's Office
[Political Section]

Subject: Declassification of files/papers on Netaji.

In connection with a request of Shri Anuj Dhar (r/o ▓▓▓▓▓ New Delhi) under RTI Act for a list of files on Netaji, it has been decided **[Flag-X]** with the approval of the Principal Secretary to undertake declassification exercise as most of the files on Netaji are classified.

2. It has been desired that the papers be scrutinized keeping in view the decision taken about declassification while sending papers to Mukherjee Commission or in relation to Court case as well as with regard to the provisions of Section 8 of RTI Act. A group comprising of SO(Ddak), SO(Pol) and SO(NGO) has also been formed to scrutinize the records. The files of Political Section were submitted for declassification earlier, but it was desired that the matter be submitted with a detailed statement about the classified documents.

3. Accordingly, a statement containing details of each of the classified papers in the 27 different files belonging to Political Section is at **Flag-A**. Files figuring at S.N. **1-14 are more than 25 years old** , while others are less than that. It may also be mentioned here that photo-copies of all these 27 files were made available to Justice Mukherjee Commission of Inquiry for their reference.

[A declassified PMO note from 2006 refers to declassification exercise undertaken as a result of an RTI application filed by Anuj Dhar. National Archives, New Delhi]

On 23 January 2016, the birth anniversary of Subhas Bose, Prime Minister Modi personally released the first lot of 100 files, containing over 15,000 pages—all scanned and put up on a dedicated website launched by the National Archives. In so far as transparency and declassification is concerned, India never had an event of such magnitude and scale. We all grew up knowing about India's obsession for dark secrecy. But the authors, working in tandem with the Bose family members, have changed that situation forever. Our actions have led to the release of more than 1000 previously secret files, of which 304 have been released by the Modi government.

Once these files were declassified, we undertook a close study of all the papers. When we started putting together the insights from these documents with evidence obtained from people associated with the case, the pieces of the jigsaw puzzle started falling in place. And that's how we have been able to unravel the mystery surrounding 'Gumnami Baba'.

We would be happy if the Allahabad High Court takes note of our findings, because if it wasn't for them the whole story would have been successfully suppressed back in 1985 itself.

We end this preface with a caveat which has been detailed in this book but warrants emphasis here. This book is a piece of detective work to unveil the identity of a person who took extreme care to keep his existence an absolute secret. Given the nature of information available, there are several questions to which we do not have answers. We can confidently say that answers to such questions will not be available without access to much larger resources and unfettered access to all intelligence files. In other words, the Government (preferably under the supervision of court) will have to sponsor this investigation in all sincerity and the resources at its command to fill all the gaps. The central thrust of our research has been to establish the identity of the man of mystery. Everything else flows out of this core issue.

It is for legal experts to opine whether the collective evidence presented by us qualifies to be called 'clinching'. What we can say on our part is that the current stand of our Government regarding Netaji's fate—that he died on 18 August 1945—is based on interpretation of circumstantial evidence in the absence of direct proof. This was admitted by our first PM Jawaharlal Nehru, who understood legal nuances, in a letter to Netaji's elder brother Suresh Chandra Bose in 1962. As such, the official position of our Government itself is based on circumstantial evidence. The following chapters furnish far stronger evidence—eyewitness, documentary and forensic—and hence clinching.

No.704-PMF/62

(277)

May 13, 1962.

Dear Shri Suresh Bose,

I have your letter of the 12th May. You ask me to send you proof of the death of Netaji Subhas Chandra Bose. I cannot send you any precise and direct proof. But all the circumstantial evidence that has been produced and which has been referred to in the Enquiry Committee's report has convinced us of the fact that Netaji has died. In addition to this, the lapse of time now and the extreme probability of his being alive secretly somewhere when he would be welcomed in India with great joy and affection, adds to that circumstantial evidence.

Yours sincerely,

[Document obtained under the Right to Information Act]

ONE

A SLEEPY TOWN
SHOOTS INTO FAME

O N 1 FEBRUARY 1986, an order of the district judge of Faizabad[1] to open the locks of the Ram Janmabhoomi–Babri Masjid complex set off a chain of explosive events. The passions ignited by the order—both for and against—completely submerged another set of events that had erupted just about four months back in the sleepy town which, by the beginning of 1986, threatened to acquire much larger proportions had the mandir–masjid dispute not intervened.

As Dr Raghunath Prasad Mishra, former surgeon at the district hospital in Faizabad, settled down for dinner with his family on the evening of 16 September 1985, someone started banging on the door. He opened it to find Saraswati Devi Shukla, a lady in

---

1   The Faizabad district comprised the twin towns of Faizabad and Ayodhya. Since November 2018, the district is known as Ayodhya.

her mid-fifties, breathless and highly agitated. 'Bhagwanji is very unwell, please come quickly,' she blurted out. Leaving his meal half-eaten, Dr Mishra rushed to 'Ram Bhawan', a spacious house located in the posh part of the town. The honorific 'Bhagwanji' was used for a reclusive *sanyasi* (holy man), the spiritual mentor of Mishra, who he had brought from Ayodhya in 1983 to live as a tenant in Ram Bhawan, owned by Gurubasant Singh. The holy man had become a sort of a curious fixture in the gossip circles of the town because of his habit of living behind a curtain, never showing his face to visitors. Since the chances for any outsider of getting an audience with him were negligible, a new entry into his circle of followers took place mostly through recommendations from the existing network.

The other option was to submit a written request, with full details of the seeker's background, to the man behind the curtain. The chances of success in both methods were far from certain. Only a handful of his disciples from nearby areas and occasionally a group from Calcutta came to meet him. They were the only people who knew his antecedents. Among the many rumours about him, it was said that he was a spiritual powerhouse who knew the past and could see the future like no other. It was also said about him that he was equally conversant with national and international politics, as if he was a participant, an insider aware of minute details far beyond the limits of public knowledge.

The holy man was now seriously ill and his attendant Saraswati Devi was running around to get help. She also ran to inform Dr Priyabrata Banerjee, a well-known homeopathy practitioner in the town, who was intimately known to Bhagwanji ever since his late father Dr TC Banerjee began treating him from the mid-1970s. All efforts by the two doctors to save Bhagwanji proved futile. Late on the evening of 16 September, it emerged from Ram Bhawan that Gurubasant Singh's inaccessible, unseen tenant was dead. The news spread to his other disciples, but Dr Mishra made sure that no one outside the immediate circle comprising Saraswati Devi, and her son Rajkumar came close to the body. Their guru's wish to remain unknown and unseen was to be followed even after his death. For two days after he was gone, Bhagwanji's body remained under the constant guard of the family of Dr Mishra, the man in charge. Mishra told the rest of the local disciples that the wait was for the Bengali followers of Bhagwanji who had been notified of his death.

Public curiosity began to mount in the meantime. A crowd gathered outside Ram Bhawan, demanding to know the identity of the unseen *sanyasi* and to see his body. When it became clear that no one from Calcutta would turn up for inexplicable reasons, Dr Mishra manoeuvred the crowd by announcing that the body was being taken to Ayodhya for cremation. After aimlessly driving around for a while, a Matador van carrying the body was swiftly re-routed to Faizabad cantonment, to a secluded place on the banks of the River Sarayu near Guptar Ghat—a spot considered sacred in the Ramayana tradition[2]—on the evening of 19 September. A funeral pyre was erected within minutes. Present at the cremation site were thirteen disciples including Dr Mishra,

---

2 It is believed to be the spot where Lord Ram took Jal Samadhi.

Dr B Rai (an anaesthesiologist at the district hospital), Ravindra Nath Shukla (a resident of Faizabad), Dr Banerjee, Panda Ram Kishore Mishra (a priest from Ayodhya who once had Bhagwanji for a tenant) with his two sons, and Rajkumar Shukla (son of Saraswati Devi). As the flames wrapped the mortal remains, the disciples were consumed by an emotional turmoil. They had all given their word to Bhagwanji to keep his identity secret. Now the man was gone. Panda Ram Kishore was the first to bewail: 'We are only thirteen here to see him off on his last journey. There should have been thirteen lakhs.'Like everyone who came in contact with him, Panda Ram Kishore was drawn to Bhagwanji for his unusual ways. Nearly a decade ago on a wintry night in Ayodhya, suddenly realising that the septuagenarian holy man must be very cold, Kishore offered him the brazier he was using, only to be told, 'This body has lived in Siberia. It does not require warmth.'[3]

The urban legend of Bhagwanji would have remained a subdued, localised affair had it not been for the subsequent incidents. While rumours about the holy man's identity engulfed the town, a few broke into Ram Bhawan and started grabbing whatever article they could lay their hands on. A dispute also emerged among his disciples over the custody of Bhagwanji's belongings. In order to prevent the ransacking of his belongings, Dr Rai, Dr Mishra and Saraswati Devi barred the door of his room with three locks. Soon Panda Ram Kishore Mishra added

3   Kingshuk Nag, 'Siberian survivor to secretive sadhu... Netaji mystery lives on,' *The Times of India*, 8 September 2015.

fuel to the fire by becoming the first of the disciples to go public, breaking the shell of secrecy. The deceased holy man, he claimed, was none other than Netaji Subhas Chandra Bose. Forty years after he was incontestably last seen in Saigon, the trail of Subhas Bose, in a manner of speaking, thus appeared in Faizabad. If you believe the believers, this dusty north Indian town—not the salubrious Taipei, not some snowy expanse in Siberia—was where the endgame of India's longest running political controversy actually played out.

In September 1985, there was no way that the unfolding events could have escaped the notice of the authorities. Ram Bhawan was at a walking distance from the residences of the who's who of local officialdom. A body, reportedly covered in the national flag, had been cremated on a piece of land falling within the remit of the Army—without any intimation to and permission of the military or civil authorities, who were, according to eyewitnesses, keeping a hawk's eye on the developments. Cops trailed the van which carried Bhagwanji's body. An FIR was lodged against all the thirteen disciples for unlawful disposal of a body at a public place. And that was the end of it. Dr Mishra was too well known and Dr Priyabrata Banerjee had inherited the good name and profession of his father Dr TC Banerjee. Both of them were socially known to local officials. Banerjee was on friendly terms with Ajai Raj Sharma, the DIG of Faizabad (would-be Delhi Police Commissioner and Director-General of Border Security Force). None of Bhagwanji's followers ever denied that they had illegally cremated a body in Guptar Ghat. Some even dared the authorities to take action against them. And yet, the police kept mum. Why? 'Because they knew he was Netaji,' reasoned Ravindra Shukla. 'If he wasn't, they would have clobbered us and thrown us into jail for spreading such rumours. Don't you know how UP police works?'

After a month of doing nothing, in response to rising public outrage, the cops swooped down on who they thought was the weakest link. Poor Saraswati Devi and her son Rajkumar were rounded up and taken to the police station. Their 'arrest' sparked anger among the disciples. The next day a local daily created a sensation. Ashok Tandon, the editor of local Hindi daily *Naye Log*, had known some of Bhagwanji's disciples. His instincts beginning to tickle, Tandon asked reporters Chandresh Srivastava and Ramteerth Vikal to make inquires. The result was the breaking news on 28 October 1985. A six-column headline on the front page screamed, 'Living incognito in Faizabad, Netaji Subhas Chandra Bose passed away!' Along with it appeared an editorial by Tandon, calling for a probe into the issue. Saraswati Devi, who had served and seen Bhagwanji for decades, now mustered courage to tell media persons that so far as she knew, Bhagwanji was Subhas Bose.

She told *Naye Log* that Bhagwanji blamed Nehru–Gandhi dynasty for his ordeal and claimed that his identity was known to many top-level personalities, who used to meet him secretly. Not all Bhagwanji's followers were forthcoming with all the details, however. They were still under the dilemma of how much to tell, or whether to say anything at all. It took one disciple—Ravindra Shukla—thirty years to divulge on oath before the Sahai Commission that one of the visitors to Bhagwanji who he had taken around Ayodhya under the holy man's instructions went on to become India's thirteenth President.[4]

The *Naye Log* story sent ripples across the town. Tandon heard about the systematic attempts to suppress the circulation of the newspaper, but the news was too big to be contained. A rival newspaper, *Jan Morcha*, began its own investigation, repudiating the view that Bhagwanji could have been Subhas Bose. The District Magistrate too rubbished out of hand the linking of the reclusive hermit—christened by media as 'Anaam Sant' and 'Gumnami Baba'—to the indomitable freedom fighter. He said that there had been an official inquiry which revealed nothing of that sort. As the state machinery adopted a wishy-washy attitude, more and more journalists started connecting the dots. The *Saptahik Sahara* in its 24-30 November 1985 edition concluded after an intense investigation that it was 'quite possible' that the holy man was Subhas Bose. The commotion then attracted the attention of Tushar Kanti Ghosh—one of the most prominent names in Indian journalism, a Padma Bhushan awardee and editor of two Calcutta-based dailies *Amrita Bazar Patrika* and *Jugantar*, and the Allahabad-based *Northern India Patrika (NIP)*. After reviewing the developments, Ghosh approved an investigative series to be published in the now defunct *NIP*. A team of Nirmal Nibedon, Vishwambhar Nath Arora and Sayed Kausar Husain, the news editor, ran the investigative series that started on 20 December 1985 and continued in seventeen parts culminating

---

4   Affidavit submitted by Ravindra Nath Shukla before the Justice Sahai Commission of Inquiry, 15 October 2016, Faizabad.

on 23 January, Subhas Bose's birth anniversary, next year. 'The investigations and piecing together of the exciting material, painstakingly collected, with enormous efforts night and day, led us to the inescapable belief that the man (Bhagwanji)...was one of the greatest personalities India ever had,' read the *NIP* editorial on 20 December 1985. The series that traced down a number of people spread across different cities who came in touch with Bhagwanji, ended with interviews of five key dramatis personae in Ayodhya and Faizabad who had known Bhagwanji for long— Dr RP Mishra, Saraswati Devi, Panda Ram Kishore Mishra, Pushpa Banerjee (widow of Dr TC Banerjee) and her son Dr Priyabrata Banerjee—aiming to settle the question of the holy man's identity.

Dr Mishra deflected most questions put to him. Rumours about Bhagwanji being Netaji were just that—rumours. The unambiguous reply on his identity was: 'He is an Indian and Shiva personified: Lord Shiva himself.'[5] Despite living with Bhagwanji for over two decades, the first time Saraswati Devi saw, so she claimed, his face was in 1981, when he slipped in the bathroom and broke his femur. Even her father had not seen his face. Betraying the dilemma on coming clean on Bhagwanji's identity which most disciples suffered from at this point, Saraswati Devi reversed her position from what she had told *Naye Log*. She told the *NIP* reporters, 'People said he was Netaji but I do not know,'

---

5   Nirmal Nibedon & Vishwambhar Nath Arora, 'A Doctored Version,' *Northern India Patrika*, 19 January 1986.

was her take on his identity.[6] 'It was useless and futile' to discuss his past, Bhagwanji had told her. In contrast to the denial and vagueness of Dr Mishra, and the vacillation of Saraswati Devi, Pushpa Banerjee harboured no doubt about Bhagwanji's identity. She had witnessed the power of Bhagwanji which fell in the realm of the paranormal and so had other members of her family. There were many reasons for her to believe that he was none other than Subhas Bose—which were primarily based on deductive reasoning—but the biggest and unmistakeable proof was her own memory. She had seen Subhas Bose in Lucknow in 1933 and again in 1939. She could not mistake the man whom she was seeing now for anyone else. She tested the man to be doubly sure. She deliberately told him the wrong year of the second meeting. Bhagwanji didn't disappoint her. He corrected her immediately.[7]

The last installment of the *NIP* series on 23 January 1986 was headlined, in quotes, 'The Man was Subhas Bose.'

The *NIP* reports on 'the man of mystery' pushed the people of Faizabad into a vortex of emotions. But the instant reaction of the state government was to float a conspiracy theory that the Janata Party and the BJP were behind the public outcry. The truth was that the public discontent was spontaneous, with every section of the society, including local Congress leaders, pitching in. The man who had in a sense let the cat out of the bag—Panda

---

6   Nirmal Nibedon & Vishwambhar Nath Arora, 'The Last Days,' *Northern India Patrika*, 20 January 1986.

7   Nirmal Nibedon & Vishwambhar Nath Arora, 'The Last Days,' *Northern India Patrika*, 20 January 1986.

Ram Kishore—was in fact a well-known Congress party leader of Ayodhya.[8]

Responding to a petition by local political leaders, the District Magistrate asked the police to conduct an investigation into the matter. In early November, the local police was entrusted to find out the identity of Bhagwanji and prepare an inventory of his belongings. The inventory-making process spread over three days stunned the local populace as news spread about the items discovered in Ram Bhawan. The witnesses to the process— the lawyer Satya Narayan Singh (president of the Faizabad Bar Association), Omprakash Madan of *Naye Log*, journalist VN Arora, lawyer Madan Mohan Pandit, leader of BJP Anil Tewari and leader of Janata Party Ram Prakash Singh issued a public statement asking for a high-level judicial inquiry for a clear and final conclusion on the identity of Bhagwanji as they felt that the letters, books, newspapers and magazines, other documents and items appeared to be related to Netaji Subhas Chandra Bose.[9] The political uproar gathered further momentum, with political leaders of all shades joining in the melee.

Meanwhile, alarmed by the reports that the authorities were contemplating auctioning the belongings Bhagwanji had left behind, Sayed Kausar Husain persuaded activists Dr MA Haleem and Vishwa Bandhav Tewari to approach the District Magistrate

---

8   Panda Ram Kishore Mishra's sons proudly pointed out to the authors the prominently displayed photos at their residence, showing him in close proximity to Jawaharlal Nehru and Indira Gandhi.

9   Ashok Tandon, 'Way Netaji nahin thay to kaun thay?' *Ganga*, April and May 1987.

on 30 January 1986. Their letter, copies of which were marked to the Foreign Secretary in Delhi and a disinterested Uttar Pradesh (UP) Chief Minister ND Tiwari, called for an inquiry.

> An important English daily of Uttar Pradesh, *Northern India Patrika*, has after months of enquiry and investigations come to the conclusion that the saint was none else than Subhas Chandra Bose. The most important evidence which the paper has cited is based on the records, documents and materials found in his residence of which an inventory was prepared cursorily by a police officer of a lower rank.... We, therefore, submit to you that the documents and other materials found in the said house should remain sealed and preserved for the purpose of inquiry, and the guards posted there should continue to remain there in the national interest. We would like to be informed of the steps you propose to take in the matter.[10]

The response from the District Magistrate (DM), however, was only silence. Before long, Lalita Bose, daughter of Subhas Bose's elder brother Suresh, rushed in from New Delhi. Her arrival put paid to the allegation that the BJP and others were causing the commotion as Lalita was a member of the Congress party at that time. In early 1986, she met Vir Bahadur Singh, the new Chief Minister of Uttar Pradesh, and found him 'helpless'. Lalita's request to have a proper catalogue of the belongings and correspondence left behind by Bhagwanji, made by a senior police officer or advocate-commissioner, was turned down. On the sidelines, Lalita carried out her personal inquiry. In talks with

10   Copy of the letter shared by Vishwa Bandhav Tewari with Anuj Dhar in 2001.

many locals and media persons, she would break down, telling them that Bhagwanji was turning out to be her missing uncle. To the *Hindustan Times* she would tell that Bhagwanji 'was of the same age, size and colour as Netaji. His accent was Bengali. His notes on books in English and Bengali looked like the writing of Netaji'.[11]

Lalita took the next logical step on the advice of Sayed Kausar Husain, whose behind-the-scene activities were going to prevent the authorities from covering up the issue. On 10 February 1986, Lalita Bose, Dr Haleem and Vishwa Bandhav Tewari moved the Lucknow Bench of the Allahabad High Court against the state of UP, the Chief Minister, the state's Home Secretary and the District Magistrate of Faizabad. Their lawyer was legal luminary Robin Mitra, about whom former Chief Justice of India AS Anand would write that, 'those who practiced with him at the bar, bear testimony to the fact that he was respected both by the Bench and the Bar for his advocacy, hard work and fairness'.[12] Describing the enquiry by Nibedon–Arora–Husain team as 'a great national service', the petitioners lamented that despite interest evinced by the public, the District Magistrate was merely 'sitting tight over the matter'. They stated how perfunctorily the police had made an inventory of the items left by Bhagwanji. To pre-empt the state government's plan to auction Bhagwanji's belongings, they argued

---

11 'Bose niece wants mystery solved,' *Hindustan Times*, 24 October 1989.
12 Justice Dr AS Anand, 'Delay in justice and low rate of conviction are major flaws,' *Hindustan Times*, 9 January 2006.Accessed from: https://www.hindustantimes. com/india/delay-in-justice-and-low-rate-of-conviction-are-major-flaws/story-qm2MRFPiOsO8lfmbLny1IP.html.

that the petitioner Lalita Bose 'being the niece of Netaji Subhas Chandra Bose has a right to the property, if the nameless saint is found to be Netaji'. They even suggested that Bhagwanji's books, correspondence, etc. could be sent to the National Archives in New Delhi. The court's intervention was sought as there was 'no other alternative remedy available' due to 'the callous inaction of the opposite parties', especially the Chief Minister, who had been 'absolutely unreasonable'.[13]

Making up for the state government's inaction, Justices SS Ahmad and GB Singh announced an interim relief on the same day. The state was called upon by the judges to file a counter-affidavit within six weeks (although it took thirteen years before the government responded). The main request was agreed to by the court—and thus the Bhagwanji matter was saved for posterity. The DM of Faizabad was ordered to oversee the preparation of an elaborate inventory, giving details of and about the items found from Bhagwanji's room at Ram Bhawan and then keep all these in his safe custody. The High Court order should have made news across the nation but it didn't. The event was overshadowed by the Ram Janmabhoomi–Babri Masjid dispute triggered by the order of the district court passed ten days earlier. It is widely held that the dispute at this time was revived by a deliberate political move of the Rajiv Gandhi government in Delhi. Suddenly, an appeal on this matter was filed at the district court in Faizabad in January

---

13   Writ Petition No 929/86 by Lalita Bose, Dr MA Haleem and Vishwa Bandhav Tewari against the State of UP, the CM of UP, the Home Secretary of UP and the District Magistrate, Faizabad.

1986 to unlock the temple–mosque complex. The petitioner was not a party to the dispute but the judge allowed his prayer promptly. This act came in for severe criticism under the 2010 order of the Allahabad High Court. 'There was absolutely no occasion to show such undue haste. The appeal was filed on 31st January 1986 and was allowed on the next day i.e. 1st February 1986. At least the reason for this extreme haste is not mentioned in the judgment,' wrote Justice SU Khan.[14]

The Bhagwanji matter came up for a brief discussion in the UP Legislative Assembly. On 25 February 1986, Krishanpal Singh and Nityanand Swami, (who would be the Chief Minister of Uttaranchal in future), asked about Bhagwanji and Jagdambika Pal of Congress—now in BJP and in Lok Sabha—too spoke about the need for an extensive probe, even though he saw no Bose link. Standing in for the government, Finance Minister Baldev Singh Arya stated that an inquiry had revealed that Bhagwanji was not Subhas Bose. The lawmakers wanted to see the inquiry report, but the minister refused to oblige them.

The process of cataloguing Bhagwanji's belongings commenced on 23 March 1986 and lasted till 23 April 1987. During this period, 2,673 mostly invaluable items left by the holy man were taken over officially and described in an inventory. While it was happening, Lalita Bose was there for a while. She told *The Pioneer* on 1 April 1986 that the personal effects of

---

14 Judgement delivered on 30 September 2010 by Justice SU Khan, Lucknow Bench of Allahabad High Court, in the matter of Other Original Suits No 1, No 3, No 4 and No 5 of 1989.

Bhagwanji 'were in one way or the other related to the kith and kin of Netaji'.

By having the holy man's belongings secured, Lalita Bose and others met with partial success only. After the inventory had been prepared, all the items recovered from Bhagwanji's room in Ram Bhawan were sent to the district treasury and stored in sealed boxes. As the court case lingered on for years, the people concerned gradually lost steam. Nirmal Nibedon, who had made a name for himself as an acclaimed writer on North-East insurgency, died in an accident, which some thought was linked to his interest in Gumnami Baba. Lalita Bose was last heard making a public pitch for resolving the issue in October 1989. Addressing the media in New Delhi, she 'demanded to know why the Government was not serious to find out whether "Gumnami Baba" of Faizabad was Netaji as a section of the Press had suggested'.[15] Meanwhile, Ashok Tandon had put together a cogent analytical narrative, as opposed to the pieces of news reports, based on more information than he had been able to present in *Naye Log*. This was published in nineteen installments in the *Ganga* magazine, starting April 1987, ending in October 1988. The series was titled *Way Netaji nahin thay to kaun thay*? (If not Netaji, who was he?) All installments except the last one: 'Kya way Netaji hi thay?' (Was he indeed Netaji?) of Tandon's articles were edited and approved for publication by the magazine's editor Kamleshwar—the famous writer, and the scriptwriter for classic Hindi movies such as *Aandhi, Mausam* and *Chhoti si baat*.

---

15 'Bose niece wants mystery solved', *Hindustan Times*, 24 October 1989.

Despite his own precarious financial condition, co-petitioner Vishwa Bandhav Tewari picked up the threads in the 1990s. MA Haleem had passed away. Tewari wrote to the Prime Minister, Home Minister, Speaker, Governor and Chief Minister of UP and the Forward Bloc in Calcutta, but all in vain. In 1997, he was told that the file of Lalita Bose's 1986 petition was untraceable in the court records. At that juncture, Dr Alokesh Bagchi, a surgeon from Gorakhpur, came to his rescue. Sincere but credulous, Bagchi felt attached to Subhas Bose because his grandfather had hosted him once. His and Tewari's efforts led to a judicial injunction in May 1998. Justice Brijesh Kumar of the UP High Court ordered for the re-creation of the file. Bagchi found that in the court record someone had fraudulently entered 'case resolved' against Lalita Bose's petition so that no response would be needed from the state government. It was due to Bagchi's lobbying efforts that the state government had to file a counter-affidavit in the court in 1999, when the central government was coming under increasing pressure to initiate a new judicial inquiry into Subhas Bose's fate. The state government, however, through its counter-affidavit, dismissed Lalita Bose's demand for a proper inquiry. 'No reliance can be placed on any news published in the newspaper without verifying the authenticity of the same,' it asserted.

Another thirteen years would pass before the situation would take a dramatic turn. In the intervening period, while it was left to be buried under the sands of time for a gradual death, the matter was miraculously revived when one morning in 2001, Justice MK Mukherjee stepped into Ram Bhawan. The trail was at the same time fortuitously picked up by *Hindustan Times (HT)*. In an investigation of its own, in which the co-author of this book, Anuj Dhar, was the lead investigator, the newspaper's web portal pieced together available information regarding the entire Subhas Bose mystery. The *HT* probe in its first phase concluded in 2001 that 'on present evidence it would seem improbable that Bose died on August 18, 1945'. No national daily had ever ventured out to take such a definitive stand on this controversial issue. The *HT* probe was a runaway hit on the internet. A worldwide audience became aware of the intricacies of the Bose mystery for the first time. A major chunk of hits on the *HT* stories came from the United States, home to a large number of people of Indian origin as well as expats.

Thereafter, prompted by inputs from a source with direct access to a highest-level contact in the Government, Dhar turned his attention to the Bhagwanji matter. It was, he was told, 'India's best-kept secret'. Till this happened, unaware of the *NIP* and *Ganga* series like most Indians, Dhar had a completely closed mind on the very possibility of Netaji having been alive in the guise of a sadhu for all the years he was presumed dead. In November 2001, Dhar travelled to Faizabad to attend the Mukherjee Commission's hearing there and, helped by Alokesh Bagchi and Supreme Court lawyer Bijan Ghosh, queried the main characters in the Bhagwanji narrative.

Going forward from where the *NIP* and *Ganga* series had left off, Dhar managed to connect more dots and upheld the Bose–Bhagwanji link. The introductory editorial for *HindustanTimes.com* Netaji probe phase-2 in April 2002 read:

We do not fear the inference that the hermit may be Netaji Subhas Bose, but we do gasp at the conclusions that will be drawn from the writings and letters that have survived this man. Taken even on their face value, they have the potential to change Indian history the way we know it. We tremble even as we release the evidence…but we do so in the belief that Indians have the maturity and the strength of mind to handle the truth, however stark it may be.[16]

On 31 January 2013, the Allahabad High Court finally gave its decision on Lalita Bose's petition, now clubbed with a recent petition filed by Shakti Singh, son of the owner of Ram Bhawan. The credit for obtaining the order clearly went to Shakti Singh and his lawyers Bulbul Godiyal and Madhumita Bose, daughters of Lalita Bose's counsel Robin Mitra. Justices Devi Prasad Singh and Virendra Kumar Dixit surveyed the entire Bose death mystery matter and chided the state as well as central government for their acts of omission. Justice Mukherjee's inquiry commission too was faulted for not carrying out a proper inquiry into the Bhagwanji episode. The authorities were also questioned for not responding to the inquiry made by the *NIP* team and the co-author of this book (which we hope is not too immodest to quote):

Efforts made by Anuj Dhar, learned author, to find out the truth behind the alleged accidental death of Netaji in plane crash seem to be genuine and based on relevant material, that too when the finding recorded by the learned author has not

---

16   The investigation website has now been taken down by the *Hindustan Times*.

been controverted by the Government of India or government of West Bengal. ...The effort made and finding recorded by the learned author (supra) with due extensive tour of various places with regard to survival or death of Netaji Subhas Chandra Bose including Gumnami Baba must be attended by the Government of India with due sincerity to expose the truth.

More pertinently, the court observed:

The articles/items of late Gumnami Baba raise reasonable curiosity for a probe to find out his identity. The celebration of the birthday of Netaji Subhas Chandra Bose on 23rd January every year, books, documents and material relating back to the period when the alleged death of Netaji took place in the plane crash, including the books with regard to war crimes and materials collected by Anuj Dhar in his two books as well as a series of 17 articles published in *Northern India Patrika* from 20th December, 1985, to 23rd January, 1986 with regard to Gumnami Baba alias Bhagwan Ji prima facie makes out a case for a probe into his identity. The State and Central Governments should look into it to remove doubts with regard to Gumnami Baba by holding appropriate enquiry.

The court said it was a 'duty cast upon the [state] government to preserve the articles/household goods of such person at appropriate place/museum scientifically, so that coming generation may not be divested from its right of access for research work or otherwise'. In view of this, the court ordered that Bhagwanji's belongings 'may be kept scientifically, under the supervision of a qualified person (curator)' at a museum in either Faizabad or Ayodhya. Also, the state government was directed to appoint 'a committee consisting of a team of experts and higher officers, headed by a retired judge of High Court, to hold an enquiry with regard to the identity of late Gumnami Baba alias Bhagwanji'.[17]

Given the complex nature of the matter and the fact that the Netaji mystery was yet to turn into a major national issue, the High Court verdict wasn't received too well in the media. Lobbying by Anuj Dhar in coordination with Shakti Singh and five-term MLA Akhilesh Singh of the Peace Party were not successful in persuading the state government to fully implement the court order. Due to the efforts of Akhilesh Singh, however, an adjournment notice criticising the state government for failing to implement the order was moved in the state assembly on 14 March 2013 by MLAs of several parties including the Congress, BJP and Quami Ekta Dal. In the discussion that followed, leaders of all political parties sank their differences—a feat that one doesn't see too often in caste politics-driven Uttar Pradesh—and put across their views in a most dignified way.

The Leader of Opposition, Swamy Prasad Maurya of the BSP (who since then has joined the BJP and is currently the deputy chief minister of the state), said that Netaji was next only to Mahatma Gandhi in the freedom struggle and remarked that it was 'unfortunate for the country that the causes of Netaji's death have not been known'. Hukum Singh of the BJP insisted that the constitution of the inquiry commission should not be delayed. Even Anugrah Narain Singh of the Congress party asked

17   Order of the Lucknow Bench of the Allahabad High Court, Miscellaneous Bench No 929 of 1986 delivered on 31 January 2013.

the government to set up a commission to settle the Bhagwanji mystery.[18] But despite all these efforts, the state government wouldn't take any decision. It was only after the snooping scandal turned the Bose mystery into a hot topic that the state government could be approached at the highest level by Lucknow-based educationist Adheer Som[19]. On 13 February 2016, three members from Subhas Chandra Bose's family, Shakti Singh, Som, the authors and others met Chief Minister Akhilesh Yadav at his residence-cum-office.

For good measure, before we met him, Yadav had, in deference to the court order, sanctioned Rs 1.5 crore for the transfer and preservation of Bhagwanji's belongings to the Ram Katha Museum in Ayodhya. We requested the Chief Minister to take the next natural step. If Bhagwanji's belongings were going to be displayed in a museum dedicated to Lord Ram, the least the nation needed to know is who he really was. In March 2016, when the process of transferring select belongings of Bhagwanji commenced, the nation for the first time became aware of his story to an extent. Recovery of the Bose family pictures among the belongings received considerable media attention. However, there was no reaction from the Central government or even the ruling party.

---

18 Atiq Khan, 'UP Opposition demands panel to identify 'Gumnami Baba,' *The Hindu*, 15 March 2013.
19 Som has since then come out with a compendium titled *Gumnami Baba: A Case History*.

[*The Times of India*]

Three months later, making good on his promise to us, Akhilesh Yadav decided to set up a commission of inquiry to ascertain Bhagwanji's identity. Justice Vishnu Sahai, former acting Chief Justice of the Allahabad High Court and someone deemed 'close' to the ruling Samajwadi Party, was appointed its chairman. The Central government, which must have been made aware of the development, made no comment as if the unfolding events concerned someone of zero consequence to India.

TWO

A HOLY MAN APPEARS

BY THE END of 1988, the two major investigative series run by the *Northern India Patrika (NIP)* and the *Ganga* magazine had largely been able to reconstruct the broad contours of the past two-and-a-half decades of Bhagwanji's extraordinarily secretive life in various parts of Uttar Pradesh. What rendered this account incomplete was the absence of inputs from Bhagwanji's associates in Calcutta—their recollections and letters and notes exchanged for over two decades. Our access to the papers of the Kolkata disciples (the importance of which we elucidate in a later chapter), extensive interaction with the witnesses still alive and the audio recordings of the witnesses whom the *NIP* journalists interviewed (none of whom are alive) have helped us fill in the gaps with far greater detail and build on the foundation laid by Nibedon and Tandon. To this must be added the information gleaned from the proceedings of the Justice Mukherjee Commission of Inquiry.

The earliest that Bhagwanji's presence can be traced back definitively is 1957, when he lived in Lucknow. This is based on documents recovered from Ram Bhawan. As Rajkumar Shukla recollected before the Mukherjee Commission and us, around 1955/56, his widowed mother Saraswati Devi and he moved in with her father, already in the service of Bhagwanji. Mahadev Prasad Mishra, a Sanskrit teacher, died in 1970, taking all his secrets with him. Saraswati Devi died in 2000, just before she could depose before the commission.

From the talks Bhagwanji had with his disciples from Kolkata, it would appear that he was in Uttar Pradesh (UP) from the early 1950s. One person who was aware of Bhagwanji's presence from that time was Surendra Singh Chaudhary, an aristocrat from Etawah. Known as 'Raja saab', with an unusual degree of credulity over matters paranormal[1], Chaudhary claimed to have met Bhagwanji for the first time in 1953. At that time, he was living in the small town of Mainpuri, approximately 130 km east of Agra and about 350 km southeast of Delhi when Chaudhary got in touch with him. If the choice of the city was odd, even more so was the specific location within the city where he was found living—at the house of the then Deputy Superintendent of Police (DSP), as a monk. Chaudhary found striking similarity between Swami Vivekananda and a clean-shaven Bhagwanji in ochre robes, complete with a *safa* (turban). Chaudhary claimed that he

---

1   All information ascribed to Surendra Singh Chaudhary in this book, unless otherwise specified, is based on his interview with Syed Kausar Husain of *NIP*. We are in possession of the audio recording of the interview.

was accompanied by Pandit Jyoti Shankar Dikshit, who was the secretary of the provincial Congress committee of UP in the mid-1920s and later an activist of the Hindu Mahasabha. Chaudhary had never seen Subhas Bose, but Dikshit had witnessed his rise in the Congress and knew him closely. Dikshit had no doubt who he met at Mainpuri.

While no mention of Dikshit is found again in the narrative, Chaudhary met Bhagwanji at the same place after two years. They remained in close contact for the next six to seven years. The time Chaudhary spent in close proximity of Bhagwanji helped him get an idea of his early years in India. Chaudhary's chronology started with Bhagwanji becoming the spiritual guru of the Rani of Rijor in Etah district of UP (a branch of the Chauhan dynasty had settled here). After the death of the queen, he moved to a place called Umarpur, from where he again moved back to Etah district to a village called Sakit. From Sakit, Bhagwanji moved to Mainpuri from where, after a stay of over two years, he moved to Shikohabad, another small town not very far to the west of Mainpuri. If Chaudhary's account is to be believed, it places the starting point of the Bhagwanji story at around 1950 or 1951. No information, however, is available from Chaudhary's account on how and exactly when Bhagwanji reached India. On the other hand, Mahadev Prasad Mishra is said to have helped Bhagwanji enter India from Nepal in an unspecified year. Bhagwanji himself narrated to someone who became his confidant subsequently that he re-entered India from Nepal.

It is not possible to independently verify Chaudhary's narrative of Bhagwanji's early years fully, but bits of Bhagwanji's later discussions with his Calcutta followers validate parts of it.

> I reached Uttar Pradesh as a yogi, *sanyasi*. I have been attached to yoga, *sadhana* and mysticism consistently from my childhood. Being a bona fide *sanyasi*, I can train people in practical yoga. Over time I acquired a few disciples, chiefly from the elite and aristocratic families. I was clean shaven at that time and my health was much better too. One day three gentlemen came, one of them carrying a framed photograph. Many people had gathered that day to do obeisance to the 'Sadguru' of the Rani and to hear his religious advice. The gentleman placed the framed photo in such a manner that it was visible to everyone present. *The Statesman* had published the news of the air crash with a photograph up to the hip. This person had cut the photo out and framed it nicely. People who had gathered there looked at the photo and then at my face. Perplexed, many of them asked the gentleman, 'When did you click the snap of Bhagwan Guruji? Please give us a copy too.'... The gentleman then revealed that the photo was of Netaji. Imagine my intolerable situation!...He opened the frame with a knife and showed the clipping to everyone...The seniormost officer of the UP government was deputed to verify the truth. On his second visit he became my disciple...I left that place.[2]

Thus, at least initially, Bhagwanji used to sit face-to-face with his disciples giving commentaries about mysticism and yoga, till his identity was exposed. Also clear from this incident is that from early on, he started facing the problem of being identified and of his local associates talking about his identity, starting a whisper

---

2   Charanik, Oi Mahamanaba Ase, Jayasree Prakashan, 2010, pp 333-4. Translated
     from Bangla by Chandrachur Ghose.

campaign that often led to intervention by the local authorities. It was a pattern that would occur again and again. According to Chaudhary and validated by Bhagwanji himself, the first of such interventions happened in Rijor. As the news of a strange monk who looked and talked like Subhas Bose spread in the area, the state government asked the District Collector to investigate. The collector went in with the Superintendent of Police, resolute to break up a sham, but instead they became disciples of the holy man. The matter died there. It was in Mainpuri, Chaudhary claimed, that Bhagwanji started the practice of meeting people from behind a curtain. That, however, did not end his movements outside his residence. Rajkumar Shukla, Saraswati Devi's son, indicated to us that Bhagwanji at times went around and intermingled with people in religious places. Of course he did this on the sly, and till such time his 'cover' was blown. In subsequent years, he mostly ventured out at night with his face wrapped up like an Egyptian mummy. Perhaps that was just as well because he described himself as a 'ghost who walked'.

From Shikohabad, Bhagwanji shifted to Lucknow, where Chaudhary found a house for him at Singar Nagar, in the southern part of the city about half-an-hour away from the heart of the city at Hazratganj. The house exists to this day; the grandson of the Sikh gentleman who was Bhagwanji's landlord now lives there.

Lucknow was in an entirely different league from the small towns where Bhagwanji had been taking shelter until now. Apart from being the seat of the UP government, it was the playground of the who's who of Indian politics. It was a place with which Subhas Bose was familiar and was given a public reception when he was the Congress president and again later when he toured the country to consolidate his Forward Bloc. Among those who had organised his reception, one was now the Chief Minister and a few others would go on to occupy the state's highest political seat in the coming years.

A year or so before Bhagwanji set foot in the city, the then Chief Minister of the state, Govind Ballabh Pant, Subhas Bose's bête noire, had moved to New Delhi as the Union Home Minister. Pant was replaced by the scholarly and deeply spiritual Dr Sampurnanand. It is not known how, he and Bhagwanji got in touch. By all available accounts, Sampurnanand was the person who consistently made necessary arrangements for Bhagwanji, whose real identity he knew. Bhagwanji spoke about Sampurnanand and his younger brother Paripurnanand to his followers and referred to them in his letters. The Sampurnanand papers kept at the National Archives in New Delhi testify to the Congress stalwart's long and close association with Subhas Bose and a deep interest in the paranormal, a pet area of Bhagwanji. But it was in his book *Memories and Reflections*, which he finished writing in 1961 when he was no longer the UP chief minister, that Dr Sampurnanand devoted an unusually laudatory chapter about Bose and the INA. Referring to Bose, he wrote:

> He was one of the greatest fighters for freedom this country has known…Jawaharlalji always enjoyed Mahatmaji's confidence to an extent which no one among the younger men in the Congress did, but there was always a section of Congressmen who beleived that Subhash (sic) was much the abler of the two.[3]

---

3   Sampurnanand, *Memories and Reflections*, Asia Publishing House, pp 133-134.

Sampurnanand went on to recount that he had voted for Bose in his contest for Congress presidency in 1939 against Gandhi's nominee Pattabhi Sitaramayya. Later, when Bose travelled across the country to mobilise support for his Forward Bloc, 'I myself had the honour to be his host for three days in Lucknow.' Bose's former comrade was bitingly sarcastic about the top Congress leadership and their attitude towards him and his INA. Referring to Bose's fervent appeal to Gandhi, seeking his 'blessings and good wishes' for the war he had launched, Sampurnanand wrote:

> This was not to be. He received neither. There was universal appreciation in the country for his patriotism and courage. Even those leaders who had always tried to keep him at arm's length could not withhold their grudging need of praise when the news of his death arrived but not an iota of moral support had been extended to him from such quarters.[4]

Curiously enough, when the official line of his party and the central government was that Subhas Bose was dead, Sampurnanand wrote that 'what happened to Subhas Bose is still wrapped in mystery'.

> He is reported to have met his death as the result of an air accident but, among those who cherish his memory with respect and affection, there are some who believe that he is still alive and will someday come to India to lead the country to greater glory and prosperity.[5]

Dr Sampurnanand and Subhas Chandra Bose had entered

4   Ibid, p 138.
5   Ibid, p 138.

politics around the same time and both had joined the pro-changer camp of Chittaranjan Das, whose premature death robbed India of a top-rung leader, and rendered Mahatma Gandhi the undisputed leader of the country. Through Sampurnanand most likely, another person who became aware of Bhagwanji's presence in Lucknow was renowned Sanskrit scholar, philosopher and *tantra* expert Gopinath Kaviraj.

One day—so reads the diary of a Bhagwanji follower—Sampurnanand asked Bhagwanji: 'Do you know Tripathi?' Bhagwanji replied that he had heard his name. Sampurnanand then said: 'Tripathi's guru Gopinath Kaviraj has told him about you.' The reference was to the then home minister of the state and a would-be Central minister Kamalapati Tripathi, another believer in *tantric* rituals, who is said to have been a great influence in Indira Gandhi's quest for spirituality.

One can only conjecture what had actually made Sampurnanand broach the question of Subhas Bose's fate—as was claimed by a former Intelligence Bureau (IB) official—with Clement Attlee when the former British Prime Minister visited Lucknow in October 1956.

In 1982, retired IB official Dharmendra Gaur made a sensational claim that Attlee, who was PM from 1945 to 1951, told an inquisitive Dr Sampurnanand that he did not believe that Bose had died in any crash and that he had escaped to the USSR.[6]

---

6   Dharmendra Gaur, 'Netaji to Roos gaye thay—to fir?' *Amar Ujala*, 4 April 1982. Gaur also referred to it in his book *Mein Angrenjon ka jasoos tha* (Vijay Goel Publishers). In 1990, Gaur gave a detailed account to writer Ranjeet Panchalay, who relayed the information, including a signed note by Gaur, to Anuj Dhar.

Gaur further claimed the talk was bugged and the tape sent to the IB head office. There's no way to prove late Dharmendra Gaur's words, though he has left his version in writing.[7] At the same time, there's no doubting that Attlee did display an extraordinary candour during his visit to India. From Lucknow, Attlee proceeded to Calcutta, where on 22 October, he met Prime Minister Nehru at the Raj Bhavan. During his stay at the Raj Bhavan, Attlee told the acting Governor, who was Chief Justice of the Calcutta High Court, in the course of an informal talk that his deciding to set India free had more to do with Bose's activities than Gandhi's peaceful persuasion.[8]

While being provided with support by the Chief Minister of India's largest state was a remarkable development, the sketchy details available from the accounts left by Bhagwanji or his associates do not indicate an equally remarkable, if not more, development—the extent of his contact with the UP political establishment. Documents recovered from Ram Bhawan when read in the context of the state's then political situation, make us wonder about the magnitude of silence on Bhagwanji, which can't be but deliberate.

One of the letters discovered from Bhagwanji's belongings was a short one written by Banarasi Das on 15 July 1957. Born in 1912, Babu Banarasi Das had joined the freedom movement

---

7   Ibid.

8   Justice Phani Bhushan Chakravartti described his interaction with Attlee in a letter dated 30 March 1976, to Sureshchandra Das, publisher of historian Dr RC Majumdar. Subsequently in 1978, a facsimile copy of Chakravartti's letter was published by Dr Majumdar in his autobiographical book in Bengali, *Jibaner Smriti Deep*.

in his youth and worked his way up to the provincial leadership of the Congress party. According to an unconfirmed source, Das had joined the Naujawan Bharat Sabha (NBS) in 1928. Given the close connection between NBS and Subhas Bose (he presided over NBS conferences in Karachi in 1929 and in Mathura in 1931), it is not unlikely that their paths had crossed before he left the country. Das's letter—in which he tried to convince Bhagwanji of the necessity of a security perimeter and assured that such cover would be provided—gives away the fact that he knew the real identity of the mysterious monk. When he wrote to Bhagwanji, Das was only a parliamentary secretary in the UP government, and clearly not in a position to make such an arrangement on his own without alerting the senior ministers in the government, especially the minister in charge of police—Kamalapati Tripathi, the state home minister who had already been informed by Gopinath Kaviraj. Therefore, it is more likely that he was just the conduit for conveying their message to Bhagwanji, since this was not an official offer. It is needless to point out that it is not for any ordinary person that the high and mighty of a government offer to set up a security perimeter in such secrecy. There is no record or any witness account to suggest that Bhagwanji agreed to the proposal of a security perimeter. His interactions with Sampurnanand continued to be focused entirely on the spiritual. In fact, apart from a few instances of accepting minor non-religious logistical help, it appears that Bhagwanji wasn't ready to take up any debt of favour.

It wouldn't be irrelevant to mention that both Das and Tripathi went on to become chief ministers of UP. While Tripathi, who remained Chief Minister from April 1971 to June 1973, later served as the Railway Minister under Indira Gandhi, Banarasi Das headed the UP government from February 1979 to February 1980.

It is quite possible that another top politician in the state at that time would have known about Bhagwanji's presence. Although his name doesn't feature in any of the available documents from Ram Bhawan (much of which had been destroyed by Bhagwanji himself and same taken away after people gained access to Ram Bhawan), it can be said with reasonable amount of confidence that it wasn't possible for him to have remained in the dark. At the time of writing the letter offering security arrangements to Bhagwanji, Das served as the parliamentary secretary to Chandra Bhan Gupta (better known as CB Gupta)—Sampurnanand's opponent in the state Congress party, who eventually brought down his government. It defies reason that Das would do so without informing Gupta. Incidentally, one of the organisers of Bose's reception in Lucknow on 20 November 1938, who was also a member of the Uttar Pradesh Legislative Assembly at that time, was none other than Gupta. In 1939, Bose had deputed Gupta to resolve the inter-party conflict in Ajmer.[9] Gupta went on to serve thrice as Chief Minister—December 1960 to October 1963, March to April 1967 and finally from February 1969 to February 1970. Reporting on the birth centenary celebrations planned for Gupta in Lucknow in 2001, *The Times of India* saw it

---

9   *The Selected Works of Subhas Chandra Bose*, ed Ravindra Kumar, Atlantic Publishers & Distributors, Vol 1, pp 87, 102-104. It appears from the correspondence that Gupta could not take up the responsibility due to his prior engagements.

fit to describe him as 'an ardent follower' of Bose.[10]

Besides these four chief ministers, another piece of evidence indicating Bhagwanji's connection with a fifth one was found among the material recovered from Ram Bhawan. This innocuous looking piece of paper wasn't a letter and at first glance one could mistake it for details of a five-year deposit scheme, calculations for which were scribbled on one side. On the other side, however, was a rough sketch drawn by hand of the then Chief Minister's house at the city's posh residential area of Mall Road. The name of the politician wasn't written on the note, but the only chief minister to have been living in that area was Chaudhury Charan Singh, who headed the government twice—first from April 1967 to February 1968 and from February to October 1970—before going on to become first the Deputy Prime Minister and then the country's fifth Prime Minister. Many Bhagwanji followers have publicly claimed since 1985 that Charan Singh frequently visited him. Bhagwanji praised Singh's ideas and efforts about improving India's agrarian output. Thus, five chief ministers either knew about Bhagwanji's identity or were in contact with him. The remarkable thing about these connections was that Bhagwanji in no way seemed to have benefitted from the politicians—very unusual in a country where relationships between holy men or women and politicians have rarely been devoid of murky deals. In exchange for divine grace, such holy men almost invariably

---

10   CB Gupta Centenary Celebrations, *The Times of India*, 10 December 2001, https://timesofindia.indiatimes.com/city/lucknow/CB-Gupta-centenary-celebrations/articleshow/432367191.cms.

benefitted materially. But not Bhagwanji. He chose to refuse to be in proximity to power and the powerful.

The story of political connections does not get over yet. Another name that features a few times in the letters of Chaudhary and other pieces of paper found at Ram Bhawan is that of Raj Narain, freedom fighter, socialist and also the Leader of the Opposition in the UP Assembly. Narain later shot to national fame by winning the case of electoral malpractice against Prime Minister Indira Gandhi and later in 1977, by defeating her in the general elections. How much he knew exactly is not clear, but Chaudhary's letters mention some of Bhagwanji's associates meeting him. As the local newspapers started discussing the identity of Bhagwanji in October 1985, journalist Ashok Tandon had a surprise visitor one evening. Raj Narain questioned him for two hours on the details of his findings. He had rushed from Delhi, Narain told Tandon, only to find out more about Bhagwanji and had come over to him after meeting local officials. He promised to raise the issue across the country until the Government was compelled to establish the holy man's identity.[11] In what seems inexplicable now, the Foreign Broadcast Information Service (PBIS), an arm of the CIA found it important enough to pick up a news item published in the *Patriot* newspaper of Delhi to include in its foreign news compilation of March 1986. The published news had reported on 13 February 1986 that:

---

11   Ashok Tandon, *Gumnami Subhas*, Om Prakashan, 1986, p 138.

Mercurial and ebullient [sic] chief of the All-India Socialist Party Raj Narain, now convalescing in local Balrampur Hospital, today gave a seemingly bizarre explanation for his current illness. Mr Narain firmly believes that one Gumnami Baba who died at Faizabad was none other than Netaji Subhas Chandra Bose, and according to a local eveninger, the erstwhile 'Hanuman' has sufficient proof of this fact. The sad demise of the Baba, the report quoting the leader says, has 'shell-shocked' Mr Raj Narain to the extent that he had to be hospitalised.[12]

Nothing more happened on this front. Raj Narain was dead by the end of the year.

What then was Bhagwanji's nature of relationship with these political leaders? It is difficult to speculate. However, one thing is clear—that Bhagwanji was not contemplating any kind of material benefit—not even political ones. In turn that implies that the man of mystery wasn't even remotely interested in the partisan politics that he witnessed. Had he been, it is inconceivable that he wouldn't try to contact the most stringent opponents of Jawaharlal Nehru and Indira Gandhi—the Gandhian socialists Ram Manohar Lohia or Jayaprakash Narayan (JP). The Congress Socialists had let Subhas Chandra Bose down in 1939 when he had stood up in rebellion against the Congress high command, but JP had been one of the last persons with whom he had discussed organising a revolution before he left the country. Seeing the naked power struggle, the dog-eat-dog state of leadership, Bhagwanji meant every word when

---

12   Near East/South Asia Report, JPRS-NEA-86-040, Foreign Broadcast Information Service, p 99.

he castigated his followers, 'Indian politics! Ugh! It stinks!'

In Lucknow, Bhagwanji again faced the risk of his identity being blown in public, an incident he narrated to his Calcutta followers. Needing a new pair of glasses, Bhagwanji checked into BN Baijal Opticals—a famous optician's shop in Lucknow's Ameena Bagh that in the past had for a client Mahatma Gandhi himself.[13] While trying out a round-rimmed one, Bhagwanji, clean-shaven like a Buddhist monk, removed his headgear and looked into a mirror. In an instant, his shaved bald pate and familiar-looking visage stunned another customer. 'Netaji!', he whispered. In an instant, two young men threw themselves at his feet. Bhagwanji had to make a hasty retreat. 'This is why I now keep this moustache and beard,' he summed up the moral of the story to the Calcutta followers a few years later.

Although he survived a dire situation by the skin of his teeth, this incident does bring us some important details: that he would venture out of his residence, even if occasionally, and that a chauffeur-driven car designed to hide the passenger had been put at his disposal by some unknown persons.

Chaudhary claimed that he arranged a meeting between Bhagwanji and then Railways Minister Lal Bahadur Shastri. According to Chaudhary, Shastri came down to Singar Nagar to meet Bhagwanji without knowing his true identity. They discussed only spiritual matters, sitting on either side of the curtain. Like many of Chaudhary's other claims, there is no way to verify if

13 Neha Shukla, 'Bapu wrote to us thanking us for making his specs,' *The Times of India* (Lucknow edition), 3 October 2017.

there is any truth to this one.

Bhagwanji himself admitted in a letter written many years later to one of his key disciples that he used to be visited by the Chief Minister, other Ministers, members of royal families, including some descendants of the last Nawab of Awadh.[14]

Yet, it is clear that although many of the top political leaders and government functionaries in Uttar Pradesh, including the Chief Minister, knew about Bhagwanji, they maintained complete silence as long as they lived. As we go along, we will probe further Bhagwanji's connections with those in power.

Before long, however, a new trouble disrupted the relative stability of Bhagwanji's life. Being annoyed by the time and money invested by Chaudhary on Bhagwanji without receiving any material benefit for their family in return, his brother-in-law approached a senior bureaucrat of the state complaining that Chaudhary was being duped by a Bengali mendicant who pretended to be Netaji. The bureaucrat, according to Chaudhary, had him taken into custody by Hazratganj police station for interrogation and Bhagwanji had to leave the Singar Nagar residence, apprehensive of the possibility that under pressure Chaudhary might give out secrets that were so vital to him.

Bhagwanji shifted to the house of a Muslim gentleman in Khadra, on the other side of the Gomti river for a couple of weeks and from there moved again to a house on the banks of the river. One day, Chhotelal Dwivedi found a monk at his doorstep asking

---

14   Bhagwanji's letter to Pabitra Mohan Roy, September 1975.

for a place to stay for a short period. Dazzled by the personality of the monk, a spiritually inclined Dwivedi immediately agreed to let him stay in a vacant quarter of his house without charging any rent. Dwivedi would watch Bhagwanji sit quietly on the steps leading to the river and doing puja in the adjoining Shiv temple and the in-house temple for hours. Just as he came, Bhagwanji decided to leave suddenly informing Dwivedi only a few days prior. At the time of leaving he gave enough hints to Dwivedi about his identity. Wherever Bhagwanji stayed, his unusual ways aroused suspicions and this place was no exception. The reason for his leaving, he told his landlord, was that as news about his identity was spreading, more people were getting curious. It was time to find a new place. Understanding what he was dealing with, Dwivedi never said a word about this period to anyone except his son.[15]

Between Singar Nagar and Dwivedi's house, Bhagwanji had to spend some time on a ghat—most probably the Devraha Ghat—on the banks of Gomti under a temporary shelter of tarpaulin, as he couldn't find shelter anywhere.[16]

In the entire saga of Bhagawanji, people came and left, some visiting occasionally, some through letters while others just vanished. Barring a few minor gaps, only one person stayed with him till the end, running the household wherever they moved,

15 Discussion with OP Dwivedi, son of Chhotelal Dwivedi, who works in the office of DGP, Lucknow. Chhotelal Dwivedi died in 2002. The credit for finding out the house from old photographs goes to Adheer Som.
16 Deposition of Rajkumar Shukla to the Justice Mukherjee Commission of Inquiry, Faizabad, 13 August 2001.

protecting him from unwanted interference of outsiders and taking care of the disciples when they visited. To Bhagwanji, she was 'Matushri Jagadamba' or mother of the universe (Jagadamba in the vocative case). Saraswati Devi Shukla was a young widow when she joined Bhagwanji as a domestic help. Accompanying Saraswati Devi was her six-year-old son Rajkumar and her father Mahadev Prasad Mishra. While Rajkumar stayed with his mother, Mishra would occasionally visit Bhagwanji. Saraswati Devi told the reporters of *NIP* that it was in Nepal where he used to teach that Mishra learnt about Bhagwanji's existence. Mishra had access to a royal priest of Nepal, and it has been claimed that the Nepal royals knew about Bhagwanji. Apart from a small amount of Nepalese currency recovered from his room in Ram Bhawan, this connection would come up in Bhagwanji's discussions with some of his followers in Calcutta.

Time was up in Lucknow after spending about two years. With Chaudhary, Bhagwanji left for Naimisharanya (now better known as Neemsar, located in Sitapur district) during the Navaratri (September/October) of 1958. If Lucknow epitomises the urbane heritage of the Nawabs, the British Raj and finally the political elite of free India, the rustic Neemsar is one of the most important symbols of India's mythological past. Chaudhary arranged their stay at a dharmashala; meals came from a local Bengali hotel. After staying there for a few months, Bhagwanji shifted to a Shiv temple very close to the famous *chakra teertha*. According to local history, the temple is about 800 years old.

Saraswati Devi had been away from Bhagwanji when he had lived at Dwivedi's house in Lucknow and it appears Chaudhary again arranged for her and Rajkumar to join Bhagwanji at Neemsar. Mahadev Prasad Mishra, who accompanied them, left strict instructions with his daughter never to leave Bhagwanji's service.[17] Chaudhary left Neemsar around the same time that Bhagwanji moved into the Shiv temple.

Bhagwanji's strange ways had already started drawing the attention of the small-town populace which was a few thousands at that time: people had started talking about the holy man purportedly with great powers who remained confined in his room. Panda Shiv Narayan, the priest of the temple and his wife whom Bhagwanji addressed as 'Durga Ma' were in awe of their guest. As news spread, visitors started coming in to talk to the mysterious holy man. Sitting on the terrace of the building adjoining the temple, Bhagwanji would address the visitors on religion and philosophy, across a curtain. As time passed by, the number of visitors kept increasing and the whispers among locals about the Bengali baba started getting stronger.

There were obvious security risks with the way things were going. As a preliminary measure, Bhagwanji had *amla* and mango saplings planted in the courtyard to prevent the unhampered view of the temple. Trouble erupted soon from two directions. Driven by their animosity towards the relatively better-off Shiv Narayan whose prestige had been enhanced by the presence of a crowd-pulling mystic, other priests in the town started plotting to pry Bhagwanji away to their respective ashrams and temples.

---

17 Bhagwanji's letter to Pabitra Mohan Roy, September 1975. Rajkumar Shukla has no memory of how he reached Neemsar along with his mother and maternal grandfather.

To add to this problem, Chaudhary's sister appeared on the scene, determined to oust Saraswati Devi so that she could take her place. She threatened that she would make public the secret that Bhagwanji was none other than Subhas Chandra Bose. The two forces soon combined, escalating Bhagwanji's problems. Matters soon reached a stage where intruders raided the temple in the dark of the night to physically harm Saraswati Devi and Rajkumar. To their shock, they found Bhagwanji standing in the way. The sight of the unarmed elderly *sanyasi* made them scramble for safety, but not before dealing a few unintended blows on him.

With the situation threatening to go out of control, both Durga Ma and Jagadamba took matters in their hand. They descended on the other priests as well as Chaudhary's sister with a fiery tongue lashing to keep them away from causing further damage. But some damage was already done. The growing whispers of 'Netaji' living in the temple in disguise, coupled with the machinations of the priests and Chaudhary's sister brought the local police to Bhagwanji's doorstep. When the sub-inspector who came first to investigate failed to go beyond a fierce Saraswati Devi who wouldn't let him go anywhere close to Bhagwanji, he returned the next day with the station officer and a team of constables, accompanied by around fifty to sixty of Shivnarayan's opponents.

'This fellow received a good thrashing from the hands of my mother,' Bhagwanji told his Calcutta associates later. What followed was a repeat of a similar situation in Rijor a few years ago and would occur again. Bhagwanji called the station officer inside and spoke with him for half an hour. By the time the officer emerged from Bhagwanji's room, he had become a disciple.[18]

The whispers had reached the office of the District Magistrate too. However, his request for an investigation was promptly turned down by Lucknow. He was told not to disturb a *sanyasi* who was not involved in any unlawful activities, merely on the basis of rumours. The magistrate was given strict instructions not to pay any heed to rumours of Netaji being around.[19] Curiously enough, this information was shared by Bhagwanji himself with his followers. The question that naturally arises is—how did he know about official confidential correspondence? It wouldn't be unreasonable to guess that the same powers that stopped the magistrate from meddling also informed him of what was going on.

Bhagwanji also claimed that following these incidents, the District Magistrate, the Sub-Divisional Officer and the Superintendent of Police offered him police protection, but he refused. He knew accepting such an offer would only make matters worse: the rumours would fly faster and farther with a grave risk to his anonymity.

One of the regular visitors to the Shiv temple who was mesmerised hearing Bhagwanji chant Sanskrit hymns with flawless pronunciation and melodious voice was Shivnarayan's brother-in-law Srikant Sharma. He approached Saraswati Devi for permission to meet Bhagwanji, 'so that I can see him and I can take his shelter'. Sharma was allowed to talk to Bhagwanji, but

18   Charanik, Oi Mahamanaba Ase, Jayasree Prakashan, 2010, pp 338-340.
19   Ibid, p 341.

only from beyond the curtain. Before long, however, Srikant was going to get luckier.[20]

During Subhas Bose's tour of the United Provinces in 1939, Sharma had seen him at Sitapur, Sidhauli and Biswan. When he did get to talk to Bhagwanji, his curiosity was further aroused.

In the summer of 1962, Professor Atul Sen—a freedom fighter who had been acquainted with the top leaders of his times— Gandhi, Nehru, Bose included—fainted while touring some remote area in Naimisharanya. He was brought to the temple complex where he conversed with Bhagwanji. On his return to Calcutta, Sen told his friend Dr RC Majumdar, the historian, that he had spoken with Subhas Bose.

Confused, Dr Majumdar would go on to write in 1966 in a Bengali magazine that while the holy man did not appear before Sen (whom the historian did not mention by name), he told him many past episodes which were not likely to be known to others. 'Highly educated and respected gentleman really believed that the person with whom he had conversed with was Netaji,' wrote Majumdar.[21] Meanwhile, ignoring Bhagwanji's caution, Prof Sen wrote to Prime Minister Nehru on 28 August 1962:

Dear Jawaharlal Ji,
I take the liberty of addressing these few lines to you in the matter of the widely prevalent belief that Netaji Subhas Chandra Bose

---

20 All information attributed to Srikant Sharma is based on his deposition to the Justice Mukherjee Commission of Inquiry which took place on 14 August 2001 at Faizabad. Anuj Dhar also spoke to him at length.

21 This was narrated by Sunil Das before the Khosla Commission. A freedom fighter and Bhagwanji follower in secret, Das was also the editor of *Jayasree*, the magazine in which Dr Majumdar had written about Atul Sen's experience.

is not dead. Mine is not mere belief but actual knowledge that Netaji is alive and is engaged in spiritual practice somewhere in India. Not the Sadhu of Shoulmari, Cooch-Behar, in West Bengal about whom some Calcutta politicians are making a fuss at this moment. I deliberately make the location a little vague because from the talks I had with him for months together not very long ago I could understand that he is yet regarded as Enemy No 1 of the Allied Powers and that there is a secret protocol that binds the Government of India to deliver him to allied 'justice' if found alive.

If you can persuade yourself to assure me that his information is not correct or even if it is correct your Government shall resist any action by any of the said powers against the Great Patriot I may try to persuade him to return to open life.[22]

Nehru's response was somewhat odd. One, in view of his own repeated pronouncements that Bose had died in 1945, he shouldn't have taken kindly to Sen's claim that Bose was alive. Two, the bit about a secret protocol was so patently absurd that it warranted a contemptuous dismissal. Since Nehru had a marvellous intellectual capacity to personally dictate cogent responses to the numerous letters he received from all over the country each day, it cannot be assumed that he did not apply his mind while responding to Sen's seemingly nonsensical posers on so important an issue. But Nehru's 31 August reply to Sen didn't even touch upon the main issue of Bose being alive, as if he wanted to avoid any discussion on it. Nehru, however, was

---

22 Copy of this letter and Jawaharlal Nehru's response were obtained by the authors from the Ministry of Home Affairs through the Right to Information Act of 2005.

emphatic in his denial of the alleged secret protocol. 'Even if any country asks the Government of India to hand him [Bose] over, it is not going to be agreed to.'

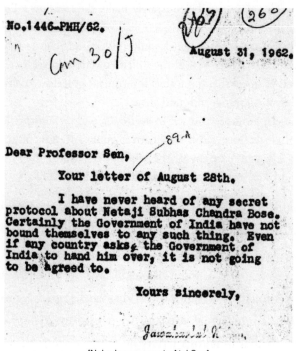

No.1446-PHH/62.

August 31, 1962.

Dear Professor Sen,

Your letter of August 28th.

I have never heard of any secret protocol about Netaji Subhas Chandra Bose. Certainly the Government of India have not bound themselves to any such thing. Even if any country asks the Government of India to hand him over, it is not going to be agreed to.

Yours sincerely,

[Nehru's response to Atul Sen]

Sen would never get to be in touch with Bhagwanji again, but the word about his meeting 'Netaji' reached a small group of people in Calcutta. They were former members of the old revolutionary group Anushilan Samity, which at one point of time included in its fold even Bhagat Singh and Dr Keshav Baliram Hegdevar, who would set up the Rashtriya Swayamsevak Sangh (RSS) later. The veterans called a secret meeting and decided to send Dr Pabitra Mohan Roy, to verify Atul Sen's claim.

[Dr Pabitra Mohan Roy]

Nothing on his ordinary, bespectacled face told of Roy's daredevil past in the service of the nation. A medical doctor by training, he had followed Subhas Bose to SE Asia for the cause of India's freedom. Riding on a Japanese submarine, Roy returned to India in 1944 as an INA secret service operative. But his mission was doomed by betrayal. A fast-track trial under the Enemy Agents Ordinance against Pabitra, fellow spy Americk Singh Gill and Haridas Mitra, who had dared to shelter them, commenced in May and by June-end their execution orders were out. The sentence was eventually commuted and Roy was released in 1946. At the time he made his journey towards Neemsar, he was also serving the last year of his term as a member of the state's Legislative Assembly (See Appendix B for a biographical sketch of Pabitra Mohan Roy).

Pabitra undertook the visit to meet Bhagwanji at a time when a sensational claim that Subhas Bose was not only alive but he was in India in the guise of a holy man in Shaulmari pocket of the Cooch Behar district of Bengal, had created a commotion in the state. This was despite the Nehru government officially declaring in 1956 that Bose had died in Taiwan following a fatal air crash. The official stand was based on the findings of free India's first official inquiry into Bose's fate, headed by Shah Nawaz Khan, former INA man and a hero of the Red Fort trials. SN Mitra, an ICS officer then serving as the Chief Commissioner of Andamans represented the government in the committee, and Suresh Bose, Netaji's elder brother, the Bose family.

It had all begun with a showdown in Calcutta on 6 September 1955 during a meeting of Netaji memorial committee. As a participant, Shah Nawaz, now a Congress leader, inadvertently triggered a backlash against the Government by telling the gathering that the Prime Minister was not ready for any official probe into Bose's death. It resulted in the adoption of a resolution envisioning a public-funded inquiry into the mystery. If it had come into being, this civil society-led unofficial committee would have had Justice Radha Binod Pal as its head. Pal enjoyed an iconic status in Japan due to his dissenting pro-Japan judgment at the Tokyo war crimes tribunal. The judge already had some idea about the Bose death issue. He had been dramatically informed by a fellow American judge that the Taipei crash was 'possibly a myth'. Pal discussed it publicly more than once. 'The whole thing demands a thorough investigation,' he wrote in 1953. 'Statements by individuals made here and there will not convince me as to the truth of the story given out. I have reasons to doubt its correctness.'[23]

In pursuance of the Calcutta resolution, Shah Nawaz Khan met Prime Minister Nehru. He was thereafter never seen again by the side of those who doubted the crash theory. Gone was the man who had himself believed that his former leader never

---

23   Letter to AM Nair. Facsimile appended in Suresh Bose's Dissentient Report.

perished in any air crash, as the following 1948 intelligence report
released by Bengal government shows:

Place and attendance.	Organized by.	President.	Speakers.
4. Curzon Park (100).	India Tomorrow Club.	KARTICK CHANDRA BASU.	1. BIREN BASU, 2. JYOTISH CH. DUTTA, 3. President.

At No.1 SHAH NAWAZ said that he believed Netaji was
still alive and that his return depended on the
international situation, He stressed the need for
giving military training to the youths to make
India strong.
A poster exhibition was held at 86B, Gopinath Dutta Lane. It was organized by the Bangiya
Bandhab Samity and opened by SRI KSHITISH CHANDRA
BASU. Pictures depicting the Sepoy Mutiny, the
march of the I.N.A. at Imphal, the famine of 1943
and the photos of BHAGAT SINGH, KHUDIRAM BASU were
exhibited.

The Nehru government suddenly woke up to Shah Nawaz's
eminence. There was a shift in the official position, which had
till then remained stridently opposed to a proper investigation.
'I have said that the question of Netaji Subhas Chandra Bose's
death is, I think, settled beyond doubt. There can be no inquiry
about that,' Nehru had stated in September 1955.[24] But on 13
October 1955, he minuted in an official note that in consultation
with the Indian ambassador in Japan, BR Sen, and Bengal Chief
Minister Dr BC Roy, he had decided to set up the Shah Nawaz
committee to probe Bose's death. Nehru also noted that he did

---

24   Suresh Bose, Dissentient Report.

not 'think it necessary' to 'consult Shri Subhas Chandra Bose's wife in Vienna'.[25] The PM defined the task before the official inquiry panel in the following words: 'The purpose of the inquiry will be to find the circumstances of the death.' The Indian embassy in Tokyo thereafter took up the issue with the Japanese foreign ministry. The director of Asian Affairs Division told AK Dar, the point man in the Indian embassy, that the Indian government's proposal to inquire into Bose's death was 'acceptable to the Government of Japan in the terms in which the proposal was made by the Indian Ambassador to the Foreign Minister [of Japan]' at the specific instruction of Prime Minister Nehru. Dar's subsequent note for New Delhi threw further light on 'the terms' and their implied meaning:

3.   Mr. Nakagawa added that the Government of Japan hopes that there would be no departure from the main objective in view and extraneous enquiries and aside researches would not be made.

[National Archives, New Delhi]

To ensure that there was 'no departure from the main objective in view', the terms of reference for the Shah Nawaz Committee came preloaded with the assumption that Bose had died following an air crash.

---

25 All official quotations, unless specified otherwise, are from the files declassified by the Government of India since January 2016. These files can be accessed from: http://www.netajipapers.gov.in/.

[From left: SN Maitra, Shah Nawaz Khan, a Japanese witness and Suresh Bose during the course of their inquiry. National Archives, New Delhi]

The committee examined 67 witnesses in India and outside. Day one of its inquiry was rather dramatic. Subhas Bose's close aide Muthuramalingam Thevar appeared as the witness No 1. His claims, which didn't make much sense to most people, sent Suresh Bose and the Government on a collision course. Thevar charged that the terms of reference of the committee reflected a foregone conclusion. He gave Shah Nawaz a piece of his mind and then held a press conference in Delhi on 3 April. Making a most unbelievable claim that he had met Subhas Bose in China recently, Thevar told the media that he would furnish conclusive proof that Bose was alive if the inquiry committee was reconstituted under Dr Radha Binod Pal's lead. 'The Government must make it known categorically to the public whether Netaji's name is still in the list of war criminals and if not, when it was removed and how?'[26] Thevar's bizarre claims did not have any takers except for Suresh Bose, who took them up with the Prime Minister. Nehru subsequently recorded:

---

26 'Story of meeting Netaji last February,' *Hindustan Standard*, 4 April 1956.

Our effort should be to get as many facts as possible about Netaji Subhas Chandra Bose's last days—the disappearance or death or whatever it was. Apart from direct evidence which we have thus far received and which may further be obtained, it seems to me almost inconceivable that Netaji should be alive. Over ten years have passed since the aircraft accident. Even if he had escaped then I cannot conceive how he could possibly remain silent during all these years when it was very easy for him to communicate in various ways with India.

Senior Pakistan government official Habibur Rahman's deposition before the committee in New Delhi marked his first and last appearance in India since Partition. As the most important witness to Netaji's 'death' in Taipei, he was expected to make a long statement and a comprehensive one he did make in support of the air crash theory. In graphic details he described Subhas Bose's death. But, after he had recorded his official version, Rahman spoke indiscreetly to Suresh Bose's right-hand man Sunil Krishna Gupta: 'Let them declare that Netaji is dead. It will be our double gain when he returns!'[27] Rahman's interrogation reports of 1945-46, now declassified, show that his version of Bose's death was not believed by his interrogators. 'Throughout the protracted questioning, resentment was visible from ...[his] face and he made no bones about it,' the Intelligence Bureau was informed in April 1946.[28]

---

27   Sunil Gupta in conversation with Anuj Dhar. He also referred to his meeting
       with Rahman in his testimony before the Khosla Commission.
28   Re-interrogation of Capt Habibur Rahman, File 400/INA, 9 April 1946,
       National Archives of India, New Delhi.

In July 1956, the committee members discussed their respective findings. Suresh Bose enumerated a number of discrepancies and contradictions he had detected in the air crash narrative and Bose's death in Taiwan. He rested his case saying he was veering towards the conclusion that there had been no plane crash at all. Shah Nawaz told Suresh Bose that in that case he would have to write a separate dissenting report. The last meeting Suresh Bose had with Shah Nawaz as a member of the Netaji Inquiry Committee was on 16 July. Shah Nawaz frowned and asked him to vacate the committee's office. 'Spoilsport' Suresh was now at the receiving end of the government officer's tantrums. As per his account, he was humiliated, compelled to leave Delhi and 'not a single piece of important and relevant paper or exhibit from the record' was officially provided to him for writing his report. On 29 July, Suresh Bose received a communication from Shah Nawaz demanding he should submit his dissenting report in two days. He saw the Government's hand behind the pressure tactics. A few days later, the Shah Nawaz–Maitra findings were leaked out to a Calcutta newspaper. Suresh immediately sent a letter to Shah Nawaz with a copy to the Prime Minister. The PM's 13 August reply brought him little comfort. Nehru theorised that the leak 'was some kind of an intelligent guess by some reporter or some clerk in our office here. Obviously, the chairman of the inquiry committee had nothing to do with it'. Angered, Suresh Bose wrote back:

> When the chairman curtly turned down my request for relevant papers, I suspected that without inspiration from higher ups, he would not have had the audacity to decline the legitimate

request of his colleague. My opinion has now been confirmed.[29]

Nehru did not respond to this scathing attack accusing his government of trying to muffle Suresh's views. After some days, Bengal Chief Minister Dr BC Roy, an old political supporter-turned-rival of Subhas Bose, started backchannel manoeuvres. Those were rainy days for Dwijendra Bose, son of Satish Chandra Bose, the eldest brother of Subhas. The Chief Minister spoke to him over the phone. 'Hello! Dwijendra, I am in search of you. Why are you afraid of seeing me? Come here [to my office].' The discussion (as recalled subsequently by Dwijendra) continued in the chief minister's office. 'What are you doing in this business, earning a thousand here or a thousand there? How will you keep your family prestige with this paltry income?...I will give you business.' Dwijendra wasn't averse to the idea. 'You are a friend of the family—[rather] you were in the 30s [and] in the 20s. If you are in love with the family again, I am here, you can give me business. I will take it.'

Clearly it was not love. Roy gave out that it would have to be a trade and the price to be paid by Dwijendra was, 'You get the report of Shah Nawaz signed by Suresh and I will give you whatever business you want.'

'Not at that cost! I will never ask my uncle,' Dwijendra was blunt in his response.[30] Roy then had Suresh Bose come over to the Writers' Building. As Suresh entered his chamber, Roy confronted

---

29   Suresh Bose, *Dissentient Report.*
30   Record of examination of Dwijendra Nath Bose at the GD Khosla Commission of Inquiry, 8 August 1972, Proceedings of the Khosla Commission, Vol XI, pp 3314-15.

him. 'Subhas is dead. How come you are stating to the contrary?'

'Who told you that Subhas is dead?' Suresh shot back. Roy recounted the statements of some witnesses and Suresh discounted them citing the findings of intelligence agencies. Thereafter, Roy asked Suresh if he would like to be a Governor. This led to an exchange of heated words. Suresh Bose would allege that if he had signed the official report, his 'reward would have been the governorship of Bengal'.[31]

Unlike this particular episode, it can now be proven with the aid of official records that the Nehru government resorted to the doctoring of records to shore up evidence in favour of the official line. As it happened, the then Director, Intelligence Bureau (DIB) BN Mullick supplied Shah Nawaz a dossier of the British-era intelligence reports. The selection was made in such a way so as to tip the needle in favour of the air crash theory. The first report in the dossier was from PES Finney, IB Assistant Director before Independence. Dated 5 September 1945, this report comprised 10 points. The conclusion of the report looked as if Finney was fully backing the air crash theory:[32]

telegrams; along with numerous other documents, must have been purposely left where the British would find them. But in that case one would have expected some report from the Staff Officer to be on the file, whereas the series is incomplete. Although at this stage one cannot rule out the possibility of Bose being still alive, and of these telegrams being part of a deception plan regarding himself, (particularly in view of his previous intentions of escaping to Russia), the general impression gained from the study of these documents and the talk with Isoda and my informant is that Bose did actually die as stated.

.   .   .   .   .

Sd. P.E.S.Finney.
Assistant Director,
Intelligence Bureau,Govt.of India.
Attached I.A.U. 7 Division
Bangkok.

[National Archives, New Delhi]

31   Record of the examination of Suresh Bose before the Khosla Commission.

32   Copy of the report supplied by the Ministry of Home Affairs under the Right to Information Act, 2005.

The four dots at the end of the para represented deletion. What was deleted? On checking recently declassified documents, we found that points 11 and 12 were left out of this truncated document. These points overturn the impression generated by the doctored document that Bose had died. After outlining the general impression, Finney had actually detailed a further line of investigation to assess its validity and suggested circulation of 'any conclusive information, one way or the other' because he could foresee that the inquiry would take a long time. Here's how the report actually looked like in the uncensored copy:

whereas the series is incomplete. Although at this stage one cannot rule out the possibility of Bose being still alive, and of these telegrams being part of a deception plan regarding himself, (particularly in view of his previous intentions of escaping to Russia), the general impression gained from the study of these documents and the talk with Isoda and my informant is that Bose did actually die as stated.

11. The following line of investigation is suggested :
(a) tracing and examining of staff officer TADA in Japan.
(b) examination of Swami in Penang.
(c) Further examination in detail of Lieut. Gen. Isoda.
(d) examination of Hikari personnel in Saigon.
(e) search of Hikari documents in Saigon.
(f) examination of Chief-of-Staff or other staff-officers of Southern Army in Saigon who know about these telegrams.
(g) tracing and examination of Col. Habibur Rahman.
(h) search of photographs, remains or ashes, etc. of Bose in Saigon, where they may have been sent, or in Tokyo.

12. Considerable time is being spent on these enquiries, and it is therefore requested that any conclusive information, one way or the other, should be circulated as soon as possible.

Sd/-
Asst. Director,
Intelligence Bureau,
Govt. of India,
attached I.A.U.
7 Divn.
Bangkok.

[Last part of original report by PES Finney, Assistant Director, IB. File 273/INA, National Archives, New Delhi]

On 3 August 1956, the Shah Nawaz report (ghost written by SN Maitra) was handed over to the Prime Minister. It concluded that 'Bose met his death in an air crash, and that the ashes now at Renkoji temple, Tokyo, are his ashes.' The report recommended that the ashes should be 'brought to India with due honour, and a memorial erected over them at a suitable place'. The Union Cabinet approved the majority report on 9 September. According to an official record, 'the Cabinet also decided that question of bringing over Netaji's ashes to India might be left for future consideration'. On 11 September, a reassured Prime Minister placed the report before Parliament. Newspapers the world over carried the news prominently the next day. 'Anti-British Indian dead, inquiry finds,' was *The New York Times* headline. At home, *The Hindu* lead story was: 'Death of Netaji established: Overwhelming evidence obtained.' In the Rajya Sabha, the Prime Minister adroitly fended off the few discontented lawmakers. 'Mr Nehru said the Government felt that the evidence put forth in the report was adequate and no reasonable person who read it could come to any other conclusion. If a person had an unreasonable mind, it was difficult to reason with him.'

Afterwards, helped by secret records Sunil Krishna Gupta had obtained surreptitiously, Suresh Bose went on to write his *Dissentient Report*. In it, he accused Shah Nawaz of carrying out his inquiry 'not with the intention of arriving at the truth, but to fill up the gaps in the evidence and for explaining and reconciling discrepant and contradictory statements that stood in the way of his coming to the conclusion that the plane had crashed and that Netaji had died'. He stated that the evidence he had come across as member of the committee proved that Subhas had escaped to the USSR.

> It would have been an act of extreme meanness and downright treachery on the part of the Japanese government to have handed over Netaji, their erstwhile friend and collaborator, to the Anglo-Americans, and of this they were incapable, as a self-respecting and a cultured nation. The only other alternative, therefore, was to broadcast his death after he had left, and continue to support it with manufactured and tutored evidence... They could not very well say that Netaji had escaped from their territory to an unknown destination, as they would have been accused of aiding and abetting the flight of a man who, in the eyes of the Anglo-Americans, was a war criminal.

Suresh Bose concluded his report with an 'appeal to my countrymen'. His demand for transparency in the matter was an impossible act to follow then. He called on the people not to accept either his or Shah Nawaz–Shankar Maitra report and instead,

> make a demand to our Government to place at their disposal the whole evidence that was made available to the committee and... form their own opinion after a careful perusal and consideration of the same, and, if the general opinion be that the aircraft accident did not take place and that Netaji Subhas Chandra Bose did not die, as alleged, to demand an impeachment of all those who have taken part in this nefarious game.

Suresh Bose's report was not accepted by the Government. The relevant declassified file[33] shows that Nehru took the decision without reading it.

PRIME MINISTER'S SECRETARIAT

I did not know that Shri Suresh Chandra Bose's dissentient note had been received by us. In any event, I think we should place it on the table of the House. As a matter of fact, the Hindustan Standard is going to publish the whole of it serially.

2.   I have no idea how big the report is. It does not appear necessary to get it printed. It should be enough to place, let us say, two copies on the table of the House.

3.   I think that one answer should be framed to all these questions. It should state (1) that a separate report has been received from Shri Suresh Chandra Bose. This will be laid on the table of the House. (2) The Government of India have accepted the findings of the majority of the Netaji Subhas Chandra Bose Enquiry Committee and find no reason to vary that decision. (3) As has been previously stated, the question of bringing the ashes to India is dependent not merely on the Government's wishes, but on other factors. In view of this fact, no steps can be taken at present either to bring the ashes to India or in regard to a suitable memorial.

J. Nehru
(J. Nehru)
5.11.1956

[Jawaharlal Nehru's memo on Suresh Bose's *Dissentient Report*. Source: National Archives of India]

---

33   File No 24 (20) – FEA/56, Ministry of External Affairs, National Archives of India. The Committee functioned under the MEA and Nehru was the External Affairs Minister.

Shah Nawaz and SN Maitra were allegedly 'rewarded' for their good work. One became a deputy minister and the other flew out on a plum diplomatic assignment. Shah Nawaz remained in the limelight as minister and head of several government entities for the rest of his life. Hailed as an embodiment of 'truth, integrity and patriotism' by Prime Minister Indira Gandhi following his death in 1982, Shah Nawaz in his lifetime had to endure barbs from Bose's near and dear ones for his 'betrayal,' his 'command performance' for Nehru. *Kya bhaijaan, deputy ministership ke liye aapne Netaji ko maar diyya!* (Brother, you killed Netaji for deputy ministership!) Suresh Bose's daughter Shiela Sengupta taunted him once.[34]

The Government made its position official, but the Shah Nawaz Committee report went largely disregarded and disbelieved. The matter lay dormant for a few years until a new sensation erupted from a small village in north Bengal in the early 1960s just as the country was being thrown into the vortex of India–China war.

---

34   Shiela Sengupta in conversation with Anuj Dhar.

THREE

A SADHU HERE AND A SADHU THERE

RUMBLINGS IN THE Bengal press began early in 1962 adding the Shoulmari dimension to the Bose mystery. All of a sudden, some people with links to Subhas Bose in the past began propagating that the mysterious Swami Saradananda living in an ashram in a remote village in the Cooch Behar district of north Bengal called Shoulmari was Subhas Bose himself. Rumours spread thick and fast, and by early 1962 the 'Sadhu of Shoulmari' was the talk of the entire state. The way the Bengal government reacted to this scenario was baffling. The state police and intelligence apparatus were rattled by the claim, no matter how preposterous it appeared on the face of it. Completely ignoring the fact that Subhas was officially dead, the state government machinery went into an overdrive to find out who Saradananda really was. As early as 1961, the police had laid a secret siege to the Shoulmari ashram. On 6 September 1961, the Deputy Commissioner of Police, Cooch Behar, informed the state's Home Secretary, 'Careful watch has been kept by the police on the ashram, but so far it has not been possible for the police to locate and identify the sadhu.'

In spite of the veil of secrecy around Saradananda and his identity, it became clear early on that there were some ambitious plans to expand the activities of the ashram when the ashram administration advertised in newspapers for recruitment of legal advisers, teachers and other administrative officials at high salaries. Appeals for donations to the ashram were also issued.

Amidst this confusing state of affairs, a key member of the ashram's administration who was very close to Saradananda, Haripada Basu, added fuel to the fire by sending telegrams to both Prime Minister Nehru and Chief Minister Dr BC Roy to the effect that Saradananda was none else than Subhas Bose.[1] Haripada was promptly expelled from the ashram and a denial was issued, but given his standing in the area, local people lent a high degree of credence to his claim. 'It is hereby emphatically announced that the founder of the Shoulmari Ashram is not Netaji Subhas Chandra Bose nor had he any relationship with Shri Netaji…I respectfully request my countrymen not to put any credence to this myth,' read a declaration issued a few days later by Ramani Ranjan Das, secretary of the ashram.

In March, more information was unearthed by the police. Reporting to the Deputy Inspector General of police, the

---

1   Copy of a report dated 11 February 1962 of a district intelligence officer, Jalpaiguri.

Superintendent of the Government Railway Police, Sealdah, wrote that Saradananda appeared in Falakata, a town about sixty kilometres from Shoulmari in early 1959[2] and approached Usha Rani Das, wife of Dr Ramani Ranjan Das. Dr Das gave up his practice from the day he met Saradananda and donated all his assets for the purpose of setting up the ashram at Shoulmari. He also gave up his post as a secretary in the local Congress party. Dr Das's father, however, confided to a relative who worked in the police department that although he hadn't met Saradananda, he believed that the monk was Netaji. The ongoing investigation revealed that Saradananda was brought to Falakata by a local tobacco merchant from Sonapur Chowpatty, about fifteen miles away from the town. Soon, a more detailed denial of any linkage between Saradananda and Subhas Chandra Bose was issued by Dr Gope Gur-Bux, the ashram's public relations officer. There was no mystery around the ashram and thousands of people had met Saradananda, he claimed.

Gur-bux's special ire was reserved for Satya Gupta, who was at the forefront of the group of people in Calcutta who were convinced that Saradananda was Subhas Bose. 'Sri Satya Gupta has neither any right nor any reason to be associated with the ashram by any stretch of imagination. "Mystery" may be in the minds of such people (but not within the bounds of the ashram),' Gur-Bux declared.

After spending about four months in the vicinity of the ashram

---

2   An official note of 2 August 1962 takes back the date to 1957.

from October 1961, 'Major' Satya Bhushan Gupta announced in February 1962 that after meeting Saradananda, he didn't have the slightest doubt that the sadhu was Subhas Bose. Gupta's claim generated more curiosity. The reason that some importance was given to his statements to the press and to those made at numerous public meetings lay in his background as a revolutionary who was close to Subhas. Gupta joined Bengal's revolutionary movement as an associate of Anil Roy, the leader of Dhaka's Sri Sangha. Eventually, Gupta broke away from Roy and along with a few others formed the Bengal Volunteers group dreaded by the British administrators. At the Calcutta Congress of 1928, Gupta, who had a large group of followers, was suspended for a year from taking part in the activities of the volunteer organisation that was set up under Subhas's command for insubordination.[3]

As the situation heated up, Haripada Basu who had been expelled from the ashram for communicating to Nehru and BC Roy that Saradananda was Subhas Bose, had a sudden change of heart within two months, and in a public meeting at Falakata in April 1962 declared that he had been wrong. Accompanied by Niharendu Dutt Majumdar, a barrister who was once a close political aide of Subhas Bose and later a minister under BC Roy for some time, Basu revealed his epiphany to a crowd of over one-and-a-half-thousand. Majumdar had got in touch with the ashram in August 1961 following which he also started providing legal

---

3   *Terrorism in Bengal: A Collection of Documents*, AK Samanta (ed), Vol II, Govt of West Bengal, pp 999-1000.

advice to the ashram administration (Siddhartha Shankar Ray, another barrister who was to later become the state's chief minister had also appeared in the courts on behalf of the ashram for some time). He had been interacting with Saradananda very closely since February 1962 and had issued a categorical statement that Saradananda was definitely not Subhas Bose. Despite these open declarations, the public mood was far from assuaged. Meetings continued to be held demanding a settlement of the controversy over Saradananda's true identity.

In their quest, the police even obtained Saradananda's handwriting sample and ran it through a CID expert who could spot differences between it and Bose's handwriting, even though the samples were not sufficient to draw a conclusive inference.

```
twists and nicer aspects of the writings are lost. Even then, the
general pictorial look of the two writings are slightly suspicious,
so far their general look is concerned. There are lots of differences
as well between the two writings. I have also considered the
difference of age between these two writings.

        Under the circumstances, it becomes very much difficult
to come to a conclusion without consulting actual script writings
of the writer.
```

Sd/- Promod Sen
23.4.62
HANDWRITING EXPERT, O.I.D.,
WEST BENGAL.

On 25 April 1962, the state government finally made a public statement through a press note. It declared that 'so far as the government is concerned, it has had no approach to Srimat Saradanandaji and therefore it is not in a position to make any statement' regarding his identity, but insisted that the sadhu was not Subhas Bose since the secretary of the ashram had said so. The press note made no reference to all the investigations till then and their findings, but issued a strict-sounding warning that the government wouldn't tolerate any movement in the Shoulmari area, and if there was any, it would be strictly dealt with. In issuing an official communication, the government, in effect, concealed more than it revealed. The warning also did not seem to have had any impact, as meetings continued and posters with pictures of the sadhu and leaflets suggesting he was Subhas Bose continued to circulate widely.

Meanwhile, numerous intelligence reports were received in Calcutta and New Delhi. On 26 April, for instance, the IGP of West Bengal was informed that one of the visitors to Shoulmari was, of all people, Shah Nawaz Khan himself. Among other visitors named by the secret police reports were PK Sehgal, Ashrafuddin Ahmad Chowdhury,[4] a group belonging to Gopal Mukherjee (also known as Gopal Patha),[5] and Nirmal Chandra Das, son of Beni Madhab Das, the teacher of Subhas Bose about whom he had written with much respect in his autobiography. Saradananda, however, did not meet with any of them. In June arrived Lalita Bose with the spiritual leader Balak Brahmachari.

---

4   Secretary of Bengal Congress when Subhas Bose was the president. Worked with Bose to set up Forward Bloc and was a member of the first working committee of the Bloc. After partition, he opted to live in East Pakistan, where he served as Education Minister.

5   Gopal Mukherjee shot to fame during the riots of the Direct Action Day of Muslim League on 16 August 1946 when he took charge of defending Hindu families and retaliating with violence.

She was treated with courtesy at the ashram but it appears Saradananda did not meet her either. Her cousin Dwijendranath Bose (Subhas's nephew and a freedom fighter) who had visited the ashram earlier wasn't any luckier. The Subsidiary Intelligence Bureau reported that Balak Brahmachari offered his help to the ashram and donated some money too.[6]According to some other sources, yet another person visited Shoulmari and interacted with Saradananda in such secrecy that if Saradananda himself hadn't given it out, no one would have known. The person was NG Swami, the main moving force behind the secret service of Netaji's INA. Swami never gave any public statement, but allegedly broke down in tears on meeting Saradananda.[7]In 1965, Hiralal Dixit, a person claiming to have known Subhas Bose from 1928, met Saradananda in Shoulmari and proclaimed him to be Bose.

Through July and August of 1962, some other members of Subhas Bose's old revolutionary network too landed at Shoulmari. Sunil Das, Pabitra Mohan Roy, Samar Guha—all leading lights of the Praja Socialist Party—arrived to find out the truth about Saradananda. The police reported that even Leela Roy, their leader and firebrand revolutionary and social worker was planning to visit the ashram (although eventually she didn't).

The controversy reached another level when another former associate of Subhas Bose arrived at the Shoulmari ashram. Uttam Chand Malhotra, who had sheltered Bose in Afghanistan in 1941

---

6   The information in this paragraph is compiled from various police and
     intelligence reports generated during the second half of 1962.
7   Shri Avijit, *Taihoku Theke Bharate*, Firma Labanya jyoti, 3rd Ed, 1995, pp 254-5.

held a public meeting on his arrival on 30 July. Before reaching Shoulmari, he had declared himself an agnostic as far as this matter was concerned but upon arrival, summarised his impression in a public meeting from whatever he had heard till then by saying that although he was a vastly learned and pious man, Saradananda wasn't Bose.[8] Following his meeting with Saradananda, Uttam Chand clarified in another public meeting that he held on to his views and that he had visited the ashram only at the insistence of Satya Gupta.[9]

The Intelligence Bureau (IB) continued to monitor the developments not only at the ashram and its vicinity, but kept a watch over related people and political organisations. The IB, for instance, collected information from a 'secret source' that after the Forward Bloc had instituted a ten-member enquiry committee 'to probe into the identity of the Shoulmari Sadhu' that included leaders like Hemanta Bose and Kanailal Bhattacharya, the general secretary of the party, RK Haldulkar had written to the ashram seeking a meeting with Saradananda. A meeting with the committee members collectively was denied by the ashram but Haldulkar was told that individuals desirous of meeting Saradananda should apply with their respective photographs.[10]

By 1963, the matter was being discussed at the national level. Atal Bihari Vajpayee asked PM Nehru in the Rajya Sabha on

8   Copy of a report of a district intelligence branch officer dated 2 August 1962 sent to the Special Superintendent of Police, IB, CID, West Bengal.
9   Report of the Superintendent of Police, DIB to the Special Superintendent of Police, IB, CID, West Bengal, dated 24 August 1962.
10   Extract from a Secret Source of IB dated 17 October 1962.

22 August 'whether any inquiry has been made?' The PM replied that 'inquiries we have made and the Government of West Bengal have made have conclusively established that Swami Saradananda is not Netaji Subhas Chandra Bose, and he himself denies it absolutely'.One such inquiry had been carried out by Rajya Sabha MP Surendra Mohan Ghose, once a close revolutionary associate of Subhas Bose who had fallen out with him later, switching loyalty to the Congress high command with whom Bose clashed. Ghose went to Shoulmari to find out whether Saradananda was Bose when Prime Minister Nehru personally directed him to do so—another inexplicable instance of Nehru's behaviour in direct contradiction to his proclaimed belief that Bose was long dead. Ghose went to Shoulmari ashram on 11 September 1962, met Saradananda face-to-face and grilled him for days. Ghose asked Saradananda who he was before he renounced the world. 'I cannot give my identity of *purbashram* (earlier life). But why should people make such a mistake? You can see for yourself that I am not Netaji,' Saradananda said. 'Can anybody mistake me for Netaji?' he asked again, and Ghose replied, 'Not he who saw Netaji alive and knew him.'Saradananda nodded and said 'nobody would deny his own father' and he was 'not the son of Janaki Nath Bose'. After he was done, Ghose sent a telegram to minister Morarji Desai in London, who was on a standby just in case the holy man turned out to be Bose. On 4 October 1962, Ghose submitted his report to the Prime Minister.

In the meantime, some remarkable changes in opinion held by important players in the matter had taken place. Gope Gur-Bux, who had come down heavily on Satya Gupta, quit the ashram

This man is not Subhash Bose. I wonder, how he could be confused with Subhash by people who knew him. One thing, I find that some people are bent upon to make a political Capital out of this Sadhu's presence there. It would have been much better for the Sadhu himself to disclose his antecedents. However, I have no doubt in my mind that this Sadhu has nothing to do with Subhash Bose.

              With kindest regards,

                                        Yours sincerely,

Shri Jawahar Lal Nehru,   *S. m. Ghose*
      Prime Minister of India   (S.M.GHOSE)
Prime Minister's House,
NEW DELHI-1

[Conclusion of Surendra Mohan Ghose in his letter to Jawaharlal Nehru. Obtained from Ministry of Home Affairs under Right to Information Act]

sometime in the middle of 1962 and started living with Balak Brahmachari, the spiritual guru who became a strong votary of the claim that Netaji was alive. Brahmachari was no run-of-the-mill guru. He had Presidents, Prime Ministers and other top political leaders genuflecting before him in public. 'Netaji is alive and he will return as the leader,' Brahmachari insisted (which became a standard slogan of the Santan Dal, the organisation established by him). By the end of the next year, Gur-Bux's journey to the other end of the spectrum was complete. At a public meeting held at the Calcutta maidan, he announced that if the Prime Minister announced in unambiguous terms that Netaji's name was not in any war criminals' list, he would take it upon himself to produce him in public. In December 1963, he announced at another public meeting that Saradananda was none else than Netaji. He gave a call to Saradananda to appear in public and assume the presidentship of the country.

Uttam Chand Malhotra too came out with a changed opinion soon after leaving Shoulmari. He had relieved himself of all doubts regarding Saradananda being Netaji, he announced. Next year, he published a book recounting his experience and arguing that the two persons were the same.

Whatever it's worth, it must be noted that the ashram did not hesitate to contact the highest echelons of the Government when required. When a man was nabbed with a gun inside the ashram premises in August 1963 threatening to eliminate Saradananda, the secretary of the ashram Ramani Ranjan Das wrote to Nehru seeking greater security. A cursory assurance from the Prime Minister's Secretariat—by itself not a small matter that the PMO should respond to a complaint which fell under the ambit of the local enforcement authority—enraged Das. He wrote back to Nehru squarely putting the blame of the attack at his doorstep since the assailant purportedly used the Prime Minister's name. In the same letter, he drew Nehru's attention to the fact that the ashram was able to ward off allegedly spurious lawsuits due to the personal intervention of the then Bengal Chief Minister Prafulla Sen.

By the end of 1965, the public frenzy and interest of the press had largely subsided. Plagued by huge debts and increasing litigation, the ashram hadn't reached anywhere close to its original ambitious plans. Saradananda was reported to have left Shoulmari for Ukhimath (in present Uttarakhand) in April 1966, where he started living in a camp with a handful of followers. Sometime later he moved to a place near Guptakashi.

The decline in the fortunes of the ashram and the petering out of the controversy, however, did not stop the sadhu being tailed by intelligence officers. On the contrary, documents from this period show that more than one state was keeping an eye on him. A note dated 21 November 1966 from the Special Branch in Lucknow informed West Bengal: 'We have been maintaining a watch on the said Baba of Shoulmari Ashram.' Saradananda was back to Shoulmari in mid-October 1967 with his faithful secretary Ramani Ranjan Das who had accompanied him. The district intelligence branch, however, picked up a news that befuddled them and when the news spread, the public. The elder of the two daughters of Das, both of whom were unmarried, had given birth to a baby girl about three months ago when they were living with Saradananda. The sadhu of Shoulmari explained this away as a matter of immaculate conception; the baby, he said was conceived through spiritual power and that she was the goddess Mahamaya herself. 'Situation is under watch,' reported the district intelligence branch to Deputy Inspector General of Police at the end of October. Saradananda left the ashram again in early January 1968. In July that year, he was found camping at Amarkantak in Madhya Pradesh. Informing the Bengal Intelligence Branch that by the end of the year he had reached Bilaspur (now in Chhattisgarh), the central Intelligence Bureau sought a report on the recent activities of Saradananda. In October 1969, the IB again contacted Bengal's Intelligence Branch, informing them that the IB had lost track of the sadhu after February 1969 when he was last seen at Amaravati in Maharashtra.

SECRET/IMMEDIATE

No:6/DG/68(6)
INTELLIGENCE BUREAU
(Ministry of Home Affairs)
Government of India
—

New Delhi-11, Dt. the

MEMORANDUM

Please refer to our Memo. No.6/DG/68(6) dated 17.9.69.

It is now reported that Baba Saradananda of Shoulmari Ashram stayed in a temple on Dharni Road, near Ghatang, Amravati (Maharashtra) from November 1968 to February 1969. At Amravati he collected a very large amount of money and then proceeded to some place between Nainital and the Nepal border. However, he has not been located after February 1969.

We should be grateful if you could please trace the whereabouts of the Sadhu. We may also please be kept informed as and when anything of interest about the Shoulmari Ashram comes to your notice.

(SARATH CHANDRA)
ASSISTANT DIRECTOR

The Supdt. of Police,
Int. Br., West Bengal,
CALCUTTA.

The cat and mouse game of Saradananda's frequent change of place and the intelligence officers following him and often losing sight of him came to an end in January 1977, when the Intelligence Branch in West Bengal was informed by the Superintendent of Police, Dehradun, that he had passed away.

What had started with a loud bang, ended in a whimper barely heard.

Shoulmari remained a mystery in people's minds as the authorities never gave it out publicly that the identity of the sadhu had been cracked by them a decade-and-a-half before his death in faraway Dehradun.

The Superintendent of Police had reported his findings on Saradananda's identity to the Deputy Inspector General, Intelligence Branch, in Calcutta on 31 January 1962. Speaking to various sources, he summarised the physical attributes of Saradananda. With a stout and muscular build, he sported a 'long beard and unshaped moustache'; was about five-feet, ten-inches in height (a later report claimed he was five-feet-six-inches); eyeballs were black; there was a cut mark above the right eye; a tumour on the right foot made his walk a little 'defective'; the nose was sharp and the complexion was fair. He was a Hindu Bengali, but his speech had an intonation typical of 'Comilla–Tipperah–Mymensingh belt'. Saradananda, a chain smoker (later investigations reported that he smoked five packets of Capstan Navy Cut daily), was thought to be about fifty-years-old.

The more important part of the officer's report was the precise identification of Saradananda. One of his sources identified Saradananda as 'Jatin Chakrabartti' of Comilla (Bangladesh) who had once been the principal of the Comilla Victoria College. He was also a former member of the Anushilan Samiti and 'was charged for the murder of Mr Davis, District Magistrate, Comilla, and since the murder he has been absconding'. About the meeting of his source with Saradananda, he reported:

> On seeing the sadhu he cried out 'Jatinda Na' (Isn't that Jatin da!) and the sadhu became visibly moved. The holding of the cigarette in the mouth also appeared to the visitor to be of the same pattern as that of Jatin Chakrabartti. A few minutes after identification he was ordered to quit the ashram.

There were alternative theories too, and the superintendent

reported one of them in the same report referred to above.

> There is, however, one alternative theory that he is not Jatin Chakrabartti, but Abinash Bhattacharji of the Anushilan Party. Physical features of both being in many ways similar this confusion has arisen. But the major part of available evidence goes to prove, but not conclusively, that the Sadhu of Falakata is Shri Jatin Chakrabartti, a political absconder.

As far as the government was concerned, not only had it confirmed that Saradananda wasn't Subhas Bose in disguise, but also established his true identity. While it announced the first half of the information repeatedly, it kept the latter part of the information a closely guarded secret.

The description of Saradananda also varied according to people who met him. Niharendu Dutt Majumdar described him, in contrast to the intelligence reports, as a man about six feet half –inch tall and dark complexioned.[11]

Dwijendra Nath Bose later recounted the experience of another person who had examined Saradananda closely. Kabiraj Kamalakanta Ghosh, a famed ayurvedic physician was called by the ashram, purportedly on the advice of Dutt Majumdar, to examine Saradananda when he had developed a cold and cough. Before Ghosh's visit, Dwijen told him to check for specific identity marks on the body of Saradananda—marks on the body of Subhas Bose were known to his family members. Ghosh didn't find any of those marks. Moreover, he reported back that Saradananda had

---

11   Record of examination of Niharendu Dutt Majumdar at the GD Khosla Commission of Inquiry, 22 September 1972, Proceedings of the Khosla Commission, Vol XII, pp 3893.

hair on the frontside of his head and was bald only at the back of the head (a contradiction of some reports which claimed that Saradananda was bald in the frontside of his head).[12]

The discrepancies also led to a rumour that Saradananda wasn't Subhas Bose; that the real Subhas Bose remained hidden in the ashram while Saradananda occasionally made appearances in front of his followers. Prafulla Sen, the then Bengal Chief Minister, is also alleged to have said that there was more than one sadhu living in the ashram.[13]

A revolting view subsequently emerged that the Shoulmari sadhu had been propped up at the Nehru government's behest to befuddle the public, to take their attention away from the Bose mystery. When Dwijendra visited Shoulmari ashram, to his utter shock, he found a number of central intelligence officers including IB Director BN Mullik snooping around in person. Dwijen claimed that one SC Mukherjee, an administrator of the ashram, was an intelligence officer too. All those cases of sadhus who claimed themselves to be Netaji were being financed by the central government, Dwijen went on to allege.[14]During his journalistic investigations, young Barun Sengupta, the would-be founder of the Bangla daily *Bartaman*, was also told the same by local political leaders. But every claim was being keenly followed

---

12   Record of examination of Dwijendra Nath Bose at the GD Khosla Commission of Inquiry, 8 August 1972, Proceedings of the Khosla Commission, Vol XI, pp 3388-89.

13   Shri Abhijit, *Taihoku Theke Bharate*, Vol 2, Firma Labanyajyoti.

14   Record of examination of Dwijendra Nath Bose at the GD Khosla Commission of Inquiry, 8 August 1972, Proceedings of the Khosla Commission, Vol XI, pp 3356, 3399.

by the central and state intelligence departments.[15] 'I was told by so many intelligence officers working in the eastern region of the country that it is Mr [BN] Mullick who looks after all these things,' he would disclose in the course of his deposition before Justice GD Khosla.

Saradananda, the sadhu of Shoulmari may have created a sensation in the press and among public, but this was not the only case of a holy man either claiming himself or being claimed by his followers to be Subhas Bose in disguise. Dwijen described a few instances of his family's run-ins with such lesser-known claimants. In about 1959 or 1960, a sadhu by the name of Hanuman Gir, along with a couple of his associates, visited Suresh Bose when Dwijen too was present. The associates of the sadhu claimed that Hanuman Gir was Netaji. But Dwijen found him to be an 'ugly looking fellow' with a 'ghostly appearance'. Even as the associates tried to explain the appearance by claiming that Netaji had changed his face, Dwijen found his handwriting to be different from that of Subhas Bose.[16]

Countless such stories have emerged over the years and continue to do so even to this day. One story, however, needs a passing mention here—a story recounted by Dwijen. He was told about 'another gentleman in Uttar Pradesh' called 'Parda Baba'. 'Some people say that he is Netaji,' said Dwijen. Parda Baba's

15   Record of examination of Barun Sengupta at the GD Khosla Commission of Inquiry, 6 July 1972, Proceedings of the Khosla Commission, Vol IX, p 3009.

16   Record of examination of Dwijendra Nath Bose at the GD Khosla Commission of Inquiry, 8 August 1972, Proceedings of the Khosla Commission, Vol XI, pp 3355-56.

handwritings were shown to Dwijen, 'but that handwriting did not tally'. The handwritings were shown to him by a person named Kumar Bishwanath Roy. As we will see in the subsequent chapters, Dwijen told only part of the story and hid the larger part.

FOUR

ALL THE NETAJI'S MEN

IT WAS THE second time within a span of a few months that Pabitra Mohan Roy had travelled out in his quest for Netaji. As he set foot in Neemsar with an associate and follower of Subhas Bose, Amal Roy[1], Pabitra couldn't help but recollect his disappointment at Shoulmari. Meeting Saradananda from the distance of a few feet on two consecutive days had dispelled all his doubts; the man was definitely not Netaji. And now, in a vastly different land, he was chasing another lead. He had held on to his hopes of Netaji's survival, remembering the emphatic claims of Gandhiji and Sarat Chandra Bose. Above all, Netaji's last words to him as he prepared to enter the submarine on his way to India: 'Don't be disheartened if you hear any surprising and depressing news. We will meet again.'

---

1   A wealthy follower of Subhas Bose, who contested the 1962 state elections against Dr Bidhan Chandra Roy on Jana Sangh ticket.

After some enquiry, Pabitra and Amal were able to track down the location of the Bengali sadhu, but gaining an audience with him took about two months. Bhagwanji finally spoke with Pabitra in December 1962. Having tested Pabitra's patience for long, Bhagwanji now opened his heart and 'secrets' to him. A black curtain blocked his view, but not his stentorian voice. As that voice addressed Roy as 'my intelligence officer', unforgotten memories of someone who had 'died' seventeen years earlier flickered in Roy's mind's eye. For him, there was no mistaking that it was Subhas Chandra Bose speaking from the other side of the curtain.

'You cannot even understand under what awful, abnormal mental stress, bodily pain and circumstantial handicaps I am living here.'

The condition in which Pabitra found his leader whom he had continued to search for over two decades broke his heart. Pabitra wanted to stay on to serve him better but Bhagwanji declined. After he returned to Calcutta, Bhagwanji reiterated:

> I am going through all these terrible troubles and hazards of my life only for the final consummation of the mission for which I am. You have in your own way suffered quite a bit. I do not for the present want to take you away from your family's tender circle. Please remember my humble self to your good wife. I wish she could feed me with '*Ilisherjhal-bhat, Daccai Parota, Aloor dam* and *Kalia*'.[2]

---

2   Bhagwanji's letter to Pabitra Mohan Roy, 22 December 1962.

And then came his most vital order. No one was to know that Bhagwanji—a 'Dead Man' to the world—was at 'N' (Naimisharanya, also known as Neemsar).

> From this moment you must not mention me and 'N' to any one, whatsoever and whoever. When you shall meet in the future, you must not even by the slightest indication give out that you contacted me at 'N'. You shall sacrifice your head but keep your lips sealed. Only when you shall be ordered in clear verbal tones 'Your seals are off now', then you can. Similarly, tell others of this present phase. Let no one come to me. If anyone asks about__ turn a complete blank. Keep a true and factual scrutiny of persons and parties.[3]

Over a period of time, Pabitra was given a surreal lowdown on Bhagwanji's 'post-death' activities. The 'ghost of the dead' had been 'floating in and floating out' of India, appearing in different places 'like Erebus', the Greek god of darkness. Occasionally, Bhagwanji would lose himself in nostalgia reminiscing about his childhood, about Beni Madhab Das, about Hemanta Sarkar and many others.

That a young Subhas Bose had run away from his home on a spiritual quest, or that Beni Madhab Das was his school teacher and Hemanta Sarkar his childhood friend, or that Deshbandhu Chittaranjan Das was the one who had initiated him into politics, were matters of common knowledge. Just because someone

---

3   Ibid. Bhagwanji also wrote: 'Only a handful of picked persons know me at "N".' Whenever Bhagwanji had to refer to Subhas Chandra Bose, he would write an underscore or just write S. During conversations, he would use 'your dead ghost' or 'your S' or simply 'this body'.

regurgitated all that did not mean he was Subhas. Anyone could have lifted these details from any standard biography or collected works of Subhas Bose.

But wouldn't a former INA secret service man, trained in espionage, see through it all? And what about someone else who had known Subhas Bose since the 1920s? And yet others who got to work closely with Bose at different phases of the freedom struggle?

Back to his Dum Dum residence from his surreptitious trip to Neemsar, Pabitra Mohan Roy was a troubled man. He had received a letter from Bhagwanji listing out a number of articles—strange ones at that—which he needed. Pabitra was at a loss on how, with his modest means, he was going to arrange the articles Bhagwanji had instructed him to bring by the end of January 1963. The list included items like a 'chronometer wristwatch which must give absolutely correct time, without fluctuating a second'; a pair of binoculars which must be the 'most powerful, highest powered, longest range, utmost clarity, to be used by hands only'; a transistor, 'extremely powerful in shortwave and midwave'; cigars and a Fowler's Dictionary.

For a while Pabitra couldn't think of anyone trustworthy he could go to for help. Then it struck him that *Didi*, the then chairperson of the Praja Socialist Party of which he was a member, could be approached. A sisterly figure for old revolutionaries, Leela Roy (nee Nag) was treated by Subhas Bose as something of an equal. Her portrait in Parliament House—unveiled in 2008 in the presence of Prime Minister Dr Manmohan Singh—evidences Roy's exalted position among the pantheon of freedom fighters. Daughter of a wealthy Rai Bahadur, who retired as Deputy Magistrate of Dhaka district, Leela excelled early in life in academics as well as sports and became the first woman to earn a Master's degree (in English) from the Dhaka University. In future, Roy would become the first women detainee under Bengal Ordinance Act from the city. At the university, she met her future husband Anil Roy—the suave, erudite and radical young man who was in the process of building the underground revolutionary organisation that later came to be known as Sri Sangha—and followed him into the revolutionary fraternity. Preetilata Waddedar, a martyr of Chittagong armoury raid had been recruited by Leela Roy. A feminist, Roy presented a paper on history of women's movement in Bengal at the Calcutta Congress session of 1928. She founded several schools for girls and started a magazine called *Jayasree*, with the blessings of Rabindra Nath Tagore. She was jailed several times between 1931-38 and 1942-46. Elected to the Constituent Assembly in 1946, Roy resigned opposing Partition of India. Thereafter, she devoted herself to rehabilitating refugees and bringing succour to victims of communal violence, Hindus as well as Muslims, for which Gandhi had praised her.

Just over three years younger than Subhas, Leela Roy had known him from the 1920s. The political association between them became stronger with Roy being appointed to head the women's sub-committee of the National Planning Committee formed by Subhas as president of the Indian National Congress in 1938. Leela and Anil Roy took the responsibility of organising the Forward Bloc when Subhas formed the party after resigning as the Congress president in 1939. As Subhas languished in jail after his arrest in July 1940, he named Leela Roy as the second editor of his party mouthpiece *Forward Bloc*. He summoned Roy to meet him before escaping from home internment in 1941 but the meeting failed to take place. When *The Statesman* started a virulent campaign against Subhas in 1942, Leela Roy rose in his defence in a scathing attack on the government of the day and the Communist Party. Soon, she was back to prison. Subhas wanted her in the southeast Asian theatre, but his attempts to reach out to her as the Indian National Army entered the Indian soil also did not bear fruit. His message reached her too late. By the time she was released from jail in 1946, Subhas was lost in mystery.

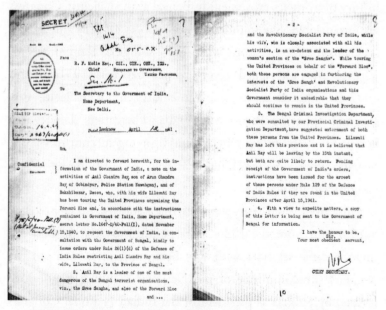

[UP Chief Secretary's note seeking ban on entry of Anil and Leela Roy into the United Provinces in 1941. (Source: File No 75/9/41, Home Department. Courtesy National Archives of India)]

Roy had sent Pabitra to find out the truth about Saradananda. It was, therefore, only natural that he would tell her about the real truth which had turned his world upside down. On 7 January 1963, Pabitra let Leela Roy into the secret—that he had met 'Netaji' at Neemsar. Stunned, Leela Roy recorded in her personal diary that evening:

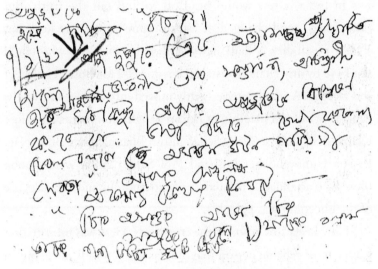

[Diary entry of Leela Roy on receiving the news of Bhagwanji from Pabitra Mohan Roy. Courtesy Bijoy Nag, Jayasree Prakashan]

আজ দুপুরে এক অত্যাশ্চর্য সত্য উদ্ঘাটিত হোলো।অভাবনীয় তার সম্ভাবনা, অচিন্তনীয় তার আনুষাঙ্গিক সবকিছুই।আমার অনুভূতিকে বিশ্লেষণ করতে বা ভাষা দিতে চেষ্টা করবো না।কেবল বলবো হে অঘটন পটিয়সী দেবতা আবার দেখলাম অকস্মাৎ কোথায় কি ঘটে—চির অসম্ভব আসে চির সম্ভবের বেশে. যাদের বল্লাম তাদের নানা বিচিত্র প্রতিক্রিয়া।

(A bewildering truth was revealed today afternoon. Unfathomable are its possibilities; everything associated with it is unthinkable. I won't try to analyse my feelings or put words to them, but would only say: 'O God of making the impossible possible, I saw again what can happen all of a sudden, the eternally impossible appeared in the form of the possible.' Received strange and varied reactions from all those I informed.[4] [Translation by Chandrachur Ghose])

Several in the former revolutionary circles had disbelieved the official story of Bose's death in 1945. Wherever they heard of any news that sounded like a lead, even the claims that Bose was in India, a few would head off to find out the truth. But now things stood changed; it was no more an obscure lead, but a clear possibility, a hard news verified by someone who could not have by any chance mistaken anyone else for Bose. The effect was electric. A small coterie swiftly moved into action. Hurriedly, Leela Roy called a meeting of her Sri Sangha confidants and close relatives. Sunil Das, Shaila Sen, Santosh Bhattacharya, Bijoy Nag, Basana Guha and her husband Prof Samar Guha were among those who attended. The anxiety of expectations and the suspense of the uncertain was palpable.

Now Leela Roy stood at the crossroads. Here was information from a most reliable person that Subhas was not only alive, but in India. Countless questions swarmed her mind. There was so much to tell him; there was so much to hear from him; there was an unfinished mission. To find answers to her questions, Roy arrived in Neemsar on 23 March 1963, accompanied by Shaila Sen, Samar Guha and Anil Das. Anil Das, who belonged to the same village as Leela Roy, had been with the INA and had interacted with Subhas Bose on multiple occasions. Samar Guha, another

---

4   Charanik, *Oi Mahamanaba Ase*, Jayasree Prakashan, 2010, p 427.

staunch follower of Anil and Leela Roy, had joined the freedom movement in the mid-1930s while still in his late teens. Following his leaders, he joined the Forward Bloc. Subhas Bose became the guiding star of this accomplished scholar in Chemistry.

The first day did not go well, however, putting brakes on her heightened expectations, she noted in her diary:

> Arrived destination at 12-30 noon on 23/6/63, and was lodged in Dharamsala wherein medium [the intermediary to liaise between Roy and Bhagwanji] and his friend stayed; cooked and ate by 2 pm and went out to see the area in the evening and discovered that neither the Leader nor his doorkeeper [Saraswati Devi] are here. Was greatly depressed and felt halted, decided to leave the place next morning.[5]

Putting aside the impulsive decision the next morning, she decided to stay on till the time she got a chance to meet the 'Leader'. Within the next few hours, she was informed that Saraswati Devi had returned. Samar Guha, Anil Das and Shaila Sen rushed to meet her, followed by Roy. Notwithstanding all their efforts to 'ingratiate themselves' with Saraswati Devi, a meeting with Bhagwanji didn't materialise. Roy was 'mortified' and returned with a sense of 'deep humiliation'. On the morning of 25 March, Shaila Sen met another intermediary and 'got very very useful information from him, in such details that I was almost sure he has got the news of our presence'. The intermediary came to meet Roy again on the afternoon of 26 March, this time to convey a

---

5   Charanik, *Oi Mahamanaba Ase*, Jayasree Prakashan, 2010, p 427.

message from the elusive man; Roy felt that the purpose of his visit was to assess her reaction. The message delivered was, 'When I reappear, you will be the first one that I will meet.'

The message failed to satisfy Roy. For her, this was not a personal issue. The question troubling her was what she and her colleagues were to do. 'My mind has strangely become unreactive despite the various analyses, speculations of the people around me,' she wrote in her diary on 28 March. The same day, she sent a letter to the man she was anxious to meet telling him that she would leave on 30 March if her staying back didn't serve any purpose. Along with her letter she sent two books—*Last Days of the British Raj* by Leonard Mosley and the first volume of R C Majumdar's *History of Freedom Struggle*. Much as she might have desired, no request to prolong her stay came from the other side. She decided to leave on 30 March. On the evening of 29 March, however, she had two unexpected guests: Srikant Sharma and Saraswati Devi. For Sharma, this had turned out to be a happy occasion. Acting as a go-between, he had been allowed inside Bhagwanji's room for the first time. He saw an 'older Netaji' behind the curtain. He carried from him a set of a cup and saucer as a parting gift for Leela Roy, and a message asking her to visit the Shiva temple before she left.

Prodded by Roy, Sharma conveyed the crucial question to Bhagwanji: how could she ascertain that he was Subhas Bose? Remaining silent for some time, Bhagwanji started reminiscing the stories of the yesteryears—about the occasions when he had interacted with Roy—stories that weren't part of the standard knowledge about Subhas Bose. With the usual warning about not giving out his presence in Neemsar to people came an unusual observation, Bhagwanji asked Sharma to convey to Roy that his coming out in public was neither in the interest of the country nor of himself. For reasons unexplained, he believed that his coming out would pitch the nascent republic against the UN and the 'big powers' which might lead to a third world war. Sharma was asked to advise Samar Guha to give up his obsession about 'knowing the whereabouts of Netaji' and work instead to spread Netaji's ideology and philosophy across the country.[6]

Finally, as the much-awaited call to meet came, Roy went to the temple the next morning and from there to the railway station. Whatever followed thereafter caused torrents of tears to flow.

***

AS THE TRAIN screeched to a halt at the Howrah station, Leela Roy found Sunil Das and Bijoy Nag waiting to receive her. A former revolutionary from Sri Sangha who was much younger to Anil and Leela, Das was her closest follower. Nag was her adopted son, her brother's son by birth. Both had waited anxiously to hear about her experience and findings. Roy was, for now, somewhat

---

6   Record of witness examination of Srikant Sharma at the Justice Mukherjee Commission of Inquiry, 14 and 16 August 2001, Faizabad. Sharma had no prior information about Leela Roy and gave no indication that he was aware of the details that emerged about Subhas Bose's post-1941 life after 1945. As a result, while talking to the Justice Mukherjee Commission at the age of 94, he made a few mistakes in remembering what Bhagwanji said to Leela Roy. Clearly, had these mistakes been made by Bhagwanji himself, Leela Roy would have instantly known that she was dealing with an impostor.

convinced that the man she had met in Neemsar was Subhas. 'He has done so much for the country. He is suffering even now,' she told Nag. 'Her sole aim after she returned was to ensure that Bhagwanji had the basic comforts of life,' Nag told us.

The first thing Leela Roy did then was to dispatch alternative medicine practitioner Kamalakanta Ghosh to Neemsar to take care of Bhagwanji's immediate medical needs. Ghosh, the same person sent by Niharendu Dutta Majumdar to treat Saradananda at Shoulmari, was no ordinary physician. He had joined the revolutionary movement inspired by Anil Roy and was arrested in 1930 on charges of plotting the murders of the Governor of Bengal and the Viceroy.[7] 'This Kamalakanta was a close follower of Leila (sic),' noted the Bengal government in a secret report of 1935.[8] The immediate ailments of Bhagwanji that Ghosh had to treat were varicose veins and piles. Bhagwanji had been suffering much pain due to these problems. Riding on horses for a considerable period of time was stated by Bhagwanji to be the reason for causing the problem of piles.

Thereafter, Roy started informing a few select people about the return of 'Netaji' to India. Topping the list was Subhas's eldest surviving brother Suresh Chandra Bose. Then came his friend Dilip Kumar Roy. (Subhas's childhood friend Hemanta Kumar

---

7   Amiya K Samanta (ed), 'Report on the Activities of Terrorists in Bengal During the Period April to December 1930,' *Terrorism in Bengal, A Collection of Documents on Terrorist Activities from 1905 to 1939 Vol I*, Government of West Bengal, 1995, p 625.

8   File No 43/42/35-Political, 1935, Home Department, Political Section, Government of India. National Archives of India.

Sarkar had expired.) Also on the list were political compatriots Trailokya Nath Chakravarty, Hem Chandra Ghosh, Satya Ranjan Bakshi, Maulvi Ashrafuddin Ahmed Chaudhury, Hari Vishnu Kamath and Swami Asimananda Saraswati Maharaj. Historian RC Majumdar also figured on the list. Not everyone was going to believe Roy. She was rebuffed when she tried to reach out to the Bose family members other than Suresh Bose.

The message for Dilip Kumar Roy was conveyed through a hand-delivered letter. Born a day before Subhas, Dilip was one of his closest friends from his Presidency College days—a friendship that continued till the time Subhas was in India. The later become a famed musician (Bharat Ratna M S Subbulakshmi being his disciple) and eventually a holy man.

[The picture on left was taken at Cambridge University in the early 1920s. Dilip is sitting on the left and Subhas is standing on the right. The other picture shows Dilip around mid-1970s in Haridwar. Courtesy: Hari Krishna Mandir Trust, Pune]

Her heart in turmoil and her body wrecked by a recent stroke, Leela Roy wrote with a shaking hand to Dilip...

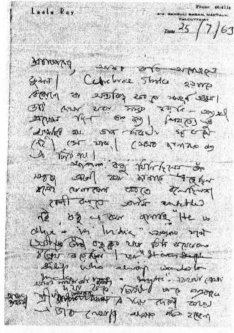

[Exhibit 221, Mukherjee Commission]

I wanted to tell you about your friend. I am not entitled to speak much, but I can only inform you that "**He's alive—in India.**" He has mentioned about your friendship with him many times. For example, "**It was Dilip who always wanted to make me a mystic.**" For this reason, this letter is important... If you trust me, then it is 100 per cent fact. No one else should know about it—this is a stern injunction on me. [Translated from Bengali, except the words emphasised]

Reaching Trailokya Nath Chakravarty was not easy for he was in East Pakistan, the present-day Bangladesh. The revered 'Maharaj' of revolutionaries had troubled the British during the freedom struggle so much that they had kept him locked up for thirty unimaginable years in all—more than ten of which were in the notorious prison hell in Port Blair. Recent media reports and books, including one written by Congress stalwart Mani Shankar

Aiyar, have cited Trailokya's grit in an attempt to try and minimise Veer Savarkar's sufferings in the Cellular Jail—where both were lodged at the same time once.

Leela Roy asked former revolutionary Sailendra Roy to sneak into East Pakistan and deliver her top secret message to Trailokya. It was a high-risk mission. Passport and visa were arranged hurriedly for Sailendra—himself from East Bengal—who took the help of his old contacts in Dhaka to reach Maharaj. Chakravarty had been put under continuous police surveillance by the then East Pakistan government, and any stranger visiting him was a suspect, especially if he was found to be an Indian. Sailendra faced the possibility of being incarcerated or even hanged as an enemy agent, if he was caught. He reached his destination under the guise of a servant to the family. It was a brief but dramatic meeting. On hearing who had sent him and the purpose of his visit, Maharaj asked Sailendra not to speak but to write down whatever he had to say, lest anyone overhear their conversation and report it to the police. As Sailendra wrote each page, Maharaj read and burnt it.[9]

The formidable revolutionary was completely shaken up after he was briefed. A letter of his was located among Bhagwanji's belongings at Ram Bhawan in 1986. 'The person with whom I was lodged in Mandalay Jail, played tennis and participated in Durga Puja—I have not forgotten him. I'm still with him,' he began. He recalled older days: 'In Delhi, in the year 1940, at Shankar Lal's residence I was accompanying him.' Shankar Lal was Forward

---

9   Diary of Sailen Roy, Justice Mukherjee Commission of Inquiry Exhibit No 148 (c).

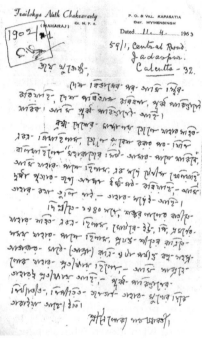

[Exhibit 151, Mukherjee Commission]

Bloc general secretary. 'I was by his side while we toured United Province. On a chilling winter night in the Agra ground, hundreds of people were waiting for him till nine at night.' Then, a dash of emotion, a yearning to see 'him' again: 'I am eagerly waiting for the same person. The oppressed and tortured people of East Pakistan are waiting for him.'

Without writing 'Subhas', Trailokya made it clear it was him that he had in mind. It was at Shankar Lal's Delhi residence in 1940 that Trailokya had last met Subhas. He was also with Subhas when he was bundled off to the dreaded Mandalay Jail in the 1920s.

After he was ousted from the Congress in 1939, Subhas Bose had tried to create a broad platform by bringing diverse groups (Leftists, Hindu leaders, Muslim League) together. At his behest, Trailokya had then met old friends—Keshav Baliram Hedgewar, Pandit Paramanand (another revolutionary to have undergone nearly three decades of incarceration in British India), Veer Savarkar and his younger brother Ganesh in an attempt to organise a revolutionary upsurge across the country. The response was not encouraging but Maharaj persisted.[10] However, before long, Bose and his key associates were back in jail. Post-1947, the indefatigable Trailokya would go on to play a part in the Bangladesh liberation movement as well. In 1970, he visited New Delhi and was on 8 August felicitated at a reception attended by Prime Minister Indira Gandhi, Lok Sabha Speaker G S Dhillon and several MPs. In the wee hours of 9 August, Chakravarty passed away. The Prime Minister, who out of her deference for the 83-year-old Anushilan stalwart had personally served him sweets, was shell-shocked at his sudden demise. 'Meeting him was a moving experience,' she said.[11]

Leela Roy also introduced to Bhagwanji a person Subhas Bose had known when he was subsequently in South East Asia. Former INA secret service man Anil Das had accompanied Roy to Neemsar in March 1963 but had not been able to get in touch with the mysterious man behind the curtain. His turn came a little later. Declassified in 1997, and now available at the National Archives in New Delhi, is an intelligence report which reads that on his last night in Bangkok in August 1945, Subhas Bose talked to Anil Chandra Das about the underground work after the Japanese surrender. Another report speaks of the officials' anxiousness to nab him, as Das had gone missing after Bose's reported death.

---

10   Jele Trish Bochhor O Pak Bharater Swadhinata Sangram, Trailokya Nath Chakraborty, Maharaj Trailokya Nath Chakraborty Smritirakkha Committee.

11   Lalit Kumar Sanyal, Biplab Tapas Maharaj Trailokya Nath.

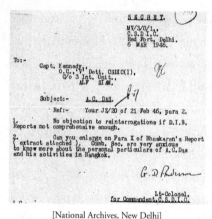

Yet another record shows Bose writing to Hikari Kikan—the Japanese military organisation liaising with Azad Hind Government—to hand over to AC Das fifty revolvers, some wireless sets and some British currency for post-war work. None of these documents were in the public domain so long as Das lived. But his letters recovered among the possessions of Bhagwanji add to the account given in the official records. Das's first letter to Bhagwanji in 1964 was something of an aide-memoire, vetted and approved by Leela Roy. Das had recapitulated his role in the freedom struggle, beginning in the 1930s and lasting beyond 1945.

> On the night before he left Bangkok, Netaji took individual interviews of a number of people. I was one of them. When Netaji called me, it was half past 2 am. He told me about the post-war work and cautioned me against getting arrested. He gave me a letter addressed to Hikari Kikan. ...Netaji said that wherever he may go, he would remain in contact with us via wireless....When I heard the news of the crash of Netaji's plane, I knew such news would come and it would not be true. I waited for over a decade and in 1956, I visited India and told everything to auntie [Leela Roy]. In 1961, I left Bangkok for good and last year, auntie sent me to Naimisharanya and thereafter, whatever small or big news I wanted to know, I came

to know from her. Now I am waiting for your orders. [Loosely translated from Bengali]

After perusing this letter, Bhagwanji specifically asked Das about what had really happened after 16 August 1945 and what sort of statements were given by the captured INA personnel. Das elaborated in another letter that he

received 2 wireless sets and a few revolvers, pistols and stenguns from Hikari Kikan. They could not give me British currency. Then I went underground. Within 6-7 days the British Military reached Bangkok...First Debnath Das surrendered before British military authority, and he was let off after his statement was taken. [Loosely translated from Bengali]

Through Leela Roy only, her foremost aide Sunil Das was to become one of the many eyes and ears of Bhagwanji. Several of Sunil Das's letters to him read like intelligence reports. Everything and anything concerning Subhas Bose was digested and sent for the information of Bhagwanji.

An average-looking person, Sunil Das wasn't an average politician. Bright enough in his student days to have his paper published in *The American Journal of Physical Chemistry*, he chose to be a freedom fighter like his siblings, all three of whom died for the nation, unsung. His elder brother was beaten to death while in police custody in 1932. Das himself was first put in jail in 1931 on charges of attempting to assassinate the District Magistrate of Dhaka. He was arrested again in 1933 on charges of conspiring to murder the District Magistrate of Midnapore. This time he was detained in several prisons without trial till 1938. He was back in jail in 1942 and was not out till 1946. Post-independence, he was elected to the Bengal assembly. He would go on to resist the Emergency and edit the Bengali volumes of collected works of Subhas Bose as editor of Jayasree publication. So long as he lived, Sunil Das kept his mouth completely shut about his Bhagwanji connection, even though he was active in intellectual circles in Calcutta and elsewhere.

The closest Das came to discussing the Bhagwanji matter was in 1972 when he was being examined before the Khosla Commission. This commission had come into being due to the singular efforts of a follower of Leela Roy. After he had accompanied Roy and others to Neemsar to meet Bhagwanji, former revolutionary and chemistry professor Samar Guha chalked out the main agenda of his public life—recognition for Netaji and negation of the air crash theory of Bose's death. In his maiden speech in the Lok Sabha on 3 April 1967, he made an issue of the absence of Bose's portrait in the Central Hall of Parliament among those of the other makers of India. He charged that 'it was not an omission but... a deliberate and calculated act on the part of the Congress government to minimise the position of Netaji and relegate him to secondary leadership in the history of national freedom'. With the

Indira Gandhi government unwilling to consider his demands, Guha gathered like-minded persons—Atal Bihari Vajpayee and Madhu Limaye being the most prominent—in and out of Parliament and formed a 'national committee'. Together, they also sought a fresh inquiry into Bose's fate and found ample support among the MPs from all parties. Consequently, on 11 July 1970, orders were issued for the formation of a one-man commission. Nine months later, Justice G D Khosla, a former Chief Justice of the Punjab High Court, took over as its chairman.

Khosla was a newsmaker in his own right. He had graduated from Cambridge and excelled in the judicial branch of the ICS. Seen from the eyes of his best friend Khushwant Singh, the writer, Khosla was an archetypal brown *sahib*, who 'made it a point to wear a dinner jacket when he sat down to dine'.[12] As a judge, Khosla had already earned a footnote in history as the sentencing judge in the Mahatma Gandhi assassination case. In 1947, after he moved from Lahore to Shimla, Khosla was asked to head the fact-finding organisation to investigate cataclysmic communal violence following the partition of India. He went on to record his findings in his first book. First published in 1949, *Stern Reckoning* continues to be in circulation till date. Its brilliant prose and graphic description of the darkest period of modern Indian history have made it one of the most well-read books for that period. But Khushwant Singh thought Khosla justified the Hindu–Sikh violence against the Muslims as a 'legitimate

---

12   Khushwant Singh, 'End of a Long Friendship,' *The Telegraph*, 25 June 2011.

retaliation'. 'I was not aware of the anger that he harboured in his person,' he wrote of the negative trait in his friend's personality in *The Telegraph* of 25 June 2011.

The most infamous instance of this anger spewing out had occurred soon after Khosla's retirement from the Punjab High Court in 1961. Denied a ceremonial send-off by the Bar, Khosla gave vent to his frustration by writing a snide newspaper article titled 'The snake: A fable for grown-ups.' His targets were the unassuming Advocate General of Punjab S M Sikri and his wife. Cambridge-educated Sikri asked Khosla to make amends but he refused. Thereafter, Sikri filed a criminal complaint against Khosla. The former judge reacted by escaping to London. It was a question of his honour, so Sikri wouldn't give up the chase. Eventually, Khosla did apologise publicly and the criminal complaint was withdrawn by Sikri in larger interest of the judiciary. Just the sort of conduct one would expect from a man who rose to be the Chief Justice of India in 1971.

Post-retirement, Khosla became a full-time writer, wielding his pen with equal ease with fiction, history, travelogue and mythology interpreted for the modern times. His writing style earned him many admirers, one of them being L K Advani. Above all, Khosla got to share his literary interests with Jawaharlal Nehru. In Manali, both spent a 'good deal of time together trekking through the forests and hills', wrote historian V N Datta in *The Tribune* of 19 August 2001. Nehru wrote the foreword for one of Khosla's books. The proverbial fly in the ointment was the backdrop of a public slight Khosla had endured during his only meeting with Subhas Bose at Cambridge in the early 1920s, when both were young ICS aspirants. Khosla happened to be passing by when Bose was explaining to his fellow Indian students of his decision to quit the heaven-born service. Khosla thought there was nothing unpatriotic in Indians substituting Englishmen in the service. Bose, in Khosla's own words, gave him 'a withering look of contempt'.[13] V N Datta, a former president of Indian History Congress, commented that this experience 'was bound to rankle in Khosla's heart'.[14]

At his residence in Calcutta, an ailing Sunil Das tendered before the commission his account of his association with Subhas Bose and what he made of the controversy surrounding his fate. Amar Prasad Chakraborty, the counsel for Forward Bloc and a would-be Member of Parliament, tried to get his secrets out:

> The point that I want to ask from you is that you knew Netaji intimately so as not to mistake his identity?
>
> His identity? So far as I am concerned, good heavens, never. How can I mistake his identity?
>
> Do you think that if Netaji is really alive, there is something really insurmountable which would prevent him from coming into the arena when the country is in utter confusion and chaos?
>
> Your question has two parts. Regarding the first part of the question my reply is, I believe that Netaji is alive. Regarding the second part I have no competence to go into it.

---

13   G D Khosla, *Last Days of Netaji*, Thomson Press, p 3.
14   V N Datta, 'Did Netaji actually die in 1945?' *The Tribune*, 19 August 2001.

How many times do you think Mrs Leela Roy met Sarat *babu*?

I think almost every day.

Were there any discussions regarding Netaji's alleged plane crash?

As far as I remember, Sarat babu [Subhas and Suresh's elder brother] never believed it.

Did Didi [Leela Roy] ever write regarding the disappearance of Netaji?

There were occasions when this subject cropped up in editorials [in her magazine *Jayasree*] after 1963. I should say, we noticed a change in her—within herself. Although I happened to be her closest colleague and in many matters she shared counsel with me, as you know, we had been trained in the crucibles of secret revolutionary politics, and we have developed a code and we maintain the code in this way. Unless I am specifically told, if somebody in the hierarchy wants to keep something within himself or herself, we do not try to get it. That has been our training. Up till now I carry that thing with me.

[Right to left: Sunil Das, Sunil Krishna Gupta, Amar Prasad Chakrovarty in suit, and Bose family lawyer N D Mazumdar. Source: Jayasree Prakashan]

The list of such persons of impressive background who took Bhagwanji to be Subhas Bose contained many more names because several people secretly met him over the years. Around forty people of Leela Roy's group in Kolkata were aware of his existence. Not everyone, of course, got to meet him or even exchange letters. One of the older revolutionaries who was part of the team that decided to send Pabitra to Neemsar was Ashutosh Kali (surname spelt with the variants Kahli and Kahilie), an Anushilan Samiti veteran who went on to become one of the trusted associates of Rash Behari Bose, and recruited Rajen Lahiri of Kakori Conspiracy fame.[15] Kali's History Sheet prepared by the British Indian police after his first arrest in 1916 observed, 'In 1910 he came in contact with Makhan Lal Sen of Sonarang, one of the most prominent figures in the annals of revolutionary crime, and from that time onward...he was in contact with the most important members of the revolutionary party.'[16] Like Maharaj, Kali too had been prevented by long years in prison from playing a bigger role in the freedom struggle. His arrest in 1940 came after he threw in his lot with Subhas Bose's organisational work for consolidating the radicals. In May 1963, he offered his services to Bhagwanji.

> The moment we received your instructions, we started maintaining secrecy. ...I am determined not to allow any laxity on our part...any danger to your existence is not just so for you, but also for us all. It can result in a great disaster as well as immense damage to the nation. [Translated from Bengali]

---

15   S P Sen (ed), Dictionary of National Biography Vol II, Institute of Historical Studies, Calcutta, pp 277-278.
16   History Sheet of Ashutosh Kahilie alias Master, Home Political, March 1918. National Archives of India.

Before he died in a tragic accident in 1965, Kali visited Bhagwanji in May 1963. This is what he wrote to him:

> Ever since we got news of you, all of us, the entire Anushilan group, have been yearning to gain from your guidance and work under your instructions. ...I have crossed the age of seventy (but) the idealism that I imbibed from the valiant revolutionaries, the courage with which I fought everything is still burning bright within me. ...If you give the clarion call, even at this point of life, I will not hesitate to join the movement. I wanted to inform you that Basanti Devi is desperate to receive news of you. She has requested us to let her know about your whereabouts. [Translated from Bengali by authors]

The reference to Basanti Devi in Kali's letter was probably to Subhas's mentor Chittaranjan Das's wife, a motherly figure to him, who lived to a ripe old age.

After being tipped-off by Leela Roy, Suresh Bose directed his confidant Sunil Krishna Gupta to go to Basti and find out the truth. Gupta returned from his first visit undecided, but it didn't

[Suresh Bose is seen paying homage to Leela Roy (died 1970)]

take long for his scepticism to be washed away. He would also meet the man behind the curtain face-to-face. Without offering any details, Suresh Bose went on to assert before the Khosla Commission in 1971 that his brother was alive at that time. Asked to 'take this commission into confidence and to say what are the reasons for believing this,' he curtly said, 'There is no reason why I should take this commission into confidence.'[17]

Suresh Bose passed away in 1972, but Sunil Krishna Gupta lived up to 2010 to tell his incredible tale of being in touch with 'Netaji' secretly.

Sunil Gupta went on to become one of the closest disciples of Bhagwanji. As the Khosla Commission worked in the early 1970s to investigate Subhas Bose's fate, Gupta along with Samar Guha kept a hawk's eye on the people involved and the work of the commission. He and Samar Guha were in Taipei when Justice Khosla landed there. In fact, it was Samar Guha's efforts that made the Commission's visit to Taipei possible. With Shah Nawaz Khan not being allowed to visit the place where the reported air crash involving Netaji had taken place on the lame pretext of India not having diplomatic relations with Taiwan, there was all the more pressure on Justice Khosla to undertake this visit. 'We cannot officially approach the Taiwan government in this matter,' read a 1970 Ministry of External Affairs (MEA) note following the receipt of a request from the commission. 'The alternative is to make discreet and unofficial enquiries with Taiwan's diplomatic Missions in Hong Kong or Japan or Bangkok,' further reads the declassified note.

---

17   Record of witness examination of Suresh Chandra Bose at the G D Khosla Commission, 17 August 1972, Alipore. Vol XII, p 3621.

SECRET

Ministry of External Affairs
(East Asia Division)

Subject:- Visit of the Netaji Enquiry Commission
to Taiwan.

Reference:- *Letter No. 8/1/70-NIC dated 31.8.1970
from the Secretary, Netaji Enquiry
Commission.

        We cannot officially approach the Taiwan
Government in the matter.

2.   The alternative is to make discreet and unofficial
enquiries with Taiwan's diplomatic Missions in Hong Kong
or Japan or Bangkok.

3.   Our experience with Taiwan's representative
stationed in Hong Kong has not been satisfactory. He
has proved to be a difficult man. He made numerous
attempts to establish contacts with officials of the
Indian Commission in Hong Kong and, when this proved
fruitless, insisted on an official request from the
Commission being addressed to him before he could conside
a particular visa application from any Indian national
desirous of visiting Taiwan.

[National Archives, New Delhi]

The MEA, however, opined that any attempt to reach out to the Taiwanese representative in Hong Kong would be 'counter productive' as he was 'believed to be one of their seniormost intelligence officers'. Similar apprehensions had been cast in 1956 when Shah Nawaz Committee desired to approach the Taiwanese. 'It is unlikely that the Formosan government will give any facilities. In fact, they may put obstacles and suggest degrading conditions,' read a declassified telegram from that time. Facts on record, however, show that each time Taiwan authorities were approached, in 1956 and thereafter, they offered cooperation without any strings attached. It's our people in New Delhi who smelt a conspiracy due to their own hidden fears. The stalemate over Khosla Commission's visit to Taiwan eventually forced an intervention by Samar Guha and the other lawmakers. A joint letter

to Prime Minister Indira Gandhi signed by twenty-six of them—
Atal Bihari Vajpayee's name appearing prominently—demanded
that the commission 'should be given facilities to visit Taiwan'.
It was pointed out that 'many Indian government officials visit
Formosa every year, even though India has no diplomatic relations
with the island'. When the Government still did not concede to
their demands, Guha had to play hardball. In a private meeting with
Indira Gandhi, he threatened to take the lid off India's intelligence
links with Taiwan. It worked, for the time being, and in July 1973,
G D Khosla landed at Taipei's Songshan airport. Guha beseeched
him right there to contact the Taiwanese authorities only to be
informed that the MEA had already instructed the judge not to.
'Why have you come over here, then? Why did you not tell us this
in Delhi?' Guha shouted.

'Why have you come to Taipei after twenty-seven years?'
people asked Guha and Gupta. Somehow, they obtained
permission from the Taiwanese authorities to inspect the out of
bounds, unused old airstrip from where the Japanese bomber
had allegedly taken off and crashed. But persuading Khosla to
go there proved trickier. After he reached there, Khosla acted up.
He wouldn't get out of his car and when he did, he began gazing
at the sky, his arms crossed on his chest, a clear sign of negative
body language. Guha tried to draw his attention to the apparent
mismatch between the topography of the area and the one seen in
the pictures of the plane debris furnished by the Japanese to prove
Bose's death. The pictures showed the debris strewn near a hill,
whereas according to the survivors, and a sketch confidentially
provided by the Japanese foreign office to its Indian counterpart

in 1956, the plane had crashed just next to the runway.

The hills, as Guha and others noted, were miles away even from the new runway. Apparently the Japanese had fobbed off to the Allies pictures of debris of some other plane. His adrenaline running fast, Guha turned to G D Khosla, 'Look at the pictures! Look at the hills in the background! They don't match! These pictures were planted!'

'What am I to do with these pictures?' Khosla flew off the handle. 'I have nothing to do with them.'[18] Then turning away, he barged into his car. He was treating the pictures as 'inadmissible in evidence' because of the legal technicality that Habibur Rahman, the single most important eyewitness to Netaji's reported death in 1945, had not appeared before him to testify 'to what they depict'.

What appeared to others at that time as a strong desire on the part of Sunil Gupta to know the truth had a deeper meaning. He would reveal it nearly three decades later in 2003. When questions were raised regarding his letters to Bhagwanji, found at Ram Bhawan, Gupta told the Mukherjee Commission: 'I went there [Taiwan] to participate in the Khosla Commission of Inquiry. Whenever I used to go to participate in the said Inquiry, I used to meet Bhagwanji for his advice. After return also, I used to apprise him of the proceedings held.'

All of Sunil Gupta's siblings were freedom fighters with nephew Dinesh Gupta (elder to him in age) being one of the legendary Benoy–Badal–Dinesh trio. In a heroic tale not too well-

---

18   Samar Guha, *Netaji: Dead or Alive?* Calcutta Book House, 1997 edition, p 54.

known outside Bengal, the three teenagers in 1930 made a daring
entrance into the Writers' Building and shot dead a top cop for he
had mistreated Subhas Bose and others. Today statues of the three
martyrs are a popular landmark outside what used to be the seat
of power in West Bengal until a few years ago when large-scale
renovation took government offices out. Sunil Krishna Gupta
assisted Amar Prasad Chakraborty, the Forward Bloc counsel
before the Khosla Commission. Many of Chakraborty's posers
for the witnesses evidently came from Sunil and they certainly
did not fit in the present-day Forward Bloc's confused worldview,
which doesn't see Subhas Bose emerging alive out of the USSR.

In the 1990s, Sunil Gupta was the moving force behind
Rudra Jyoti Bhattacharjee's PIL leading to the formation of
the Mukherjee Commission in 1999. An article in the *TIME*
magazine described Sunil Gupta as someone who 'demands no
recognition and even refuses to be named'.[19] Because he died in
penury, even some Bose family members who knew him have
trouble recalling Sunil Gupta's name today. Records declassified
in 2016, however, testify to Gupta's credibility. It wasn't always
so. Writing to the then Prime Minister V P Singh to make the
point that the story of Bose's death was far from established, one
of Subhas's grandnephews, Ashis Ray acknowledged that he had
to depend on, of all persons, Sunil Krishna Gupta to put together
his note (Ray's belief has undergone a complete turnaround since
then).[20] Earlier, on 17 August 1956, Intelligence Bureau Deputy

19   Meenakshi Ganguly, 'Keeping the Faith,' *TIME*, 19 April 1999.
20   Note accompanying letter of Ashis Ray to V P Singh, 19 August 1990 in PMO
      File No 800/6/C/1/90-POL, Netaji Subhash Bose – Bringing in the ashes of…

Director S Balakrishna Shetty—the officer in charge of the matters relating to Subhas Bose—wrote to the Home Ministry: 'We reliably understand that some of the Top Secret papers of the Government of India made available to the Chairman of the Netaji Enquiry Committee are now in the possession of one Sunil Krishna Gupta.... He appears to have obtained them through his friend Mr [Suresh] Bose....'

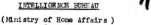

INTELLIGENCE BUREAU

(Ministry of Home Affairs)

SECRET.

We reliably understand that some of the Top Secret papers of the Government of India made available to the Chairman of the Netaji Enquiry Committee are now in the possession of one Sunil Krishna Gupta, 25/A, Kristo Dass Pal Lane, Calcutta. He appears to have obtained them through his friend Mr. Bose who was a member of the Netaji Enquiry Committee and intends to show them to Mr. Muthuramalinga Thevar his freind.

For information and for the consideration of the Ministry of Home Affairs if any action is to be taken against S.K. Gupta.

Sd/-

S. Balakrishna Shetty
DEPUTY DIRECTOR

M.H.A. (Shri A.V. Pai)
D.I.B. U.O.No.31/DG/56 dated, 17 August 1956.

[National Archives, New Delhi]

Actually, it was the other way around. It was Gupta who had obtained the papers for Suresh Bose to enable him to write his *Dissentient Report*. All the same, following an investigation, then Bengal Chief Secretary S N Ray had this to say through his 10 June 1957 Top Secret letter:

Sunil Krishna Gupta…is well educated, possesses considerable cultural attainments and is intimately known to the Bose family. All the members of Sunil's family, including his two grown up sisters, were associated with the political movement in the Far East sponsored by the late Subhas Chandra Bose.

Sunil Gupta was not the only member of his family devoted to Bhagwanji. His elder brother Atul kept in touch. Their nephews Jagatjit and Surajit Dasgupta (both of whom passed away recently) visited Bhagwanji for the first time in 1979 and also in 1982 and 1983, and at some point, had a chance glimpse of the mystery man's face. None of them were ever in any doubt about the true identity of the man.

More names were added to the list of people sent to Bhagwanji by Leela Roy and Pabitra Mohan Roy over the years. One of the earliest ones who was not from one of the revolutionary groups was Kumar Bishwanath Roy, an affluent man who had the financial means to provide for Bhagwanji's many requirements. For Kumar, there was no beating around the bush—he was as direct as one could be regarding Bhagwanji's identity. 'I was a boy of twelve years when you had come along with Deshbandhu to campaign for Bidhan Roy in 1923 at the field adjacent to my house. Attracted to your personality, I had resolved to become someone like Subhas Chandra when I grew up,' he wrote. Kumar 'reminded' Bhagwanji that he had worked with Subhas from 1935 to 1941 and along with Sarat Bose, was elected to the legislative council of Bengal in 1945, but turned from politics to spirituality after India's partition. Going by another note of Kumar, Mahamaya Prasad (most probably Mahamaya Prasad Sinha, who went on to join

Charan Singh in forming the Bharatiya Kranti Dal and becoming Bihar's first non-Congress Chief Minister) was expected to lend support to Bhagwanji's group through Gopal Sastri of Gaya, a former Congress activist from the pre-independence days. It is not known whether they made it to the inner coterie or if contact was established.

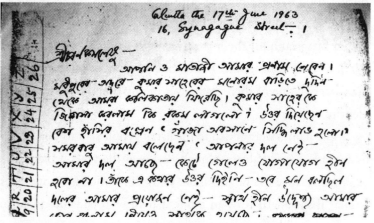

[A letter from Amal Roy to Bhagwanji. A Netaji aficionado, Amal used to spent significant time with Bhagwanji along with his friend Pabitra Mohan Roy]

In 1965, Leela Roy sent another of her ardent followers Dulal Nandy (who passed away in early 2018) to meet Bhagwanji. On reaching his destination, a building known as Lal Kothi, Nandy found Amal Roy, Sunil Gupta and Gopi Krishna Bandopadhyay already present there. Bhagwanji took a great liking to Dulal. Over the years he came to be addressed by him as 'Braja Nandan' or simply 'Nandan'. Dulal, who visited Bhagwanji every year from 1965 to 1985 except 1973, played an important role in moving the holy man from one location to another, but claimed never to have seen his face. His compatriot and another Leela Roy aide, late Santosh Bhattacharya, who had served Bose as young party worker in the late 1930s, was luckier for he did. He identified Bhagwanji as Bose.

Also to meet Bhagwanji in 1965 and get convinced that he was Subhas Bose was Apurba Chandra Ghose. He had interacted with Subhas Bose many times prior to 1941, and later worked as the manager of *Jayasree* magazine from 1951 to 1974. Standing in front of Justice Mukherjee at the age of 94, Ghose had a few interesting tales to tell:

> In 1939, Netaji stayed at Manikganj for one day only in the kutcharibari [office building] of a Zamindar. In the same kutcharibari, Leela Roy, Prof Jyotish Chandra Ghosh, Anil Roy and the Private Secretary of Netaji also stayed on that day. I was in charge of that kutcharibari. When I first met the Bengali *Sanyasi* at Basti, he asked me about my native place. I replied that I hailed from Manikganj in Dacca district, which was then in East Pakistan. He then asked me whether I was the man who had offered him a hair comb when he came out of the bathroom in that kutcharibari after having his bath.
>
> I replied in the affirmative. He then asked me whether I could remember that he smiled when I offered him the comb. When I replied that I had noticed him smiling, he told me that he smiled because I made a silly mistake while offering him the comb. He told me that I should have offered the comb on a plate or dish instead of offering it with my bare hands.
>
> He also enquired about Bahadur who was a durban in his Elgin Road residence while he lived there. I told him that I knew Bahadur and that it was Bahadur from whom I used to take the key for entering the living room of Netaji. He then asked

me whether I had seen a calendar with a picture of the Goddess Kali in that room; I replied that I had seen that calendar in that room.[21]

Bijoy Nag visited Bhagwanji for the first time in 1970 and continued to meet him every year till 1977. Not everyone was sent to Bhagwanji at the same time. Also, there is no way of knowing for sure who all kept in touch with him believing he was Subhas Bose. All those who met him were sworn to secrecy, and Bhagwanji would destroy much of his correspondence. Former revolutionaries were very carefully conveyed the news of the 'return of Netaji', at least the most prominent among them. If some of them believed the news (and consequently verified the truth themselves) knowing that Leela Roy wouldn't contact them with unfounded claims, some turned her away. To a great extent, this distrust was based on antagonism among revolutionary groups as well as personal rivalries going back two to three decades.

Hem Chandra Ghosh presents one of the examples of this category. Ghosh was the erstwhile leader of the feared Bengal Volunteers revolutionary group that emerged from Subhas Bose's volunteer group of the 1928 Calcutta Congress. Ghosh, one of the founders of Sri Sangha broke away from Anil Roy after a long-drawn dispute over revolutionary policy. Roy's growing influence soon led to a personality clash and Ghosh broke off from both Roy and Leela (then Nag) and joined the Bengal Volunteers of

---

21   Record of witness examination of Apurba Chandra Ghose at Justice Mukherjee Commission, 12 May 2003, Kolkata.

Satya Gupta who too was a former member of Sri Sangha.[22] Gupta was the same person who campaigned that Saradananda of Shoulmari was Subhas Bose. It has also been hypothesised that in portraying the revolutionary protagonist Sabyasachi in his famous novel *Pather Dabi* (proscribed in the British era), Sarat Chandra Chattopadhyay drew inspiration from Ghosh.[23] 'Bar-da' or 'Hem-da', as he was fondly called by his younger comrades, including Subhas (Bhagwanji also referred to him as such), was the brain behind many a revolutionary upsurge.

Credentials of Ghosh were presented to Bhagwanji for his approval to accept the former revolutionary in the close inner circle. A note recovered from Faizabad read: 'He is an ardent follower of yours. He avoided active politics in your absence, and will not do anything until you issue specific directions to him.... He did not believe Saradananda of Shoulmari.' Ghosh, however, was not enthusiastic in his response. The available correspondence indicates that this could have been due to his conviction that if Subhas ever came back, he would personally contact his 'Hem-da'. The response of Satya Ranjan Bakshi, one of the earliest comrades of Subhas who swore by Deshbandhu and who continued to believe that Subhas was alive was in similar strain.

There were others who would neither believe what they were told, nor would they completely reject it. Leaders of Forward

22   Amiya K Samanta (ed), 'Report on the Dacca Sri Sangha up to 1929, REA Ray, Bengal Government Press, 1932,' *Terrorism in Bengal: A Collection of Documents Vol II*, Government of West Bengal, 1995 pp 975, 991.
23   Sankari Prasad Basu, *Vivekananda O SamakalinBharatbarsha*, Vol VI, Mandal Book House, pp 160-61.

Bloc—Ashok Ghosh (who remained the West Bengal state general secretary of the party from 1946 till he breathed his last in 2016), Kanailal Bhattacharya (who became a minister in the Left Front government of the state) and Amar Prasad Chakraborty—were informed. Although the Forward Bloc claimed to be the party founded by Subhas Bose, it went through a major split in the late 1940s when the Marxist group in the party gained dominance and aligned with the Communist Party. The other (anti-communist) faction to which belonged Anil Roy, Leela Roy and their followers formed the Subhasist Forward Bloc and eventually joined the Praja Socialist Party, becoming political rivals. Although the Forward Bloc leaders held Leela Roy in immense respect, the political differences probably came in their way of going along with her.

Once Pabitra Mohan Roy confronted Ashok Ghosh, to be told that, 'Now that he has become a sadhu, what purpose will be served in going after him?'

'Please ask him when was I a sadhu (dishonest)?' was Bhagwanji's repartee on hearing Pabitra's report.[24] When Chandrachur Ghose asked Ashok Ghosh about his opinion on Bhagwanji in an interview conducted in 2007, he admitted knowing it all but had no explanation for his inaction or non-response.

Bhagwanji was constantly kept updated about the people who were being contacted by the Kolkata group, but he was paranoid about masking his identity. 'Tell them that he is alive, nothing

---

24   Authors' interview with Ranendra Mohan Roy, son of Pabitra Mohan Roy.

more,' was his standing instruction for those who he felt could be allowed in the outer circle of his trust. Yet, there were people who either chanced upon him, or met him after coming to know about him from other sources. In an intriguing letter, he wrote to Leela Roy:

> Sometime ago three people, one after the other, came to meet me. I don't know how they landed up here. One among them was a person who Deshbandhu [CR Das] had himself introduced, in his drawing room, to the 'dead man' after his return from England as an ICS. All the three people were in constant contact till the 'end' [probably a reference to January 1941]. They said that 'You are alive despite the Shoulmari controversy only because you are living like this in UP. If you were in Bengal, it would have been impossible to live incognito. It would not be possible for you to remain hidden even if you lived in a house surrounded by seven walls....' [Translated from Bengali by Chandrachur Ghose]²⁵

Breaking down in tears, these people told Bhagwanji, to his shock, that his manner of talking had remained unchanged. Anyone who had known him for some time would immediately identify him. 'The way you talk hasn't changed a bit. Your Bengali vocabulary and diction are exactly identical to those in the past. The same little stammer, with a little drawl, frequent use of same words such as *korto* [used to] and *kore ache* [has done] remains the same.' ²⁶ Bhagwanji did not disclose the identities of the men who met him. Neither did they disclose anything about Bhagwanji

---

25   Charanik, *Oi Mahamanaba Ase* (2010 edition), Jayasree Prakashan, p 431.
26   Ibid.

after their return to Calcutta. Like much else they remained as shadows hovering around the man of mystery, probably assisting him in ways that would never be known.

Dwijendra Nath Bose, nephew of Subhas, was also sounded out, but exact details were not divulged. A note found in Faizabad, in all probability written by Kumar Bishwanath Roy, describes Dwijen's attitude:

> Dwijen has now started believing that 'he' has returned to the country. He told me, 'I don't know where he is,' and asked me to inform him if I ever contact 'him'. He asked me to convey that 'I will do everything for him. Although I am staunchly anti-Communist, I am ready to go against my own ideas if he so desires.'

Such emphatic assertion to Roy indicates that the story Bose's nephew gave to the Khosla Commission about 'Purdah Baba' didn't end where his narrative stopped. Dwijen asserted before the Khosla Commission on oath in 1972 that his uncle Subhas was alive but refused to elaborate. All he would say was:

> If I give a clue in this committee, that would be made public and the Government will know of it and that is dangerous to Netaji. It is for him (Netaji) to decide when that should be made public or when he should return to India.[27]

Despite the closeness of the network, it was not always foolproof. Whispers of Bhagwanji's presence and identity did

---

27   Record of witness examination of Dwijen Bose at the G D Khosla Commission.

leak out at times to people outside the closely-knit inner circle. Leela Roy once reported to Bhagwanji that some workers of Forward Bloc had got wind of his existence and were planning to gatecrash. However, the system of double-filtering—first at the level of the followers and then by Bhagwanji himself on the basis of credentials submitted by them—managed to keep him isolated from unwanted visitors.

People from Kolkata or Uttar Pradesh, however, formed only a part of Bhagwanji's network. In total secrecy, many were getting in touch with him from different corners of the country. One of those names would give goosebumps to the RSS–BJP rank and file—if not their top leaders who are giving the Congress leaders a run for their money in eulogising Mahatma Gandhi. The *Guruji* of the entire current top brass of the Sangh Parivar—former Prime Minister Vajpayee, former Deputy PM Advani, former HRD Minister Dr Murli Manohar Joshi, RSS chief Mohan Bhagwat, his predecessor the late K S Sudarshan and, above all, Prime Minister Narendra Modi—maintained a contact with Bhagwanji. Here is a letter written in late 1972 by Madhav Golwalkar to Bhagwanji testifying that he held the latter in the highest esteem. The handwriting was identified by Dr Joshi, who has for years spoken out and taken steps towards resolving the Netaji mystery matter.

Golwalkar starts his letter, part of the inventory prepared by the Allahabad High Court's order, with the salutation: 'I bow before you a hundred times.' The contents of this letter, coupled with Bhagwanji's utterances make it clear that Golwalkar, who ran India's biggest social organisation, was taking instructions and words of advice from a seemingly non-descript, mostly-unseen holy man. Bhagwanji scribbled 'Dr Hedgewar' at the top of the letter. On its backside, he appeared to have made some astrological calculations about Golwalkar, who was rather unwell at that time. When he passed away a few months later, Bhagwanji felt shattered. 'No one will ever know or understand what a loss this has been for me,' he told Pabitra Mohan Roy.

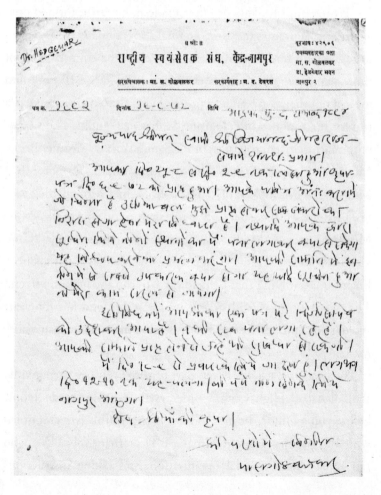

While it is not known whether Narendra Modi ever met Golwalkar, in his 2008 book *Jyoti Punj*, which is about 16 persons who inspired him, the essay on 'Pujniya Shri Guruji (Revered Shri Guruji)' is the longest.

Many names pop up at various places in the Bhagwanji narrative in a momentary flash only never to be heard of again: there was a certain Aulia *Saheb*, who knew who Bhagwanji really was and helped him. Bhagwanji did once mention about his secret stay at Nizamuddin Dargah in Delhi. He wrote letters, probably anonymously, to Balasaheb Thackeray and ABA Ghani Khan Choudhury, the late Congress leader from Malda. He would even say that 'his men' were 'in every key place (here and overseas)'; in military, government and in intelligence. 'Their garb is legal. They simply cannot be touched or detected.'

Bhagwanji attracted people across all divides. A certain Abdul Hafiz wrote to 'respected secret sadhu' in Hindi that he prayed to the Almighty for fulfilment of Bhagwanji's desires. 'Please take your original form at the earliest!' It is not very common for Hindu holy men to have Muslim followers. Bhagwanji had a Muslim attendant at Ayodhya. And he often quoted from the Bible. 'To everything there is a season, and a time to every purpose under the heaven.' A descendent of Guru Nanak Dev, Gurucharan Singh Bedi from Dera Baba Nanak in Gurdaspur, sent Bhagwanji a copy of the *Guru Granth Sahib* and wrote: 'Crores of Indians have put their eyes upon you.' There was a letter from Calcutta likening Bhagwanji to the invincible Bhishma, the grand old man in the epic *Mahabharata*. Bhagwanji once drew the same analogy for himself, saying he was the 'legal inheritor of this earth but was stepping aside from the path of ruling'.

Yet another letter in broken English by Gurucharan Singh Bedi read: 'People say you are Mother India's best son Netajee himself.' Bhagwanji himself used the metaphor for himself. 'I am a son of the motherland,' he wrote in Hindi in an undelivered letter to Vibhuti Narayan Singh, former Chancellor of Banaras Hindu University and last king of Kashi. Given his unusual structuring of sentences and preponderance of Bengali and Urdu words, Hindi was clearly not Bhagwanji's first language.

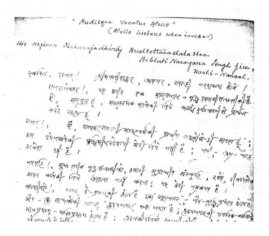

Also found at Ram Bhawan was a postcard written by one B K Kaul, who lived in Delhi, in November 1971. It appears from his letter that Kaul pledged all his wealth for 'the goodness of Man's service', and was anxious to meet Bhagwanji. Of course, not everyone who wanted to meet Bhagwanji got the chance. He was highly selective and at times took years before granting an audience.

At some point in time, political activist Manu Bhai Bhimani—who had been associated with Gandhi, Subhas and other leaders before 1947—came in contact with a Bhagwanji follower. The follower assessed Bhimani and made a short note for Bhagwanji's perusal.

> He [Bhimani] came in contact through a common friend. He talks too much. He says that:
> 1. If Netaji is in India why does he not appear or broadcast? All the people will accept his leadership at once.
> 2. ….
> 3. He helped Shri Sarat Chandra Bose all the time till he was alive.
> 4. He helped Netaji when he escaped from Calcutta to Kabul. Sisir and Manu Bhai went with him. He has a special white bag which he used when he accompanied Netaji.
> I verified the points 3 and 4 from Sisir Bose—Point 3 is correct, but point 4 is not correct. Bhimani also sent me a letter which has been sent for your kind perusal.

'He has lied,' Bhagwanji commented. He dismissed as 'false' Bhimani's claim that he had helped Sarat Bose until his death in 1950. He crossed out both points 3 and 4 and wrote: 'You don't know facts. *Mejda* helped him. Everyone knows this except you fool.'

In front of his very few most trusted followers, Bhagwanji addressed Sarat Bose and Suresh Bose as *Mejda* and *Sejda* respectively—just as Subhas used to. He referred to Subhas's mother as his own, and treated with veneration an umbrella that was said to be of Janaki Nath Bose, Subhas's father.

Efforts were also made to bring a certain Panna Dasgupta (most likely a former revolutionary and then leader of the Revolutionary Communist Party of India), but his behaviour was not considered worthy of further persuasion. 'He was found bragging about how he is exploiting me in the name of Netaji,' says a report to Bhagwanji from Kumar Bishwanath Roy. Once Roy also reported to Bhagwanji about a conversation he had had with Central minister Ashoke Sen:

> He (Sen) asked me: 'Well, does your gurudev live in India? Was Shoulmari sadhu Netaji himself?' I took stock of the situation and replied, 'I heard from Niharendu Dutt Majumdar that this sadhu was not Netaji.' I avoided the first question and slipped out. I doubt he knows something. You should be vigilant. [Translated from Bengali by authors]

Ashoke Sen, who became the Law Minister in Rajiv Gandhi's government, most likely knew something about Bhagwanji. As Bijoy Nag told us after checking Leela Roy's papers, a problem faced by Bhagwanji with the local official in Neemsar was resolved by Sen. Ranendra Mohan, Pabitra's son confirmed this incident. Evidently, Bhagwanji shared his secrets with his followers on the need-to-know basis.

At some point in time, the news of Bhagwanji's presence trickled down in Bengal to Balak Brahmachari, founder of the cult group called Santan Dal. Its members thereafter started a vociferous public campaign to proclaim that Subhas Bose was alive with the apparent motive of boosting their own prospects. Graffitis across the state announcing 'Netaji is alive' and 'Netaji will return as the leader' were a common sight until the 1990s. Some are seen even now. In December 2017, such a poster was spotted even in Lucknow Cantonment. On social media too, Brahmachari's supporters continue their campaign fired by their flights of fancy. In a poster circulated by them, Brahmachari is given a pride of place along with Bose, Homi Jehangir Bhabha, Air Marshal Subroto Mukerjee and even Adolf Hitler, all of whom died in mysterious circumstances. Incidentally, Brahmachari's own death in 1993 was followed by a controversy whipped up by his followers. They claimed that their dead guru had merely entered into a 'nirvikalpa samadhi' and would come back to life. After a 55-day stand-off and international media coverage, Brahmachari's body was seized by the police and cremated.

Papers recovered from Ram Bhawan throw light on how Brahmachari came to think about the idea of a living Netaji. Kumar Bishwanath Roy was summoned by Brahmachari—the connecting link between the two was Barindranath Ghosh, the former revolutionary and younger brother of Sri Aurobindo. Tears rolled down his cheeks as he clasped Roy's hands and told him in a choked voice, 'I don't want the rule of thieves under Atulya Ghosh and Prafulla Sen…I promise to extend every possible help to you in carrying out all work of Netaji; many of my disciples will contribute financially too.' Brahmachari did not get access to Bhagwanji although Roy wrote in his report to him that he came to trust Brahmachari. The letter is undated, but since Prafulla Sen was Bengal's chief minister from 1962-67, it can be guessed that it was written during this period. The authors have seen or heard nothing to suggest that Brahmachari came in contact with Bhagwanji. On the contrary, Bhagwanji told someone very close to him that he did not fancy Brahmachari much. The cult members, of course, have their own set of mostly unverifiable claims. One of these is that Pranab Mukherjee took *diksha* from Balak Brahmachari.

[Pranab Mukherjee paying respect to Balak Brahmachari. Source unknown to authors]

Come to think of it, the former President's name is intertwined with the entire Bose mystery. It figures in the context of all three theories of Bose's death. Mukherjee is one of the foremost votaries of the air crash theory, for which he doesn't have much fan following among several Netaji admirers and Bose family members, excluding those with links to the Congress party. Twice, Mukherjee was publicly heckled by those who did not agree with him. In the first instance, high drama unfolded on 23 January 1996 in Kolkata when Mukherjee was speaking at a programme to commemorate Netaji's centenary birth anniversary. Barely had

Mukherjee referred to Netaji in past tense, when a mob led by a man in a saffron robe started shouting slogans. One person climbed on to the stage and lunged towards Mukherjee, but was apprehended in time by guards. Mukherjee left the venue in a huff.[28]

Years later, Pranab Mukherjee was described in the Justice Mukherjee report as one of the seven witnesses who had testified before the commission in favour of the story of Bose's death in Taiwan. The rest included a fellow Congressman and Nehruite Natwar Singh who did not know much; a former INA veteran who lied under oath and a prejudiced journalist known to Mukherjee. In an ironical twist, Mukherjee, having returned to power in 2004, then sat in judgment on the commission report along with his other Cabinet colleagues. Since the chances of minister Mukherjee taking an objective view of justice Mukherjee's report were dim, there were murmurs of protest. Pranab was accused of trying to scuttle the commission's inquiry and that probably led to his facing the 'mob fury in Kolkata', while his car was entering a hotel on 18 June 2006.[29]

Behind the scenes, Mukherjee had as the External Affairs Minister in the Narasimha Rao government dealt with issues relating to the Bose mystery, including the demands that New Delhi take up the issue with Moscow. Declassified records show that the joint secretary in charge of Europe East Division (JS [EE])

---

28   Sudhir K Singh, 'Netaji diehards drum it into Pranab with bamboo sticks,' *The Pioneer*, 24 January 1996.

29   'Pranab faces ire over Netaji report', *Hindustan Times*, 18 June 2006, Accessed from http://www.hindustantimes.com/Pranab-faces-ire-over-Netaji-report/ Article1-110907.aspx.

in the Ministry of External Affairs made a realistic assessment of the situation. R L Narayan—who had had two stints in Moscow and would be an ambassador shortly afterwards—admitted that the official Russian response since 1991 to the Indian approaches was not satisfactory. Narayan clarified that a recent official Russian denial about not knowing anything about Bose was not based on the 'Stalinist period (KGB archives)'. He explained: 'Papers relating to the Stalinist period (KGB archives) are kept separately and have so far not been accessed by foreign and even Russian scholars.' Narayan recommended issuing a démarche (a petition) to the Russians seeking a search of the KGB archives for 'any evidence of Netaji's stay in the Soviet Union'.

by foreign and even Russian scholars, with the exception perhaps of very limited and selected scholars like the late historian Volkogonov, who has published biographies of Lenin and Stalin on this basis. Papers relating to the post-Stalinist period fall into two categories - governmental and Central Committee/Politburo (these are again kept separately). The Russian Foreign Ministry's Note Verbale suggests that their disclaimers about Netaji may be based essentially on perusal of these latter archives.

6.   It would be unrealistic for us to expect the Russian authorities to allow our scholars access to KGB archives.   What we can do is to request the Russian authorities to conduct a search into these archives and let us know if there is any evidence of Netaji's stay in the Soviet Union.

7.   It is recommended that we may request our Ambassador in Moscow to make a suitable demarche to the Russian authorities on the above lines.

(R.L. Narayan)
Joint Secretary(EE)
January 12, 1996

[National Archives, New Delhi]

Narayan's note was seen by Mukherjee, who then directed Foreign Secretary Salman Haidar to discuss the issue with Narayan 'urgently'.

EAM F.S and J.S (EE) my pl discuss || urgently.

Pm.
14/1/96

The outcome of the meeting became apparent with the events that followed. No démarche was ever issued. Making an about-turn, Narayan in his next note dropped his sympathetic line. In March, he made the following conclusion:

9.   In the circumstances, it is felt that it would not be appropriate for Government of India to make a formal request to the Russian Government to open their KGB/Presidential archives to the Asiatic Society scholars.   This would amount to our disbelieving the Russian Government's categorical and official statement on the subject.

(R.L. Narayan)
Joint Secretary (EE)
7.3.1996

In 2016, Pranab Mukherjee's name was dragged into the Gumnami Baba matter as well. A follower of Bhagwanji, Ravindra Shukla, stated before the Sahai Commission in October 2016 that around 1981-82, he was instructed by Bhagwanji to accompany a Bengali gentleman to the local market. The Bengali gentleman, according to Shukla, was Pranab Mukherjee.[30] It is difficult to

---

30   Written submission of Ravindra Nath Shukla to Justice Vishnu Sahai
     Commission, 10 October 2016, Faizabad.

imagine that a Union minister (Mukherjee held Commerce and Steel & Mines portfolios around that time) would go around like this. But then, the whole Bhagwanji saga itself is incredible. He did receive many visitors, and, going by his accounts and those of his followers, top level people met him on the sly. And, we have another follower telling us that once Bhagwanji praised Mukherjee for his sharp memory. The man behind the curtain was not in the habit of commenting for a lark.

In August 2014, Prime Minister Modi remarked that 'a half-an-hour talk with Mukherjee is like reading a good book'. He heaped praise on the then President, who, he said, 'can remember dates and times of historical events'. He wondered 'what software his brain is made of'.[31] But this was not the impression of those who witnessed Pranab Mukherjee give evidence before the Mukherjee Commission. He entered New Delhi's Vigyan Bhawan on 15 October 2001 with nervousness writ large on his face. Why would such an eminent person of such exalted stature, unmatched experience and boundless wisdom be so anxious at such a low-key occasion no media was interested in covering? From barely two meters away, Anuj Dhar (witness No 50) observed Pranab Mukherjee (witness No 48) closely as the commission examined him. Mukherjee answered Justice Mukherjee's questions with his face flushed, his fingers twitching.

31   'Prime Minister Narendra Modi Misses Wit and Humour in Parliament', NDTV, 13 August 2014, accessed from: https://www.ndtv.com/india-news/prime-minister-narendra-modi-misses-wit-and-humour-in-parliament-648589.

'Mr Mukherjee, in 1995 you were the Minister in charge, External Affairs, Government of India?' Justice Manoj Mukherjee asked him. 'Yes,' Pranab Mukherjee answered. 'In that capacity, did you deal with the issue of bringing the alleged ashes of Netaji Subhas Chandra Bose kept in the Renkoji temple to India?' the judge further asked. On getting an affirmative response, the judge put the next query: 'Does not that necessarily mean that you were in firm conviction that Netaji was dead?'

'No,' Pranab Mukherjee replied instantaneously. It meant that it was not Pranab Mukherjee's personal conviction that Netaji had died in 1945. Pausing a little, he elucidated this: 'At that time, the position of the Government of India was that the ashes were of Netaji.' Therefore, what Pranab Mukherjee tried to do in 1995 was in deference to the Government of India's stand, which he, as a minister, was duty bound to follow. More telling was his dodging of the last question put to him by Justice Mukherjee. 'Is there any documentary or other evidence within your knowledge, which is relevant to the terms of reference [assigned to this commission]?' He answered: 'Except the earlier two reports of the committee and commission as stated earlier, I have no other material.'[32]

Considering the deep reverence he says he has for Netaji, it is inconceivable that Pranab Mukherjee's insight into Netaji's fate should be restricted to merely possessing two reports any college student could have easily found in public libraries. In recent years,

---

32   Record of the oral evidence tendered by Pranab Mukherjee before the Mukherjee Commission.

the former President has written volumes dealing with a whole gamut of issues relating to Indian politics which he came across in his long and illustrious career. There is no mention whatsoever of any of the many matters relating to Subhas Chandra Bose that he personally handled—for which numerous official records are now available, thanks to the declassification undertaken by the Modi government when he was the President. In an op-ed article in *The Indian Express* on 26 July 2017 to mark the end of Mukherjee's tenure as the thirteenth President of India, Prithviraj Chavan, former Maharashtra Chief Minister and MoS in Dr Manmohan Singh's PMO, narrated his 'good fortune to work with and closely observe Pranab*da* since 1991'. Vouching for his 'razor-sharp memory', Chavan recalled how Mukherjee 'would keep us spellbound with his vast knowledge of history of modern India'. The discussions, Chavan wrote, 'would often carry on for hours'. In contrast, the Pranab Mukherjee who appeared before the Justice Mukherjee Commission of Inquiry was taciturn, reserved and foxed. His answers were short and he made no attempt to get into details. Chavan in his *Express* article had this telling anecdote:

Pranab*da* is very good at keeping secrets. In fact, Indiraji used to say, 'Whenever Pranab*da* is given any confidential information, it never comes out of his belly. What comes out is only the smoke from his pipe.'

FIVE

THE ROAD TO FAIZABAD

IN THE DEAD of the night, a car stopped outside the Shiv temple at Neemsar with two trucks following. Panda Shiv Narayan and his wife stood looking with bewilderment as the car and the trucks sped off. They had no idea where to. It was June 1964.[1]

The arrival of Pabitra Mohan Roy, followed by Leela Roy, Sunil Krishna Gupta and their handpicked team of faithfuls changed not only the material condition of Bhagwanji, but also the nature of information related to him. Till then, no one had recorded his thoughts and his activities in any manner. Now, with meticulous notes of meetings being taken down by most of the visitors

---

1   *Jayasree*, Magh 1419 (Jan-Feb 2012), based on a letter written by Anil Das to Leela Roy. However, Srikant Sharma claimed that Bhagwanji moved out of Neemsar in July.

from Calcutta and large volume of communication, it gradually became possible to create an analytical profile of the man of mystery. Others too recorded their recollections and impressions with journalists and also with the Justice Mukherjee Commission. However, before we delve into that analysis, it is important to complete the chronological account of his movements until he reached Ram Bhawan in 1983, his last known residence. As dates available from various sources are not always accurate, we have tried to rely primarily upon documentary evidence in the form of notes, diaries and letters and accorded recollections of Bhagwanji's followers secondary importance.

The stay at Neemsar had started getting too eventful for Bhagwanji's comfort. The feud of the Pandas, tantrums of Chowdhary's sister and finally the arrival of people from Calcutta had put him in the middle of much attention that he wanted to avoid at all costs. Added to these was a visit of the high-profile spiritual guru Anandamayee Ma who held a much publicised Samyam Mahavrata Saptah (a week-long resolve to practice self-control) followed by a another week of *Bhagavad Purana* recital in October and November 1960 which was attended by hundreds of her disciples including bureaucrats and politicians from across the country.[2]

Bhagwanji narrated to his Calcutta followers that Anandamayee Ma insisted on meeting him. It is not possible to say for sure what exactly she knew about his identity at that point

---

2   'Shree Shree Anandamayee Sangha,' *Ananda Varta*, Vol VIII No 4, pp 175-190, Varanasi.

of time, but with the local Panda network joining her, she must have picked up the whispers. Rajkumar recalls that a road was laid down overnight to connect the Shiv temple with the main road to facilitate her arrival. Bhagwanji, however, refused to meet her.[3]

By August 1963, Bhagwanji made up his mind to move out of Neemsar. Finding a new location wasn't easy and it was nearly a year before he shifted to Faizabad.[4] Anil Das, Kamalakanta Ghosh and Santosh Bhattacharya executed the stealthy shift, which was the first of a series of frequent moves over the next year.

Protecting his identity and maintaining his security were of paramount importance. Bhagwanji therefore traversed the distance of over 200 km from Neemsar to Darshan Nagar crouching on the floor between the two rows of seats in a car, while Saraswati Devi and Rajkumar remained seated on the backseat.[5]

The new residence—Shankar Niwas in Darshan Nagar village, about 6 km to the east of Faizabad town—was soon found to be unsuitable for living, being damp and swamped with insects, but more importantly with only one route for entry and exit which went against Bhagwanji's security plan in choosing accommodation. Early in August 1964, the support team from Calcutta settled the new residence of Bhagwanji at Lal Kothi in Ayodhya's Baksaryia Tola, owned by Lucknow entrepreneur and proprietor of Speed Motors, Vishnu Narain. The *NIP* team

---

3   Charanik, *Oi Mahamanaba Ase*, Jayasree Prakashan, 2010, p 341. Interview of Rajkumar Shukla by the authors.

4   Witness examination of Srikant Sharma at the Justice Mukherjee Commission, 14 August 2001, Faizabad.

5   Interview of Rajkumar Shukla by the authors, 2016.

succeeded in tracking down Narain and getting his version of the story. The whispers in the town were that the 'Swamiji' who had taken shelter in his property 'was a very big personality'.

> More than two decades ago a Bengali person aged about 50 years approached me for accommodating a Swamiji in one of my kothis in Ayodhya. I allowed him to live in Lal Kothi. While he stayed in Lal Kothi, the Swamiji never appeared before anybody and always remained within the cloistered quarters of his room. The behaviour of the inmates did lead me to believe that he was a mysterious man indeed.[6]

At Shankar Niwas, the *NIP* investigation found out,

> The Man had a very close shave with the world around him. One morning, the villagers around climbed the high trees around Shankar Niwas to catch a glimpse of him. But strangely for a man who had ostensibly renounced this world, the security system was tight. A man wielding an automatic weapon sprang out from nowhere and threatened that he would not hesitate to shoot to kill if the intruders did not retreat immediately. Like chattering monkeys, the villagers scampered down the trees and fled.[7]

Such an incident is bound to draw attention in a small town, especially when it involved a *sanyasi* living mysteriously. Perfect food for gossip. The police arrived here too, but there was no

---

6   Nirmal Nibedon and Vishwambhar Nath Arora, 'A Fair Lady Comes at Midnight,' *Northern India Patrika*, 22 December 1985.

7   Nirmal Nibedon and Vishwambhar Nath Arora, 'I Pledge to Keep this Secret,' *Northern India Patrika*, 23 December 1985.

encounter. Even before the police could see him, Bhagwanji was gone. The *NIP* team reconstructed the event based on their interviews:

> The Swami's meticulous planning and yearning to live apart from the world once again aroused the curiosity of a person, a policeman for a change. The then inspector in charge of Ayodhya kotwali, Mr Jitendra Bahadur Singh, was a visitor to Mahant Vaidei Raman Saran of Hanumat Niwas some 50 yards away from the Lal Kothi where three roads met. Mahant Saran managed to send a discreet message to the escorts of the man that the Inspector wanted to meet the Swami face-to-face, come what may. No reply was received at the Hanumat Niwas. The Inspector wanted to live up to his name and planned a raid. He was determined to unmask the man in one swift, lightning strike; a counter-ambush of sorts, not knowing that the ground had already been vacated for any such eventuality. The Bahadur Inspector stormed in one night along with his posse, only to find empty rooms.[8]

According to Bijoy Nag's estimate based on the dates of letters exchanged, Bhagwanji stayed at Lal Kothi less than a year—from August 1964 to March 1965. The next destination was farther away, in Basti, 70-90 km east of Ayodhya, depending on the route. The quick change in residence continued in Basti too, with Bhagwanji leaving the first residence in just about a couple of months. The move to a lawyer's house at Pathan Tola in Purani Basti was organised by Sunil Krishna Gupta, where Bhagwanji

---

8   Ibid.

lived from early March to late May in 1965. However, the accommodation proved to be too small for his requirement.

The next move was to Sharista Kothi at Raja Maidan in Purani Basti—property of the royal family of Basti (which now lies in ruins), planned and executed by Dulal Nandy and others. Here, Bhagwanji would spend the longest time among all the places that he lived—over ten years, from May 1965 to September 1975 [or 1974].

The key new person to make an entry into Bhagwanji's circle of trust at Basti was a local lawyer, Durga Prasad Pandey. As in other places, rumours started flying thick and fast in Basti about the real identity of the monk in hiding. Groups of unknown Bengalis visiting him, the postman delivering letters and magazines like *The Illustrated Weekly of India* and *TIME* magazine (American) in big piles in a back of beyond town had the local rumour mill spinning. After many unsuccessful attempts to get an audience with Bhagawanji, Pandey finally wrote a letter to him on 10 February 1967. 'Here at Basti, I have been constantly keeping my watch while your honour had been residing in Sri Roop Kishore Vakil's house and now shifted to Raja Basti ka Hata,' Pandey wrote. Pandey's letter documents how the local people were intrigued by the unseen monk: 'the letters, the telegrams, the purchases in the market and buying standard English magazines and periodicals are another side of the coin to dazzle and puzzle the mind of the beholders about your mystery'. Then he broke the secret source of his information: 'An old and very religious ex-Revenue Officer, late Sri Jwala Prasad Misra, told me as to your honour's identity while breathing his last (sic).' Without mentioning the recipient's name, Pandey didn't leave any scope for doubt that he knew who he was writing to:

> You had been an ex-ICS of profound scholarship and far reaching command over English marked with an enormously beautiful and elegant handwriting, deep deep religious thinking and far reaching command over English...January 23rd was celebrated as your birthday here, the most auspicious day of the country, when the immortal words 'Jai Hind' resounded through and through all the flora and fauna on the Indian soil...I pledge to keep this secret as long as I am in this world.

Pandey's imploring met with this evasive response:

> I am a bonafide *dashnami sanyasi* and you will know that a man under the holy orders incurs death according to the civil laws and a *sanyasi* is dead to his former life.

As an afterthought, Bhagwanji added:

> In passing, you shall find cogent answers to all your hypotheses, queries, thoughts...both as expressed in your letter, and which remain unexpressed in your heart. Peruse with your heart calmly, quietly, lovingly. Every word, phrase, sentence and their constructions are pointers for you; they are pregnant with possibilities. Seek and thou shall find.

Pandey's persistence would pay off nonetheless. He was gradually allowed the access only a few had. Eventually, he even saw the man, almost daily, for nine years. About three decades later, an eighty-four-year-old Pandey told the Mukherjee Commission that the man he saw behind the curtain in 1967 was the same person he had seen from a very close distance making a two hours long speech in 1940 at the *Ganga* Prasad Memorial Hall in Lucknow.[9] That was the only time Pandey had seen Subhas Chandra Bose.

Pandey stuck to Bhagwanji for the remaining years of his stay at Basti and remained in contact in the subsequent years. Through the years, Pandey never wavered from the promise he made Bhagwanji—to keep his identity under wraps. When the police team investigating the 'Gumnami Baba case' approached him towards the end of 1985, Pandey burst forth in anger. 'If I answer your questions the whole country will be on fire,' he told the investigating officers.[10] He would speak only if he failed to withstand a third-degree torture or in front of a proper commission of inquiry, he insisted.[11]

While Bhagwanji lived in Basti, momentous political events were taking place that went a long way in changing the political identity of India. India emerged victorious in the 1965 Indo-Pak war; by January 1966 Prime Minister Lal Bahadur Shastri was dead immediately after signing the Tashkent Pact initiating the era of Indira Gandhi. 1971 saw the next Indo-Pak war and ascendancy of Mujibur Rahman as the leader of a new nation—Bangladesh. While these went on, people noticed unusual things happening around the mysterious guest. As the local investigation by the team of *NIP* journalists found, 'strange events transpired only in darkness...heavily curtained cars of all makes, Indian

---

9   Witness examination of Durga Prasad Pandey at the Justice Mukherjee Commission, 8 August 2001, Faizabad.
10 Ashok Tandon, 'Way Netaji nahin thay to kaun thay?' *Ganga*, May 1987.
11 Letter from Durga Prasad Pandey to the Justice Mukherjee Commission of Inquiry, dated 12 April 2001.

and foreign, city sahibs in three piece suits' would appear all of a sudden and vanish equally suddenly.[12]

Not surprisingly, these events piqued the curiosity of the local police, as it had at other places. This time, the Station House Officer tried to 'bust the mystery of the nameless Man', but his insistence to get an audience with the man got him 'summarily transferred the next day itself'.[13] Increasing public attention and threat to his cover meant it was time to move again.

This time, however, the responsibility to secure a new place fell on Pandey. For the first time after Neemsar, the Calcutta disciples were not involved. Pandey selected the Prahlad Dharmashala, owned by Panda Ram Kishore Mishra. On the day of Dhanteras in 1974, he took Bhagwanji to Ayodhya in a Maruti car (which belonged to his friend) and his twenty-five trunks in a truck.[14] An initially reluctant Mishra had agreed to rent out his accommodation when Pandey pleaded that his aged Guruji was having difficulty in finding a place to stay and agreed to pay the rent for the two months that he would live there in advance.[15]

The other departure from the usual was that Saraswati Devi didn't accompany Bhagwanji to the new place. She stayed back at Basti. Pandey had found a replacement, a Muslim attendant, to take care of Bhagwanji's daily needs.

Mishra went to meet the new tenant who he had been told

12   Nirmal Nibedon, with Vishwambhar Nath Arora, 'I Pledge to Keep this Secret,' *Northern India Patrika*, 23 December 1985.

13   Ibid.

14   Letter from Durga Prasad Pandey to the Justice Mukherjee Commission of Inquiry, dated 12 April 2001.

15   Audio recording of Ram Kishore Mishra's interview by *NIP* team.

was a Sant Mahatma after a few weeks, once the Kartik Mela was over (end of November). He had already been told that the monk did not meet anyone face-to-face and therefore wasn't surprised when he had to speak with his tenant from across a closed door. When Mishra visited again after a couple of days with his wife, Bhagwanji established a connect with them which both would fiercely protect till the end of their lives. 'You are my Nanda baba and she is my Yashomatimaiya. Now that I am in your shelter, it is up to you to protect me from any disturbance to my *sadhana*,' he told the visiting couple, referring to the tradition of Krishna. The discussion left the couple convinced that they had come across a person of a very high calibre. From his Hindi pronunciation, it was clear to Mishra, who hosted people from all regions of the country, that the Sant was a Bengali, but at the same time, the frequent use of Urdu words intrigued him.[16]

As had been agreed, Bhagwanji left Prahlad Dharmashala after two months. The new destination was a house in front of the Gurudwara Brahmakund in the same town. Again, it was Pandey who took charge of transporting Bhagwanji (in the same car in which he had been brought to Ayodhya from Basti) and his belongings late one evening. Mishra and his wife kept up their regular visits.

The next few years—January 1975 to May 1978—when Bhagwanji lived at Ramkot Ward, Gurudwara Brahmakund, were troublesome ones. To start with, the landlord Gurubaksh Singh Sodhi soon started creating trouble. When all was over, the *NIP*

16   Ibid.

team tracked down Sodhi and spoke with him.

> The owner of the house, Gurubux Singh Sodhi [sic], then
> already nearing 64, confirmed the peculiar characteristics
> of the Man. 'He was always in hiding, being called upon by
> strange people at night in cars of all sizes and shapes, with
> an extraordinary voice and sources of income which were
> unknown. Yes, some people said he was none other than Netaji
> Subhas Chandra Bose,' said the retired teacher, who today,
> along with his wife, runs a private school in the same premises
> where once sojourned the Man.
>
> Almost all the disclosures of Gurubux Singh Sodhi [sic] were
> confirmed by his observant children. His son confirmed to us
> that among the many strange vehicles was a flag car, which
> came in regularly...The grand-daughter of Mahant Narain
> Singh, the elder brother of Sardar Gurubux Singh Sodhi
> was another youngster who was drawn towards the Man.
> Miss Harpreet Kaur, lovingly called 'Lovely' wanted to learn
> English from the Man. The Man willingly imparted lessons
> in the English language, the standard of which made the girl
> spellbound. Lovely, 23, now an executive in a bank, recalls the
> resonant voice, the likes of which she never heard again.[17]

Current chief priest of Gurudwara Brahamakund Sahib,
Gyani Gurjeet Singh Khalsa, caught sight of Bhagwanji's as a
17-year-old. 'The radiance on his face was astounding. It cannot
be explained in words,' he told *The Times of India* in 2015.[18]
Another person to have come face-to-face with Bhagwanji was

---

17   Nirmal Nibedon and Vishwambhar Nath Arora, 'The Lame Law Lurks,'
     Northern India Patrika, 27 December 1985.
18   Subhro Niygo and Saikat Ray, 'Netaji, The Saint?' *The Times of India* (Kolkata
     edition) 14 October 2015.

Sodhi's grandson Charanjit, who was then a student of class eight. To this day, Charanjit vividly recalls the glow on the face of a bearded Bhagwanji that he saw when the curtain of his room was blown away by wind one morning as he carried milk for the old monk. Another aspect that he remembers was the regular visits of government cars and jeeps at night.[19]

Things started turning sour soon. As in the instances of the previous towns, gossip soon started flowing thick and fast. A local Hindi weekly *Swapna Rekha* carried a report on 3 July 1977 with the title 'Woh Sant ke Roop me Kaun?' The newspaper speculated that the hidden saint was 'so great a person that if he comes out in public his identity might bring a political storm in the country'. Sodhi himself got swept into the identity question, first filing a report on the suspicious activities of the mystery man with the police and then with the district magistrate and the state's home secretary. Undeterred by the administration's rebuff and threat to sue him for breach of peace in the town, Sodhi finally filed an eviction suit against Bhagwanji. The case was settled out of court and Bhagwanji moved on to the next accommodation at the nearby Lucknow-wali Hata (also called the Lucknow Kothi) near the Chhoti Devkali temple.

If Bhagwanji's stay at Brahmakund was marked by unwanted attention drawn to him by external troublemakers, it also saw the entry of a few people who would stay with him till the end. Among these were Dr T C Banerjee, renowned homeopath of Faizabad

19   Interview of Charanjit Singh Sodhi by the authors, Ayodhya.

(and eventually his family), Dr Raghunath Prasad Mishra, the district surgeon, Dr B Rai and Krishna Gopal Srivastava, an art teacher at the Rajkaran Vaidik Pathshala Inter College of Faizabad.[20] Saraswati Devi too was back to take up her usual role.

Dr T C Banerjee arrived on the scene when Bhagwanji's health had suddenly deteriorated and he was suffering from much pain in the joints and concomitant fever. Dr Banerjee passed away in 1983, but the *NIP* team got the first-hand account from his widow Pushpa Banerjee:

> In the year 1975, when the Man was living in Brahmakund Gurudwara complex in the house of Gurbux Singh Sodhi in Ayodhya, Saraswati Devi Shukla alias 'Jagdambe Ma' came to the late Dr TC Banerjee around noon one day with a request that the doctor should visit an ailing '*Sanyasi*'. The doctor, reluctant to go out, refused and asked the lady to bring the '*Sanyasi*' to his dispensary. But as the lady insisted, the doctor agreed without knowing that the visit would give him an unforgettable reward. On reaching the Man's place, he was not made to remain behind the curtain. Instead, the main doors of the apartment were opened for him.

It was an experience of a lifetime for the doctor who was astounded at the first sight of the Man. Awe-struck, he stood staring at the spectacle—unthought of and unbelievable. Though the bludgeonings of time had their effect on the physical self of the Man, his salient features remained unchanged. Prominent forehead, the glow of the eyes, the moonish face and resounding

---

20   Nirmal Nibedon and Vishwambhar Nath Arora, 'The Ultimate Refuge,' *Northern India Patrika*, 5 January 1986.

voice were all there intact for the doctor to perceive. Mrs Pushpa Banerjee clearly remembers that day when her husband remained in the room of the Man for hours together and came back excited over the turn of events, and full of remorse for the irony of history.[21]

Dr Banerjee unburdened his emotions in front of Ram Kishore Mishra. Once, when Mishra reached Gurudwara Brahmakund, he found Dr Banerjee standing outside. After the usual discussion about Bhagwanji's health, Mishra recalled, Dr Banerjee couldn't restrain himself anymore. 'Aap dhanya hain jo ke Subhas babu ki seva mein kuch samay de paatey hain (you are blessed to be able to spend some time in serving Subhas babu),' he blurted out. Mishra was dumbstruck for a few minutes.

Before long, Pushpa Banerjee and her son and daughter-in-law Dr Priyabrata Banerjee and Rita Banerjee were allowed into the inner precincts, where they interacted with the man sitting right in front of him. Other kin also managed access denied to most. Gorakhpur-based insurance agent Dilip Kumar Mukherjee, a nephew of Dr T C Banerjee, unexpectedly got lucky after years of persistent trying. He entered the room to feel Bhagwanji's penetrating glance from behind silver-rimmed glasses. Overwhelmed by the unimaginable spectacle of seeing 'Netaji' right in front of him, Dilip burst into tears. After he regained composure, he managed a conversation. A favourable comment on Communists invited scolding from Bhagwanji. 'What do you know about them? I have seen them from close. I have been to

21 Syed Kauser Hussain, Nirmal Nibedon and Vishwambhar Nath Arora, 'The Man was Subhas Bose,' *Northern India Patrika*, 23 January 1986.

Russia. I saw how a few luxuriated while the rest suffered. I went to their grand palaces. This body [of mine] even endured torture in Siberia.'[22]

Although Bhagwanji shifted his base, by now the people of Ayodhya had been alerted to the presence of the mysterious man. The thread of investigation out of curiosity was picked up by Virendra Kumar Mishra, a journalist representing the *Current*, a weekly published from Bombay. He approached the Superintendent of Police Gyaneshwar Jha with a detailed letter suspecting a big cover-up. After one unsuccessful visit, however, the invisible hand came into play again with Jha being transferred immediately to another district.

The problem of piles was still causing much pain to Bhagwanji. With the Banerjees away, one of the disciples called Dr Dashrath Prasad Tomar, an Ayodhya-based homeopath for his treatment. Dr Tomar, a graduate from the Calcutta Homeopathic Medical College and Hospital who speaks fluent Bengali was awestruck by the saint's deep knowledge of homeopathy. His surprise was even greater when the 'saint' behind the curtain asked him whether he could use Hamamelis for treatment of piles, which he said he had contracted many years ago due to continuous horse-riding spanning over twenty hours a day. Bhagwanji complained that earlier the famous homeopathic institution C Ringer and Company of Calcutta used to send him medicines, but they had now stopped sending.[23]

---

22   In conversation with Anuj Dhar in 2001. 'I spoke to him in Bangla. He followed every word of it, but replied in Hindi,' Mukherjee added.
23   Interview of Dr D S Tomar by the authors, Ayodhya.

Dr Tomar touched a chord in Bhagwanji's heart when he told him that his teacher in Calcutta was Bijoy Kumar Bose, a revolutionary-turned-physician.[24] The conversations often veered around history and politics, when they were not discussing homeopathy.

Misfortune struck another blow in 1981 when Bhagwanji broke his femur from a fall in the bathroom, confining him to a wheelchair for some time. His movements, however, became restricted after the accident and he had to depend on Saraswati Devi entirely. It was in this condition that he made his final move. This time, the responsibility was taken up by Dr R P Mishra, the district surgeon, who had by now become a close confidante of Bhagwanji.

With the move to Ram Bhawan in Faizabad town under the cover of night began the final phase of the anonymous act.

24   Bose, son of an additional judge, joined the anti-partition movement of Bengal in 1905 and was soon in the list of wanted revolutionaries. He fled to France to avoid arrest and to learn bomb-making and also to acquire arms. He had to flee France too after the French authorities were hot on his pursuit under pressure from the British government. Finally he arrived in the US and under the guidance of Dr J T Kent, widely considered the forefather of modern homeopathy, devoted himself completely to the discipline. Dr Mahendra Singh, *Pioneers of Homeopathy*, B Jain Publishers Pvt Ltd, 2006, Delhi, pp 30-32.

SIX

FORENSIC FRAUD

MYSTERY MAN BHAGWANJI'S movements, activities and the happenings surrounding him over a span of three decades intrigued everyone who came to know of his existence. Extraordinary he was without an iota of doubt, but was he really Subhas Chandra Bose in disguise? Several other questions will follow from this central query. What was the need for all this secrecy? Why didn't he come out in the open? Addressing these follow-up questions will make sense only if we are able to address the central question of identity convincingly. And to be able to do that, we will have to assess the evidence available—direct and circumstantial, categorised into two classes—forensic and non-forensic. In this chapter, we assess the forensic evidence, and subsequently we shall go on to evaluate if the forensic evidence stands in conflict with the non-forensic, direct and circumstantial.

The question that first emerged in a scattered manner in the vernacular press in Uttar Pradesh gathered steam when it was brought to the notice of the Justice Mukherjee Commission of Inquiry. Even though the origins of the commission went back to the PIL filed by Rudrajyoti Bhattacharjee at the behest of Sunil Krishna Gupta, Bhagwanji's closest followers took no initiative to apprise the commission about his existence for reasons we shall delve into subsequently. The commission's attention towards this matter was drawn by Bose enthusiast, Dr Alokesh Bagchi, former journalist Ashok Tandon, Ram Bhawan owner's son Shakti Singh and Faizabad resident Kailash Nath Jaiswal—all of whom filed affidavits before the commission in response to the statutory notification issued by the commission in May 1999. Instructed by Mukherjee, commission staffer and retired sessions judge N K Panja visited Faizabad and took evidence from Bhagwanji's followers in UP. Afterwards, the former Supreme Court judge himself arrived in Faizabad in November 2001.

The belongings of Bhagwanji were inspected by Mukherjee in the district treasury. Some 700 items, mostly letters and books, were selected to be taken to the commission's office in Kolkata. Most important among them were the specimens of Bhagwanji's writings and a matchbox containing a few teeth said to be his. No photograph of his was available as he never allowed anyone to capture him on camera. Surreptitious attempts by followers to even record his voice never succeeded either. The handwriting samples and the teeth were sent by Justice Mukherjee for scientific examination. The handwriting samples went to one independent expert and two government laboratories, and the teeth to two government laboratories. The results, it was assumed, would provide incontestable evidence to prove or disprove the contention of many that Bhagwanji and Netaji were the same person.

The handwriting and DNA reports received by the commission in sealed covers were opened by Justice Mukherjee at a public hearing in Kolkata in 2004. The independent handwriting expert identified Bhagwanji as Netaji whereas Central and Bengal government experts ruled it out. One DNA report was negative and the other inconclusive. Based on these findings, Justice Mukherjee went on to write in his report made public in May 2006 that while there was 'no reason for not acting or relying upon the evidence' of certain witnesses 'who had seen Netaji before 1945 and also met Bhagwanji/Gumnami Baba face to face on a number of occasions', there were 'other formidable facts and circumstances on record' which stood in the way of this commission in arriving at a conclusive finding that Bhagwanji/Gumnami Baba was none other than Netaji'. The report then summarised the negative findings of the government DNA/handwriting experts and concluded that 'in absence of any clinching evidence to prove that Bhagwanji/ Gumnami Baba was Netaji, the question whether he (Netaji) died in Faizabad on September 16, 1985, as testified by some of the witnesses, need not be answered'.

In 2010, four years after his core finding that Subhas never perished in any air crash was dismissed by the Central Government, Justice Mukherjee burst out during a casual discussion while a documentary was being filmed. This was inadvertently recorded. A portion from this recording was then shown in the media. The authors chanced to see the entire recording. Blasting the Central

Government in language he could not have used in his report, Mukherjee could be heard hinting at a forensic fraud. He asserted more than once that he was '100 per cent sure' that Bhagwanji was Subhas Bose, adding that he was not able to prove it due to the Government's shenanigans. The retired judge has since then repeated his personal opinion in private conversations with the authors as well as some members of Netaji's family.

Be that as it may, for many, the results of the DNA sealed the debate. While the report of the Centre for DNA Fingerprinting and Diagnostics (CDFD) in Hyderabad, which examined two out of the seven teeth, reached no finding, as the teeth 'did not yield DNA suitable for complete analysis',[1] a year later, the Kolkata-based Central Forensic Science Laboratory (CFSL) which examined the remaining five, categorically ruled out any match after comparing the DNA from the teeth with that obtained from Subhas Bose's relatives.[2]

However, the foundation of the scientific certainty of these tests becomes highly questionable when the settings of the examinations are scrutinised and their relative placement is assessed vis-à-vis established judicial principles pronounced

---

1   Letter of S P R Prasad, Senior Technical Officer, Centre for DNA Fingerprinting and Diagnostics, Hyderabad to P K Sengupta, Secretary, Justice Mukherjee Commission of Inquiry, Kolkata, 23 June 2003. Samples were delivered to CDFD on 4 March 2003.
2   DNA Profiling Test on Teeth: Genetic Identity of Alleged Source-Gumnami Baba, Report by the National DNA Analysis Centre, Central Forensic Science Laboratory, Kolkata, to The Secretary, Justice Mukherjee Commission of Inquiry, Kolkata, 11 June 2004. The teeth and three blood samples were delivered to CFSL on 15 October 2003 and two more blood samples in December 2003.

through judgements of the Supreme Court and a number of high courts. The lessons that can be drawn are comparable to international experience. In other words, the results produced by the government labs become untenable.

To start with, although all seven teeth were made available to the CDFD, for some inexplicable reasons, the five remaining teeth were not used for meeting the desired concentration of DNA. More so because this wasn't a case of distributing the teeth between two laboratories. The decision to send the remaining teeth for a second round of tests was taken by the commission only after the receipt of the inconclusive report.[3]

The commission formally asked the CFSL to conduct the DNA tests through a letter dated 22 December 2003. Strangely, a day before, on 21 December, Bengal's top daily *Anandabazar Patrika (ABP),* which had had a history of scoffing at the entire Bose mystery, published a report claiming that the results of the DNA test had proved that 'Gumnami Baba was by no means Netaji'. The commission regarded the publication of this report as prejudicial 'to the progress of the inquiry' and complained to the Press Council of India. *Anandabazar Patrika* contested this through their legal cell head, who told the Press Council on record that the story represented what was 'a scoop in journalistic parlance and they were satisfied about its genuineness'. It was submitted that 'the information was substantiated by the official reports

---

3   Anuj Dhar, then a journalist, heard from the commission officials that there was a telephone call from the CDFD to the commission that the DNA had in fact matched. Since we cannot reveal the identity of the sources, this information is being placed here as a footnote only.

subsequently issued' in June 2004 when Justice Mukherjee had made the DNA reports public. The Press Council consequently ruled in favour of *Anandabazar Patrika*: 'To say that the press should not publish any information till it is officially released would militate against the spirit of investigative journalism and even to an extent the purpose of journalism.'

ডিএনএ পরীক্ষায় মার্কিন সেনার কেন্দ্রে আর্জি জানাবে নেতাজি কমিশন

নির্মাল্য মুখোপাধ্যায়

জাপানের রেনকোজি মন্দিরে রাখা দেহাবশেষের ডি এন এ পরীক্ষা করানোর জন্য মার্কিন সেনাবাহিনীর ডি এন এ গবেষণা কেন্দ্রের কাছে সাহায্য চেয়ে ফের যোগাযোগ করবে নেতাজি কমিশন। কমিশনের সচিব পি কে সেনগুপ্ত এখনই বিষয়টি বিশদ ভাবে জানাতে রাজি নন। মঙ্গলবার তিনি বলেন, "এখনই বিস্তারিত ভাবে কিছু বলব না। শুধু এটুকু বলতে পারি যে, সাদ্দাম হুসেন ধরা পড়ার পরে নিশ্চিত ভাবেই ইরাকের পরিস্থিতি বদলাবে। আমরা আশা করি, এর পরে মার্কিন বাহিনীর ডি এন এ গবেষণা কেন্দ্রের সাহায্য পেতে অসুবিধা হবে না।"

কিছু দিন আগেই ওই মার্কিন গবেষণা কেন্দ্রের পক্ষ থেকে কমিশনকে জানিয়ে দেওয়া হয়েছিল, ইরাক নিয়েই তারা ব্যস্ত, তাই দেহাবশেষের ডি এন এ পরীক্ষার ব্যাপারে কোনও ভাবেই সাহায্য করা যাবে না। তার প্রধান দু'টি কারণ ইরাকে মার্কিন সেনার অবস্থিতি এবং সাদ্দাম হুসেনের নিখোঁজ হওয়া। তখনও পর্যন্ত ধরা পড়েননি সাদ্দাম। দু'দিন আগেই ইরাকের তিকরিতে সাদ্দাম পাকড়াও হওয়ায় পরিস্থিতির পরিবর্তন হয়েছে বলে মনে করছে কমিশন। তাই কমিশন মার্কিন বাহিনীর ওই ডি এন এ গবেষণা কেন্দ্রের সঙ্গে নতুন ভাবে যোগাযোগ স্থাপন করতে উদ্যোগী হয়েছে। ধরা পড়ার পরে ওই কেন্দ্রের সাহায্যেই সাদ্দামের পরিচয় নিশ্চিত করতে ডি এন এ পরীক্ষা করিয়েছে মার্কিন বাহিনী।

মার্কিন বাহিনীর ওই ডি এন এ গবেষণা কেন্দ্রের ব্যাপারে কমিশনকে খোলা সার্টিফিকেট দিয়েছে ওই বিষয়ে ভারতের তিন গবেষণা কেন্দ্র— হায়দরাবাদের সি ডি এফ ডি এবং সেন্টার ফর মালিকিউলার বায়োলজি (সি এম বি) এবং কলকাতার সেন্ট্রাল ফরেন্সিক সায়েন্স ল্যাবরেটরি (সি এফ এস এল)। ওই তিন সংস্থার পক্ষ থেকে কমিশনকে জানানো হয়েছে, মার্কিন বাহিনীর ডি এন এ গবেষণাগার বিশ্বের অন্যতম শ্রেষ্ঠ। সেখান থেকে দেহাবশেষের ডি এন এ পরীক্ষা করালে যথার্থ ফলাফল জানা যাবে।

তবে ইউরোপ ও আমেরিকার বিভিন্ন সংস্থার কাছ থেকেও এই ব্যাপারে ইতিবাচক সাড়া পেয়েছে কমিশন। তাদের বিষয়টিও খতিয়ে দেখা হচ্ছে। বার্মিংহাম স্টেট ফরেন্সিক সার্ভিস থেকে ডি এন এ পরীক্ষার দায়িত্ব নেওয়ার জন্য সেখানকার প্রতিনিধিরা ভারতে আসতে আগ্রহী বলে জানানো হয়েছে। ব্রিটেন, জার্মানি থেকেও এই ব্যাপারে আগ্রহ প্রকাশ করে বেশ কয়েকটি চিঠি এসেছে।

চলতি বছরেই দেহাবশেষের ডি এন এ পরীক্ষার কাজ শুরু করতে চায় কমিশন। নেতাজি বলে প্রচারিত উত্তরপ্রদেশের ফৈজাবাদের 'গুমনামি' বাবার ব্যবহৃত জিনিসপত্রের ডি এন এ পরীক্ষায় সুভাষচন্দ্র বসুর সঙ্গে কোনও মিল পায়নি কমিশন। গুমনামি বাবা যে কোনও ভাবেই নেতাজি নন, তা প্রমাণিত হয়ে গিয়েছে। কমিশন ডি এন এ পরীক্ষার জন্য নেতাজির মা প্রভাবতী দেবীর বংশের তিন জনের এবং বাবা জানকীনাথ বসুর বংশের দু'জনের রক্তের নমুনা সংগ্রহ করেছে।

রেনকোজি মন্দিরে রাখা দেহাবশেষের মধ্যে দাঁত এবং কিছু হাড়ের খোঁজ পেয়েছে কমিশন। সেই ছবিও তুলে নিয়ে এসেছে তারা। ডি এন এ বিশেষজ্ঞদের মতে, কেবল ছাই থাকলে ওই দেহাবশেষের কোনও গবেষণামূলক পরীক্ষা করা সম্ভব হত না। কারণ, ছাইয়ের ডি এন পরীক্ষা হয় না।

[The *Anandabazar Patrika* report of 21 December 2003]

Investigative journalism is a jolly good thing, but can one investigate something that's yet to come into existence? Reports do get leaked out, findings of commissions are reported before they are made known officially, but only after they have been drafted or the conclusions have been reached. One cannot know the findings of a DNA test before it is completed. It's an argument that no legal eagle can twist because the 'secret' DNA report that according to the newspaper justified their reporting was signed and sent to the commission by CFSL director Dr V K Kashyap on 6 June 2004—a full six months after the *Anandabazar Patrika* got what they thought was a 'scoop'.[4]

From the morphological examination and analysis of SRY gene, mt DNA (HVS I & HVS II), and Y-STR loci in the forwarded Exhibits 1-10, it can be concluded that forwarded teeth – (Exhibits 2 to 4) belong to a single human aged male individual – (alleged Gumnami Baba). The individual – source of the teeth does not belong to either maternal or paternal DNA lineage of Netaji Subhash Chandra Bose, therefore, can not be of Netaji Subhash Chandra Bose.

The remnants of teeth (Exhibits 1-5) & blood samples (Exhibit 6 -10) are returned in close sealed packet. The impression of specimen seal used in remnant packets is affixed below:

(IMPRESSION OF SPECIMEN SEAL)

(V.K. KASHYAP, Ph.D., FNASc.)
DNA Expert*
DIRECTOR, CFSL, Kolkata

Encls:
i)   Photographs: I, II-a, II-b, III & IV
ii) Table – I & II
iii) Appendix – I to V
iv) Annexure I to VI

DIRECTOR
Cum-Chemical Examiner
Central Forensic Science Laboratory
Directorate of Forensic Sciences
Ministry of Home Affairs, Govt. of India
Kolkata - 700 014

* C.V. enclosed (Annexure-VII)

[Exhibit 222A, Mukherjee Commission]

---

4   'The respondent stated that Gumnami Baba's DNA report was made public at Mukherjee Commission's hearing on June 23, 2004 where the Commission's Chairman, Hon'ble Justice Manoj Mukherjee unveiled the DNA report pointing out that Gumnami Baba and Netaji are two different persons and there is no match between the two. The content of the news item and the report which was made public on 23.6.2004 appeared to be identical.' Decision rendered by the Press Council of India at its meeting held on June 28, 2005 at New Delhi, http://presscouncil.nic.in/OldWebsite/Decisions/decision05/41.htm.

The commission set aside the CDFD report because it was inconclusive but asked Kashyap to appear before it at its Kolkata office. Kashyap, also based in Kolkata, did so only after summons were served on him thrice. He had also ignored the commission's repeated directions to let them know whether it was possible to lift latent fingerprints from Bhagwanji's belongings. The little research that we did about this aspect tells us that it was possible. Dr G S Sodhi, coordinator of the Forensic Science Unit at SGTB Khalsa College, Delhi, elucidated the following on detecting fingerprints on old manuscripts:

> Fingerprints are the crisscross lines on the bulbs of fingers and thumbs. The pattern of these lines on each finger of a person is so unique that it is not repeated on another finger of the same person or on the fingers of any other person. The crisscross lines, called ridges, are studded with small holes called sweat pores. As the name implies, sweat continuously oozes out of these holes. When fingers touch any surface (like paper, glass, plastic, metal, etc.), the sweat from these pores is deposited, providing a mirror-image of the ridge pattern. However, we cannot see the ridge pattern because sweat is colourless. Hence this deposition is called latent (meaning hidden) fingerprint.
> Sweat is composed mainly of water, but has a host of other chemicals too. Some of these may be transformed into coloured derivatives by treating the latent fingerprint with specific reagents. The fingerprint then becomes visible or—in technical language—developed. Amino acids are an important class of chemicals present in sweat. These react with a reagent called ninhydrin to produce a purple coloured derivative named Ruhemann's purple (named after the scientist who first standardised this reaction). Thus, the colourless amino acids in a latent fingerprint are converted into purple colour

and become visible. This is the best method for detecting fingerprints on paper and paper items.

Amino acids neither react with chemicals present in paper, nor do these diffuse within the capillaries of paper. Therefore, ninhydrin method allows for the detection of latent fingerprints which are many years or even many decades old. In fact, this technique is recommended to a person who wishes to know whether or not a particular notebook/ book belonged to or has been handled by his father or even by his grandfather. Even after years, the fingerprints come out intense and clear. In case these are faint, they may be rendered sharp by further chemical treatment. This is a non-destructive method, meaning that the paper of the manuscript does not degrade though it may acquire a light background colour.[5]

Not just that, Kashyap was quite gung-ho about the feasibility of a DNA test on the presumptive remains of Subhas Bose kept at Tokyo's Renkoji temple. This was something that the other top experts—from Sir Alec Jeffreys (a pioneer of forensic use of DNA) to Lalji Singh—had ruled out completely. Amazingly enough, as early as 2000, Kashyap was talking of a scientific 'breakthrough'. According to a *Times of India* report, 'the scientists here [at CFSL] claim to have hit upon a more sophisticated version of DNA testing, which, they said, could help them prove conclusively if the remains kept at the Renkoji temple in Japan are actually of Netaji Subhas Chandra Bose'.

'Recently we have mastered the technology, and with this breakthrough we are now able to do what forensic centres

5   Personal communication to Anuj Dhar.

in Washington in US or Birmingham in UK are doing,' was Kashyap's tall claim.[6]

CFSL scientists claim breakthrough in DNA

New test could identify Netaji's ashes

By Saikat Ray

CALCUTTA: Scientists here claim to have hit upon a more sophisticated version of DNA testing, which, they said, could help them prove conclusively if the remains kept at the Renkoji temple in Japan are actually of Netaji Subhas Chandra Bose. Dr V.K. Kasyap, deputy director at the Central Forensic Science Laboratory, said that the CFSL achieved the breakthrough during the last six months after unsuccessful attempts to develop the technology since 1997. The new "mitrocondrial DNA test-

for a mitrocondial DNA testing," he added.

Kasyap, assistant director Rajni Trivedi and a team of scientists consisting Ranjan Dutta and Prabal Chatterjee inspired by encouraging results of mitrocondrial DNA testing produced in the US and the UK, started researching in CFSL, Calcutta, to develop the same kind of testing.

"Recently we have mastered the technology and with this breakthrough we are now able to do what forensic centres in Washington in US or Birmingham in UK are doing," Kasyap said.

[*The Times of India* on 14 April 2000]

There is no doubt that the process of DNA testing is scientific and beyond reproach. But humans can err, or pull wool over others' eyes or can become a victim of trickery. Moreover, a verifiable track record of suppressing matters related to the Subhas Bose mystery does not merit any official claim to be accepted at face value. Both the CFSL and CDFD labs work under the government. The credibility of DNA testing process in India itself has been called into question over matters nowhere as politically significant as the Bose mystery. For example, in 2003, three police officers and two doctors were found guilty of 'fudging the DNA

6   Saikat Ray, 'CFSL scientists claim breakthrough in DNA,' *The Times of India* (Kolkata), 14 April 2000.

samples of five innocent civilians' killed in a 'fake encounter' in Jammu and Kashmir in 2000.[7]

Two unimpeachable authorities testified that we have little to tom-tom about our state-controlled forensic labs. A secret April 2006 US government record leaked by Wikileaks said: 'Forensics is weak in India—only two DNA labs service the entire country.'[8] Our Government is aware of that. On 1 February 2010, Home Minister P Chidambaram admitted that the 'state of forensic science as well as the state of the Central and State Forensic Science Laboratories "leave much to be desired".'[9] An illustration of it appeared in an article titled "Could better DNA testing facilities in India have saved the Talwars?" in *Firstpost.com*:

> Over the last decade, the use of DNA tests to solve crimes has seen a significant rise in crime investigation in India. But forensic experts warn that the absence of standard practices, quality checks and regulation has resulted in irresponsible and inaccurate application of the technology. The use of outdated technology and lack of expertise to competently collect and analyse DNA samples from the crime scene has compromised investigation and led to instances where courts have rejected DNA evidence as being unreliable or inconclusive.[10]

---

7   '"Fudged" DNA samples,' *The Hindu*, 24 July 2003.

8   'Secret channel between U.S. embassy and Delhi Police "highly improper",' *The Hindu*, 18 December 2010, https://www.thehindu.com/news/national/Secret-channel-between-U.S.-embassy-and-Delhi-Police-lsquohighly-improper/article15599572.ece.

9   'Government appoints team to examine state of forensic science,' *Daily News & Analysis*, 1 February 2010, https://www.dnaindia.com/india/report-government-appoints-team-to-examine-state-of-forensic-science-1341982.

10   'Could better DNA testing facilities in India have saved the Talwars?' Firstpost.com, 11 October 2012, https://www.firstpost.com/india/could-better-dna-testing-facilities-in-india-have-saved-the-talwars-486172.html.

G V Rao, DNA analyst and formerly chief staff scientist at CDFD, told the reporter that India was 'very much behind the rest of the World in upgradation of technology as required'. He added: 'The recent example of Bhanwari Devi case, where the CBI had to send the victim's bones to FBI, USA for identification to get it identified. This is a sad reflection of the present status of DNA technology in India.' Rao also pointed out that 'No proper records of the tests conducted are being maintained for production in a court of law for its inspection.'[11]

Leaving the tall claim of the CFSL director aside, Indian government forensic labs are certainly not in the league of the labs in the US or Europe that one can take their word as final on issues that have political ramifications. Around 1999, the CFSL performed a DNA test on the remains presumed to be of Paul Wells, a British national kidnapped along with others by terrorists in J&K. According to a report published in *The Independent* of London in January 2000, the J&K Police 'announced that scientists in the Central Forensic Science Laboratories in New Delhi and Calcutta had confirmed through DNA testing of samples of bones and other body parts that this was indeed the body of Mr Wells'. To verify the claims made by the CFSL labs, the British carried out their own tests. The Foreign and Commonwealth Office later announced that 'British police forensic scientists had decided that the remains were neither those of Mr Wells nor of any of the other hostages.'[12]

---

11   Ibid.
12   Peter Popham, 'DNA tests rekindle mystery of kidnapped British trekkers,' *The Independent*, 28 March 2000. https://www.independent.co.uk/news/world/asia/dna-tests-rekindle-mystery-of-kidnapped-british-trekkers-282444.html.

Asked to choose between the Indian report and the one from London, ordinary citizens like us may want to pick *our* report out of a misplaced sense of patriotism, but throughout the world, everyone will go with the British report. Even our own elites—politicians, top bureaucrats, soldiers, intellectuals, journalists, spooks, just about everyone—whose children's favourite destination for study, work and permanent domicile is more likely to be London or New York than Mumbai and New Delhi—won't give a fig for a report from an Indian lab when another one from the West is at hand. Every time there is some forensic test involved in some high profile contentious matter in India, the parties involved try to seek opinion from foreign experts as they are regarded not only as more learned but also far more credible considering the high corruption levels in India.[13] That's the reason why in the recent Sunanda Pushkar case, such tests were carried out in the UK and in America.

Recall the Bhanwari Devi murder case of 2012. This was about a woman who had disappeared after her extra-marital affair with a Rajasthan government minister became public knowledge. An inquiry was carried out in right earnest. The CBI sleuths actually went all over Rajasthan with a fine tooth comb and managed to dig out from a remote village, pieces of bones thought to be hers. These bones were then sent all the way to the United States, so that the Federal Bureau of Investigation (FBI) could find out if these

---

13   According to corruption watchdog Transparency International, India continues to be among the most corrupt countries in the world in 2018. https://www.transparency.org/news/feature/corruption_perceptions_index_2017.

indeed were of the missing woman. The FBI later confirmed that the remains were hers and the case was cracked. The very fact that the authorities in India have moved heaven and earth for the sake of truth and justice in cases involving ordinary mortals, but have done nothing in the Subhas Bose matter speaks volumes about their bona fides in the matter. Why didn't we seek FBI help in ascertaining if those really are Bose's remains at the Renkoji temple?

Determined in our pursuit to take this matter to its end, we revisited the issue of DNA and handwriting tests in the course of writing this volume. First, we took up the CFSL and CDFD reports with the DNA experts who had both professional knowhow to assess them as well as sufficient inside knowledge of the workings of these labs. The CDFD report was seen by Dr Maharshi Krishna Deb, a scientific researcher at Stanford University, who works at Stanford Institute for Stem Cell Biology and Regenerative Medicine in California. Dr Deb felt somewhat amused. The test, to his mind, was 'most likely politically conjugated to truncate its normal inference' for reasons beyond his comprehension.

> No reason has been cited for not being able to amplify other 6 loci. The Genescan Analysis lacks loading control. A ubiquitously expressed gene like (GAPDH) should have been used to rule-out any ambiguity towards the loading of equal concentration of DNA for each sample. As such without a loading control, change or lack of DNA band can potentiate a dubious inference. The band intensity of Amelogenin in each of the 5 lanes (samples) raises such conviction of scientific misconduct. Amelogenin is a marker commonly used for sex determination in forensic studies (although there are scientific evidences that Amelogenin can't unequivocally infer the sex of

an individual). In this study as all the 5 DNA samples were obtained from male (XY) individuals, the band intensity of Amelogenin should have been equal.

The Genotyping data shows that none of 9 microsatellites (STRs) could be amplified, besides the Amelogenin signal. Hence this sample holds no biological or experimental relevance. This implies that DNA sample from 1 tooth (of the concerned individual) has been used in this study making this entire episode highly unscrupulous as same sets of STR ought to be amplified from 2 DNA samples (2 teeth) at the minimum to draw a scientifically relevant conclusion, which otherwise should be refuted as baseless and thus cannot substantiate any evidence. [Emphasis added by authors]

This observation received supporting evidence from an unexpected quarter in October 2017 as the Allahabad High Court pronounced its judgment in the sensational Aarushi Talwar–Hemraj murder case. Coming down heavily on the CBI for deliberately tampering with a most crucial piece of evidence indicating who could have been the murderer, the court in its order recorded that a pillow was recovered from the house of Krishna, the Talwars' compounder. This pillow bearing some suspicious-looking spots was sent to CDFD Hyderabad. CDFD returned a finding that DNA of Hemraj was found on the pillow. But three years later, CDFD stated that due to a typographic error, it had mistakenly reported this particular finding. The officer who reported this and the finding earlier was the same Senior Technical Examiner who had furnished the Gumnami Baba teeth report.

This officer's, rather CDFD's credibility over the Aarushi matter was blown to smithereens in the court order. 'There was no possibility of any mistake creeping in into the report,' it stated. What had really happened was that a letter had been mysteriously handed over to CDFD by the CBI's case investigating officer. 'It was virtually suggested by the said letter of the Investigating Officer that there was a typographical error.' The court further said that 'the CDFD Hyderabad simply abided by the cryptic suggestion given by the Investigating Officer on 17.3.2011 and virtually satisfied his requirement.'[14]

Earlier, a CBI Judge in Delhi awarded rigorous imprisonment to two former Principal Scientific Officers of CFSL Delhi in 2013 under the Prevention of Corruption Act.[15]

The most damning indictment, however, came in August 2018, when the Delhi High Court ordered the CBI to conduct an inquiry into the working of the Forensic Science Laboratory in Delhi, particularly with respect to DNA tests. The Court suspected widespread commission of offences 'under the Prevention of Corruption Act, Indian Penal Code, etc. if thoroughly investigated'.[16]

So much for scientific testing!

Skimming through the CFSL report about Gumnami Baba, another expert (who works in one of the CFSL labs and

14   Judgement delivered by Hon'ble Bala Krishna Narayana, J. on Criminal Appeal No. - 293 of 2014 along with Criminal Appeal No - 294 of 2014, Allahabad High Court, 12 October 2017.

15   'Court sentences two Central Forensic Science Laboratory scientists in corruption case,' *Daily News & Analysis*, 11 October 2013, https://www.dnaindia.com/india/report-court-sentences-two-central-forensic-science-laboratory-scientists-in-corruption-case-1902307.

16   Apoorva Mandhani, 'Delhi HC Orders CBI Probe Into Irregularities In DNA Reports Submitted By Forensic Science Laboratory, Delhi,' LiveLaw.in, 7 August 2018, https://www.livelaw.in/delhi-hc-orders-cbi-probe-into-irregularities-in-dna-reports-submitted-by-forensic-science-laboratory-delhi-read-judgment/.

therefore cannot be named) noted that a most vital component of it was missing. 'Where is the electropherogram?' we were asked. An electropherogram is a chart depicting DNA analysis during the process of enabling the sorting of molecules. It is on the electropherogram that the DNA experts base their findings. While the CDFD report contained an electropherogram, the CFSL report submitted to the Mukherjee Commission had none. It defied reason that it was not attached with the report, when CDFD had no problem in enclosing theirs with their report even though they claimed that they could not draw any conclusion.

So, as advised by the DNA expert consulted by us, we sought 'certified copies of the Electropherogram of all the 8 analysed Exhibits used during the so-called 'Operation Abhigyan'—the title given to Gumnami Baba test by CFSL, under the Right to Information Act. Since CFSL had concluded that Baba was not Netaji—which means he was a nobody—they should have had no hesitation in providing us the electropherogram as nobodies are of no consequence to anyone. However, CFSL refused to give us the copy of the elusive electropherogram saying they could not do so as it 'pertains to a third party and is confidential in nature'. What 'third party' and what 'confidential nature'? Finding no sense in the CFSL's response, we filed an appeal as mandated by the RTI Act. CFSL Director Priyankar Ghosh this time himself answered to say that previous reply was 'correct'. 'The information sought by you cannot be disclosed as it comes under RTI Act Rule 11(1).'

The third party in this instance was the Mukherjee Commission to which the CFSL report was given. But the commission wound up more than a decade ago. Its report was made public in 2006.

All its records including the CFSL report were transferred to the National Archives in 2010 by the Ministry of Home Affairs under whose aegis the commission functioned. This made the MHA the successor third party. Clause 11(1) of the RTI Act reads that despite reservations from the third party, information can still be given 'if the public interest in disclosure outweighs in importance any possible harm or injury to the interests of such third party'. The 'third party' in this case clearly faces no harm in case the disclosure is made—as long as everything is fine with the electropherogram and its reading.

Following the lack of credibility and the apparent shortcomings in the DNA tests conducted on the seven teeth found at Faizabad, we need to look at how such evidence is treated at the courts in order to gain a fuller picture of the evidentiary value produced and claimed.

On the point of reliability of medical evidence when it contradicts ocular evidence, the Supreme Court in July 2009 upheld the verdict of the Karnataka High Court that 'in a conflict between the ocular evidence and the medical evidence, if the testimony is acceptable, trustworthy and reliable, the same should be preferred to the medical evidence'.[17] In another case in 2010, the Supreme Court held that:

> where the medical evidence is at variance with ocular evidence, it has to be noted that it would be erroneous to accord undue

---

17   Mallappa Siddappa Alakanur & Ors vs State of Karnataka, Criminal Appeal No 1055 of 2002,Supreme Court of India, Judgement delivered on 7 July 2009, https://indiankanoon.org/doc/424859/.

primacy to the hypothetical answers of medical witnesses to exclude the eyewitnesses' account which had to be tested independently and not treated as the 'variable' keeping the medical evidence as the 'constant'. Where the eyewitnesses' account is found credible and trustworthy, a medical opinion pointing to alternative possibilities cannot be accepted as conclusive.

However, where the medical evidence goes so far that it completely rules out all possibility of the ocular evidence being true, the ocular evidence may be disbelieved.[18]

Clearly, none of the DNA test results can be said to have completely ruled out 'all possibility of the ocular evidence being true' in this case. Rather, quite the opposite. The ocular evidence according to even Justice Mukherjee was reliable and consistent. According to the principle laid down by the Supreme Court, therefore, that evidence gains primacy over the doubtful medical evidence.

The observation of the Allahabad High Court in 2013 is also in line with this principle. While delivering its judgement on the cases filed by Lalita Bose in 1986 and Shakti Singh in 2010, Justices Devi Prasad Singh and Virendra Kumar Dixit observed:

From the aforesaid material discussed by Mukherjee Commission, there appears to be no room for doubt that there was substantial oral and documentary evidence which prima facie makes out a case for scientific investigation with regard to identity of late Gumnami Baba.

The Commission had disbelieved the theory on the ground

---

18   Abdul Sayeed vs State of MP, Criminal Appeal No 1399 of 2007, Supreme Court of India, Judgement delivered on 14 September 2010, https://indiankanoon.org/doc/126399/.

that DNA test of five teeth found in Ram Bhawan could not tally with the DNA of blood collected from descendants of Netaji....

After careful reading of the Commission's report, it appears that the Commission has based its finding on the DNA test of five teeth out of nine found in Ram Bhawan, Faizabad. Commission has not discussed any evidence or recorded a finding that five teeth found in Ram Bhawan sent for DNA test were of Gumnami Baba or Bhagwan Ji and who were the persons who retained the teeth of Gumnami Baba after cremation. Even little doubt with regard to the veracity of teeth will compel a man of common prudence not to ignore the oral and other documentary evidence, that too when there was difference of opinion with regard to handwriting of Netaji compared by the experts.[19] [Emphasis added by authors]

The DNA results from CFSL clearly did not pass muster according to the High Court judges.

A scrutiny of the results of handwriting analysis on which the commission based its findings also shows a similar pattern—an unusual haste by government experts to prove that the handwritings did not match.

Before taking up this scrutiny, it is important to understand the context—we are dealing with the handwriting of a person who was extra careful not to blow away the cover to his identity.

As his old faithfuls came in contact with him at Neemsar and the volume of letters written by him increased, his handwriting

---

19   Miss Lalita Bose & Others vs State of UP & Others (Miscellaneous Bench No 929 of 1986), connected with Subhas Chandra Bose Rashtriya Vichar Kendra, Faizabad vs State of UP (10877 of 2010), Lucknow Bench of Allahabad High Court, 31 January 2013.

became his first point of attention. Although, by his own admission, he was writing in Bengali after nearly two decades, he received feedback from old colleagues that his writing style and usage of phrases were very much identifiable. Even his diction.

Soon after Leela Roy met Bhagwanji, he wrote to her:

Sometime back three people came to meet me, one after another. I don't know how they got my contact information. Among them was one who was introduced by Deshbandhu [CR Das] himself in his drawing room when the 'dead' returned from England after becoming an ICS...They told me, 'You have survived despite Shaulmari only because you are living in these conditions in UP. Had you been in Bengal it would have been 100% impossible to avoid being found out, even if you lived in a house protected by seven layers of walls. Your way of talking hasn't changed a bit...Those who have been with you can never make a mistake...the way you speak Bengali with a lisp, prolonging the utterances, has remained exactly as before.' I nearly stopped breathing on hearing this...Today you are also saying the same. Le style, C'est L'hommemême (The style is the man himself)—this French dictum is true. Therefore a change is absolutely essential. No chance, no risk, no failure. Please do something to help your 'dead'—please write down along with your comments a number of long, long passages which are diametrically opposite to my manner of writing, use of language and talking. I will start thinking, talking and writing accordingly.[20] (Bengali parts of this paragraph translated into English by Chandrachur Ghose)

It cannot be said with certainty, but most probably Roy did follow up on Bhagwanji's request. One of the items recovered from

20   Charanik, *Oi Mahamanaba Ase*, Jayasree Prakashan, 2010, pp 431-432.

Ram Bhawan was a notebook which had twenty-four different types of writing styles and handwriting patterns. In addition, Roy started writing even routine letters to him in different styles—parts in Bengali, parts in Bengali mixed with English.

So paranoid was he about his letters being intercepted by the government agencies that he wrote to everyone, including Leela Roy, in disguised handwriting. When he wrote in Bangla, he used Nagari script, and when he wrote in English, he used capital letters. Leela Roy wasn't pleased. 'Write the letters in English and Bangla. It is nearly impossible to read and understand your letters,' she wrote back. But the practice continued. The only exception to this rule was Pabitra, to whom he wrote in flowing hand in Bangla and English from the beginning to the end. However, even to him, the style of writing was very different. Only the first few letters were written in the old Subhas Bose style, most of which were returned to Bhagwanji after copies by hand of the letters were made usually by the recipient.

[Courtesy: *Times Now*]

The first proper analysis of Bhagwanji's writing was carried out in 2002 for *Hindustan Times* by B Lal, a former Additional Director of the National Institute of Criminology and Forensic Sciences, Ministry of Home Affairs. Co-author Anuj Dhar had approached Lal on behalf of the newspaper, where he was working at that time, after he gathered that Lal was India's topmost handwriting expert.

During his service years, which included a stint as Chief Government Examiner of Questioned Documents, Lal had honed his skills in several forensic labs in the US, the UK, Germany and Switzerland. Post-retirement, he was taken on the panels of several government departments and banks, such as the State Bank of India and Citibank. Post retirement, he continued to receive cases from the police. He also delivered lectures to security officials and even judges on the aspects of handwriting testing. At the 87th Indian Science Congress in 2000, he was awarded the lifetime achievement award in forensic sciences.

B Lal gave a positive report to *Hindustan Times*—a newspaper which had no axe to grind over the Subhas Bose disappearance matter. Following the publication of a news story in *HT* based on Lal's report about Bhagwanji's handwriting samples in English Dhar had obtained from Ashok Tandon and others, the Mukherjee Commission hired Lal's services. Later, working on different sets of English and Bangla samples provided by the Commission, Lal produced two definitive reports stating that Bhagwanji and Bose were one person.

Applying the fundamentals of the forensic testing of questioned documents as enumerated by Albert S Osborn (the father of the science of questioned document examination) and Wildon R Harrison (another noted American expert), Lal concluded that the English samples picked up from Ram Bhawan (questioned documents) were 'written by the same person' who wrote the admitted handwritings of Subhas Bose. He found that 'in spite of the time gap there are fundamental similarities'.

> Through intense comparison of admitted writings of Netaji Subhas Chandra Bose...it has been shown that he is a skilful writer having at his command more than one variety of letters.

Such pattern...is also found in the relevant questioned English writings and such similarities are quite characteristic in nature and have great identifying value.

Regarding the Bangla handwritings, he wrote in a separate report:

The questioned Bengali writings are having a time gap of few years when compared with the date of execution of admitted Bengali writing. ...Even having time gap, the relevant questioned Bengali writings and relevant admitted Bengali writings are showing characteristic similarities with natural variations and the collective occurrence of such similarities may not be found in the writings of two different persons as a matter of chance. The collective occurrence of significant similarities can only be explained by the fact that both the writings belong to one and the same person.

He further pointed out that as in the English writings, in Bengali also, Bhagwanji was in the habit of writing in 'small-size letters utilizing every available space'. This is a sort of idiosyncrasy, he added, which was evident in Subhas Bose's writings as well. Lal further highlighted that both Bhagwanji and Bose were in the 'habit of giving a peculiar sign when making insertion of certain words'. This peculiar caret was described by him as having a 'very high identifying value'. The following combo image (next page) illustrates the point. First is a specimen of Bose's writing in 1936, and below it is a portion from a letter Bhagwanji wrote in the 1970s:

Lal's conclusion was not that of the government experts. They reported that Bhagwanji and Bose were two different persons. One report came from Dr S K Mandal, senior scientific officer at

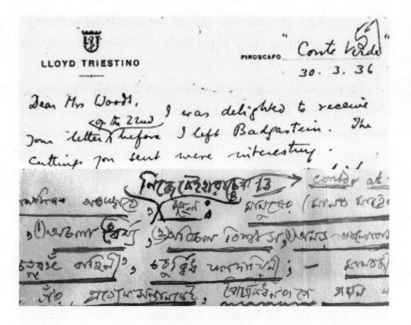

the Forensic Science Laboratory, Kolkata. While giving a report, a handwriting expert is supposed to state reasons for drawing the conclusions. But Mandal's report merely stated that the writings were of two different persons. Annoyed, Justice Mukherjee chided him, but was powerless to take any action as he was heading a commission of inquiry, not a court. To our mind, Justice Mukherjee would have nevertheless done well to bring on record the shoddy manner in which the government experts made their case, in stark contrast to the professionalism shown by B Lal.

The second report came from Amar Singh, Government Examiner of Questioned Documents, and M L Sharma, Deputy Government Examiner of Questioned Documents. 'We have carefully and thoroughly examined the original documents of this case in all aspects of handwriting identification and detection of forgery, with the scientific aids in the Government of India Laboratory at Shimla,' they stated while explaining the reason for their opinion.

This Central government report admitted that Bhagwanji's writings 'do not show any sign of imitation or forgery in them'. This was the only common ground between them and B Lal. In his report to *Hindustan Times*, Lal had noted that Bhagwanji tried to conceal his identity by overwriting the strokes and writing in the capitals, but failed. It is not possible for a writer to change his writing habits completely, Lal explained. 'Even in an effort to hide his identity, the writer is not able to leave his individual characteristics and other peculiarities found in his handwriting. There is such a faithful reproduction of some peculiarities that even a gap of time to the extent of decades cannot hide them.'

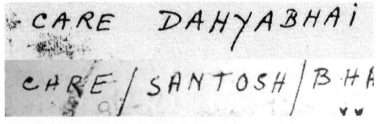

[Subhas Bose (above) and Bhagwanji (below)]

Lal's conclusion on this point was that he found 'no evidence… that the questioned writing has been made by a writer other than Shri Subhas Chandra Bose by imitating/copying the writing of Shri Subhas Chandra Bose'. But if you believe the Government of India laboratory report, the resemblance was merely cosmetic.

Both the handwritings in their pictorial appearance appear to bear a marked resemblance to each other at the first instance, which is due to similar style and class of writing. However, the analysis of the structures of the letters, the study of the 'master pattern' of the letters, in words as well as range of variations on close observation shows that the two writings are quite distinctive and different in their origin and are written by two different authors.

The report gave some details and at the end showcased a 'juxtaposition chart' highlighting 24 instances of differences between the two handwritings.

That was not very impressive. Lal's report was supported by 460 large size photographs accounting for each and every alphabetical letter appearing in the handwriting samples given to him. He also dwelt at length on the issue of 'natural variation' in handwriting.

Every genuine writing has got natural variation since the human hand is not an exact reproducing machine and it is very important to consider this natural variation for a correct conclusion regarding authorship of a writing. If natural variations are taken as differences then there would be error in the identification.

His finding was that Bhagwanji's handwriting showed 'natural variations which are additional symptoms of genuineness and there exists significant similarities'.

That the Central government experts were not confident of their report became clear when they chose to ignore the commission's summons to appear before it in New Delhi. This was on the same day when B Lal was also to be examined. They lost their nerve, probably at the prospect of being questioned in the presence of their former boss. Amar Singh never turned up before the commission. After skipping the Delhi hearing, M L Sharma went all the way to Kolkata from his office in Shimla to make the Government's case. As state expert Mandal was being examined, Sharma, flouting the rules, sneaked into the venue and made a note of the questions Mandal was being asked by Justice Mukherjee.

Both the experts made contradictory statements during their examination. Mandal was asked by Justice Mukherjee: 'Do you agree that to study the writing habits of the author of a document the shape of punctuation marks, their position and frequency, the choice of a peculiar punctuation sign, the mark of a caret, underscoring and bracketing need to be considered?' He answered, 'Yes.' Then he was asked: 'Did you consider all those factors before arriving at your conclusion and have those factors been reflected in your report?' Mandal responded: 'I considered all the above factors but none of those factors have been reflected in my report.'

M L Sharma too was asked by a deponent: 'Do you agree that a mature writer can have a habit of using a peculiar or unique sign or insertion in a line, which is rare?' He replied: 'Yes, it may have.' Later he was asked: 'Do you agree that such a sign has a very high identifying value in examining a writing?' Knowing the repercussions of answering in the affirmative, Sharma now said: 'I do not agree.' At the end of the examination, he could not conceal the truth. 'Do you agree that such a sign falls within the category of individual characteristics?' He said: 'Yes.' He was asked: 'Do you agree that individual characteristics of a handwriting are the most

important factors to determine the authorship of a document?'
Answer: 'Yes.'

A fresh DNA test outside India by an independent expert was
not feasible for us, but a handwriting test was. It became possible
when US citizens Deepak Nijhawan and Abhishek Bose offered to
get it done during Anuj Dhar's lecture tour in the US in September-
October 2016. The tour was funded and organized by a group
of Americans of Indian origin (Abhishek being the coordinator),
some of whom were most eager to help in determining the truth.
It was decided to let Deepak, a businessman in Kentucky, and
Abhishek, a management consultant based out of Maryland,
handle this particular matter.

Deepak and Abhishek shortlisted a few
experts and eventually hired the services
of Curt Baggett, a leading, independent
handwriting expert in the US with over
40 years of experience. A skilled authority
in document examination, Texas-based
Baggett (picture) has completed over 5,000
cases. He has examined documents and/or
testified in court cases as a handwriting expert in all fifty states in
the US, Washington, Canada, England, Ireland, the Netherlands,
New Zealand and other countries. Baggett has been a consultant
as a forensic document examiner for the Number 1 rated television
show, 'CSI: Crime Scene Investigation', and has appeared as a
handwriting expert on *CNN*, *CNBC*, Inside Edition, *CBS*,
NBC, *FOX*, and shows 'Judge Alex' and 'Texas Justice'. Baggett's
education and training in document examination and psychology

include the following: US Army, Military Police Officer's School, BA and MEd from McNeese State University, Lake Charles, Louisiana, and postgraduate studies at the University of Houston.

On our part, for the test, we selected two specimens of Bhagwanji's handwriting in English he had written to Pabitra Mohan Roy after their meeting in the late 1962. These were made available to us by Roy's son Ranendra Mohan Roy, along with several other letters.

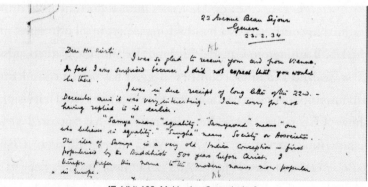

Copies of Subhas Bose's handwriting came from different sources, including letters supplied to the Mukherjee Commission by the Netaji Research Bureau of Kolkata.

[Exhibit 102, Mukherjee Commission]

All these samples were then forwarded to Curt Baggett by Deepak Nijhawan. We did not figure in the picture as we did not want the expert to know what the test was all about. We ensured complete caution so that Baggett had no way of knowing that these samples were related to Subhas Chandra Bose. Nijhawan did not tell him either, and nor did Baggett ask anything. 'This forensic document examiner was asked to conduct an examination of questioned handwriting of an Anonymous Author/Person to determine authenticity of the questioned handwriting by comparing the questioned handwriting to known,' he wrote in his report. That Baggett did not know who the test was about placed him in a different league than the experts in India who examined the Bhagwanji samples knowing that the matter was about Subhas Bose. So, his impeccable reputation and professionalism notwithstanding, there was absolutely no chance of Baggett entertaining any pre-conceived notion or prejudice.

All Baggett was told was that the matter pertained to a 'highly successful politician' in India a long time ago. Some background information was provided, such as the vintage of different handwriting samples. We thought it pertinent to inform him (through Deepak Nijhawan) that there was considerable time gap between the handwriting samples and the circumstances in which they were written by their respective writers. Our brief to him read:

> The questioned writings were written in 1963 by a man in his mid or late sixties. He was living in isolation, constrained by lack of access to basic comforts of life, practically living a life

of an ascetic. He had very limited financial capability, would have been full of anxiety, troubled by physical illnesses such as severe arthritis in his knees and piles. He lived a secretive life, interacting with only a handful of people—very few of them literate and even fewer who could read or write proper English....The admitted writings are formal and carefully written as the writer knew they would be preserved; whereas the questioned writings formed letters written confidentially to someone who was not supposed to share them with anyone. On the contrary, these documents were supposed to be destroyed after being read.

Baggett provided us his expert opinion through a fifty-nine page report in February 2017. 'I am willing to testify to facts herein stated in a court of law and I will provide to the Court exhibits to show that my testimony is based on sufficient facts or data and that my opinion is correct,' he affirmed in a sworn statement before a Notary Public in the State of Texas.

Professionally written as it was, the report provided legal data, including quotes from court verdicts in the US, 'to support accuracy of skilled handwriting experts at 93.5%'. For the test involving the samples sent by us, Baggett employed a methodology said to be used by the FBI. In addition to this, Baggett had a second independent examination done by a qualified handwriting expert. His report reads:

> The scientific methodology used in this examination consists of the 'ACE' method, which means 'Analyze, Compare, and Evaluate'. The FBI, US Treasury Department, and the US Postal Services reportedly use this reliable method in their questioned document laboratories.

ASTM recommends this method as the standard in this field. This method was also accepted and affirmed by the District of Columbia Court of Appeals in Case No 08-CF-1361, Pettus Vs United States. In addition, this examiner adds the Peer Review Methodology, which requests a second independent examination by a qualified handwriting expert. The State and Federal Court qualified expert I selected to peer review this case confirmed my opinion.

Baggett confirmed that the samples provided to him were genuine pieces of natural, free-flowing writing: 'No indications of forgery were noted on the questioned handwriting....' The process of handwriting identification was explained in Baggett's report in these words:

> Handwriting is not only handwriting, but also 'brain' writing. Handwriting is formed by repeated habits of writing by the author, which are created by neuron-pathways established in the brain. These neuron-pathways control muscular and nerve movement for writing, whether the writing done is by the hand, foot, or mouth. An examination of handwriting includes establishing patterns of writing habits to help identify the author.
> The handwriting on the Q [questioned] documents were enlarged and examined scientifically in a side-by-side comparison to the known samples, under a microscope and on a light table. Measurements of letter height, lateral expansion, angles, slant and line quality were examined under a microscope. Significant similarities of the handwriting characteristics displayed in the questioned handwriting were revealed when compared to the known handwriting. The questioned handwriting, when compared to the known handwriting, displayed similar and

regular line quality, flow, size, shape, slants, positions of letters, stops and starts, end and beginning strokes.

Baggett added that his 'examination revealed significant similarities, not likely seen by an untrained or poorly skilled examiner'. In substantiation, the report listed similarities between the two sets of handwritings. These thirty-four instances were supported by enlarged exhibits.

Before drawing his conclusion, Baggett emphasised that 'the leading forefathers of document examination in the USA agree that one significant difference in the fundamental structure of a writing compared to another is enough to preclude common authorship'.

> [Ordway] Hilton stated: 'It is a basic axiom of identification in document problems that a limited number of basic differences, even in the face of numerous strong similarities, are controlling and accurately establish nonidentity.'
> [Wilson R] Harrison made similar comments: 'Whatever features two specimens of handwriting may have in common, they cannot be considered to be of common authorship if they display but a single consistent dissimilarity in any feature which is fundamental to the structure of the handwriting, and whose presence is not capable of reasonable explanation.'
> [James VP] Conway expressed the same theme when he wrote: 'A series of fundamental agreements in identifying individualities is requisite to the conclusion that two writings were authored by the same person, whereas a single fundamental difference in an identifying individuality between two writings precludes the conclusion that they were executed by the same person.'
> [Albert S] Osborn and others have generally agreed that despite

numerous similarities in two sets of writings, a conclusion of identity cannot be made if there are one or more differences in fundamental features of the writings.

With this backdrop, Baggett wrote that Bhagwanji's handwritings did not 'display many distinguishable differences' when compared to the known handwritings of Subhas Chandra Bose. 'Normal variations exist in all handwriting,' he clarified, adding that no 'unexplainable significant differences' were noted by him in the handwriting of Bhagwanji. Baggett's final conclusion was:

Based on a significant number of similarities of identifiable handwriting characteristics among the questioned handwriting, it is my professional expert opinion that the same person authored the handwritings of the Anonymous Author/Person on the Q documents. (**See extract from the report in the following pages.**)

The US expert's report hence exposed the forensic fraud perpetrated by the *sarkari* handwriting experts. Given the circumstantial data discussed in the foregoing paragraphs, it wouldn't be unfair to conclude that the DNA tests performed at government-controlled labs were fudged too.

CURT BAGGETT'S

HANDWRITING EXPERT REPORT
EXAMINATION OF QUESTIONED HANDWRITING OF
Anonymous Author/Person
AND
BASIS AND REASONS FOR EXPERT OPINION

EXAMINATION REQUESTED

This forensic document examiner was asked to conduct an examination of questioned handwriting of an **Anonymous Author/Person** to determine authenticity of the questioned handwriting by comparing the questioned handwriting to known.

EXHIBITS

Documents examined were transmitted via Internet and printed from an HP printer. The documents included two (2) pages with purported handwriting of an Anonymous Author/Person, labeled herein as 'Q1' and 'Q2' which contains the questioned writings of an Anonymous Author/Person. All documents are exhibited with clear numbers for reference and for identification and there is no need to describe each document individually.

OBSERVATIONS, DESCRIPTIONS AND/OR LIMITATIONS

The identification of any signature/handwriting is based on the agreement, without unexplainable difference, of the handwriting characteristics displayed. These characteristics include the form of the letters, the beginning, connecting, and ending strokes, the proportions of letters, both inter-letter and intra-letter, the slope, size, and curvature of the writing/printing. The outstanding significant features of the writing are other factors used to analyze, compare and evaluate. The elimination of an author is based on a lack of some or all of the above-noted characterizations.

The quality of documents and handwriting were sufficient for examination. The exemplars of known samples of the handwriting were compared one to another to verify that the same person authored each sample and to determine the natural variation in the regular normal design of handwriting. The patterns of writing were verified under the microscope and by using other scientific instruments such as metric measuring devices, light table, and handheld magnifying devices. The handwriting characteristics displayed in the known handwriting are all very similar. Original documents were requested, no originals were immediately available. I would like to examine originals if possible.

Handwriting is not only handwriting, but also 'brain' writing. Handwriting is formed by repeated habits of writing by the author, which are created by neuron-pathways established in the brain. These neuron-pathways control muscular and nerve movement for writing, whether the writing done is by the hand, foot, or mouth. An examination of handwriting includes establishing patterns of writing habits to help identify the author.

The handwriting on the Q documents were enlarged and examined scientifically in a side-by-side comparison to the known samples, under a microscope and on a light table. Measurements of letter height, lateral expansion, angles, slant and line quality were examined under a microscope. Significant similarities of the handwriting characteristics displayed in the questioned handwriting were revealed when compared to the known handwriting. The questioned handwriting, when compared to the known handwriting, displayed similar and regular line quality, flow, size, shape, slants, positions of letters, stops and starts, end and beginning strokes.

No forensic lighting examination was conducted on the questioned documents since no originals were provided and no ink or paper examination could be conducted.

Indented writing is an impression created by the pressure of a writing instrument on a page on top of the questioned item. These impressions may be deciphered using various techniques, which include side lighting and electro static processing. No ESDA machine was used in this examination since no originals of the questioned documents were provided.

Some limitations are imposed on the examiners when originals are not available for an examination. However, the size, shape, form, beginning, ending, spacing, curves, angles, height, width, added or missing letters, or an absence of regular writing habits all can easily be detected from clear copies. No indications of forgery were noted on the questioned handwriting in the size, shape, line quality, letter distortion, and shaky starts and stops.

METHODOLOGY

A Meticulous examination of the questioned handwriting to the known handwriting was conducted using a side-by-side comparison with the unaided eye, handheld magnifying loupes, microscope, photocopy enlargements, grids, a light table, and metric measuring devices. The scientific methodology used in this examination consists of the 'ACE' method, which means 'Analyze, Compare, and Evaluate'. The FBI, U.S. Treasury Department, and the US Postal

Services reportedly use this reliable method in their questioned document laboratories. ASTM recommends this method as the standard in this field. This method was also accepted and affirmed by the District of Columbia Court of Appeals in Case No. 08-CF-1361, *Pettus V. United States*. In addition, this examiner adds the Peer Review Methodology, which requests a second independent examination by a qualified handwriting expert. The State and Federal Court qualified expert I selected to peer review this case confirmed my opinion.

EXAMINATION

The questioned handwritings were examined and noted to have significant similarities present between the size, height, width of letters, angles, and connecting strokes when compared to the known handwritings.

My hypothesis was formed without bias as to authorship of the questioned documents. My examination revealed significant similarities, not likely seen by an untrained or poorly skilled examiner. My conclusion was logical and based on results of the above described reliable methodology, analysis, comparison and evaluation.

All tests were done with accepted scientific methodology, techniques, and scientific instruments, which I relied on to assist me in my decision to the questioned handwriting.

My scientific examination revealed the same author in the questioned handwritings of the Anonymous Author/Person. The measurable distinctions of each letter, pattern, angle, and slant, and the results of my tests indicate that the Anonymous Author/Person was the author of both the 'K' and 'Q' documents.

CONCLUSION

The leading forefathers of document examination in the USA agree that one significant difference in the fundamental structure of a writing compared to another is enough to preclude common authorship. *Handwriting Identification, Facts and fundamentals*, Ray A. Huber and A.M. Headrick, CRC Press LLC, 1999, pp 50-51:

[Ordway] Hilton stated: "It is a basic axiom of identification in document problems that a limited number of basic differences, even in the face of numerous strong similarities, are controlling and accurately establish nonidentity."

[Wilson R.] Harrison made similar comments: "...the fundamental rule which admits of no exception when handwritings are being compared...is simple – whatever features two specimens of handwriting may have in common, they cannot be considered to be of common authorship if they display but a single consistent dissimilarity in any feature which is fundamental to the structure of the handwriting, and whose presence is not capable of reasonable explanation."

[James V.P.] Conway expressed the same theme when he wrote: "A series of fundamental agreements in identifying individualities is requisite to the conclusion that two writings were authored by the same person, whereas a single fundamental difference in an identifying individuality between two writings precludes the conclusion that they were executed by the same person."

And finally,

[Albert S.] Osborn and others have generally agreed that despite numerous similarities in two sets of writings, a conclusion of identity cannot be made if there are one or more differences in fundamental features of the writings.

The questioned handwritings of the Anonymous Author/Person do not display many distinguishable differences when compared to the known handwritings of the Anonymous Author/Person. Normal variations exist in all handwriting and none of the Anonymous Author/Person's have any unexplainable significant differences. I find all handwriting on the Questioned documents match the handwriting on the Known documents.

Based on a significant number of similarities of identifiable handwriting characteristics among the questioned handwriting, it is my professional expert opinion that the same person authored the handwritings of the Anonymous Author/Person on the Q documents.

I have applied the generally accepted Questioned Document Examiner principles and methods reliable to the facts in this case.

I am willing to testify to facts herein stated in a court of law and I will provide to the Court exhibits to show that my testimony is based on sufficient facts or data and that my opinion is correct. My Affidavit and Curriculum Vitae are attached and incorporated herein by reference.

Respectfully Submitted,

Curt Baggett

Forensic Document Examiner

State of Texas)

County of Dallas)

The above Letter of Opinion was sworn and subscribed before me this 21st day of February 2017.

Patricia J. Hale

Notary Public – State of Texas

SEVEN

THE MAN WHO WASN'T THERE

UNRAVELLING ANY MYSTERY requires pooling of relevant pieces of information from diverse sources, followed by their validation and putting them together in a meaningful way. The conundrum of Bhagwanji has been doubly difficult to unravel as at the centre of it is a personality who was determined to suppress his identity. He was a meticulous planner with an eye for the minutest of details and brooked no deviation from a plan once laid down. He was adept in gathering intelligence and in using it in his planning. In addition, he was surrounded by people who had bound themselves to him by an inviolable oath of secrecy. Others were apprehensive of the consequences of getting entangled in a matter they thought had serious political ramifications and hence decided to stay lost in the crowd, never coming forth to share the incredible experience they had.

Even politicians and bureaucrats, with a few exceptions, who claimed in private interactions to have known something about the mystery man, would just drop a hint here or a bit of information there. Nothing more. If Nirmal Nibedon had encountered these hurdles in 1985, we found not much changed in our times. One surviving follower of Bhagwanji in Kolkata, for instance, told us in no uncertain terms that the main reason why he could not share information beyond a limit because of our differences in approach. While we treated this as a historical mystery, for him it was a live matter.

It was a matter of faith for him that the mysterious monk, far from being dead, was alive and active in spiritual endeavours; that he would emerge in public one day, soon, to start a new order in the country. Several notable people in Uttar Pradesh are reticent about the information they hold. Some among them will never speak in public, but admit only in private conversations what they know; some won't even do that. They stand completely apart from those who have shed all inhibitions and freely pour forth whatever they know. But that too comes in stages, not at one go. Revelations are made in phases spanning years.

Yet, we have doggedly persisted with the leads, interviewing the key associates. The perseverance has yielded results but not entirely satisfactory results. Many of Bhagwanji's associates started opening up very gradually and there is still much to be uncovered. In such a situation, the mainstay of our investigation has been documents: letters, diaries, notes, scribblings on loose sheets, newspapers and books and published material.

Unfortunately, the place where much of these have accumulated—the district treasury of Faizabad where the belongings of the mystery man are stored—is out of bounds for researchers. That is definitely a roadblock, but opening up of other sources prevented it from becoming a cul-de-sac. Ashok Tandon was farsighted enough in 1986 to take photocopies of some of the documents found among Bhagwanji's belongings. And, through a decade, the followers of the mystery man in Kolkata, Bijoy Nag and Surajit Dasgupta, gave us access to their diaries and letters—only a very small part of those, but enough to allow us a deeper insight than what was known to the outside world. These diaries were notes of discussions that took place when they visited the 'Man', taken down by several persons over the decades. The 'Man' wrote frequent letters to his followers, sometimes daily—a volume and frequency often not matched by them. After a point, however, they stopped. The remaining papers, by their judgment, were too sensitive to be shared.

Part of what they refused to divulge reached us, thanks to the Ministry of Home Affairs. The Kolkata followers had submitted a number of diaries and letters to the Mukherjee Commission they felt were not meant for our eyes. Whatever the other consequences of Justice Mukherjee's work, one crucial measure he took was to list all affidavits and relevant documents which were submitted to him as 'exhibits' to his report. These were obtained by Chandrachur Ghose after a four-year long effort under the Right to Information Act. Thus, we gained access to numerous writings of the mystery man (which were collected as handwriting samples by the Commission), diaries and letters of the followers, the detailed inventory prepared of the man's belongings and other relevant papers—running into thousands of pages. The insights and leads these provided have been invaluable. Although these documents were listed as exhibits by Justice Mukherjee in his report, he did not analyse their contents. It is therefore for the first time that a fullest possible reconstruction of the phenomenon still known to most people as Gumnami Baba, based on all these documents and the interactions with people linked to him, is being published.

Another significant source that has been utilised is one that is available in the public domain. It is an obscure book named *Oi Mahamanaba Asey* (*Here comes the superhuman!*). This is essentially a compilation of a series of articles published in the Kolkata-based *Jayasree* magazine. A number of enlarged editions of the book have been published since its first appearance in 1973. Authored by 'Charanik', the articles are based on the notes and diaries of Gumnami Baba's followers and his letters to them.

Jayasree is today hardly known in Bengal, what to speak of India. But it has a glorious history behind it. The magazine was first published from Dhaka in May 1931, established and edited by Leela Roy. Rabindranath Tagore named the magazine and Nandalal Bose painted the cover page of the magazine's first issue. With Roy's arrest in December 1931 because of her revolutionary activities, publication of the magazine became irregular, coming to a stop entirely in 1935. It reappeared again from June-July 1938, this time from Calcutta, welcomed back by Jawaharlal Nehru, Subhas Chandra Bose, Kaka Kalelkar, Kamaladevi Chattopadhyay and Vijaya Lakshmi Pandit, among others. After the death of Leela Roy in 1970, the magazine was edited by

Sunil Das, followed by Samar Guha and, currently, the septuagenarian Bijoy Kumar Nag.

Jayasree started dropping hints about Subhas Bose being alive and in India from the late 1960s. It was in its January 1969 issue that the magazine started publishing Bhagwanji's discourses without naming him. Soon the term 'Mahakal' was coined to denote the speaker whose quotes were being published. Bijoy Nag started the storytelling with Bhagwanji's quotes as Charanik, and continues to publish his column till this day. He followed Bhagwanji's instructions. To those who read the column patiently they clearly hinted at Subhas Bose being alive, but no more specifics were given. Bhagwanji was presented as the superhero who moved as a shadow behind global events of far-reaching consequence. As a man who was capable of moving global powers with his schemes, he was portrayed as full of sorrow at the state of his motherland and angry with the way political leaders conducted their business.

The columns were never written in plain narrative Bangla. The text is highly cryptic with unconnected quotes carrying deep meaning (often not apparent) sewn together with lamentations or wonder of the narrator. Several layers of clues, suggestions and incoherent messages written in a near-cryptographic usage of the language makes the text mysterious and frequently incomprehensible. Real situations are often juxtaposed with imaginary ones, facts are often mixed with unverifiable conspiracy theories creating a fantasy zone where anything is possible. It is a volume of text created by a fanatical believer; those who believe can get a nebulous sense but never a concrete framework. For the sceptic, it is gibberish.

We have tried our best to deconstruct the mystifying text through numerous interactions with its author, but specific answers to hard questions were not the norm. We have therefore relied upon only those parts which we know can stand scrutiny.

It is, however, a surprising and completely unexpected discovery of a new source of information by the authors that takes all those listed above to a different dimension. This discovery at one level provides an astounding view of the working of the mystery man's mind and his way of life, but at another level takes the vexatious information gaps to a new height pointing at scintillating possibilities. Probably the most significant finding till now consists of a tranche of about a hundred-and-thirty handwritten letters from the man at the centre of so many controversies to his Man Friday—Pabitra Mohan Roy—in Bengali and English in free-flowing handwriting.

It would be pertinent to recall Roy's version of Bhagwanji's letters to him when investigating officers from Faizabad visited him in Calcutta in November 1985, in their quest to discover the true identity of the monk behind the curtain. The police interrogation was tape recorded and the transcript published by the *Northern India Patrika*.

> Q: You must be having letters from Swamiji? Please show them to us.
> A: *Ekdo chiththi aata tha, nahin rakha, phenk diya* (I received a letter or two, didn't keep them and threw them away).[1]

---

1   S Kausar Husain and Vishwambhar Nath Arora, 'The Ultimate Feedback,' *Northern India Patrika*, 18 January 1986.

Clearly, Roy hadn't given up his role of being Netaji's secret service man. Many of the letters he received from Bhagwanji had been handed over to Sunil Krishna Gupta while others were copied and the originals destroyed. Yet, hundreds of original letters have survived along with journals of Roy where he faithfully noted down whatever he heard from Bhagwanji.

No one knew about the existence of these letters except those in whose custody they were. Ranendra Mohan Roy was kind enough to search his father's papers and make available to us every extant letter written by the holy man. Reticent and shy by nature, Ranendra (71) has all along remained out of the picture. He shared nothing when Anuj Dhar first met him in 2002, nor did he appear before the Mukherjee Commission. Nevertheless, he quietly followed our efforts over the years. Ranendra learned about Bhagwanji from his father and first met him when his father took him to UP. However, he was restrained by his obligations towards his large family, with financial difficulties, and his concern for his growing children, from publicly espousing or supporting the efforts made to unravel the Bhagwanji mystery. He chanced to do it only now as the authors approached him following some persuasion by his US-based daughter Indrani. In a changed scenario, Ranendra decided to share the information he possessed. He was all set to appear before the Sahai Commission but thought otherwise when we informed him of our impression that the retired judge demonstrated no intent to try and understand this exceedingly complex matter.

Even with all this information, we have only been able to scratch the surface. The question of Bhagwanji's identity may be now answered more clearly, but the detailed contours of life and activities during the nearly three decades from the mid-1950s until 1985 are still nebulous. That said, this is the fullest assessment possible at this moment.

EIGHT

HIDE-AND-SEEK

THE ORGANISATION WHOSE job is to keep tabs on everything and anything of slightest significance within India would like us to believe that it knows nothing about the controversy surrounding Bhagwanji. But then, this isn't surprising in the least, considering the unflattering track record of the Intelligence Bureau (IB) over the entire Bose mystery matter.

A fragile, bespectacled man with an avuncular persona behaved before the Khosla Commission as if he had been living in a cave when the whole of India was discussing the Bose mystery. Bhola Nath Mullik was the undisputed czar of the Indian intelligence for an incredible fourteen years, when the IB had not been bifurcated to form separate entity of R&AW. These days the term for the IB director lasts only for about two years. Mullik was one of Nehru's closest confidants, and he almost worshipped the former prime minister.[1] Post-'retirement', Mullik was something of a national security adviser. He finally called it quits in 1968. Yet, as a witness before the Khosla Commission, this man trotted out one lie after another about the IB's handling of the Bose mystery. And this wasn't the first time he had behaved mischievously. When the charade of the Shah Nawaz's inquiry was on in 1956, Mullik provided Shah Nawaz a dossier of the British-era intelligence reports. The selection was made in such a way so as to dip the needle in favour of the air crash theory. The first report in this dossier had been tinkered with to conform with the official stand on Bose's death.

'IB doctored reports on Netaji's death'

TIMES NEWS NETWORK

TDI Archives

Bose visiting Port Blair in 1943

New Delhi: A new book on Netaji Subhas Chandra Bose, whose disappearance still remains a mystery, says the Intelligence Bureau doctored British intelligence reports to support the Nehru government's claim that he died in an air crash in Taipei on August 18, 1945.

After being sidelined in the Congress, Netaji mysteriously disappeared from India, went to Germany to strike an alliance with Hitler, and later got Japanese assistance to establish the Indian National Army that fought its way almost up to the northeast of India.

The book, 'India's Biggest Cover-Up' by former journalist Anuj Dhar, claims that in 1955, then IB director B N Mullik sent a dossier to the Shah Nawaz Committee that had been set up by the government to probe Bose's 'death'. The first document in the dossier was a report from Phillip Finney, an assistant director with IB who had been sent to southeast Asia to ascertain facts. The copy of the November 1945 report supplied by the IB appeared to confirm the Japanese announcement of Bose's death, just at a time when the British were preparing to arrest him.

The Shah Nawaz Committee and later the Khosla Commission used Finney's report to claim that inquiries by British officers had concluded that the Japanese announcement was correct.

Dhar claims that Finney's report in the IB dossier had been censored to expunge its last three and most crucial paragraphs — that he was actually not sure of Bose's death. He found the full original report in the archives of a declassified defence ministry file.

Dhar also accuses Mullik of lying on oath when he was summoned by the Khosla Commission as witness in 1970. When repeatedly asked if the IB ever snooped on Shaulmari baba, a hermit who many believed was Netaji, he said the government never asked the IB to track the hermit because it "did not concern national security".

There has been no conclusive proof that Baba was indeed Netaji, but Dhar reproduces formerly top secret IB records to show that Mullik personally supplied information on him to Nehru.

The author also claims to have collected information from the Taiwan government to rule out the 1945 crash.

[*The Times of India* on 11 July 2012 reporting Anuj Dhar's finding]

---

1   Regarding his weekly meetings with Nehru, Mullik wrote in his memoir, 'I must admit that these were the greatest moments of my life and I used to drink deep at his feet. On these occasions he appeared to me like the sage of the Upanishads explaining the Truth as realised by him to his disciple.' B N Mullik, *My Years with Nehru*, Allied Publishers, p 65.

If this was not enough, serving and retired intelligence officials appearing before Shah Nawaz Khan and GD Khosla made misleading statements.[2]

Appearing before the Khosla Commission on 12 June 1971, Mullik demonstrated the art of skilful evasion of cross-examination. Pretending to fight bouts of forgetfulness and going in loops when asked questions, the former Director of Intelligence Bureau (DIB) kept stonewalling the experienced lawyers trying their best to extract a straight and coherent response from him. If his intent was to project the impression that the Intelligence Bureau wasn't concerned about Subhas Bose, he emerged largely successful. The sum and substance of Mullik's sworn testimony was that 'anything concerning the security of India would bring the Intelligence Bureau into the picture'. And since neither the Bose mystery nor the Shoulmari episode had anything to do with national security, they were not looked into by IB. 'The only time I had a talk with Pandit Nehru about Netaji was in 1950-51,' Mullik claimed. His assessment of the pre-1947 intelligence reports on Bose's disappearance was:

> When there was a sustained agitation about Netaji, I wanted to see the reports in the Intelligence Bureau. Then I saw these reports which were made during the time of pre-Independence days and I gathered the impression that at that time the Intelligence Bureau came to the conclusion that Netaji had

2   For instance, H K Roy, an inspector attached to the Finney–Davies team, told the Shah Nawaz Committee that Finney's report 'was definite that Netaji was dead'. Available reports belie this claim. Finney and others received inputs that Bose could be in Soviet Russia after his 'death', and so they were not able to draw a clear conclusion.

died as a result of a plane crash. So, one day, I talked to Pandit Nehru that these agitations are happening and we had this report in the Intelligence Bureau. He said he knew about this but he had been requested by Sarat Chandra Bose not to make it public due to family complications.

Sarat Bose died in 1950 thinking that his brother was alive. One need not be the Director of Intelligence Bureau to see through a white lie coming from Nehru—unless Mullik himself was coming with one.

In a flash of inquisitiveness, Khosla Commission's senior counsel T R Bhasin tried to extract from Mullik that the IB must have looked into the gamut of issues linked to the Bose mystery, especially the claims that he was alive and in India.

> Shri TR Bhasin: Now, when you joined as Director of Intelligence Bureau in July 1950, and from there onwards, is it correct that the question of Netaji's alleged death continued to agitate the public mind?
> Shri BN Mullik: It did.
> Shri TR Bhasin: Did the Intelligence Bureau deal with this aspect?
> Shri BN Mullik: No. During the entire period that I was Director of Intelligence Bureau, we were never asked to make an inquiry about this aspect.[3]

He repeated the same line when questions specifically related to the Shoulmari sadhu were put to him by Bhasin: 'We made no

---

3 Oral evidence of B N Mullik at the G D Khosla Commission of Inquiry, 8 August 1972, Netaji Inquiry Commission (1970), Record of Oral Evidence, Vol XI, p 3290.

inquiries about the Baba of Shoulmari. I am talking about my time,' he asserted.[4]

```
SHRI B.N. MULLICK:  We made no enquiries about the Baba of
                    Sholmari.  I am talking about my time.
SHRI T.R. BHASIN:   Supposing if there was responsible
                    statement made on the floor of the
                    Parliament that Director of Intelligence
                    has submitted report, that would be
                    incorrect.
SHRI B.N.MULLICK:   In my time, it would be incorrect.
```

Mullik repeated his assertion when Bhasin rephrased the same question.

Q: May I then take it that about the Baba of Sholmari (sic) an enquiry made either by the State Government or by the State Intelligence was passed on to you?
A: I do not remember. It must have occurred after I left the IB.[5]

This was not a casual statement. On oath, he repeated his position again after sometime when questioned by Forward Bloc's counsel A P Chakravarti.

Q: And the Shoulmari ashram situation had created such a thing in Bengal and Uttar Pradesh and in other parts of India, here also, did you not receive any report in these circumstances?
A: I do not remember to have received any report about the Shoulmari ashram.[6]

---

4   Ibid, pp 3292-93.
5   Ibid, p 3304.
6   Ibid, p 3319.

Mullik probably never ever thought that one day the classified records might see the light of day. Previously Top Secret records obtained by persistent efforts of the authors in a single stroke removed the veil of obfuscation weaved by Mullik. The first tranche of such records declassified under the instruction of the Central Information Commission in 2007, following our appeal, included a letter from K Ram, Principal Private Secretary to Prime Minister Nehru to Mullik, dated 23 May 1963.

> Please see the enclosed letter which has been addressed to the Prime Minister by Shri Ramani Ranjan Das, Secretary, Shoulmari Ashram. I should be grateful if you will kindly have suitable inquiries made into this matter and let me have a report for the Prime Minister's information.

On 12 June 1963, Mullik sent Ram his reply, marked Top Secret. He enclosed an investigation report received from the Bengal CID, on one miscreant who had attempted to kill Saradananda.

On 7 September 1963, K Ram wrote another Top Secret letter asking Mullik to throw light on the Shoulmari case, simple and straight. In his Top Secret response (see image on next page), Mullik left no room for any doubt that IB not only inquired about Shoulmari Sadhu[7] but also kept a watch on the Bose case; a completely different stance from what he would claim under oath a few years later.

---

7   As discussed in Chapter 3, Intelligence Bureau kept an eye on Shoulmari Sadhu till he died in 1977. Reports filed by top IB officials are now available. Here, we are discussing the case of Mullik only.

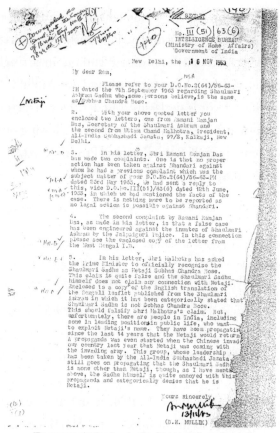

[Document obtained under the Right to Information Act]

Now, what was the need to mark this innocuous correspondence 'Top Secret'? If the Bose mystery or its offshoots like the Shoulmari affair were so irrelevant that Mullik did not feel the need to discuss them after 1950, as per his sworn statement before the commission, why make use of the highest level of security grading? That's because, contrary to what Mullik gave out, the Bose mystery indeed was a highly volatile and hence a Top Secret issue—details about which could not be given out to anyone, courts of law and commissions included. If Mullik had told the Khosla Commission that the IB was indeed trailing Bose after his death, it would have exposed the hollowness of official statements that Bose had died in 1945.

Ace journalist Barun Sengupta's evidence to the commission in this regard was quite revealing. Sengupta suggested that Shoulmari sadhu had been set up by the Intelligence Bureau itself as some sort of diversionary tactic. Sengupta told Justice Khosla: 'I had no belief in this from the very beginning, but as a reporter I had to go and investigate. I went to the local intelligence people, the State Intelligence Bureau as it is called, the intelligence branch of the West Bengal Police. I asked one of the chief men who was supposed to be dealing with this section, "What is this about Shoulmari?"'

Sengupta was told that B N Mullik was 'also entrusted with the Netaji inquiry affair'.

I was told by so many intelligence officers working in the eastern region of the country that it is Mr Mullik who looks after all these things…I never talked to Mr Mullik and I knew that Mr Mullik will not tell me anything. …Mr [BP] Chaliha, Mr PC Sen and Dr BC Roy knew certain things. There are certain things which do not go beyond the Chief Minister's level.

The crux of Sengupta's enquiry was that the IB knew 'fully well... about many saints and monks masquerading as Netaji' and that it was on a constant lookout for a 'dead' Bose.

Whenever there is a rumour or a story, the central intelligence people and the state intelligence people go and investigate into it. They also come to us [journalists] for further enlightenment and to know whether we have any information.[8]

The then director of the IB, the handsome and swashbuckling Atma Jayaram, too, appeared before the Khosla Commission. It then emerged that much before Sir Humphrey Appleby in the British satirical series *Yes Minister* employed the truism 'He that would keep a secret must keep it secret that he hath a secret to keep' to explain the official secrecy scenario in the United Kingdom, our own Intelligence Bureau had been practising it in letter and spirit.

'Has your department been dealing with the subject of Netaji Subhas Chandra Bose?' was the simple question put to Jayaram.

Jayaram's answer should have been an emphatic 'No'. The government's stand was that Bose was dead, and since the matter did not concern national security, the IB had no reason to even deal with it as it had scores of other pressing issues to look into. This was precisely what Mullik had explained before the commission.

Instead, Jayaram went into a long-winded waffle: 'As director of intelligence branch, I can only say that the intelligence department has wide possibility and whatever the Government wishes to know, we will do it, but it is difficult for me to say what we do or what we do not [do].'

It isn't difficult to understand that Jayaram was merely trying not to say 'yes'.

---

8   Oral evidence of B N Barun Sengupta at the G D Khosla Commission of Inquiry, 6 July 1972, Netaji Inquiry Commission (1970), Record of Oral Evidence, Vol IX, p 3002-3040.

At this point, Khosla took over.

Q: Can you say that the intelligence department has not at all been dealing with any news concerning Netaji?

A: I cannot say that but we have presented whatever material we have...

Q: ...have you ever, your department, done any inquiry?

A: Not that I know of.

Q: Can you say that your intelligence department has never conducted any inquiry into the baba of Shoulmari Ashram?

A: I can only talk from my memory. This subject did come up some years ago and when we use the word inquiry, not in the form of police inquiry.

Q: I am talking as a layman!

A: Inquiries would be done by the police organisation. In this particular case by West Bengal government and they would send their reports or pass their reports both to the Government and to us.

Q: There were certain inquiries?

A: Certainly.[9]

This little acknowledgement by Jayaram, albeit in a backhanded manner, knocked off the smokescreen that Mullik had carefully created just a day ago. Inadvertently, by admitting that the West Bengal government shared information with the IB on the Shoulmari case, he also demolished Mullik's position that the IB didn't consider the disappearance mystery as a matter of national

---

9   Oral evidence of Atma Jayaram at the G D Khosla Commission of Inquiry, 9 August 1972, Netaji Inquiry Commission (1970), Record of Oral Evidence, Vol XI, pp 3415-16.

security. Mullik himself had explained the principle on the basis of which a state government shared intelligence with the IB.

> In many case(s) the State Special Branch consults the Intelligence Bureau otherwise things are done in the States which the Intelligence Bureau may not know. If it affects the security of India, then the Intelligence Bureau would know and the State Branch would report to the IB but in a matter like Netaji where no security was involved, there was no such compulsion for the State Branch to report to the Intelligence Bureau. (sic)[10]

The partial disclosure provoked Bhasin to put a very logical query to Jayaram: 'When the Government of India has accepted Shah Nawaz Committee's report that Netaji is dead then how is it that the intelligence department goes after every news when it appears that Netaji is not dead but he is alive?'

Jayaram wouldn't say anything cogent in response. It was only in 2015 that we got an inkling why.

At the National Archives in Delhi in December 2014, Anuj Dhar stumbled upon (among freshly released Ministry of Home Affairs [MHA] records, as a result of our RTI quest), the photocopies of two West Bengal Intelligence Branch files detailing how Subhas's nephews were snooped on for more than two decades by local sleuths. The findings of this elaborate exercise were regularly shared with the top IB officials, such as

---

10   Oral evidence of B N Mullik at the G D Khosla Commission of Inquiry, 8 August 1972, Netaji Inquiry Commission (1970), Record of Oral Evidence, Vol XI, p 3301.

R N Kao, the would be founder chief of R&AW, who were evidently receiving similar inputs from other parts of the country as well. It was obvious that these Intelligence Branch papers had made it to the public domain due to an oversight because their originals remained locked up in Kolkata. So, thanks to the 'mistake' on the part of the MHA, we discovered that Amiya and Sisir, one a barrister and another a paediatrician, both freedom fighters in their own right, died never knowing that files bearing their names had been maintained in strict secrecy by the Director, Intelligence Branch, West Bengal.

So thorough was the interception that letters the Bose brothers received from their acquaintances in Japan, Europe and America—like historian and Bose biographer Leonard Gordon and Indian American historian Damodar SarDesai—were opened, read, copied and kept on file.

Copy from F.No. 1372/64(American)(Cal.) Page No. 57.

SECRET

A casual agent reports on 2.11.64 that Damodar R.SarDesai, 1043, West 35th Street, Los Angeles 7, California, U.S.A., communicated on 28.10.64 with Dr. Sisir K. Bose, General Secretary, Netaji Research Bureau, Netaji Bhawan, 38/2, Elgin Road, Calcutta-20, as follows :-

[National Archives, New Delhi]

Also intercepted were the letters Emilie Schenkl wrote to her nephew Sisir Bose. A note by the intelligence department on a 1955 intercept described Emilie as the 'alleged wife' of Bose, rather than 'widow'. It was a giveaway that, never mind what the government had given out for public consumption, for the sleuths Subhas Bose was still living.

Comment

The addressee is evidently the alleged wife of Sri SUBHAS CHANDRA BOSE.

[National Archives, New Delhi]

More damaging information came to the fore in September 2015 after Bengal Chief Minister declassified 64 Intelligence Branch files relating to Bose as a direct fallout of the nationwide outrage over snooping following *India Today*'s expose' based on the National Archives files that saw the light of day because of the efforts made by the authors. Now it became crystal clear that the snooping was much more extensive and covered not just Bose's kin but also INA veterans and journalists. A major focus was on finding out more about Bose. 'Deb Nath Das, an ex-INA leader who is actively engaged in anti-Congress propaganda, is preaching in political and party circles that Netaji Subhas Chandra Bose is alive and is somewhere in Manchuria, China, at present,' read a 1948 report. 'I told you that I heard in 1946 from Japanese sources that your brother is still living,' read an intercepted 1949 letter to Sarat Bose from Lilly Abegg, a Swiss journalist who grew up in Japan. Most incredible was the case of a fifteen-year-old school boy named Pirthi Lal Subba. He was snooped upon after he wrote a letter to Sarat Bose, Subhas's elder brother, in November 1949, inquiring whether Subhas Bose was still alive. Luckily for the boy, 'nothing against him politically or otherwise' was found by the intelligence branch.

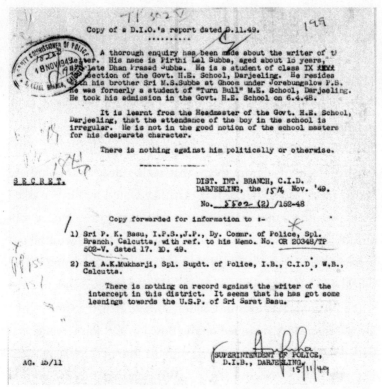

Copy of a D.I.O.'s report dated 8.11.49.
....

A thorough enquiry has been made about the writer of t
letter. His name is Firthi Lal Subba, aged about 15 years,
late Dhan Frasad Subba. He is a student of class IX
section of the Govt. H.E. School, Darjeeling. He resides
with his brother Sri M.S.Subba at Ghoom under Jorebungalow P.S.
He was formerly a student of "Turn Bull" M.E. School, Darjeeling.
He took his admission in the Govt. H.E. School on 6.4.48.

It is learnt from the Headmaster of the Govt. H.E. School,
Darjeeling, that the attendance of the boy in the school is
irregular. He is not in the good notion of the school masters
for his desparate character.

There is nothing against him politically or otherwise.

S E C R E T.   DIST. INT. BRANCH, C.I.D.
                                      DARJEELING, the 15th Nov. '49.

                           No. 5502 (2) /152-48

        Copy forwarded for information to :-

1) Sri P. K. Basu, I.P.S.,J.P., Dy. Commr. of Police, Spl.
   Branch, Calcutta, with ref. to his Memo. No. OR 20348/TP
   802-V. dated 17. 10. 49.

2) Sri A.K.Mukharji, Spl. Supdt. of Police, I.B., C.I.D, W.B.,
   Calcutta.

        There is nothing on record against the writer of the
        intercept in this district. It seems that he has got some
        leanings towards the U.S.P. of Sri Sarat Basu.

                              SUPERINTENDENT OF POLICE,
AG. 15/11   D.I.B., DARJEELING.
                                          15/11/49

The conclusion drawn by a visibly shaken Mamata Banerjee
on the day of the release of the files was that Bose might have been
alive after 1945. BJP national spokesperson M J Akbar, a former
top journalist and later the Minister of State for External Affairs,
had already told *India Today* that there was 'only one reasonable
explanation for this long surveillance'.

> The government was not sure whether Bose was dead, and
> thought that if he were alive he would be in some form of
> communication with his family in Calcutta.[11]

---

11   Sandeep Unnithan, 'When Nehru spied on Netaji,' *India Today*, 20 April 2015.

To Chandra Kumar Bose, the spokesperson of the Bose family, it was 'clear that the Government knew Netaji was alive and thought that he might establish contact with family members. There was a fear that he would return,'[12] he added.

In spite of such a background, at no point in time did the Intelligence Bureau feel the need to inform either the Khosla Commission or the Mukherjee Commission, which repeatedly sought information from them, that such a thing was going on. Perhaps they did so out of fear that they would be further asked what prompted this surveillance in the first place. Not a soul outside the intelligence machinery came to know a word about it even as free India heralded in a golden era of snooping. More shockingly, evidence thrown up by a file declassified in late 2014 at the National Archives in London showed that the fruits of the illegal surveillance mounted on the Bose kin and former aides was shared by the Intelligence Bureau with the former colonial masters.

[7 October 1947 letter from SLO, Delhi, forwarding report about Bose to MI5 chief]

Wanting to get to the bottom of the spying saga, the authors filed an RTI application with the Intelligence Bureau in February 2015. 'Who authorised the snooping on the Netaji family members and for what purpose; how long did it continue; how many states were party to it and

---

12   'Revealed: Shocking scale of snoop on kin,' *The Times of India* (Kolkata edition), 19 September 2015.

who were the family members placed under surveillance?' the application by Anuj Dhar, inter alia, asked. However, IB curtly refused to disclose anything saying it was exempt from giving any replies to RTI applications. Our submission that the exemption was not applicable in cases of 'allegations of corruption and human rights violations' was set aside even after we filed a review application with the appellate authority in the bureau. Snooping on ordinary citizens was neither a violation of their rights, nor is it a corrupt practice, the IB would have us believe. And if there was indeed a reason, the bureau wouldn't divulge it to us.

The silence of the IB notwithstanding, the following four characteristics of the large-scale spying provide a clear answer towards its raison d'être when viewed in perspective of the national security principle elucidated by B N Mullik.

1. Correspondence to and from the Bose family were intercepted, read, and copies made. Family members, journalists, historians, as well as ex-INA soldiers were tailed and meticulous reports were filed. In fact, anyone with remotest link to Netaji, including a child showing interest in his death mystery, was not spared.

2. Available records show that the snooping continued from 1946 to at least 1971. Going by the statement of a nephew of Netaji, his father was under surveillance till he passed away in 1984.

3. The surveillance was carried on at a multi-state level and must have incurred massive expenditure in one of the poorest nations in the world.

4. All the states reported the resulting intelligence to the central IB.

Now let's recall Mullik's words quoted in the previous pages, again.

In many case(s) the State Special Branch consults the Intelligence Bureau, otherwise things are done in the States which the Intelligence Bureau may not know. If it affects the security of India, then the Intelligence Bureau would know and the State Branch would report to the IB.

Why were all these people snooped upon across States and why was the IB being reported to? According to Mullik's explanation the exercise must have concerned national security. But, by no stretch of imagination can they be categorised as threats to national security. Therefore, the only logical conclusion that can be drawn is the common thread binding them was considered a national security issue, which, in this case was Subhas Chandra Bose.

Neither Sisir nor Amiya were political hotshots or mass leaders who posed any threat to the ruling party. If they could be tailed, would it be unreasonable to expect that the more politically active followers of Subhas Bose were spared? Leela Roy was a top-level political leader; Pabitra Mohan Roy and Sunil Das were legislators and Samar Guha and H V Kamath were parliamentarians. They were not only the most vocal among the activists who demanded the government of the day come out with the truth regarding Netaji but had connected with one particular mysterious figure living in Uttar Pradesh. It is inconceivable that the intelligence establishments wouldn't have any documents on them.

Not one of the 304 files declassified by the Modi government since 23 January 2016 originates from any of the intelligence organisations, though in some files we come across IB records. Important though every single declassified record is to any researcher, the released files are merely a collection created as a result of regular bureaucratic collation. From day one, the authors have stressed the need for the release of the intelligence records as a prerequisite to cracking the Bose mystery. References to seventy-seven IB files are already there on record. While we don't think they contain anything explosive, they might lead us to other hidden or destroyed records. The description of one among the seventy-seven known files illustrates this point:

File No.25/DG/70 (S.No.69 in IB's list ibid)	This file contains a note on the issue whether Netaji is dead or still alive. Some leaders and parties in India, it appears from the file, still believe that Netaji is alive and that is why the Khoshla Commission was constituted by the Government of India under the Commissions of Inquiry Act, 1952 in order to get the mystery unraveled.

[National Archives, New Delhi]

In 2006, R&AW (carved out of IB in 1968) responded to our RTI application that it did not have 'any information pertaining to Netaji'. The authors were tersely reminded that the intelligence agency was 'under no obligation to provide this information under the Right to Information (RTI) Act, 2005'.

I am directed to refer to your letter dated 21.12.2006 addressed to AS(SR) and appellate Authority, Cabinet Secretariat, Bikaner House(Annexe), New Delhi on the subject mentioned above and to inform you that the R&AW does not have any information pertaining to Netaji. As such no list as requested by you in point 2 can be provided. It might be added that we are under no obligation to provide this information under the Right to Information(RTI) Act, 2005.

Yours faithfully,

(P.N. Ranjit Kumar)
Deputy Secretary to the Govt. of India

We are not inclined to take this response as truthful. That's because we have a copy of a 2001 affidavit filed before the Mukherjee Commission by then Home Secretary Kamal Pande. This affidavit lists out several Top Secret/Secret records about Bose, whose disclosure was likely to harm India's 'relations with friendly countries'. Among these listed records, one originates from the R&AW: An Under Office note of 1994 vintage dealing with certain articles published in a Russian journal on the basis of classified KGB records. This particular record, and the file from which it originates, are not to be found among those declassified by the Modi government and made public through the website http://www.netajipapers.gov.in/.

Document originating from Cabinet Secretariat (R&AW)

Sl. No/ Page No.	File No.	Details of documents
1. 95/c	No.I/12014/27/93-IS(D.III)	Cabinet Secretariat (R&AW)'s UO No.11/1/94-IC-2829 dated 25.3.1994 regarding articles published in 'Asia and Africa Today' on Netaji Subhas Chandra Bose– summary of two Articles published in the September-October, 1993 issues.

(KAMAL PANDE)
Home Secretary
Government of India
New Delhi.

All that the declassified files have revealed are some snippets giving us some insight into the working and the mindset of those at the helm of Indian intelligence. Two pertinent instances revolve around Iwaichi Fujiwara, a retired lieutenant general in Japan who had helped form the Indian National Army during the war. In 1967, a sword presented to Subhas Bose by a Japanese leader was brought to Calcutta by Fujiwara, who had retained contacts with his old INA compatriots. The sword was handed over to Sisir

Bose at a function chaired by then governor of West Bengal. A few months later, a group of MPs, including M L Sondhi, Samar Guha and Madhu Limaye, sought support from the Prime Minister so that the relic could be brought to Delhi. Notwithstanding the fact that it's illegal to spy on MPs, IB wasted no time in finding out what these people's representatives were up to. The opening para of the first IB report for the PM's office read that the MPs were seeking an inquiry into Bose's disappearance. In 1974, Fujiwara was invited to attend Netaji's birth anniversary programme in Imphal, Moirang. This invite by Sisir Bose prompted the Indian Embassy in Tokyo to do a thorough background check on Fujiwara, his pro-India antecedents notwithstanding. The Embassy staffers, evidently linked to Indian intelligence, were able to obtain records in Japan by secret means. P J Rao, First Secretary (Inf), started to connect the dots...

> I place herewith a sheet containing the names, careers, and areas for intelligence gathering against each Director of what is known as Fujiwara Asia Institute. This is headed by General Fujiwara who, during the last war, was in charge of military intelligence operations in Asia and was the main liaison with INA. ...General Fujiwara and directors do travel to areas in Asia where they have established contacts. Their operations naturally require considerable funds. My information is that the funds come from various agencies including SDF, extreme right-wing organisations and some business houses. Whether they have any connection with the CIA is not known.[13]

---

13   Ministry of External Affairs file no C/121(39)73-JP, 'Visit to Imphal—Japanese delegation in Jan 1974—Netaji birth anniversary,' National Archives, New Delhi.

If only such fabulous expertise had been employed to find out the truth behind the less than satisfactory account of Subhas Chandra Bose's reported death offered by the Japanese!

Given this backdrop and that the Intelligence Bureau, the world's oldest spy agency, has had deep penetration into every nook and corner of India, it is inconceivable that the Bhagwanji matter escaped their notice. In fact, local journalists who investigated the matter before and after 1985 came across tell-tale signs of IB's unseen presence. V N Arora, part of the *Northern India Patrika* team that investigated the matter in 1985-86 and a former principal of Saket Postgraduate College in Faizabad, narrated to us how his only chance to meet a living Bhagwanji was thwarted by an IB officer. In 1978, desirous of meeting the holy man, he had left a written application with Saraswati Devi, who asked him to come the next day at 4 pm. Arora's chance never came. He was visited by one N P Tiwari, an IB officer of the rank of deputy superintendent of police, who, Arora told us, 'seized my time from 2 pm to 6.30 pm and persuaded me not to disturb a saint who is practising meditation for self realisation far from the public eye'.[14] Arora repeated the entire incident in his affidavit to the Sahai Commission in 2016.

> On my enquiring from Mr Tiwari as to why he had come, he told me that he had come to make a social call since I was an important person in Ayodhya. At about 3 pm, I told Mr Tiwari that I had to leave as I had an appointment at 4 pm. He asked

---

14   Interview with Dr V N Arora by the authors, Faizabad, 2014.

whether my appointment was with Parde Wale Baba. I asked
Mr Tiwari how he had come to know that I was going to meet
Parde Wale Baba. He replied that since yesterday he had found
my scooter parked outside Lucknauwa Kothi so he thought
that I was going to meet Parde wale Baba. I asked Mr Tiwari
whether I or Parde Wale Baba or both were under surveillance.
He gave an evasive reply and said that since in Ayodhya town
there were only a few scooters, he had recognised my scooter.
He told me that Parde Wale Baba was just an ordinary sadhu
who was living in disguise and if I was under the impression
that he was Netaji Subhas Chandra Bose then I was under a
big delusion. He succeeded in persuading me to believe that he
was an ordinary sadhu living under disguise and was certainly
not Netaji Subhas Chandra Bose. Consequently, I never visited
Parde Wale Baba alias Bhagwanji.[15] (sic)

Sayed Kauser Hussain, the former *NIP* news editor, testified
before the Mukherjee Commission that 'there were four
investigations at the instance of the central government'. The
police inquiry report of 1985 itself states that when Bhagwanji
'was in Basti he had become a matter of inquiry and it is reported
that some central intelligence agency had conducted a thorough
inquiry about him'.

Where are those inquiry reports now? No such report was
made available to the Mukherjee Commission by IB or the
Ministry of Home Affairs, under which it officially functions. We
are given to understand that Justice Sahai never asked IB or the
state CID for anything.

---

15 Affidavit of Dr V N Arora to Justice Vishnu Sahai Commission, Lucknow,
    2 December 2016. Dr Arora shared his affidavit with the authors.

Available lists of the IB files concerning Bose do not show anything about Faizabad, though there are references to reports about Shoulmari and 'persons who were taken as Netaji'. Available records show that every time an absurd claim was made that Subhas was in the guise of a holy man, the IB lost no time in cross-checking it.

INTELLIGENCE BUREAU
(Ministry of Home Affairs)
• • •

Our enquiries reveal that the original name of Sant Tulsi, who has issued pamphlets in the name of 'Veer Subhash Seva Sangh', is Ram Sunder Tiwari, xxxxxx at present working as an Assistant Engineer in Asthapana Khand, Okhala, New Delhi on a UP Government project. He has recently formed 'Veer Subhash Seva Sangh' in Allahabad, which has no following. He believes that Nemai Chand Goswami of Varanasi is Subhash Chandra Bose. Tiwari is known to to be a fadist and nobody takes him seriously. Similarly, Amarnath Sharma, who has asserted that Subhash Chandra Bose is alive, is a whimsical man and people do not pay attention to his claims.

(A. V. Karnik)
Assistant Director

[National Archives, New Delhi]

But the bureau seemed to have looked the other way whenever the Bhagwanji issue was flagged, not even when a direct reference to the unseen holy man was made in a letter to PMO. One Swami Amalananda wrote a stinker to Prime Minister Indira Gandhi on 12 December 1974 with regard to Parda Baba (Bhagwanji was also known as such at that point in time).

Your taunt to Samar Guha in Parliament 'the entire House

would be happy if you can tell us where Netaji is' forced me to write this letter. …Secondly, why a batch of intelligence service was posted at Naimisharanya during 1964/65 to watch 'Parda Baba'? And when he left Naimisharanya for the garden house of Raja of Ayodhya at Darsan Nagore, why the intelligence service followed him like a ghost?[16]

It may be recalled that Swami Asimananda Saraswati (former Bengal revolutionary-turned-ascetic who worked with Subhas Bose), one of the people Leela Roy had sounded after she met Bhagwanji had a disciple called Amalananda. But we cannot say that this and that Amalananda were the same person.

Is it therefore possible to reconcile with the official position of India's intelligence establishment that despite there being so much going for the Bhagwanji angle, they did not look into the matter or generate a single record? We don't think it is. It becomes all the more unbelievable when even the CIA had been collecting information on Subhas Bose's post-'death' activities.

One of the CIA documents obtained by us under the American Freedom of Information Act shows that the American intelligence agency received reports from sources within India about Bose's possible survival, once in 1950 (in Siberia) and then in 1964 (in India).

Something curious happened in 1964 in the CIA's office at Washington, DC. Under the order of a top official, an unnamed

---

16   Letter of Swami Amalananda to Indira Gandhi, 12 December 1974, PMO File No 2/64/78-PM.

source was called in February 1964 for an interview related to Subhas Bose. That such an interview would be conducted by the CIA regarding a man who did not feature anywhere in its domestic or foreign policy considerations is, by itself, a matter to wonder about. The interviewing officer, who had little idea who Subhas Bose was, made note of the fact that the unnamed source was 'dressed neatly in a business suit,' conversed intelligently and 'did not appear to be alarmed or emotional about his story'. The source came in with the information that 'there now exists a strong possibility that Bose is leading the religious group undermining the current Nehru Government'.[17]

We have already seen that the Foreign Broadcast Information Service (FBIS)—an open source intelligence gathering component of the CIA which is now called Open Source Center—had not failed to note a news item concerning Bhagwanji which should have been of no consequence to the US.

To come back to the point, all the information discussed above clearly establishes that there is much more information in the custody of our intelligence agencies than is given out either by them or by the government. Our intelligence agencies must be holding Bhagwanji-related classified reports whose very existence is being denied for fear of havoc their disclosure would unleash.

But how can that be possible? How can a government, in a

17   Document No C00022904, Subhas Chandra Bose, Central Intelligence Agency, 27 February 1964. It was part of the records released in 2014 by the agency in response to a Freedom of Information Application filed by Abhishek Bose at the request of Anuj Dhar. Reference No F-2014-00375. From Michele Meeks, Information and Privacy Coordinator, CIA, to Abhishek Bose, 28 January 2014.

democracy, where the rule of law is supreme, keep secrets in such a way? Well, let alone records, governments can even deny the existence of projects, departments and even massive organisations. In Britain, the land of the Westminster model which we are still trying to learn from, the formal acceptance that its external intelligence agency MI6 actually existed came more than eight decades after it was formed. Our Government did not accept that an entity such as R&AW existed for quite some time after it was formed. In 2013, *The Guardian* revealed the discovery of a secret archive at a high-security government communications centre in Buckinghamshire, north of London. 'Foreign Office has unlawfully hoarded more than a million files of historic documents that should have been declassified and handed over to the National Archives,' the paper reported.[18]

If disclosure of something is not deemed to be in the interest of a nation or its ruling class—democratic or otherwise—it shall not be told. Not until enough time has passed by to nullify any damage the disclosure would entail. As reported by the *BBC*, Japan revealed in March 2010 that for forty years, it had kept a lid on the very 'existence of a secret Cold War deal, allowing the transit of nuclear-armed US vessels through its ports'. The hi-voltage disclosure—Japan is the only nation to have suffered a nuclear Holocaust—came after decades of outright denials by officials.[19]

---

18   Ian Cobain, 'Foreign Office hoarding 1m historic files in secret archive,' *The Guardian*, 18 October 2013, https://www.theguardian.com/politics/2013/oct/18/foreign-office-historic-files-secret-archive.

19   Japan confirms secret pact on US nuclear transit, BBC, 9 March 2010, http://news.bbc.co.uk/2/hi/asia-pacific/8557346.stm.

Not that such things don't happen in the land of the biggest moral giants of them all—Mahatma Gandhi and Pandit Nehru. To the rest of the world, we are the nation of Buddha and Gandhi. This impression is reinforced to the visitors when they arrive at New Delhi's international airport and see imagery and artefacts linked to Buddha and Gandhi. Little do they know that there is another side as well. One of the most famous modern Indian catchphrases—'Buddha is smiling'—denotes the secret (so secret that even our Defence Minister had no clue) detonating of our first nuclear device in 1974, when we fooled the CIA among others. Sitting under Mahatma Gandhi's portrait in the South Block, our successive defence ministers have turned India into the biggest importer of weapons in the world. Most cunningly, we have successfully projected a holier-than-thou image of our leaders even though the real fact of the matter is that someone like Richard 'Tricky Dick' Nixon was an incompetent blunderer by our standards. Imagine not been able to pull off a thing as simple as snooping! The Watergate scandal was nothing but the outcome of a botched-up attempt at snooping on the opposition at Nixon's behest. And here in India, we were able to do it for decades, without ever getting caught! Of course, some human ventures are bound to fail. Giani Zail Singh saw through it as President of India, and so did Tony Blair, going by the account of his Director of Communications and Strategy at 10 Downing Street. During a visit to Delhi, MI6 bug detectors found two eavesdropping devices in Blair's bedroom at a top hotel. 'We decided against making a fuss,' wrote Alastair Campbell in *The Blair Years: Extracts from the Alastair Campbell Diaries.*

Those who'd still like to think that our Government can never fudge the truth or conceal it from us as it believes in the Gandhian percepts would do well to pursue the following paras carefully.

In 1963, US President John F Kennedy revealed to Sudhir Ghosh, an eminent Gandhian and ambassador-at-large for Indian interests since pre-independence days, that the Chinese attack of the previous year had made Prime Minister Nehru beseech the US for military support. Two years later, on 15 March 1965, Ghosh stated during his speech in the Rajya Sabha that 'the father of nonalignment asked for American air protection' and the US President 'did respond and order one of the American aircraft carriers to proceed to the Bay of Bengal'. Though his aim was to laud Nehru for giving precedence to national interest over the principles he talked about, Ghosh's statement had an opposite effect. He was charged with attempting to sully the former PM's good name. Communist and Congress MPs mauled him in the House on March 19. Communist leader Bupesh Gupta led the charge against Ghosh, accusing him of making up fiction at the behest of Americans:

Our party led a delegation to the late prime minister [Nehru] and we met him. I was there. It is said that the matter was discussed in November 1962. He had said no such thing. He absolutely denied it to us. The delegation was led by our party chairman, Comrade Dange. I was there. He said no such thing. He had not made any such request. I do not know of any such thing. ...Therefore, today I remember. I am in a position to say that the prime minister has not said any such thing. I find the Congress member making a serious statement. It has serious international repercussions. I ask whether he has been put up, advised by some American friends and so on, to say such a thing. I do not know that. But I think the government should come out and immediately make a statement.[20]

Lal Bahadur Shastri summoned Ghosh to his chamber. In the presence of Home Minister Gulzari Lal Nanda and Foreign Secretary C S Jha, Shastri told Ghosh that there was nothing on record to suggest that Nehru had ever made such a request to Kennedy. Since Ghosh had heard it straight from Kennedy, he stood his ground and requested Shastri to ascertain the facts from the US Ambassador in New Delhi before making a statement in Parliament. He said if he was proven wrong, he would apologise publicly. A day before the PM was to make a statement in Parliament, Ghosh learnt from his American sources that Jha had been told by the US Embassy that the US Government did have the letters from Nehru. Thereafter, Ghosh marched into the PM's office to see Shastri. Now the PM was unwilling to meet him, because he had by then discovered that the copies of Nehru's letters were indeed available with the government somewhere.

The PM went on to state in Parliament that '[Ghosh] had said that at the time of the Chinese attack on India in 1962, a US aircraft carrier equipped with supersonic planes was present off Calcutta just outside the territorial waters of India and that the aircraft carrier was there at the request of the late Prime Minister Nehru. Neither of these statements is correct.' Shastri was playing with words, and Ghosh was not willing to play ball. Having lost

---

20   Rajya Sabha debate on 'Reference to certain remarks by Shri Sudhir Ghosh,' 19 March 1965.

face, he shot off a personal letter to Shastri, telling him that his clarification made no difference to the substance of his statement that India had sought military support from the US. Ghosh repeated that Nehru's letter to Kennedy, personally delivered by Ambassador B K Nehru, had sought '16 squadrons of fighting aircraft', which was much more than a carrier.[21]

In his reply, Shastri—whose name is a byword for honesty in present-day India—asked Ghosh to let the matter rest. Ghosh would have perhaps let that be, but he was publicly humiliated when the US State Department backed Prime Minister Shastri's statement that Nehru did not ask for an American aircraft carrier, leaving out the other vital details. Ghosh then used his formidable connections and goodwill with the US lawmakers, and managed to corner Secretary of State Dean Rusk during a public hearing in the Senate in 1966. Rusk was evasive at first and then said it was not proper for him to discuss correspondences between the two heads of governments.

Ghosh died in 1967 when he was barely fifty-one. Two Top Secret letters of Nehru hand-delivered to Kennedy by the Indian ambassador proving Ghosh's contention remained classified at the John F Kennedy Presidential Library and Museum in Boston—'allegedly in part at the request of the Government of India', according to former Central Intelligence Agency (CIA) analyst Bruce Riedel.[22] It was only in 2010 that they became available. In

21 Sudhir Ghosh, *Gandhi's Emissary*, Rupa and Co, 1967. See p 331 and 334-336 for Ghosh's account of the controversy.
22 Bruce Riedel, *JFK's Forgotten Crisis: Tibet, the CIA, and the Sino-Indian War*, Harper Collins, 2015, p 135.

these, Nehru is found to be asking for 'a minimum of 12 squadrons of supersonic all-weather fighters', 'modern radar cover', and United States Air Force personnel 'to man these fighters and radar installations'. Going further, with a view to attacking the Chinese bases, Nehru is seeking 'two squadrons of bombers of B-47 type', plus training for Indian pilots and technicians in the US.

B K Nehru, the ambassador, Prime Minister Nehru's cousin and Kennedy's friend, never discussed this correspondence with anyone but told veteran journalist Inder Malhotra—a reputed biographer of Indira Gandhi—that he had 'locked them up in a safe that only the ambassador could open'.[23]

This leads us to the issue of ultra-secret information and how governments hide them. Within governments the world over, information of grave sensitivity is secured separately from the other Top Secret records. In America, conspiracy theorists think of this class of information as falling in the 'Above Top Secret' category. In the Central Intelligence Agency, the term used is Sensitive Compartmented Information (SCI)—information which is so sensitive that it requires special, separate handling.

In India, the land of truth and *ahimsa*, such information is usually entrusted to the Officers on Special Duty, kept under the personal custody of ministers and other top officials, placed in secretive 'T branch' of the Home Ministry or handed over to intelligence agencies for safekeeping. Intelligence agencies have a variety of places, including safehouses and bank lockers, to

---

23   Inder Malhotra, 'Letters from the darkest hour,' *The Indian Express*,
       17 November 2010.

store sensitive stuff whose existence they won't admit. Another advantage with them is that they can work beyond the periphery of the law. Incidentally, several Bose-related papers declassified by the Modi government originate from T Branch, which is abbreviation of Top Secret Branch.

MINISTRY OF HOME AFFAIRS
गृह मंत्रालय
T. BRANCH
टी शाखा
TOP SECRET
परम गुप्त
N. G. O.

[National Archives, New Delhi]

Throwing light on the working of the T Branch, its former head B S Raghavan wrote the following in *The Hindu* of 6 December 2010: 'The behaviour of my second-in-command in the "T" branch used to remind me of the story circulating about the US Secretary of State, Dean Rusk, who came to meet the US President, Lyndon B Johnson, one day in his Oval Office and told him, "Mr President, I have come with something that is so top secret that one of us must leave this room before I bring it up!"'

Vappala Balachandran, former Special Secretary, R&AW, wrote in the *Indian Express* on 23 January 2016 that R N Kao had commissioned the writing of an official chronicle detailing the intelligence agency's role in the 1971 war. Then he made this pertinent revelation: 'This task was completed sometime in 1984 or 1985, but the volumes were kept in sealed envelopes in the personal custody of the R&AW chief's staff officer. ... In January 1986, I inherited these sealed envelopes when I became the staff officer. I handed them over to the late B Raman, who took over from me in September 1990. Since then, these envelopes must have been mechanically handed over and taken over by relieving officers.'

IB's own secret archive is said to be holding a fabulous collection, a veritable Aladdin's Cave of secrets. Every time former IB chief and National Security Advisor M K Narayanan teased people with his 'I have a file on you'[24] jibe, he was unknowingly paying a compliment to the richness of the documentation in the possession of India's spy agencies.

While for obvious reasons we can't produce any ultra-secret record from our intelligence agencies, we can indirectly prove their existence. A relevant portion from B N Mullik's November 1963 Top Secret report discussed earlier in this chapter is zoomed here:

```
unfortunately, there are people in India, including
some in leading positions in public life, who want
to exploit Netaji's name.  They have been propagating
since the last 14 years that the Netaji would return
A propaganda was even started when the Chinese invad
our country last year that Netaji was coming with
the invading army.  This group, whose leadership
```

As any junior-level intelligence officer can tell, the IB Director's personally signed notes such as this one are distilled from heaps of material. So, for this one document, there must be several reports detailing each and every aspect mentioned in it. The IB must have

24   Sahil Makkar and Probal Basak, 'I have a file on you: M K Narayanan,' *Business Standard*, 5 July 2014, accessed from https://www.business-standard.com/article/current-affairs/i-have-a-file-on-you-m-k-narayanan-114070400684_1.html.

several reports regarding the 'propaganda' during the Chinese attack that 'Netaji was coming with the invading army'.

The most secret records of them all are held directly by the Prime Minister of India, who is not answerable to any court of law. The records produced before a court or commission usually come from the bureaucrats in the Prime Minister's Office in South Block, which has something like 30,000 classified files. All the PMO files concerning Netaji that have been declassified by the Modi government are from the PMO record room. Only the PM himself knows what is there in his personal safe, at his residence, etc. National interest necessitates this sort of secrecy because there have been instances when top officials have betrayed India's secrets to other nations.

Secret

PM's House

PM's desires to see the Top Secret file on "Netaji Subhash Chandra Bose". This may be made available to me urgently

(Shakti Sinha)
PS to PM
10.4.99

Section Officer (NGO), PMO

The following four T.S. files on the subject, have been sent to PS to PM (Shri Shakti Sinha) separately.

10/4/99 (i) G-12(18)/74-NGO
(ii) G-4(2)/95-NGO
.... G-... 15F-NGO and

[National Archives, New Delhi]

How we wish Justice Sahai Commission had made an attempt to extract information from the intelligence agencies! In our affidavit before it, we had specifically requested for 'a full accounting of Intelligence Bureau's insight concerning Netaji mystery, including Gumnami Baba angle'. If the commission had gone along this line, we would have advised it to start with consulting retired intelligence officers—because only they know the system well enough to get things out of it. It would be better if somehow the Centre and UP State governments could be persuaded to make a declaration through the *Gazette of India,* freeing all serving and retired government officials, especially those with the intelligence services, from the provision of Official Secrets Act and other regulations so that they may freely share information about Subhas Bose with the commission as well as the public, through the media. Since Subhas Bose died in 1945, officially, and ours is the nation of truth and *ahimsa*, there should have been no opposition to this demand.

The Sahai commission could have sought from the intelligence agencies all information available in any format—electronic, paper, picture or microfilm. There would be no room for word play or any other stratagem. Release of information could have been followed by written, unqualified, sworn declarations by the intelligence chiefs that the disclosure was full and nothing that they personally knew of had been concealed. Given the past instances of skullduggery, they cannot be trusted.

Specifically, the commission could have sought access to intelligence agencies' databases, after having acquired a good understanding of the databases with the help of retired intelligence officers. Details of all current and historical databases could have been ascertained, including how the systems had developed and changed over time. Full access could have been enabled by the agencies, even if it meant giving access to Justice Sahai in person. All incoming and outgoing communications from or to Faizabad/ Lucknow area between September 1985 and February 1986, when the Allahabad High Court passed the interim order, could have been searched for specifically.

NINE

ALL IN THE FAMILY

FOLLOWING THE UNRAVELLING of the snooping scandal in 2015, national spotlight fell on Subhas Bose's family. Anyone who could lay claim to the epithet of 'Netaji kin' became an overnight expert on anything and everything related to Subhas Bose, airing their views which were more often than not grossly uninformed. A number of these 'Netaji kin' made best possible use of the situation in whose build up they had played little or no role. Different individuals hold different opinions but tend to converge on one point when it comes to the Bhagwanji issue. The central argument that they take recourse to for denying the possibility of Bhagwanji and Netaji being the same person is: 'Why wouldn't he contact my father/mother/family if he really was Netaji?' It, therefore, becomes imperative to understand this phenomenon called 'Netaji kin' and trace its history since Netaji's disappearance in order to be able to answer this question.

The importance of dynastic and family element in Indian politics and social life can hardly be overstated. Special benefits invariably accompany the association with famous names. The Bose family has been no exception. And it is largely through this privilege that a number of family members have been able to exercise influence on political parties and governments, riding on the wave of popularity that Subhas Bose enjoys in the country, even seven decades after his disappearance. Consequently, their views have usually been taken into account in the decisions of the government, depending on their political affiliations.[1]

In the pre-independence era, the British Intelligence noted that within the family, Subhas's three nephews 'functioned as his principal lieutenants'—Ganesh and Dwijen (two sons of his eldest brother Satish) and Aurobindo (son of Suresh).[2] While Ganesh passed away in 1943, both Dwijen and Aurobindo were arrested as security prisoners in the 'Bose Conspiracy Case' and were released towards the end of 1945. Both Dwijen and Aurobindo (as also his brother Kalyan) played important roles in the student movement in the 1930s and actively helped Subhas organise his Forward Bloc. In 1941, both of them were involved in the execution of Subhas's escape from home. Dwijen was meted

---

1   Hitting out at a section of the family with his characteristic sarcasm, Nirad C Chaudhury, uncle of the current chairperson of the Netaji Research Bureau told *The Asian Age* from his home in Oxford that Subhas had become 'a good business proposition' and 'all that they can do is encash on their *Rangakaka* (uncle Subhas)'. Pranab Mukherjee, 'Netaji's marriage a cultivated myth, says Nirad Chaudhari,' *The Asian Age*, 12 January 1996.

2   Home Department: Political (Internal), File No. 44/8/44-Poll (I), National Archives of India.

out particularly harsh treatment during his incarceration.

Among Sarat's sons, Asoke entered student politics as a leader of the Bengal Provincial Students' Association (BPSA) but left shortly for higher studies in Europe in 1931. On his return, Asoke's role was largely restricted to assisting Subhas in his correspondence and other political work in a personal capacity. Asoke accompanied Subhas to Haripura in 1938 and played a crucial role in his escape from India in 1941. Younger brother Amiya was off to Cambridge in 1937 and got involved in the UK chapter of India's freedom struggle, helping to organise his uncle's visit to London in 1938. Amiya returned home towards the end of 1944, and after Sarat's release in September 1945 took up the responsibility of the INA Relief Committee work in Calcutta. Sisir was too young to be involved in Subhas's political life and his first major involvement came in the form of driving Subhas out of his Elgin Road house on the night of his escape.

As in the case of many large families, the Bose family too wasn't a monolith. Riven by disputes and rivalries of various sorts, relations within the family weren't always cordial. Following Sarat's release after the war, a dispute over 38/2 Elgin Road (later Netaji Bhawan) arose when children of Suresh Chandra Bose claimed that Subhas had left behind a letter passing on his share in the house, including furniture and other belongings, to them. They also claimed that Janaki Nath Bose, too, had created a will transferring the house to the children of Suresh Bose 'as he believed that Suresh Babu was not a responsible man and would ruin everything in speculation'. The matter reached Mahatma Gandhi for intervention.

Sarat responded through a scathing handwritten letter to Mahatma Gandhi, written on 25 May 1946, spanning sixteen sheets, demolishing the claims and making no secret of the state of family relations. Sarat indicated that the letter purportedly written by Subhas on the basis of which the claims were made was a piece of forgery. He named his [and Subhas's] sister Kanaklata Mitra as 'one of the persons responsible for the bickerings that arose between some members of the family living at 38/2 Elgin Road'. With regard to Subhas's relations with his nephews, Sarat was categorical:

> It is not true that he loved Suresh's sons the most. The fact is that among his nephews he loved Amiya and Sisir (my sons) most and used to confide many things to them. He never confided anything to Ranjit and Kalyan (Suresh's elder sons). To Aurobindo (Suresh's third son) he confided very little indeed. He loved Dwijen (Satish Babu's son) and confided many things to him.

Sarat also reacted strongly to insinuations against Suresh Bose by his children and stoutly defended his brother. 'Suresh never indulged in speculation,' he wrote, 'though it is true that he is not successful in business. Father did not consider him irresponsible.' He further threw light on the relations between Suresh and his children—and this explains why although Suresh was in contact with Bhagwanji, they remained oblivious to it:

> Suresh has always been anxious to educate his sons properly and marry his daughters, but his wife and children never listen to him. They insult him frequently and have even threatened him with personal violence. He is not allowed food from their

kitchen, not even a glass of water. Bose's factory belonged and belongs to Suresh but the whole of the income from the factory is being appropriated by his wife and children. I shall not say anything about their so-called love and respect for Subhas but it is obvious that their love for the latter's properties is more.[3]

On being apprised of the situation by both sides, Mahatma Gandhi replied to Sarat on 16 July.

I had long chats with Bela [Mitra] and Arvind [Aurobindo]. They feel deeply aggrieved by your treatment of them. It is not, as I could see, so much a question of money as of ill-treatment. They feel too that Amiya is the evil genius…. They seem to have discussed the matter with Jawaharlal and Sardar. They appear to have said they can do nothing…. The issue is purely moral. This you should be able to fix up without any difficulty. They ought not to be cut off from the family, if they have been.[4]

New problems arose as the existence of Emilie and Anita became known to the family. The name of Emilie Schenkl had been familiar to those associated with Subhas with the publication of his book *The Indian Struggle* in 1934, where he acknowledged her assistance in writing the book. Emilie's article 'Winter in Badgastein' was also published in *The Modern Review* in February 1938. Before going into these, however, it is important to assess

---

3   These documents are now available among the Patel papers preserved in the National Archives, some of which have been digitised too.

4   Mahatma Gandhi's letter to Sarat Bose, 16 July 1946, *The Collected Works of Mahatma Gandhi* (Electronic Book), New Delhi, Publications Division Government of India, 1999, Volume 91, p 292.

the question of Netaji's 'marriage' to Emilie Schenkl and put it in the proper perspective, as a significant section of people in Bengal still do not believe that Subhas Chandra Bose could have married and have had a child. The primary reason is the image of Subhas as a man who not only sacrificed his personal life at the altar of the country's freedom, but the importance in which he held brahmacharya (abstinence) as part of his spiritual quest. According to one 'Netaji kin', 'Popular misconceptions of Subhas Chandra Bose's asceticism stem from an overemphasis on values and attitudes he may have held very early in his youth.'[5] This has to be viewed as part of the many myths that a number of family members have tried to create to explain away complex situations. Writing to Amiya Nath Bose in February 1934, Subhas, then 37 years of age, advised his young nephew at the end of his teens, 'Whether you practise Brahmacharya after marriage or not, you must do it now.'[6] He then went on to explain the types of Brahmacharya and the ways to undertake the practice based on his own experience. This streak of asceticism never left Subhas as we will discuss in more detail in a subsequent chapter. In fact, it got stronger with time.

The second factor that has contributed to a very large extent to the confusion about Subhas's marriage is the perplexing behaviour of the family over this matter. This started with the news of Subhas's alleged marriage reaching India. The first person

5   Sisir Kumar Bose and Sugata Bose (ed), *Subhas Chandra Bose: Letters to Emilie Schenkl 1934-42*, Permanent Black, p xviii.
6   Copy of the handwritten letter in possession of the authors.

to hear of her was not Sarat, as would be normally expected, but Jawaharlal Nehru. Dr Abdul Hafiz Akmat and his wife had met Emilie through Subhas in 1940 and grew close to her. After the war was over, he got in touch with Nehru to inform him that Subhas and Emilie were married. Nehru informed Vallabhbhai Patel while asking Akmat for more detailed information. Akmat sent more information to Nehru on 22 June 1947 through a note which stated among others things:

I have been able to get the following information, which is quite reliable.

1.   The late Mr SC Bose has left his testament with the mother of the child and it now appears that she was married to him. She has this testament with her and probably a copy of it can be had, but of course it is not quite easy to get it through the post.

2.   The child is now 4 ½ years old. About the parentage of the child there is no doubt on account of the great resemblance which the child bears to the father, the testament and the confirmation of the mother of the child.

...

5.   ...At present she is living with her family in a very pitiable state. Her father is already dead. The grandmother and the mother of the child are sacrificing everything in order to keep the child alive and healthy, but in spite of it the position of the mother and the child is precarious. They need immediate help.

The memory of the late Mr SC Bose can only be honoured if India helps without delay his wife and his only child. It should not be forgotten that she was his most trusted friend, companion and co-worker during the most trying periods of his life.

According to the latest information I have received just now, it seems that some months ago Mrs SC Bose sent a copy of this testament together with a letter to Mr Sarat Chandra Bose, but as she has received no answer, it seems very likely that these have not reached their destination. The whole affair is so tragic and I cannot help adding and asking whether it is the fault of the poor faithful girl to have to have faithfully worked with the late Mr Bose for India for which she has now got into this tragic state. I am quite sure that you will take immediate steps to help this deserving soul.[7]

Nehru forwarded the note to Patel, asking him to depute Nathalal Parikh 'who is in Antwerp and ask him to inquire into the matter and arrange help if necessary'.[8] Patel wrote to Parikh on the same day asking him to find out if the information was correct and if it was, to make arrangements to help Emilie and Anita. On receiving the initial information from Dr Akmat, Nehru had also got in touch with ACN Nambiar, who was Subhas's second-in-command at the Free India Centre in Nazi Germany, to find out more. Nambiar confirmed the facts to Nehru through his letter dated 12 August 1947. 'I am able to affirm that B[ose] was very

7   Dr Abdul Hafiz Akmat to Jawaharlal Nehru, 22 June 1947, Sardar Patel papers, National Archive of India.
8   Jawaharlal Nehru to Vallabhbhai Patel, 7 August 1947, Sardar Patel papers, National Archive of India.

deeply and seriously attached to S[chenkl] and in Europe no other woman entered his life the same way. S was to my knowledge intensely devoted to B,' Nambiar informed Nehru. He also wrote that 'B, it would appear, has given a note to S, prior to his departure from Europe, affirming a sort [sic] of Hindu marriage with S useful for an eventual legitimation of fatherhood'. He pointed out that Subhas did not want any publicity about his marriage and fatherhood at the time of his secret departure from Europe (in a submarine), constrained by the prevailing German laws and also due to 'other considerations, both of a family character and political nature'. Nambiar also told Nehru that he had hinted about the matter and a responsibility in regard to the child to one of Subhas's nephews.[9] Recently released documents in the British archives indicate that this nephew was Amiya Nath Bose, to whom he wrote three letters hinting about Emilie and Anita but claimed to have not got any response.

Unknown to Nehru, Nambiar and Amiya, all this correspondence was intercepted by the Intelligence Bureau and shared with the Indian Political Intelligence (IPI) in the UK. Post-Independence, IB dutifully passed on this intelligence to MI5. Nambiar, however, divulged none of this to Leonard Gordon, American biographer of the Bose brothers Sarat and Subhas, when he wrote to Gordon decades later that 'I cannot state anything definite of the marriage of Bose referred to by you, since I came to

9   ACN Nambiar to Jawaharlal Nehru, 12 August 1947, Sardar Patel papers, National Archive of India.

know of it only a good while after the end of the last world war.'[10] While the statement appears true, the picture of Subhas and his relationship with Emilie that Nambiar portrayed during his interrogation by Captain Naurang Singh Bains of the Combined Services Detailed Interrogation Centre (CSDIC), run by the British War Office, MI9 and MI5, was pretty bleak. He told his interrogator that Subhas decided to keep the fact that he had a child with Emilie without marriage a strict secret, and that Emilie hoped that 'with the success of his mission he would regularise their relationship'. Subhas, according to Nambiar, had decided to marry her, against the advice of his associate Auto Faltis, 'accepting what he considered to be the inevitable consequence of retirement from his political career, when the story should become known to his followers in Europe and India. I believe that with the failure of all his plans Bose will now give up political activity in order to be able to rejoin Frl Schenkl and his child,' he concluded.[11]

The CSDIC described the relationship between Subhas and Emilie in the most demeaning manner in a note appended to Nambiar's interrogation report:

> She first came into contact with Bose in 1933 in Vienna where she worked as Bose's typist. Bose fell in love with her and kept her as a mistress. She accompanied Bose on most of his tours. After Bose's departure to India in 1937, she remained in touch with him through correspondence. When Bose arrived in

---

10   Leonard Gordon, *Brothers Against the Raj*, Viking, 1990, p 345.
11   Statement of ACN Nambiar to CSDIC, File KV2/3904, The National Archives, Kew, UK.

Vienna in 1941...(Emilie) stayed throughout in his house as his wife.[12]

Although the CSDIC report indicated marriage, it included no details on it.

Back in India, Sardar Patel informed Sarat of Subhas's marriage, enclosing the note received by Nehru from Dr Akmat through his letter dated 7 August 1947. Sarat's response was one of indignation and disbelief. Referring to the report on Emilie and Subhas's marriage, he wrote a week later:

> I have read the enclosure to your letter very carefully. I cannot accept the report contained therein as true. I wish you had referred the matter to me before writing to Nathalal. I do not think Nathalal has the training necessary to make enquiries of this nature and he may do more harm than good. After all, if Subhas left a family (which I do not believe) it is up to me and not to Nathalal to assist the family.[13]

On 29 August, Sarat wrote to Patel again informing him, 'I am making enquiries and if I feel satisfied about the truth of the report, I shall certainly do the needful.' Around the same time, Nehru also forwarded Nambiar's note to Sarat, and in November Parikh sent a photocopy of Subhas's 'testament' mentioned by

12   Appendix B to Statement of ACN Nambiar to CSDIC, File KV2/3904, The National Archives, Kew, UK.

13   Vallabbhai Patel to Sarat Chandra Bose, 7 August 1947; Sarat Chandra Bose to Vallabhbhai Patel, 14 August 1947. Durga Das (ed), *Sardar Patel's Correspondence, Vol 5*, Navajivan Publishing House, pp 86-88. Patel's letter was also intercepted by the West Bengal Special Branch. File No CP 513.

Dr Akmat, which in reality was a letter from Subhas to Sarat, written on the eve of his voyage to Southeast Asia, informing him that he had married Emilie and that he had a daughter.[14]

Sarat finally wrote to Emilie nearly four months after the receipt of these pieces of information on 10 April 1948. Unknown to Sarat, Emilie had already written to him with all details nearly over two years ago. Not receiving a response to her letter dated 12 March 1946, she sent the same letter two more times—on 15 April and again on 1 August 1946. Unfortunately, none of the letters reached Sarat. Emilie wrote to Patel thanking him for sending Parikh to find out how they were doing. As a gesture of thanks, she sent with Parikh a photograph of Vithalbhai Patel, Sardar Patel's elder brother who'd recommended her to Subhas for secretarial work, that was in her custody. Emilie also shared with Patel the letter she had written to Sarat and a note containing some additional information about her and Subhas. The note cleared the legal position on their marriage:

> According to law I am not married to [be] Mrs Subhas Chandra Bose. I am therefore still bearing maiden name. It is only the custom here that a woman having a child is entitled to call herself Mrs instead of Miss, whether she is married or not. (sic)

She also made it clear to Patel that, 'We are living under somewhat poor conditions, but this is only due to the fact that

14   Sarat Chandra Bose to Emilie Schenkl, 10 April 1948, in Madhuri Bose, *Bose Brothers and Indian Independence: An Insider's Account*, Sage, p 237.

the situation in Austria is desperate and we are not worse off than all the other people of Austria.' Thus, 'I have never asked for any financial help.'[15]

After corresponding with Emilie for some time, Sarat travelled to Europe towards the end of 1948 to meet her (accompanied by his wife and their three children), and welcomed her into the family. Henceforth, Sarat was Emilie's *Mejdada* too, as her letters to him show. Sarat's children too started writing to their 'Aunty'. As far as Anita was concerned, Emilie wrote to Chitra (Sarat's daughter) in June 1949, 'It still seems funny to her that all of a sudden she has got so many sisters and brothers.'[16]

Yet, quite strangely, even after clearing up his own doubts and accepting Emilie and Anita into the family, Sarat never spoke publicly about Subhas's marriage although the news, mostly in distorted forms, had started making appearances across the country. This is all the more perplexing because he was not unaware of them—people known to him brought them to his attention. Some of these letters were intercepted by the state intelligence departments and it can't be ascertained whether they reached Sarat, but some certainly did. Therefore, maintaining secrecy over the marriage couldn't have been a reason, since the government and the people already knew and they were talking, often in uncharitable ways. The best way to stop that would have been to provide the complete picture. It wasn't a family matter

15   Note appended to Emilie Schenkl's letter to Vallabhbhai Patel (undated), Sardar Patel papers, National Archive of India.
16   Copy of intercepted letter from Emilie Schenkl to Chitra Bose, 23 June 1949, Special Branch File No TP502/49 IV.

either. Subhas was a major public figure and an attempt to draw an artificial line claiming his marriage to be a family matter was unreasonable.

On 21 April 1949, MR Vyas who worked under Subhas at the Free India Centre in Germany informed Sarat about a story published in a Gujarati bi-weekly of Ahmedabad called *Hindu Samaj* which reported that Subhas had a nine-year-old son by his (civil) marriage to a 'German lady' and that she would be visiting India soon. Vyas wrote that this was not an isolated case of reporting as one of his friends had seen a similar report in a British newspaper.[17] Around the same time, Abid Hasan, Subhas's close aide in both Germany as well as SE Asia, sent Amiya Nath Bose a paper cutting of an Urdu weekly published from Pune called *The Sadaji Vijai* that also reported the existence of an eight-year-old son of Subhas.[18]

When Ramgati Ganguly, general secretary of the UP Forward Bloc asked him about the authenticity of a news published in the Hindi daily *Sanmarg* that reported Sarat's meeting with Emilie and also the existence of an eight-year old son, Sarat's response was cryptic and puzzling. 'You should completely ignore such articles,' Sarat replied, without providing any further insight.[19]

---

17   Intercepted letter of MR Vyas to Sarat Chandra Bose, 21 April 1949, File TP 502/49 II, Special Branch, West Bengal.
18   Copy of intercepted letter of Abid Hasan to Amiya Nath Bose, 18 April 1949, File TP 502/49 II, Special Branch, West Bengal.
19   Photostat copy of Sarat Chandra Bose's letter to Ramgati Ganguly, dated 28 April 1949 published in booklet *Liu Po-Cheng or Netaji?* by Shiva Prosad Nag, pp 10-11.

Needless to say, one public statement from Sarat Bose would have been enough to clear all confusion and conspiracy theories regarding the marriage of Subhas.

More confusion was created around the date of the marriage, and this came from Emilie herself. When she wrote to Sarat for the first time, Emilie described to him the circumstances of their marriage:

> Your brother has (sic) come to Europe again in 1941 and asked me if I could come and join him in Berlin to work with him. I agreed and joined him in April 1941 and we worked together till Autumn 1942.
>
> Your brother asked me when I was in Berlin, if I would accept his proposal to marry him. Knowing him since years as a man of good character and since there was a mutual understanding and we were very fond of each other, I agreed. The only difficulty was to get the necessary marriage permission from the German government. Though Austrian by birth, I had at that time been [a] German subject and, therefore, [had] to obey German laws. And it was very difficult for a German to get the permission to marry a foreigner. Since we both did not want to beg for a favour and wanted also to avoid making an affair of the whole matter, we decided to settle it between ourselves and got, therefore, married according to Hindu fashion in January 1942. The whole thing was kept a secret, only two friends knowing about it.[20]

This version remained the 'general story in the [Bose] family' as has been explained by another Netaji-kin recently, until Emilie

---

20   Copy of Emilie Schenkl's letter to Sarat Chandra Bose dated 12 March 1946 appended to her undated letter to Vallabhbhai Patel, Sardar Patel papers, National Archive of India.

gave an entirely different story to Bose biographer Leonard Gordon and the director of the Delhi-based Nehru Memorial Museum & Library (NMML) sometime in the 1980s.[21] According to the new version, Emilie and Subhas got married in Badgastein on 26 December 1937.

Public reaction was also influenced to a great extent not only by Subhas's silence on his marriage, but by his direct public denial on many instances. His behaviour in this matter, however, is understandable and perhaps justifiable. From 1938 onwards, he was on the national scene as never before. Following his split from the Congress and going on virtually a warpath with the colonial government, any talk about his personal life would have been a massive distraction. It would not only have provided an opportunity to his detractors for spreading salacious rumours, given the unusualness of his relationship, but would have spelt danger for Emilie and her family. What's inexplicable, if Emilie's amended version of their marriage is true, is Subhas not sharing such an important development in his life with at least Sarat. If it had to be kept secret, Sarat was one person who could. That Subhas didn't doubt this is evident from his sharing his escape plan in 1941 with his elder brother.

However, there is at least one instance where one of his close associates has claimed that he confided in her his anxiety over the marriage issue. 'I have done something that I don't know whether people in India will be able to understand,' Subhas told Lakshmi Sahgal in a post-dinner conversation. 'Do you think people in

---

21   Krishna Bose, *A True Love Story: Emilie and Subhas*, Niyogi Books, pp 25-27.

India will understand?' he asked her again.[22]

Emilie soon got mired in a feud over Subhas's published and unpublished works. It is unnecessary to go into the details of it, but the declassified files containing intercepted letters of the Bose family show, that as early as in 1948, a dispute erupted between the sons of Suresh Chandra Bose and Amiya Nath Bose over the publication of and copyright over Subhas's works.

Things didn't go well between Amiya and his younger brother Sisir too. Towards the end of 1967-68, the Sarat Bose Academy, whose general secretary was Amiya, was ousted from the premises of the Netaji Bhawan and in 1977, he was expelled from the Netaji Hall Society in a meeting called by Sisir, a meeting which Amiya could not attend.[23]

Sarat's demise in 1950 removed the force of a great personality who had held the family together despite differences. There was no one who could step into his shoes and the next generation went their different ways. As far as politics was concerned, with the Socialist Republican Party becoming defunct after Sarat's death, they opted from the options available. Dwijen, to best of our knowledge, remained with the Forward Bloc, and Aurobindo veered away to join the Indian National Trade Union Congress (INTUC), the trade union wing of the Congress party.

In a surprising move, Amiya Nath Bose met Nehru and joined the Congress party in 1955. Conveying his decision to Emilie,

22   Peter Ward Fay, *The Forgotten Army: India's Armed Struggle for Independence 1942-45*, The University of Michigan Press, pp 311-12.
23   Madhuri Bose, *Bose Brothers and Indian Independence: An Insider's Account*, Sage, pp 251-252.

he explained, 'The present policy of the Congress is completely in line with the policy uncle has been advocating since 1938.'[24] This was in a way odd, particularly in the context of Subhas and Nehru's attitude towards each other post-Tripuri Congress of 1939. In fact, it was to Amiya that Subhas wrote on the aftermath of the Tripuri Congress that:

> Nobody has done more harm to me personally and to our cause in this crisis than Pandit Nehru. If he had been with us— we would have had a majority. Even his neutrality would have probably given us a majority. But he was with the Old Guard at Tripuri. His open propaganda against me has done me more harm than the activities of the 12 stalwarts. What a pity![25]

Even Sarat's relation with Nehru, Patel and the Congress high command had turned bitterly adversarial 1947 onwards. That despite the presence of a strong Left movement in the state he would turn to Nehru in search of socialist politics is indeed baffling. Anyway, Amiya changed camps in 1967 when he successfully contested the Lok Sabha elections with the support of the Forward Bloc. By 1971 he had moved away from the Forward Bloc and in that year's Lok Sabha election was defeated while contesting as an independent candidate. Again, he shifted to the Janata Party which stormed to power in 1977 and was appointed as India's ambassador to Burma. Amiya's younger brother Sisir, an

---

24 Copy of intercepted letter from Amiya Nath Bose to Emilie Schenkl dated 17 May 1955, Special Branch File No 606-39.
25 Letter from Subhas Chandra Bose to Amiya Nath Bose dated 17 April 1939, *Crossroads*, Asia Publishing House, p 113.

admirer of Indira Gandhi, was elected to the state assembly on a Congress ticket in 1982. The connection was severed before long, with the assassination of Indira in 1984. Miffed by Rajiv Gandhi's behaviour and attitude towards the Bose legacy, Sisir joined ranks with Pranab Mukherjee who had formed the breakaway Rashtriya Samajwadi Congress (RSC). His next attempt to get elected to the state assembly as an independent in the 1987 elections was unsuccessful. Anyway, Pranab was back in the Congress by 1988. The mantle passed on to Sisir's wife Krishna who successfully contested the parliamentary elections on a Congress ticket in 1996 from Jadavpur, and thenceforth on Mamata Banerjee's Trinamool Congress (TMC), another breakaway group of the Congress, in 1998 and 1999. Sisir and Krishna's son Sugata contested and won the Lok Sabha seat from Jadavpur on a TMC ticket in 2014. The youngest brother of Amiya, Subrata, joined the Forward Bloc and was elected to the Lok Sabha in 2004. Only the eldest, Ashoke, never showed any keenness to join politics. Chitra Ghosh (Sarat's daughter), too, has remained associated with the Forward Bloc.

Despite the differences, views of the family members converged on the issue of Subhas's disappearance, at least until about 1965, when Sisir was convinced by his own research that Subhas had indeed died in the alleged plane crash of 1945. None of Sarat's children ever backed the air crash theory. In fact, none of Subhas Bose's 11 siblings believed the air crash theory. For instance, Sisir's brothers—Ashoke, Amiya and Subrata wrote to Prime Minister VP Singh on 4 May 1990 that:

> During the lifetime of our youngest uncle, late Shailesh Chandra Bose, a statement signed by him and all sons of every

one of Netaji's brothers was issued to the Press at Calcutta stating that the 'ashes' at Renkoji temple were not the 'ashes of Netaji'. [26]

Today there are, broadly speaking, two sections of the Bose family, divided between the theories of Subhas's death in the plane crash and his death in the former Soviet Russia. Interestingly, after the declassification of the secret files when nothing about Russia came to light and, on the other hand, Gumnami Baba matter started hitting headlines, the family members, who had all along backed the killed-in-Russia theory, suddenly changed tack and started leaning towards the air crash theory. Only a very small section among Bose family members—children of Asoke Nath Bose (Sarat's eldest son), Jayanti Rakshit and Arya Bose being most prominent—are open to exploring the Bhagwanji angle.

The face of the first group, that is those who back the air crash theory, is Prof Sugata Bose, currently a Member of Lok Sabha from TMC and a history professor at the Harvard University. Sugata's stand that Bose died in an air crash is repeatedly cited by Congress party leaders and supporters to dismiss the other theories. According to them, it is most credible because Sugata is not only a grandnephew of Subhas and a Harvard University history don, but also the executive director of the Netaji Research Bureau, the most well-known institute in the memory of Subhas, being run from the house where he lived, in Kolkata. The main arsenal in their inventory is Sugata's Netaji biography *His Majesty's*

---

26   Copy of the letter in possession of the authors. It also appears in a declassified file.

Opponent, which, at the time of its release in 2011, was touted as 'an authoritative account' of Netaji's untimely death in a plane crash which would 'put to rest rumors about the fate of this "deathless hero"'. Unfortunately that hasn't been the case, for obvious reasons.[27]

Looking back at the change of Sisir's views, his sister Chitra spoke with much bitterness to *The Times of India* in April 2015. She said that 'the entire family, including Sisir, was united in the belief that Netaji had not died in the plane crash. Then something happened in the mid-1970s that led to Sisir changing his stance,' continued Chitra as she for the first time publicly spoke about her brother. 'It coincided with his moving closer to the Indira Gandhi-led Congress.' Chitra further alleged that Sisir and his family toed the Congress line on Netaji solely due to the financial aid that the Netaji Research Bureau had received from successive Congress governments.[28]

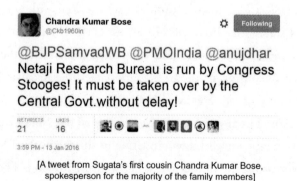

Chandra Kumar Bose
@Ckb1960in   Following

@BJPSamvadWB @PMOIndia @anujdhar
**Netaji Research Bureau is run by Congress
Stooges! It must be taken over by the
Central Govt.without delay!**

RETWEETS   LIKES
21   16

3:59 PM - 13 Jan 2016

[A tweet from Sugata's first cousin Chandra Kumar Bose,
spokesperson for the majority of the family members]

---

27   For a critique of the book and other details, see *India's biggest cover-up* by Anuj Dhar.

28   'Family rift widens over Netaji files,' *The Times of India* (Kolkata edition), 23 April 2015.

When the Mukherjee Commission was set up, it was expected of Sisir and the Harvard professor to file affidavits like the other family members to help the commission and the nation in overcoming the controversy. When Sisir did not, the commission summoned him. He refused to appear. He actually stated this through a letter: 'I have no personal knowledge as to the issues referred to the commission. I am therefore not competent to depose in this matter.' Krishna Bose too implored the commission to excuse her 'from any personal appearance as a witness'. At the same time, Sisir, Krishna and Sugata kept on telling the media that Subhas had died in Taipei. This trait of telling one thing to the media and another to an official inquiry is a peculiarity seen in many Bose family members.

The Mukherjee Commission also summoned Sugata Bose, but he never turned up. However, after Justice Mukherjee submitted his report, Sugata opened a front against him. In his book, he characterised MK Mukherjee as a 'retired Bengali judge' to impute partiality to him.

Significantly, Sugata Bose in his book dramatised his grandaunt Emilie Schenkl's obvious reaction to the 1945 radio announcement of Subhas's death. Later he quoted from another letter to insinuate that she believed in Subhas's death in that air crash. A possible motive behind misrepresenting Emilie's real views was that the professor did not want to embarrass his late father's good friend, senior Congress leader and our former president—Pranab Mukherjee.

Pranab Mukherjee's name has been intertwined with the Bose mystery matter. In late 1995, Mukherjee went on a world-wide, never-before quest to exorcise the ghost of the Bose mystery. After meeting the Japanese Foreign Minister in Tokyo, he flew to Germany.

[From a declassified file: Clipping of a 22 October 1995 news item in *HT*]

There is a letter in a declassified PMO file which might hold a possible motivation for this mission. DN Sinha, a Nehru acolyte and president of Mahatma Gandhi Institute of Ayurvedic Research and vice president of All India Freedom Fighters organisation, wrote to Prime Minister PV Narsimha Rao to express freedom fighters' gratitude to allow Mukherjee to confirm Bose ashes. 'It should fetch you additionally 10 to 20 per cent votes in the Lok Sabha election,'[29] reasoned Sinha (see image on next page). These are the same set of people who often accuse others of doing politics in Netaji's name!

On 20 October 1995, from Augsburg, an agitated Emilie Schenkl rang her grandnephew Surya, Germany-based eldest son

---

29   File No 870/11/P/11/95-Pol, Disappearance of Netaji Subhas Chandra Bose, Prime Minister's Office, National Archives, New Delhi.

D. N. Sinha
President:
National Council of OISCA in India
All India Qaumi Ekta Committee

Vice-President:
OISCA International, Tokyo
All India Freedom Fighters Organisation

Fax   : 011-3343421 Telex : 31-6304
        Off. : 3732730
Tel.   : 3733175
        Res. : 6910923

5/125, Jeevan Tara Building,
Parliament Street,
New Delhi - 110 001

October 30, 1995

Dear Respected Prime Minister,

I beg to refer you to our earlier representations regarding giving a new life to the Congress Party under your dynamic Leadership.

In one of the points, We proposed that Netaji Subhash Chandra Bose's sacred ashes kept at the Renokaji Temple in Tokyo now for 45 years be brought to India and taken round the Country to enable the people of India to pay their homage and then kept in a memorial to be built at the Freedom Fighters' Colony on Prof. N.G. Ranga Marg, New Delhi-110 068.

We, the Freedom Fighters now express our gratitudes to you to allow the Foreign Minister Sri Pranab Mukherjee to confirm that the sacred ashes of Netaji kept in a gold casket, as we saw recently at Renokaji Temple in Tokyo, would be brought to India after 45 years from Tokyo. This would also please the Japanese who preserved them for us so respectfully now for over 4 decades.

It should fetch you additionally 10 to 20% Votes in the Lok Sabha election and the party's success could be assured.

[National Archives, New Delhi]

of Amiya Nath Bose. She told Surya (Sugata's first cousin) that 'Mr Pranab Mukherjee was coming…to convince her and Anita to give their approval [in writing] for bringing the so-called "ashes" of Netaji to India'. Ever since his arrival in Germany in 1973, Surya had heard his grandaunt telling him of her disbelief in the air crash theory. She had told as much to the other family members, including Subhas's nephew Pradip Bose (now deceased), grandniece Jayanti Rakshit and grandnephew Chandra Kumar Bose.

In Germany on October 21, Pranab Mukherjee sat down with Emilie Schenkl for an important meeting. Also in attendance was her daughter, Dr Anita Pfaff, Anita's husband, Martin Pfaff and India's ambassador to Germany, SK Lambah. Mukherjee, the master strategist, started building the whole thing up by telling

Emilie that the Indian government was keen to 'bring back Netaji's ashes' to India at a suitable time, provided the controversial issues were resolved. Ambassador Lambah stated that the Japanese had reacted negatively to the proposal of transferring the ashes to Germany. The only option left was to take them to India.

Emilie was put off by the suggestion. She reacted angrily to Mukherjee's proposal that she should sign on a paper, approving Subhas's death in Taiwan. According to a sworn affidavit filed subsequently before the Mukherjee Commission by Surya Bose, 'she did not believe that Netaji had died in a plane crash...and that those "ashes"... had nothing to do with Subhas' because she was of the opinion that 'Netaji was in the Soviet Union after 1945'.[30]

Never the one to give up easily, Pranab Mukherjee tried to convince Emilie that Subhas was never in Russia. He showed her an official communication from the Russian government, purporting to claim that Moscow had no record of Bose's presence in the Soviet Union during or after 1945. Emilie saw through it all. She refused to go by Pranab's persuasive words. After she made it clear that she could not even tolerate his presence there, Anita and Martin Pfaff took Mukherjee out to thrash out the matter over lunch.[31]

---

30 Affidavit dated 6 March 2000 filed by Surya Kumar Bose before the Mukherjee Commission. Copy with authors.

31 Another version of this meeting was given by Anita to the Bangla magazine *Desh*. In an interview published in the 20 January 2001 issue of the magazine, Anita recollected: 'When Pranab Mukherjee came here, the Ambassador in Bonne informed us what he wanted to discuss. My mother did not want to engage in any controversy at that time. She was present at our meeting with Mukherjee but did not show any interest or enthusiasm in the discussion.' Suman Chattapadhyay, 'Father is dead, let his ashes be brought back to India immediately: Anita', *Desh*, ABP Ltd, 20 January 2001, p

Surya called his grandaunt after a few days, when an Indian daily carried a news item claiming that Emilie had given her approval to the Government of India's plans for bringing the 'ashes' to India. Emilie became furious as she reiterated that she 'had approved of nothing'. She charged that 'Pranab Mukherjee was propagating an untruth for reasons best known to him'.[32] She passed away in March 1996, believing that Renkoji ashes were not of Bose. This was the reason why, as long as she lived, she neither visited Renkoji temple, nor did she allow the ashes to be brought over to India. But despite Emilie's categorical 'No', Pranab Mukherjee twisted facts in a Top Secret note he filed on 28 October 1995. He wrote that both Emilie and Anita had 'agreed to bringing the ashes of Netaji to India'.[33]

For reasons only she can explain, Anita agreed to Mukherjee's proposition against the wishes of her family members, excluding those linked to the Congress party. In February 1998, she wrote a letter to Prime Minister IK Gujral. In this she requested Gujaral to transfer the Renkoji remains to India—something that many of her cousins, like her dead mother, thought was an 'an act of sacrilege'.[34] While it is an open secret that Nehru did little for

---

32   Affidavit dated 6 March 2000 filed by Surya Kumar Bose before the Mukherjee Commission. Copy with authors.

33   File No G-16(3)/95-NGO, 'Proposal to bring mortal remains of Netaji Subhas Chandra Bose from Japan to India,' Prime Minister's Office, National Archives, New Delhi. On 21 August 1998, Krishna Bose, then an MP, wrote to Home Minister LK Advani that 'Netaji's wife and daughter agreed with the view [of Pranab Mukherjee] that arrangements should be made to bring Netaji's ashes back to India.' There is no record in declassified files to show that Emilie had agreed to any such proposal.

34   Letter to Prime Minister VP Singh from brothers Ashoke, Amiya and Subrata, May 1990. Copy with us.

Bose's legacy, Anita went on to tell *The Times of India* in February 2000 that she 'dismissed the popular perception that Jawaharlal Nehru looked upon Netaji as a rival and that Nehru and Indira Gandhi had ensured that Netaji's role was ignored'.[35]

Declassified documents show further that in spite of the Government's long-standing position that ashes kept in Renkoji temple were Bose's, Mukherjee, as the External Affairs Minister, did not give a go-ahead to their DNA testing in the mid-1990s. 'I am afraid any step to conduct DNA test may precipitate controversy which may not be desirable,' Mukherjee noted on an official record of 7 February 1996. 'We suggest that this matter may rest where it is now.'

Anita's role in the matter has been questionable. In January 2016, a day before the Narendra Modi government started the process of declassifying the Netaji files, Anita was approached by the media for her reaction. In a nutshell, this is what it was:

follow us: f y g+ 🖂 **hindustan**times

india world cities opinion sports entertainment lifestyle tech photos videos

monsoon session | 25 years of change | smartphone survey | movie reviews | ht paathshala

Netaji's daughter convinced he died in crash, wants DNA test of remains

Prasun Sonwalkar, Hindustan Times, Augsburg (Germany) | Updated: Jan 22, 2016 09:26 IST

---

35   Mahendra Ved, 'Daughter believes Netaji died in crash,' *The Times of India*, 28 February 2000.

Speaking to *India Today* a few days later, she commented that such a DNA test 'would put the case to rest' for 'at least the rational people'. However, according to a declassified memo signed by then foreign secretary Salman Haidar, Anita opposed such a DNA test in 1995 when the Government discussed its feasibility for the first time. In 2001, she explained her opposition by saying that although it might appear to be an attractive proposition from the scientific point of view, a DNA test wouldn't be able to bring around those who don't believe in the story of the plane crash. She was doubtful if a categorical conclusion could be reached even if a test was possible, and worried about the way the ashes had been preserved for all these years.[36]

```
VIEWS OF NETAJI'S DAUGHTER

12.  Ms. Anita Pfaff, Netaji's daughter from his German
wife, had visited Delhi for discussions with other members
of the family and been in touch with the Japanese Ambassador
in Delhi in February 1995.  She had also written to some
associates of Netaji, including Hayashi.  EAM met her in
Germany in October 1995.  During discussion with EAM, she
expressed her willingness to go along with the proposal of
bringing back the ashes to India but did not approve of the
DNA test.

VIEWS OF OTHER IMPORTANT MEMBERS OF NETAJI'S FAMILY

13.  While Dr. Sisir Bose supports the idea of bringing back
the ashes, Late Amiya Nath Bose, Netaji's nephew had been
the most vociferous skeptic of the  air crash episode and
had opposed any proposal of bringing back the ashes.


14.  This issues with the approval of the External
Affairs Minister.



                              (Salman Haidar)
                              Foreign Secretary
```

[National Archives, New Delhi]

---

36   Suman Chattapadhyay, 'Father is dead, let his ashes be brought back to India immediately: Anita', *Desh*, ABP Ltd, 20 January 2001, p 51

The idea behind seeking a DNA test in 2016 was to perhaps make light of, or even discredit, the movement seeking declassification of the Bose files, in which Anita played no role whatsoever. In that respect, her stand was only a shade better than that of Sugata Bose who was openly hostile to the idea. But after it became apparent that Narendra Modi was going to declassify the papers, both grudgingly started making qualified statements about the declassification. Incidentally, during his Lok Sabha election campaign, Sugata used to highlight his blood relation to Subhas Bose. However, after becoming a Member of Parliament, he did not ask even a single question relating to the Subhas Bose matter. According to the data available on the Lok Sabha website, he, however, asked a question about the preservation of the Mahatma Gandhi papers at the National Archives in New Delhi.

Another Netaji kin who has of late started making headlines for his pro-crash line following the declassification drive undertaken by the Modi government is Ashis Ray, son of one of Sarat Bose's daughters. Former journalist and cricket commentator, Ray's background is impressive. Declassified files reveal that he was espousing the cause of settling the issue of Bose's fate from the late 1980s, if not earlier. In 1990, Ashis wrote a letter to then Prime Minister VP Singh. He opened it by informing the Prime Minister about his grandaunt Emilie's view on the Renkoji temple remains 'since certain individuals are…attempting in a seemingly clandestine manner to transship them here'.

Her answer was categorical. She remarked: 'I do not want these ashes to be brought to India. You cannot be sure they are uncle's

(Netaji's). That is my opinion.' I asked her if I may convey this to you. She gave me her consent to do so.[37]

Seeking an end to the controversy by raising points, most of which were logical, Ray attached with his letter 'a note on the alleged air crash' for the PM's scrutiny. He wrote that he hoped that the note 'will convince you that a lot more evidence is required to drive home the claim that Netaji died in the reported air crash'. Ray's letter ended with the appeal that 'it would be nice if we took into account Emilie Schenkl Bose's sentiments on the subject'. The attached note outlined the case against Bose's dying in Taipei. At the end, Ray noted that he was 'deeply indebted to Sri Sunil Gupta for the guidance and information provided by him on the subject'.

```
As recently as 1966, a panel of Japanese war time aeronautical
experts, after carefully examining
the evidence of those who described themselves as survivors of the
plane crash in question, observed: "The entire Japanese air operation
before and during the Pacific War did not record any case of a
propeller falling out during take-off (which is what the disaster was
attributed to). If the plane dived to the ground (as was claimed),
it could have smashed itself into bits, killing all aboard instantly."

---------------------------------------------------------------------

The author of the above note is deeply indebted to Sri Sunil Gupta
for the guidance and information provided by him on the subject.
```

[National Archives, New Delhi]

This was Sunil Krishna Gupta, Bhagwanji's man. Gupta's kin confirmed to us that Ashis Ray used to sit with him for hours in order to understand the nuts and bolts of the Bose mystery matter.

37   File No 800/6/C/1/90-Pol, 'Netaji Subhas Chandra Bose – Bringings in the ashes of,' Prime Minister's Office, National Archives, New Delhi.

With the return of the Congress party to power in 1992, Ray's view began undergoing change. He now started gravitating towards the finality of the air crash theory. In 1994, he pressed to an indulgent Foreign Secretary that it would give him 'enormous satisfaction if we could silently and skillfully "clear" up the mystery once and for all'.

ASHIS C. RAY
F-162 Malcha Marg
New Delhi - 110021.
Phone: 301 3520

7 September, 1994.

Dear Foreign Secretary,

Enclosed herewith is a copy of a note I submitted to the PM and Arjun Singh, following a suggestion from the latter that I should do something to try and bring the "ashes" at Tokyo's Renkoji temple - said to be Netaji's - back to India.

In fact, I received a very encouraging reply to my memo from Amar Nath Varma, a photocopy of which is being sent with this as well.

Incidentally, I have kept Prakash Shah and Ranjit Kalha posted on the matter.

Your kind interest is most heartening. I should like to emphasise that I seek no credit or publicity on the issue either now or later. It would, however, give me enormous satisfaction if we could silently and skillfully clear up the "mystery" once and for all.

I take this opportunity to congratulate you on the long term planning and implementation you have introduced as Foreign Secretary. It is a pleasure to observe your stewardship of the MEA. And I wish you continued success.

With best regards,

Yours sincerely,

Mr Kris Srinivasan
Foreign Secretary
Government of India
3 Circular Road
New Delhi.

[National Archives, New Delhi]

On its part, the Government extended Ray a helping hand. Over the years, he travelled to different places around the world to collect information to substantiate the Taipei death theory and plant stories in the media.

भारत का राजदूतावास, टोकियो
Embassy of India,
2-11, Kudan-Minami 2-chome,
Chiyoda-ku, TOKYO 102
Telex: 2324886 INDEMB J
Phone: 03(3262)2391
Fax: 03(3234)4866

AMBASSADOR

No. TOK/102/2/92   May 19, 1994

Dear Ashish,

You had requested for certain unclassified papers in regard to the question of Netaji Subhash Chandra Bose's ashes. I send you an English translation of the death certificate issued in 1945 and given to us by the Japanese Ministry of Foreign Affairs in the name of Ichiro Ikura.

It is indeed possible that since the death of Netaji was at that time kept strictly confidential, the certificate may have been issued in a fictitious name. I also enclose a copy of report of Shri S.A. Ayer on the air crash of Netaji Subhash Chandra Bose at Taihoku on August 18, 1945.

With reference to your request for xray of the urn containing Netaji's ashes and a letter or certificate from the Government of Japan in regard to the death certificate, you had mentioned that you would have further discussions in Delhi and let me know the position.

With regards,

Yours sincerely,

(Prakash Shah)
o/c

[National Archives, New Delhi]

Despite holding much information relevant to the terms assigned to the Mukherjee Commission of Inquiry, Ray, like his cousin Sugata, made no effort to assist the commission formed on court's orders. Nor did he offer any assistance as the declassification movement picked up steam with several members of his family, including his octogenarian mother, joining it. As the declassification process kicked in, London-based Ray suddenly resurfaced and began flashing the findings of his 1990s research undertaken with the assistance of then Congress government. He was successful in planting several pro-air crash stories in the media. The Press Trust of India flashed each of his press releases. At the same time, in his comments and tweets, Ray made no bones about his visceral hatred for Prime Minister Modi and liking for the Congress party. In time, Ray started rooting for Congress openly. In early 2018, he came out with a book titled *Laid to Rest,* which, like the one written by his cousin Sugata, was claimed to be the last word on the Netaji death issue. Despite unprecedented marketing, including release functions attended by retired MEA officials and top journalists, the book hasn't become the last word.

The authors have had the pleasure of knowing for years that Netaji kin opposed the air crash theory. From them we learned many things, gained a wider perspective and received support in variety of ways as all of us collectively endeavoured to bring about a closure to the matter. Our relations were very cordial, even though most family members were not on the same page as us on the issue of Bhagwanji. We thought we had agreed to disagree on this point.

This association entered a new phase in late 2012 with the release in Kolkata of *India's Biggest Cover-up*. The book laid out, for the first time, a methodical approach to ending the Bose mystery by way of declassification and other related steps. This was the consummation of Mission Netaji's strategy—to re-brand the Netaji mystery as a matter of transparency—a larger issue which no right-thinking person could sidestep. The family, most graciously, said good things about Dhar and his book and offered support since declassification was something they had been demanding as well, though not in a structured way.

Outline of an action plan was chalked out in November 2012 at Kolkata. This was at a function organised by Chitra Ghosh to felicitate Dhar.

THE TIMES OF INDIA, KOLKATA *
SATURDAY, NOVEMBER 24, 2012

TIMES CITY

Netaji kin demand end to secret files

New Book Rekindles Long-Standing Plea

Subhro Niyogi | TNN

Kolkata: Around 30 members of Subhas Chandra Bose's extended family will meet on Sunday to demand declassification of all files on Netaji. While no one doubts that Bose is dead by now — almost 67 years after his disappearance from Taihoku in present day Taiwan — an inquiry commission and many researchers have found enough evidence to question the theory that he had died in a plane crash.

"Time has come for the Indian government to lift the veil of secrecy over Netaji's disappearance. Though it has been a long-standing demand of the family, the Centre has opposed it citing the sensitive nature of the information, whose public disclosure may lead to a serious law and order problem. This stand is untenable. Now, a new book on Netaji has thrown fresh light on the mystery and

many startling revelations, exposing top-secret documents and photographs that prove the existence of Bose till at least 1985. The book also points a finger at top politicians, bureaucrats and the Indian Intelligence Bureau, which allegedly tried to suppress the truth.

According to the author, who has been unable to gain access

Subhro Niyogi

Anuj Dhar with his book, India's Biggest Cover-up

been out. This is the fittest case for trial by media for the government will not declassify the files unless there is pressure," said Dhar, who has published 220 images of rare documents, 90 of which are still classified, in the book.

Though there is no count on the number of secret documents on Bose that is with various government departments, the PMO, while replying to an RTI query, had recently declared that it had 33 classified files, seven of which were top secret and three confidential.

At Sunday's meeting, Bose's family members will get together with Dhar to demand a line of action to resolve the Netaji mystery in national interest, suggesting, among other things, replication of the JFK Records Act. In 1994, the US cleared the air about John F Kennedy's assassination by declassifying the records. They will also consider re-

[*The Times of India* on 24 November 2012]

At the meeting, Mission Netaji members and their well-wishers in Kolkata impressed upon the family members that the only realistic chance of getting the files declassified lay with a powerful leader who would not co-exist with the Congress party, and was a nationalist to the core. Only one man fitted the description—the then Gujarat Chief Minister Narendra Modi. Most members of the Bose family reacted rather sharply to this suggestion, as they felt—due to their association with the Left Front and Trinamool Congress in Bengal—that Modi was 'communal' and so they were not ready to approach him. Since the family wouldn't agree to write to Modi at that moment, it was agreed to approach Mamata Banerjee. So, a letter was sent to the West Bengal Chief Minister by Bose's nephew Dr DN Bose on behalf of the Bose family. Banerjee was requested to ask Prime Minister Manmohan Singh to declassify all secret Bose-related files.

Side by side, the family members also tried to seek an appointment with the Chief Minister so as to press the demand in person. These efforts did not succeed. Further attempts by the authors to access details about seventy-or-so classified files on or about Subhas Bose being held by the Bengal government under the RTI act did not succeed as well. The family's appeal to Naveen Patnaik, the Chief Minister of Odissa, met with no response. Meanwhile, Mission Netaji and the family members and admirers of Bose in Kolkata had begun organising marches and press conferences to sensitise the people about the need for declassification. Cousins Chandra Kumar Bose and Abhijit Ray, both grandsons of Sarat Bose, played a most prominent role in building up the momentum. Chandra became the family spokesperson and the face of the movement.

Thanks to these activities in Kolkata, the BJP in Bengal under

Rahul Sinha, who knew Chandra Bose, started supporting the declassification demand. Sinha helped by writing a letter to party president Rajnath Singh about the need to flag the Netaji issue. Eventually, the Bose family was brought around to the idea of reaching out to Narendra Modi by Chandra Bose. In April 2013, Chandra met the then Gujarat Chief Minister. Modi was handed over a letter approved by two dozen children and grandchildren of Subhas's brothers—Sudhir, Sunil, Sarat and Suresh. In the letter—drafted by us—the kin underlined the reason why the Chief Minister of Gujarat was being approached over the declassification issue:

> Netaji belonged to the entire nation, so we extend our appeal to you for your kind support in demanding from the Prime Minister that the Central Government must release in the public domain, all records to help unravel the mystery about his fate and bring a closure to the issue. It goes without saying that as long the Government of India continues to sit on secret records about Netaji's fate, it would not be able to take up the issue of secret records held by foreign governments.

As a result of many such lobbying efforts by us and the Bose family, the word went around. On 23 January 2014, then BJP president Rajnath Singh flew to Subhas Bose's birthplace in Cuttack to make a solemn promise there that if the BJP was voted to power in the General Elections, the party would try and resolve the matter.

By the end of 2014 the narrative of the Bose mystery had been overhauled by us. Mission Netaji's RTI quest, pursued vigorously for four years by Chandrachur, led to the declassification of around 10,000 pages related to the previous inquiries into Bose's fate. The declassification was ordered (under compulsion) by the Manmohan Singh government. The records eventually reached the National Archive in 2012 and were opened to researchers in November 2014.

Dhar visited the archive in December and spotted among the released documents, the photocopies of two West Bengal Intelligence Branch files on Bose's nephews, Amiya Nath Bose (father of Surya, Chandra and Madhuri) and Sisir Bose (father of Sugata Bose). Without wasting much time, Dhar wrote about the snooping in his online column in *Swarajya* and then on *The Daily O* of the *India Today* group. At personal level, the writers tried to sensitise the family members to take the matter up as it was serious. The initial response of the family was subdued as some members said that such things were not unusual and happened in every nation.

The situation changed dramatically when *India Today* ran a cover story on the snooping issue in April 2015. Overnight, the snooping scandal put national spotlight on the Bose family and matters relating to the disappearance of their celebrated ancestor. It was in this scenario that Mamata Banerjee decided to release 64 intelligence files in the custody of her government. By this time rumours were going around that Modi was in the process of doing something. The efforts of TMC Parliamentarian Sukhendu Sekhar Ray in favour of declassification also help build up the crescendo. On 17 September, Mamata gave a massive boost to the declassification demand by releasing 64 classified files. Their reading convinced the chief minister that Bose had perhaps not died in 1945 and the earlier snooping reports were correct.

The sensational disclosure received massive public attention, reflected in yet another round of unprecedented media coverage. On 18 September 2015, Chitra Ghosh told *The Times of India* of her assessment that 'Nehru … knew that the plane crash was a hoax and feared that Netaji was confabulating with his family from abroad'.[38] Her cousin Dr DN Bose added: 'I am surprised to find that police continued to snoop on the Bose family till 1971. This makes me believe that the Government wasn't sure about Netaji's whereabouts till then.'[39]

The Bose family began getting calls from the PMO. Within days, Prime Minister Narendra Modi himself announced that he was going to meet the delegation led by the family members in October. The Bose family was then approached to give a list of people to be included in that delegation. At this point, certain

38   'Revealed: Shocking scale of snoop on kin,' *The Times of India* (Kolkata edition), 19 September 2015.
39   'Bose speakers,' *The Times of India* (Kolkata edition), 19 September 2015.

members of the Bose family were so overwhelmed by the sudden
importance thrust on them that they started objecting to including
the names of Mission Netaji members in that list. They started
to say that only the Bose family members should meet the PM.
The consideration of gaining political mileage out of this sudden
celebrityhood also lurked in the air. In one swoop, they forgot
their own repeated statements in numerous press conferences
that 'Netaji belonged to the entire country' not just to his blood
relatives. They also forgot that the attention coming their way was
because of Mission Netaji.

Five members of Mission Netaji (MN) were eventually taken
in as a result of intervention by Surya, Madhuri and Chandra, who
till then had worked in close association with the authors since the
past many years. However, the members of MN were cautioned not
to raise the Bhagwanji matter. Some of the MN members almost
decided to not go on that condition, but eventually realised that
opting out of the meeting at 7 Race Course Road was not going to
do the issue any good. The family also did not accept MN's advice
that they should demand acceptance of Justice Mukherjee's report
and formation of an inquiry to probe the snooping. The reasons:
they did not like following their pro-Bhagwanji comments and
they feared an inquiry would lead to unearthing of factoids which
might be embarrassing to some of them.

Over a period of time, as Mission Netaji endeavoured to get
an inquiry constituted to ascertain the identity of Bhagwanji, the
rest of the family members turned more and more hostile towards
them. All of a sudden, they appeared to wake up to the fact that
MN had always considered the Bhagwanji angle a plausible one.

The family's discomfort reached a new level as Asoke Nath Bose's children, Jayanti and Arya (joined by Jayanti's husband Amiya Rakshit) broke the ranks to join MN in meeting the Chief Minister of UP Akhilesh Yadav in February 2016, seeking an inquiry into Bhagwanji's identity, as directed by the Allahabad High Court.

[Pic courtesy: UP Chief Minister's Office]

The family refused to appreciate MN's stand that in view of divergent claims, including theirs in private talks that Netaji was killed in Russia and that Bhagwanji was an impostor, a fair inquiry was required. In fact, in our written submission to the Chief Minister, all of us (Amiya, Jayanti, Arya included), clearly stated that 'the terms of reference of this inquiry should include investigation of long-standing and often-repeated *allegations that said Baba was an imposter and/or a foreign spy and/or a 'dummy' set up to misguide the people of India, and if these allegations are found to be true, to identify the perpetrators of such abominable criminality.* (Emphasis supplied). Whatever the family members were saying in private talks, we brought on record as we wanted (and still want) to know the unadulterated truth about what really happened to Netaji. Nothing else.

When the Justice Sahai Commission was eventually formed, the family had all the intentions to ignore it completely; the possibility that the former Judge might conclude that Bhagwanji and Netaji were the same person alarmed them. This led 17 family members to write to Justice Sahai on 10 October 2016 that:

> …we would like to convey to you the conclusions of the Justice Mukherjee Commission (JMC) regarding the disappearance of Netaji. In the course of the investigations the Commission obtained samples of blood from 3 nephews and niece of Netaji. The blood donors on the paternal side were Subrata Bose (former Member Lok Sabha) & Dwarka Nath Bose and on the maternal side, Nirupam Som, Tripti Nag and Sadhan Kar. Comparing the DNA of these members with the DNA obtained from the teeth of Gumnami Baba, it was conclusively proven through the tests conducted by Central Forensic Laboratory, Kolkata, that there was no match with either the maternal or paternal side of his family. These details are given on the pages 121-122 of Vol I of the JMC Report. As you are fully aware there can no surer method of identification than comparison of DNA. Thus a case has been proved incontrovertibly that there is no connection between Gumnami Baba and Netaji Subhas Chandra Bose.
>
> Further there is documentary evidence that the documents and photos of the Bose family found in his house were brought over to him at his request by a visitor who has stated this publicly. There is no existing photograph of the Baba who did not appear in person before visitors before he passed away in 1983. Some journalists are passing off a morphed photo of Subhas Chandra Bose as Gunmani Baba by superimposing a beard—a reprehensible act defaming a National Leader.

It is instructive to read these contentions in conjunction with those appearing in an article co-authored in June 2016 by siblings Surya and Madhuri Bose titled 'The dishonesty of those who exploit and abuse the name of Netaji'.[40] Inter alia, the following arguments were made in this article in *The Wire*:

> The imposters have come and gone.... One such character claiming to be none other than Netaji was actively pursued publicly and legally by our father Amiya Nath Bose, Netaji's nephew. After threatening defamation proceedings against father, the man fled and was never heard from again. Others beat a path to the door of the Bose ancestral home at 1, Woodburn Park in Kolkata, purportedly carrying messages from Netaji for his old pair of spectacles and other personal items. Upon father's request for a written message from Netaji, they too disappeared. Father never gave any credence to any 'sadhus' or 'babas' pretending to be his uncle Subhas, and given his astute legal brain, rejected such assertions or speculations as utterly false and mischievous.
>
> The persistence of such claims must be strongly challenged with rational arguments and scientific evidence where possible. Surely they cannot be based on the 'belief' of a select number of individuals, even of those who had known and worked with Netaji during the freedom struggle, and are persons who are widely respected and admired.
>
> Netaji, the father of modern economic planning in India, driver of communal harmony, a warrior who led from the front—is this a man who would choose seclusion over involvement, allowing access only to a select few and not members of his family closest to him?

40   Surya Kumar Bose and Madhuri Bose, 'The dishonesty of those who exploit and abuse the name of Netaji,' 13 June 2016, https://thewire.in/history/the-dishonesty-of-those-who-exploit-and-abuse-the-name-of-netaji-subhas-chandra-bose.

Surya and Madhuri have inherited much of their worldview regarding their granduncle from their father, the late Amiya Nath Bose. Described by the siblings as someone possessing an 'astute legal brain', Amiya was evidently given to believing in hearsays, as long as they had a touch of the glamour of international politics. For instance, in 1990, he called media persons to tell them that a Swedish diplomat had told him over the phone from Geneva that he had 'some very bad news about Subhas Bose dating back to 1947'. The diplomat was 'not prepared to disclose anything more over the phone and urged Mr Bose to fly to Europe as early as possible to help him in making further enquiries'.

THE TIMES OF INDIA,' NEW DELHI, MONDAY, SEPTEMBER 3 1990 **5**

'Fresh clue on Netaji's death'

The Times of India News Service

CALCUTTA, September 2: THE controversy over the mystery of Netaji Subhas Chandra Bose's death was revived here yesterday when Mr Amiya Nath Bose, a nephew of Netaji, claimed that he had received fresh information that Netaji did not die in an air crash at Taihoku airport on August 18, 1945, but something very bad had happened to him in 1947.

mystery surrounding the last days of Netaji in the Soviet Union.

He said American intelligence reports clearly stated that there had been no air crash at Taihoku airport in Formosa in August, 1945 and that Netaji was able to reach safety his "pre-determined destination", which, according to Mr Bose, was Manchuria. He pointed out that Manchuria was occupied by the Soviet Union from Japan after atom bombs were dropped on

Amiya was willing to giving credence to and read much into a short telephonic call but was not willing to repose such faith in the words of those in India who had been raising their voice for Subhas against all odds for decades. This included Amiya's good friend Samar Guha. The vague examples of certain characters reaching out to Amiya and his chasing them away, cited by the siblings in their article, have nothing to do with either Bhagwanji or his followers. Niharendu Dutt Majumdar, the Bose family lawyer, in front of the Khosla Commission, however, presented a different picture. According to Dutt Majumdar, the Shoulmari ashram filed a contempt petition against Amiya at the Jalpaiguri court and also at the Calcutta High Court for certain comments he allegedly made against the ashram. In return, when Amiya filed a counter petition against the ashram for contempt of court, it was turned down by the High Court.[41]

The fact of the matter is that no member of the Bose family told either the Mukherjee Commission or the previous Khosla Commission and Shah Nawaz Committee that Subhas was killed in Soviet Russia. It is only in private and before the media that the family members circulated the theory of Bose's imprisonment and probable death in the erstwhile USSR. All that Surya Bose would tell the Mukherjee Commission was that his grandaunt Emilie believed that Netaji was in Russia after 1945, something that Bhagwanji's followers concur with.

On 23 January 2016 in New Delhi's National Archives, soon after Prime Minister Modi released the first tranche of classified files, Surya Bose told *Times Now* that in 2013, a former *New York Times* correspondent of British origin asked him: 'Mr Bose could you tell me, when I came to Japan in 1964 why was MI6 still looking for Subhas Chandra Bose?'[42] Earlier, Surya's father Amiya

---

41   Oral evidence of Niharendu Dutt Majumdar, Netaji Inquiry Commission: Record of Oral Evidence, Vol XII, 22 September 1972, pp 3894-95
42   'Intelligence files will solve the Netaji mystery,' *Times Now*, 24 January 2016. Accessed from: https://www.youtube.com/watch?v=VVlAkt-66iY

told press reporters in 1990 that Sarat Bose received information that Subhas 'might have been executed in Soviet Russia or he had been held in custody in a concentration camp'. We have not come across anything which might suggest that Sarat received any such info or that he believed it, assuming he did receive it. Sarat Bose died in early 1950, months after proclaiming that his brother was in China. Bhagwanji also claimed to be in China at that time.

Astonishingly, Amiya made no such claim during his deposition before the Khosla Commission. In fact, he was tentative at the time of deposing before the commission. Never stoutly contesting the story of the plane crash, he told Justice GD Khosla in December 1972, 'What I always felt is if it is established that he did die in that air crash and these ashes are Netaji's ashes, I think we have shown scant respect to the ashes of the greatest Indian leader.'[43] Furthermore, he tried to block the most well-known proponent of 'imprisoned in a Soviet gulag' theory of the day, former MP Satyanarayan Sinha, from being allowed to present his case before the commission because 'the entirety of his evidence is hearsay'.

But in his later years Amiya started backing the Russia killing theory. On 22 January 1996, some time before he passed away, Amiya sent a letter to his friend and then Leader of Opposition Atal Bihari Vajpayee. The letter was hand delivered by their mutual friend Samar Guha, a follower of Bhagwanji. The letter, whose copy we possess, reads: 'Recent findings have given a clear

---

43   'Fresh clue on Netaji's death,' *The Times of India*, 3 September 1990.

indication that Subhas Chandra Bose was in the former Soviet Union in 1946. The so-called "ashes" at the Renkoji temple have nothing to do with Subhas Chandra Bose.'[44]

After 2010, when Justice Mukherjee's personal views about Bhagwanji and his disapproval of the Bose family member in its context became known, almost overnight the very Bose family members who used to publicly praise him for having led the fairest inquiry into Netaji's fate turned against him. As stated earlier, this is the reason why they did not demand from Prime Minister Modi during the meeting at his residence that Justice Mukherjee's report should be accepted. The golden opportunity was wasted for sheer ego.

The family's claim that the Bhagwanji saga is absurd is in itself preposterous. It is astonishing that despite such a formidable background to the case, Surya and Madhuri Bose failed to refer to the Allahabad High Court verdict, or even their aunt Lalita Bose, in their *The Wire* article. At the same time, they engaged in a banal rhetoric that claims of the Bhagwanji angle 'must be strongly challenged with rational arguments and scientific evidence'.

This naturally raises the question that if some Bose family

---

44   In his comments to *Times Now* in 2016, Surya Bose emphatically stated that in the presence of his father his grandfather Sarat was informed by Alfred Wagg and then Justice Radha Binode Pal that there was no air crash. Amiya himself narrated this in his letters to Prime Ministers VP Singh and Narasimha Rao. However, while giving evidence to the Khosla Commission in 1972, Amiya presented a much more mellowed down version of what Radha Binode Pal told Sarat Bose. 'According to him [Pal] the American intelligence reports were not conclusive,' is all that he told Khosla.

members had rational arguments and scientific evidence against the Bhagwanji angle, what prevented them from presenting such arguments and evidence before Justice Mukherjee? Not one Bose family member challenged this theory on record. On the other hand, sworn statements made by certain family elders and the family lawyer (no longer alive to present their case before the media), coupled with the other material on record, show that the Bose family, from late 1940s to the time of the functioning of the Khosla Commission, felt that Netaji was alive then. In hindsight, this appears to be linked to Bhagwanji as we shall now see.

Appearing on behalf of the Bose family before the Khosla Commission, former law minister of Bengal Niharendu Dutt Majumdar pressed the family's view that Subhas Bose was yet regarded as a war criminal. To quote GD Khosla, 'Mr Mazumdar has, on behalf of the family of Bose, argued with considerable vehemence and persistence that the government of India has deliberately suppressed or destroyed evidence which would have proved that Bose's name was included in the list of war criminals who were to be tried by the War Crimes Tribunal.'[45]

The family told the Khosla Commission that the charge that Bose was still a war criminal was the 'most important, if not the only reason, for his remaining incognito'[46] in early 1970s.

This position is nothing but an amplification of utterances of

---

45   'Report of the one-man commission of inquiry into the disappearance of Netaji
      Subhas Chandra Bose,' Ministry of Home Affairs, 30 June 1974, New Delhi, pp
      56-57.
46   Ibid, p 58.

Bhagwanji. If Subhas Bose had been killed in a Siberian gulag, there was no question of his being treated as a war criminal as late as 1971 as the family counsel argued the following before the commission.

```
limitations for prosecution of War Criminals.  I am
wondering what was the special urgency or occasion
for India at this time to make such a ratification
and what was India's special interest in this matter,
unless India has somebody in view or may be for
reasons not known to me.  Now the question therefore
arises that whether in the fitness of things, this
Hon'ble Commission should not have a copy of such a
Convention placed before it by the Government of India.
```

[Record obtained under the Right to Information]

Why would Bhagwanji allow access 'only to a select few and not members of his family closest to him', ask his siblings. How do they know that Bhagwanji did not reach out to 'his' family? As far as we know, at least two members of the Bose family were in some sort of contact with him.

Suresh Bose was Subhas's elder brother, and the most relevant person in the context of the death mystery considering that he was part of the Shah Nawaz Committee set up in 1956 to inquire into his brother's fate. From 1963, the year he came to know about Bhagwanji, Suresh Bose made repeated public statements that Subhas was alive. Making this position legally tenable is his 1972 assertion before the Khosla Commission under oath that Subhas 'is alive even today'. This was soon before Suresh died. The following comes from Volume XII of the record of oral evidence before Khosla Commission accessed by the writers under the Right to Information Act in 2007.

```
Q:23-Did you make a statement on 20.2.66 ax that Netaji
     was alive and that he would come in 1966 in the
     Amrita Bazar Patrika and Hundusthan Standard dated
     7.3.66 ?
A:   I have no knowledge about it but I have already been
     convinced that Netaji did not die as alleged and is
     alive even kdm today.
```

But Suresh Bose wouldn't give any more details. Bhagwanji did not want the world to know about him in 'national interest'. Bluntly, Suresh Bose told the Khosla Commission in response to a poser: 'There is no reason why I should take this commission into confidence. I want to know why should I do it and for what purpose?'

Can someone in the Bose family explain why Suresh Bose said so?

When Bhagwanji's belongings were being inventorised, a copy of Suresh Bose's testimony and the original summons sent by Khosla Commission to him were located at Ram Bhawan. Also found was a photograph of Suresh Bose, carefully wrapped in Bengali silk, indicating reverence. Lalita Bose, Suresh Bose's daughter thereafter revealed in April 1986 to the media that her father used to confabulate with a rustic-looking visitor from Basti (where Gumnami Baba lived in the 1960s) to take messages from 'Subi'—his brother Subhas.[47] She rued the fact that she did

---

[47] NK Singh, 'Questions Miss Bose would like to be answered,' *The Pioneer*, 1 April 1986.

not believe her elderly father then. Sunil Gupta, Suresh Bose's right-hand man, was of the view that Suresh Bose did not trust his children over Bhagwanji (refer to Sarat Bose's view on their relations, detailed towards the beginning of this chapter), which explains why they could never clarify why their father insisted that his brother was alive.

Also located from the belongings of Bhagwanji was a copy of the record of oral evidence before the Khosla Commission by Subhas's nephew Dwijendra Nath Bose. In his examination before the Khosla Commission, Dwijendra was asked if he had indeed made a statement on March 6, 1966 in Thiruvananthapuram that 'Netaji was still alive and was working in a place very near the borders of India'.

'Yes I did say,' Dwijendra affirmed. Asked why Bose was still in hiding, Dwijendra retorted that, 'It was not correct to say that. He is still working for India. He will come out... at the appropriate time....'

'Netaji still alive', says nephew

TRIVANDRUM, March 6.
Mr. Dwijendranath Bose, General Secretary of the All-India Forward Bloc, and a nephew of Netaji Subhas Chandra Bose, reiterated here today that Neaji was still alive and was working in a place very near the borders of India.

'I can tell you that last September, Netaji had an attack of pneumonia and was examined and treated by some very eminent doctors, whom I know, but I won't name, Mr. Bose told reporters.

Mr. Bose also stated that a staff reporter of a Calcutta daily had gone to the place where Netaji was staying, and had returned convinced that he was alive. The reporter, of course, could not meet Netaji.

Asked why Netaji was still in hiding, Mr. Bose replied that it was not correct to say that he was in hiding. 'He is still working for India. He will come out into the open and enter India at the appropriate time in such a way that he can establish a new order in the country,' Mr. Bose

[An *Amrita Bazar Patrika* clipping from a declassified file]

Q: You will excuse me for putting an annoying question. Government is spending so much upon this Inquiry Commission and the subject matter of the inquiry is to disentangle the mystery about Netaji's disappearance. So, do you think that possessing the knowledge about Netaji being alive so far as the members of Netaji family are concerned is not unfair to the people and the Government to allow this inquiry to go on when you have positive knowledge and you are not prepared to disclose?

A: If I give a clue to this committee, that would be made public and the Government will know of it and that is dangerous to Netaji. It is for him (Netaji) to decide when that should be made public or when he should return to India.

Q: I am now putting it to you finally—Can it be possible under any condition for you and others who know that Netaji is alive to disclose this to this Hon'ble Commission?

A: There are two things. Men like me can only disclose things about Netaji leading to where he is or where he was at a particular time if we are ordered by Netaji himself and nobody else. The other thing is that the Prime Minister should make a situation conducive for this and should broadcast a message to Netaji, "Wherever you are India welcomes you and the Government welcomes you".[48]

A letter written by Pabitra Mohan Roy, recovered from Ram Bhawan (see images on next page), indicates that Dwijen's stand might have been the result of the hints given to him by Leela Roy or Pabitra himself. 'Dwijen has started believing that "He" is now back in the country. He told me that he doesn't know where "He" is and requested me to let him know if I can put him in touch,' Pabitra wrote in the undated letter. Pabitra recommended Dwijen to be taken into Bhagwanji's inner circle, along with Hem Chandra Ghosh and Satya Ranjan Bakshi.

Strangely, children of Dwijen Bose and grandchildren of Suresh Bose signed the letter that was sent to Justice Sahai by the family. Justice Sahai would have done well to question them

48   Oral evidence of Dwijendra Nath Bose, Netaji Inquiry Commission: Record of Oral Evidence, Vol XI.

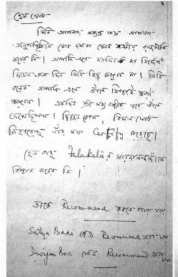

about the statements of their father/grandfather on record. The grandchildren of Suresh Bose could have also thrown some light on the fact as to why their uncle Pradip Bose told Justice Khosla that former Bose aide turned diplomat N Raghavan had tried to impress upon the Nehru government that Subhas was in East Asia, and was therefore posted as India's ambassador to China to find out whether Subhas was really there.

Of all the Subhas Bose kin, the name that stands tallest is that of Sarat—Subhas's elder brother, father of Chitra Ghosh (the No 1 signatory to the Bose family letter to Justice Vishnu Sahai) and grandfather of Surya, Madhuri, Sugata, Ashis, Chandra, Abhijit Ray, Jayanti Rakshit and others. If Subhas had not died in 1945 and was in a position to communicate, the one person he would have reached out to was his brother Sarat. It so happened that before he passed away in 1950, Sarat made a public assertion that

Subhas was alive and in China. It defies imagination why Sarat's own children and grandchildren are pretending not to know about their grandfather's stand. Is it owing to the fact that it doesn't support either the air crash or the Russia killing theory? Sarat made repeated assertions about Subhas being alive. Declassified West Bengal government intelligence files contain reference to many.

NETAJI ALIVE–BELIEVES SJ. SARAT BOSE

"He Would Appear Again In Appropriate Moment"

By A Staff Reporter

The belief that Netaji was alive was expressed by Sj. Sarat Chandra Bose addressing a public meeting in Calcutta on Thursday.

Sj. BOSE said that though he had no information of Netaji yet he had this belief that Netaji was alive and perhaps due to some reason best known to him he was not emerging from his secluded life.

It would be futile on their part, Sj. Bose said, to conduct any search for him or to try to secure any news of his present whereabouts. When proper time would come and when Netaji would think the moment appropriate for his emergence he would appear again and would come to his motherland to fulfil his unfinished task.

Not only that, Sarat, according to an intelligence report, met Deputy Prime Minister of Vietnam 'and requested him to help Netaji's reappearance in the East through the independent State of Vietnam'. In response, Dr Pham Ngoc Thach said,

> If Netaji would personally appear before him at Vietnam, he and his people would certainly do their best to protect and shield Netaji against UNO's trying him as a war criminal.

3. On 25.2.48 SARAT CHANDRA BOSE received the Deputy Premier, Viet Nam, at a tea party and requested him to help Netaji's reappearance in the East through the independent State of Viet Nam.. The Deputy Premier, who is confident about Netaji's death, assured Sarat Bose that if Netaji would personally appear before him at Viet ....d his people would certainly do their best to protect and shield Netaji against U.N.O.'s trying him as a War Criminal. Sarat Bose agreed to make Netaji appear before Dr.Thantch.

So it leaves one wondering if the kin of Sarat would level the same charge of dishonesty and abuse of Netaji's name against their grandfather in their keenness to appear morally superior. The bigger question is why they have chosen to remain silent about these utterances of their elders. Is it incidental or deliberate?

The current generation of Netaji kin like to point out that the belongings of Bhagwanji were brought over to him at his request by a visitor who has stated this publicly. Of course, all those books, Bose family pictures, etc. were sent by the followers to Bhagwanji over the years. It has never been asserted by anyone associated with Bhagwanji, including us, that he carried all these goods from China into India. All we did was to wonder why Bhagwanji was collecting such material and why people with past association with Netaji were obliging him?

Lastly, some Netaji kin have charged that some journalists are passing off a morphed photo of Subhas Chandra Bose as Gunmani Baba by superimposing a beard. We do not know which journalists the family allude to, but the 'morphed photo' referred to is surely the following:

 This visual, purporting to show Bhagwanji (Gumanami Baba) has been published in innumerable newspapers, websites and even shown on TV channels. The visual was created as an identikit in 2002 when *Hindustan Times* was releasing the findings of Anuj Dhar with regard to the Bhagwanji angle. Illustrator Siddharth Ghosh modified a picture of Subhas Bose on the basis of a description of Bhagwanji's face by Dr Priyabrata Banerjee (since deceased). Since

Dr Banerjee (who had by then duly deposed before the Mukherjee Commission) said that Bhagwanji looked exactly like Bose (stated by others as well), an existing picture was used as a base. The final visual, showing both the original Subhas Bose image as well as the artist's impression, was used with a story attributed to Anuj Dhar. This is how it appeared on *HT's* website:

Illustration: Siddharth Ghosh

Artist's impression of Bhagwanji based on eyewitnesses' accounts. On the left is a late 1930s picture of Netaji Subhas Chandra Bose.

The print edition of *Hindustan Times* on 24 April 2002 carried the same story with the Bhagwanji visual in a box. The description read: 'An artist's impression of Bhagwanji' (see image on next page).

At no point did either *Hindustan Times* or Anuj Dhar make a claim that the picture was genuine. The picture does not appear in *India's Biggest Cover-up*, which has more than 220 images. Nor have the authors in their articles and hundreds of social media posts used this visual as a picture of Bhagwanji. It would seem that at some point in time someone picked up the *HT* combo image, took out the Bhagwanji identikit and posted it after removing the caption that it was a mere visual representation of a Subhas Bose lookalike. This is how the visual gained currency in the age of internet. The point the family tried to make was much ado about nothing.

Was the Faizabad hermit Netaji in disguise?

Anuj Dhar
www.HindustanTimes.com

THE RENKOJI shrine in Japan may or may not be the repository of Subhas Chandra Bose's ashes, but a few teeth kept in the Faizabad district magistrate's treasury for the past 16 years could finally establish the truth about Netaji's disappearance.

Bose's relatives and INA associates say Netaji spent his last years disguised as Bhagwanji, a hermit who lived in a rented room in Faizabad. They say the teeth were Bhagwanji's. DNA tests were conducted to examine the claim that he was Bose. Bhagwanji died in 1985 at the

Two faces of the same man?

BHAGWANJI HAD a striking resemblance to Netaji. He was as tall as Netaji and was of the same age. He too had gaps between his teeth, a scalpel mark on his abdomen and wore round-frame spectacles and an Omega gold watch. The hermit treasured many rare and original pictures of Netaji's parents and had among his followers many of Netaji's old associates, including INA Secret Service sleuth Pabitra Mohan Roy.

An artist's impression of Bhagwanji

age of 86 — Bose would have been the same age that year.

Also found in Bhagwanji's house were documents, photographs and souvenirs, reportedly belonging to the Bose family. B. Lal, a handwriting expert pointed by HindustanTimes.com, says the writing samples of Bhagwanji and Bose do

match, implying the texts must have been written by the same person. All the writing samples are dated after 1945 — the year Netaji reportedly died. However, while a handwriting analysis could be significant, the finding is not conclusive.

After Bhagwanji's death, when word spread that he may have been Bose, the Allahabad High Court sealed his belongings and sent them to the Faizabad treasury. Last year, the seal was broken so that the Mukherjee Commission, which is probing Netaji's disappearance, could examine them.

A commission member said select items from the Faizabad

treasury would reach Kolkata in the first week of May. "We may then go in for handwriting analysis and a DNA test," he said.

Officially however, Netaji has been consigned to the X-files. The Government has continued to stonewall efforts to get to the bottom of the mystery and has refused access to its Netaji dossier.

Home Secretary Kamal Pande explained this stance to the Mukherjee Commission, saying "I have examined the documents...the disclosure will lower Netaji's image...hurt the sentiments of the people at large. Diplomatic ties with friendly countries may also be adversely affected."

An artist's impression of Bhagwanji

TEN

INTERREGNUM

WHETHER OR NOT a plane crashed at Taipei on 18 August 1945, one thing indisputably came to an end—the public life of Subhas Chandra Bose. While this absence of his was turned into one of the arguments in favour of his death in 1945 by the government, a game of shadows had begun beyond the public gaze, even as theories, hypotheses, conjectures were constructed one after the other in the public arena.

Starting with Pandit Nehru, the Indian government exuded absolute confidence that Bose was dead (a line maintained by successive governments, including the NDA government under Narendra Modi). At the same time, popular disbelief in this version remained in vogue, with several unanswered questions. Yet, the sceptics didn't have any credible alternative version to explain what exactly happened to Bose. If the 'evidence' for Bose's death was not definite, nor were the alternative theories. Even those, like Suresh Bose, who were certain that the story of Subhas's death in the plane crash was absolutely false, were unable to say what had happened to him, other than claiming that he could have gone to Soviet Russia. Barring other claims such as those of Muthuramalingam Thevar and Sarat that Bose was in China in the late 1940s and early 1950s, all that was definitely known in the 1960s was that he was, at the time of his reported death, headed towards Manchuria—a territory occupied by the Soviet forces, which also had the presence of the defeated Kwantung army and the Chinese.

Logically, Bose's journey to Soviet Russia made the greatest sense among all the probable scenarios in the immediate aftermath of the Japanese surrender. That's the scenario he had been preparing for. Claims and counter-claims continue to emerge, but till today Bose's presence in Russia has not been established beyond doubt. Above all, the Russians have consistently denied having to do anything with Bose's fate.

It was, therefore, natural that the question of what had really happened in and after August 1945 would be at the top of their mind when Pabitra, Leela Roy and others established contact with Bhagwanji in 1962-63. They were, however, so overwhelmed to have found their lost leader living in extremely difficult conditions and the urgent need to ensure some basic level of comfort for him that the enquiry about the past became of secondary importance. If the need for absolute secrecy prevented free discussion, the personality of Bhagwanji was another obstacle. It was he who set the agenda for the conversations. Most of his visitors didn't dare ask direct questions. Instances of asking questions were rare, and when asked, the questions were more about his views and in the nature of seeking clarifications. The discourses became more relaxed only with the passage of a number of years. Hence, the information emerging from available letters and minutes of conversations is not in the form of a cohesive narrative, but a collation of snippets spoken at different points in time to different persons. Apart from non-availability of the full set of documents from Bhagwanji's disciples, another serious obstacle to getting a coherent narrative is the gap between what he spoke and what his followers noted down. They struggled to comprehend the flow of his talks, especially those in accented English, and names of places and characters. A scrutiny of the available journals throws up a number of such instances. In fact, Bijoy Nag himself recorded a chiding by Bhagwanji for failing to accurately write down what he said.

> You have forgotten to write about the trip to China a few days after arriving in Tokyo. You have also missed mentioning the fact of staying as a guest at the house of a powerful personality after becoming 'Mrita Bhoot' (dead ghost). You have omitted the incident of receiving a special request through a special person. On granting of the request, the arrival of a delegation of a country at the house of the host and tendering an invitation—you have forgotten to write. You haven't written about the existence by two different names at two different places.[1]

1   Charanik, *Oi Mahamanaba Ase*, Jayasree Prakashan, 2010, pp 315-16.

The 'last days'

The established narrative of Subhas Bose's first leg of his 'last' journey is that he arrived at Bangkok from Singapore on 16 August. From there, he flew out the next morning to Saigon with his associates in two planes. Flying in one of them were Habibur Rahman, S A Ayer, Pritam Singh and a Japanese officer, besides Bose himself. In the second flight were Gulzara Singh, Abid Hassan and Debnath Das, along with General Isoda (the chief of Hikari Kikan) and Hachiya Teruo, the Japanese Minister-designate to the Azad Hind Government. In his book *Unto Him a Witness*, Ayer, Subhas Bose's information minister, described the scenario on reaching Saigon and named a not so well-known Indian Independence League (IIL) person:

> ...here we were at the Saigon aerodrome on what Netaji described as 'an adventure into the unknown'. Netaji saw a solitary Indian in the distance. He wanted to know who it was. The Indian turned out to be Mr Chandra Mal, Secretary of the Transport Department of the IIL in Saigon. He had learnt that Netaji was coming and he had come to the aerodrome to see whether he could be of any service to Netaji.... We drove in two cars to the outskirts of Saigon and arrived at the house of Naraindas, Secretary of the Housing Department of the IIL Saigon.... Officers of the League had dispersed. None of them, except Chandra Mal, knew that Netaji was in their midst right at that moment.[2]

Bhagwanji had a startling comment on this little-heard of Chandra Mal—that he was a British agent. The flight to Saigon

---

2   SA Ayer, *Unto Him a Witness*, Thacker & Co Ltd, Bombay, pp 66-67.

was a closely held secret, yet Chandra Mal was there at the airport—how could he reach there before 'He' arrived, Bhagwanji asked. His pointer was not only towards Chandra Mal, but towards Ayer as well.

The infiltration of the IIL, as well as the Japanese intelligence machinery by British spies, was one aspect that Bhagwanji spoke on many a times. If he was proud of the INA, he was also acutely aware of the extent of the rot in the revolutionary army. Recorded history of the Provisional Government and the INA, as well as the memoirs of those close to Subhas Bose, clearly show just how deeply he was affected by the instances of desertion and espionage. 'Half of the Intelligence Section of the Japanese Foreign Office maintained links with the British intelligence,' Bhagwanji told Pabitra. The capture of the assets withdrawn from the Azad Hind Bank by Attavar Yellapa, the Governor of Azad Hind Bank at Taunggyi, under Bose's instructions was another instance which occurred due to treachery of a British agent in the INA, Bhagwanji claimed.

Bhagwanji claimed that one Gopal Singh, who had raised money for 'Netaji Fund', siphoned off Rs 4 crores and escaped to Siam (Thailand), a fact that he said was known to the Indian and Thai governments. Within the IIL, he named Chandra Mal, Ghulam Ahmed and Taru Khan to have been covertly working for the British. Ghulam Ahmed, he said, previously worked with the British police force in Hong Kong.[3] Along with Taru Khan, he was

---

3   The case of Ghulam Ahmed has also been recorded by Major General A C
      Chatterji in his book *India's Struggle for Freedom*, Chuckervertty, Chatterjee &
      Co Ltd, 1947, pp 289-91.

recruited by Major General A C Chatterji. These two, he claimed, were also close to Anand Mohan Sahay. Among the better known in the Azad Hind and Japanese establishments, Bhagwanji said that Rama Murti and General Araki were traitors, and worked in connection with Col Figgess and Col Wilson of the British army. Bhagwanji pointed out that Sahay and Ayer[4] had links with the Japanese Imperial Headquarters and the British Intelligence in Tokyo.

It is intriguing that documents declassified by the Modi Government show that not only the INA treasure was looted, the perpetrators were also allowed to go scot-free in free India. Munga Rama Murti, the head of IIL in Tokyo, and S A Ayer were accused in the official records of the Indian government for having made away with the war chest Bose had created with public help to sustain the freedom struggle. Assisting the duo was Colonel J G Figgess, the military attaché at the British embassy.[5] He is now remembered in the UK as late Sir John Figgess (OBE), soldier, diplomatist and oriental porcelain expert.[6]

---

4   Both Sahay and Ayer joined government service after Independence.
5   Ministry of External Affairs file 25/4/NGO-Vol 1 deals with the issue of the
     missing INA treasure. Munga Ramamurti, the head of Indian Independence
     League (IIL) in Tokyo, Bose's propaganda minister S A Ayer and Colonel
     J G Figgess were indicted by the Indian mission in Tokyo.
6   This allegation of collusion between Figgess and Ramamurti was present in
     Indian circles in Japan too. Writing to the Shah Nawaz Committee in May
     1956, A Seth, who had been residing in Japan for 25 years, accused Ramamurti
     to be an informer to the Japanese 'about the activities of Indians and after the
     war he renewed his business, but on behalf of [the] British'. In a note dated
     1 November 1951 for Foreign Secretary, which was seen by Prime Minister
     Nehru, R D Sathe, Joint Secretary in MEA, wrote that there was a reported
     invitation from Figgess to Rama Murti to settle down in the UK. (MEA File
     No 25/4/NGO - Vol 1, National Archives of India).

Lt General Sadao Araki was tried for war crimes after the war, given a life sentence but was released in 1955 for health reasons. He died in 1966.

Bhagwanji also turned his attention to Shah Nawaz Khan, who became a celebrity as soon as he returned to India from the South-eastern theatre, on the back of the public protests against the Red Fort trials. At the same time, there were rumours floating around that Shah Nawaz had turned himself over to the British and that he had promoted himself to the rank of a Major General. Bhagwanji claimed both were facts. What was the exact nature of betrayal, he did not elucidate, but said that when the Azad Hind Cabinet, on receiving news of Khan's 'betrayal' decided to arrest and court martial him, 'I gave my final signature on that order, but it was too late. He had fled.' It was General A C Chatterjee who first got wind of Khan's betrayal and when he did, he rushed to inform his leader. Bhagwanji claimed he told a shocked Chatterjee (referring to him in the old Bengali style—Chatterjee *mohashoi*) that he had prior information, but had kept quiet. Why? An exasperated Chatterjee demanded an explanation. What if this had led to greater danger? Bhagwanji's response was stoic: 'I have taken up something [the INA] which has been built by others. If I start pruning, then many people will have to be thrown out. I have kept quiet to stop that from happening.' On the matter of Shah Nawaz claiming the rank of Major General, Bhagwanji's amused response was that after their return to India, many INA men had escalated their ranks because they had nothing to worry about being challenged openly.

There is no official document that the authors know of

suggesting that Shah Nawaz betrayed the INA. His interrogation report, available at the National Archives in New Delhi, on the contrary shows him to be staunchly loyal to the INA. All that we are aware of are allegations, including those made by some of the Bose family members. With regard to Suresh Bose, it can be safely assumed that he amplified Bhagwanji's thoughts. In his deposition before the Khosla Commission, Suresh let loose a volley of allegations, describing Shah Nawaz as 'a dark specimen of an unparalleled treachery to Netaji'.

> Shah Nawz Khan falsely coined his rank as Major General instead of his correct rank as Colonel in the Azad Hind Fauj... he fought well in the initial stage of the war but subsequently played Netaji false.... He was rightly suspected of passing over some INA secrets to his brother and others in the British Indian Army opposing them for which he was given an important assignment away from Netaji's headquarters. Some loyal officers were placed with him for reporting about his conduct and he was not allowed to meet Netaji during his last four and half months' stay in South East Asia... the order of court-martial was passed against him but it was not carried out as the war suddenly came to an end.[7]

Again, nothing on record is available to support these contentions. Memoirs and available war time documents paint quite the contrary picture. According to his own account, Shah Nawaz Khan along with three others met Netaji for the last time on 7 March 1945 in Rangoon, as they started to join the battle at Popa. Shah Nawaz surrendered along with the

---

7   'Shahnawaz played Netaji false,' *Hindustan Times*, 18 November 1970.

troops under his command, including Colonel G S Dhillon on 18 May.[8] Col Dhillon later testified to Shah Nawaz's reluctance in surrendering to the British forces and commended 'his large-heartedness in surrendering his prerogative of a commander to the combined will of the officers and men under his command'.[9] In view of these, Suresh Bose's views on Shah Nawaz appear to be without any foundation.

One of the characteristic features of Subhas Bose that he learnt from the revolutionary groups was the art of keeping secrets. The cardinal principle of these groups was to share information strictly on a 'need-to-know' basis, following a chain of command where an individual wouldn't know the identities of others involved in the execution of a plan. Subhas demonstrated the same characteristic when he consulted his team on whether he should accept the lone seat offered by the Japanese on the flight from Saigon. In Ayer's words, 'But where was Netaji going? We did not ask him and he did not tell us.' Bhagwanji went a step ahead. He said that he knew much in advance that Japan would surrender and had started planning accordingly, but never told anyone about his future plan. Disappearance, he said, was planned long before the Japanese surrender. Then he said something utterly striking. He said he had made a secret trip to the Soviet Union much before the Japanese surrendered. He claimed to have spent a month and a half there.

---

8   Shah Nawaz Khan, *My Memories of INA & its Netaji*, Rajkamal Publications, 1946, pp 194-195.
9   G S Dhillon, *From My Bones: Memoirs of Col Gurbakhsh Singh Dhillon of the Indian National Army*, Aryan Books International, 1998, p 346.

The generally accepted position is that in the last few months before the war ended, Bose did not even visit Tokyo, let alone undertaking a secret visit to USSR. The Shah Nawaz Committee report reads that 'in October 1944 Netaji visited Japan for the third and last time'. However, available at the National Archives is an intelligence report stating that Bose visited Tokyo in December that year to discuss with the Japanese government a possible rapprochement with China and Russia.

SACSEA Commission No 1 report of 6 November 1945 opens with the statement that 'in December 1944, Subhas Chandra Bose suggested that it would be expedient for the Japanese government to come to terms with Chiang-Kai-Shek and further seek friendship with Russia'. Where and when he said that is made clearer subsequently: 'There are indications that the Japanese government evinced a keen interest when Bose put forth these suggestions and in fact, plausible as these looked to them, it was in this connection that Bose visited Tokyo on Dec. 44 [sic].'[10] Yet another record in the archives even speaks of a rumour about Bose's secret visit not just to Tokyo but to Russia.

> In November 1944 there was a general rumour…that SC Bose was preparing to leave for Moscow in order to place all information about the Indian freedom movement before the leaders of the USSR. It was also said that Col SA Malik would follow SC Bose to Moscow. …In December 1944, Lt Sadhu Singh of HQ, 1 Div, INA, was acting as QM of the YE-U rest Camp, informed B 766 that SC Bose had left for Moscow and was soon expected back in Tokyo.[11]

---

10   File No INA 400, National Archives, New Delhi.
11   File No INA 249, National Archives, New Delhi.

For reasons we can now appreciate in hindsight, Suresh Bose made a similar claim before the Khosla Commission. A *Times of India* report dated 6 November 1970 quoted him saying that Bose's plan to go to Russia 'was drawn up in early 1944 and it was accepted by the Japanese government'. In pursuant of this plan, what Subhas did next according to Suresh was reported by *Hindustan Times*:

> In December 1944, when the Azad Hind Government was functioning and the INA was engaged in the battlefields, Netaji was absent from there for about a fortnight. During this period, Netaji had been to Russia and had probably met Marshal Stalin.[12]

On 17 August 1945, while Habibur Rahman climbed into the plane with Bose, they were seen off by Ayer, Debnath Das, Gulzara Singh, Pritam Singh, Abid Hassan, Isoda and Hachiya. They stood at the aerodrome and saw the plane taking off and vanishing in the horizon. All of them gave their versions of what transpired at Saigon on that day, either through their statements to the official inquiries or through their memoirs or statements to the press, which are fairly consistent. Bhagwanji, however, gave a different twist to the story, introducing a new character at the Saigon aerodrome—a certain Kimura. He said there were two bombers—the first one was a dummy flight which was publicised to be carrying him, Kimura and others.[13]

---

12   'Shahnawaz played Netaji false,' *Hindustan Times*, 18 November 1970.
13   Charanik, *Oi Mahamanaba Ase*, Jayasree Prakashan, 2010, pp 308-309.

Could 'Kimura' mentioned by Bhagwanji be General Heitaro Kimura? Was he also in some way involved in the ploy to save Bose's life? A superior officer to Tsunamasa Shidei, Kimura had led the Japanese–INA charge against the Allied forces during the Burma Campaign in the South-East Asian theatre of the war. Post-1945 he was tried as 'Class A' war criminal at the International Military Tribunal for the Far East and hanged in 1948. Shidei, on the other hand, was claimed to have died along with Bose in the plane crash, though the evidence of his death was even sketchier. Or was it some other Kimura? We can't tell. None of those present, however, mentioned Kimura. Everyone, on the other hand vouched for the presence of Shidei. By 1956, the sequence of these events was well-known, thanks to press statements of the INA members and the report of the Shah Nawaz Committee, and it would be difficult for anyone even cursorily familiar with the relevant details to make such a statement. The sole reference to Kimura was made in the course of Shah Nawaz Committee's inquiry by Lt N B Dass of the INA. Dass, however, claimed that Netaji and Kimura boarded a flight in Bangkok while Habibur Rahman and some other Japanese officers boarded another plane. The two planes subsequently flew in two different directions.[14] The committee rubbished his claims on the basis of Debnath Das's (Adviser to the Provisional Government of Azad Hind) statement that Dass wasn't even posted in Bangkok.[15] Debnath Das went

---

14   Evidence of Lt N B Dass to the Shah Nawaz Khan Committee, 23 April 1956, Ministry of External Affairs, Annexure to File No PS-56/NEC.

15   Netaji Inquiry Committee Report, 1956, p 37.

underground in September 1945, as instructed by Netaji before his departure, on being assured by a staff officer of the Japanese Army that the story of the plane crash was concocted.[16]

The 'real' bomber carrying him, Bhagwanji claimed about his 'escape', left for an unknown destination later. He indicated having remained in the vicinity of Saigon, where a few days after the 'crash', he was accidentally spotted by several Anglo-American soldiers and Japanese petty officers. The Japanese General who was reported dead in the 'crash' signed the peace treaty, according to Bhagwanji.[17] He further said that he instructed Habibur Rahman on what to do and what to say subsequently, and also informed him that he had confided his plans to two Japanese Generals.

A crucial part in this escape plan was played, Bhagwanji hinted, by the Genyosha (the Black Ocean Society) of Mitsuru Toyama.[18] Toyama and his ultra-nationalist society (as also the Kokuryukai or the Black Dragon Society) was a powerful organisation with deep connections in the Japanese government and military establishments. Toyama had played a crucial role in protecting Rash Behari Bose from being handed over to the British in the earlier decades and there is at least one known instance of a meeting between him and Subhas Bose.

Bhagwanji's narrative opens a whole new avenue in the story

---

16   Evidence of Debnath Das to the Shah Nawaz Khan Committee, 5 April 1956, Ministry of External Affairs, Annexure to File No PS-56/NEC.

17   General Kimura led the surrender ceremony in Rangoon on 24 October 1945.

18   Charanik, Oi Mahamanaba Ase, Jayasree Prakashan, 2010, p 92.

of 17 and 18 August, leading to the alleged plane crash. According to his version, he didn't even travel to Taiwan, but took his escape route from Saigon. By extension, it therefore could not have been possible for him to have a first-hand knowledge of what really transpired on the island. But he could definitely point out to the loopholes in the Taiwan story, even if it meant taking cues from investigation carried out by others. That is exactly what he did.

The ideal course of action for him would have been to step out publicly and tell the story as it really happened—the route of escape he took, where he went, what he did for all these years and so on. Or at least to let his followers like Pabitra announce before the Khosla Commission that he was living in Basti. Why he didn't or couldn't do it constitutes the subject of another chapter, but for now, his sole object was to disprove the story of the crash. As he minutely followed the proceedings of the G D Khosla Commission and helped his followers strategise, the strict instruction to them was *restrict yourself to disproving the air crash theory.* However, his view about the commission was that it was a ploy by Indira Gandhi to be sure about his status and to make sure that he wouldn't become an obstacle in her political career.

Both Pabitra Mohan Roy and Sunil Das appeared before the Commission in September 1972. While the statement of Das was recorded on 6 September, Pabitra's turn was on 25 September. Bhagwanji was duly informed about their schedule; he received Pabitra's letter on 4 September, and his detailed response was received by Pabitra just four days before his deposition. There was probably no exchange with Sunil Das on the talking points, and Bhagwanji hoped he had been able to keep secret what he came to know between 'N' (Neemsar) and 'B' (Basti, where Bhagwanji was residing then). Das told the Commission that he believed Bose was still alive and yet dodged the questions arising out of his assertion.

Bhagwanji asked Pabitra to prepare his statement in consultation with Sunil Krishna Gupta. However, he outlined some pointers for him. Pabitra's background would be known to the 'enemy', Bhagwanji wrote to him—if it isn't, it means that 'either they are inefficient or don't care'. Anyway, Pabitra should start his story from the time of his involvement with the 'terrorist' groups, extending up to the events till his release in 1946 and mention the roles played by Rash Behari and Subhas. Pabitra would stick to the script on this aspect when he appeared before the commission. However, Justice Khosla did not allow him to speak further, with the result that he could not elucidate the rest of the pointers. If he had been given more time, Pabitra would have, as advised by Bhagwanji, alluded to a statement attributed to Rafi Ahmed Kidwai that Subhas was alive and that he would return. This was based on a letter published in a newspaper from someone in Lucknow, who was close to Kidwai, and to Bhagwanji as well. Bhagwanji had further pressed that 'to doubt the statements of a righteous and high-principled person like Muthuramalingam Thevar' was unfair. In the same breath, he added that 'the views expressed by a jurist like Radhabinod Pal cannot be false'.

The next pointer related to the arrest of Subhas Bose's youngest brother, who resembled him, at Gandhiji's ashram months after the news of the air crash. 'The Government of the day knew that the story of the plane crash was a smokescreen of lies. That is why forces were deployed at the border to ensure strict vigil and the police and the intelligence apparatus were on the alert within the country too. The result was the arrest of Sailesh [Bose],' Bhagwanji wrote. He further asked Pabitra to recall how he along with a few other ex-INA persons were 'offered a highly lucrative job in the intelligence department by a very senior officer under Sardar Vallabhbhai Patel'. However, at the final stage of signing the contract, when Pabitra and the others asked a clause to be added that they would never be asked to investigate about Netaji's whereabouts, the offer was dropped. 'This confirmed that the Government knew that Bose was alive and their only effort was to know about his current location and activities.'

Bhagwanji referred to a statement of Lal Bahadur Shastri that 'if he comes back he will be given a hero's welcome' and asked, 'Does it make any sense to talk of a scenario of the return of someone who is confirmed dead?' He drew attention of Pabitra to the claim of two members of Parliament that they had seen him at an airport in France. This was rather intriguing. Mukand Parekh, personal secretary to Deven Sen, a Member of Parliament from 1967, testified before the Khosla Commission that in 1946, Sen and K N Joglekar (a convict of the famed Meerut Conspiracy case and later general secretary of Forward Bloc), saw Subhas Bose at Marseilles airport. As they tried to speak with 'Bose', who was in military attire, he indicated them to keep mum by placing his finger on his lips. On their return to India, Sen related his account to Sarat Bose. Chaplakanta Bhattacharyya, a former editor of *Anandabazar Patrika,* also testified before Justice Khosla that Deven Sen confided in him the same account. 'Mr Deven Sen and Mr Joglekar are both dead and their story is no more than hearsay evidence. The story itself does not carry conviction,' Khosla subsequently observed in his report.[19] By sheer coincidence, the day Bhagwanji's letter containing the pointers reached Pabitra, was also the day when Mukund Parekh deposed before the Commission, recounting the experience of Deven Sen—who had died soon after his press conference in December 1970.[20]

For any inquiry to be complete, Bhagwanji then added, the scene of the incident must be investigated. 'Consulting the logbook at the Taihoku airport will prove that there was no plane crash on that day. It will not be easy to track the logbook.' He also underlined that the commission needed to adopt a very friendly approach towards Taiwan in order to access relevant information. 'A strictly official approach and behaviour will not help alleviate the indifference that has resulted from India's attitude towards Taiwan,' he cautioned. But the Government of India, as discussed previously, had no intention of adopting a friendly attitude towards Taiwan. On 11 July 1973, G D Khosla landed at the Taipei Songshan Airport, which had come up on the site of a much smaller Matsuyama aerodrome. Waiting for him there were Samar Guha and Sunil Krishna Gupta. According to Guha's account, he

19   Report of the One-Man Commission of Inquiry into the Disappearance of Netaji Subhas Chandra Bose, 1974, p 97.

20   Bhagwanji reconfirmed this incident to Bijoy Nag during his conversation on 26 September 1971 at Basti. 'In 1945/46 I had to go on a flying visit crossing through Europe...During my flying visit in my uniform two Indians saw me, with their eyes popping out. For about eight days I did not hear whether they had talked about it here. They are probably MPs now, I am not sure.' Unpublished diary of Bijoy Nag, shared with authors. Translated from Bengali by Chandrachur Ghose.

implored Khosla to contact the Taiwanese authorities only to be informed that the Ministry of External Affairs had advised the judge against it. 'Why have you come over here, then? Why did you not tell us this in Delhi?' Guha protested. 'Why have you come to Taipei after 27 years?' people asked Guha as he went around the Taipei city making enquiries about the reported air crash. The word spread and soon the Taiwan government knew of a foreign judge on their territory, carrying out an inquiry without any notification. Had Guha and Gupta not intervened, Khosla would have been booted out of Taiwan.

Bhagwanji also wanted Pabitra to tell the commission about what had transpired when Gandhi had come to see him [Pabitra] at the condemned cell. 'Mahatmaji had gone there to meet you. When you asked him about the plane crash, he smiled and said, "*Bhala Subhas kya mar sakta hai? Pehle pehle to woh* plane crash *ki khabar sunkar bahut dukh hua tha, magar uske bad jana ki woh khabar udai gai hai.* Subhas has so many resources...I am now fully convinced that Subhas is alive"' (*Can Subhas die? Initially I was deeply saddened to hear the news of the plane crash, but later I came to know that it was a deliberately spread false news*).

Lastly, Bhagwanji wanted Pabitra to vouch for that generally known fact that Netaji always wore a large, round gold watch, a present from his mother. 'You have seen it many times on me... None of you know that the watch was not a mere watch but more a protective amulet, blessed by the love and affection of my mother.' This was in the context of Habibur Rahman furnishing a square burnt watch with the claim that it had been removed from the person of Bose after the crash. But everyone agreed that

Bose wore a round watch in his last days. Dwijen Bose during his testimony before Khosla said that he had noticed that the mark left by the fastener on the leather strap indicated that the square watch was worn by someone whose wrist was bulkier than his uncle's. After grilling Rahman, Dwijen concluded that he gave him a hint that the air crash was a ruse and he (Rahman) was carrying out an order.

As another letter written to Pabitra in 1971 reveals, Bhagwanji kept a keen watch on Dr Satyanarayan Sinha and the Bengali journalist Barun Sengupta, who was writing articles on Netaji mystery in *Anandabazar Patrika*. Bhagwanji asked Pabitra to consult the articles written in the *Hindustan Standard* by Sinha which apparently claimed that he had seen the logbook himself in Taiwan (Sinha's book *Netaji Mystery* which was a compilation of his series of articles contains no such claim). Later on, Bhagwanji would egg on his Calcutta disciples to discretely talk to Sinha and impress upon him that it would be a great loss of face if he could not produce the concrete evidence of the claims made in his book. Barun Sengupta is an 'adept' journalist, Bhagwanji observed. He was impressed with the way Sengupta was pointing out the loopholes in the functioning of the Khosla Commission. 'It appears from his articles that he has an investigative mind and wants to reach the bottom of the problem,' Bhagwanji wrote to Pabitra. Bhagwanji was aware of Sunil Gupta's close connection with Sengupta. 'Does he have similar views like you?' he asked, and suggested that both Gupta and Pabitra should meet him privately to get insights from him on points that could be used to build pressure on and influence the commission. The suggestion, however, came with the strict note of caution that under no circumstances would they divulge his presence within India, or that they 'know the real secret'. They were free to tell Sengupta that he was alive, but outside India, something that Subhas Bose's nephew Dwijen would say in his deposition before the commission. 'Be very careful! Never allow yourself to be off guard at any moment. You cannot be frivolous about someone's life,' was his warning.

After his return from Taiwan in 1973, Sunil Krishna Gupta met Bhagwanji in Basti to share his experience in detail. Discussions went on from 8pm to 2am on the night of 27-28 August and from 8pm to 1am on the night of 28-29 August. The briefing was followed by planning for the argument sessions of the Khosla Commission which were to commence from the second week of September. Gupta noted down the crux of Bhagwanji's instructions in his diary:

> After detailed discussion on Formosa [Taiwan], [he] gave extensive instructions on which points needed to be established before the Commission. He said, the first thing to be established is that no plane crash took place on that day at that location. Even if there was a crash, Netaji was not in the plane. Next, the statements of various witnesses must be analysed to demonstrate that a number of people saw him alive at different places even after the so-called plane crash.

As the argument session of the Commission was about to begin in September 1973, Gupta informed Bhagwanji that a former member of the legislative assembly from Dhaka had written to the commission and asked whether they should refer to that letter during the arguments.[21] Not having any idea about the contents of the letter from Dhaka, Bhagwanji asked Pabitra to inform him in detail, but as a matter of general principle, he had no problem as long as the letter did not compromise his 'safety and security' by divulging his location and activities.

From September 1973 to June 1974, when the Khosla Commission report was submitted, there is a gap in availability of information. Although no direct documentary material is available on his observations, what Charanik has written in *Oi Mahamanaba Ase* (OMA) is in line with what Bhagwanji wrote to Pabitra. According to Charanik, Bhagwanji had predicted unambiguously what would be the verdict of the Commission: 'His (G D Khosla's) hand is the hand of the Head of the country; his fingers are the fingers of the Head. Therefore, the judge is holding the pen of the Head. That is, this is a command performance.'

In another undated letter to Shiva Prosad Nag which was recovered from Ram Bhawan, Bhagwanji wrote:

কিন্তু অদ্ভুত, অতি অদ্ভুত, তোমরা এবং তোমাদের গভর্নমেন্ট: যে ব্যক্তি 'সর্বস্বীকার্য রূপে প্রমাণিত ভাবে মরে গেছেই, সেই নিশ্চিত মৃতকে, মরেছে কি না মরেছে জানিবার তরে 'লোডেড ডাইস কমীশন' বসাও বারে বারে? ক্যানো?! তোমরা সবাই হচ্ছো এর কারণ: 'POPULUS VULT DECIPI' It is strange, very strange, that you and your government repeatedly set up loaded dice

---

21   We are not in a position to verify this because most of the documents, etc. exhibited by Khosla Commission have vanished and only about 91 were made available to the Mukherjee Commission and subsequently the authors, who sought them under the Right to Information. The more sensitive ones were reported 'unavailable' by the Government.

commission in order to find out whether the man who has been proven by all to be dead, is really dead or not. Why? You all are the reason. *Populus vult decipi* (people wish to be deceived). [Translated from Bengali]

As it happened, Khosla submitted his report-cum-political testament against Subhas Bose in June 1974. In it, Subhas Bose was depicted as a 'puppet' of the Japanese. Almost simultaneously, Khosla released a hagiographical biography of Prime Minister Indira Gandhi, and a book on Bose's fate based on his report and experiences as chairman of the commission. Its very title revealed Khosla's gut feelings as to where he placed Bose in history. *Last days of Netaji* was clearly paraphrased on Hugh Trevor-Roper's *The last days of Hitler.*

The crux of the story that can be filtered from all of Bhagwanji's stories, snippets and claims is that Subhas Bose managed to hoodwink the Allied Forces, as well as many Japanese and Indians, into thinking that his plane went to Taiwan, whereas he really broke journey in Saigon.

After the 'plane crash'

The most popular narrative about Subhas Bose's escape from the South-East Asian war theatre in August 1945 has invariably remained focussed on his arrival in the Russian-controlled territory. The debate thereafter has primarily revolved around whether he emerged from the Soviet land alive or was eliminated there. If clues provided by Bhagwanji are true, then this narrative has all along missed an important element in the chain of events.

Bhagwanji indicated to Bijoy Nag that sometime after his

'death', he was hosted by a powerful political personality.[22] A couple of papers with random jottings recovered from Bhagwanji's room in Faizabad in 1986 might be pointing towards another secret move. It is difficult to say with certainty, but from writing patterns they do look like Bhagwanji's handwriting. Scribbled on the papers are:

> *1945 Hanoi Anami Government*
> *2.9.45 Hanoi*
> *Japanese surrender 4 days [illegible]*
> *Liu Pocheng (Mr X)*
> *Anami Government later became Ho Chi Minh's North Vietnam Government Mr Alfred Wagg, an officer of the American Military Intelligence, knows this He informed his own Government*
> *1945 October*
> *General's guest in South China*
> *Contact with Anami Government*

Alfred Wagg, then associated with the *Chicago Tribune*, had caused a flutter on 29 August 1945 when he dramatically interrupted a press meet of Jawaharlal Nehru to claim that he had seen Bose near Saigon (now Ho Chi Minh City) a few days after the reported death. On 1 September, London's *Sunday Observer* picked up Wagg's claim and added that the Japanese report was 'not believed in British and American military circles'. Wagg went on to repeat his claim in private talks with many top Indian leaders, Gandhi downwards. On 25 September 1946, the *Indian*

---

22   Charanik, *Oi Mahamanaba Ase*, Jayasree Prakashan, 2010, p 315.

Daily Mail (published from Singapore) quoted Wagg as saying that Bose is 'still alive and is expected to reappear on the political scene at the psychological moment'.

'Liu Pocheng', rather Liu Bocheng, a well-known Chinese marshal does fleetingly figure in the annals of the Bose mystery. A booklet titled *Liu Po-Cheng or Netaji?* was published in 1956 by Shiva Prosad Nag. A school headmaster, editor of a newspaper and Bose admirer, Nag made a most farcical claim that Bose was living in China in the guise of Bocheng. Bhagwanji appeared to have denied this in a letter to Pabitra even though he maintained a contact with Nag subsequently. His booklet contains no credible information and more or less falls in the same league as another and slightly better known booklet titled *Netaji Mystery Revealed* (1954). Its writer S M Goswami, a former government officer, didn't seem reliable either, going by his unsubstantiated volley of claims. He reproduced some poor quality pictures purporting to show 'Bose' in China in the early 1950s. One of them turned out to be of Lee Ke Hung, superintendent of the Peking University Medical College, as per the information supplied by the foreign ministry of China to India.

However, a fascinating lead about Subhas Bose's presence in Vietnam soon after his reported death was unearthed by Adheer Som, author of *Gumnami Baba: A case history* in December 2016. On Som's request, eminent historian and Vietnam expert Prof Christopher Goscha shared his note on a French report on Japan's war-time South-east Asian Special Services, based on Japanese sources. According to the report, 'Chandra Bose was reported to be present at the end of November at a conference in

Hanoi where six nations were represented. Chandra Bose would have since left for Russia via Yunnan. The Russian government would have taken charge of him from the frontier (onwards).'[23] In July 2017, this received a boost from Paris-based historian, Jean-Baptiste Prashant More, who, as widely reported in the Indian press, stumbled upon a French intelligence report at the National Archives of France stating that 'Bose's present whereabouts were unknown as late as December 1947', implying that rather than accepting the story of his 'death' propagated by the Japanese, the French were still looking for Bose. The French report, according to More, was written for the 'Haut Commisariat de France for Indochina' under the title: 'Archival Information on Subhas Chandra Bose.' French Indochina corresponds to today's Vietnam, Cambodia and Laos. More told *The Times of India* that the report read that Bose 'escaped from Indochina, though it does not state how'.[24]

'Captive' in Russia?

Of all the claims that have been made about Subhas Bose's presence in Soviet Russia after his reported death, the closest to a direct evidence was rendered by a former chief engineer with the Heavy Engineering Corporation (HEC Ltd). A postgraduate in mechanical engineering from the UK, Ardhendu Sarkar, for good

---

23 Pravin Kumar, 'French file: Netaji was in Hanoi in November 1945,' *The Times of India* (Lucknow edition), 21 December 2016.

24 M T Saju, 'Netaji didn't die in air crash, says secret French report, *The Times of India*, 16 July 2017.

measure, testified on oath before the Mukherjee Commission. Later, in his plush, high-rise apartment home in Kolkata, he would unassumingly recall his experience to Anuj Dhar. This happened in the early 1960s at Gorlovka machine building plant, near Donetesk in Ukraine, then part of Soviet Russia. Sarkar's superior officer at the plant, B A Zerovin, became friendly towards him after he learned that he hailed from Bengal. In a moment of camaraderie, Zerovin let it slip that Zerovin was not his real name. He was actually a German Jew who had been brought to the USSR after the Second World War, sent to a Siberian gulag for indoctrination, given a new identity and was married to a Russian. Then to Sarkar's horror, he said that he had met Subhas Bose in Berlin, and 'again in 1948' in a gulag somewhere beyond the end of Trans-Siberian Railways in the vicinity of the Ural Mountains. He said that Bose was apparently being treated fine, given a car and was moving around with two guards. In their short exchange, Bose told Zerovin that he expected to go back to India soon.

Soviet Russia, Siberia, gulags and Russian leaders figured heavily in Bhagwanji's talks with his close followers and also in his letters and their notes. He said he spent quite some time in a gulag in south central Siberia, somewhere in the vicinity of Lake Baikal and the Ural Mountains. 'Stalin did not treat me like an enemy, my own people did,' he said during a conversation with Sunil Gupta.

If only hints are given by Bhagwanji on Bose's stay in Vietnam till September 1945, his discussions and writings on Bose's presence in the Soviet territory are comparatively much more forthcoming and definitive. The overall narrative again topples the theory in currency since many decades—that Bose was imprisoned in the USSR and probably was assassinated or simply died there.

According to Bhagwanji, he was not only present in the erstwhile USSR, but his presence was coveted by their top leadership. Soon, he was put in touch with the Chinese by the Russians. Moreover, he claimed to have operating bases somewhere in the Central Asian region where he frequently travelled to. The initial days, he indicated, were not easy. 'Of course they didn't treat me like a son-in-law,' he later revealed to Pabitra.[25]

However, not before long, he was 'absolutely and entirely free and independent' in his sphere of activities over 'far flung regions (territories) the major portion of which do not come either in Russia or China'. This area, he claimed 'has been notified as prohibited region under international laws'. There was an 'extremely important & vital secret base there', where even Russian 'aircrafts do not fly over'.

Interestingly, Bhagwanji indicated how the story of his imprisonment in Siberia gained currency in India. In summary, he claimed that he was part of a secret mega-project undertaken by Russia in a huge uninhabited area of Siberia, along with other 'experts'. Large-scale machinery was set up for the project and the area was declared out of bounds for even government officials. Arrangements were made for accommodation of the heads of the several divisions of the project, and for him too. Bhagwanji

25   Interview with Ranendra Mohan Roy by authors, Kolkata, 2016.

claimed that he was accompanied by several men from the Azad Hind government.[26] This news somehow reached the Indian ambassador Vijaya Lakshmi Pandit (India's first ambassador to Russia, 1947-49), who went there. Bhagwanji also mentioned that K P S Menon (Ambassador from 1952 to 1961) too heard about him and asked the Soviets for permission to visit the area, but probably was denied permission. Menon, according to him, heard it through the grapevine that 'he' had many scientists from many countries including India working under him, and came to know about his men from the Azad Hind government too.

If this sketchy narrative is true, then Bose was in Russia for a few years after Independence. Bhagwanji mentioned that he was grateful to Pandit and Menon, although he didn't elucidate any further. In a reference to Menon, who was junior to Bose by a year when studying in the UK (Bose was in Cambridge while Menon was in Oxford), Bhagwanji mentioned that he had done a favour to Menon as a student, which Menon returned.[27] Regarding Vijaya Lakshmi, Nehru's talented younger sister and free India's first representative to the USSR, a conspiracy theory

26   In April 1946, intelligence officers probing the death of Subhas Bose sat down in New Delhi to ponder over intelligence pooled in from multiple sources. Helping the discussion was a three-page note, whose copy is available. Inter alia, the note referred to a claim by Russian Vice Consul-General in Tehran that 'Bose was in Russia where he was secretly organising a group of Russians and Indians to work on the same lines as the INA for the freedom of India'. Copy of note numbered C-4, Part IV, dated 8 April 1946. File no INA 273, National Archives, New Delhi.
27   Various letters from Bhagwanji to Pabitra Mohan Roy, note of conversations with Bhagwanji by Surajit Dasgupta, October 1982.

goes that after her return from Moscow, she made a statement that she had 'some information which if disclosed would electrify India and the resultant happiness would be greater than what the people had experienced on 15 August 1947'. Rai Singh Yadav, a former Director of the erstwhile Information Service of India of the Ministry of External Affairs, told Anuj Dhar that he had once asked Ambassador Pandit about this 'important statement of hers' but she sidestepped the issue. She also sent an affidavit to the Khosla Commission stating that 'she had never met Netaji Subhas Chandra Bose in any connection after he left India'.[28]

Bhagwanji explained that as news of his presence in the Siberian project leaked out and spread through rumours, people assumed, because of the place's notoriety for hard labour camps, that if he was in Siberia, he must have been a prisoner. However, he pointed out, that not many know that there are many civilian cities, towns and villages in Siberia. About Siberians, he commented that they are the tallest among the Russians—and the most innocent too. Many years later, when a newspaper clipping of a letter to the editor of the *Hindustan Standard* of 15 July 1965 citing Netaji's last known speeches to demonstrate his inclination towards the Soviet Union, arising from the growing conflicts between them and the US and UK, and hypothesing about his subsequent seeking of help from them was shown to Bhagwanji, he appreciated the comments of the writer. 'It must be admitted that the writer has

---

28   Report of the One-Man Commission of Inquiry into the Disappearance of Netaji Subhas Chandra Bose, 1974, p 48.

sharp observation power within his limited sphere,' he scribbled on the margins. But when the writer concluded that 'Whatever is the truth, this much is certain that nothing definite will be known about the fate of Netaji who might still be breathing somewhere in the Siberian wastes at this very moment, unless someone in the External Affairs Ministry in Delhi or at the Kremlin speaks out,' Bhagwanji acerbically commented, 'Oh wishful sentiments! Who do you have to speak out?'

While no reference about the possibility of Bose's presence in Siberia is to be found in the Nehru era files declassified by the Indian government, a CIA report accessed by the authors under the Freedom of Information Act does show that as late as 1950, rumours that Bose was in Siberia and waiting to make a comeback were floating in New Delhi circles. Indian intelligence files, provided they were not destroyed like some other Bose-related papers, are likely to contain relevant information, but have been kept out of the purview of the declassification drive undertaken by the Modi government.

To his followers, Bhagwanji described in detail the layout of the Siberian prison camps which indicate his intimate knowledge of the area. This was before Aleksandr Solzhenitsyn's classic *The Gulag Archipelago* provided a ringside view for the first time.

Concentration camps of central Siberia contain male and female labourers, farmers, craftsmen, authors, scientists and teachers—from 5 to 25 thousand in each. Not one or two, there are almost 49 concentration camps. They are manufacturing ultra-modern goods for daily use. These are transported to the retail outlets in the main cities. Those who buy those products do not know that they may have been manufactured by their parents, brothers, sisters or other kin. If you came to know what goes on there you would run for your life. Driven by hunger people have gone to the extent of eating their own flesh. A new camp was being constructed, so the soldiers took 10,000 prisoners with them. But there was no hut there. Their duty was to install pillars by digging 12 feet holes in the ice to surround themselves. "Keep your back hot by heavy work"—anyone who does not follow this will freeze and die.[29] [Translated from Bengali]

Decoding Bhagwanji's coded letters to Pabitra, a hazy storyline of how he gained influence in the Soviet land emerges. From Stalin's days, Russia had been trying to do something in that area in absolute secrecy against China, in a way that no one would suspect its involvement, but had failed repeatedly despite its power and resources. Thereafter, when Bhagwanji arrived, he took over and helped the Russians succeed. The area of operation was vast and inhabited by five or six different races. This success triggered some sort of upheaval, twice, in quick succession, and helped Bhagwanji establish himself at the high tables in Moscow; it led to the Russians holding him in high esteem, which gradually turned into 'affectionate love'. Russia was extremely grateful to him for the things he had done for them, he claimed. A sort of non-aggression and non-interference deal was struck: that Bhagwanji would not act against Russia and the Russians would give him a free hand in his 'mission'.

---

29   Charanik, *Oi Mahamanaba Ase*, Jayasree Prakashan, 2010, pp 92-93.

No way to return

When he left Soviet Russia around 1949 at the close of the war crimes trials, Bhagwanji did not have an immediate plan to return to India, because he felt—or was given this impression—that India was still not a free country. That under some secret pact the colonial rulers had with the Indian leaders at the time of the Transfer of Power in 1947, he was to be tried and handed over to the Anglo-Americans as a 'war criminal'. For such a sordid state of affairs, he blamed Nehru, chiefly. 'He shall always rave, spew and curse the English for hours and hours—but shall always act just the opposite.'

The authors have suffered the mortification of outlining the revolting charges Bhagwanji levelled against India's first prime minister for the sake of bringing about a closure to the entire matter. 'Truth will out,' goes the old English proverb. We deem it our duty to furnish all the available details relevant to the subject matter that we have researched with the sole purpose of arriving at the truth—whatever it is. So, Bhagwanji alleged that Pandit Nehru (referred to by him as 'JN') was a 'compromised' man by the time he was released from Ahmednagar Fort prison on 15 June 1945. 'JN and his men knew the fact that he was released and fully backed up by USA+UK.' In a soliloquy, he added: 'Only because of you'. (By 'you' he meant himself.) 'Because they know and know fully well that, you shall never-never compromise and Gandhi+Patel+JN+others have always compromised.' In a letter to Pabitra, he posed: 'Shall your Mother Bengal, Janani Janambhoomi's 'S_' ever be USA-UK-JN's? Can he? Can you... even think 'S_' is capable of being such a turncoat? Has he come down on this earth of Mother Bengal to be this? Has he sacrificed his whole life to this end?'

'S_' was Bhagwanji's way of writing 'Subhas'.

From Bhagwanji's point of view, Nehru frittered away India's interests by making her part of the British Commonwealth of Nations after independence. Worse, he implied that India's long-term strategic interests were made subservient to those of the world powers, and that if it were not for what he [Bhagwanji] did post-1947, India would turn into a battleground for the cold war.

> JN has played his treacherous game (of Mir Jafar, Jaychand, Vibhishan) with the people of India in such a manner and has manipulated the whole thing in such a way that any miscalculated step by them might make simple and innocent India and her people victims of the most horrible and undesirably hellish (game of) war! That is the crux of all.

In 2006, Narendra Singh Sarila, who was aide-de-camp to Lord Mountbatten at the time of the Partition and later served as India's ambassador to different countries, came out with a shocking inside account. Relying on his first-hand understanding of the events and declassified records in the UK and the US, Sarila in his book *The Shadow of the Great Game: The Untold Story of India*[30] revealed that Britain had insisted on the partition of India, mainly because of its fears over Soviet expansion into the region. 'This story has been told as a tale of heroes (Nehru and Gandhi)

---

30   Narendra Singh Sarila, *The Shadow of the Great Game: The Untold Story of India's Partition*, HarperCollins Publishers India, 2005.

and villains (Jinnah and Churchill), but Sarila presents it as a series of blunders by Nehru and the Congress Party,' wrote British author Jad Adams in his review of the book in *The Telegraph*.[31] Sarila charged Congress leaders with 'arrogance', 'inconsistency', 'poor political judgement' and a fatal lack of interest in foreign affairs and defence.

Bhagwanji even claimed that as and when all the documents concerning the Transfer of Power in 1947 are made public, Indians would know why he had to go into hiding. While most Transfer of Power records are now in public domain and they do throw some light on Subhas's fate—that he might have not perished in Taiwan and was probably in Soviet Russia—there are some more records that are still being held classified by the British government. Whether or not those still secret records are about Bose we cannot tell. In December 2012, the Foreign and Commonwealth Office (FCO) in London turned down a Freedom of Information Act request filed by Chandrachur Ghose to disclose one file it was holding. The FCO said the file 'remains sensitive' and 'its release could compromise our relations with the countries concerned'. In May 2013, the Ministry of External Affairs in New Delhi revealed, in response to a Right to Information request filed by well-known RTI activist S C Agrawal, that the historic records relating to India's joining the Commonwealth of Nations in 1949 were, quite unbelievably, untraceable. Efforts were made

---

31   Jad Adams, 'The ill-fated battle for Indian independence,' *The Telegraph*, 28 August 2006. Accessed from: https://www.telegraph.co.uk/culture/books/4201192/The-ill-fated-battle-for-Indian-independence.html.

to locate in the UNP Division and Europe West Division—the two divisions which have dealt with Commonwealth Affairs—correspondence, file notings and documents dating back to India joining the Commonwealth in 1949, the MEA said. Sanjay Rana, Director of UNP, replied that:

> Enquiries were also made with the High Commission of India in London to locate the relevant records and documents. However, these efforts did not yield the correspondence/ file-notings/documents, etc. dating back to India joining the Commonwealth in 1949 as sought by the applicant. Further, no information was found as to where such records/documents might be located.[32]

Some valuable insight is nevertheless available. Legendary T N Kaul, former Ambassador to the USSR, the US and Foreign Secretary, wrote in his memoirs that even after independence Russians 'still looked upon India as a colony of Britain' and 'could not understand why we still wanted to remain in the Commonwealth when we had suffered so much at the hands of British imperialism'.[33] Strong words from a man the *India Today* described in the review of his book *Reminiscences, Discreet and Indiscreet* as 'a self-confessed unrepentant Nehruphile'. According to the MEA's declassified record of the conversation between Joseph Stalin and Sarvepalli Radhakrishnan, then Indian Ambassador

---

32   'Mystery in history: What forced Nehru to remain under Queen's umbrella even after independence?' *India Today*, 5 May 2013, accessed from: https://www. indiatoday.in/india/story/india-clueless-about-circumstances-which-forced-it-to-join-commonwealth-after-independence-161844-2013-05-05.

33   T N Kaul, *Reminiscences discreet and indiscreet*, Lancer publishers, 1982, p 150.

in Moscow, on 15 January 1950, 'Stalin asked several questions regarding India's position in Commonwealth and seemed anxious to know if she was more or less independent than, say, Canada'.[34] Russian journalist Valeriy Kashin recapitulated in an article in *Russia Beyond the Headlines* in 2012, that the transfer of power in India in 1947 was nothing more than a 'political farce' for the Soviet Union. 'Out of 19 English major generals, 16 remained in India, and out of 280 brigadier generals, 260 would remain in support of the idea that India retained military and political allegiance with its former mother country.'[35]

Viewed from this perspective, when it had come to the crunch, all vows of attaining *Purna Swaraj* (complete independence)—something that Mahatma Gandhi was never in favour of—were discarded by the Indian leadership of the day. 'They got Independence in a begging bowl,' was Bhagwanji's pet peeve. Subhas Bose never wanted India to remain in the Commonwealth. In 2012, British historian Perry Anderson observed:

> There was no overthrow of the Raj, but a transfer of power by it to Congress as its successor. The colonial bureaucracy and army were left intact, minus the colonisers. In the mid-1930s, Nehru, denouncing the Indian Civil Service as 'neither Indian

34 'Record of the Conversation between IV Stalin and Sarvepalli Radhakrishnan,' 15 January 1950, History and Public Policy Program Digital Archive, NMML, JN (S 4) Vol No 34, 286-287.
Available on Revolutionary Democracy website on 11 December 2010.
http://digitalarchive.wilsoncenter.org/document/119261.
35 Valeriy Kashin, 'What Stalin thought of Gandhi and Nehru,' 3 May 2012, Russia and Beyond, accessed from: https://www.rbth.com/articles/2012/05/03/what_stalin_thought_of_gandhi_and_nehru_15660.

nor civil nor a service', declared it 'essential that the ICS and similar services disappear completely'. By 1947, pledges like these had faded away as completely as his promises that India would never become a dominion. The steel frame of the ICS remained in place, untouched.[36]

Winston Churchill, the most anti-Indian among the colonial British, gave his thumbs up to the Transfer of Power in 1947 only after being convinced by Lord Mountbatten. Thereafter, on 21 May 1947, Churchill wrote to Prime Minister Attlee that if 'there is an effective acceptance of Dominion status for the several parts of a divided India, the Conservative Party will agree to facilitate the passage of this session of the legislation necessary to confer Dominion status upon such several parts of India'.[37]

On 4 July, Attlee wrote back to clarify the meaning of Dominion Status:

Dominion Prime Ministers constantly stress the point that they are independent States within the British Commonwealth. They bear allegiance to The King who is The King of all the Dominions. The insistence on independence does not touch the point of allegiance, but emphasizes the complete freedom of every member of the Commonwealth from control by any other member. I think this is a most valuable counter to the demand for independence outside the Commonwealth as it shows that this demand can be satisfied within it. This is, in fact, the meaning of Dominion Status.[38]

---

36   Perry Anderson, *The Indian Ideology*, Verso; Reprint edition (5 November 2013), p 105.
37   PREM 8/565, The National Archives, London.
38   CHUR 2/43 B, The Sir Winston Churchill Archives Trust.

Kunwar Natwar Singh, arguably the greatest Nehruphile of our times, was compelled to admit in an op-ed article in *The Hindu* on 14 November 2008 that 'Nehru throughout the freedom movement was vigorously opposed to independent India having anything to do with the British Commonwealth' and that 'there is little doubt that the Mountbattens talked him into changing his mind'.[39] A slightly different light was thrown upon this by Alex von Tunzelmann, the author of *Indian Summer: The Secret History of the End of an Empire*: 'When all others had failed, Edwina persuaded Nehru in May 1947 to accept a period of dominion status for India rather than to hold out for full independence....' Lord Mountbatten even wanted the Union Jack on the upper canton of the Indian Tricolour—a proposition that Gandhi and other Congress leaders supported to the hilt. Gandhi actually took a swipe against those who were opposed to it. 'But what is wrong with having the Union Jack in a corner of our flag? If harm has been done to us by the British, it has not been done by their flag and we must also take note of the virtues of the British. They are voluntarily withdrawing from India, leaving power in our hands,' he said at his Prayer Meeting of 19 July 1947.[40]

Bhagwanji, reflecting disapprovingly in 1963, stated that 'it is death to compromise on principles'.

---

39   K Natwar Singh, 'Nehru & the Mountbattens,' *The Hindu*, 14 November 2008.
40   Alex von Tunzelmann, 'An affair to remember,' *The Los Angeles Times*, 23 September 2007.

In the early 1970s, Mountbatten described to writers Larry Collins and Dominque Lapierre how he had ensured that India remained a part of the Commonwealth even after the Transfer of Power. 'They would keep the same uniform [in the armed forces], merely putting the three lions on their shoulder instead of the actual crown...they would keep the white ensign with the red cross of St George, just as in the Navy.... They must owe some common allegiance to the King....'[41]

And allegiance to the King of India did pay beyond 'independence'. On 15 August 1947, President of the Constituent Assembly Rajendra Prasad requested Mountbatten to convey to the British monarch 'a message of loyal greetings from this House'. That message will serve as an inspiration in the great work on which we launch today, he added. 'I hope and trust that the interest and the sympathy and the kindness which have always inspired His Majesty will continue in favour of India and we shall be worthy of them.'

George VI signed the letters of credence and appointment of Indian ambassadors after August 1947. Even Natwar Singh saw too much of 'Raj phraseology' in Nehru–George VI correspondence. All of this is so much against the impression given in India years after Independence, depicting Congress leaders as non-compromising fighters taking on the evil British empire with the force of *ahimsa*.

---

41   Larry Collins and Dominque Lapierre, *Mountbatten and the Partition of India*, Vikas Publishing House, 1982, p 54.

PRIME MINISTER,
INDIA.

New Delhi,
28th April 1948.

JAWAHARLAL NEHRU presents his humble duty
to Your Majesty and has the honour to submit, for
Your Majesty's approval, the proposal of Your
Majesty's Ministers in the Dominion of India that
Sri Chakravarty Rajagopalachari, Governor of West
Bengal, be appointed to be the Governor General of
India on the demission of that Office by His Excellency
Rear Admiral the Earl Mountbatten of Burma, K.G.,
P.C., G.M.I.E., G.C.V.O., K.C.B., D.S.O.

Jawaharlal Nehru

PRIME MINISTER
OF THE DOMINION OF INDIA.

'Free' India remained a no-go area for the Dead Ghost. The chiefs of the Indian Air Force and the Navy were still British, and many of their Indian subordinates were more British than them. Indians did not head the Indian Army, Air Force and Navy until 1949, 1955 and 1958. 'The first Commander-in-Chief of the Indian Navy [after India became a republic in 1950] was Adm Sir Edward Parry, KCB, who handed over to Adm Sir Mark Pizey, KBE, CB, DSO in 1951. Adm Pizey also became the first Chief of the Naval Staff in 1955, and was succeeded by V Adm S H Carlill, CB, DSO,' reads a little-known fact on the official website of the Indian Navy. It was only in 1958 that an Indian—V

Adm R D Katari—became the Chief of Naval Staff.[42]

[President Rajendra Prasad with the services chiefs, two of them British, in 1953. Image taken from http://rashtrapatisachivalaya.gov.in/]

In March 1948, Prime Minister Nehru told Parliament that the INA men would have no place in the Indian Army. 'To reinstate them would lead to many complications, both practical and psychological, and the unity of the Army might be affected,' *The Times* of London reported him as announcing.[43] In 1949, the Army Headquarters (HQ) is alleged to have issued a circular against displaying the picture of Subhas Bose 'at permanent places, in canteens, quarters, etc.' The same HQ continued to insist for

42   Genesis of the Indian Navy, Official website of the Indian Navy, https://www. indiannavy.nic.in/node/1410.

43   'Indian National Army: Long controversy ended,' *The Times*, 30 March 1948.

decades that an official history of the INA commissioned by the army should not be published, as doing so would affect the 'morale of the soldiers'.[44]

[The Straits Times]

Such were the state of affairs that India's national security structure did not undergo any change after the British left. 'The framework Lord Ismay formulated and Lord Mountbatten recommended was accepted by a national leadership unfamiliar with the intricacies of national security management. There has been very little change over the past 52 years,' the Kargil Review Committee report of 1999 flatly accepted. In the wake of the disastrous war with China in 1962, India was compelled

---

44   Excerpted from the record of Dr R C Majumdar's deposition before the Khosla Commission on 5 December 1972.

to overhaul her military. Consequently, Mountbatten and top British commanders visited India in May 1963 at Nehru's invitation. In the intelligence arena, British suzerainty continued till the late 1960s, if not beyond. The MI5 itself made this known to the entire world a few years ago, even as the nation which propagates the ideals of truth and ahimsa (non-violence) to the world continues to resort to great secrecy. The British intelligence agency's official website informs us:

> Indian independence in 1947 set an important precedent for the rest of British decolonisation. **The government of Jawaharlal Nehru agreed to the stationing of an MI5 Security Liaison Officer (SLO) in New Delhi after the end of British rule.** For almost a quarter of a century, relations between MI5 and its Indian counterpart, the Delhi Intelligence Branch (DIB), were closer and more confident than those between any other departments of the British and Indian governments. In other newly independent Commonwealth countries, as in India, **the continued presence of an SLO became a significant, though usually undisclosed, part of the transfer of power.**[45] [Emphasis by authors]

Writing in *The Times of India* on 12 April 2015, in the wake of the Bose snooping scandal, a former Special Secretary of R&AW agreed: 'An unwritten agreement during the Transfer of Power in 1947 was the secret positioning of a security liaison officer (SLO) in New Delhi as MI5's representative,' wrote V Balachandran. By

---

45   Christopher Andrew, 'The British empire and Commonwealth,' accessed from: https://www.mi5.gov.uk/the-british-empire-and-commonwealth.

this time, startling details had appeared in the authorised history of MI5 by Prof Christopher Andrew, which revealed on the basis of the official records that in March 1947 deputy head of MI5 Guy Liddell obtained the agreement of the Nehru government for the stationing of the SLO. The first SLO was Lieutenant Colonel Kenneth Bourne, who was supplied with information pertaining to Bose by the Intelligence Bureau.[46]

[The *Mail Today* on 12 April 2015]

According to Balachandran and Prof Andrew, IB played second fiddle to MI5 post-1947 with great enthusiasm— and with great pleasure, as it used to in the good old days of the Raj. Former IB and police officers of the Raj era were made SLOs. All the Indian IB chiefs, beginning with Sanjeevi Pillai, made their obeisance to the MI5 bosses in London. Details given in *The Defence of the Realm* prove that the DIBs had opened their hearts

---

46   Christopher Andrew, *The Defence of the Realm: The Authorized History of MI5*, Penguin Books, 2010, pp 442-444.

and archives to MI5. Walter Bell, the SLO in 1952, described IB boss B N Mullik as 'the fount of all knowledge that I wanted'. Following a request by Mullik, an MI5 officer was sent to India in 1957 so that IB's counter-intelligence operations against the Soviet Union could be improved upon. Humbled by the 'help' the IB had received from MI5, Mullik told his counterpart Roger Hollis that he never felt that he was 'dealing with any organisation which was not my own'. When the last SLO left India in the late 1960s, 'they did so not at India's behest, but as consequence of swinging cuts forced on the Security Service [MI5]', wrote domain expert Paul McGarr in the *Journal of Imperial and Commonwealth History* in 2010.[47] The then IB Director, S P Verma, wrote to his counterpart in London that he didn't know 'how he'd manage without a British SLO,' added Balachandran in his *Times* article.[48]

If all this could have been kept secret for so long (India is officially completely silent till date), what if there is more to it? What if there were other secret, unwritten, undisclosed agreements as power was transferred to those Indians who were amenable to the British proposals? In our endeavour to get to the bottom, we filed an RTI application with the Prime Minister's Office. Usually, RTI applications filed with the Government are poorly drafted. They are often whimsical, containing little or no contextual background, which might make the job of government officials

---

47   Paul M McGarr, 'A Serious Menace to Security: British Intelligence, VK Krishna Menon and the Indian High Commission in London, 1947–52,' *The Journal of Imperial and Commonwealth History*, 9 August 2010.

48   V Balachandran, 'IB played junior partner to MI5 well after 1947,' *The Times of India*, 12 April 2015.

difficult as they undertake search for relevant information among heaps of files. To avoid the problem of lack of clarity emanating from such missing context, the following application was sent by Chandrachur Ghose:

> As has been recorded in history, on 20 February 1947, His Majesty's Government in London announced their intention of transferring power to Indian hands by June 1948. It is also a matter of common knowledge that the working committee of the Congress met on 3 June 1947 and approved the plan for the transfer of power in India. On the same day, Lord Mountbatten made an announcement to the same effect. While many books, compilations of official documents discuss the process, discuss the relevant events, no proper documentation regarding the actual Transfer of Power agreement is to be found anywhere to best of my knowledge. It is only recently that a fresh clue regarding its existence was revealed by the MI5, the British intelligence. Please see this link from the official MI5 site: https://www.mi5.gov.uk/the-british-empire-and-commonwealth. Also attached are relevant pages from the authorised history of MI5.
>
> The MI5 informs us that the government of Jawaharlal Nehru agreed to the stationing of an MI5 Security Liaison Officer (SLO) in New Delhi after the end of British rule and that the continued presence of an SLO became a significant, though usually undisclosed, part of the transfer of power. As such, I request you to provide the following documents/information:
>
> 1. Was any agreement signed between the British and the Indian governments (or Indian leaders and representatives) to give effect to the Indian Independence Act and any other associated legislation, or to create a framework for the transfer of power. If yes, please provide the copy of such agreement/s or plan/s which formalized the passing of

power to the Indians. Please make sure the copy provided to me is in full and contains all terms, points, conditions, etc. (including the undisclosed ones) agreed upon by those who signed/executed this agreement/plan. If the copy of such a Transfer of Power agreement or plan is not available with the Government of India, especially the PMO, kindly state that clearly.

2. Provide names of all those who signed/executed/ratified the Transfer of Power Agreement/Plan (or by whatever nomenclature it is known in the official files).

3. Information whether any files or documents concerning the transfer of power or the transfer of power agreement are still kept secret by the Government of India, including the PMO. If yes, a descriptive list of such records, files available with the Government.

4. Please specify under which law, rule or executive order a Security Liaison Officer (SLO) of British intelligence (MI5), usually a Raj era intelligence officer, was allowed to function in India for two decades after Independence. Please provide a copy of the relevant Act, Rule or Order.

The application evidently ruffled some feathers in the PMO. Rather than appreciating that the application was submitted with proper research and diligence, the PMO ticked us off for making a 'sweeping, generic and vague' request which 'does not highlight specific information' sought from the Government.

Sir,
    Reference is invited to your application (51446) dated 18.4.2017, on the subject mentioned above. It is informed in respect of this office that your request is sweeping, generic and vague in nature. It does not highlight specific information, you intend to seek from this office. However, your application also stands transferred online to M/o Home Affairs. You may approach the transferee public authority for information, if any.

2.   For the purpose of Section 19 of the Right to Information Act, 2005, Shri Syed Ekram Rizwi, Director, Prime Minister's Office, South Block, New Delhi (Tel No: 011 – 2307 4072, E-mail ID: rti.appeal@gov.in) is the appellate authority in respect of this office.

                                        Yours faithfully,

                                        (Parveen Kumar)
                                        Under Secretary and
                                        Central Public Information Officer

From Russia to China and Tibet

Not approving the state of affairs in India in the late 1940s, Bhagwanji, rather than return home, went over to China on a covert mission to help his Soviet benefactors in return for their generosity in giving him shelter. The Russians, he claimed, held him in 'awed esteem'. The Chinese contacted him mostly through Russia, but at times unilaterally. Why and how he became associated with the Chinese he never described, but had high praise for them.

> China is a past master in war strategy, craftiness, war diplomacy, statecraft, all sorts of war and their execution, most shrewd calculations, etc. They have been so for thousands of years. Their becoming communist does not mean that they have lost their heritage.

China considered him their equal in these qualities, Bhagwanji told Pabitra. They knew that he was capable of tilting the balance either way in their tussle with Russia, and they 'fervently' wished that he tilted the balance their way, 'though temporarily living with Russia'. Going by his claims, Bhagwanji's movements were not restricted to Russia and China alone. As discussed above, he endorsed the claim of Deven Sen that he and K N Joglekar saw Bose at the Marseilles airport. But no explanation is available to us for what purpose he had to visit France in 1945-46.

Leaving aside Bhagwanji's claims, fantastic by all means, there is definitely a Chinese angle to the Bose mystery. All those who talk about Bose's dying in Russia, including some of his outspoken family members, know of it as well, but refrain from alluding to it for an obvious reason. If Subhas Bose was in China in 1949 and afterwards, he was certainly out of the USSR—alive. And so the theory that he was imprisoned and subsequently killed there cannot be true.

For a background, India's relations with China began turning sour from the time the dragon devoured Tibet and turned to our lands. Prior to that, almost all of our top leaders shared warm vibes with China. Subhas Bose even wrote an article in *Modern Review*, where he denounced Japan's assault on China. Records declassified in 1997 show that with the end of the second World War in sight, Bose weighed his options. On 21 March 1946, INA's Chief of Staff, General J K Bhonsle, was interrogated at Red Fort on the subject of 'last plans of SC Bose'. Bhonsle told his interrogator: 'Bose had also decided that in case the Japanese Govt did not agree to taking up his case with Russia, he himself would try to get to Shanghai and from there try to contact the Russians through the Chinese Communists.'[49] Azad Hind Government minister Debnath Das told the Khosla Commission that one of the escape plans for Bose was to go 'to Yunan, the headquarters of Mao Tse Tung, who would help him carry on his campaign against the British'. He even had Ho Chi Minh on his mind. Anand Mohan Sahay was actually sent to Hanoi, and he forged a life-long friendship with the Vietnamese statesman.

In 1949, rumours began to do the rounds in India and elsewhere that Subhas Bose was in China. So much so that when the pro-Soviet Bombay-based tabloid *The Blitz* carried a sensational news headlined 'British report Bose alive in Red continent' on 26 March 1949, the American Consul there transmitted its text to the Secretary

---

49   File No INA 400, National Archives, New Delhi.

of State under the subject 'Ghost of Subhas Chandra Bose'.

[National Archives, Maryland]

The Blitz story had made a string of claims:

> The British government is rumoured to be very much perturbed over confidential information that has come into its possession, quite recently, that Netaji...is alive...This sensational news... was originally transmitted to the British Foreign Office from the British embassy in Turkey and is reported to have been confirmed since from Anglo-American secret agents in the East. It is not known whether the news of the living Bose is based upon positive evidence of his whereabouts—suspected to be in Red China or Soviet Russia, or upon what is described as the 'negative' evidence of the failure of the best brains of the Anglo-American security services to dig up slightest evidence in confirmation of the story of Bose's death....

Anglo-American sources, haunted by the bogey of the Red Peril, seem to see the hand of Bose behind every Communist offensive in South East Asia and the Far East.

Forward Bloc general secretary R S Ruiker told the media in July 1949 that Bose 'who is presumed to be in Red China, may come back to India provided the ban on his entry into the country is withdrawn'. A bombshell was then dropped by Sarat Chandra Bose, Subhas's elder brother. No one disputes that if Subhas were alive, and in a position to communicate after 1945, the one person he would have reached out was his *mejda*. Sarat Bose made a public declaration (now wished away by the majority of the Bose family members), fitting well with Bhagwanji's narrative. On 7 October 1949, Sarat Bose's paper *The Nation*, ran this frontpage story:

'Netaji in Red China', was the top headline in *The Nation*. A person of Sarat's standing and intelligence would not have published this in such a manner, without being sure about it. The story quoted him claiming 'that the Government of India was in possession of definite information that Netaji Subhas Chandra

Bose was in Red China of Mao Tse Tung'. When asked why Subhas was 'not coming to India', Sarat Bose replied, 'I don't think the time is ripe for his coming back home.' In 1956, came another shocker. Close Subhas Bose associate Muthuramalingam Thevar, whose statue now stands in the Parliament House precincts in New Delhi as a tribute to his eminence, told newspapers, such as *Hindustan Standard*, that he had secretly visited China on Sarat Bose's instruction.

Thevar said that towards the end of 1949, when Sarat Chandra Bose was ailing, he went down to Calcutta to meet him. He saw Bose on December 7 and stayed with him for ten days. They had consultations on the matter as Bose apprehended that he was going to die. After these talks, Thevar said, he left India incognito on December 17. He crossed the Burma border and entered China, where he stayed almost the whole of 1950. He met Netaji in January, but where, he would not divulge. He returned to India in October 1950. He said that the Government of India knew that he had visited China but if it doubted that he could prove that he had been to China.

It is not possible that Chinese attention was not drawn to numerous claims about Subhas's presence in their country. Even the Americans, who had nothing to do with Bose in the Cold War years on the face of it, couldn't skip mentioning it. The February 1954 issue of the magazine *National Republic* carried an article

'Jawaharlal Nehru and the Red threat to India'. Its author, Elliot Erikson, wrote that there was a 'strong possibility that Bose is alive'.

> At the end of the war, when the Japanese front collapsed in Burma, Bose, if he showed himself, ran great risk of being prosecuted as an international war criminal. If Bose is still held prisoner in Communist China, he could be sprung as the leader of a Red "liberation" of India from capitalism. The most strongly anti-Communist Congress leaders admit that if such an event happened, Indian resistance to China would collapse immediately.

In January 2011, Priyadarsi Mukherji, professor in Chinese & Sinological Studies Centre at the Jawaharlal Nehru University, met Professor Wang Bangwei, Director of the Indian Studies Centre, Peking University. He asked him about the possibility of Bose's contacts with Mao after 1949. Evasively, Wang said that both Bose and Mao had the same objective of achieving liberation of their countries by armed struggle, so it was natural for them to be close. Asked about documents related to Bose in the Research Cell of the Chinese Communist Party (CPC), Wang commented that it was impossible for foreigners to get access to the cell, when many Chinese did not have the privilege.[50]

Between his anecdotes and commentaries on Russia and China, Bhagwanji would often regale his followers with the tales of his travels in the mysterious and mountainous terrain in the Roof of the World in the 1950s. While much of his association

---

50   Prof Priyadarsi Mukherji gave this account to Anuj Dhar.

with Tibet appears to have been spiritual in nature, he made an astounding claim with relation to the most sensational political event that has characterised the relation between India and Tibet, with long-term implications for the Indo–China ties. He guided the Dalai Lama out of the land increasingly coming under Chinese occupation into India, he said. Not only that, Bhagwanji said that he trained in guerilla tactics the local warrior tribes that rose in revolt and made way for the Dalai Lama's escape.

Referring to the losing struggle waged by the Tibetans, Bhagwanji claimed that the Dalai Lama had written to Nehru asking for 50,000 rifles but was refused. This refusal made Bhagwanji livid. 'What can be a greater betrayal and meanness?' a visibly angry Bhagwanji asked his followers many years later. It was then, he said, that he intervened to convince him to escape to India:

> When he was helpless, not able to see a way to protect himself, then one General Death told him, 'As a representative of India I am showing you the way; you go to India; the Indian public will accept you and give you shelter.' Nehru was compelled to give him shelter under the pressure of public opinion.[51]

General Death was also known as General Shiva, and the interchangeability was rooted in their religious connotations:

> Shiva—the father of ghosts. When the ghosts are let loose after giving flaming torches in their hands then people get scared— those who know him call him death— both names are true.

---

51   Notes of conversation with Bhagwanji by Dulal Nandy, January 1965.

It was in 1965 when Bhagwanji spoke to his followers about the Dalai Lama incident. By then a number of well-regarded accounts had appeared around the world. If *The Flight of the Dalai Lama* by Noel Barber (1960), *Tragic destiny* by George N Patterson (1959) published from London and *The Dalai Lama* by Lowell Thomas Jr (1961) published from New York told the story in great detail, the *Time* and *Life* magazines covered the developments with their top notch brand of journalism. None of them, however, mentioned any role played by a mysterious individual in the Khampa (or Khamba) rebellion or in helping the Dalai Lama to make his decision. None, except Lowell Thomas Jr. At a secret meeting of the rebels in Lhasa around 1955 or 1956, Thomas wrote, the 'most prominent' was:

> a spokesman for the Khamba tribesmen in the region of Kham. His identity has never been revealed. He called himself General Siva, a threatening title, for Siva is the god of destruction in the Hindu religion. We may call him General Death as the nearest English equivalent....He was the professional military man of the group, and so the others looked to him to give them their strategy. He had come with a precise plan, which he now outlined in detail.[52]

General Death organised the Khambas to escort the Dalai Lama as he moved out of the Norbulingka in the dead of night. They then held the charge of Lhasa for the next few days against

---

52   Lowell Thomas Jr, *The Dalai Lama: A Biography of the Exiled Leader of Tibet*, Duell, Sloan and Pearce, 1961, pp 95-96.

Chinese onslaught until he received the message that the spiritual leader was well on his way, safely. No more of this mysterious man was heard. The Dalai Lama has never referred to him. Even the author, Thomas Jr was unable to provide any further information about him, when asked by Anuj Dhar via email. 'I regret to tell you that I cannot help identifying the one who called himself General Shiva. A total mystery to me.'

The year was 1959. Three years later, Atul Sen found Bhagwanji in Neemsar. And India stood on the verge of a war.

ELEVEN

A PHANTOM'S HOMELAND

'YOU HAVE BEEN to so many places around the world. Which is the most beautiful place you have ever been to?' asked a starry-eyed Bijoy Nag. 'If you are asking about countries, then it has to be India,' the man behind the curtain responded instinctively. 'There is no other country in the world like India. Not only does it have the prototype of climates of all countries, but it has much more which is not to be found in any other country.' Then, thoughtfully, he added in his deep voice, 'But if only scenic beauty is considered, then the place dearest to me is the *Tulsimancha*[1]...I don't know of anything more beautiful than the conjunction of day and night when mothers and sisters in every house light the lamp and blow the conch shell in front of the *Tulsimancha*.'

---

1   A raised earthen platform placed in the lawn of many Hindu households, especially in rural areas, where the Tulsi plant is worshipped by showing an oil lamp and blowing of conch shell.

In his confabulations with his followers from Kolkata, mostly in monologues, Bhagwanji was invariably lost in the memory of the days he had left behind. Here was someone who missed Bengal dearly. During an evening discussion in Basti, Bhagwanji, overwhelmed by nostalgia, painted to Sunil Krishna Gupta what he longed for:

> I want a place surrounded by bamboo fence where there will be three to four *atchala* huts on an elevated ground in the middle; two more *atchala* huts at a little distance to serve as kitchen. There should be banana, guava, and pomegranate trees around the fence. On the roof of the huts *lau, kumro* and *jhinge* plants, and *puishak,* etc. There will be a Tulsi plant in a slightly isolated place within the compound where the mothers and sisters will light the lamp every evening and blow the conch shell, praying for sisters, brothers, husbands, children by doing a *sashtangpranam,* putting the *anchal* around the neck. Everywhere there will be a deep atmosphere of peace. This is the true form of my incomparable Mother Bengal. This is my dream. This is what I am doing my *sadhana* for.[2]

It was thus a cruel tragedy that he had to remain outside Bengal. Much as he pined for his beloved Bengal, he just couldn't risk living there. The land that he loved more than his life wouldn't let him have the cover of anonymity. Yet, the memory of Bengal was always in his heart and he would find out ways to stay connected to it whenever possible. One of the items that featured regularly among the long list of goods sent by his followers was *Ganga Mrittika* (soil from the banks of the Ganga), which he carried with him while travelling. 'What this homeless, penniless beggar

---

2   Record of conversation by Sunil Krishna Gupta, 27 August 1973.

thinks, says and prays sitting in front of the lump of soil cannot be shared,' he wrote to Pabitra. The words of Michael Madhusudan Dutt resonated at the depth of his heart, Bhagwanji wrote:

রেখো মা দাসেরে মনে   সাধিতে মনের সাদ,
ঘটে যদি পরমাদ,
মধুহীন করো না গো   তব মনঃকোকনদে[3]

(Remember this servant, O Mother, I plead at your feet. If I commit a mistake in following my heart, do not forsake me. [Translated from Bengali]).

After repeated requests of Leela Roy to accept something for his personal use, Bhagwanji reluctantly asked her to send some shirts and vests made in Bengal. 'If I wear clothes made in Bengal, I will always feel the loving touch of Mother Bengal especially when travelling abroad,' he wrote to Roy. 'If I die wearing these clothes, I will die with the knowledge that I am dying in the lap of Mother Bengal.'[4]

He asked for gramophone records of Shyama Sangeet, Nazrul Geeti, Rabindra Sangeet, songs of Ram Prasad Sen and other Bengali songs along with a record player in a crashproof and waterproof airtight box. The reason he gave for asking for the player with those particular specifications was beyond belief: The music would give 'me the feel of my Mother Bengal beyond the Pamirs', a topic to which we will return in the next chapter.

Although he stayed away from Bengal and from public life in general, Bhagwanji followed the developments around the

---

3   Copy of letter to Pabitra Mohan Roy, 20 February 1963.
4   Charanik, *Oi Mahamanaba Ase*, Jayasree Prakashan, 2010, p 310.

country, apart from the global ones, and would often offer his analyses and insights into the past and present of his homeland.

Four overarching themes can be discerned from what Bhagwanji said and wrote about Bengal which was the centre of his being: (a) he could never recover from the deep sense of hurt stemming from the lack of response from Bengal when the INA entered India; (b) he held the *Bhadralok* class responsible for the fall of the province from its past glory; (c) the partition of India and especially Bengal, the brutalisation of women in particular, devastated him, and (d) he accused the British and subsequently Nehru for debilitating the province in order to eliminate any serious challenge to their hegemony.

The fact is that a *sanyasi* doesn't get alms in his own village[5], although he might be honoured like a king at other places, an upset Bhagwanji blurted out. 'I had great hope that as soon as I cross Burma, Bengal would rise up like a single person,' he recalled. According to him, at the battle of Imphal the British commander was about to surrender but four people defected to the British and informed them that the INA forces were in an unenviable position. As a result, an order not to surrender was sent out to the front and the wheels of destiny turned. The beggar went back getting no response after knocking on the door.

Bhagwanji's claim that the British Indian Army contemplated surrendering to the Indian National Army is backed by the memoirs of INA veteran Colonel Gurbaksh Singh Dhillon.

---

5   A Bengali idiom.

> The 14th Army of the enemy was on the verge of surrender. ...
> It was at this crucial stage that two of our important officers,
> Major Prabhu Dayal and Major JBS Garewal, not being able to
> endure thirst and hunger any longer, went over to the enemy.
> ...It was from these two deserters that the enemy learnt that
> the INA and the Japanese were in a poor state in respect of food
> and ammunition. ...At such a crucial juncture, orders went to
> the 14th British Indian Army to postpone their surrender.[6]

Dhillon, a firm supporter of the air crash theory of Netaji's
death with no known links to Bhagwanji, added that post-
Independence, both the INA defectors were given higher ranks
in the Indian Army. While Garewal was murdered shortly
afterwards, Prabhu Dayal became a brigadier and seemed to have
led a luxurious life as other traitors did in free India.

Bhagwanji's observations on the past of Bengal were a veritable
lecture on the history of the province and its people. Once upon
a time, he reminded his followers, Bengal was the conqueror of
Simhala in the south,[7] reached out culturally and economically
to the Khmer lands (Kambuja), Java, Bali in the east, awakened
the great China in the north and her influence spread up to
Mongolia, the lands of the present Mecca and Medina. 'Go to
Tibet, Kazakhstan, and Uzbekistan—there you will find Bengal's
dance forms, *alpana* (designs made outside Bengali houses) and
other cultural remnants of Bengal...The Egyptians don't know
where their ancestors went—at the margins of their deserts it is

---

6   GS Dhillon, *From My Bones: Memoirs of Col Gurbakhsh Singh Dhillon of the Indian National Army*, Aryan Books International, 1998, p 346.

7   An allusion to the story of Prince Vijaya conquering Sri Lanka as told in *Mahavamsa*.

only the culture of your Sadhus.'[8]

'পবিত্র, আমি বুড়ো হয়ে পড়েছি, তবু এখনও মরিনি৷ শুধু আমাকে বলে দাও কোথায়
গেলো আমার সেই বাংলা মা! কোথায় লুকিয়ে আছেন আমার বাংলা মা! শুধু বলে দাও!
বলে দাও৷ যদি নরকে গিয়েও খুঁজে পাই, ফিরিয়ে আনতে হয় – তাও একবার, আর
একবার চেষ্টা করে দেখবো৷' ('I have become old, but haven't died
yet... Tell me, where has that Mother Bengal of mine gone? ...
If I can find her even in hell, and have to bring her back from
there, I shall try again!').[9]

The partition of Bengal in 1905, the reorganisation that came
with its reunification in 1911-12 and the final partition of 1947
were vividly etched in his mind. 'Mother Bengal was vivisected (I
am getting goose bumps!)'—one piece became Bihar, another was
joined with Orissa, another with Madras and then another piece
became Assam. Even what remained of Bengal was not spared,
and the 'dagger of the secret assassin repeatedly fell on Mother's
chest' to give away half of that truncated Bengal.

With acid dripping from his pen, Bhagwanji indicted the
intelligentsia and the political activists of Bengal for what he saw as
their cacophonous effeteness. When Bengal was cut into two and
a part given away to Pakistan, when lakhs of *maunds* of rice were
thrown into the river by the British 'scorched earth' policy, when
boats worth crores of rupees were burnt resulting in a 'man-made

---

8   Bhagwanji appears to have been keenly interested in the ancient connection
     between Egypt and Bengal, a controversial theme in current academic field. For
     more details on this topic, see Projit Bihari Mukharji, 'The Bengali Pharaoh:
     Upper-Caste Aryanism, Pan-Egyptianism, and the Contested History of Biometric
     Nationalism in Twentieth-Century Bengal,' *Comparative Studies in Society and
     History*, Volume 59, Issue 2, April 2017 , pp 446-476.
9   Copy of Bhagwanji's letter to Pabitra Mohan Roy, 5 February 1963.

[Some orphans who survived the Bengal famine of 1943. Source: Kalyanee Bhattacharjee (ed), *Bengal Speaks,* Hind Kitabs, 1944. Taken from *Wikipedia*]

famine and epidemic' which killed 50 lakh people, 'were these packs of jackals sleeping then?...Where had their heroism vanished?' His bitterness knew no bounds when he accused the Indian government of discrimination against the refugees from East Pakistan. He alleged that 'the refugees from West Pakistan were not only 'paid 1.25 to 1.5 times the value of the land they left behind', but compensated on the basis of the exaggerated claims they made. On the contrary, the people fleeing East Pakistan were not considered refugees only on the excuse of some technical point.

> 40-50 lakh refugees from East Bengal have not been paid a single penny. Why? As if doing charity, Rs 40-50 crore has been doled out for providing shelter and feeding them. But not one penny for compensation! And to add insult to injury, all this is being done through the hands of a Bengali dog who is himself an East Bengal refugee! The refugees of East Pakistan left a very prosperous state of affairs. They came bereft of everything...I say, they came bereft of everything, even of the courage they had...Oh! These people were left on their own—deserted both

by God and man. After all partition was not their fault. Why should they suffer! Daughters, sisters, mothers were keeping their soul in their body by white (?) slavery! In Bengal! Oh! Pabitra! Can't write anymore. I will probably go mad![10]

Reminiscent of the observations of Lord Curzon and Andrew Fraser on the political benefits of partitioning Bengal,[11] Bhagawanji pointed out that the British realised that it would not be possible to rule over India unless Bengal—the most prosperous part of the country—was weakened, drained of its spirit and turned into an inanimate object. Bhagwanji reminded Pabitra that the liberation movement against the British started in Bengal by what they called the *Sanyasi* Rebellion (1760s onwards)—'We *Sanyasis* led that movement.' (মনে রেখো – ইংরাজের বিরুদ্ধে একেবারে প্রথমে বাংলাতেই মুক্তি সংগ্রাম হয়েছিল৷ Lead করেছিলেম আমরা সন্ন্যাসীরাই) 'Bankim babu based his *Anandamath* on the government records which he read.' The British understood that if Bengal is weakened then the 'root

---

10   Ibid. The Displaced Persons (Claims) Act of 1950 and The Displaced Persons (Compensation and Rehabilitation) Act of 1954 limited the benefits to refugees from West Pakistan only. The stark contrast in rehabilitation and compensation provided to the refugees from East Pakistan vis-à-vis West Pakistan has been discussed in detail in Pallavi Chakravarty's, 'Post-partition refugee rehabilitation in India with special reference to Bengal 1947 to 71,' PhD thesis submitted to the Delhi University, 2011, http://shodhganga.inflibnet.ac.in/handle/10603/28325. These laws either defined displaced persons as those coming in from West Pakistan or stipulated compensation for them only. Bhagwanji put the blame at Nehru's doorstep: 'If this was done by an alien government, it could be understood. But the use of such a technical plea on own people—mother, father, brother, sister— who are fleeing to save their self-respect, lives, religion!...But who is that devilish person who has closed the door of technical plea so ruthlessly?' (কোনও Alien Govt যদি এই technical plea-এর দোহাই দিতো তো কিছু বোঝাও যেতো৷ কিন্তু নিজের দেশের, নিজেরই Govt নিজেদেরই দেশের মা-বাপ-ভাই-বোনের লজ্জা, ইজ্জত, মান, ধর্ম-প্রাণ বাঁচাবার জন্যে মৃত্যুর মুখের মধ্য দিয়ে পালিয়ে আসছে, আর তাদেরই জন্য technical plea!...কিন্তু কে? কে ঐ পৈশাচিক-পাশবিক দানব যে technical plea-র 'দরোজা' বন্ধ করে নির্মম হয়ে দাঁড়িয়ে আছে?) Copy of Bhagwanji's letter to Pabitra Mohan Roy, 12 February 1963.
11   See Sumit Sarkar, *The Swadeshi Movement in Bengal 1903-1908*, Permanent Black, 2011.

of the disease' would be removed. This was achieved by making Bengal forget its glorious past.

In his letters and discourses, Bhagwanji would occasionally travel back to the days of the freedom struggle where, unavoidably, his relations with and thoughts on Gandhi and Nehru would be the predominant component. Sometimes, these stories would be recounting of well-known episodes of Subhas Bose's life, such as his meeting with Mahatma Gandhi on his return to India after resigning from the civil service. 'He satisfactorily answered a couple of questions,' but he could not convince "your man" on the remaining and "more crucial questions".

He reminisced about the conflict between his political guru CR Das and Gandhi that led to the formation of the Swarajya Party. Gandhi was afraid of Das, he claimed.

> The guru of this very Bengal—Deshabandhu—and his disciple '___' had the strength to throw the gauntlet to Mr Gandhi and Jawahar, and to defeat them repeatedly in an open fight. They did not forget the humiliation of that defeat.

Subhas Bose had quoted British parliamentarian Ellen Wilkinson to write in *The Indian Struggle* that 'Gandhi was the best policeman the Britishers had in India'. Bhagwanji took it to another level claiming that the British government regarded Gandhi as their 'stooge'. According to him, the British government dealt with 'a group of busybodies' whenever they faced the pressure of mass movements and revolutionary upsurge. They treated these busybodies as 'a conglomeration of doubtful qualities' with whom they could deal anytime on their own terms,

Bhagwanji continued, and in times of trouble when they contrived to contain the 'thunder', they at once got out these busybodies to get 'their deal' through.[12]

The assessment of Gandhi wasn't only political. There was a deep-seated personal aspect too, which reflected the ambiguity that was once evident in Subhas Bose too, most acutely after the Tripuri crisis of 1939. As historian Amalesh Tripathi has pointed out, 'It is strange that Bose failed to understand that his struggle was neither with Pattabhi [Sitaramayya] nor with the Working Committee [of the Congress], it was with Gandhi himself.' Yet, after all his opposition to Gandhi from 1922, he faltered at the time of decisive action.[13] Gandhi's bias towards Nehru hurt Bhagwanji. On one of the rare occasions when he vented his raw emotion, Bhagwanji went into a soliloquy recalling Nehru and the blessings he received from Gandhi:

> Oh! Give him his due! Affection...and don't feel miserly at that...for affection was his. Of course, I know—as others do—much of his drummed-up 'legend' shall not endure. Honest historians and critics, judging in retrospect shall not give marks for 'achievements', both foreign and domestic. Still—affection was his...May be you [Subhas] very aptly and correctly said, 'He is non-Indian...with his head and heart in England and only his feet in India. He shall always plan grandiose, which shall always fail...He shall always rave, spew and curse the English for hours and hours—but shall always act just the opposite'...

12   Copy of Bhagwanji's letter to Pabitra Mohan Roy, 6 February 1963.
13   Amalesh Tripathi, *Swadhinata Sangrame Bharater Jatiya Congress (1885-1947)*, Ananda Publishers Pvt Ltd, pp 258-265. Translated from Bengali.

May be, Oh—may be many 'things' more…Still affection was his (personal and in abundance).[14]

In the final count, however, Bhagwanji appeared to have reconciled his feelings for Gandhiji. He said he had no ill-feelings towards the Mahatma:

> He has no rancour for Bapu. Though Bapu (because Bapu got twice defeated in his fight against him was so rattled that he gave up his Congress membership and also started a whispering campaign against your Dead Man) and Congress thought otherwise. Your Dead Man has no rancour because Bapu at last turned a volte face and preached fighting for freedom and honour (which was your right creed); and because hearing and becoming stimulated and emboldened (he was a mere figure-head and marionette in the hands of___) by the radio exhortations of your Dead Man, he stoutly opposed partition, and during the last fateful meeting he wept like a child before them and sobbed out praying against partition (this *faquir* has documentary evidence) but he was overridden roughshod. Also it has been kept a secret that your Dead Man went with Bapu's full blessings and concurrence of the inner committee. No your Dead Man bore no rancour.[15]

The extreme bitterness and critical outlook towards Nehru, however, remained till the last. Yet another instance which according to Bhagwanji irked Nehru was the public appeal by Rabindrnath Tagore addressing Subhas as the *Deshanayak* (the hero of the nation) and appealing to him to take up the leadership of the country. Bhagwanji pointed to Nehru's article which he

---

14   Charanik, *Oi Mahamanaba Ase*, Jayasree Prakashan, 2010, p 54.
15   Ibid, p 246.

wrote in 'Ramanandababu's [Ramananda Chatterjee's] *Modern Review*—if someone really wanted to understand him [Nehru]. In November 1937, a month before the Congress session in which Nehru was expected to be chosen the party chief, an article appeared in the Calcutta-based *Modern Review*. Profiling Nehru, its writer, a certain 'Chanakya', cautioned that men like him were 'dangerous' and potential 'dictators'. 'He calls himself a democrat and a socialist and no doubt he does so in all seriousness... but a little twist and he might turn into a dictator.... His conceit is already formidable. It must be checked. We want no Caesars.'

Later, it turned out that it was Nehru himself who had written this article. If Bhagwanji found the article to be narcissistic and conceited, commentators on modern Indian history have seen it in a much more positive light. Alex Von Tunzelmann, author of a book on the end of British rule in India (who also labelled Subhas Bose as 'extreme right-wing'), finding in it reflections of a great personality has commented, 'Introspection, honesty, wit and mischief—few other politicians in history could have written such a lucid essay in self-deconstruction.'[16] According to Bose biographer Mihir Bose, Nehru later explained that he wrote the article to avoid becoming the president of Congress for a third consecutive term, eventually leading to the selection of Subhas Bose as the new Rashtrapati in 1938. Writing in *The Telegraph*, Ramachandra Guha commented that 'Nehru's Caesarist

---

16   Alex Von Tunzelmann, *Indian Summer: The Secret History of the End of an Empire*, Pocket Books, 2007, p 105.

tendencies were kept in check by his own self-awareness'.[17] Political commentator Inder Malhotra pointed out that Nehru went on to disprove what he wrote in the article. 'Far from becoming a dictator—which he could have done easily, like his two contemporary leaders of freedom movements, Sukarno in Indonesia and Kwame Nkrumah in Ghana—he built India up as the world's largest democracy,' commented Malhotra.[18]

As far as MA Jinnah was concerned, Bhagwanji held both Nehru and Gandhi responsible for his turn towards a hardline position. 'The only reason that Mr Jinnah moved away and joined the Muslim League with great sense of hurt was Jawahar. Jawahar turned him into a fanatic for Pakistan,'[19] he told Pabitra. This accusation in all likelihood was based on the views of Maulana Abul Kalam Azad referring to the falling out between the League and the Congress after the 1937 elections for which Azad put the blame on Nehru. Bhagwanji also remembered Jinnah's opposition to the Khilafat movement. He apparently warned Gandhi that Gandhi was sowing the seeds of a poisonous tree that would destroy the country. Bhagwanji opined that Gandhi had many weaknesses, but 'the worst among them was an inferiority complex'. He would either dominate a person or otherwise wouldn't allow him to be in the Congress. That was the reason,

17   Ramachandra Guha, 'Dangers of Hero Worship—Reading Ambedkar in the Time of Modi,' *The Telegraph*, 3 May 2014, https://www.telegraphindia.com/opinion/dangers-of-hero-worship-reading-ambedkar-in-the-time-of-modi/cid/186946.

18   Inder Malhotra, 'A most wanted man,' *The Indian Express*, 13 November 2014, http://indianexpress.com/article/opinion/columns/a-most-wanted-man/.

19   Copy of Bhagwanji's letter to Pabitra Mohan Roy, 5 February 1963.

according to him, why Gandhi never allowed Jinnah to rise in the Congress or to occupy any responsible position.

Bhagwanji also laid the blame for Partition on the Congress leaders. He deeply appreciated the efforts of Maulana Azad to prevent the Partition, and recalled Gandhi's 'stout' opposition to the Partition despite which he was 'overridden roughshod'. In Bhagwanji's view, 'there was no better nationalist in the Congress than Maulana *sahib*'. Although Cyril Radcliff was opposed to the idea of Partition, he was convinced by Louis Mountbatten who pointed at the Congress leaders. 'How does it matter to you and to me when they are themselves ready to destroy their own country?' was Bhagwanji's version of Mountbatten's argument. However, he absolved Gandhi from the transfer of power negotiations. 'Gandhi had no role in the transfer of power,' he later told Bijoy Nag.

As the undisputed leader of the Congress and as the prime minister, Nehru was able to work his way because 'he knows very well the gullibility of the Indian masses'. 'It is on their cheated votes that he is in the chair. And he is a past master in guiles.'

In Bhagwanji's view, post-independence, being 'fanatically anti-Bengal and everything Bengali', and having 'a free hand to consolidate', Nehru would do everything to destroy the state as that was the only place from where an effective opposition to him could come up. This, however, he would do subtly, trying to conceal his true intention. Bhagwanji gave the example of Nehru electing himself to be the Chancellor of Visva-Bharati (Tagore's university) to present a benevolent face. He called the central legislation on Visva Bharati that brought the university under the control of the Congress-ruled central government a death blow to it. Strangely, he also accused that not a single Bengali was appointed to any critically important position, especially in the defence service, despite Air Marshall Subroto Mukherjee becoming the first Commander-in-Chief (later Chief of Air Staff) in 1954 and General Jayanto Nath Chaudhuri becoming the Chief of Army Staff in 1962. Another of Bhagwanji's grudges was that no strategic establishments were set up in Bengal. Although 'Bengal has the greatest number of FRS (Fellows of the Royal Society) and is far ahead of other scientists in the field of physics—none of them was entrusted with atomic undertakings,' he complained. Despite repeated statements in Parliament that encroachment of even one inch of Indian land by Pakistan would be considered an act of war and would be resisted by the entire force of the government, parts of Bengal were being given away, he alleged. This, he said, the government did not have the courage to do in Punjab or Bikaner.

Another reason for his worry was the decline of the Calcutta port. Thousands of crores of Rupees were being invested to create major ports out of lesser, insignificant inland ports in the ruse of economy and importance, but the underlying objective was to turn the Calcutta port insignificant, he accused. 'Arguments are being woven to fool the public while strangulating the port of Calcutta—it is being allowed to be silted. Not only the port of Calcutta, but the harbour and the Hugli river too. Already port handling has declined by 40% by their diabolical conspiracy.'[20]

---

20   Copy of Bhagwanji's letter to Pabitra Mohan Roy, 6 February 1963.

The economic decline of Bengal has been, and still is a sensitive topic in the state's politics. De-industrialisation in the region and policies such as freight equalisation that deprived the state of its locational advantage have been hotly debated in the press as well as academic publications. In 1971, a few years after Bhagwanji made the charge that Bengal was deliberately squeezed in by the Central government, a book provided data to the same effect. First published by Anandabazar Patrika Pvt Ltd, *The agony of West Bengal* by journalist Ranajit Roy furnished evidence which overturns the general perception that Bengal's decline started after Communists took over the reign of power. Roy wrote that on the very first day of independence, the West Bengal government discovered that the Centre had, on the stroke of 12 o'clock the previous night, slashed the state's share of jute export duty. A second blow was struck the same night. Her share of the divisive pool of the income tax was reduced from 20% to 12%, while Bombay's share was pushed up from 20% to 21% and the composite Madras state's share from 15% to 18%. The money saved at the cost of West Bengal enabled all the other States to get more.

During a debate in the Parliament in 1971, Tridib Chaudhuri, former Anushilan revolutionary, later a stalwart of the Revolutionary Socialist Party and member of Parliament warned the Central government by saying, 'You are confronted in West Bengal with nothing short of a revolution.'[21] Roy made a series of disturbing charges, backed by economic data, covering various fields, all

---

21   Ranajit Roy, *The Agony of West Bengal: A Study in the Union-State Relations*, New Age Publishers Pvt Ltd, 1973.

showing a step-motherly attitude towards the state. But Roy offered no clue as to what could have been the motive. Bhagwanji, on the other hand, attributed it to Nehru's fear of the 'real Bengal and real Bengalee' who had the potential to become the obstacle to his plans. At the back of their mind is fear, Bhagwanji wrote. 'They know extremely well what shall happen when "The Ghost-who-walks" appears! So it is but natural, that, he should take everything to "set the stage" before the ghost's possible appearance.'

Bhagwanji minced no words in holding Nehru responsible for the death of Syama Prasad Mookerjee. He alleged that Mookerjee was 'murdered' because of his fallout with Nehru over Bengal and treatment of Hindu minority in East Pakistan, not Kashmir as is generally understood. He described a Cabinet meeting where an argument between Nehru and Mookerjee was on the verge of developing into a scuffle. It was only years later in 1968 that veteran Congress leader Narhar Vishnu Gadgil, a minister in Nehru government, for the first time, made public that such a thing had occurred. In his book *Government from Inside*, Gadgil provided the inside account that 'there was much heated exchange between him [Nehru] and Shyama Prasad Mookerjee on the problems of West Bengal...I tried to pacify both Nehru and Shyama Prasad and requested them to resume their seats. Both of them had stood up surcharged with emotion and I was afraid something untoward would happen.' Following the resignation of Shyama Prasad from the Cabinet, Vallabhbhai Patel asked Gadgil to go and try to persuade him to reconsider his decision. 'But Shyama Prasad was adamant. He said that Nehru's policies had ruined Bengal. Nehru, he thought, was not interested in justice for the [Bengali] Hindus,' Gadgil reminisced.[22]

In a mysterious language, Bhagwanji indicated that Nehru could undertake two crucial measures with regard to the Liaquat–Nehru Pact of 1950 about the rights of minorities in India and Pakistan only with the help of Mookerjee, who agreed 'after months of persuasion and solemn (false) promises in writing'. When Mookerjee found that the promises had been broken he threatened to expose Nehru and to do his utmost to undo the wrongs as far as possible. 'He paid for this…you know, how?' was Bhagwanji's suspenseful comment. Correspondence between Nehru and Mookerjee available at the National Archives, however, show that the latter had mellowed down after the confrontation.

Bringing Mookerjee in the picture with regard to the Netaji death controversy was his nephew who we reckon was in contact with Bhagwanji. In 1972, Dwijendranath Bose testified before the GD Khosla commission that 'Syama Prasad Mookerjee told me that your uncle is alive,' and that he would go public with his claim 'at the opportune moment'. Mookerjee died in mysterious circumstances in Kashmir on 23 June 1953. There were demands for an inquiry but the Prime Minister turned them down. Accompanying Mookerjee to Kashmir was his young secretary, Atal Bihari Vajpayee. So long as Vajpayee was the Prime Minister he did nothing to get into the causes of his mentor's death. But after stepping down, he made a shocking claim that Mookerjee was 'killed in 1952 as part of a "conspiracy" between

---

22   NV Gadgil, *Government from Inside*, Meenakshi Prakashan, 1963, p 142.

the then Jawaharlal Nehru-led Central government and Jammu and Kashmir government'.[23]

'Sheikh Abdullah was and is JN's man,' Bhagwanji would say. The context was the agitation over the Constitutional relation between Jammu and Kashmir and central government. His many utterances reflect an abhorrence for Abdullah's politics, which he claimed was condoned by Nehru.

Contrary to the consensus view on Nehru's ideological inclinations and what would appear contradictory to the subsequent political developments in the country, Bhagwanji was emphatic in charging that Nehru was a 'confirmed communist' in disguise, and the Communist Party of India (CPI) thrived only because of him. This, he argued, was evident from the plethora of legislations being passed, which were 'more forward' than the laws of communist Russia. 'In order to usher in Communism he has been juggling with words and phrases all these years to whitewash Communism with the brush of socialism and welfare.' The Indian communists, he was of the opinion, were wearing the mask of 'utter fanatic patriotism'.[24]

---

23 'Nehru conspiracy led to Shyama Prasad's death: Atal,' *The Times of India*, 7 July 2004, accessed from: https://timesofindia.indiatimes.com/india/Nehru-conspiracy-led-to-Shyama-Prasads-death-Atal/articleshow/768217.cms.

24 In his *Nehru: A Biography* (Asia Publishing House), Frank Moraes has presented a number of incidents which paint a completely different picture from what Bhagwanji indicated. 'Nehru, who in a parliamentary speech had described the Indian Communist party as "the most stupid party among the Communist parties of the world," not only utilised the full force of the governmental machinery against the Reds but also called upon the people to resist their call to violence' (p 418). During the election campaign of 1951, 'Greeted at one centre by a parade of red flags, he turned angrily on the shouting, gesticulating Communists. "Why don't you go and live in the country whose flag you are carrying?" he asked.' (p 413)

Bhagwanji described an incident that would appear straight out of international political thrillers. According to this version, Nehru reluctantly agreed to consider a motion in the Parliament to ban the CPI, under severe pressure from other political parties and legislators ('He always plays to the gallery, he has been doing so throughout his life,' commented Bhagwanji). However, on the day a decision by the Parliament was expected, a car of the Russian ambassador reached Nehru's place and left within ten minutes. When the prime minister reached Parliament, it seemed as though the anger he had shown earlier against the CPI had vanished. He ended up with only 'moderate criticism'. 'JN is the main strength of CPI,' was Bhagwanji's surmise.[25]

On the topic of the communists' blind imitation and practice of taking orders from Moscow and Beijing, Bhagwanji mocked that if the Indian communists are sent to live in China and Russia for six months, they would be straightened out. Time and again, he recounted anecdotes about how the Communist party in Russia ensured productivity of the workers, contrasting that with the labour unions in India, which, according to him, were only interested in increasing their pay and power of negotiation, while neglecting the issues of increasing production and productivity.

Nehru's non-alignment was a myth—a mere bluff, Bhagwanji held. For him, it was an effort to play both Russia (on whom the government was completely dependent for protection and for operating big industrial units) and the US (from whom Nehru

<hr>

25   Copy of Bhagwanji's letter to Pabitra Mohan Roy, 12 February 1963.

had no qualms in borrowing funds and food).[26] They (the US and the UK) are no idiots, Bhagwanji wrote: They see this game through without batting an eyelid, laugh in their sleeves and carry on. 'But blinded by selfish interest the rulers don't even realise that the very purpose of giving aid to India was to keep her in the state of *Trishanku* (a character from Indian mythology who represents a state of neither here nor there).'

The US and the UK, in his view, knew fully well about Nehru, but they had no choice now. Although they had propelled him to the top spot and had been propping him up ever since, they were helpless as foreigners now. They understand that Nehru had manipulated the situation in such a way that any miscalculated steps on their part could lead to a war in the region. Nehru was released from jail (in 1942) and received full support from the US and the UK only to stop Subhas, because they knew that the latter would never compromise. In contrast, Bhagwanji wrote, Gandhi, Patel, Nehru and others always compromised. 'It is death to compromise on principles.'

Nehru has thus succeeded in handing over a fait accompli to the US and the UK, Bhagwanji added. The line of argument taken by Nehru for not coming out openly in the camp of the US and the UK is that such a step would allow Khrushchev to openly

---

26   As India's ambassador in Moscow KPS Menon succinctly put it down, 'it was "entirely consistent" with India's foreign policy to encourage "a little competition" between the Soviets and the West when it came to furnishing India with technical assistance and economic aid'. Paul M McGarr, *The Cold War in South Asia: Britain, the United States and the Indian Subcontinent, 1945-65*, Cambridge University Press, 2013, p 35.

align with Mao—a situation that is undesirable to them. If the US openly intervenes in favour of Nehru in the war with China, then Russia might decide to supply arms to China, following which China is certain to bomb India. It is also possible that if the US gets involved in a conflict with China then Russia will make it its own war and escalate the conflict within the region. Nehru has impressed upon them that all these consequences are of course equally negative. Although annoyed with Nehru, both the US and UK have no choice but to agree to these arguments, he said.

On the basis of documents declassified in the recent decades in archives across the UK and the US, Paul M McGarr's 2013 book *The Cold War in South Asia: Britain, the United States and the Indian Subcontinent, 1945-65* throws fresh light on how the Nehru government negotiated its balance of power with the UK, the US and Russia. 'Working with Nehru and his government promised to advance Soviet interests in the developing world, Khrushchev noted later, and had little bearing on the underlying perception in Moscow that the Indian leader was essentially a Western flunky,' notes the author.[27] On the other hand, in private talks with the British and American diplomats the prime minister confided that in the event of a world war, India 'would not side with the Communists'.[28] The author also cites an incident which demonstrates how amenable Nehru could be to British persuasion. In 1963, at the height of Indo-Pak dispute over a

---

27   Paul M McGarr, *The Cold War in South Asia: Britain, the United States and the Indian Subcontinent, 1945-65*, Cambridge University Press, 2013, p 33.

28   Ibid, p 45.

settlement on the Kashmir problem, it took one trip from Louis Mountbatten to change Nehru's fierce stand on not allowing any third-party mediation. 'By the time he [Mountbatten] had talked for a couple of hours with N[ehru] about Kashmir, we were in a different India,' noted Paul Henry Gore-Booth, the then British High Commissioner to India.[29]

The government in New Delhi, Bhagwanji claimed, was corrupt as well with more than 60% of all foreign aid and loans going into the pockets of the leaders (something, he said, was corroborated in the US Senate). Yet, if the global financial institutions wanted to send experts to oversee the utilisation of the aid funds, the Indian government screamed that it was an insult. 'Of course, they could not siphon off funds if the global experts were present to monitor implementation of the projects,' Bhagwanji was quite assertive, especially the close friends and relations of Nehru who have made huge fortunes. Being a godless man, Nehru did not have any 'qualms of conscience'.

> He is a Janus-faced man. He is a communist with a vengeance. He has nothing to lose and everything to gain. All his near and dear ones and other relatives have got huge fortunes; all of them have been extremely well and highly placed. About a crore is being spent on his own self. He has but a few years to live. So, what does he care what happens to India or the world after his death? He does not believe in God. He is a Godless man. So, why shall he feel the qualms of conscience?

Bhagwanji ridiculed the government's propensity to take the

---

29   Ibid, pp 208-209.

moral high ground while bargaining for international aid and loans; in fact, the very attitude that made them queue up for aid. 'I have a sad smile on my face when I see you trying to browbeat the Western world by shouting, giving statements to newspapers, etc. that if they don't give you the alms you have asked for then they will be destroyed.' Pointing at the smaller European countries which are similar to a district in India, he asked who did they take loans from to rise to the current level of development, that apart from financial aid they are able to provide help on technical, scientific and war capabilities? Countries like Germany, Russia and the US became great countries by their own hard labour and not by begging, he continued. From being settled on a desert land, Israel had developed into a green country. He had himself seen how Russia turned a barren stretch of desert land into a five hundred mile long canal where boats and steamers plied, with trees lining both banks. 'The crux of what I am saying is that you stand on your feet, become self-reliant. Who has ever become great by depending on others?'

According to Bhagwanji, the US and the UK were inextricably entangled with Nehru for fear and anxiety of his (Bose's) reappearance and were pressing Nehru very hard to settle the Bose problem once for all. They could start a final showdown with Nehru, Russia and China only when the Bose problem was completely settled. But, as matters stood in March 1963, they knew Bose was alive, and naturally they were jittery.

His overall assessment of Nehru's regime was that the state in which he has left India 'might well require God's own intelligence' to revive her.

Bhagwanji appeared to be relatively more favourably oriented towards Indira Gandhi ('she is the best option when compared to Nehru and Shastri'), but her imposition of Emergency enraged him. Those dark days figured heavily in Bhagwanji's talks with his Calcutta followers. He was disturbed the way Jayaprakash Narayan (JP) was being treated, though he felt JP was 'still not free of his sympathies for the communists'.

> Where can you find greater depravity and bankruptcy than this—the same person who the father honoured, now the daughter is abusing in the lowliest terms, calling him thief, etc. What greater misfortune can the country have?

A note of his conversation taken by Bijoy Nag in October 1976 shows him mocking the people for not standing up to the government's oppression: 'If the British government did this, they would have ruled for 100 more years. You would have submitted. You know to submit only, not how to fight. Three quarters of those who knew how to fight are dead. The remaining are inactive.' A month earlier, he ticked off the grandson of CR Das for the role he was playing. 'A sycophant like Siddhartha Shankar Ray is difficult to find.' On 24 January 1977, he credited the Western press for the lifting of the Emergency. 'This election wouldn't have taken place if not for the unrelenting criticism by *BBC*, European and American press. Nobody criticised this except the Western countries. All the Arabian countries, SE Asia (Indo China), Africa, Latin America and all communist parties and countries rather praised it…for this you should kneel down and thank the Western press. *BBC* exerted the maximum pressure.' The villain of Emergency, Sanjay Gandhi, came under severe castigation. Bhagwanji alluded to his assaulting his mother and spoke about his alleged illegal financial transactions: a meeting in a Delhi hotel, a few sealed boxes leaving the country, and his depositing 'Rs 300 crore and plenty of gold in a Swiss bank'. Bhagwanji even dragged in Indira's name. Talking to Surajit Dasgupta in February 1983, he claimed 'Now Indira Gandhi has a cash deposit of Rs 400 crore—but none of it is with her or in her house. They are kept in two foreign embassies—one has been transferred to a foreign country. It was transferred overnight by Dhirendra Brahmachari by the truckload.' Brahmachari, the Yoga guru of Indira, is remembered in certain circles as an Indian version of Rasputin.

Going by his claims, Bhagwanji appeared to have been receiving definite information of surreptitious dealings by the government with foreign powers and infiltration by foreign agents. Even in the area of aid and trade, he warned, if Russia gives Rs 3, it will ensure a return of Rs 3,000, because 'Russia is like an octopus'. Whatever it does, it does for its own interest. Making an astounding claim, Bhagwanji said that although both the Russian and the Indian governments publicly denied it, he knew that there were 23 points along the Indian coast to facilitate the Russian navy. He also claimed to have definitive knowledge about India's resources. You can supply the whole world with 'the reserve of nuclear fuel that is present in your country', he said, but 'your scientists do not have the power to extract them'.

When it came to discussing the state of Indian politics, Bhagwanji's words were laced with utter contempt. Free India's politics had solely become the pursuit of power, with the fire of idealism extinguished. Bengalis do not have the determination, perseverance and the strength to follow an ideal, he said. The determination to achieve the ideal even if it meant sacrificing one's life wasn't there anymore. Climbing the throne by any means was the only objective. Stinging words came out of his mouth when a follower broached the topic: 'Statesmen are a rarity in this world, but in India there is no statesman at all. Naturally, stability is a mirage in this country where the number of despicable, mean, self-seeking political parties is astronomical, and where politicians number by legions. The vagaries of wayward politicians have debased the very life and look of India, let alone Bengal.'

Several factors, in his view, resulted in this debasement. One of them was neglect of the country's past. 'You are so enamoured by the present that you have completely forgotten the past, which is now a burden to you. For you religion is ancient and fossilised,' he chided his followers. The axiomatic truth for him was that a nation which cannot bind itself to its history and culture cannot ever win. He cited Kenyan anti-colonial activist and politician Jomo Kenyatta as an example who silenced critics by stoutly defending the customs of his country by explaining them on the basis of sociology, geography and local climate. 'But you should know that religion is your pivot. Bind yourself behind your back. There is an ocean of unbounded energy from which you have sparked off. Men can struggle only when there is this power behind them—they can struggle and make progress. That is why you need unbounded faith. Man can't live without religion.' The other factor, which to Bhagwanji was India's gravest tragedy, was the nation's purported lack of military thinking. India's misfortune was that the country hasn't had a national military thinking since the last two thousand years, he lamented. Apart from the strength of ideology, it is military strength that has determined the history of nations through the ages. He wished that every citizen of the country should know about military strategy and speak in terms of military strength. The culture of political correctness was clearly an anathema to the man. 'I do not believe in universal love. It is bunkum, a cliché,' he announced. The concept of universal love was meaningless unless one had a strong and secure home, a place to stand. 'Can you practise universal love in a vacuum? ...What utter nonsense! You must have a centre to radiate yourself,' he explained.[30]

The presence of separate personal laws for different religious communities irked Bhagwanji. Laws must be made universal; Hindus and Muslims cannot have separate laws, was his emphatic view. He came across as a strong critic of the Indian policy of secularism. Secularism implies anti-religion, he pointed out. Even the country which taught India the concept of modern democracy, which had the mother of all Parliaments, didn't hesitate to make Christianity the state religion in their democratic polity, he argued. What then stopped Nehru from making Hinduism the state religion and rule of law the state policy? That would have assured everyone that Hinduism wouldn't be imposed on non-Hindus. According to Bhagwanji, it was under pressure from the British that Nehru was compelled to give a twist to the original meaning of the term through Radhakrishnan and others. The British had

---

30   Charanik, *Oi Mahamanaba Ase*, Jayasree Prakashan, 2010, *passim*.

realised that unless secularism, with its modified meaning, can be implemented in India it wouldn't be possible to maintain the practice of divide and rule. Additionally, it would pose a threat to Christian missionary activities.[31]

He was, however, acutely aware of the political atmosphere in the country. In the current age of depravity, if anyone tries to talk about Swami Vivekananda's Call to the Nation, then people will tell him that those are only for showcasing in bookshelves. 'If someone uncompromisingly follows the ideal of nationalism, then you Bengalis and Indians will start seeing the spectre of chauvinism,' he observed sarcastically.

As the World Happiness Report 2017 ranks India 122nd among 155 countries ranked on the basis of a happiness index, Bhagwanji's words, spoken in the 1960s, appear to be ominous in retrospect. 'India's biggest casualty is happiness: no one is happy, people appear very sombre,' he wrote. 'The leaders are giving sermons on radio day and night. The radio does not have any lively programme—everything is insipid. The leaders are busy hearing their own voices.'[32]

31   Ibid, pp 56-57.
32   Ibid pp 57-58

TWELVE

DER ÜBERMENSCH

T HE QUESTION THAT inevitably follows the first question of why Bhagwanji, if he was Netaji, did not come out in public to reclaim his place, is what he was doing in all those years. Our assessment is that all the multifarious activities that he was involved in can be grouped into three main categories. These categories also reflect three aspects of his personality, which at some levels are confusing, if not contradicting each other.

Firstly, Bhagwanji claimed that while remaining stationed in India, he surreptitiously moved across several countries and continents. He took part in the powerplay of international politics, mostly as a strategic advisor at the highest levels, influencing the outcomes of world events more often than not. According to his fantastic-sounding claims, his zone of play was spread across several conflict-ridden countries such as Israel, Palestine, Arabic, African, Central and Southeast Asian countries, apart from China and Russia. This, he said, he was doing in India's interest. Secondly, after taking *sanyas* formally, he delved deep into spiritual practice. According to many of those who came in touch with him, he appeared to be a spiritual powerhouse, possessing various *siddhis* mentioned in the scriptures. Thirdly, he spent a large amount of time in UP in confinement, often plagued by serious illness and mostly spending days in utter penury. In this chapter, and the two subsequent ones, we take a close look into each of these aspects.

The terrible poverty in which Bhagwanji lived and his physical sufferings were clear to both Pabitra Mohan Roy and Leela Roy from their initial interactions. That he was living the life of a monk was also apparent, especially with Bhagwanji's main identity in his surrounding areas being that of a holy man. However, as interactions increased, the façade of a holy man in disguise started coming apart. The spiritual aspect of Bhagwanji was overpowering, but around it was woven an identity that was intensely political, though not in the ordinary sense.

In spite of the strictest secrecy maintained by him, Bhagwanji opened up to Pabitra and Leela Roy, with a word of caution:

> You cannot comprehend, to what end your Dead Man is working and with what Powers. Your imaginations will be awed, your brain will reel, if even by chance you could come to know even a fractional part of his present activities.

Over a period of time, Bhagwanji started providing glimpses into his secret world, revealing much, but withholding crucial bits, just as a spymaster would. He would speak and write about his work and plans, but always without giving away the precise details. In letters and discourses, especially during the early years and less frequently as the years went by, he sketched the broad outlines of his objective and a vague picture of how the goal would be attained. For Leela Roy, the language became a hurdle. The code names and oblique references to places, characters and events would often befuddle her. Not one to accept an unfavourable situation silently, she raised the issue with Bhagwanji, drawing a sharp reaction from him. He wouldn't be able to give more precise details than whatever he had already told her because that would mean giving out the identity of his 'horizon'—his sphere of action and influence—and his modus operandi, he wrote to her. However, he believed that he had given her enough details and if she couldn't comprehend, it was because she hadn't paid diligent attention to what he had said.

> If you had cared to select the key parts from the numerous letters that contained all sorts of discussions and compile them into a separate notebook whenever you received each letter, you would have easily understood. If these letters fall in the hands of the 'other side'; if they read each letter diligently, cull out and put together those 'special' messages from the large mass of letters, then they will get a clear picture of the objective of the Dead Man's *matri sadhana* and its final shape. Reading the predictions perfectly matching the 'incidents' that have happened from 'then till now', they will understand what the completion of the remaining ones means and will thus get the God-sent opportunity to take pre-emptive action to save and sustain themselves. They will be elated that where they were groping in the dark in the search of the dead, now they have light.
> Despite all these, of all people, you complained....[1] [Translated from Bengali]

---

1   Bhagwanji's letter to Leela Roy, undated, quoted in *Jayasree*, February 2015, pp 457-458.

Based on the available fragments from the documents generated over two decades by Bhagwanji, it is possible to reconstruct only an approximation of the 'plan' that he started discussing with Leela Roy and Pabitra—a plan that concerned not only India but spanned across wider geographies and had armed conflict as a prominent component. The components of the plan, the evolving strategy and the means deployed to make the plan successful are available in bits and pieces in letters written to and notes taken by different people at different points of time. It is a complex jigsaw puzzle where one would be lucky to find the pieces, let alone fit them together to get the full picture. If anything emerges with a semblance of coherence, it is the end objective. Bhagwanji's clear goal was to reunify India and, in the fullness of time, make her a world power.

As the Second World War drew to its end, all Subhas Bose could do was to implore helplessly both the Congress and the Muslim League not to bring about the 'vivisection of India'. It was but natural therefore that the partition of the country was a development that devastated him. He could never reconcile with it.

'A monstrosity shall be wiped off the map,' Bhagwanji wrote to Pabitra. 'Know it as the unalterable truth that the divided, wretched motherland (*Janani Janmabhumi*) will get back her undivided form, and if "someone's" mental state so reacts to the situation then, the undivided motherland can take a larger form too,' he wrote to Leela Roy with the fire of suffering burning in his heart (*see the image of the letter*). Most importantly, not only did he assure her of his presence during the reunification—'*Bhoot* (the ghost) will still be around'—but assured Roy that all this would happen while she was alive. He asserted that there wasn't a shred of doubt about any of the developments he predicted. 'These are as certain as life and death.' In 1963, he would write to Pabitra that in the next twenty years,

> A completely new, refulgent, glorious Bengal-India shall be astride. And, also, in all humility, I might tell you that the world shall reap the harvest of peace for a millennium[2], with Divine mother *Jagadamba Durga* and God's grace. It is not for nothing that your Dead man is 'Dead' and is staking all his brain-and-worth towards this end. You shall live to taste the fruits of his most laborious endeavours. It is now God's own will. Do not feel even a shadow-of-doubt about this Truth.[3]

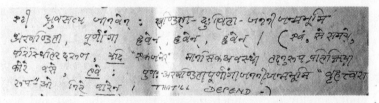

[Bhagwanji's letter to Leela Roy, undated, 1963. Courtesy Bijoy Kumar Nag. (এটি ধ্রুবসত্য জানবেন: খণ্ডিতা-দুঃখিতা-জননী জন্মভূমি অখণ্ডিতা, পূর্ণাঙ্গা হবেন, হবেন, হবেন (এবং, সে সময়ে, পরিস্থিতির দরুন, যদি "একজনের" মানসিক অবস্থা তদনুরূপ প্রতিক্রিয়া কোরে বসে, তবে: পুনঃ অখণ্ডিতা পূর্ণাঙ্গা জননী জন্মভূমি "বৃহত্তরা রূপ"-ও নিতে পারেন)]

The goal was articulated with a tone of finality and an assurance of having invincible forces at his command. Bhagwanji must have given more details on the fantastic plan—which was rather unbelievable, coming as it did from a man who had confined himself to a small temple, did not meet anyone around and had extremely modest means. But those details are not available to us.

---

2   To Leela Roy also he indicated that the scheme of things that he was about to establish would last for centuries.

3   Bhagwanji's letter to Pabitra Mohan Roy, 1 January 1963.

He called it 'the greatest secret of the era'. Before Leela Roy made contact with Bhagwanji, Pabitra, he said, was the only person to know anything about it 'outside the cadre who are entrusted with the execution of the plan of stratagem and strategical orders and the oncoming military operations of "concentration",—"dispersion",—"distribution", as finally approved and ordered into operation by your Dead Man in India'. The man knew his Sun Tzu.

One of the registered letters in which Bhagwanji discussed some of his ideas with Leela Roy, however, never reached her; it was lost, or stolen. That was not the only time—his letters went missing a few times making him extremely worried. He kept a keen eye on the letters being delivered to detect signs of tampering (see image of letter to Pabitra Mohan Roy). It is not improbable that communications to and from Leela Roy and Pabitra were under intelligence scanner, the way those of the near and dear of Subhas Bose were. It is far more likely that the two leading followers were being shadowed in the way Sisir and Amiya Bose were, in view of their known links with Subhas Bose. In fact, Leela Roy's stature was not matched by any 'Netaji kin' other than Sarat Bose. The letter was important as it contained details of his plans, of course written in language that would be unintelligible to anyone without the knowledge of the context.

Bhagwanji summarised the major points in a subsequent letter. To Leela Roy, his strict instruction was to rise above all considerations of 'party, sect, political ego, personal ego' for none of these would matter in the new scheme of things that he envisioned. Accordingly, she should not allow any political

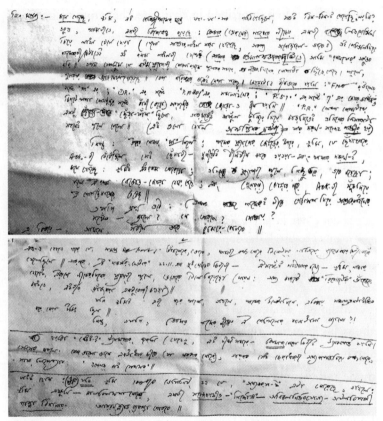

[Bhagwanji's letter to Pabitra Mohan Roy, 19 January 1972, discusses in great detail why he suspects that Pabitra's letter to him might have been opened and read. He also explains how censoring of letters was done in an obvious reference to the days of the British Raj]

party or politician of any sort to come within a hundred miles of her activities. *Janani Janmabhoomi* should be the only reigning queen in her existence, replacing all thoughts of party politics. He wanted Roy to play a prominent role in the new order—what exactly, he didn't spell out, but described it as 'a Job's job'—and wanted her to 'prepare and gear up from now onwards'. Roy was his first choice and he did not want anyone else to assume that role: 'I'll be mutely mortified in that case,' he wrote to her.[4] For Bhagwanji, his aim was equivalent to his *Matri Sadhana* (mother worship). War, he argued, was not 'an emotional business', but a 'cold, calculated affair'.

> Whether war should be brutal, cathartic or a human business is besides the point. Everyone knows that no war can be conducted and fought with kid gloves. Modern war, especially, takes an appalling toll both of human life and property. No civilized nation risks it lightly, but when it is forced on it, it has to be waged in a manner that makes the opponent wince. This is done not in any vindictive spirit but in a cold, calculated manner to break the opponents' morale so that he is forced to sue for peace. Abstract principles have nothing to do with the waging of war.[5]

Although Bhagwanji assured both Leela Roy and Pabitra about his presence during and after the planned operation, he also indicated that the operation had been put on a self-propelling mode and would not stop even if he wasn't around.

'If you wish for peace, understand war,' was his suggestion. Ignorance in this matter leads to disarmament of the peace-loving people who are subsequently neither able to prevent war nor control its course. The central strategy of warfare was, according to him, captured in the sequence of 'concentration-dispersion-distribution', which he explained to Pabitra. 'The whole principle of war is condensed in this one single word "concentration",' he wrote soon after India's humiliation in 1962. It was nothing less

---

4   Bhagwanji's letter to Leela Roy, undated, 1963.
5   Bhagwanji's letter to Pabitra Mohan Roy, 1 January 1963.

than a lecture on the art of warfare that deserves to be quoted extensively.

> Abstract principles have nothing to do with the waging of a war. You (also mentors and policymakers of India) must grasp this elementary fact and apply the mind without further delay to the understanding of war…Basically, the approach is simple: The enemy must be made to disperse his forces under pressure and should be kept in the dark about the point or points where a concentrated attack will be made to bring about disorganisation. To ensure success, two major problems must be solved—disorganisation and exploitation. One precedes and one follows the actual blow. You must somehow wrest the initiative from the invader and aim at bringing about disorganisation of his forces in some vital sector in the frontline as well as on his home front. The more you make it clear that you shall fight only at the places of his choosing and disperse your forces at his dictation, the more you shall place yourselves at a disadvantage. You have to parry the enemy on all fronts including the home front. The so-called wise men of the world say, and hope, 'War will have no future.' But experience suggests that war has some purpose that is beyond the ambit of human reason, despite its palpable unreasonableness as a way of settling human issues. That purpose may be as a corrective to greater evil, as a cleansing of the spirit of a people and age from corruption and sins.[6]

The Chinese, he said, were following to the letter the elementary rules of strategy laid down by 'experts in warfare' and 'JN (Jawaharlal Nehru) and his henchmen who are seeking approach to Peking' should be made aware of it. And then he

---

6   Bhagwanji's letter to Pabitra Mohan Roy, March 1963.

himself laid down the key principles to Pabitra.

The Dos and Don'ts for strategists and tacticians by world famous master strategists and tacticians in classical works are 8 in all:

Dos

- Adjust your ends to your means...It is folly to bite off more than you can chew, and the beginning of military wisdom is to know what can't be done. So, learn to face facts while still preserving faith.
- Keep your object always in mind while adapting your plan to circumstances.
- Choose the line (or course) of least expectation.
- Exploit the line of least resistance.
- Take a line of operation which offers alternative objectives. For you will then put your opponent on the horns of a dilemma, which goes far to assure the chance of gaining one objective at least—whichever he guards least—and may enable you to gain one after the other.
- Ensure that both plans and dispositions are elastic or adaptable.

Don'ts

- Don't lunge whilst your opponent can parry. The experience of history shows that no effective stroke is possible until the enemy's power of resistance or evasion is paralysed.
- Don't renew an attack along the same line or form.[7]

Read out of context, these could appear to be the words of someone obsessed with armed conflict but war was just one of the many options that he discussed. If anything, these words show

---

7   Ibid.

that he possessed a mind that understood both the art and horror of war.

Bhagwanji made it clear that he was very much aware of the downsides of getting entangled in a prolonged war. 'I believe that the brute terror of war is like a major surgery, which should be taken up only when absolutely necessary,' he explained. It should be no more than a temporary measure, following which the 'surgeon' must step aside. Bhagwanji's utterances on war were neither a theoretical exposition nor restricted to India's China war in its reference. He mentioned to Leela Roy that he would do his best to achieve his goal through minimum bloodshed within and outside the country, but if that proved inadequate and if he was forced, then he,

> ...shall shuffle his final pack-o'-cards and, play-in his four aces, without a shadow of doubt...and, in that case...the world shall witness...the unbelievably–most terrible thing (the world has ever seen, or for that matter, shall ever see) of the last 4-5 centuries...

For the onlookers in the country and outside, the indicator would be a series of small-scale conflicts that were going to occur in different phases with increasing frequency. 'Shocks, kicks, thumpings, blows (many sided and from inside too) shall be coming' [on to India] he wrote. And then, within a year—at the most with a variation of a few months—there will be a great multipronged shock that will throw the country into a state of panic. The Government won't have the courage to take the steps that would be desired by the whole country. At that time, he indicated, he would need to travel to his 'gyrating centres' at least some of which were outside the country. As the situation peaks, he said, 'somewhere—somethings shall be done', and it will be seen that both sides are equally powerful. Things will be shoved under the carpet again.[8]

If the purpose of writing in this style was to throw off any suspicion about his identity and plans, it must have worked wonders. What probably made sense to Pabitra or Leela Roy (sometimes with great difficulty) would appear gibberish to any outsider. Yet, as would become clear eventually, Bhagwanji was throwing hints about the two major wars that India would face within the next ten years—the wars of 1965 and 1971—the alignment of other countries and India's failure to leverage its victory in both.

If Bhagwanji asked Leela Roy to prepare for a future leadership role in his scheme of things, he had more meticulous instructions for Pabitra over a longer period of time, and a cautionary message:

---

8   Bhagwanji's letter to Leela Roy, undated, March 1963.

Your task operation must not be found lagging at the proper hour. You have been finally commissioned for three task works:

- getting the things as wanted 'item by item'
- getting your Force ready for 'The Task'
- getting, preparing, collecting, sorting and keeping irrefutable facts, proofs, dates, information on persons, groups, and parties whose outlook and activities are 'ANTI' __ without sentiments. (sic)

The first task assigned was in regard to procuring the items Bhagwanji had listed to Pabitra in one of his earliest letters, and the third of these stipulated tasks was something that Pabitra carried out till the time Bhagwanji remained in touch with him. The most curious part, however, was the instruction to get a 'force' ready. Was he asking his former intelligence officer, who was now a politician, to raise an army? It would appear so; more of a guerrilla force. The nomenclature used by Bhagwanji—'force of reoccupation', 'army of reunion', and at times, '*Bharat Suraksha Bahini*' (sounding similar to future *Mukti Bahini* of Bangladesh liberation war), seem to indicate that the force was to be used in the context of a conflict with Bangladesh. If so, it is an astounding move predating the formation of the Mukti Bahini by nearly eight years.

The 'force' was not to go beyond a Division in size and not lesser than four thousand. In his letters, Bhagwanji gave sketchy details of the force he had in mind, of which the important ones were that it was to comprise 'handpicked', 'tested', and 'fanatic fighting material' from among non-Muslim men who were to be deployed in the border areas of East Pakistan. Pabitra drew up a list of such areas and obtained Bhagwanji's approval. Bhagwanji asked him to focus on the traditional fighters of Bengal—the Rajbanshis,

Doms, Bagdis and the Namashudras. It was not surprising, in view of his opinion about Indian communists, that he instructed Pabitra to ensure that none of the chosen people, or anyone from their families, was associated with the Communist Party.

One of the tasks planned for this proposed force was to stop trespassing and infiltration of non-Hindus from across the East Pakistan border. 'In the not very distant future,' the force's 'task' would expand to making 'sorties' across the border; localities on the other side were to be selected for overnight operations. He named Pabitra its Field Commander. When action began, he assured, Pabitra would operate and lead his men 'independently (with his own officers)' and 'shall not be placed under a Corps commander'. On the V-Day, with his force Pabitra 'shall be recognised and proclaimed as "the only commander from inside India" to lead his own army of reunion'.

Raising a force was easier said than done. Bhagwanji was aware that in view of Pabitra's public visibility as a politician, any such effort was bound to attract attention. He therefore advised him to utilise the current situation. Following the China war, the Government was focusing on reorganising the home guards and civil defence; NCC (National Cadet Corps) training was made compulsory. 'With a little manipulation you shall be able to create your army in the guise of above-mentioned bodies,' Bhagwanji advised Pabitra in March 1963. There would be no apprehension on the part of the authorities and he could openly carry out his activities posing as a patriotic citizen responding to the call of the Government. He goaded Pabitra to fully utilise all avenues open to him, starting from his membership of the Praja Socialist Party

(PSP), which could come in handy in approaching those in power to obtain government funds allocated for this purpose. He was free to use the central office of the INA in Delhi, and in the name of Netaji's ideals even approach J K Bhonsle, INA's chief of staff and later a junior minister in Nehru's government, and other former soldiers of the INA who had not joined the Congress government or taken favours from it. Bhagwanji suggested that he should contact (in secret) Y B Chavan, the then Defence Minister, who 'is very much inclined towards INA' and is 'a worshipper of Shivaji'.

Quoting the Spanish proverb *Hurtar para dar por Dios* (to steal, in order to give for God's sake) Bhagwanji reminded Pabitra that the motherland was the only God.

Eventually, nothing materialised. Like many other social and political tasks that Bhagwanji would assign his followers, this plan too remained a non-starter.[9]

These forward-looking plans and milestones, however, were not the starting point of his activities in the subcontinent. They were only meant to have his old revolutionary associates involved—cautiously, slowly, but surely. His first major involvement in the subcontinent appears to have come with the Chinese invasion of 1962. He claimed to have intervened to have the People's Liberation Army (PLA) back off.

Atul Sen had informed Nehru about Bhagwanji in August 1962. Pabitra landed in Neemsar soon, but had to wait for a

9 'I have been exhorting you for the past several years and you have done nothing,' Bhagwanji chided his followers later. Charanik, *Oi Mahamanaba Ase*, Jayasree Prakashan, 2010, p 303.

couple of months before he could contact Bhagwanji sometime in November. The reason for the prolonged waiting was Bhagwanji's absence from Neemsar. 'This old *faquir* had to go out twice, while here. Once for about 5 ½ weeks before Nov, and once for about 7 weeks (a month before that). A "certain" of your comrade officer-in-arms, brought critical information, and I had to go at a moment's notice (the result is before you all),' Bhagwanji wrote to Pabitra in one of his earliest letters, written in December 1962. He went out, he claimed, to manoeuvre his way through the Chinese leadership in order to ensure the withdrawal of the PLA. To Leela Roy, he mentioned that the unilateral ceasefire was announced within fifteen days of his return.[10]

[Bhagwanji's letter to Pabitra Mohan Roy, 21 September 1972, outlining his role in unilateral ceasefire declaration by the PLA. Bhagwanji suggested to Pabitra that he should bring this to the attention of the inquiry of then ongoing Khosla Commission]

The earliest available commentary of Bhagwanji on the war comes from a letter he wrote to Pabitra on 22 December 1962, just a month after the ceasefire in the Sino-Indian war. His take on

---

10   Bhagwanji's letter to Leela Roy, undated, quoted in *Jayasree*, February 2015, p 458.

the India-China war was similar to what the experts came to hold years later as a chastened India repulsed the Pakistani offensive in 1965. In his letter to Pabitra, Bhagwanji gave his overall views on the conflict:

> The government stand self-condemned and have been forced to admit and confess the falsehood, and double-talks and Himalayan blunders. The government stand branded as traitors. Take it from me, this aggression is the greatest blessing Mother India could invoke for her children.

On the face of it, calling the Chinese attack a blessing would sound anti-national, when the atmosphere in the country was charged with patriotic fervour, anger and grievance against the intruders. But what Bhagwanji indicated was that the attack exposed the serious breaches in India's political, military and administrative set up, as much as the role played by the political parties.

Opening the battle on 20 October, the Chinese forces invaded Ladakh, and across the McMahon Line in the then North-East Frontier Agency. That the invaders continued their march unopposed worried Bhagwanji when he rushed out of Neemsar, crossed the Indo-China border, and confronted the Chinese leaders. 'When "he" came to know that the Chinese have moved in, "he" was angry and stationed himself just outside the border to explain the terrible consequences of the aggression, to stop the unopposed progress of the victorious forces and to have them declare ceasefire unilaterally, he wrote to Pabitra about his activities. This, according to Bhagwanji was a result of greed overtaking the original Chinese plans. The lack of resistance and the cooperation of the fifth columnists[11] in India was too tempting for their forces not to push forward their march: the onward march of the PLA was the result of overenthusiasm of certain factions within the Chinese army, but 'fifteen days after my return, the aggression was stopped unilaterally'.

With the knowledge of an insider, he described some of the instances of betrayal that helped bring on the Chinese onslaught. 'A son of Bengal had sent an expert report to JN on measures that needed to be taken at key positions to prevent incursions by enemies across the Himalayas, but JN was not allowed to receive the report,' Bhagwanji wrote in a letter in the mid-1960s. In a scandalous allegation, he claimed that the report was smuggled out of the Defence Ministry to Pakistan and from there to China. China used exactly the same routes marked in the report, he claimed.

While there is no information on any report despatched by a Bengali officer as Bhagwanji claimed, in 2012, *India Today* accessed a Top Secret 1960 assessment by Lt-Gen SPP Thorat (a Maharashtrian), then army commander, Eastern Command, on the looming threat of China. Was it the one alluded to by him? It was written after a year-long study of the Chinese build-up across the McMahon Line. The Army even war gamed Chinese incursions and India's response in the form of Exercise Lal Qila in 1960. The magazine quoted former vice-chief of army staff Lt-Gen Shantanu Chowdhary saying, 'Had effective preparations

---

11   'Their dogs in this country had provided them with all information and facilitated their advance,' were his words.

been done when Lt-Gen Thorat warned, the situation would have been very different.'[12]

Bhagwanji kept writing about the Chinese invasion and Indo-China relations now and then in his letters, but one place where he jotted down his thoughts and reactions was the book *Himalayan Blunder* by Brigadier J P Dalvi, first published in 1969. A copy of the book recovered from Ram Bhawan was found to be densely underlined and replete with comments on the margins. It was one of the samples of handwriting that led B Lal to conclude that Bhagwanji was none other than Subhas Chandra Bose (see images on next page). Writing comments on the margins was indeed an old habit of Subhas Chandra Bose.

Evidently, he admired Dalvi's account. Against Frank Moraes's comment in the book's foreword that 'It is the great merit of Dalvi's book that while he evidently has sufficient dynamite to blow some political and military reputations sky-high, he refrains from doing so merely for the heck of doing so,' Bhagwanji remarked, 'too true'.

He wrote that he was a witness to Brig Dalvi's imprisonment in a prisoner of war camp in Tibet. The Chinese were '100% correct students of Maharshi Kowtilya'. On Nehru's decision to refer the Kashmir problem to the UN, Bhagwanji wrote, 'A humiliating reptilian study of a stupid clown—posing statesmanship.' On Dalvi's criticism of India's non-alignment hope that 'vague diplomatic promises and hopes would be our safeguard to ward

---

12   Gaurav C Sawant, 'Lt-Gen Thorat's 1962 warning on Chinese intrusions went unheard,' *India Today*, 16 October 2012, https://www.indiatoday.in/india/north/story/lt-gen-thorat-1962-warning-on-chinese-intrusions-went-unheard-119084-2012-10-16.

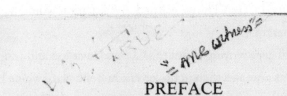

[Very very true. Me witness]

PREFACE

THIS BOOK was born in a Prisoner of War Camp in Tibet on a cold bleak night.

On the night of 21st November, 1962, I was woken up

The Uneasy Lull—1950 to 1955

[100% correct student of Maharshi Kowtilya]

THE CHINESE began to consolidate their hold on Tibet with customary thoroughness. On 9th September 1951 they entered Lhasa "peacefully". In political matters they were patient, and did not force the pace of change. They used the existing political system and the immense authority of the Dalai Lama to implement the famous Seventeen-Point Agreement.

In the early years their primary aim appeared to

...network of communications and stationed large garrisons

136

[Only the Indian Govt. is adept in empty boasts of JN—the then PM. He was wicked through and through].

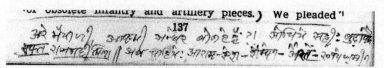

[अरे भैया जी, आप भी अंधेर बोलते हैं?! सोचिये सही: बुढ़ापे मे मुफ्त राजगद्दी मिला। अब चाहिये: आराम–ऐश–शैम्पेन–औरतें–रुपये–ज़मीन
(O brother! What nonsense! Think about it: in old age he [Nehru] has ascended the throne without having fought for it. What does he need now? Comfort, luxury, champagne, women and wealth)]

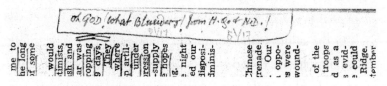

[Aren't your high praises sentimental? I know Gen. Prasad only as a 'yesman-lapdog' to the High Command and the political bosses. He never possessed strength of character to take up command, when the necessity arose. He was afraid]

[Oh God! What blunders! From HQ & ND!]

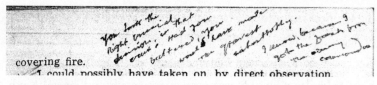

[You took the right crucial decision in that event. Had you battered, you would have made the gravest catastrophy (sic). I know, because I got the facts from the enemy commander]

off the Pakistani danger', Bhagwanji commented in Hindi, *'Oh! Ve jante nahin? Baaton ki vajra prahar se hi qila fatah kar loonga!'* (Don't they know? I will capture the fort with the might of my words!).

'Arrey Mian Sahab, apne kya soch rakhe hain? Hamari mahan half-Muslim leaderon ne sharab pi kar philosophy ki ek hi theory se un saare napaakon ko bhasm kar denge. Apne philosophy jaante hain?' [You have preconceived notions, my dear. With one theory of philosophy conceived after getting drunk, our great half-Muslim leaders will destroy all obstacles. Don't you know philosophy?] he remarked sarcastically in his broken Hindi on the then government's neglect of India's frontiers and the armed forces. On Nehru's announcement to the Parliament that India was lodging protests against repeated Chinese incursions, his take was *'Haan ji! Protest ki golabari se sab ke sab Chini hafiz ki prostate gland phat gaya hai! Sab bhage! Samjhe MPs?'*

On the soldiers facing hardship, Bhagwanji wrote, 'Ah, dear simple honest sons of India.' 'God, save these sons who are, thus, sacrificed for those politicians chairkeeping only,' he lamented. For Lt Gen Umrao Singh, he wrote, 'I make my humble bow to thee.' Reacting to Dalvi's point on lack of intelligence appreciation on the Chinese intentions, Bhagwanji wrote, *'Nautanki ke raj me aisa hi hoga; us se chaunkte kyon ho?'* He marked Chief of Army Staff General P N Thapar and Chief of the General Staff General B M Kaul as 'guilty men'. He was particularly harsh on General Kaul: 'He had a nervous breakdown and ran away at the first shooting from the Chinese side,' he wrote. On Major General Niranjan Prasad he commented, 'He is no general in the real sense of the word.' Later, he again made an assessment of Maj Gen Prasad as if he had seen him closely: 'I know Gen Prasad only as a "yes man lapdog" to the High Command and the political bosses. He never possessed strength of character to take up command when the necessity arose. He was afraid.'

On Jawaharlal Nehru, Bhagwanji was unrelentingly scathing. Reacting to the Indian government's promise of recovering 'every inch' of occupied territories in Ladakh, he noted, 'Only the Indian Govt is adept in empty boasts of JN—the then PM. He was wicked through and through.' At a more personal level, he remarked, *Arre bhaiyyaji, aap bhi andher bolte hain? Sochiye sahi, budhape me muft raj gaddi mila. Ab chahiye araam, aish, champagne, auratein, rupaye, zameen.'* [You are talking nonsense. Think about it. In the old age, he has got reigns of the country without having to struggle for it. Now he needs comforts, luxuries, champagne, women, money, property]. 'J No 1 *kayar aur charitraheen tha,'* he commented at another place. [Nehru was a coward and characterless]. The prime minister's handling of the entire conflict drew the comment, 'Oh, suckling baby PM!'

To Dalvi's observation that 'Public opinion in India had become inflamed at the Government which made brave statements but appeared to take no action,' Bhagwanji remarked, 'Government *hi to public ko, jhoot, fareb bazi, gaddari aur chhipav se bilkul hi gumraah kiya tha, apna apna kursiyan bachaye rakhne ke liye.'* [The public was misled by the Government that engaged in lies, intrigue and treachery. This was done to safeguard political interests.]

When Dalvi explained his reasons for not opening fire on the Chinese forces in the Tseng-Jong battle, Bhagwanji fully endorsed his reasons. 'You took the right crucial decision,' he scribbled on the margin of the page, 'I know because I got the facts from the enemy commander.' As the author expressed his apprehension that 'my troops were likely to be sacrificed through the stubbornness of others', Bhagwanji remarked, 'You realise this now! I've been trying to make you understand this all the while till now!' One point on which he disagreed with Brig Dalvi was over his resignation—Bhagwanji believed that the Brigadier should have resigned after the debacle. 'You are a great soul Brig Dalvi,' he wrote. 'God blessed you for your nobility, humility and honesty. He saved you from sure death and brought you back to your people.'

Scores of such comments which could only be written with full insider's knowledge fill up the pages of the book, leaving one to wonder as to how he could gather all this inside intelligence. (*See the compilation of images from the book*).

Although his views on China were unambiguous, Bhagwanji wouldn't put the blame of the war on the neighbouring aggressor country. According to his reading of the developments, China was not to be blamed as ostensibly it had no intention of grabbing Indian territory initially. It was Nehru who made China aggressive by his bravado, referring to which Bhagwanji commented that it is 'suicidally foolish and sheer meanness to underestimate and make fun of one's adversary'. According to him, every historian and war expert knows that China is really a past master in game of geopolitics for thousands of years. Rather than mocking the enemy, a worthy and noble fighter always admires and appreciates the shrewdness and fighting abilities of his adversary, and tries to match him. Now that Nehru stood defeated in the war, it was sheer hypocrisy and utter stupidity to bemoan and bewail India's weakness and unpreparedness. The game of war is about vanquishing the enemy through his unpreparedness. To complain to the world that the enemy is unscrupulous, unkind, brute, and does not give prior information about his intentions "is crass nonsense". 'It is your enemy's business to befool you in all respects.'[13]

Given the opportunity (which according to Bhagwanji was nothing but an open invitation in this case) any conquering nation would embark on a conquering venture. The Chinese knew that Nehru was no match for them, the monk said. Writing in early 1963, Bhagwanji predicted that although the war had ended and even if diplomatic negotiations made progress, China would still remain in possession of Indian territory, 'not to speak of Tibet'. 'What India needs is not cursing the enemy, but matching him in his skills squarely and beat him at his own game,' was his suggestion for the way forward.

The 'intelligence' shared by Bhagwanji on the post-war period was even more sensational. He indicated that he had prevailed upon the Chinese to make a top secret conciliatory offer to Nehru—an offer that China agreed to make only out of deference to him, even at the cost of losing some standing in the global communist order. Along with the proposal went a message from the Dead Ghost, 'I want to come back.' But there was no response. The message was sent a second time through a mutually known and respected foreigner, and then again for a third time through an Indian. Each time the message was met with silence.

---

13   Bhagwanji's letter to Pabitra Mohan Roy, March 1963.

The Chinese had apparently predicted that Nehru would rebuff both their offer and Bhagwanji's message, but went ahead due to his insistence. Now they were proved right and Bhagwanji was mortified. That was probably the first time he tried to surface with the help of the Government. Bhagwanji mentioned that after Nehru's death, Lal Bahadur Shastri too remained silent about his desire to return to India.[14]

In hindsight, Bhagwanji speculated that the silence of Nehru was probably to be expected because taking him back would mean throwing the blunders of the Government wide open to public view, which would result in severe public reprisal. 'One day,' he hoped, 'when the people of India come to know about the background of the disaster and all that is kept secret now, they will be shocked to shame.' The question, however, that will remain unanswered is why did Bhagwanji ask Nehru to aid his return?

Bhagwanji's purported influence on the Chinese probably led Pabitra to question the possibility of his involvement in the 1962 attack. This resulted in a sharp and furious retort: 'It is preposterous, nay, it is blasphemous even to dream that [he] shall lead those thrice cursed infernal Han lords. Never say such words again.'[15] Whatever the relations between China and India, Bhagwanji's good relations with the Chinese remained intact. He was open in admiring certain traits of the Chinese. Once, he lamented that India would do better to follow in their footsteps instead of blindly imitating the West. 'Never forget that

14   Bhagwanji's letter to Leela Roy, undated, quoted in *Jayasree*, February 2015, pp 458-459.
15   Bhagwanji's letter to Pabitra Mohan Roy, March 1963.

irrespective of the perception of other countries regarding China in terms of their relations, ethics, etc.—whatever it has done till now—all rights and wrongs, mistakes, misdeeds, managing their internal and external affairs, building its army, fighting wars— has been on its own steam, without taking any external aid,' Bhagwanji wrote to Pabitra. He further explained in a letter dated 27 November 1971:

> Whatever China is doing and is going to do, it alone will be responsible for that. It is not dependent on others on any matter. It is competing with Russia as an equal in infiltrating all small and big countries in the world—among their students, workers' unions, schools, colleges, universities, professors, the educated class, labourers, farmers and politicians. Working secretly among them, the Chinese are fomenting dissatisfaction, unrest, terrorism, strikes, demonstrations, rebellions and sabotage. Russia and China are doing these in your country too. The Chinese are proving equal to the CIA also.[16]

That the Chinese could wrest control of Aksai Chin from India and parts of Pakistan-occupied-Kashmir from Pakistan was to Bhagwanji an indicator of the 'high calibre of its diplomatic capability'. India needs to give due respect to its abilities and make itself stronger by learning from them, was his advice. India's foreign policy, he said, should aim to avoid a conflict over India between either of the communist States of China or Russia and the Western superpowers, especially the US. Speaking at a time prior to China's development of the atomic bomb, Bhagwanji

---

16   Bhagwanji's letter to Pabitra Mohan Roy, 27 November 1971. Translated from Bengali.

painted the possible scenarios that might emerge if India accepted military intervention from the US in the event of another Indo-China conflict. In such an eventuality, Russia might lend atomic bombs to China, which China would surely use on India. Another possibility was that Russia might project the US intervention in an Indo-China conflict as a war between the US and China, and declare a war against the US. India's aim, therefore, he said, was to ensure that 'China must not be provided with a valid reason to force Khrushchev's hands' to give them the bomb or 'a chance to fight' the US 'for and over India'.[17]

Bhagwanji claimed direct relations with the Chinese leaders up to the early 1970s. Not only did he favour China's demand for becoming a permanent member of the UN Security Council, but on 27 November 1971, a month and two days after Communist China was admitted to the Security Council, Bhagwanji wrote

---

17   The Soviet Union did side with the Chinese during the 1962 war, driven by the Cuban missile crisis, and as we saw in chapter 10, Nehru did seek help from Kennedy. The situation had changed by 1971. The apprehension of India getting embroiled in the rivalry between Soviet Union and China came up during the Indo-Pak war of 1971, but from another source. To assuage the feelings of the US government over the Indo-Soviet friendship treaty, India's ambassador to the US, L K Jha met Henry Kissinger on 25 August 1971. Kissinger told Jha that 'he could not understand why India would want to be drawn into the Sino-Soviet rivalry, or why it would deliberately antagonize the US.' According to the US version of the minutes of the meeting, Jha told Kissinger that Indira Gandhi was not at all pro-Soviet, but gave in to the pressure exerted by former foreign minister Dinesh Singh (who Jha alleged to be on the payroll of the Russians), P N Haksar and foreign secretary T N Kaul. *Foreign Relations of the United States, 1969–1976*, Volume XI, South Asia Crisis, 1971, eds Daniel J Lawler and Erin R Mahan (Washington: Government Printing Office, 2010), Document 134. According to diplomat Maharaja Krishna Rasgotra, Jha gave an opposite report, stating that it was Kissinger who suspected Dinesh Singh of having taken money from the Soviet Union. Maharaja Krishna Rasgotra, *A Life in Diplomacy*. Penguin Books Ltd Kindle Edition.

to Pabitra that responding to requests from the Chinese, he had helped them in framing their arguments in support of their demand. Bhagwanji described in detail what exactly happened when he visited China:

The Chinese have had some long-standing grievances for which they have been demanding redressal. For a long time they have been discussing among themselves the ways and means of ensuring that their demands are met. Their topmost leaders then asked the 'very special person' for his views. 'He' told them that it was their internal affair and advised them, that 'first dehusk the paddy yourselves, without me. Once that is done, I will provide you with a draft based on my own assessment, and you can then compare both our versions'. Their 'very own person' then left, to return at a later date. Their leaders had in the meantime prepared their draft. Their 'own person' handed over his version of the rough draft which he had prepared for them and asked 'will this serve your purpose?' Their leaders rushed with the draft to a place for secret consultations, while 'their own person' went to dose off for some time in the garden. He woke up with a jolt from a noise that sounded like a series of large sea waves breaking off. The leaders carried him off on their heads among deafening applause of a thousand more party workers to the meeting hall of the celestial palace. There he was swamped with hugs, embraces and kisses. Thereafter very strong drinks started flowing, although the 'own person' restricted himself to a refreshing sherbet and light snacks.

After the initial euphoria subsided it was announced loudly for informing all leaders, workers, soldiers of the people's army and citizens of the celestial country, 'Oh! our thoughts and considerations are so narrow! It is astonishing to see how refined the thoughts of "our own person" are. He has added 15 arguments more than what we could put together, and each one of the demands is based on historic truth.' Those points were accepted. Armed with around two dozen such demands, the Chinese leaders made their way to the permanent membership of the Security Council.[18]

It is impossible to determine the veracity of these claims. Although the US had opened channels of communication with communist China leading to Henry Kissinger's visit to China in July 1971, it was still the biggest stumbling block to communist China's permanent membership of the Security Council. By the end of June, Richard Nixon admitted to the US Ambassador to Taiwan that replacing Republic of China with communist China in the Security Council was a certainty, but his administration would not support any move to throw Taiwan out of the UN.[19] The US continued its old strategy of blocking communist China's entry by moving the resolution requiring two-thirds majority votes in the UN General Assembly, which was rejected on 25 October. Thereafter, a resolution sponsored by Albania, Algeria and other twenty-one countries proposing restoration of the 'lawful rights' of communist China in the UN and expulsion of the representatives of Chiang Kai-shek was passed.

Prima facie, Bhagwanji's support to the Chinese would appear to be contradicting his avowals of serving his motherland. How could he assist the powers that he knew had designs on his *Janani Janmabhoomi*? At the same time, he was definitely not ungrateful.

---

18   'We are forever grateful to you for making possible what we failed to attain even after trying 10-12 times,' Mao told him later, Bhagwanji claimed. *Oi Mahamanaba Ase*, Jayasree Prakashan, 2010, p 237.
19   'Getting To Beijing: Henry Kissinger's Secret 1971 Trip,' University of Southern California, http://china.usc.edu/getting-beijing-henry-kissingers-secret-1971-trip

The burden of debt on him towards Russia and China was very real. He was resentful too, towards India. He blurted out at an angry moment: 'Russia and China have given me everything. They have put everything at stake to keep me alive and have not shown the slightest intent of interfering. Should I be theirs or India's who has abandoned me?'[20] Yet, there was a larger reality beyond all his apparent support to Russia and China. He had no illusion about their ambitions. 'Don't think I am with all that China is doing,' he told Bijoy Nag in 1973. His debt of gratitude didn't cloud his vision, or his intent. Even a decade earlier, Bhagwanji's assessment of the nature of relations between India and China clearly weighed on India's side. He wrote to Pabitra that China 'with its present policy is and shall remain your arch enemy'.

'China is dreaming that it will re-establish the Central Celestial State that it once was, and the garb of communism is only a fencing for the outside world,' he told Nag during one of their meetings. Both Russia and China desired communism to take over in India, but their approaches differed. While Russia preferred a takeover in a 'peaceful constitutional manner', China, 'which had far-reaching designs', would adopt any method it found suitable. To this day, the Chinese consider all countries and races outside their celestial empire to be inferior and barbaric except the more ancient India, Bhagwanji held.

China can never conquer India, he assured. 'If ever she so forgets herself (and "someone") and takes "such a lunge"—she shall be hamstrung and shall be made to cry halt.'

---

20   Journal of Jagatjit Dasgupta. Notes of conversation on 16 December 1979.

Comparing the attitudes of Russia and China towards India, he wrote to Pabitra in 1963, 'Until now, Russia has done nothing to antagonise India; on the other hand, Russia has antagonised China for India's sake.' He also claimed to be playing off Russia and China against each other. In this context, he characterised himself as Shakuni, the crafty king of Gandhara in the epic *Mahabharata*. China, he claimed in 1963, when the relations between the two countries were on the wane, has a 'completely secret' geopolitical goal. 'That objective is…somehow to get a war started' between Russia and the West. 'If they can get this done, then it will be a windfall for them,' he explained to Pabitra. It is an ongoing geopolitical manoeuvre in which 'China plays such a game of underhand, backdoor diplomacy that often Russia's position becomes precarious.'

Although Bhagwanji, going by his claim, worked closely with the Chinese leadership, he was particularly attached to Mao Zedong. On multiple occasions, he fondly narrated his conversations with Mao to his devoted listeners from behind the curtain. Based on the Bengali pronunciation of Mao's surname (Tung), Bhagwanji referred to Mao by the pseudonym Tungabhadra. 'Whatever you think of him or say about him, he is not at all a bad person. In fact, he is really great, a true leader of his people,' he said.[21] An embodiment of charm in the best traditions of the country, according to him, Mao represented the ideal of the ancient tradition and character of the country, 'who has been working out each problem of diplomacy absolutely

---

21   Charanik, *Oi Mahamanaba Ase*, Jayasree Prakashan, 2010, p 379.

correctly'. According to Bhagwanji, China and India were similar as far as losing their culture and ancient traditions as a result of colonial plunder was concerned. While a much shorter period of suffering under colonial rule than India has given China the chance for a faster reawakening, due to the prolonged slavery-induced state of intoxication, India is still not showing any sign of renascence. Bhagwanji's assessment was that the 'real driving force and reason' behind China taking the path of communism was only to 'recapture their ancient glory-cum-splendour'. Only communism would allow a fanatically inspired small group to concentrate all power to dominate over a country and its people in their hands. It was really nationalism in the garb of communism.[22] This, however, 'was their most stupendous blunder'.

With the insight of someone who has seen it all happen in front of his eyes, of someone who could see beyond the obvious, Bhagwanji narrated how Mao became the victim of the means he had adopted as the shortcut to attain greatness of his country: how he became a megalomaniac dictator driven by a 'Godless creed', his 'madman-like obsession' with his own revolutionary theories, his tactical retreat in the face of criticism within the party, leading to the rolling out of the cultural revolution movement from 1966. From his narratives, it is clear that he was in familiar

---

22   In an editorial obituary after Mao's death, *The Times* made strikingly similar comments. 'To the end he remained an untiring revolutionary, though the success he had as a revolutionary would have been beyond his reach had he not first won the loyalty of his countrymen as a nationalist, dreaming…of a glorious era when a regenerated China would compel the admiration of all the world. He gave China confidence and restored its pride…Essentially, Marxism was a tool to be exploited, a foreign import to be used and cast aside when it had served its purpose.' *The Times*, 10 September 1976.

territory in China, with access to secret and sensitive places. In the December 1978–January 1979 issue of *Jayasree*, Charanik's column described an underground city in Beijing. The column quoted Bhagwanji: 'With great surprise I saw that a complete city with all modern amenities, commercial and residential areas has been beautifully built deep underground which cannot be destroyed by ten atom bombs.' Since Charanik's columns always have had a time lag between Bhagwanji's conversations that are reported and the actual time of the discussion, it can be safely assumed that the story of this underground city was narrated by Bhagwanji much earlier. Even if it was not, it was nonetheless outstanding that Bhagwanji could describe Dixia Cheng—the underground city of Beijing equipped with facilities such as restaurants, clinics, schools, theatres, factories, and warehouses,—whose construction, starting in 1969 was concluded in 1979. The city remained unknown to the outside world till it was opened officially to tourists in 2000.

In all this, Bhagwanji claimed that he acted as Mao's intimate and secret advisor. He recounted how Mao acknowledged, time and again, his country's debt for all his help. He lamented to Bhagwanji that he [Mao] was punished by God for his sins in the form of loss of his son (Mao Anying). For Bhagwanji he admitted having the deepest admiration mixed with a tinge of fear of a person who had forsaken everything for a larger cause. Bhagwanji, in return, had the kindest words for him. 'I have tears when I recall how much they have done [for me]. Irrespective of whether anyone remembers, I will never forget the invisible flow of compassion inside his gigantic frame.'[23] On a lighter note, he commented on Chou En Lai, 'Although he drinks extremely stiff alcohol for hours, I have never seen him losing control or making a mistake.' Maotai, the Chinese liquor with up to sixty per cent alcohol content drew global attention when in 1972 Chou En Lai used it to raise a toast with Richard Nixon. Bhagwanji also recalled some personal habits of Mao: that he was a chain smoker, preferring very strong tobacco which was grown in his own garden; that he suffered from constipation; and that he had a slight lisp, pronouncing 'trick' as 'tilk'. Again, taunting Nehru, Mao supposedly told Bhagwanji, with reference to the highway constructed between Xinjiang (Sinkiang) and Tibet, passing through Aksai Chin:

> What kind of foolish ruler would one be who doesn't have an idea about the geographical border of his own country? I hope you don't need to be reminded that when after taking over 33,000 miles [sic] we constructed the six lane highway in that completely uninhabited region, your country's leader didn't even know about it. He got to know about it six years later when he heard about it from the traders. To cover up his incompetence, he said on the floor of Parliament that no one goes to that region, not even a blade of grass grows there. In other words, there is no harm even if that region is lost. And the members of your Parliament clapped for him.[24]

The Xinjiang Highway was constructed between 1951 and 1957. In a discussion with Henry Kissinger on 12 August 1971,

---

23   Charanik, *Oi Mahamanaba Ase*, Jayasree Prakashan, 2010, p 206.
24   Ibid, p 238.

Chou En Lai said that Nehru had no idea about the road even three years after its construction. He recalled his talks with Nehru in 1956, when he told the latter, 'You didn't even know we were building a road in the last three years, and now you suddenly say it is your territory.'[25]

One specific example of the extent of his influence on Mao which Bhagwanji gave many times was that he instigated the Chinese leader to roll out the Cultural Revolution leading to the death of millions. He convinced a marginalised Mao that if he delayed action, then he would lose all power soon. Bhagwanji vividly recollected the day the purges started: 'There was blood on the roads up to ankle height.' At the sign of Mao's nervousness at the scale of death, Bhagwanji claimed that 'there was someone behind him to prop up his courage'. Once, in Bhagwanji's presence, 'non-stop, indiscriminate firing went on in a city...300 trucks carried out dead bodies through the night. The dripping blood from the trucks filled the city roads'. Comparing his situation to that of Yudhishthir, who was compelled to witness the horrors of hell despite his being truthful all his life, Bhagwanji commented, 'Mother [Kali] made your man see hell too. My head swirls when I recount those scenes to you,' he told Bijoy Nag.

If this claim is true, the natural question that follows is whether Bhagwanji genuinely believed in or supported a programme like the Cultural Revolution. From what he said, it is certain that he

---

25   Top Secret Memorandum of Conversation held on 10 July 1971, The White House, 12 August 1971. Nixon Foundation. https://cdn.nixonlibrary.org/01/wp-content/uploads/2017/01/19110003/Polo-I-MemCon-July-10-1971-Part-2.pdf.

didn't: his action was a part of the larger goal of weakening China, to prevent it from becoming too powerful to pose a threat to India. The anonymous man of Basti made clear his thinking before Dulal Nandy. The guiding principles of his life were—steadfastness in oath like Bhishma, adeptness in diplomacy (*kutniti*) like Shakuni, and living by the principle of righteousness (*dharma niti*) like Shivaji.[26] 'Mao didn't realise that his person was really a Shakuni.' Again, 'they have no other beloved *matul* (maternal uncle—a reference to Shakuni) and strategical adviser like me. They can't even imagine that their strategical adviser *matul*—General Death—is behind the five or six uprisings that have taken place (in Tibet).' If Bhagwanji referred to himself as Shakuni in the game of politics, Mao, driven by megalomania became Duryadhana for him. The same went for Russia too. According to Bhagwanji, he was perhaps the only one who knew 'the very innermost thoughts and activities of both the camps, without their suspecting even in their wildest dreams' that he was 'their Anti'.

Yet, his affection and admiration for Mao was genuine. He considered Mao as perhaps the single person whom he could feel one with. He was deeply saddened when the news of Mao's death after prolonged illness reached him. When Bijoy Nag, Santosh Bhattacharya and Dulal Nandi visited Bhagwanji at Basti during the Durga Puja that year (1976), he poured his heart out to them. 'Do you know what the disease is like?' he asked them, and went

---

26   Notes of conversation with Bhagwanji taken by Dulal Nandy, January 1965. The other characters that he named as his role models included King Krishnachandra and the ancient sage Vishwamitra.

on to describe the symptoms of the disease. 'For example, if you are writing, your hand will stop suddenly; you will come to a sudden stop while walking,' he told the group, which as usual was furiously taking notes.[27] *The New York Times* reported on 10 September that Mao 'was widely believed' to be suffering from Parkinson's disease.[28] The Chinese official announcement had not specified Mao's illness. Knowing what was not in the public domain was Bhagwanji's forte. Information about Mao's death was no exception. 'Both Mao and I knew about this disease,' he said. Although Bhagwanji suggested allopathic treatment, Mao was unwilling as according to his assessment, the dosage of the medicine was yet to be fixed and hence it could not be considered the proper medication. 'The pioneer of this medicine was a Greek,' Bhagwanji enlightened his listeners.[29]

As with China, Bhagwanji's link with Russia continued. It was important to maintain that link. 'Russia is playing with Asia, Latin America, America, Europe and Africa,' he said. So is China, while the US is 'matching its game with them'. In the game of global politics, these three were the movers and shakers according to him. 'Let people say whatever they want but the result will depend on the games being played by these three countries,' was

---

27   Notes of conversation with Bhagwanji taken by Bijoy Kumar Nag, 1 October 1976.
28   'Mao Tse-Tung Dies In Peking At 82; Leader Of Red China Revolution; Choice Of Successor Is Uncertain,' *The New York Times*, 10 September 1976.
29   Bhagwanji probably referred to the Greek-American scientist George Constantin Cotzias and his breakthrough in treatment of the disease by using dihydroxyphenylalanine (see *George Constantin Cotzias: A Biographical Memoir*, published by the National Academic Press, Washington, DC).

his view. Both Russia and China take advantage of democracy in other countries to extend their control and supremacy, he held.[30] In India, 'Thousands of people are working in the garb of patriots on behalf of both Russia and China,' Bhagwanji told Bijoy Nag. 'They have infiltrated many places.'[31]

Communist Russia was crueller than the Tsarist regime, Bhagwanji shared his insight with his followers.[32]

Soon after getting in touch with them, he asked both Leela Roy and Pabitra to keep track of what was going on in Russia and China. 'I have been informed of the possibility of some sudden incident in Russia,' but that would not impact the plan for the subcontinent. Similarly, he claimed to have received intelligence that just after the Russian incident, China would do something (what that is he did not specify) that at present is considered by others to be an impossibility. No one can say what Bhagwanji referred to, but two major events took place soon after. On 14 October 1964, Nikita Khrushchev was deposed, bringing into power Leonid Brezhnev and Alexei Kosygin. Two days later, China conducted its first nuclear test. Who can say that Bhagwanji didn't refer to these?

To Pabitra, Bhagwanji gave a detailed account of what he claimed to have seen in Russia as far as its communism was concerned:

---

30   Notes of conversation with Bhagwanji taken by Pabitra Mohan Roy, 29 December 1968.

31   Notes of conversation with Bhagwanji taken by Bijoy Kumar Nag, 30 September 1971.

32   Notes of conversation with Bhagwanji taken by Pabitra Mohan Roy, 22 January 1973.

Remember one thing: Communism, as was understood by dogmatists, IS NO MORE IN 'R'! Yes. It is a fact. 'R' has got, now, five distinct social classes or strata:- (1) The very uppermost class (2) The upper or elite (3) The privileged Bureaucracy-cum-Party cadre (4) The middle class and (5) The common people (just like here). Now the 'Govt & Party' is vigorously encouraging and inviting women of 'R' to look more sleek and thin and cultivate and have figures like the sophisticated West! ...'R' is now being governed by oligarchy and just like the conspiracies, secret plans, secret killings, open massacres of the old times of *maharajas*, *samrats* and *badshahs* all these are happening in 'R'. Hundreds of common people gathered to share their story of suffering and complain against the inhuman, terrible suffering and privations. They have been sprayed with bullets en masse.[33]

He repeatedly predicted the demise of Communism. It would die in the land of its birth, he wrote to Leela Roy in early 1963, and eventually it shall disappear as a political force 'on both sides'— probably a reference to the Soviet Union and China. 'Diabolical Godless Communism shall be buried 1,000 fathoms deep, never to rise.' In another possible reference to a loss of territory for China, he predicted that only 'China proper (shorn of her skirt frills) shall live sans Communism,' and 'Russia-without-Asia-team shall be happy (sans Communism)'. It appears he was predicting in 1963 what would take place in 1991 (see image on next page).

While his machinations with China and Russia continued at several levels, very soon India was plunged into another war. If the China war was treated as a blessing in disguise by Bhagwanji, the

---

33   Bhagwanji's letter to Pabitra Mohan Roy, March 1963.

DIABOLICAL - GODLESS - COMMUNISM SHALL BE BURIED 1000 FATHOMS DEEP, NEVER TO RISE. (ON BOTH SIDES). ONLY CHINA - PROPER (SHORN OF HER SKIRT - FRILLS) SHALL LIVE, SANS COMMUNISM.

. राख्या- उड़िया्त - इंडिया- देश -SHALL BE सुखी (SANS... Communism)

. BENGAL, THAT IS INDIA : LIGHTS — OUT.

war of 1965 with Pakistan and the subsequent developments left him disappointed with the Indian leadership. Yet again, speaking on the subject like someone who had top level intelligence inputs from several sources, Bhagwanji claimed that Pakistan plunged into the incursion with tacit encouragement from the UK.[34] The Pakistan army decided to go for the jugular, Bhagwanji wrote to Leela Roy, at a time when the prestige of the Indian Army had taken a beating after the 1962 China onslaught. In fact, he referred to a conversation between Ayub Khan and Lal Bahadur Shastri in London where the former apparently told the latter that, 'I can walk over to Delhi, any hour I want to, you know?' leaving Shastri speechless. He went on to claim that Ayub spoke in similar vein many times in Pakistan, showing great contempt towards Hindus. 'These *dhotiwala* Hindus, what do they know of fighting? They

---

34   Probably Bhagwanji had in mind the fact that Britain had brokered the ceasefire and the international arbitration over the Rann of Kutch dispute that gave an advantage to Pakistan, a development that encouraged the latter. His views might also have been informed by the role played by Britain during the conflict. When India retaliated by crossing the Indo-Pak border in Punjab, however, Britain supported the Pakistani contention that it was a graver act than the Pakistani aggression. The British prime minister accused India for escalation of the hostilities and asked Lal Bahadur Shastri to ensure that weapons given by Britain to safeguard against a Chinese attack were not used. See Paul M MacGarr, *The Cold War in South Asia*, Cambridge University Press, pp 303-322.

know only to lose and run away from the battlefield. They only know how to be good slaves.'[35] As it came to be known much later, Ayub Khan did send his army chief General Mohammad Musa a Top Secret order (Annexure G to GHQ letter no 4050/5/MO-1 dated 29 August 1965): 'As a general rule, Hindu morale would not stand for more than a couple of hard blows delivered at the right time and the right place. Such opportunities should therefore be sought and exploited.' [36]

Taking a dig at India's political leaders, Bhagwanji retorted, 'Whatever the Pakistanis thought and said is the bitter truth—but those truths are applicable only to the politicians, not to the Indian Army.' He took great pride in the fact that the then Army Chief Jayantababu [Jayanto Nath Chaudhuri] is 'the son of *Janani Janmabhoomi*'. Bhagwanji gave strong hints of not only sending messages to a few unspecified persons in the military establishment 'through some roundabout/convoluted channels', but also claimed to have moved around places inside Pakistan which would be impossible without the help of the Indian Army. However, he was disappointed with the end result. His cues, he rued, were 'not used to the hilt'. Later, he wrote to Leela Roy.

> Blast it all, Lee! Lahore was completely evacuated by the civilians. Pak military were fleeing Lahore like squirrels. It was a matter of punching—taking ...Sialkot, Muzaffarabad and 1/3rd of Kashmir were a matter of one week. 'Someone' was

---

35   Bhagwanji's letter to Leela Roy, undated, published in *Jayasree*, March 2015, p 460.
36   Brian Cloughley, *A History of the Pakistan Army: Wars and Insurrections*, Carrel Books, 2016. For Ayub Khan's derogatory language towards Shastri, also see Paul M MacGarr, *The Cold War in South Asia*, Cambridge University Press, p 307.

there himself. Someone crossed and re-crossed Ichogil. Thrice had been in Shalimar! Hell of Hells, that thumbnail area of Chamb could be literally turned into a veritable inferno and not a soul to call Allah! Dash it all! They behaved (both sides— India, Pakistan) just like copybook puppet soldiers. Both sides stuck to the set pattern of Sandhurst [British military academy] manoeuvres. The generals of each side could anticipate the next move of the other side. Yet something more would have happened (in seven more days the Kashmir problem wouldn't be there, Lahore would have been yours) if LB [Lal Bahadur Shastri] didn't wilt at the scolding of the 'others'. I couldn't imagine that Jayantababu would get entangled in politics.[37]

Seven years later, while discussing international politics with his followers, Bhagwanji again picked up the thread of the 1965 war and said something astonishing:

[Jayanto Nath] Chaudhuri was disappointing. Not once, but five times it was explained to him thoroughly that Sialkot, Lahore and Muzaffarabad could be easily taken, almost without any shock. He was even given a tour of Shalimar Bagh by 'someone' along with a few soldiers. Everything was shown to him. Lal Bahadur himself had said 'I want Lahore and Sialkot.' But he wet his pants. Nasser had also written to take Lahore. I was livid. If he had taken those three places, leave alone Field Marshall, he would have become Marshall of the Realm. The problem is that neither Indian public nor parliamentarians have any knowledge or understanding of military matters.[38]

The disappointment over the Indian Army not pushing it to the end continued for Bhagwanji, who viewed the Tashkent agreement as the result of a diplomatic game of the US, the UK

---

37   Bhagwanji's letter to Leela Roy, undated, published in *Jayasree*, March 2015, pp 460-461.

38   Notes of conversation with Bhagwanji, taken by Pabitra Mohan Roy, 25 January 1973.

and even the Soviet Union. The contents of the Tashkent proposal were prepared secretly without letting India know about it, he said, driven by Pakistan's fervent appeal to the UK for help. The UK, in turn, influenced the US on the contours of the agreement. The Soviet Union too came to Pakistan's rescue, according to him, while appearing publicly as India's sole friend. Bhagwanji claimed that he conveyed his information regarding these developments to Shastri, asking him to be on guard. His suggestion to Shastri was to invite the Russians to India for the negotiations, instead of going to Tashkent. But Shastri 'lost his head', according to him. Again, 'before leaving for Tashkent, it was properly conveyed' to Shastri that the Soviet Union was considering some policy shifts with regard to India and the Arab world. Bhagwanji claimed that after he sent across the messages, feelers were sent back to him, probably from the government. He felt that Shastri 'responded to these words of caution and signals at 5-6 mammoth meetings and 2-3 times in Parliament'. He also wondered if his messages were the reason for what (he was given to understand) Shastri remarked during the unveiling of Netaji's statue in Calcutta before he left for Tashkent. Things might have turned out differently if he had acted fully in line with the words of caution conveyed to him, Bhagwanji wrote remorsefully. Like everyone else, he was jolted by Shastri's sudden death in Tashkent.[39]

Describing a scene of sweet revenge in Tashkent, as if he had his men reporting to him from the site, Bhagwanji described how Ayub bowed before Shastri.

---

39   Shastri death controversy has been dealt by Anuj Dhar in *Your Prime Minister is Dead*, Vitasta Publishing, 2018.

When LB and Ayub met each other in a separate room, Ayub told him in Urdu *Ab to rahem karo, jo ho gaya so ho gaya*. He said many things to LB to show himself as the younger brother and India as the more powerful elder brother. Then he said, 'How can I explain to you how helplessly I am trapped....' [40]

'What happened in Tashkent is thuggery,' was Bhagwanji's opinion about the developments. He hoped that one day or the other the real information would be out in the public domain and 'You will be shocked. Dead Ghost himself was shocked on being told in a roundabout way.' Referring to Pakistan's reaction to the treaty, Bhagwanji appreciated that the country had 'spoken its mind honestly'. There were widespread protests against the Tashkent agreement. Bhagwanji wrote to Leela Roy. 'Know this for sure that every person in West Pakistan is now one with the Pakistan government in desiring the destruction of India.' At the same time, he was deeply distressed to see what he termed the Indian government's effort at creating 'such hype over celebration of the ghost of Tashkent and... shamelessly try[ing] to sell the treaty to the people of the country and the parliament'. Even more surprising to him was that the people of India bought the propaganda. 'This means, whoever says whatever, the country hasn't awakened. Therefore, it is imperative to open their eyes forever with the rudest kick.'

Writing to Leela Roy in a letter (undated, but written shortly after the Tashkent incident), Bhagwanji made an astonishing prediction. In East Pakistan, the agitation over the 'six point formula' demanding provincial autonomy had just commenced

---

40   Ibid, pp 461-462.

from June 1966, led by Sheikh Mujibur Rahman. There was, however, no indication yet of the magnitude of the political eruption that would shape up in the next few years, tearing the eastern part of Pakistan to form a new country. There was nothing in the air to indicate the extent of military suppression that East Pakistan would be subjected to. It was at this time that Bhagwanji wrote to Roy that...

> A terrible situation is being created in East and West Pakistan because of which Ayub will have to become Nadir Shah in order to trample down East Pakistan. If Ayub cannot fully become Nadir Shah for fulfilling the goal only then there shall be found another one, to take his place, to become full Nadir Shah.... Indian Govt's security shall stand jeopardised, but adequate arrangements have been made to ensure that other powers are not able to join in.[41] [Translated from Bengali]

The scenario that Bhagwanji painted was about five years away, before Yahya Khan took on the mantle of Nadir Shah. So much so that even the general sent out by him to run down East Pakistan, Tikka Khan, came to be known as the 'Butcher of Bangladesh'. Bhagwanji's aim, as mentioned above, and as he told to Dulal Nandy too in January 1965, was a unified Bengal. It won't even occur in the dream of the global powers that the two 'pieces' will reunite. And the way to achieve that was only possible through a war. His advice to Leela Roy (and her team), however, was not to raise any demand for a united Bengal just yet, but allow the developments to play out.

---

41   Bhagwanji's letter to Leela Roy, undated, published in *Jayasree*, March 2015, pp 508-509.

Muslims of East Bengal have been so primed as to be in no mood to be united with Hindu West Bengal. They want to taste independent Muslim Bengal. Let the Muslim East Bengal get it, seemingly on their own gas first. The next 'stage' shall crop up thereafter. This is tactical.

This was not all. In no uncertain terms, Bhagwanji predicted that the conflict would be a localised affair without any intervention from foreign powers. 'Various diversions will be created so that the other powers cannot concentrate on one issue only,' he wrote. While China will stand behind Pakistan, the UK, and due to its influence, the US, will remain aloof contrary to the Indian government's expectations. Declassified US government documents, however, clearly show that the Nixon administration tilted towards Pakistan. Wanting to avert what he feared was going to be total annihilation of Pakistan, Nixon successfully pressured the Russians to prevent India from going into West Pakistan after the victory in the East. Kissinger's personal approach to China to threaten India seemed to have not succeeded, though. Bhagwanji's further claim was that India would seek Russia's help and intervention, but Russia too would not come forward. He indicated that China and Russia would engage in a confrontation in a different place which would keep both powers out of the India-Pakistan conflict.[42]

---

42   While there was no confrontation between the two powers at this time, Maharaj Krishna Rasgotra, former Indian Foreign Secretary points out in his memoirs that the 'Chinese were apprehensive of an attack by the Soviet Union whose one million heavily armed troops were deployed on the border.' He was informed by an official of the US State Department, he has written, that the Soviet Union had the capability to 'easily detach Xinjiang and Tibet from China and the Chinese knew that'. Maharaja Krishna Rasgotra, *A Life in Diplomacy*. Penguin Books Ltd, Kindle Edition.

The astonishing thing to note is that all these were spoken and written by him much before the conflagration in East Pakistan took the secessionist form. In his evidence before the Khosla Commission on 6 September 1972, Sunil Das recalled that in 1965 Leela Roy had forewarned her close associates that 'something was likely to happen on the Indo-Pakistan border— between India and East Pakistan' which would result in the influx of about 50-60 lakh refugees. Roy, along with her colleagues spent hours moving across villages along the border. 'In March 1971, Indo-Pak conflict came about...when one crore crossed the border from East Pakistan to India....Whether this was a hint sent to her or whether it was a divine disclosure, I do not know,' Das said, not breathing a direct word about Bhagwanji as he and others had been ordered by the man behind the curtain.[43]

Bhagwanji kept a keen eye on the developments as the Bangladesh movement gathered steam. As the Indian Army started training the Mukti Bahini, Bhagwanji wrote to Pabitra in July 1971, 'Match carefully all that I explained to you in Naimisharanya [with the current developments]....This is the beginning of the fulfilment of the last two phases of my divine promise.' When Bijoy Nag reached Basti in September 1971 to spend the days of Durga Puja, Bhagwanji was more specific: 'It will be a line written in history that this area was known for a short time as Pakistan.' He pointed to the play of a greater force when he told Nag that the freedom for Bengalis in East Pakistan will not

---

43   Record of Oral Evidence: Netaji Inquiry Commission (1970), Vol XII, Oral Evidence of Sunil Das, 6 September 1972, pp 3796-97.

'come through you (India) but with the help of others. Someone's actions will lead to tumult in the UN. It will be forced to get free Bangladesh established.'[44] Incidentally, George H W Bush, later the 41st President of the US and then the ambassador to the UN, introduced a resolution for ceasefire in the UN just about three months later. During the same visit, all of a sudden Bhagwanji started talking about the strategic importance of Jessore to Nag. 'Have you seen the Jessore fort? I know its layout,' he said, and then went on to describe the fort (cantonment):

> On the top at the *agnikon* (south east) is the barrack of the Baluch Regiment—a huge armoury beneath that; towards east from there are the officers' area; in the *ishankon* (north east) the Pathan Regiment—there is a huge oil reservoir underground, like a lake—at the middle there is a huge pillar; on the north west—a huge runway. This could have been captured during the days of the heavy monsoon. The fort can be taken in three days.

Even more strikingly, Bhagwanji went on to say that there were three ways in which the cantonment could be taken without any resistance.

The date of the discussion was 29 September. Confined to a decrepit room of a dilapidated building in a back of beyond small town in north India, a man in the garb of a *sanyasi* was talking casually about the military importance of a town in another country, whose importance would be known to the country more than two months later.

---

44 If Yahya had any understanding of statecraft he could have managed the situation better, was Bhagwanji's observation. 'But statesmanship is in extreme short supply in the current world.'

On 7 December 1971, Jessore—'a division headquarters and the military linchpin of the western half of East Pakistan'—became the first city of East Pakistan to be cleared of Pakistani forces by the Indian Army, without any resistance. As reported in *The New York Times*, just after Jessore had fallen, General Sam Manekshaw issued a message for Pakistani troops: 'Lay down your arms before it is too late. Time is running out. Indian forces have encircled you. Your fate is sealed.'[45]

While discussing the Bangladesh liberation war, Bhagwanji indicated several times that he had been moving in and out of the country, both before and after the war. Writing to Pabitra on 28 July and again on 3 August 1973, he recounted the story of a *faquir* passing repeatedly through the road in front of a house where Mujib and Trailokya Nath Chakravarty were in the midst of a discussion. 'Maharaj was immersed in a discussion with Mujib and kept looking out of the window again and again.' The old *faquir*, bent under the burden of age, passed many times, saying a prayer in Urdu. Bhagwanji had told the same story to Bijoy Nag too in September 1971, with the addition that Mujib commented, looking at the *faquir* that 'this fellow is from Pindi [Rawalpindi, the headquarters of the military intelligence establishment of Pakistan] and I will finish all of them,' implying that the *faquir* was a Pakistani agent. 'I asked myself—is this the man who will liberate his country with this kind of ability of identifying men?' Bhagwanji told Nag, clearly pointing to the fact that the passing

45   Sydney H Schanberg, 'India Claims Capture of Jessore, Admits a Mile Kashmir Retreat,' *The New York Times*, 8 December 1971.

faquir was none other than himself. Apart from this, Bhagwanji's letters in the middle of 1971 are replete with references to travels abroad all hinting towards these being related to the developments in Bangladesh.

Of the many letters from Bhagwanji written during this period, the most astounding was one written to Pabitra on 11 November 1971. The substance of the letter was incredible but what made the letter stand out was the paper on which it was written. It was embossed with the official emblem of the Indian government. 'Today I am somewhere else,' he wrote, with the 'responsibility of many keys and levers in these hands'.

> I am on my way to explain the indications and directions of some special tasks with far reaching consequences. I will travel on my exclusively own magic carpet. If I don't return, this is my last letter to you. After this it will be eternal silence. My life is not my own. There is nothing personal in this life... But if I do return, I will have to go hundred per cent flawlessly underground in order to accomplish a very special task. I will not intimate the others (Mukul [Sunil Das], Santosh [Bhattacharya], Paltu [Bijoy Nag], Dulal [Nandy] and Param Pujaniya [Suresh Chandra Bose]) about this now. You must ensure that they do not get wind of this plan.

How did Bhagwanji have access to a government letter pad with the national emblem embossed on it? Apparently, this was not the only time. Leela Roy too had once received a letter from him in an envelope marked with the address of Rashtrapati Bhavan, according to Bijoy Nag.

Pabitra received another letter from Bhagwanji around the same time, most probably after the letter of 11 November. In this letter, Bhagwanji informed Pabitra that he had returned to Basti after undertaking a few missions abroad, and that until the further specified tasks were accomplished, he would have to remain in the background. The aim of the mission was to 'disintegrate P[akistan] and to ensure that India stands to gain from its military intervention[46] 'if no mistake is committed out of fear, as [General J N] Chaudhuri did'. The letter also refers to some of the identities by which he was known to different involved parties.

Going by the followers' recollections of what Bhagwanji had told them, Sam Manekshaw was aware of Bhagwanji's existence.

---

46   On 6 December, a CIA operative leaked out India's 'war objectives' to the agency. Prime Minister Indira Gandhi informed her top ministers that, apart from liberating Bangladesh, India intended to take over a strategically important part of Pakistan-occupied Kashmir (PoK) and go for total annihilation of Pakistan's armed forces. The CIA went on to assess that fulfilment of India's war objectives might lead to 'the emergence of centrifugal forces which could shatter West Pakistan into as many as three or four separate countries'. As a direct result of the operative's information, the Nixon administration went on an overdrive to save West Pakistan from a massive Indian assault. For an overview of this episode, see Anuj Dhar, *CIA's Eye on South Asia*, Manas Publications, 2009.

It started before Manekshaw was elevated as the Army Chief. When he was GOC-in-C of the Eastern Command, Manekshaw would secretly confabulate with Bhagwanji's emissary, goes one of the claims. Even as one attempts to swallow this, comes another, that in the dead of night, like a scene from an espionage thriller, Manekshaw would join Bhagwanji in a secret place to take stock of the war. It is further claimed that bombing of the Governor House in Dhaka one day before Pakistan eventually surrendered was at Bhagwanji's instance. Not only Manekshaw, some of the followers claim that the legendary R N Kao too was in touch. Ravindra Shukla, a follower in Faizabad, told the Sahai Commission that the day Indira was assassinated, he heard Bhagwanji ruing that his repeated instructions to Kao to increase Indira's security were overlooked. 'No one should ever hurt a woman,' Bhagwanji said, bristling in anger. In 1984, R N Kao was the Prime Minister's security advisor; in 1971, he was heading the R&AW. There was no love lost for Indira but Bhagwanji nonetheless admired her courage and held that she had a better sense of national security than her father and Shastri.

While the focus of the world was on the war going on in East Pakistan, the Bay of Bengal and the Indian Ocean had their share of action in the form of a standoff between the US and Soviet naval forces. Some of the letters exchanged between Bhagwanji and Pabitra point towards Bhagwanji's presence in the vicinity of the Indian coasts.

Towards the end of December, Pabitra sent Bhagwanji copies of a Bengali newspaper *Jugabani*, which reported the movement of a speedboat and probably linked it to rumours of Subhas Bose being sighted. When he responded in mid-January, Bhagwanji didn't refute the news. Instead, he wrote, 'I read the news, but my personal carrier was not a speedboat.' Can this be taken as an affirmation of the news report with a small modification regarding the type of vehicle? Probably, and beyond, because what Bhagwanji narrated thereafter takes the matter to the realm of high-end military science, comparable to the depictions in latest James Bond or other sci-fi superhero movies.

> It was a midget man o' war[47], a gunboat with the superstructure of a luxury State yacht, capable of undertaking multiple known and unknown tasks, with the awesome, terrible power of destroying, cutting, vaporising, with different types of rays, using electro-magnetic and gravitational science. It is an automatic boat that can perform all its functions on its own. The midget can travel on different types of water bodies— from the smallest of rivers to a rough ocean with ease. It has been built by the government of a country that is extremely advanced in scientific research. Many boats, carrying people, can be launched from the midget like torpedoes travelling at high speed. I was on the carrier that is the fully developed version of this midget.[48]

The only hint about the location of the super-specialised and high-tech carrier given by Bhagwanji was that it was at that time travelling in the 'Chinese sea area,' a possible reference to

---

47   An armed naval vessel, a warship. He wrote more about the carrier—'Germany, Russia, China, the fleets of the US, UK, Japan know about the carrier. It doesn't have any particular ensign or flag, but is often seen traversing the international waters. The only thing that these countries do not know is where the carrier is berthed, or serviced.'

48   Bhagwanji's letter to Pabitra Mohan Roy, 19 January 1972. Translated from Bengali.

[Parts of Bhagwanji's letter to Pabitra Mohan Roy describing the marine vehicle that he claimed he was travelling in during the Bangladesh war, 19 January 1971] the South China Sea. His letters of this period mention sending two emissaries from the strange carrier—one person to Madras to deliver letters to someone close to Sunil Das (nickname Mukul), who would in turn forward the letters to Das, and another emissary to Mujibur Rahman. Bhagwanji's letters to Das were considered so secret that the emissary had them sewn in his underwear. The instruction was that the letters could be read only by Das, Bijoy Nag (Paltu), Santosh Bhattacharya and Pabitra, following which they should be burnt to ashes, after copying the contents. When the emissary failed to trace Das's contact in Madras, he sent the underwear by registered post to Basti. These were forwarded to Das by Bhagwanji sometime later.

The original letters sent by Bhagwanji through his emissary are not available, and we have to depend on subsequent letters written to Pabitra where he summarised the key points. These included his plans for East and West Pakistan, the roles to be played by the global powers, and what he was doing in such a carrier in the international waters. The letters contained the details of a masterplan which explained through which 'channels' the Pakistani leaders were advised and encouraged to act in a way that resulted in the mass exodus from East Pakistan and then the military rampage resulting in the 'death of three million'. He had written that the Hindus would account for up to seventy per cent of the casualties. 'It was my desire to keep you informed before this storm erupted so that you all do not get unduly worried by the developments,' he wrote to Pabitra. He wrote that he had sent more letters that described his prolonged movements in the midget, on two rivers of the 'other side' which eventually merge and flow through a vast area—a clear reference to Bangladesh and probably the Padma (Ganga) and Brahmaputra rivers. When Bijoy Nag met him in September 1971, Bhagwanji described his journey through the rivers of Bangladesh and how among the crowd that gathered on the banks he could not spot a single Hindu family.

His message to Mujib, he said, was a stern warning linked to his past. But when was the letter conveyed? Mujib was a prisoner of Pakistan from 27 March 1971 until he was released on 8 January the next year. On 10 January 1972, he returned to Dhaka. Since Bhagwanji was recounting an incident that had taken place earlier, in his letter written on 19 January, it is unlikely that the message was sent after Mujib's release. This implies that Bhagwanji's emissary met Mujib in Pakistan jail, possibly in November when Bhagwanji wrote to Pabitra from 'somewhere' on the paper that had the Indian government's seal embossed. That's also possibly the reason why Bhagwanji wrote that Mujib was in shock on seeing the emissary; he was completely bewildered at how the man reached him. This becomes all the more intriguing when Bhagwanji dropped hints that he or his undisclosed associates might have had a role in the release of Mujib. 'Neither the government of India nor the European governments had any means of saving Mujib. All that they could do was to appeal to the Pakistani government to release him, but everyone had come to believe that Mujib was not alive anymore,' he wrote, as usual, as someone with inside information.[49] Even the

---

49   According to Rasgotra, however, Nixon told Indira Gandhi in their meeting in November 1971 that it was under the US government's pressure that Yahya had promised not to execute Mujib. Maharaja Krishna Rasgotra, *A Life in Diplomacy*, Penguin Books Ltd, Kindle Edition.

government of Bangladesh in exile eventually came to believe in it. Bhagwanji pointed out that the internal power struggle within the government-in-exile began immediately after liberation since the leaders had started believing that Mujib had been killed. 'The person who became the first ideal of patriotism by renouncing allegiance to Pakistan, endangering his own life and his family, had the first right to become the High Commissioner to India, but was denied by his political compatriots. You think these people will remember what India has done for them?' a bitter Bhagwanji wrote to Pabitra.

Bhagwanji's attitude towards Mujib underwent a transition from the beginning till Mujib's assassination. In Mujib, Bhagwanji found the best hope for breaking Bangladesh out of Pakistan. In January 1973, he wrote to Pabitra that Mujib's position must be strengthened. However, this appears to have been a strategic decision and he didn't allow his judgement to be clouded by emotions. He would often go back to the past to judge Mujib. 'He was out and out a Muslim Leaguer, a commander of the Muslim League forces,' he wrote remembering Bengal's days of communal strife in 1946. 'Mujibur was the leading torch of the hellish story of Noakhali,'—Bhagwanji wouldn't allow the gory past to be overshadowed by the present situation. 'Mujibur abuses Jinnah, Gandhi and Liaquat Ali in filthy language, but says that "so and so" (Bhagwanji's typical way of referring to his past life) is my idol,' he however added.

If there was any single aspect in the whole story that made the monk spit fire, it was the horror inflicted on the Hindu women. He reminded Nag of the incidents where women were trafficked across villages for prostitution, were taken to Africa by ship and the countless who were pulled out of their homes and raped by hordes. 'All the women trafficked since the time of Partition in East and West Pakistan were Hindus. No East Bengali Muslim raised his voice about this kicked, driven out and despised lot. Rather, they were not unhappy,' Bhagwanji wrote in another letter. The message sent by Bhagwanji to Mujib therefore has to be read in this context. Mujib was reminded of his earlier 'Hindu-baiting', starting from the Noakhali riots of 1946, and was asked to tell the Muslims in Bangladesh to atone for their sins, which included forcing the exodus of over twelve million Hindus in the face of persecution. 'He was clearly told that the terrible acts that were unleashed, making blood flow like a river, will be withheld only after revenge is extracted,' Bhagwanji wrote to Pabitra. Mujib was told that his release would take place only after Yahya Khan moved out of the scene. How that was to happen was explained to him. According to Bhagwanji, Mujib wept silently, and uncontrollably, hearing all this. Yahya resigned on 20 December and was soon put under house arrest by Zulfikar Ali Bhutto.

The formation of Bangladesh, Bhagwanji claimed, was not part of his horizon's work. It was personal. During the September trip of Nag, Bhagwanji told him that he would set out on a trip to the Soviet Union shortly and he knew what the Russians would tell him. As all things related to him, even this account is nothing but surprising and contrary to the narrative of the Indo-Soviet relationship. In a jocular tone, Bhagwanji spoke on what he expected to hear and Nag noted it down:

Hey listen, this is between you and us: don't spill it out. We care a damn about what happens to your country…. Whether Bengal survives or dies, we care a damn. Remember, you and us have to keep in mind our common interests, but the place where you are going [Bangladesh] is more of uncommon interest. We will put up a great show of welcome [to India], but keep in mind what we told you.

On his part, Bhagwanji resented Russians' helping the Yahya Khan regime with weapons and funds. Wanting to pull Pakistan out of Chinese influence, Russia had made several overtures to Pakistan beginning 1966. Technical and economic assistance in several projects, ranging from a steel mill to a nuclear power station, was promised. But it was the Russian arms deal with Pakistan in July 1968 which 'placed a heavy strain on Indo-Soviet relations', as Verinder Grover highlighted in his book *USSR/CIS and India's foreign policy*. India had all the reasons to worry as Russian military supplies to Pakistan were not confined to harmless items such as jeeps and helicopters, but also included sophisticated weapons, including tanks. This military assistance continued till March 1970.

With both Pabitra and Sunil Krishna Gupta having their ancestral house in Bangladesh, they used to speak of the lost land often with great emotion, something that touched Bhagwanji. After the Bangladesh government was set up, he asked Pabitra for the specifics of their property, and summoned the 'people from the other side' to obtain their assurance that their property would be returned. They obliged, but for some inexplicable reason Pabitra sent him the property documents after much delay. By then, Bhagwanji, annoyed with the delay had already communicated

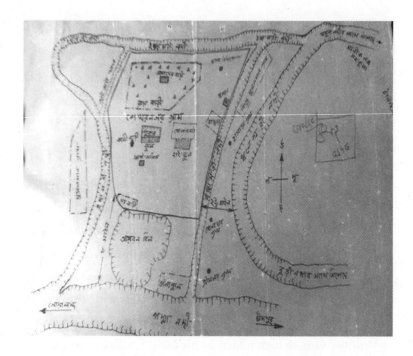

to his contacts in Bangladesh that he was no more interested in recovering the property. The map of the property in the village Shekharnagar was found among the belongings of Bhagwanji at Ram Bhawan during the preparation of the inventory.

In January 1973, Bhagwanji jotted down his summary observations in a letter to Pabitra. 'East Bengal is now a cauldron, where rice, lentils, potato, cauliflower, elephant foot yam, onion, garlic, egg, stale meat, dead fish, oil, clarified butter (ghee), turmeric, red chilly are boiling together.'[50] Mujib is trying to appease the Hindus because of his precarious position, he wrote, but he doesn't

---

50   Reference to *khichuri*, a popular dish where assorted vegetables are boiled in rice and lentil.

realise that he is 'caught in the quicksand'. Bhagwanji noted that while Mujib gave priority to the display of large photos of Huseyn Shaheed Suhrawardi, his political mentor, at the same time he was changing names of places associated with the memory of Leela Roy. Bhagwanji also commented that from the very beginning, Mujib 'has been pleading, wherever he can, to obtain a foothold in the Muslim and Arab world on the ground of religion, without understanding statecraft and diplomacy'. Bhagwanji felt angry and aggrieved that Hindus in Bangladesh were still 'fourth class' citizens and that they were living an uncertain life of the downtrodden, yet were forced by the terror unleashed on them to tell the world that they were living in peace and comfort. 'They haven't got back 90% of their property and their family (especially mothers, sisters, daughters and wives) snatched away from them,' he wrote. 'It has been suppressed that ninety-seven per cent of the refugees who were forced to leave their land after Yahya unleashed his war are Hindus,' he angrily remarked.

Bhagwanji felt that the show of affection, inclusivity and the secular outlook of Mujib was opportunistic. To demonstrate that Mujib's basic thinking was still coloured by an Islamic consciousness, he narrated an incident to Pabitra: On the flight to Pakistan after winning the general elections in 1970, Mujib apparently told a foreign dignitary that he would never forget the oppression of wicked Hindu landlords on the poor Muslim peasantry before the partition. 'These were the words of a Mujib drunk with the possibility of becoming Prime Minister of Pakistan,' Bhagwanji commented. Mujib and West Pakistan were negotiating only on a few parameters, and if they had reached an agreement, Bangladesh would today still be known as Pakistan. That, however, was not to be. 'Then the sky fell down' and being unable to stop the battering by 'blood brothers', Mujib changed tack, starting to rely on the support of the Hindus. 'From the great Calcutta killing, through Partition, till ten days prior to Yahya's pounding, all that was done with the Hindus was forgotten and they became the new brothers from the same mother,' Bhagwanji remarked caustically. For him, the joint command of the Indian and Bangladesh forces was a ruse set up by India at the request of the Bangladesh government. According to him, the entire credit and honour of liberating Bangladesh went to the Indian armed forces. Instead, all credit was being accorded to a few who had taken shelter under the Indian Army. 'If the Indian Army had not acted for another ten days, no sign of Bangladesh Mukti Bahini would have remained, and the area would have remained as East Pakistan,' was his assessment. He told Pabitra that it was really the Indian soldiers who were fighting, putting on the garb of Mukti Bahini soldiers, while training some of them. 'But, only five to six months after Indians handed over their country to them after fighting their battle and shedding blood for them, the Bangladeshis have started singing a different tune now.'

Despite these misgivings, Bhagwanji had no doubts about Mujib's stature and capability. Two years after the birth of the new country, when internal conflicts had started raising their head and a general atmosphere of political grievance had spread, Bhagwanji told Pabitra in no uncertain terms, 'In this atmosphere of distrust, when the dark clouds are gathering and storms are imminent, only one person can stand tall, with his head held high—that person is Mujib.' In view of Mujib's acknowledgement of India's help, Bhagwanji wrote, 'All praise must go to him for this.' The political squabbles notwithstanding, 'Mujib's leadership is intact.' Bhagwanji, however, noted that at a time when Mujib should increase his mass contact programme significantly to disseminate his ideology and spread the message of caution, he is being forced by political compulsions to stay silent. He warned that Mujib's silence was giving space to his detractors to poison people's minds. 'But they forget that plans of mice and men go awry in the inscrutable face of providence. And they are playing Hamlet without the prince of Denmark.'

Clearly here was a person who was on top of the developments unfolding in Bangladesh. He knew by name the key political players, their past and current political affiliations, links with foreign powers, and also the groups which had been complicit in or actively perpetrating massacre. He drew the picture of political fragmentation behind the screen of post-liberation tide of nationalism. For instance, in one letter he wrote to Pabitra, 'The communists have created well-organised cells in all the districts and sub-divisions of East Bengal, especially in the north, and in Barisal and Noakhali. The communists did not collaborate with the Awami League. Even during the liberation war their support was largely a lip service, only to fool the public. They probably haven't got financial support from China.'

It is difficult to ascertain for sure, but it appears from the available letters that a few people in Calcutta were invited by the Bangladesh government in early 1973 to visit the country, through the Deputy High Commissioner stationed in Calcutta.

Pabitra was one among the invited ones and was told that the delegates would be the personal guests of Mujib. As was usual, he immediately wrote to Bhagwanji, informing him about the people invited and asked for his guidance. Bhagwanji gave his approval for the trip, but advised caution, asking Pabitra to find out the reasons for the invitation. He asked Pabitra to stay with Mujib and his family, and drafted the lines along which he should talk while in Bangladesh. The essence of Bhagwanji's draft was praise for Mujib in general and emphasis on two specific points in particular—that Mujib's coming out of Pakistani prison was nothing short of a divine intervention, and that Mujib was the living form of Subhas Bose's ideals. 'Only the ideals of Mujib will bring the boat of Bangladesh safely to the coast, overcoming rough weather. Mujib and Sonar Bangla are synonymous,' he asked Pabitra to convey to Mujib. He also suggested that Pabitra should consult journalist Barun Sengupta to get a proper understanding of the ground situation in Bangladesh.

It would be pertinent to dwell on the connection between Subhas Bose and Mujibur Rahman. Mujib had always been an ardent admirer of Bose, the only person other than Chittaranjan Das, who he believed could have bridged the Hindu–Muslim rift in colonial India. In his *Unfinished Autobiography*, Mujib wrote about his dilemma regarding the goal of Pakistan and his admiration for Bose:

> When we listened to Subhas Bose addressing us on the radio from Singapore we used to get excited. It seemed to us then that if he managed to land his troops in Bengal it would be easy for us to oust the English. But then it occurred to us

that having him in Bengal would not bring us any nearer to Pakistan. And what would happen to the millions of Muslims of the country then? Then again I thought that someone who could leave everything in his country to spearhead a movement for its independence could never be parochial in his outlook. In my mind, my respect for Subhas Bose continued to grow.[51]

Although Samar Guha claimed that Mujib had met Subhas Bose in 1940, Mujib didn't mention it in his autobiography.

According to diplomat Sashanka S Banerjee, who was closely associated with some of the leading figures of the Bangladesh liberation struggle, especially Mujib, as early as December 1962 Mujib had clandestinely sent to Jawaharlal Nehru his plan of action for a liberated Bangladesh asking for moral and material support. After a long delay, New Delhi responded, advising him that the time for such action had not yet arrived and that Mujib should first build his support base through political action. India would come to his aid when he succeeded in building up a critical mass of support. The government communiqué probably suggested a Gandhian mode of action comprising non-cooperation, civil disobedience, and of course non-violence. Mujib was not impressed. Mujib told Banerjee that he admired Netaji's path and didn't think the Gandhian model would work with West Pakistan. Banerjee's assessment was that the 'Bangladesh leader, however, knew that he had to strike a tactical compromise as a compulsion

---

51   Sheikh Mujibur Rahman, *Sheikh Mujibur Rahman: The Unfinished Memoirs* Penguin Books Ltd, Kindle Edition.

of realpolitik given that he was dealing with Nehru, a Gandhian by conviction'.[52]

Mujib was crafty enough to deal with the stereotypical questions often raised by those who professed to be Gandhians. 'But Netaji deeply respected Gandhiji!' is an oft-repeated view. Banerjee knew Netaji's remarks of respect for Gandhi, but understood that those remarks of Netaji from the Southeast 'were in reality also tactical ploys employed by him to keep criticism on the home front at bay while the armed struggle led by the Azad Hind Fauj...continued its military campaign in full vigour against British Imperial Army'. In the final count, Mujib told Banerjee that he would 'pick and choose from Bose's model in that he would make references in his speeches, when occasion arose, extolling the virtues of "peaceful non-cooperation" with military dictatorship during the course of the liberation struggle'. According to Banerjee—whose insights have been admired by the likes of K Sankaran Nair, the second R&AW chief, Dr Henry Kissinger and David Petraeus (CIA director, 2011-12)—Mujib framed his slogan 'Give me unity, I will give you liberty,' on the basis of Netaji's rousing call 'Give me blood, I will give you freedom.'[53]

It is probably needless to point out that no published material or declassified record show any sign of the presence of Bhagwanji or of any mysterious figure. To the best of our knowledge, only one

---

52 Sashanka S Banerjee, *India, Mujibur Rahman, Bangladesh Liberation & Pakistan (A Political Treatise)*, Kindle Edition.
53 Ibid.

reference to Subhas Bose appears in the relevant declassified US records. A derisive, stray comment made in a State Department telegram originating from the US Embassy in Dacca on 3 January 1975. Referring to the reported shooting of one a political leader, the embassy telegram said that unless his body was displayed, 'there will soon grow up stories that he still lives, *a la* Subhas Chandra Bose'. This would mean that the rumour that Bose was still alive was current in Bangladesh too in that period. There is no doubt that Bose's memories were summoned during the Bangladesh liberation war period. Going by Yatindra Bhatnagar's book *Bangla Desh: Birth of a Nation,* Bose's classmate at Cambridge and later ICS officer C C Desai, who used to be India's envoy to different countries including Pakistan before becoming an MP, saw shades of his friend in Rahman's tactics. Mujib's 'directives immediately before Yahya troops struck, may be well compared with Netaji's thesis of anti-imperialist struggle and Samveda [Samyavad] propounded by him in 1933'. Mukti Bahini's war cry 'Joi Bangla' was inspired by 'Jai Hind'.

[Samar Guha (left) and Subhas's nephew Amiya Nath Bose are seen presenting a portrait of Netaji to Mujib. Courtesy: *Jayasree Publications*]

Despite Bhagwanji urging him to go to Bangladesh many a times, Pabitra failed to make a trip due to his own and his wife's ill health. His ancestors' land was lost for ever. Although Pabitra couldn't go, the other followers of Bhagwanji published a booklet written by Samar Guha, whose central theorem was that Mujibur Rahman was the living embodiment of Netaji's ideals. They also remained in touch with Bangladesh's government-in-exile, most notably, members of Mujib's family.

In the publication titled *Netaji O Bangabandhu*, Guha wrote how Mujib's political mentor Shaheed Suhrawardi recounted the story of his meeting with Gandhi just before partition, where the latter lamented that 'Only Subhas could have saved the country today.' Suhrawardi agreed. He also told Guha that he had got Bose's horoscope analysed by the Bhrigu astrologers of Banaras and they had been categorical in their assertion that Bose was alive and would return. When Mujib visited Calcutta in 1972, he made it a point to visit Bose's statue at the Red Road along with Indira Gandhi and the house he used to live in on Elgin Road. 'The creation of Bangladesh is the proof that Netaji is alive,' he was quoted as saying in the *Anandabazar Patirka* on 17 January 1972.

However, in an audio message to Dr Sisir Bose on 23 January 1972, Mujib clearly said that Netaji was 'no more, but the path of liberation struggle is flooded by light spread by him; he is immortal and eternal'.[54]

Sitting in faraway Basti, Bhagwanji was keeping an eye on the developments. A hope of a united Bengal flickered in his mind when Mujib started talking about Netaji publicly, he later said, but his hopes were soon dashed when he saw that Mujib had started toeing the line of Indira Gandhi completely. 'I understood that he had sold out,' Bhagwanji concluded.

---

54   The message can be heard here: http://www.netaji.org/nrb-archives.
      html?fbclid=IwAR1GaFHTHtDoc7K3-ZKgZl8asb5EHV8_IFs097uU_1_
      BSusp_5rp4gTyJF8.

Things were not going well in Bangladesh, however, after the initial euphoria had receded. In December 1973, Bhagwanji wrote to Pabitra a 'special secret: only for your ears.'—'A few days ago I had to travel to Bangladesh in response to a desperate appeal from there.' He claimed that around 35,000 members of the Awami League had lost their lives, although a far lower number was being publicised, in contrast to about two thousand (a few hundreds more or less) of the opposition parties. Mujib was killed on 15 August 1975. On the 27th, Bhagwanji wrote to Pabitra recalling the incident of sending a message of warning to Mujib during his incarceration. 'Mujib had agreed to follow the instructions but after following them partly, he tried to act clever. He thought he could avoid the consequences of not acting according to the instructions. The result is that he has had to pay more than the price of that disregard,' Bhagwanji wrote. He asked Pabitra not to believe everything that he read in the newspapers as there was more to come. In November 1975, he reiterated, 'Whatever is happening in Bangladesh is the consequence of the arrogance shown in disregarding someone's directions.'

In another curious incident, Bhagwanji instructed his followers not to be in Bangladesh in August 1975.

Whatever work you have, whoever you have to visit, all must be completed before the second week of the eighth month of 1975. You should not stay on the other side after 14th at any cost.[55]

Apart from the roles he played in the three major armed

55   Charanik, *Oi Mahamanaba Ase*, Jayasree Prakashan, 2010, p 197.

conflicts in the subcontinent, Bhagwanji claimed his involvement in other global affairs too. For this, he claimed to have travelled frequently. A follower told us that he possessed more than one passport. His stay at various places within India was more of a break from his travelling itinerary. These trips were, however, not ordinary ones. They were undertaken to accomplish the work of his 'horizon'. Although the word occurs frequently in Bhagwanji's discourse and in his letters, it is difficult to put a finger on what he exactly meant by it. All that can be surmised from his letters is that he used the word interchangeably—sometimes as a geographical and political spread, and at other times as a concept, indicating locations that were of interest to him.

The subcontinent and the great games of the great powers surrounding it was the focus of his horizon. However, Bhagwanji's narratives regarding his horizon, which can be pieced together from the fragmented material that the authors have been able to access, require continued suspension of disbelief. These narratives are almost always presented in symbolic language, but contain enough information to confound the uninitiated reader.

In March 1963, during the initial days of contact and just after the Indo-China war, he had written, 'After crossing over to this side, I have made 25 trips including the last two journeys. Try to understand, how much stress can this old body take?' He was referring to the frequent trips outside India he had to undertake in order to ensure the execution of his grand plan.

For as long as we have been able to trace Bhagwanji's stay in India, there appears to have been a flurry of activity related to this mysterious realm. Yet, these activities were not visible to the ordinary eyes, not even to his devoted followers or those who lived around him; sometimes they took place in secrecy and sometimes camouflaged in the routine. He divulged to Pabitra the places where he used to travel to. These places included Russia, China, Southeast Asia, Arab countries, Africa, and Europe.

> Oh, you simply cannot understand how terribly floating the Ghost of the Dead shall have to be! The Ghost of the Dead shall have to float in and out…shall have to float here and there and 'other places', like a 'spectre'…Prince Lucifer somewhere, in some Erebus, and somewhere as Gabriel…[56]

Although a complete list of his trips can't be drawn up due to the non-availability of all his letters, whatever is available gives a fair idea of how frequently he travelled, often in bad health.

1. Mentions three trips in a letter dated 1 September 1970
2. July 1971
3. August 1971
4. November 1971
5. Mentions that he was out between December 1971 and January 1972
6. December 1972
7. December 1973
8. Three trips between January and May, 1974
9. July/August 1975 for over a month
10. January 1978
11. October 1979
12. September 1980 and probably again in October

---

56   Ibid, p 177.

13. May 1981

14. October-November 1981

15. Twice again in December 1981

It is also clear from his letters to Pabitra that he would take extreme care not to let anyone except those closest to him know when he was travelling out. For this to succeed he took recourse to either of two methods: (a) planting one of his secret associates in his place for 'holding-of-post', or (b) instructing Saraswati Devi to keep pretending that he was present but to tell curious outsiders that 'Swamiji' had locked himself inside his room for his spiritual *sadhana*.

The soldiers and workers of the 'horizon' were camouflaged too, and were mostly out of sight—just like their super-secret activities. About these people and what they were doing, Bhagwanji would say this much:

> Remember, your [Bhagwanji's] men are in every key place (here and overseas). This time their garbs are legal. They simply cannot be touched and/or detected. Under their licit garbs they are working; they are in positions in all the key capitals and in the nerve centres which count—manipulating, pulling, suppressing, exploding, creating and forcing issues and policies, mystifying, clarifying and shaping—all only with a single purpose...When those men, who are working like Raktabeej[57] make their public appearance, you will be stunned.[58]

Although the horizon's focus was on one continent, its work

---

57   A mythical character who had a boon that whenever a drop of his blood fell on the ground, a duplicate of him would appear immediately.

58   Charanik, *Oi Mahamanaba Ase*, Jayasree Prakashan, 2010, pp 90, 115

was spread across 'two and a half'. The sole purpose, however, was 'Bengal, my only religion'. And to top it all, this realm of mystery included an unidentified region amid Pamir mountains between Russian and Chinese borders which Bhagwanji claimed to be his own, inhabited by people of diverse nationalities and ethnicities from all over the world. He gave an indication to Pabitra in his second letter to him towards the end of 1962:

> Your Dead Man enjoys (as his absolutely legal right) completely unhindered freedom in everything in his sphere– and–domain. Over a very vast region (not excluding portions of the Himalayas) there are absolutely no other government's men but his. The concerned Govts considered those regions as 'Dead'—useless for any and all persons. Now he has a carte-blanche over the whole.

In fact, the need for material help for his own region was what brought Leela Roy and her associates in touch with Bhagwanji. Unable to procure the items specified by Bhagwanji, Pabitra sought Leela Roy's help. The items that Bhagwanji instructed Pabitra to procure 'as a "Do or Die" missionary work' were no means ordinary.

- A transistor radio for use in the 'back of beyond'. It should be 'extremely powerful in shortwave and mid wave—widest shortwave. Most lifelike tone reproduction. Faultless, accurate tuning'. Bush, GEC and Telerand were some of the brands he suggested.
- A chronometer wristwatch.
- A telescope.
- Specified amount of money for two 'return incognito trips'.

(a) One piece, 26 yards long and 48 inches wide 'shimmering white pure silk cloth (closely and evenly woven, perfect finish)'.

(b) One piece, 26 yards long and 48 inches wide 'shimmering white pure cotton mulmul (closely and evenly woven—most perfect finish)'.

(c) 13.5 yards long and 48 inches wide pure cotton, 'shimmering white, one piece, markin or exactly similar cloth'.

• Sixty pounds 'guaranteed purest (milk) cream or butter, for a life saving medicinal purpose'.

Bhagwanji had a story to tell to explain why he needed the pieces of cloth:

When your Dead Man was in Berlin, a great German doctor-scientist became very very friendly—affectionate and attached. Dr was then experimenting with a Radar. In those years, all scientists were feverishly working to get at the secret of the Radar. This great scientist, while in a very intimate talk, was propounding on it. And in the course of his talks, he said that in his lab he found that Radar beam particles do not bounce back if they strike "….", and he (Dr) felt astounded. That Dr could not inform any of the Govts or other scientists. He was a bombing raid casualty. But your Dead Man remembers…
In one secret place, your Dead Man tested the truth of that German scientist's findings, and he found it to be 100% fact.

Now, Bhagwanji needed those cloth pieces to shield some structure in his region, located at a very high place, which could only be detected by radar. Sputnik had been launched into space, but use of satellites for espionage were decades away.

Yet another item that Bhagwanji asked Pabitra to procure was an English dictionary—either Fowler's or Oxford 'packed like a presentation set'. He needed to gift it to a 'very learned scholar, a Siberian Deputy of the Supreme Soviet', who was of ' very great help' to him. The Deputy had requested Bhagwanji several times to get it for him, as he would become a suspect if he tried to buy it directly.

When Pabitra visited him during the Durga Puja in 1972, Bhagwanji gave him some more hints about the location of his own region. Many rivers flow through the mountainous area, he said, with one of them being a famous one—so wide that there are innumerable islands within it. During the winter, the water freezes enabling even vehicles carrying eighty tonnes of goods to pass over. While there is a desert on one side of the river, the other side is fertile agricultural land. He indicated that the ancient silk route passed by the feet of the mountain range. One tributary river, which had clear water throughout the year was given the name Ganga. There, located at the highest point in the region was his own place with 'all arrangements', that included a telescope which allowed one to see scores of miles away clearly. India, Tibet, China, Arabia and the Mediterranean were visible from that place. 'I go there when I want to cut myself off from everything.'

Although he did not give out the secrets regarding his mysterious acts, Bhagwanji provided specific landmarks, developments that he predicted would certainly take place. One of those predictions was the reinstatement of the Dalai Lama, who, he claimed he had rescued with the help of magical powers, risking his own life and sacrificing the lives of thousands of others.

This prediction, however, is yet to materialise.

The Ghost floated around collecting the stories of the places he visited, international meetings where he negotiated, and palaces he visited as royal guest, taking the stories out of his bag when time and situation permitted. Russia, China, Vietnam, France were just some of the places where we have been able to reconstruct at least part of his activities. But there were other places which Bhagwanji mentioned, and no information is available on what he was doing there. 'Do you know where all this body has gone?' he asked. The question was of course asked to tease the people sitting in front of him. He was the only person who had the answers, and he spread them out through months and years, dishing them out in snippets, anecdotes, and if the mood permitted, in the form of long stories. Sometimes, only names of places were taken, or indicated (for instance, Lake Kaali in the Saaremaa island of Estonia, Angkor Vat, the fire temple of Baku, an unidentified nuclear reactor, and a volcano where he saw worms living in hot lava).

International conferences were, of course, common for him. He spoke as a man who had seen it all. 'The rule of international diplomacy is that opponent parties will put up a show in front of the world of shouting at the top of their voices, abusing each other; later, however, they secretly meet in the same room sharing a smoke,' Bhagwanji shared his experience with Pabitra. 'The rule for these kind of meetings is "no bar"—accusations, counter-accusations, banging the table—everything is allowed except killing each other.'

This was not mere theorising. He had examples to back it up. US warships were being repaired deep in the rivers of China, he alleged. Moreover, according to Bhagwanji, the US had been buying barges from China which were used in the Southeast Asian theatre. Again, although Russia and the US were on the surface constantly abusing each other, secretly they arranged meetings of their committees. Bhagwanji suspected that the news of his being alive and active was leaked to the US through one such meeting. That, he claimed, explained the 'statement' of former US Secretary of Defense Robert McNamara after becoming the World Bank chief in 1968. 'We have categorically different news regarding the publicised death story of so and so.' McNamara further stated as per this account that 'a team of expert Generals under the guidance of a "super mind" were overseeing the Vietminh's decision making on the Vietnam War'. He refused to name the "super mind". Exactly where and when McNamara said this according to Bhagwanji, the authors do not know, and have consequently not been able to verify.

On 24 January 1973, Bhagwanji described in an unusually long narrative, replete with use of coded language, a secret conference between the representatives of Russia, China and the US, overseen by (Ho Chi Minh?) 'a pride of nine generals and a shadow behind them', on the fate of the Vietnam War. He claimed that the 'shadow' advised the US representative to opt for a 'face saving ceasefire' since they had already lost the war. The 'shadow' was none other than Bhagwanji himself. The conversation in Basti took place three days before the signing of the Peace Accord in Paris that set in motion the ceasefire in Vietnam and the withdrawal of the US troops.

The devastating war in Vietnam frequently figured in sessions

Bhagwanji had with his followers from Calcutta over the years. He claimed that on his advice, Ho Chi Minh dumped free cocaine and opium in South Vietnam. 'The Americans have consumed at least a thousand tons till now—avidly. Change my name if the greatest power of the present world can win North Vietnam even in a in thousand years.' It was around 1966 when Bhagwanji told Sunil Krishna Gupta and others about the dumping of drugs in South Vietnam, where the American forces were. At this time, it was not known, or at least not understood very well, that the drugs menace would become one of the reasons the US forces would quit the region. It was only in 1971 that US President Richard Nixon's deputy assistant for domestic affairs informed him that up to 20 per cent of US soldiers were heroin addicts. According to the 2010 book *The politics of Cocaine* by William L Marcy, high-ranking US officials 'believed that Chinese communist and Soviet-North Vietnamese operators had flooded South Vietnam with heroin, facilitating the escalation of use by US soldiers'. How could a nondescript holy man (assuming that's what Bhagwanji really was) located in a remote part of India have possibly known about this in advance?

There is more to it. In late 1971, Balraj Trikha, a leading Supreme Court advocate who represented a party before the Khosla Commission, saw someone who he thought was Subhas Bose at a South Vietnamese airport. This was reported in the media. But when Justice Khosla summoned Trikha, he made himself scarce. Thereafter, Khosla called Prem Bhatia, then Indian High Commissioner in Singapore, to state on oath what Trikha had told him [Bhatia]. A British Indian Army veteran and

Anglophile, Bhatia happened to be one of the topmost journalists of the times. At present, the trust being run in his name awards India's equivalent of Pulitzer Prize for journalism. The importance of Prem Bhatia can be gauged from the fact that the trust has had for trustees luminaries such as Dr Manmohan Singh, M K Rasgotra, Soli Sorabjee, Inder Malhotra, Prof Mushirul Hasan, Shekhar Gupta, Alok Mehta, H K Dua and others. Put differently, Bhatia was too wise a man to have paid the slightest attention to a claim that even conspiracy theorists of the worst type would find hard to digest.

This very Prem Bhatia testified before the Khosla Commission that he met Trikha at the High Commission, heard his claim that he had seen someone dead for twenty-five years and yet thought it prudent to invite Trikha for dinner. 'We started talking and then I asked him over to a meal at my house and he was good enough to accept my invitation,' he told the commission. At no point did Bhatia, a man of outstanding intelligence, experience and connections, tell Trikha to consult a psychiatrist—something the authors would have done in his place. On the contrary, 'taken aback' by Trikha's statement, which he 'mentioned to more than one person', Bhatia brought it to the commission's notice through a confidential letter to his friend, Justice Khosla. The letter is now available at the Nehru Memorial Museum and Library, New Delhi.

Even more intriguing is the account of a Calcutta newspaper correspondent who in 1994 visited Vietnam to cover the visit of Prime Minister Narasimha Rao. Prabha Jagannathan, the correspondent, had no particular interest in the Bose mystery, but at a gathering she met a Vietnamese Foreign Ministry official who passed on to her a lead on the condition of anonymity. He said that Vietnam was holding some material which could shed some light on the disappearance of Subhas Bose. The official said, he had tried to speak with the Indian embassy officials but they showed no interest in the documents. The journalist filed her story, and it was carried by her newspaper, *The Telegraph*, part of the *Anandabazar Patrika* group. Since the group had supported the air crash theory, there was no way it could have lend credence to the Bhagwanji angle which was virtually non-existent in 1994. But here is how the published story read:

> There is accessible material here on Netaji's stay in Saigon in 1945.... However, the Indian government is reluctant to pursue this lead, which is likely to help us unearth some exceedingly interesting material on Netaji's disappearance since it will re-open the entire issue, said a highly placed source. ... Material on Netaji is also believed to have been accessed by the government here, while collecting archival material on both the World War II and the Vietnam War period. [From a declassified file kept at the National Archives, New Delhi]

Since the Vietnam War began years after Subhas Bose's supposed death, the very existence of some archival material concerning him from that period would be quite intriguing on the face of it. The correspondent did not appear before the Mukherjee Commission despite repeated summons. The commission, in any case, asked the Government to ascertain the facts. The Indian Mission in Hanoi thereafter took up the matter with the State Records and Archives Department of Vietnam. Its Director General wrote back in August 2003 that 'according to the reports made by all the national archives centres of the Vietnam State Archives Department, the agency in charge of archiving all material on history of Vietnam, there is no document related to appearance of Netaji Subhas Chandra Bose in Vietnam in these centres'. The authors reckon that if at all there are any such records with Vietnam, they would be available as classified material with the government and so approaching State Records and Archives Department was not the best way to go about it.

Of particular interest to Bhagwanji, apart from South and Southeast Asia was the Middle Eastern question, especially the Arab-Jew conflict and the contest between the US and Russia for influence over the region. Taking the visitors from Calcutta on a tour of the history of the Jews, Bhagwanji educated them on the works of Titas Flavius Josephus and Tacitus. For him, Jews were a race who have 'fanatically, unswerving faith in their religion and scripture', and who have kept alive their ancient culture even after two thousand years of suffering. According to him, it was their faith in their religion, their destiny, and in the Old Testament that has brought them thus far. 'What sustains a man? It is faith, do you understand? This is the difference between you and me,' he surmised.

A year after the six-day war of 1967 between Israel and the Arabian states, Bhagwanji explained his assessment of the situation to Pabitra. According to him, the Russians supported the formation of Israel and Soviet Russia was the first country to recognise the new state and it supplied arms (in contrast to the US and Britain who refused) which enabled it to face off with the Arabian countries in the 1948 war. Yet, Israel refused to join the

Russian camp belying their expectations because of the anticipated fallout of becoming a zone of Russian influence. Israel then gave a year to the US to settle its Middle East policy, arguing that this was a golden opportunity for them to gain influence before the Russians came in. The US, however, continued to dilly-dally, and taking advantage of this, Russia jumped in with aid and funds and swayed in its favour Egypt and Jordan. Once it realised its blunder, the US was compelled to come in to the aid of Israel. That is why the US helped Israel in the 1967 war. Russia broke off with Israel realising that if it pushed any harder, it might lead to a war with the US.

A few weeks after the Egyptian government under its president Anwar Sadat expelled Soviet military advisers from Egypt in July 1972, Bhagwanji commented 'it was Sadat's foolishness'. 'I have told the Russian leaders that no purpose will be served in wasting money on the Arabs in order to help them,' he went on to say. They should rather spend it on development in Southeast Asia. Bhagwanji then went into a prediction mode: 'Sadat will bring back Russia by begging and pleading with them. Then there will be war. At that time Russia will descend with all its ferocity, in full force. The Arabs will happily cause a war—after that the Russians will step back.' This course of action was decided he said in a secret conference in an 'enemy country' between representatives of four countries, one of which, it can be safely assumed was the Soviet Union. As it turned out, this prediction materialised partly. The diary of Anatoly Chernyaev, a top Soviet advisor, published by the National Security Archive (a non-governmental research and archival institution in Washington, DC) in May 2006, quotes the General Secretary of the

Communist Party of the Soviet Union Leonid Brezhnev claiming that during the Yom Kippur war the very next year, 'Sadat woke me up in the middle of the night twice over the phone saying, "Save me!" He demanded I send Soviet troops, and immediately!' But the Soviet Union refused to interfere. Sadat in fact severed ties with the Soviet Union in 1976, which were re-established eight years later by his successor Hosni Mubarak.

On Israel's future, Bhagwanji remained upbeat. Regardless of the level of opposition from the Arabian countries, Israel will not only stay on top of the game, but will emerge as a 'very strong bulwark against Islamic fundamentalism and Soviet communism' was his prognostication. The Arab powers will reach an understanding with the Jews which will make them accept the reality of Israel, he added. At his own level, however, despite the ongoing and the potential future conflicts, he said he prayed for peace between the two races.

Somehow or the other, information that was out of bounds for most people, probably even top politicians, appeared to reach Bhagwanji with utmost ease. About three years after the Soviet invasion of Afghanistan in 1979, he gave his 'behind the scenes' version. Surajit Dasgupta, who had been taken to Bhagwanji for the first time by his uncle Sunil Krishna Gupta, noted down Bhagwanji's words.

'His Highness [the Khan] of Kalat [a part of Balochistan] considered me to be a very close friend,' Bhagwanji said, adding that he 'showed me some papers' that contained information on an offer that the British had made to him. What the offer exactly was, Bhagwanji didn't specify, but he confirmed that it involved a plan to deploy armed forces [again not specified whether Pakistani or British] on the Pakistan border. Once the army was deployed, Bhagwanji said, two ministers from the British Cabinet and five members of the British Parliament were on their way to Kabul. The scheme was that on reaching Kabul they would discuss with the [Raja??] and other rich men how to develop Afghanistan, and the army would cross the Pakistan–Afghan border after two days. The news of this plan, however, reached the Russians five days prior to the arrival of the British delegation. Just 'when the Ministers were in the plane right on top of Afghanistan, the Russian army entered Afghanistan. The plane did not land—it made an about turn right away,' Bhagwanji concluded.

If Bhagwanji's knowledge of the 'real story' behind the Russian invasion was based on intelligence provided by the Khan of Kalat, he described subsequent developments which he claimed to have witnessed himself. Towards the end of the 1970s, he said he went into Pakistan twice—once near Mari Indus in Punjab and again to the West of Bannuin the North West Frontier Province (now Khyber Pakhtunkhwa). 'Something very funny is going on in Pakistan,' Bhagwanji said, probably around the same time, or sometime later. Around three million Afghans have moved in, many of them living a life of great luxury—'wining, dining, womanising, lording'. There is unlimited money, items of luxury, dangerous weapons, addictive substances (cannabis, opium, hashish, refined cocaine), etc. A huge arrangement has been set up with thousands of foreign trainers (for guerrilla warfare), observers, advisors, ordnance suppliers crowding the place. 'All this is happening inside Pakistan, but totally out of its control,' Bhagwanji pointed out.

Did Bhagwanji describe the 'Operation Cyclone', a top secret US programme to arm and fund the Mujahedeens? Probably. The question as to how he reached enemy territory and what exactly was he doing there, remains without an answer like so much about him.

He was playing a game of deception. As far as he was concerned, Bhagwanji told Leela Roy that he was applying the lessons he was 'forced' to learn through his entire life from his 'Gurus'. As with most of his other utterances, he added a touch of riddle in the form of a Bengali adage—'You can say that the lessons learnt from the Guru have been turned upon him.' This could have been a tangential reference to the British. He considered the UK to be still one of India's greatest enemies.

There were indications of things to come in Southeast Asia too, but again in code language—'the malignant boils that have been made to erupt will rupture; the malodorous puss will be cleansed' and 'the patients will remain forever grateful to the physician'. More importantly, the whole of Southeast Asia will pass into India's exclusive sphere of influence. Could this have been a pointer to the imminent end of the Vietnam War? In any case, the prediction on India's influence in Southeast Asia remains a pipe dream.

The picture of himself painted by Bhagwanji was no less than that of a superman in the shadows moving across the world, engaging different powers but all with the same purpose: to bring glory to India. All his sacrifices, hardships, travels, negotiations and interventions had a specified outcome—reunification of India.

As a result of his efforts, 'many maps will change. That's it. The Ghost of the Dead's *sadhana* will be complete'.

THIRTEEN

MORE THINGS IN HEAVEN AND EARTH

'HE WAS SHIVA personified: Lord Shiva himself,' nonagenarian Dr R P Mishra broke into ecstasy remembering his time with Bhagwanji. Back in those days, supernatural powers of the man were discussed in suppressed voices among his overawed followers. They experienced several instances when he knew what they were doing or discussing far away from him.[1] Bhagwanji predicted to Dr T C Banerjee's family that their planned trip to Calcutta wouldn't materialise. One follower from Calcutta experienced something inexplicable; that the unseen *sanyasi* could control time.

Accounts of the followers are replete with stories of

---

1   'Why were you thinking so much about this poor man this morning from 9.30 am to 10.30 am?' Bhagwanji wrote to Santosh Bhattacharya in a letter dated 25 January 1964.

supernatural interventions through which the man behind the curtain protected them from dangers. His reputation as a spiritual adept cut across religious barriers. In Basti and other places, for instance, he was known among Muslims as '*Chhote Khuda*'.[2] In Old Delhi, he referred to being a guest of a certain Awlia (saint) Sahab.[3] But there were punishments too. Once, the son of a follower planned to secretly record his voice. On his way, riding a scooter, he met with an accident that resulted in some minor injuries. On reaching Bhagwanji, he received a stern warning: 'Never try such mischief with me again. I let you off lightly this time.' In short, the man appeared to have attained *siddhis* which his followers had only heard of or read in the pages of scriptures.

In fact, Bhagwanji's earliest known associate who later recounted his experience to the investigative journalists of the *Northern India Patrika* claimed to have spotted him through supernatural means. Surendra Singh Chaudhary was a disciple of Swami Brahmananda Saraswati, the Shankaracharya of the Jyotir Math monastery, from whom he learnt *Paroksh Vidya* by which he was able to communicate with spirits of people dead and gone. Chaudhary claimed (Bhagwanji later endorsed his claim) that it was the spirit of the dead Syama Prasad Mookerjee which guided him to Bhagwanji then living in the house of DSP Shankar Lal in Mainpuri, UP.[4]

---

2   Bhagwanji's letter to Pabitra Mohan Roy, 21 September 1975.

3   Charanik, Oi Mahamanaba Ase, Jayasree Prakashan, 2010, p 295. A follower told us that Bhagwanji once secretly stayed in Delhi's Nizamuddin dargah.

4   Interview of Surendra Singh Chaudhary by Syed Kauser Husain of *Northern India Patrika*. Bhagwanji's letter to Pabitra Mohan Roy, 20 February 1963.

In one of his meetings with Bhagwanji at Mainpuri, Chaudhary conveyed a message from the spirit of Mahatma Gandhi:

> I conveyed to him a message from Gandhiji, which was very pathetic. Gandhiji said: '*Tumne mujhe Bapu mana hai, ab bhi mante ho. Hamari atma bhatak rahi hai. Tum hamare liye kuchh kar sako to kar dena.* (You have always considered me a father figure, and still do. My soul is still wandering around. Please do something about it if you can).' On hearing this, Bhagwanji's tears continued to flow for a long time.

Stories of Bhagwanji's supernatural powers are galore. His letters and other accounts of his disciples also show that he had full command over the *Itihasas, Puranas, Vedas,* and *Tantric* texts. However, very little is known about his actual *sadhana,* the practices that he undertook to attain spiritual powers. According to Chaudhary, Bhagwanji took up *Bhairav Sadhana* during his stay in Lucknow, the Bhaisa Kund cremation ground on the bank of river Gomti being the place of his *sadhana*. Something, however, went wrong and Bhagwanji, according to Chaudhary, suffered some physical damage akin to burns, for which he had to live on a boat in proximity to the river water for some time. This *sadhana,* according to his account, was completed in Neemsar.

The other detail available from Bhagwanji himself is a mode of Tantric *sadhana* that required him to conduct the rituals of the *sadhana* sitting on top of five corpses (*Pancha Shava Sadhana*). He also indicated undertaking Lalita Devi *sadhana*.[5] Some documents

---

5 Bhagwanji's letter to Pabitra Mohan Roy, 21 September 1975.

retrieved from Ram Bhawan suggest that Chaudhary's obsession with the occult and the desire to have Bhagwanji quickly elevated to supreme levels of spiritual attainment drove him to conduct certain rituals at the Datia Peeth in Madhya Pradesh.[6] Bhagwanji's approach on the contrary, as would be clear from his writings and discussions, was slow and steady—everything had its own scheduled time in his scheme of things.

In a letter to Shiva Prosad Nag, he described in detail how he received the vision of Goddess Kali while residing somewhere in the Indo-Tibetan border. Although Mother Kali is usually known by her dark appearance, Bhagwanji wrote to Nag that he saw her in the form of a blinding white flash and the realisation dawned upon him that the divine mother was protecting him and getting her work done through him. Saraswati Devi became Ma Jagdambe (Bhagwanji used to address her sometimes as Ma or at other times as Jagdambe) when he saw Lalita Devi manifested in her.[7]

The quest for spiritual salvation started early in his life, Bhagwanji said:

> I have been a *sanyasi* from birth…From my childhood I began hearing and perusing scriptures. As I grew up my mystic hunger also grew. I went through all the scriptures and philosophies again and again. In my college and University years, I used to seek out, hunt the so-called great seers and wise men of our days and I questioned them on mysticism. None satisfied me. I even left everything once in search of a true mystic Satguru

---

6 Parts of letters from Surendra Singh Chaudhary to Bhagwanji published in *Gumnami Subhas* by Ashok Tandon.

7 Bhagwanji's undated letter to Shiva Prosad Nag and Oi Mahamanaba Ase, p 399.

and searched far and wide in the country and high and low in the Himalayas.[8]

The influence of Western philosophy[9] featured rarely in his discussions with his followers or in his letters. However, on one occasion, while advising Pabitra on elevating his mental life to a higher plane, he put together a few of the thoughts of Western philosophers and theologians that had moulded his character.[10]

[Thomas] Fuller[11] laid out my path: 'The real difference between men is energy. A strong will, a settled purpose, an invincible determination, can accomplish almost anything; and in this lies the distinction between great men and little men.' His Lordship, the Lord Muskerry[12] conveyed to me 'Nothing is difficult to a brave and faithful man.' AG Bell[13] smiled and told me, 'You must become like this—concentrate all your thoughts upon the work in your hands! The sun's rays do not burn until brought to a focus.' [Henri-Frédéric] Amiel's[14] life's ideal is in front of me: 'Sacrifice still exists everywhere, and everywhere the elect (of each generation) suffers for the salvation of the rest.' I became prepared because I learnt the truth that 'Out of suffering have emerged the strongest souls. The most massive characters are seared with scars.'[15] This dead ghost of Bengal's

8   Charanik, Oi Mahamanaba Ase, Jayasree Prakashan, 2010, p 128.
9   Subhas Bose was a student of philosophy in college.
10 The quotes he wrote down in the letter were not always exact. Obviously he was writing from memory.
11 English churchman and historian (1608-1661).
12 Sir Robert-Tilson Deane (1745-1818), first lord of Muskerry. His family's motto was Forti et fideli nihil difficile (nothing is difficult to the brave and faithful).
13 Alexander Graham Bell (1847-1922), scientist, innovator, inventor of telephone.
14 Henri-Frédéric Amiel (1821-1881), Swiss philosopher.
15 Khalil Gibran (1883-1931), Lebanese-American writer.

dust particle is just that. [Benjamin] Disraeli[16] prepared me by teaching that 'Patience is a necessary ingredient of genius.' I experienced it through life that 'We know the truth, not only by our reason, but by the heart.'[17] I understood this during my childhood and have been living accordingly all my life that 'Self denial is indispensable to a strong character; and the loftiest kind thereof comes only of a religious stock.'[18] It matches with my whole life. I have learnt that: 'If one advances confidently towards the direction of his dreams, and endeavours to live the life which he has imagined, he will meet with a success [unexpected] in common hours.'[19] Because, 'The world turns aside to let any man pass who knows where he is going.'[20] The ability to make up your mind inspires self-confidence; it gives you inner power, and it commands the respect of your fellow men. In the present *sadhana* of my Ma Janani Kali, Janani Janmabhoomi, the advice of [Charles Caleb] Colton is my pole star and protective amulet: 'Secrecy has been well-termed the soul of all great designs. More has been effected by concealing our own intentions, than by discovering those of our enemy. But great men succeed in both.'[21] This advice guides me in all situations. Theodore Parker also explained to me the truth that 'Let men laugh when you sacrifice desire to duty, if they will... you have time and eternity to rejoice in.' Pabitra, I hope that you will assimilate this wisdom, which I received and followed in my life, to make your life complete and fruitful.

---

16   Benjamin Disraeli (1804-1881), British Conservative politician who served twice as Prime Minister.

17   Blaise Pascal (1623-1662), French mathematician, physicist, inventor, writer and Catholic theologian.

18   Theodore Parker (1810-1860), American Unitarian theologian, pastor, scholar, and social reformer.

19   Henry David Thoreau (1817-1862), American essayist, poet and philosopher.

20   Epictetus (50-135), Greek Stoic philosopher.

21   Charles Caleb Colton (1780-1832), English cleric and writer.

"... The real difference ... between men ... energy. A strong will, a settled purpose, an invincible determination ... can accomplish almost anything; and in these lies the distinction between great men and little men."

"His Lordship the Lord Ȝuǝkɛɐ Coronation" "Nothing is difficult to a brave and faithful man."

P. G. Bell, ... "Concentrate all your thoughts upon the work in your hands! The Sun's Rays DO NOT BURN UNTILL brought to a focus."

Amiel, ... "Sacrifice still exists everywhere, and everywhere THE ELECT (of EACH GENERATION) SUFFERS FOR THE SALVATION OF THE REST."

"out of suffering have emerged THE STRONGEST ... THE MOST MASSIVE CHARACTERS ARE SEARED with SCARS"

[Bhagwanji's undated letter to Pabitra Mohan Roy telling him about the influence of Western philosophers and theologians in his life]

The eclectic nature of his deriving wisdom notwithstanding, the centre of Bhagwanji's spiritual quest remained Goddess Kali. Goddess Durga-Kali was his driving force and he was just a machine in her hands, he said. Goddess Kali was synonymous with the motherland (*Ma Janani Janmabhoomi*). It was the divine mother inside him who made him say that 'My Mother has a particular language; she has a message, and someday the world will have to listen to that.'[22] '*Kalau Jagartti Kalika*,' he wrote to Pabitra, explaining to him that every yuga (epoch) has a specific deity in charge who governs rewards, punishments, births, deaths, attachment and salvation: in the Kali Yuga, it is Ma Adya Shakti Kalika. Thus, it is relatively easier in this yuga to attain *Kaivalya* (detachment, absolute independence) compared to other yugas.[23]

Above humans; above everything is Ma Janani Janmabhoomi.
Ma Janani Janmabhoomi is synonymous with my Ma Janani Kali...
Pabitra, in Kali Yuga, Shri Shri Kali is the only giver of kaivalya.

The quest had brought him far and he strived to pass some of his insights on to his associates and disciples. Pabitra, of course, was special. 'You are my disciple whom I have initiated into both mantra and *sadhana*,' Bhagwanji wrote to Pabitra on their Guru-Shishya relationship. The Guru is always connected with the heart

---

22   Charanik, *Oi Mahamanaba Asey*, Jayasree Prakashan, 2010, p 274.
23   Bhagwanji's letter to Pabitra Mohan Roy, 16 November 1973.

of the disciple and that is why 'I have to be constantly concerned about you'. 'Whenever required I have to assert my presence near you; if you are unmindful, or if you face any danger on road I have to alert you, startle you or give you a gentle push. I have to do this even if I am in the middle of *sadhana*,' Bhagwanji wrote. He was taking care of Pabitra with fatherly love (that did not mean Pabitra's children had become his grandchildren, he jested).[24]

[Bhagwanji's letter to Pabitra Mohan Roy, 3 April 1974]

To an ailing Sunil Das, he laid down the exercises of Hatha Yoga with the instruction to 'follow them with real religious zeal' for the rest of his life. 'Believe me, this humble *Faquir* is a pastmaster in all this,' he wrote. Then followed page after page of detailed guidelines on *Kapalbhati, Ujjayi, Bhastrika* and *Sheetali Pranayams*: how to sit down, how to control the breath, number of times to be done and the benefits of these exercises. Apart from curing diseases and adding a glow of health and spirituality, these had practical uses too. 'If you feel too cold when surrounded by ice, *Bhastrika* will help you to warm your body,' he pointed out. Das lived his entire life in Calcutta, with occasional travels to

---

24   Bhagwanji's letter to Pabitra Mohan Roy, 3 April 1974.

Delhi and a few other cities in India, and never had a chance to face such a situation.[25]

Sending rakhis to his followers in Kolkata was an annual ritual that Bhagwanji observed consistently. These sacred rakhis, conveying his blessings to his disciples, were treated with zealous reverence by the recipients. Occasionally, these arrived with instructions on the associated ritual.

> I am sending Raksha *ashirvad*. Read this mantra [think forcefully and meditate that 'this body' is standing or sitting in front of you (and other four members of your family) and tying the rakhi while reciting the mantra]

> *Yena baddho Baliraja daanavendro Mahaabalah*
> *Tena twaam abhibadhnaami rakshe maa chala maa chala*

> (I tie on you the raksha which was tied on Bali, the King of demons. Therefore, O Raksha! Do not ever fail to protect this follower, do not ever fail.)[26]

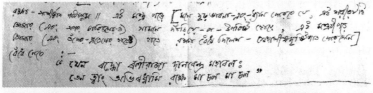

[Bhagwanji's letter of 21 September 1972 to Pabitra Mohan Roy]

When you dwell over any issue, you should not consider only its beneficial aspects or aspects that appeal to your immediate interest. While planning, a wise and thinking person takes into account the downsides too. You must think of the risks, the

25 Charankik, *Oi Mahamanaba Asey*, Jayasree Prakashan, 2010, pp 369-377.
26 Bhagwanji's letter to Pabitra Mohan Roy, 21 September 1972.

dangers and the scenario for failure. Such a person can never be surprised. Always remember this dictum.[27]

Through Pabitra, his advice to all those who wanted moral and spiritual progress was to 'set a great ideal as the pole star' and live accordingly. '*Mahajano Yen Gatah Sa Panthah*' was the advice of the scripture (Bhagavad Gita), but to it Bhagawanji added his cautionary message: 'Do not try to experiment with their teachings or judge them....*Samshaya atma vinashyati*' (the doubting self is destroyed) was the warning of God himself. There are many great characters to follow, such as Dattatreya, Jada Bharata, Rishabha Deva, Shri Ramachandra, Shri Krishna, Shri Shri Shri Balaram Jiu, Shri Shri Loknath Jiu, Swami Shri Achyutanandaji, Shri Shri Brahmananda ji, Shri Shri Chaitanya Mahaprabhuji, Shri Shri Nityananda Mahaprabhu Jiu, Maharshi Raman, Mahaprabhu Jesus Christ, Shri Shri Thakur Ramakrishna Paramhansa, Shri Shri Anukul Thakur ji, revered Lahiri Mahasaya ji and others. Perusal of their lives, however, Bhagwanji told Pabitra, makes it clear that they were never fully understood by anyone however erudite. The audacity of trying to judge the lives of such great men is unpardonable, he said. Their lives, character, work and *sadhana* are incomprehensible to gods themselves.[28]

Rituals laid down in the shastras are crucial in *sadhana*. Hence, for the benefit of his followers Bhagwanji would guide them on methods: how to do *Chandi Path* (ritualistic reading of

27   Bhagwanji's letter to Pabitra Mohan Roy, 12 February 1963.
28   Bhagwanji's letter to Pabitra Mohan Roy, 8 May 1981.

Durga Sapta Shati or *Devi Mahatmyam*), *mantra japa* (repeated chanting of mantras), follow the correct procedural components of puja, like *asana shuddhi* and *sankalpa,* etc.

If this was the ritualistic aspect of *sadhana,* explanations of the inner spiritual meanings of the sacred texts that transcended the grammatical meanings provided the substance. For '*Sadhana* is a war' and realising the deeper meaning of the texts is as important as strictly following the rules. Mechanical translations of Sanskrit without indicating the symbolic meanings, especially if they came from spiritual adepts made him angry. He would therefore guide them on which versions of the scriptures to read, and how.

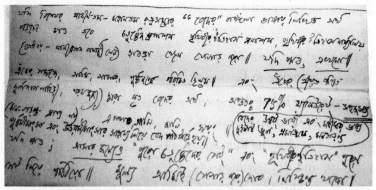

[If you want to read the most ancient and magnificent collection of gems, the Vedas, in Bengali, then collect the four Vedas published by the Prithibir Itihas office in Howrah (most probably in Kali Prasad Banerjee lane). That is, if they are still available. I was acquainted with them in my past life. I know that their interpretation of the Vedas (done by Param Pujya Durgadas Lahiri) is at least 75% accurate. The Bhashyas (interpretation and commentaries) of both Mahidhar and Ubbat are erroneous. Vedas should be read with the help of Purva Mimamsa and Uttara Mimamsa. Collect a copy of the full sets of Vedas and Prithibir Itihas (History of the World) published by them for me. I will pay the costs, you don't have to worry about that. Bhagwanji's letter to Pabitra Mohan Roy, 27 June 1977].

The spiritual path wasn't easy and everyone couldn't succeed. 'Frustration is for the general run of people,' who cannot devote themselves to their work following their in-born tendencies, Bhagwanji reminded Bijoy Nag. 'Ordinary people cannot design their lives to follow "*Karmanye Vadhikaraste Ma Phaleshu Kadachana*",' he said. By his interpretation of the Bhagavad Gita's '*Manushyanam sahasreshu kaschid yatati siddhaye, yatatam api siddhanam kaschin mam vetti tattvatah*' (Among thousands of men, rarely one tries for liberation. Among those who try for liberation, perhaps one gets to know my true nature),[29] only a specified ratio—one person per 250,000 people—can attain liberation following this instruction.[30]

He communicated with sages, old and new, Bhagwanji said. 'Many a times, while moving through the Himalayas alone, I have obtained shelter in the ashram of the Maha Pujya Agastya Dev,' he wrote to Shiva Prosad Nag. I first met Swamiji [Vivekananda] in a planchette, he said. Tara Khyapa of Tara Pith in Bengal (disciple of the more widely known Bama Khyapa) visited him at many places in his subtle body to bestow his blessings.[31] So did Sitaram Das Omkar Nath Thakur. And at times his views were quite iconoclastic.

Despite his deep devotion to Swami Vivekananda, Bhagwanji rued the fact that the Ramakrishna Mission emphasised more on his work and did not highlight the lives and work of the other disciples of Shri Ramakrishna. 'Rakhal Maharaj, Latu Maharaj, Master Mahashay were *sadhakas* of a higher level than Swamiji,' he said. According to him, 'the learned society in the US respects

---

29 Translation by Bibek Debroy, *The Bhagavad Gita*, Penguin Books, 2005, p 105.

30 Charanik, Oi Mahamanaba Ase, Jayasree Prakashan, 2010, p 136.

31 Tara Khyapa had passed away in December 1945. During his lifetime he was involved in the freedom struggle and had been in contact with many nationalist leaders. There is at least one account of his interaction with Subhas Chandra Bose, when he wrote a letter to him in religious code language, to understand which Subhas had to send an emissary to Tara Khyapa.

Swami Abhedananda more than Swami Vivekananda'. The Americans find that he used to impress with his flowery language, but its effect was temporary. In contrast, Swami Abhedananda's sayings used to make a permanent impression on the mind. Vivekananda took *sanyas* on his own as Shri Ramakrishna did not initiate him into the order of *sanyasis*, Bhagwanji reminisced. This was against the shastras (scriptures), he pointed out.

On this note, he recalled an incident when Swami Abhedananda had sent for him during his last days.

> He used to utter a few words anxiously during the last three-four days of his life. One of those was—'So-and-so is the only person in India now whose self-sacrifice is complete.' His disciples took me to him. On seeing me he stood up and embraced me although he was very ill and started saying, 'You will be victorious. Your victory is certain.'

'I will have to go to Thakur through this illness. Look, Thakur is standing over there.' Tears started rolling down my cheeks. He had one great sorrow: 'All that we wanted, and Thakur wanted, has gone astray'.[32]

---

32 Notes of discussion with Bhagwanji, taken by Pabitra Mohan Roy, 3 May 1973. Swami Abhedananda died on 8 September 1939. An eye-witness account tells us what exactly happened: 'During his illness he [Swami Abhedananda] expressed his desire to meet Sarvepalli Radhakrishnan and Subhas Chandra Bose. When Subhas Chandra Bose came to meet him, Swamiji wanted to embrace him. Subhas Chandra stood in front of him. He was so ill that it was difficult for him to stand and keep his clothes on. Somehow he managed to wrap his cloth around and said with great affection, "Come Subhas, let me embrace you."...Thereafter he blessed Subhas Chandra with all his heart, "Be victorious." He had a long discussion with Subhas Chandra regarding the present political situation. Subhas responded to his queries with the humility of a boy. Swami Shankarananda, *Jiban Katha*, Shri Ramakrishna Vedanta Math, 1946, pp 539-540. Translated from Bengali.

His criticism of Anandamayi Ma was more severe. Although no corroborating information is available to establish whether any meeting actually took place between Anandamayi Ma and Bhagwanji, one of his letters to Pabitra indicates that they did meet, or at least interact. 'Ma Anandamayi publicises herself as *Purna Brahma Sanatani*, *Purna Brahma Narayani*, so I asked her some clear and straight questions,' he wrote to Pabitra. The questions were not at all pleasant. 'It is clearly written in the *Vedas* and *Puranas* that when a *Purna Brahma Sanatani* descends on the earth, everywhere there will be peace, prosperity, and happiness,' he argued. How did then her own place of birth (in Brahmanbaria district of Bangladesh) get occupied by foreigners? Why couldn't she protect her own birth place?

I have heard you have 16-18 huge ashrams—and houses and buildings. Millionaires spend their millions at your command. That's all very well. But hundreds of thousands of women from your Dhaka, your East Bengal—mothers, sisters (I am not even talking about fathers and brothers) are roaming the streets, lanes, railway platforms of Calcutta, having become mad after losing everything, living like insects. Thousands are saving their own lives and their parents' as well by selling their body. And despite being one of them, you have come to '___' to flaunt your wealth, divinity and the being of PBS…If you really are Mother, then run to be among those who are living a hellish life. Tell them, 'Don't worry mothers, daughters and sisters; come over to live in my ashrams and houses—there will be no shortage of food and clothing…' At the same time you would have directed your millionaire disciples—'So and so, get 5 lakhs, so and so, get 2 lakhs,' etc. Is it so easy to become a Mother?

Today, I challenge you in the name of your being a woman, a mother, a sister, your motherland and your being a PBS, that if you are a true PBS then take up the Chakra and show your destroyer form. Your son is challenging you today—you rise to this challenge, take it up. If you try to shirk this by saying that this is not your work, then alright, I am challenging you that if you are PBS, then within seven days, make me, this wretched son of yours, *Purna Pratakhya Siddha*. Then you stand behind me as my mother. I will liberate your motherland from the Yavans after completing Shri Shri Ma Kali's *pratakhya siddha* and gift it to you. Now take up this challenge. I have not said anything untoward or uncivil to you—what I have said are burning issues of my heart.[33]

The talks often entered the esoteric, drawing connections between ancient insights and modern scientific knowledge. 'Because of the limitations of human beings, it is impossible for them to truly grasp the infinite and that is why the infinite appears before human eyes to symbolically represent itself.' The solar system with its unbridled pulsation is infinite for common human beings. It has, therefore, taken the same form within an atom. 'An atom is an exact replica of the solar system.' However, 'If you study Kanada[34] you will realise that the modern scientists understand only a fraction of the details laid out by him'. Atomic fission as scientists know it is only partial; a complete fission will blow the world away.

---

33   Bhagwanji's letter to Pabitra Mohan Roy, 24 February 1963.
34   Ancient Indian philosopher who propounded the Vaisheshika school of Indian philosophy.

I feel like laughing when you call the spaceships that travel to the moon, etc. *Mahakashjan*[35]—that's not *Mahakash*—it is just *Aakash*. Creation is not only one; there are innumerable creations. The space layer between each layer of creation is called *Maha Vyom*. Do you know its function? Every thought, every action is being reflected there and being permanently recorded…It is a recorder of thoughts, recorder of words and recorder of deeds.

'Vibration is the mother of all creation,' Bhagwanji said, giving an esoteric explanation of life and creation. According to him, everything around us, including us, is a collection of vibrations. It is this omnipresent vibration that is known as life force. The entirety of creation is supported, shaped, reshaped and altered by this life force, which is present in a shape somewhat like that of an egg. At the beginning there was only one sphere which was split into two by the severe intensity of vibration. Whatever is happening in one sphere is being recorded in the other. A time will come, he said, when everything will be obliterated by a huge explosion in the vibrating life force: everything will dissolve and get concentrated in a single mighty atom. All the life force converges into a point. This phenomenon, he said, is described in the *Nasadiya Sukta* of the *Rig Veda*. These can be experienced through proper *sadhana* but can never be expressed in words: they can be spoken of only allegorically. 'Even the Rishis whose feet I am not qualified to touch had to stop in the attempt to express this phenomenon and proclaim "*Avang manasa gochara*" (beyond mind or words).'

---

35   Bengali word for space vehicles. *Mahakash* is infinite space.

Bhagwanji explained the reason of having specific ways of chanting mantras too.

> If you keep repeating a mantra or a name at the same volume and modulation it will result in a vibration that will spread over your body. This will gradually reach the desired destination of the mantra. As soon as the vibration from the source is connected with the destination the power of that mantra will take form. This is what *sadhakas* mean by vision of *Ishta Devata*.[36]

Modern scientists are calling Raja Yoga the science of the ultimate, he told Dulal Nandy.[37]

'As human beings, we are, at all times radiating energy, which is soaked and stored by items around us. Even our thoughts radiate and create an electrical field which leaves an imprint on objects in the form of energy,' wrote Bhagwanji. He cited the work of one Genady Sergeyev to claim that 'every human being leaves an energetical imprint…as well as informational imprint on objects that he touches or is close to'.[38] Dr Genady Sergeyev turned out to be a prominent mathematician for the Soviet military who…devised important mathematical and statistical methods…which allowed parapsychologists to follow and depict the actions of telepathy in the brain.[39] This was stated in a 1972 Defense Intelligence Agency (DIA) report, declassified in 2004 by the Central Intelligence Agency (CIA). The report discusses

---

36 Charanik, Oi Mahamanaba Ase, Jayasree Prakashan, 2010, pp 215-217.
37 Notes of discussion with Bhagwanji, taken by Dulal Nandy, 31 January 1965.
38 Charanik, Oi Mahamanaba Ase, Jayasree Prakashan, 2010, p 261.
39 CIA-RDP96-00787R000100120001-9, Controlled offensive behavior - USSR (U), https://www.cia.gov/library/readingroom/docs/CIA-RDP96-00787R000100120001-9pdf.

Sergeyev in the context of research in Soviet Union in the area of psychokinesis (PK) or mind over matter. He conducted intensive lab research on Nina Kulagina, a Russian lady who claimed to have psychic powers. Sergeyev registered heightened biological luminescence radiating from Kulagina's eyes during the apparent movement of objects by PK'. He postulated that the 'bio-plasma' of the human body 'must interact with the environment to produce PK'.[40]

Every human being leaves an energetical imprint, as well as informational imprint, on objects that he touches on is close to.

[From a letter Bhagwanji wrote to Dr Priyabrata Banerjee of Faizabad. Courtesy Rita Banerjee]

One mystery that drew much of his attention was that of the unidentified flying objects or UFOs. *Flying Saucers Have Landed,* by Desmond Leslie and George Adamski and *Flying Saucers Farewell* by George Adamski—heavily marked and underlined, with sparse comments on the margins—were found among Bhagwanji's huge collection of books in Ram Bhawan. Although hundreds of thousands of people have sighted them, the existence of UFOs has been denied by all governments except that of Brazil, he said. Referring to Project Space Track, a US Air Force programme to track artificial satellites and space probes, that became operational in 1961, he claimed that despite the programme's base station having spotted unknown objects travelling alongside space probes its findings have not been publicly disclosed.[41] *The New York*

---

40 Ibid.
41 Charanik, Oi Mahamanaba Ase, Jayasree Prakashan, 2010, pp 141-142.

Times revealed in a report published on 17 December 2017 that the US Department of Defense had spent USD 22 million in running the 'Advanced Aerospace Threat Identification Program' from 2007 that investigated UFOs.[42]

Travelling in subtle body is made possible by the right *sadhana*: 'Once your *sadhana* reaches a stage, the *prana sharir* (subtle body) can be taken out of this *sthula sharir* (material body). After getting used to this, one can go anywhere in his *prana sharir*.[43] It isn't a difficult feat to achieve, Bhagwanji claimed; the primary requirement for attaining this power being purity of body and mind. 'I attained this ability quite easily.' Separation of the subtle body from the physical body, however, has many levels. At the highest level of attainment, one's movements even in space, among the planets and galaxies, become unrestricted.[44]

Ghosts do exist, Bhagwanji would say. So do *Gandharvas* and *Apsaras*, who belong to *Dev yoni*.

'You can hear the sound of Warren Hastings's horse cart in Calcutta if you give daily attendance. You can experience it if you stay in the balcony of the guards in the old cemetery at Gastin Road between 10 pm to 3-4 am.'[45]

If security arrangements were the biggest concern while

---

42   Helene Cooper, 'Ralph Blumenthal and Leslie Kean, 'Glowing Auras and Black Money': The Pentagon's Mysterious UFO Program,' *The New York Times*, 17 December 2017, https://www.nytimes.com/2017/12/16/us/politics/pentagon-program-ufo-harry-reid.html.

43   Notes of discussion with Bhagwanji taken by Bijoy Nag, 29 September 1971.

44   Charanik, Oi Mahamanaba Ase, Jayasree Prakashan, 2010, p 142.

45   Notes of discussion with Bhagwanji, taken by Pabitra Mohan Roy, 5 May 1973. Hastings was the first de facto Governor-General of India from 1773 to 1785.

choosing a location for staying, other worldly concerns were not any less important for Bhagwanji. Thus, when Pabitra brought the news that a house in Puri, Odisha, which he had shortlisted had a Shiva temple inside the compound, Bhagwanji wasn't happy. From the olden times, he wrote to Pabitra, it is a custom to have a Shiva temple inside a household only if it is a place haunted by harmful spirits or if there had been a murder or a suicide in the house. Otherwise, it is strictly forbidden to establish such a temple within a household. If this rule is flouted, he wrote, no one can prevent the harm that would come in the way of the family that resides in such a house. *Ganas* (attendants) of Shiva are always present in a temple where regular worship takes place and if the worship is stopped, it results in their damaging interventions. Also, any house which is left unattended for a very long time without any cleaning, purification or the fire of an oven or lamps is certain to be occupied by *Pretas* (spirits of dead human beings who are said to have not been released in the normal ways described in scriptures).

Bhagwanji listed out the religious activities that needed to be undertaken for purification of the place to Pabitra. He also recalled that there were three other houses in that locality during his youth which were known at that time to be haunted houses. He described those houses to Pabitra in detail for him to identify them.

In the same letter, he reminded Pabitra of a *Brahma Dev* (spirit of a Brahmin who died unnatural or untimely death) residing in the temple compound in Neemsar. A consequence of this was death and destruction in the family of the Pandas of the temple. Many people were witnesses to their existence. Even Saraswati Devi and Rajkumar were attacked by the spirit, who once attempted to throttle her. It was only because of his

[Bhagwanji's] presence, Bhagwanji wrote, that they emerged unharmed. The spirit was annoyed by the presence of the mother-son duo and was freed finally only through Bhagwanji's intervention.[46]

Bhagwanji was deeply interested in astrology and numerology. Serious reading of astrological books from *Bhrigu Samhita* (the real *Bhrigu Samhita* is secured by storing different volumes at different places, not in Varanasi, Bhagwanji told Pabitra Mohan Roy) to modern treatises and preparations of birth charts and making predictions based on them for many of his associates took up much of whatever free time he had. At the same time, he had a strong distaste for modern astrologers; most of them are charlatans and have no idea about correct astrological calculations, he held. *Panchangs/ Panjikas* had special importance for him. He made quite a collection of *panchangs*, going back decades, and studied them carefully. One particular matter that bothered him was the adjustment of special times—auspicious or inauspicious—during his travels abroad. 'I have to live among Hindus, Muslims, Christians, jungle tribes when I travel to China, Japan, Southeast Asia, Arabian countries, Africa, Europe and the US. How can I determine the starting time of *Amavasya* and the end of it?' he wrote to Pabitra.[47]

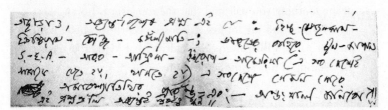

[Bhagwanji's letter to Pabitra Mohan Roy, 8 November 1975, mentioning the importance of adjusting times of astrologically significant events during his travel abroad]

46 Bhagwanji's letter to Pabitra Mohan Roy, 3 April 1974.
47 Bhagwanji's letter to Pabitra Mohan Roy, 8 November 1975.

Sometimes history and geography came alive in his words, but in very different forms than are commonly known. Jesus was a Natha Yogi, he said, and 'All of Jesus's history is in the Muth of the Natha Yogi community, but they don't allow outsiders access.'[48]

> Jesus Christ did not have a beard. The only time when he had a very small beard was when he was roaming around in our country as a *Baul*. Manuscript written by him is stored even now in the caves of Tibet. He was a Shaivite and mystic and his Guru belonged to a famous religious group in our country.[49]

'Even now a prayer to Jesus on the night before X-mas is answered, but one must not divulge the prayer,' Bhagwanji told his followers.

Pilgrimage routes of olden days too were familiar to him:

> For pilgrims/tourists in earlier days there was a road from Durjoy Linga to Amarnath, from Amarnath to Pashupatinath, from there to Kedarnath, and from Kedarnath to Badrinath. There is a beautiful pond with lotuses on that route, with steps. On the bank of the pond is a temple—on the route from Kedarnath to Badrinath. It takes only two days to cover that route. The most beautiful thing in the pond is the *Shatadal* (hundred-petalled lotus). At night the lotuses close when the water freezes. Early in the morning you will find that the top layer is frozen like a layer of glass and the lotuses are closed. When this body went on that path to Bhagawan Shri Badri Vishal Mandir, everyone kept staring at him with their mouths open.[50]

He claimed to have travelled to unknown and little-known

48   Notes of discussion taken by Pabitra Mohan Roy, 2 November 1972.
49   Notes of discussion taken by Pabitra Mohan Roy, 28 August 1973.
50   Notes of discussion taken by Surajit Dasgupta, 9 October 1982.

monasteries in Tibet and caves in the Himalayas. He recounted an out-of-the world experience of meeting an ancient Chinese saint who gave him a blue sapphire with special powers—representing God Shani—to be worn in a ring. Shani would keep protecting him, the saint assured, and help him remain behind a veil of mystery.

> No one has any idea of what's going on in three-fourth of the 350 miles width of the Himalayas, as the crow flies. I had the good luck of being able to witness probably a thousandth of that. What I saw beats the most fantastic of Arabian tales. It was in Luling and Tholing monasteries that I was told for the first about the existence of the ashram of Maharshi Agastya where people continue to live.[51]

Later, he told Surajit Dasgupta, 'The first assessment by the Thuling monastery was that I am reincarnation of Amitabha Buddha.'[52]

Dust particle of Bengal was Bhagwanji's favourite way of describing himself. However, at times he would refer to characters from the epics and Western mythology and literature to explain his position better. From India's ancient past, he described himself as Bhishma who sacrificed what was rightfully his and led a life of *Bhrahmacharya*. Bhishma was given the boon of dying only when he willed, Bhagwanji used to point out to his followers. Some painted him as Frankenstein, he said, but that was an identity 'which I neither did want nor deserve'. Another character from Western mythology with which he found resonance was one that represented fall from grace: Lucifer.

---

51 Charanik, Oi Mahamanaba Ase, Jayasree Prakashan, 2010, pp 440-442.
52 Notes of discussion taken by Surajit Dasgupta, 5 October 1982.

However, when it came to announcing his resolve to implement his plan, he repeated Krishna's promise to Draupadi in the *Mahabharata's Udyoga Parva* (modifying them a bit to suit his purpose).

Chaleddhi himavan shailo medina shatadha bhavet.
Dyauh patechcha sanakshatra na me mogham vacho bhavet.
shushyettoyanidhihkrishnena me moghamvachobhavet.
aham cha tatkarishyaami…daivaachchavidhinirmitaat.

(Even the Himalaya mountains could move; the earth would be split into hundreds of pieces, the sky with the stars would fall down, but my words would not be in vain! I will do all that through fate ordained by the creator!)[53]

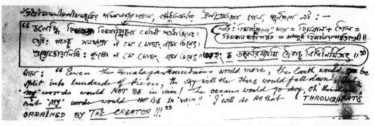

[Bhagwanji's letter to Pabitra Mohan Roy, 11 August 1971]

On one rare occasion, Bhagwanji wrote down himself what he saw as his own spiritual reality. 'I won't ever write anything like this again,' Pabitra, the recipient of the letter was informed.

'আমার' যে নিজসত্ত্বা, যাহা লইয়া, এই শরীরধারী হইয়া আসিয়াছি এবং যাহা (ঐ শাশ্বত নিজসত্ত্বা) লইয়া এই শরীরটির অধিকারী চলিয়া যাইবে; সেই 'আমার' স্বরূপ; এই সৃষ্টীর কোনরূপেরই জাগতিক সাংসারিক বস্তুর সহিত জড়িত নহে। ইহাই প্রথম জ্ঞাতব্য সত্য।
'আমার' নিজস্বরূপ মাত্র এই প্রথম (একবারই) নিম্নে আসিয়াছে কোন অত্যন্ত অতি বিশিষ্ট কারণ

53 Bhagwanji's letter to Pabitra Mohan Roy, 11 August 1971.

কার্য্যের (কর্ত্তব্যের) জন্য, এবং উক্ত কার্য্য-কারণের জন্য শ্রী শ্রী শ্রী পরমাতিপরম সত্গুরুদের, শ্রীরামকৃষ্ণ পরমহংস, এবং, তাহারও পূর্ব্বতন এবং পরবর্ত্তী গুরুবর্গের প্রোত্সাহন-আশীর্ব্বাদ-পথনির্দ্দেশ-প্রস্তুতিকরনকার্য্যে শক্তি এবং সাহায্য, অখণ্ড তৈল ধারাবৎ স্নেহআশীর্ব্বাদ প্রেম সাহচর্য্য...'আমার' এই শরীরধারণ পূর্ণা এর পরে আর 'আমার' এই স্বরূপ শরীরধারী হইবে না৷৷ ইহাই আমার পরমতত্বসত্য; যাহা অত্যন্ত গোপনীয়, গোপ্তব্য, অনধিকারীদের কাছো কারণ: ইহাতে মনুষ্যের পক্ষে অসহনীয় তীব্রতম দাহনশক্তি নিহিত আছে৷[54]

[My true self which has occupied this body and will leave it behind, that self of mine is not attached to any material item of this creation. This is the first thing that should be known about me.

My real self has come down on this earth for the first time (and only for this once) to accomplish a very special task. I have had the guidance, blessings and encouragement of Sat Gurus, the gurus preceding and following Shri Ramakrishna, and their help, love and accompaniment in the preparatory work...my taking a human body is complete. My 'self' will not take a bodily form again.

This is my ultimate truth, which is absolutely secret and should be kept from undeserving people because it has incendiary powers unbearable for humans.]

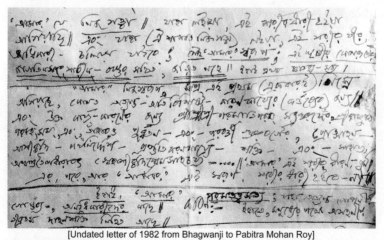

[Undated letter of 1982 from Bhagwanji to Pabitra Mohan Roy]

54 Undated letter of 1982 from Bhagwanji to Pabitra Mohan Roy.

To believe or not to believe?

There are believers, there are atheists and there are agnostics. Although we have presented the information that we have been able to put together without judgement, we are keenly aware that the reactions to it will come through these filters. While some will believe every word, some will ridicule them, others will not take any side.

It is, however, important to place information relating to supernatural phenomena and divine powers within the overall religio-socio-political context, especially when we are unravelling a tale of entwining political, spiritual and individual threads. Not being experts or adepts in spiritual practices and the powers that are said to emanate from it, where should we draw the line between the rational and irrational?

A simple search for 'astral projection' on Google yields more than three million results, compared to just over a million for 'theory of general relativity'. Similarly, a search for 'ghost' throws up about 1.4 million results against 1.1 million for an 'atom'. More results on a Google search of course do not make something truer than something else, but it does indicate the magnitude of popular reach.

The nature of belief in the supernatural gets more intriguing as one looks up to the higher echelons of society and political office.

It would be worth remembering that the belief in Subhas Bose not dying in 1945 and even remaining alive for several years thereafter has also been kept alive by statements and allusions made by some spiritual leaders with large following. A few years back, millions mourned the passing away of Sathya Sai Baba, regarded by his followers as an incarnation of God. Among those who paid their last respects to him included people as big as Dr Manmohan Singh and Sachin Tendulkar. On 2 May 2011, *The Times of India* carried an interview with former Chief Justice of India P N Bhagwati under the heading, 'Sai Baba, my god, dictated my every single judgment'. Another luminary who'd match Bhagwati's faith in Sai Baba is Shivraj Patil. One wishes the former Home Minister, who rejected the Mukherjee Commission's main finding that Subhas Bose didn't die in the 1945 Taiwan air crash, was there to hear his God publicly rejecting the Taiwan air crash theory during his 15 August 2007 discourse in praise of Bose.

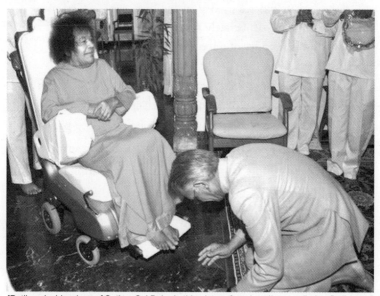

[Patil seeks blessings of Sathya Sai Baba in this picture from http://www.saibabaofindia.com]

In 2011, there was a news item declaring that Barfani Baba, a revered figure whose followers claim he is more than 200 years old, spoke of Netaji's continuing existence. Curiously, Barfani

Baba's view on Netaji has been dwelt on in a book authored by Ranjit Majumdar, a former senior Intelligence Bureau officer.

Most people will, of course, laugh at this holy man talk. But what does one do when the views offered are of someone whose circle of friends included Mikhail Gorbachev and Al Gore? Sri Chinmoy, an India-born spiritual leader who passed away in 2007 in the US, was fascinated with the Bose mystery. Unlike others, Sri Chinmoy actually wrote about it:

> Even regarding Netaji's plane crash and death, Nehru's own public pronouncements contradicted each other. Either Nehru suffered from uncertainty-nights or perhaps he deliberately wished to mould reality-day in his own way! ...God alone knows if Nehru deliberately misrepresented the truth or if he himself was a captive of uncertainty.[55]

Even as we find it difficult to believe the very idea that a person can 'move out of his body' or perform feats that are scientifically inexplicable, we have to accept that the belief in the paranormal is universal. It goes right to the top-level people, everywhere. In India, a good example is of former President Pratibha Patil. On 25 June 2007, when she was a contender for the top post, Patil made a revelation at a religious gathering that a long dead holy man had given her 'a "divine premonition" of greater responsibility coming her way'. *The Times of India* also reported the incident which revealed 'another facet of her personality, this time, of a mystic nature'.

---

55   Sri Chinmoy, Mother, Your 50th Independence-Anniversary! Agni Press, 1997, reprinted at https://www.srichinmoylibrary.com/mia

Those who will scoff at this instance would do well to keep in mind that even the most powerful people in the world, whose mental faculties and experiences are unmatched, are reported to have confronted things science doesn't agree exist. A phenomenon your smart co-worker at the office may dismiss as 'madness' might have a believer in the man who owns the company you work for. Everyone knows what sort of people line up to meet spiritual leaders. Here's one: Sadhguru Jaggi Vasudev, a yogi and mystic, writing about occult on Facebook:

Sadhguru ✓
17 mins · ✦

Occult is just technology. Today, you can pick up your cellphone in India and talk to someone in the United States. #Occult is just like this – you can talk to someone in the United States without the cellphone. It is a slightly more advanced technology.

Such instances of extraordinary people believing in, or giving credence to things science can't explain are indeed very many. One of the most well-known claims of reincarnation relates to a little girl in India of the 1930s. Shanti Devi's claim of having been born again was investigated by a committee of fifteen eminent people as advised by Mahatma Gandhi himself.

And here's an instance no one from the present generation would be able to ignore. What is common to Virat Kohli and the late Steve Jobs? Both were fascinated by a book titled *Autobiography of a Yogi*, by Paramhansa Yogananda (born Mukunda Lal Ghosh), a book in which almost every other page tells a tale of supernatural incidents. In nothing short of a miracle, it was claimed by way of a notarised letter by the director of the mortuary in Los Angeles where Yogananda's body was received, that it showed no visual signs of decay even twenty days after death.

['I love this book. A must read for all those who are brave enough to let their thoughts and ideologies be challenged,' one of the most admired persons in India wrote as he tweeted this picture]

Steve Jobs, co-founder of Apple Inc, was fascinated by *Autobiography of a Yogi* as a teenager. It stayed with him all his life and it has been reported that 500 copies of the book were handed out at Jobs's memorial. In February 2017, Virat Kohli was widely reported as saying that *Autobiography of a Yogi* had inspired him after he tweeted a picture of himself holding the book. 'The book that changed Virat Kohli and made him the success he is today' was the headline of the *NDTV* story.[56]

---

56   Sajal K Patra, 'The book that changed Virat Kohli and made him the success he is today,' *NDTV*, 18 February 2017, https://sports.ndtv.com/cricket/the-book-that-changed-virat-kohli-and-made-him-the-success-he-is-today-1660840.

As things stand today, the authors, who have no expertise in matters supernatural, have not found any reason to share Bhagwanji's and many others' belief that we have been visited by aliens using UFOs or that spirits of people long dead hover around us. And yet we know that there is this genial looking old man by the name of Jimmy Carter who holds a different view. If you do not know who he is, and are a big fan of someone who thinks that all UFO spotters are either insane or cheap publicity seekers, you should note that Carter was the President of the United States of America and he spotted a UFO himself.[57]

President Pratibha Patil is not the only important person to have communicated with a spirit. The legendary Supreme Court judge V R Krishna Iyer claimed that he spoke with his departed wife through a medium.[58] According to a book by Watergate star reporter and former *Washington Post* editor Bob Woodward, Hillary Clinton, then US First Lady, had a session with Mahatma Gandhi, thanks to Jean Houston, 'a believer in spirits, mythic and other connections to history and other worlds'.[59]

Now that you cannot laugh at this anymore, we can outline some of the things Bhagwanji talked about ghosts.

Believe me! Everything exists; e-v-e-r-y-t-h-i-n-g exists. *Pret-Pisach* all are certainly there (right at the bottom) in the layer that is adjacent to the soil). *Bhoot yoni, Zind-Pari-Yaksha-*

---

57   'Jimmy Carter may have seen a UFO,' Science Channel, https://www.youtube. com/ watch?v=QoXoYetbsds.

58   Living life king-size, *The Hindu*, 17 June, 2002. https://www.thehindu.com/the-hindu/mp/2002/06/17/stories/2002061700330300.htm

59   'Spiritual adviser aided First Lady's search, Bob Woodward, https://www.washing-tonpost.com/wp-srv/style/longterm/books/chap1/choice.htm.

Gandharva-kinnar-kinnari-Apsara-Yakshini-Gandharvi (they all are *Dev yonis*, but of low level and of common class and category); *Dikpals, Lokpals, Vasu*-and-*Rudra Rudranis*—everyone is at their own place doing their work. You can see your ancestors (*Pitr*) in the *Pitrilok*. You can know who all have been reborn (even if in a different gender due to their karmas). All these exist within the boundary of *Trilok*. *Devraj* Indra is a *Lokpal*. The expanse of *Trilok* is very small. It can be crossed by half a jump. A lot of travel and camps of the lower level *Dev Yonis* take place on this earth itself.

One Bengali *faquir* told me about a climber (herb) which keeps ghosts a 100 yards away—they can never do any harm. That *faquir* used to live in Bangladesh but came over before the turmoil of 1971. Now he lives in Ajmer Sharif for ten months in a year. The remaining two months he roams around at different places.

Only the human body has been made in a way that if used properly, ghosts, gods and goddesses, *apsaras* and *gandharvas* become visible. Only the human body can break out free of this limiting web, with the help of Siddha Purush Shri Shri Sadgurudev. Gods can't attain liberation even if they want—for that they have to take birth in a human body, do *sadhana* and then attain liberation.

There is one monastery in Tibet where no one goes because people call it the monastery of ghosts. Someone told me about the monastery and I went there with great difficulty.

Abraham Lincoln's ghost comes to the White House.

So do ghosts exist? We don't know. But in February 1987, then US President Ronald Reagan said that he would like to meet Abraham Lincoln's ghost 'which haunts the White House'. Reagan's wish was not fulfilled—the closest he came to it was noticing that his dog would not enter the bedroom Lincoln once occupied and would just stand 'glaring as if he's seeing something and barking'. His daughter and son-in-law were convinced that they had 'really seen it'—this is according to an *AFP* story published in *The Indian Express*.[60] They joined many others who are believed to have spotted a transparent person with a pinkish aura. Presidents Theodore Roosevelt, Herbert Hoover, Harry Truman, Winston Churchill...the list is long.

All that Bhagwanji said about himself or all that his followers speak of him is something worth paying attention to in case you think the foregoing narrative is fascinating. Bhagwanji said that he spent some time in Gyanganj, a mythical abode in the Himalayas. Also known as Siddhashram, Shambala and Shangri-La, this Never Never Land of the yogis has fascinated many Indians and Europeans for long, though no one could prove its existence. Most agreed that it was situated close to the Mansarover region in Tibet, but in a different dimension and, therefore, reached only by extraordinary people. Incidentally, the most well-known, recent book on Gyanganj was authored by Gopinath Kaviraj, who was awarded the Padma Vibhushan as well as the Sahitya Akademi Fellowship, the highest literary honour awarded by the Sahitya Akademi. Bhagwanji indicated that Kaviraj was aware of his existence, and it was he who informed Kamalapati Tripathi.

Bhagwanji claimed that in Gyanganj he met sages and yogis, several centuries old and capable of performing supernatural feats, like *kayakalp*—leaving one's body and entering another.

60 'Reagan wants to meet Lincoln's ghost,' *The Indian Express*, 16 February 1987.

He would call himself a *sadhak*, a practitioner in tantra. Being so, Bhagwanji said, was the consummation of a desire he had always had.

> *Shakti-sadhana* is to awaken the *kulakundalini*. The Mother is called *kulakundalini* energy. *Shakti-sadhana* is to awaken and direct this power. This is also the aim of the extremely secret *rajayoga*. On the way of awakening the *kulakundalini*, a *sadhak* has the **option** to move ahead of the point where *rajayoga* stops. He will go on if he has the courage. *Rajayogis* do not know of this path. That is the main difference between a *rajayogi* and a *tantrik*—though both their aim is to awaken the *kulakundalini*. Those who are really *tantriks* will never claim to be one. Anyone who says he is a *tantrik*, can never be one. The way of *tantriks* is very hazardous. They are bound by strict laws. The network of their organisation is spread all over the world; but India is their **nerve-centre**. A *tantrik* will never divulge their secrets even if you cut them into pieces. *Tantra-sadhana* is the **ultimate of ultimates**. [Words originally in English appear in bold]

What was the aim of his gathering these supernatural powers then?

Bhagwanji said he had been using them and would use them in future for the good of India and other nations. In one of his letters to Pabitra Mohan Roy, he stated that a 'deep, deep malign cancer is sapping out the vital saps of India', which is a 'most serious disease, fatal and malign', requiring 'more than equal diagnosis and treatment'.

'This old *faquir* of yours gives his most solemn word of honour,' he added, 'in the inviolable-and-most divine name of Mother Jagadamba, and Durga Bhavani Chandi' that 'India shall rise again in her full glory'.

Corrupt people on my Motherland's soil will be completely eliminated gradually. And after a specified period dishonest persons will not have the right to exist on Indian soil. And, our, rather your Samaritans shall lead the whole world to the fourth stage of civilization.

All we can say is that we have no competence to get into spiritual matters, much less judge them. We need *proof* in the regular sense of the word.

FOURTEEN

MENDICUS

THE GRAND PLANS, talks of international manoeuvres and the immersion in the spiritual dazzled those around him, but these were never enough to cover the deep-seated agony that kept churning inside him. 'Come Pabitra, see how the fire is burning inside the old ribs,' he wrote in early 1963.[1] As he aptly described it to Santosh Kumar Bhattacharya in a July 1967 letter, quoting from Shakespeare's Richard III, his was a 'tortured soul'.

SAY THAT AGAIN.
THE SHADOW OF MY SORROW! HA!! LET'S SEE:
'TIS VERY TRUE, MY GRIEF LIES ALL WITHIN;
AND THESE EXTERNAL MANNERS OF LAMENTS
ARE MERELY SHADOWS TO THE UNSEEN GRIEF
THAT SWELLS WITH SILENCE IN THE TORTURED SOUL;
THERE LIES THE SUBSTANCE.

[Letter to Santosh Kumar Bhattacharya, 19 July 1967.
Courtesy Bijoy Nag]

1   Bhagwanji's letter to Pabitra Mohan Roy, 5 February 1963.

Bhagwanji chose a life of hardship, but his protestations revealed more than they concealed—his consciousness that he had given up what could have been his for the asking—the highest political power, a comfortable life and admiration of a whole country in whose liberation he had sacrificed all. He wasn't interested in any of these, but the occasional outbursts of bitterness and anger, and even tears, only reflected a conflicted mind. The keen awareness of having been wronged and the despair at the nonchalance of people at the state of the country never left him. 'You have not paid the price of freedom…you have not sacrificed yourselves but forsaken those who did,' he barked at his followers.[2] Freedom came cheap for them and that's why they didn't value it. Clearly, he was never able 'to have moved on' despite his claims to the contrary. Thus, although he maintained a close emotional connect with his country and its people, he never stepped out to intervene directly in their politics. His sphere of action, he claimed, was different, and compared himself to the legendary sage Dadhichi who sacrificed his life so that evil might be defeated.

Whatever hardship came his way, he accepted, almost with a vengeance. In one of his early letters, Bhagwanji described his life to Pabitra:

> Pabitra, I—a *sanyasi* who has lost everything—have satisfied my hunger with ash. I have spent days eating leaves—boiled and then turned into paste, mixed with salt—from the tree you see near the pond on the left side of this lawn, boiled fruits of banyan and *simul* trees mixed with salt and pepper.

---

2   Charanik, *Oi Mahamanaba Ase*, Jayasree Prakashan, 2010, p 69.

Ma Jagadamba collected *Mahua* flowers from the roads in the far away villages, boiled them, made a paste and gave it to me to eat with *gur* obtained by begging. We have eaten a small bowl (*ek powa*) of boiled low quality rice for four days. Ma has collected raw and ripe mangoes—have had juice made from them. The Shivalaya is made of stone, and I have dreamt of palaces while sleeping in that. It is now that you have got a woollen wrapper (*alwan*)—until now I have spent the winters with a cotton (*sooti*) bedsheet. Why? Why? Why? I am mad, that's why. I have torn hair from the my head, hair from the beard, but still did not ask for anything from anyone. ...Tears have fallen down the dry cheeks of this old man. Sometimes I wept silently, but sometimes I howled.[3]

The contact with his old revolutionary associates was accidental and the care he received thereafter wasn't something that he had planned or expected. 'Your *faquir* did not step back into this land with any sort of expectation, however faint, in any corner of his heart, that he will be able to live in comfort or derive benefits from anyone,' he said.

Sitting in his dimly lit drawing room that doubled up as a bedroom, in his house near a market place in Basti, the sixty-six-year-old Rajkumar cried like a child before the authors remembering the days of hardship he and his mother Saraswati Devi had to endure over half a century ago. The rolling tears and the choked voice were not so much for him and his mother as much for the third person with whom they had yoked their fate. 'It is beyond belief how such a great man who had sacrificed everything for his

---

3   Bhagwanji's letter to Pabitra Mohan Roy, 6 February 1963. Translated from Bengali.

country had to live in such destitution,' he sobbed.[4]

When Rajkumar narrated the days of terrible poverty in Lucknow and Neemsar, he was reliving the pain. The heaviness of the deprivation is etched permanently in his memory. His face betrayed the feelings. The activities of the 'dead ghost' floating across the world and the supernormal feats of the spiritual maestro apart, the diaries and letters of the followers, and more importantly letters written by Bhagwanji, show us his very human side. These tell us the story of how an immensely powerful personality who, being forced to remain confined to a prison-like condition continuously, tried to transcend the worldly barriers. It is a story of the ever-present sadness of living as 'dead', the pangs of not having anyone to call his own despite having a family not too far away. It is a story of the frailties of a human body and mind, of despondence, of helpless dependence, and of odd behavioural traits. All these traits are weaved inseparably in the character of the mysterious man. Yet, large parts of this saddening aspect of Bhagwanji's life have been carefully underplayed by his Calcutta followers through the decades. *Oi Mahamanaba Asey* and the columns of Charanik in *Jayasree* have diligently avoided treading this path, focusing more on portraying Bhagwanji as a political wizard and a spiritual seer of the highest order, who suffered from occasional bouts of sadness generated by his situation.

These papers also bring out the stories of his followers— their dedication and love for the man, as much as the conflicts, jealousies and distrust of one another.

---

4   Interview of Rajkumar Shukla by the authors, Basti, 2016.

How Bhagwanji took care of his finances, or who took care of his needs is not clear until he reached Lucknow's Singar Nagar around 1955. From available accounts, it appears that Surendra Singh Chaudhary took charge of meeting the routine expenses, but bad times descended soon. Bhagwanji soon started defaulting on his rent at his Singar Nagar accommodation.[5] The result was not different from what usually happens in such situations. Not only did he have to leave the place, but had to leave behind almost everything, including a gun, as compensation.[6]

When Bhagwanji moved to live on the banks of the Gomti river under a temporary shelter of tarpaulin, set up over an area of 200 to 300 square feet, keeping him company were other homeless travellers who usually spent a few nights in that area. The penniless Bhagwanji, along with Saraswati Devi and Rajkumar would get to eat on some days, mostly out of the generosity of religious seekers, and go hungry on others.

While this happened, Sampurnanand was still the Chief Minister (he would remain so until 1960, long after Bhagwanji left Lucknow for Neemsar). Other notables had visited him too

---

5   See Chapter 2.

6   This version of events was confirmed by another follower of Bhagwanji who now lives in Lucknow. Bhagwanji himself however had a different version. He told his Calcutta followers that Chaudhary had increasingly become more interfering and inquisitive about him and tried to control his movements. As he got to know about Bhagwanji's nocturnal visits to the Bhaisa Kund crematorium for the purpose of tantric rituals, he too followed him there. According to Bhagwanji, he used to go out often for his 'own work' on the pretext of going to the crematorium, which Chaudhary soon figured out. When this interference became too uncomfortable for Bhagwanji, he left Lucknow 'at an hour's notice'. Wherever the truth lies, we can tell that Chaudhary was not the main reason for such urgent action. Had that been the case he wouldn't have been allowed to accompany Bhagwanji to Neemsar. The *Northern India Patrika* team had also found that Bhagwanji had reached Naimisharanya with Chaudhary.

at Singar Nagar. As Bhagwanji would admit to Sunil Das later, 'Intercourse with people was very convenient in Lucknow.' With such powerful men as friends, it is difficult to explain Bhagwanji's financial distress. It could mean only one thing—that he wouldn't take monetary help from his friends and followers in power.

A car was at his disposal, however, most likely organised by Chaudhary or one of his associates, as long as Bhagwanji lived in Singar Nagar. It was while he lived here that he came close to being identified publicly at B N Baijal Opticians, now 129 years old, which once made spectacles for Mahatma Gandhi.

The spell of extreme poverty continued as Bhagwanji, along with Saraswati Devi and Rajkumar reached Neemsar. At the first place of stay, in a dharmashala, all the irregularities of the hard life did him in. He contracted typhoid. Within a few weeks, he moved to the Shiva temple near Chakra Teerth. There would be days when all they would get to eat were a couple of boiled potatoes split among the three. There was no money for tea; leaves of a plant locally known as *latora*, or *lasura* (*cordia myxa*) boiled in water became the substitute. This state continued until the followers from Calcutta arrived. Bhagwanji later reminisced of this phase:

> For nearly three years, whatever I used to get as unsought alms was so little that I had to eat ashes three to four times a day. [We] used to boil and eat known and unknown leaves, fruits and flowers. Fasting was a regular thing. I was my own manual scavenger. I have spent month after month under a broken tin shade in jungles. It is better not to tell you about what else I have gone through.[7]

---

7   Charanik, *Oi Mahamanaba Ase*, Jayasree Prakashan, 2010, p 93. Translated from Bengali.

The other mundane troubles that he had to face in Neemsar have already been described in Chapter 2. The situation changed only when the Calcutta connection was established. Assistance started flowing in steadily in different forms, more in kind than in cash.

Health remained one of the greatest concerns from the beginning, as far as Bhagwanji's well-being was concerned. Piles, varicose veins, low blood pressure and fever were regular features. Leela Roy dispatched Kamlakanta Ghosh with the responsibility to bring relief to the 'Leader'. The combination of Kamlakanta's devotion and expertise did bring some relief to Bhagwanji, but the ailments kept bothering him till the very end.

Especially from the 1970s, the frequency of Bhagwanji reporting ill health increased. In November 1970, he wrote to Pabitra that he was not keeping well. In January 1973, he wrote that his physical pains were barely allowing him to continue with his *sadhana*. 'I wish I could explain to you how much I am suffering. Suffice it to say that I haven't been able to operate the radio for about a month,' he wrote. Clearly his suffering from bleeding piles continued. In July that year, he asked Pabitra to send him Pilon tablets. He also asked for Sciatin pills that are usually used for treatment of sciatica, cervical and lumbar spondylosis. In August, he complained of feverishness— 'I am in much pain for the last fifteen to twenty days.' He was annoyed with Pabitra for not being able to send ghee and fresh butter which, he said, helped in alleviating his physical pains. Durga Prasad Pandey had been unable to procure these from the local market. The medicines were, however, not providing any relief, neither from

the bleeding piles nor from sciatica. Bhagwanji asked Pabitra to
consult the famous homeopaths of Mihijam—the Banerjis—to
find out whether he could use combinations of medicines for
treating the bleeding piles from which he was suffering for many
years. Pabitra was also asked to find out if the Banerjis could give
him a single medicine to treat all his pain related problems—
sciatica, lumbago, spasms in the hip region, swelling and pain in
the knees, and varicose veins. His letters show equal keenness for
homeopathic and ayurvedic treatments, but neither was able to
provide Bhagwanji with permanent relief. His ordeal continued.

In November 1973, he complained about 'indisposed health'
which was not allowing him to write letters. Following a short
recovery, he reported illness in January 1974 that continued
through February. Even when not suffering from any illness, there
were clear indications that his health was steadily deteriorating.
Almost in every other letter of this period he complained of
his weak physical condition. Just how troubled he was with his
health problems and how desperately he wanted to be free of
them is evident from his willingness to take recourse to divine
intervention. In May 1974, he wrote to Pabitra:

> The Kali temple in Jamshedpur distributes divine amulets
> without discriminating between Hindus or Muslims. I have
> heard good things about the amulet from a few people from
> Jamshedpur. This time I also saw it mentioned in the *panjika*
> (astronomical almanac) that you have sent. You send them the
> cost of the amulet and postage so that it reaches me at once.
> Let me see if this amulet obtained from the Mother helps me
> to get rid of the sciatica, lumbago, pain in the hip and knees. I
> have never worn a divine amulet for medicinal purpose. Why

not try it and see if the pain really goes away?

On reaching Brahma Kund in Ayodhya, Bhagwanji became seriously ill, nearly confined to bed. In June 1977, he complained to Pabitra that he had been ill for the last one-and-a-half months, but despite making promises Santosh had not sent him the required medicines. 'Sick and suffering,' he wrote in September 1980. 'I am so weak that my head swirls in the effort to write the telegrams and the letters; feel so nauseous that I have to lie down as soon as I have done writing,' Bhagwanji described his physical condition thus. Walking to the bathroom was possible only with the help of Saraswati Devi. Yet, even at the slightest signs of recovery, he travelled out at this time. He would go out for the work of his 'horizon' with the consequence that his condition would deteriorate again. Early in 1981, after return from one such outing, the harsh winter of the northern plains got to him. 'Constant exposure to this biting cold has resulted in inflammation of the liver and I am in terrible pain,' he wrote in January. Regular vomiting of bile prevented his eating or even sitting for long.

Dr R P Mishra's treatment and care brought him back on his feet.

Long years of experimenting with homeopathic and ayurvedic medicine had made Bhagwanji an expert of sorts. He would often write detailed herbal remedies to Sunil Das, Pabitra and others to health them get rid of their ailments, although his own continued. When Dr Darshan Singh Tomar, a homeopath in Ayodhya met Bhagwanji, he was surprised by the depth of his knowledge of medicines. Bhagwanji's greater reliance on alternative medicine is evident from the more frequent presence of homeopaths beginning with Kamalakanta Ghosh and continuing with Dr T C Banerjee and his son Dr Priyabrata Banerjee of Faizabad and Dr Tomar of Ayodhya. He would also interact with J&J Dechane Laboratories of Hyderabad, started by D F de Souza, who combined allopathy, ayurveda and homeopathy medicine systems. 'I am usually not in favour of taking allopathic medicine,' he wrote to Pabitra. The only two allopathic practitioners of note who treated Bhagwanji were the two surgeons Dr B Rai and Dr R P Mishra, both of whom came in contact with him at a much later stage. However, it is obvious that Pabitra, an allopathic doctor, must have done his bit over the years.

The most painful blow came early next year while staying at Lucknow-wali Hata (also called the Lucknow Kothi). The eighty-five-year-old Bhagwanji slipped in the bathroom and seriously injured himself twice—first spraining the muscles of his left leg that turned the whole leg devoid of all sensation. When Saraswati Devi tried to get him out of the bathroom by carrying him on her back, he fell again. The injuries were so bad that he lost all power to move. It took her nearly six hours to drag him slowly, inch by inch, inside the house. It was in October that he gathered enough strength to sit up slowly with her help. If anything at all, this incident highlights the poor conditions of the accommodations in which Bhagwanji spent his years. These places served as good hideouts allowing a quick escape if required, but their unhealthy environment took a toll on his health. This was consistently the condition from Neemsar. From a dharmashala—his first address in Neemsar—he had moved to a temple, a place that was prone to flooding during the monsoon season, restricting his movements and increasing the risks to his health from insects, snakes and wild animals.

Although he lived for nearly a decade in Basti, he had made up his mind to leave the place by mid-1971 due to extremely poor living conditions and other extraneous factors that created an unfavourable environment for him. However, he was forced to continue at the same place until the end of 1974. This was the longest time spent at one place, of all the places that he lived. The letters that he wrote during the last four of these years with increasing desperation to move out are revealing in several aspects—the meticulousness of his planning that yet came to nought because of his helplessness, his dependence on Pabitra vis-à-vis other followers in Calcutta and his relation with Saraswati Devi and her son.

The Sharista Kothi was already in bad shape; roofs in certain parts had started collapsing. Non-stop rain during the monsoon made the compound muddy and the house damp. If the dampness was not bad enough, multitude of insects made his life a living nightmare. Especially galling were those that 'are invisible to the naked eye, but one can feel them moving on the bare body, entering the nose and ear', he wrote to Pabitra. Compounding the misery were termites all over the house, caterpillars, moths, limpets. 'Try, please, to give me relief from all these devils of crawling, flying, wiggling, leaping worms, insects, moths and trillions of other hordes,' he pleaded. Come May, and the heat too became unbearable.

The situation during monsoon became far worse within the next two years. Bhagwanji informed Pabitra that three quarters of the verandah (balcony) was filled with mud, leaving no place to sit outside the rooms which were dark, damp and had a foul smell. 'Water is dripping on my cot, on the dining table. One day, just as I sat down for supper, water poured down on my plate from the leaking roof, forcing me to go hungry that night,' he wrote. On the cover of an inland letter, he reported, 'Local people: catching fish: on the lane-road and small piece of ground just along and outside of our compound (where you all sat) and in the lane at the back of my room.' Electricity connection was also a problem, which made kerosene oil lamps essential. 'I can't see in the night at all,' he had informed Dulal Nandy soon after reaching Basti, asking him to arrange for a Petromax lamp of 100 candle power from Calcutta if possible. The lamps were provided, but a new problem arose within a few years. 'Reading and writing in the evening has become impossible,' he wrote, because adulteration of kerosene by diesel had turned the lamps unusable.

On 27 August 1971, Bhagwanji wrote to Pabitra that it was a 'crucial strategic necessity that your Satgurudev Dead Ghost and S[ubhas] should leave this link point (with and for you) for a dry place in such total secrecy that, not even the winds-of-this place can catch and retain the scent of my departure'. While travelling in November, he reminded Pabitra, 'If I do return, I will have to go hundred per cent flawlessly underground in order to accomplish a very special task.'

Therefore, from this moment onwards after critically analysing all factors, engage yourself to find out an abode which will be perfectly suitable for such a purpose. The place that you decide upon must enable fast and direct access to Dewas, Moradabad,

Barabanki, old Lucknow, Ghaziabad, Nizamuddin, and the Masjids, burial grounds and religious centres of places like Agra, etc. My being able to travel like an arrow in a direct line is the most crucial factor that you should keep in mind...Leave all other things aside and concentrate yourself with all your sagacity on this very vital and particular duty. [Translated from Bengali]

Other than reiterating that the selected place should be healthy, Bhagwanji gave broad directions regarding the layout of the house that Pabitra should look for. The foremost conditions were firstly it should have arrangement of tap water within the compound (as he no more had the strength to lift 40-50 buckets of water daily from a well) and secondly, the lavatory should be the best possible and located in a way that its odour should not contaminate the rest of the house. Following the tenets of *Vastu Shastra*, the house must not be north or west-facing. It should be safe and secure to the extent that even if he stayed away for three years, locking the house, nobody would think of entering it. There should be good hotels and restaurants nearby, apart from easy availability of eggs, fish, meat, ghee, butter and oil. And of course, the place would have to be '10000% secure', a 'dead secret' place which cannot be discovered 'in a thousand years'. His belongings would have to be taken in a truck, but that was the easy part. The 'most crucial' part of the 'manoeuvre' was to figure out how to transport him to the new place in total secrecy.

Seeing no progress, Bhagwanji wrote that he was both disappointed and saddened by Pabitra's failure to move him to a new place. 'I had really hoped that you would have accomplished the shifting by December,' he wrote in January 1972. From this point onwards, his castigations started assuming a caustic tone that intensified with the passage of time. 'You don't have that total unflinching dedication and sacrifice on the altar of your motherland and for your supremo anymore,' he wrote, accusing Pabitra of offering only lip service and being concerned only with his own well-being. These outbursts did not, however, mean that the plan was off or that Pabitra was off the hook. Rather, new names of possible destinations kept coming up. Jhansi (western UP) and Chunar (eastern UP, near Varanasi) entered the discussion. Bhagwanji wanted a considered opinion on whether these places would be suitable for him.

Claiming that his secret (non-Calcutta) associates who assisted in the work of his horizon had grudgingly given a go-ahead to Chunar as a workable option, Bhagwanji asked Pabitra to proceed. The place had both pros and cons. If he was apprehensive about the possibility of being identified by old acquaintances, the place also had the benefit of proximity to the Indo-Nepal border in a more or less straight route. The outcome for this option too was not as expected. Surprised at the lack of progress, Bhagwanji thought that lack of adequate funds was holding Pabitra back, and assured him that he wouldn't have to bear the expenses. 'Can it still be done?' he asked in September 1973. Even an accommodation with one big hall and a small room, available at a rent of Rs 50-60 per month would work. The discussion again shifted to new places, with Bhagwanji straightaway shooting down Pabitra's suggestion of a few places in Bihar. Bhagwanji was losing patience; now the search perimeter had to be widened. Wider options were to be considered. Even places such as Madras, the banks of Godavari and Narmada, Neemuch were not to be ruled out. Pleading with Pabitra to move him out by December he wrote, 'for the sake of humanity, save me!'

In December, Kathgodam (now in Uttarakhand) became the new location for consideration and in January 1974, Bhagwanji asked Pabitra to revive his links with a monk of the Bharat Sevashram Sangha in Vrindavan for finding a suitable accommodation. 'Please try to understand that I am spending the days here in great pain, burdened with tension and anxiety,' Bhagwanji urged Pabitra. In the first week of February, exasperated by the lack of any information from Pabitra, Bhagwanji wrote to him, 'It appears that you are not interested. If that is the case simply tell me. I will also know where I stand.' Within a week, Pabitra reverted with the news of having selected a house in Puri, sharing a hand-drawn sketch of the house. After a month of intense letter exchange, whereby Bhagwanji gave Pabitra instructions on arranging the house according to his requirements to the minutest details, however, the deal was called off by the end of March. Some of the features of the house, Bhagwanji discovered, were off the specifications he had outlined. Pabitra was instructed to find a replacement house immediately, in the vicinity, if possible. 'For the sake of Ma Kali, save me from the intolerability of this place Pabitra; rescue me from this place within the next 15 to 19 days,' he again pleaded.

Amidst the house hunt, Bhagwanji was also travelling out for the work of his 'horizon', which further delayed a final decision. By the middle of May, he was so desperate to shift out that he wrote to Pabitra, 'You should have taken a storehouse-like place in Puri and transported all the material from here first. I could have

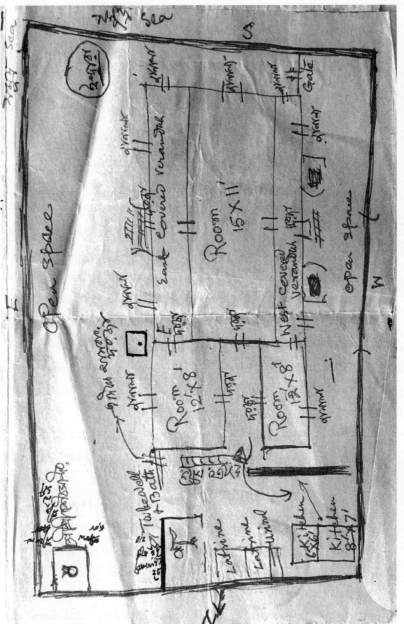

[Pabitra Mohan Roy shared the layout of a house in Puri for moving Bhagwanji from Basti, in his letter dated 18 February 1974]

stayed in one corner of that storehouse if required, till the time you found a house or an *ashram*. Now make me vanish from this place before the month comes to an end.' His caustic remarks, too, continued. 'If you cannot move me out by the end of May, then you don't need to do anything anymore for me. Anyway you have taken much trouble for this old man. Go home and relax among your family. This will be goodbye forever.'

All efforts of Pabitra came to nought. It was, however, anything but a goodbye. Pabitra, apart from being his spiritually initiated disciple, was too dear to Bhagwanji for that. Finally, on 11 November 1974, on the auspicious day of Dhan Trayodashi (Dhanteras), Bhagwanji moved from Basti back to Ayodhya again. This time it was the 'Prahlad Dharamshala' owned by Panda Ram Kishore Mishra. The arrangements were made by Durga Prasad Pandey. Most likely Bhagwanji shared his desperation with Pandey, who offered to find a house for him. For the first time in nearly two decades, Saraswati Devi and Rajkumar were now out of Bhagwanji's entourage. Her replacement was Imdad Hussain who was appointed by Pandey. Hussain, however, stayed only for a few months. Two months there and again he was shifted to the Brahmakund Gurudwara. Shortly, Saraswati Devi was back with Bhagwanji.

Apart from health issues, troubles continued in the form of the landlord and prying locals, which forced Bhagwanji to move to Lucknow-wali Hata in May 1978. It was here that Bhagwanji fell down and got seriously injured in January 1982, following which he was shifted to Ram Bhawan in Faizabad early next year under the guidance of Dr R P Mishra. One of his local disciples, Ravidra Shukla claims that here too Bhagwanji started feeling confined and uncomfortable very soon and urged him to find an accommodation in his village where he could live an easier yet anonymous life.

It was with the aim of alleviating some of the pain of these trials and tribulations on account of his ill health, poor living conditions and the strain of work that the followers from Bengal, led by Leela Roy, constantly strived to provide Bhagwanji with as much material comfort as they could afford. Sometimes, they stretched themselves beyond their ability. Occasionally it would be cash, but predominantly the aid consisted of food items, medicines, clothes, books and journals, and other items asked for by Bhagwanji. As time went by, these materials piled up. Rajkumar recalls that when moving from Neemsar to Darshan Nagar, there were barely a few boxes, but towards the end of his stay at Basti, Bhagwanji estimated that all the material that he wanted to move would fit in about 17 to 18 trunks. When she first went to meet him in Neemsar, Leela Roy took two books. Once she saw Bhagwanji's living conditions, she realised that he needed much more support and ensured that the support flowed without a break. The man had been out in the cold for far too long and was now practically a destitute. There was no way for him to be able to afford the small luxuries of life. However, what he liked or craved for was not unknown to Leela Roy. The rush to provide him with material comfort made Bhagwanji uneasy initially. 'You all are doing so much for me that I feel embarrassed. Sometimes I feel like asking you to go away,' he told Dulal Nandy. When pressed by his followers to allow them to get more stuff, he resisted: 'You are mad! *Faquir* is not going to stay here permanently, so what's the point in accumulating?' But this started changing soon.

The most crucial need for him were medicines. The followers in Bengal ensured a sustained supply of medicines through the decades for his and sometimes Saraswati Devi's treatment. The second most important supply was food. Bhagwanji was a foodie. Although he ate very little, he had the taste for the best of food from Bengal. Regular supplies included the best of confectionaries, mostly from Nahoum's, the Jewish bakery in Kolkata, variety of sweets (especially Sandesh and Rasagolla), fish, butter, ghee, tea and cigarettes. Often Bhagwanji would himself indicate what he needed and those were procured accordingly. The followers in Kolkata would then arrange the different items individually, which would be carried by one or more people when they visited him.

On the face of it, there was nothing unusual in the practice of the secret society of followers carrying gifts and other material to ensure the material comfort of Bhagwanji. For them it was already established that Bhagwanji was Netaji and they belonged to the good old revolutionary societies of Bengal (at least the elderly ones) who could have laid down their lives for Netaji. Not only doing their best, but going beyond their limits to serve the man, was therefore not surprising. Yet, one aspect of these transactions which continued for more than two decades stands out as striking. It was the tone and tenor of Bhagwanji's demands. Since we have access to only the letters written to Pabitra, it is not possible to say if he made these demands of all his Calcutta followers or only from Pabitra, but even if the former is true, the nature and frequency of these demands would no doubt have put great strain on them. Especially so, as they were men of limited means, except a few like Biswanath Roy or to some extent Santosh Bhattacharya. Financial crunch was more of a rule than exception for them. Bhagwanji was not unaware of it and often he would insist that they should not buy expensive items for him.

The fact that despite his hesitation Bhagwanji continued to ask for items he needed from his followers was probably a result of Leela Roy's insistence.

আপনার ব্যক্তিগত প্রয়োজন আমাকে জানাবেন এ দাবী করছি। আপনার devoted sister হিসেবে আমাকেও কিছু করতে দিন। দেশকে আমরাও তো কিছু সামান্য ভালবাসি। যিনি তার জন্য সাধ্যের অতীত করলেন ও করছেন তার জন্য কিছু করার আনন্দ থেকে বঞ্চিত করার মত নিষ্ঠুর হবেন না। তাতে আপনার লাভ নেই, আমাদের বড় ক্ষতি। (As your devoted sister I am demanding that you must let us serve you in some ways. You must let me know what your personal requirements are. We too love the country in whatever little way possible. Don't be so cruel as to deprive us of the satisfaction of serving the one who has done and continues to do more than what is possible for the country. You won't gain anything out of it, but it will doubtless be our loss.)

Roy reacted sharply when Bhagwanji wanted to return a few things as he didn't want that Roy and her followers would do so much for him:

জিনিষপত্র ফেরত দিয়ে দয়া করে আবার humiliate করবেননা। না যদি রাখতে চান – ওগুলো ফেলে দেবার মত জায়গা কি এ বিশাল ভারতবর্ষে নেই? কত আশা, কত বেদনা ও দরদ দিয়ে আপনার প্রতিটা কাজ আমার সহকর্মীরা করে – তা কি কিছু আন্দাজ করাও দুঃসাধ্য? সামান্য কিছু বললে তার বেশী না করে তারা তৃপ্ত হয়না। আমার সঙ্গে তাদের restrain করার ব্যাপারে রোজই বিতন্ডা হয়। তাদের যদি আপনি একথা জানিয়ে আনন্দ পান যে আপনি তাদের কোনো কাজই চাননা, পছন্দ করেননা, তাদের এই কথাই বলবো কি 'তোমাদের নেতাজীর এসবের কোন প্রয়োজন নেই···?' বলুন? (Please don't humiliate me again by returning the items. Is there a shortage of place in a huge country like ours to throw those away if you don't want to keep them? Is it so difficult to understand with what level of hope and sentiment each of your tasks is completed by my co-workers? They are never satisfied without doing in excess of whatever little you ask. I have to argue regularly to restrain them. If it makes you happy to let them know that you don't want them to do anything for you, should I tell them that 'Your Netaji doesn't need your help?...' You tell me.) (Emphasis added by authors)

Such reaction from a much admired and adored colleague was bound to put Bhagwanji in a fix.

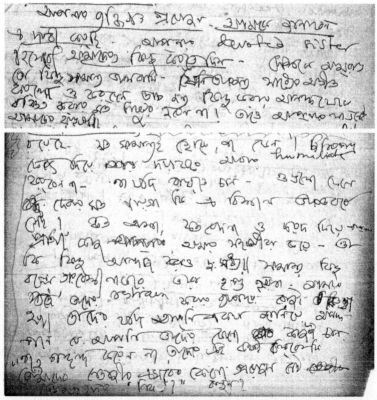

[Leela Roy's undated letter to Bhagwanji regarding taking care of his personal requirements. Mukherjee Commission exhibit obtained under Right to Information Act]

The demands were more on those who formed the inner circle of his followers than on others who reached him through these people. If he scolded someone like Pabitra for failing to procure the things that he needed, he would be extra-sensitive that those with more meagre means should not borrow money to provide for his needs. Yet, at times, his attitude was self-contradicting. Dulal Nandy's experience when he visited Bhagwanji in May-June 1965 exemplifies the contradiction. Having run out of money, but with the desire to do something for Bhagwanji, he sold his ring to have some cash for buying fruits. Bhagwanji was furious and embarrassed. After all the suffering his body had endured, he had lost the sensation of hunger and thirst, he said. Moreover, even if he had one rupee, he would never spend it for his own sake. 'You can confirm this from my co-workers, Leela, and the one respected person still alive in my family,' Bhagwanji told Nandy. At the same time, however, he lashed out at him for not being able to procure a small generator set. In most cases when his followers overstretched their financial ability, they kept or at least tried to keep it a secret from Bhagwanji.

Much of his requirements were out of the ordinary. Cleanliness was an absolute necessity. It was more so because he would eat the food item only as a *prasad*, after offering it to Ma Kali. He recounted that on two occasions, dead ants and spiders in the Rajbhog that Pabitra had brought with him made them unfit for offering to the goddess. Bhagwanji shared this with Pabitra much later and not immediately fearing that his devoted disciple would be sad if he complained. He would therefore ask that many of the prepared food items that his followers took with them should be made at home, with pure mind and body. No less an important reason for such a directive was the fact of his craving for food prepared with the touch of love of a family, of mothers, sisters and daughters. What he missed in not having his own family, he tried to compensate with the loving touch of his disciples' families. 'You know, right now I am craving for a *singara* (samosa), not bought from shops, but made at home; and *machher jhol* (fish curry) with *dal vadi*,' he blurted out to Sailen Roy during one of their evening talks. When Pabitra once arrived with pickles purchased from the market, Bhagwanji wrote to him with a tinge of pain for not following his instruction of bringing homemade pickles.

He was, of course, not concerned only about his own needs, but gave equal attention to the needs of Saraswati Devi and Rajkumar. Supplying them with clothes and other stuff was routine, but Bhagwanji would make sure that they received more than that. Thus, even at the time when Pabitra was running around to find Bhagwanji's accommodation in Puri, he asked him to get sarees for Saraswati. 'The handicraft of that place is famous. Get special sarees with fine designs for my mother from there,' he wrote to Pabitra. When Rajkumar got married, he gave her Rs 3,000 (a significant amount in those years) to arrange for the homecoming of the bride.

Inability to arrange items for Bhagwanji, and sometimes even the lack of money to travel to him would often distress his followers greatly. Cash often became a severe problem. Bhagwanji estimated in 1974 that his monthly establishment cost was around a thousand rupees. But unanticipated costs frequently took the requirement to a much higher level. Whatever the source of his money supply, on many occasions it was clearly not enough. Such sudden surges in expenses would sometimes compel him to ask for money from some in the Calcutta team. After returning from a trip in August 1971, he wrote to Pabitra that he needed to arrange for about Rs 11,000 on account of routine domestic expenses to pay off debts incurred while he was absent and also to make provisions for the next few months. Some of the Calcutta followers had visited him recently, but 'they have not been able to give much this time, rather one has secretly taken money from me'. It was a tricky situation. 'Can you arrange for Rs 11,000-12,000 for me in total secrecy, without letting anyone know?' he asked Pabitra. Not getting a reply in two weeks, he reminded Pabitra of his situation: 'I will be gratefully beholdend (sic), if you can, secretly, with your sincere actions and channels, arrange to secure and provide me with at least, the stated wherewithal, to vindicate my honour…. This has developed into a great weight on my consciousness, and this time, I am feeling very much careworn.'

He hadn't been able to pay rent from June 1970. On top of that, to save a wall from collapsing, Saraswati Devi had sold a piece of her jewellery to arrange about Rs 4,750. Pandey had to be paid Rs 1,500 for the treatment of one of his sons who suffered a serious injury, the money arranged again by Saraswati Devi. Above this, he said, he had to arrange for at least Rs 3,000 for Saraswati Devi on account of domestic costs if he had to travel out. Again, a letter of October 1980 shows that borrowing money from people around him (either directly by him or through Saraswati Devi) was not infrequent. 'I have paid off everyone to whom I owed a debt.' This, he reported, amounted to Rs 6,000. Driven probably by the constant want and acute shortage of money, Bhagwanji also tried his luck in buying lottery tickets.

In the 1970s, Pabitra started receiving regular pension from the government for being a freedom fighter, apart from being honoured with a copper plate. The amount was not that insignificant—two hundred rupees per month. It is an indication of how close Pabitra was to Bhagwanji when he rebuked Pabitra for not setting aside the money so that it could be accumulated and used to alleviate his (Bhagwanji's) financial distress. How could money be such an acute problem for someone who was trotting the globe, influencing global developments and hobnobbing with leaders of global powers? That is a natural question that would perplex anyone studying this mysterious monk's life. Bhagwanji himself answered this question only partly, and again in coded language.

> When I am engaged in the work of my Mother's *sadhana*, my expenses are taken care of by CL. That keeps my ideal intact. But I cannot use CL money when I come in, drawn by your love and affection. Doing that will be a violation of my ideal.[8]

We haven't been able to decode the meaning of CL. At another instance, he reiterated that he would never use funds from the 'exchequer', without clarifying what he meant by the word, for his personal requirements.[9] The effective point here is that while Bhagwanji admitted having financial support for the work of his

---

8   Bhagwanji's letter to Pabitra Mohan Roy, 4 October 1980. Translated from Bengali.

9   Bhagwanji's letter to Pabitra Mohan Roy, 5 January 1983. Translated from Bengali.

'horizon', when within India, he was on his own. It may well have been the usual practice, but with numerous exceptions. On many instances, Bhagwanji asked his followers to procure a number of things that were purportedly for use in his 'horizon'. It begs the question as to why he would do that, especially when he was aware of their financial condition and he anyway had financial support for work related to his 'horizon'.

[Bhagwanji's letter to Pabitra Mohan Roy informing him about the sources of his funds]

With passage of time, the number of people with access to Bhagwanji kept increasing steadily. The narrative that has existed in the public domain till now has portrayed the people to have formed a closely knit support network for him. The reality, however, was quite different. Some of those who lived around Bhagwanji and those who visited him remained interconnected, but they operated primarily as individuals and small groups. Many of these individuals barely knew each other, and often the relationship between the groups was marked by mutual jealousy and suspicion. At times, their actions and behaviour were quite opposite to their stated purpose. Thus, while a Rajkumar would remain a constant source of trouble, a Durga Prasad Pandey, while claiming to protect Bhagwanji's identity, would give out stories to the local press on the sly (so Bhagwanji suspected). A few, finding it simply too difficult to contain their excitement and the pride in knowing about the man, would blurt out information to friends and family. Most of these people remained tight lipped to the outside world and followed the unwritten code of conduct, but individual motives and inter-group dynamics remained a matter of never-ending worry for Bhagwanji.

The support group that built up in Calcutta wasn't free of these problems, although publications like *OMA* and *Jayasree* have portrayed it as a homogenous one. In fact, the people in touch with Bhagwanji formed at least three groups, led by Pabitra Mohan Roy, Sunil Krishna Gupta and Leela Roy. Of course they coordinated among themselves for planning and operations but never merged into one group. The differences surfaced soon after contact was established with Bhagwanji. Within a year of her trip to Naimisharanya, Leela Roy wrote to Bhagwanji that a disagreement had emerged between Pabitra and Amal Roy within a few months of their meeting him.

> It is my earnest request to you to please give adequate advice to Pabitra and his friend, if you too agree, that more damage than good is being done at their end. It will certainly not be wise to estrange them, but it is essential to pull them up. It is difficult to tolerate this undesirable and uncalled for mentality. I have called Pabitra two-three times, swallowing my pride, for a frank discussion and have tried to be helpful on hearing about his tiff with Amal. [Translated from Bengali]

Bhagwanji was aware of what was going on around him. 'Pabitra is not to be blamed,' he was clear. Amal Roy, according to him, had taken advantage of the fact that Pabitra was in need of money for going to Neemsar the first time. 'My life is nightmarish,' Bhagwanji was blunter when he told Dulal Nandy, 'but those who have come here have made it worse'. Irregularities in their behaviour, or liberties taken by those close to him irritated Bhagwanji no end. Thus, when he found out that a letter that he had sent to Sunil Das, with the instruction to share it with Pabitra was disregarded, he was not at all happy. The letter contained sensitive details about the Bangladesh war and his activities around it. To Pabitra, he wrote:

> Those strips also contained my blessings to Sunil as the successor of Srijukta Roy, in response to two long emotional letters he had written to me long time back seeking the inheritance of her legacy and same rights over me...But why was all this kept secret from Pabitra? Strange! My own understanding regarding this is that it was not done by Mukul...Of course the main responsibility and fault of disobeying order lies with Mukul [Sunil Das]. (Translated from Bengali).

Similarly, when Sunil Krishna Gupta landed in Ayodhya unannounced and without Bhagwanji's permission with his nephew Surajit in October 1982, Bhagwanji was extremely annoyed. This was not the first time Gupta had brought guests with him, unannounced and uninvited. 'This is the height of indiscipline,' Bhagwanji wrote to Pabitra.

At times, Bhagwanji would seek help from some of his followers, keeping it a secret from others. Such instances could be as insignificant as providing certain items, or in other cases monetary help. For instance, once he asked Pabitra, 'I hope they don't know that you send me copies of *Jugantar* from time to time? I haven't told them [others from Calcutta].' There were also instances where specific individuals would fall out of Bhagwanji's radar or would be kept out of the loop by him. The most notable instance of the latter was the effort to move out of Basti, the responsibility of which he entrusted only to Pabitra. In November 1971, while away on a trip, he informed Pabitra of his desire to shift out of Basti on his return. At the same time, he cautioned him that 'I am not writing to them (Mukul, Santosh, Paltu, Dulal, Kamal, Param Pujaniya [most respected, implying Suresh Bose], etc.) about this now. Be careful that they do not get a chance to even suspect this.' He permitted Pabitra to confide the plan only to the person whom he could trust his life with; someone who could carry the information as a secret within his heart for the rest of his life.

While the search for the house was on, Bhagwanji explained in a letter to Pabitra why he had trusted him over all the others. The differences between the camp followers of Leela Roy and Pabitra had simmered since the beginning. Referring to the general decline among Indians in term of moral and ethical values and deterioration in character, he wrote that he had never thought of Pabitra as one of those. Yet, starting with Leela Roy, all her followers had always tried to prove the opposite to Bhagwanji. 'They had their reasons, but I could never agree with them.' The others from Calcutta felt and complained to Bhagwanji that he was biased towards Pabitra. What riled Bhagwanji, however, was the possessive attitude of Leela Roy and her followers towards him, especially over a house that was built in Varanasi at the instance of her followers by 'a very generous person' at a cost of over rupees two lakhs. An old revolutionary was appointed to take care of his food and other comforts. They informed Bhagwanji that no one else had been informed about the house, not even Pabitra. 'We leave it to your discretion whether you want to inform him or not, but should you decide to inform him, please see to it that it does not create any misunderstanding,' they told Bhagwanji. He refused to move. 'No honest person can agree to such terms,' Bhagwanji said. He launched a scathing criticism of Leela Roy and her group:

> They want to keep me restricted within the boundary of their conditions? The cheek of it! ...They wanted to control my communication with others, secret movements of my messengers, but I didn't agree. They have kept the reason for this attempt to keep me constrained within the confines of their own arrangements a secret…. They just want to prove to the whole world, to the governments of the world, to political workers in India and our former revolutionaries that 'only we have had a direct contact with___. Only we had the responsibility of maintaining his secret hideout outside his horizon'.[10]

When Pabitra failed to find an accommodation for him for nearly four years, there was no end to Bhagwanji's angst. 'What have you done Pabitra?' his letter screamed, 'I never thought you would cause so much pain to me.' His letters of this time were dripping with bitter sarcasm. 'At least they have done something in my name. I had completely depended on you, but you turned

---

10   Bhagwanji's letter to Pabitra Mohan Roy, 22 May 1974. Translated from Bengali.

out to be such a miserably incompetent failure?' All the same, despite his occasional outbursts, Bhagwanji showered affection on his followers. The few exceptions were those who violated the code of conduct and endangered his position, or those whose behavioural traits he found unacceptable. He barred the entry of at least five persons from Calcutta for their troublesome behaviour, the most well-known among them being Samar Guha. Guha's crowing to Saraswati Devi in Basti once that if he let out even one word, millions would 'throng the area to see Netaji' cost Guha future visits to Bhagwanji. The others were his eyes and ears to the outside world. That helped him, but did not make them indispensable. He would forgive their occasional lapses but not forget them. A major crisis erupted when Samar Guha released a morphed picture in 1979 and claimed that Netaji was alive. A livid Bhagwanji turned incommunicado. A few months later, Pabitra mustered courage to write to him. He provided a blow-by-blow account of the photo controversy, apologised for not being able to stop Guha in time, begged for forgiveness, and reaffirmed his allegiance:

> I wish to say something—your own words—'You are my intelligence officer—and without fear or favour must act.' Now allow me to begin in a similar way. Keeping in mind Ma Kali-Deshmata-Bangajanani-Bharatmata [Mother Bengal-Mother India] and your feet, I wanted to tell you that just like in the past, I still have the same unflinching faith and love-trust; unwavering obedience; total dedication and loyalty towards you....

Perhaps the most prominent example of this forgiving nature was Bhagwanji's treatment of Sunil Krishna Gupta, who, according to Pabitra, had a role to play in the fake photo controversy. Even prior to this, for a prolonged period, Gupta had not been in touch with Bhagwanji. He ascribed Gupta's behaviour partly to his being besotted with the glamour of political power. Bhagwanji was offended, but did not cut off ties with him. 'I have to remember with a grateful heart all the generous help he has provided, the love and affection he has shown, the burden he has taken up for me,' he wrote to Pabitra. He also forgave the second, and much more serious lapse of Gupta relating to the fake photo controversy. Gupta was allowed to visit Bhagwanji in October 1980. Guha, who was completely cut off, would rue for the rest of his life his falling for a ploy devised by his political opponents, who knew of his contact with 'Netaji'.

At another level, Bhagwanji also strived to forge a better connection among his followers. 'It is your special responsibility and duty' to ensure that Sunil Das 'remains true to this faith and that no compromising tendency should affect him', Bhagwanji wrote to Pabitra in November 1980. The reason for writing this was that Sunil 'has again taken to politics'. It had been Bhagwanji's standing instruction from the very beginning to stay away from party politics. 'Politics twists the mind, intellect and sense of self. Protect him from all this,' he instructed.

If Bhagwanji instructed Pabitra to take care of Sunil Das, he also wrote to sensitise him about the affable and benevolent nature of Santosh Bhattacharya: 'He is aware of the shortcomings and complexes in you, but doesn't allow himself to be influenced or disturbed by these.' According to Bhagwanji, it was Santosh's good nature that drove him to offer compensation to Pabitra whenever the latter incurred expenditure on account of Bhagwanji. Here was one man who had no vestige of ego or an inflated sense of self-importance. 'He genuinely cares for you,' Bhagwanji told Pabitra. 'I am warning you not to trivialise it as the generosity of a rich man. You will have to face the wrath of Ma Kali if you do so.'

To what extent Bhagwanji was sensitive to the personalities and mental state of his followers is evident from his assessment of and advice for Sunil Das. Bhagwanji couldn't praise Santosh enough for the way he took care of Sunil Das during his period of crisis. According to his assessment, Sunil Das went back to party politics to find an outlet for his frustrated state of mind. It was to demonstrate to his old comrades that he was still worth something. When Sunil wrote a twenty-five page letter describing his situation and his grudges against many to Bhagwanji, the old man couldn't control his tears. He was worried any way about Sunil's failing health and now this. He wrote back a reassuring reply explaining each and every point raised by Sunil. It was a 'heart to heart, most intimate exchange of thoughts', according to Bhagwanji. Sunil's response was pleasing. 'It was like dirty clothes coming back cleaned and pressed from the house of the washerman,' was his metaphor.

One of the most striking aspects of the man was the amount of time and effort he spent discussing the minutest details regarding his followers, analysing their behaviour, their attitude, their personal problems, their physical and mental state, and how to have them stay the course. At a personal level, he had copious exchange of letters with most of them. This aspect becomes all the more remarkable in view of his preoccupation with his political and

[Leela Roy in 1946. Courtesy Bijoy Nag]

spiritual endeavours which demanded a great deal of his time and attention. Among those who entered his inner circle from Calcutta, Leela Roy's stature was undoubtedly the greatest. She was one person about whom Bhagwanji was extremely loving and caring, unusually patient and had great expectations. More than any of these, the one attribute that stands out is his respect for her. About her capability, he had a very high opinion. In fact, he held that if he could have a few more people like her, he could have done much more. All others were like children to him. 'When I look at you, all I see are young children floating around me. You may be in your fifties and sixties, but I cannot see you like that,' Bhagwanji wrote to Pabitra on a separate occasion. Except Leela Roy, who was close to him in terms of age, the others were much younger.

Pabitra was, however, the one man who stands out for his consistency in devotion, unwavering loyalty, dedication from the very beginning of the Bhagwanji saga till the end. For Bhagwanji, he was still the old intelligence officer that he used to be during the INA years. 'I have told you many times that the others are not in the habit of writing much. Therefore, you must inform me about everyone for the peace of my mind. Whether you receive any letter from me or not, you must keep providing all information until I ask you not to,' Bhagwanji wrote to Pabitra as late as August 1984. Here was a person, perhaps the only one, to whom Bhagwanji did not hesitate to divulge his weaknesses and helplessness. Throughout his communications with Pabitra, his efforts to elevate him as a person not only spiritually and morally, but also in terms of practical personality traits are noticeable. 'You must get rid of your inferiority complex,' he chided Pabitra. The man was acutely aware of the shortcomings of Pabitra and others and approached them with love and affection to make better men out of them.

Saraswati Devi Shukla was the other person who was a pillar of support and source of emotional distress to Bhagwanji in equal measures. He swore by her loyalty, but indicated that he was not keen to have her tagging along after Neemsar. 'I have asked her so many times to leave. I have even stopped talking to her for six months, but she refuses to go,' he said later. A formidable lady with a fiery temper and shrill voice, Saraswati Devi's role in protecting Bhagwanji like a wall was never in doubt. She suffered all privations without complaining, with her son which were an inevitable part of being with Bhagwanji. Before the Calcutta followers reached Neemsar, Saraswati Devi would walk miles into the nearby villages, collecting food, clothes, money from wherever she could manage with the sole purpose of taking care of the man. That was her mandate from her father when he left her to take care of him.

To see Saraswati Devi—*Jagadambe Ma*, or simply *Ma* for Bhagwanji—suffer so much was painful for Bhagwanji and that was most likely the reason that he wanted her gone. Her attitude, however, started undergoing change with time. This coincided with the coming of age of Rajkumar, her only son. According to

Bhagwanji, the boy, now growing into a man was the source of all troubles that ensued, but blinded by love, Saraswati Devi could never see any fault in her son. Barely a teenager, Rajkumar ran away from home in Naimisharanya. Overwhelmed by grief, Saraswati Devi cried so much for months that one of her eyes got damaged. From a practical point of view, this meant additional medical costs for Bhagwanji. To add to the woes, her extreme reluctance to apply medicine aggravated the problem. As Rajkumar returned after some time, his tantrums kept increasing. 'For Ma, her son is no less than Brahma,' Bhagwanji would later write to Pabitra.

Things came to a pass in Basti after Rajkumar got married in 1970. In the meantime, he had moved to his own accommodation in the same town, running a small flour mill, with financial help from Bhagwanji. By the time the first child was born to Rajkumar and his wife, Saraswati Devi had run out of patience. She wanted to be with her son, daughter-in-law and the new born grandson, but was prevented by the ailments of Bhagwanji. The man was an unavoidable burden for her. As she got to know of Bhagwanji's plan of leaving Basti, she started hoping that it would happen soon. However, as time went by without Pabitra being able to settle for a new place, she started voicing her annoyance. In fact, her sarcastic comments were one of the reasons for Bhagwanji's caustic remarks to Pabitra, taunting him for his failure to find a new accommodation. Ironically, only a couple of months after Bhagwanji left Basti for Ayodhya, she came searching for him. Saraswati Devi roamed the streets of Ayodhya searching for Bhagwanji as she did not know his new address at Gurudwara Brahmakund. Tears, apologies and repentance got her back into

Bhagwanji's household again and thankfully so, as she nursed him like a mother would do her child when he remained immobile for a prolonged period. Saraswati Devi stayed till the last with Bhagwanji. Although her minor misdeeds such as taking away Bhagwanji's utensils and other household items to give them to Rajkumar continued, Bhagwanji ignored all this in view of her dedication and service.

To sum up, Bhagwanji led a terrible life, suffered so much on account of his ill health, poor living conditions, frequent financial crunch and last but not the least, the shortcomings of his followers. The man, however, was able to rise much above these and stand tall with his convictions. Anything else would have been a disappointment.

FIFTEEN

SO'HAM

THE FIRST NECESSARY element for building up a case of contested identity is a claimant. If a *sanyasi* hadn't walked into the grounds of the palace of the Maharaja of Burdwan in 1834, or another one in 1921 to the Buckland Bund in Dhaka, the two most sensational cases of contested identity in India— those of Pratapchand in Burdwan and Ramendra Narayan Roy in Bhawal—wouldn't come into existence. The case of Bhagwanji never became such a sensation, although it had all the ingredients of becoming an edge-of-the-seat thriller, because he didn't step out to make any claim. When his followers finally did make the claim on his behalf after his passing away in September 1985, it failed to gather the momentum until nearly two decades later.

Naturally, all sorts of speculations regarding Bhagwanji's identity kept accumulating over the years among the people who neither had any access to him or to his close band of followers.

This was in fact a success of the mystery man's strategy of keeping his identity a secret. He left the world behind him speculating about his true identity. The truth remained confined to the inner circle of trusted disciples, most of whom held on to their oath of secrecy for decades after he was gone.

The forensic evidence from independent handwriting experts leaves no doubt about the identity of the man. But is the non-forensic evidence congruent with it? What convinced old comrades like Leela Roy, Pabitra Mohan Roy and scores of other followers that the man who had once fired the patriotism of millions, confronted the strongest imperial power, taken head on the established leadership of the national political organisation, was living a nondescript life, leaving everything that he held so dear? How similar or different were the traits of Bhagwanji with those of Subhas Bose?

Our access to the notes, correspondences and views of some of the followers, albeit limited, allow us to address this question from an insider's perspective.

It would be useful to take Justice Manoj Mukherjee's treatment of evidence in his attempt to settle the identity of Bhagwanji as the starting point. Since we have already dealt with the forensic evidence in his report, here we focus on other material evidence and witness accounts that he dealt with and his line of reasoning. Justice Mukherjee put the witnesses who claimed Subhas Bose lived incognito as Bhagwanji into five categories:

- *Hearsay or belief*: Five witnesses (Dr Alokesh Bagchi, Vishwa Bandhu Tewari, I B Saxena, Ramendra Pal, Kailash Nath Jaiswal), whose claim was based on hearsay or belief but no 'substantial material information'. The accounts of these witnesses were dismissed by the judge straightaway as they never came in contact with Bhagwanji.

- *Journalists*: Three witnesses (Ashok Tandon, Vishwambhar Nath Arora and Sayed Kausar Hussain), whose claim was based on their journalistic investigation. The statements of these journalists were also left out of consideration by the judge.

- *Those who were around but did not see Bhagwanji*: The judge discounted the witness accounts of six people who constituted this group (Gur Basant Singh, Shakti Singh, Nirupam Mishra, Ravindra Nath Shukla, Nandalal Chakrabarti and Dulal Nandy).

- *Those who saw Bhagwanji, but did not see Subhas Chandra Bose*: This group included people who frequently interacted with Bhagwanji over many years and saw his face but had never seen Subhas Chandra Bose. Dr Priyabrata Banerjee and his wife Rita Banerjee of Faizabad, Rajkumar Shukla (son of Saraswati Devi), and some of the followers from Kolkata, such as Sunil Krishna Gupta, Bijoy Nag, Surajit Dasgupta, Jagatjit Dasgupta and Tarun Mukhopadhyay comprised this group.

- *Those who had seen both Subhas Chandra Bose and Bhagwanji*: This group, comprising Durga Prasad Pandey, Shrikant Sharma and Apurba Chandra Ghosh represented the strongest evidence to Justice Mukherjee. However, Bithi Chatterjee (mother of Rita Banerjee) who had seen both Netaji and Bhagwanji could not be sure if both were the same. Unfortunately, a key witness who had seen Subhas Bose in 1939 and again in Ayodhya in 1976— Pushpa Banerjee, wife of Dr T C Banerjee—had passed away before the Mukherjee Commission began its investigation.[1]

---

1 Mrs Banerjee told the *Northern India Patrika* investigators in no uncertain terms that Bhagwanji was indeed Subhas Chandra Bose. 'She said that once she told the Man that she last met Netaji in Lucknow sometime in the year 1938—giving the wrong year deliberately, the Man immediately corrected her that it was 1939.' S Kausar Hussain with Nirmal Nibedon and V N Arora, 'The Man Was Subhas Bose,' *Northern India Patrika*, 23 January 1986.

While the accounts of Priyabrata Banerjee and Rita Banerjee were dismissed by Justice Mukherjee on the ground that they were based on hearsay and were only belief, for the remaining witnesses in groups D and E, he had the following to say:

> Apparently, there is no reason for not acting or relying upon the evidence of the last two categories of witnesses particularly of the category who had seen Netaji before 1945 and also met Bhagwanji/Gumnami Baba face to face on a number of occasions, more so when their evidence regarding the frequent visits of some freedom fighters, eminent politicians and former members of INA on January 23 and during the Durga Puja festival is supported by the fact that letters written by some of them including Prof Samar Guha, Dr Pabitra Mohan Roy and Ms Leela Roy were found in 'Ram Bhawan'.

Thus, at least the witness accounts of those who had seen both Subhas Bose before 18 August 1945 and Bhagwanji were valid evidence. 'But,' the judge stated, 'there are other formidable facts and circumstances on record which stand in the way of this Commission in arriving at a conclusive finding that Bhagwanji/Gumnami Baba was none other than Netaji'. In other words, in absence of those 'formidable facts and circumstances', this category provided credible evidence that it was indeed Subhas Bose who lived as Gumnami Baba.

The 'formidable facts and circumstances' that came in the way were:

- Although Sunil Krishna Gupta, Surajit Dasgupta, Jagatjit Dasgupta, and Tarun Kumar Mukhopadhyay submitted a joint affidavit in response to the public notification issued by the inquiry commission, they remained 'conspicuously silent about the entire episode of Netaji's living in disguise as a saint'. Other witnesses claiming Bhagwanji to be Netaji in disguise 'did not even file any statement before this Commission in support of their such claim'.

- The fact that witnesses like Sunil Krishna Gupta did not divulge to the G D Khosla Commission the fact that they had definitive information about Netaji being alive defies reason. Their explanation that they were under an oath of secrecy is 'extremely difficult to rely on' especially when 'he has now divulged that fact in spite of that oath'.

- Forensic evidence did not add up. While experts differed on their opinion with regard to the analysis of Bhagwanji's handwriting, the Central Forensic Science Laboratory, Kolkata, clearly opined that the DNA of a set of teeth recovered from Ram Bhawan did not match with 'either maternal or paternal DNA lineage' of Subhas Bose.

As a result, because of these hurdles, the evidence which he found credible could not be considered 'clinching' by Justice Mukherjee. Yet, the tonal difference in drawing the conclusion in his report is notable when compared with other claims such as the Shaulmari sadhu and the sadhu of Sheopur Kalan. While there was no 'reliable evidence' in the case of the former, the latter was 'rejected outright'. In contrast, the claim of Bhagwanji being Netaji showed only 'absence of clinching evidence'.

As far as the non-forensic part is concerned, Justice Mukherjee found the oath of secrecy and its treatment by the Calcutta disciples to be the main obstacle in relying upon the evidence provided by them. Justice Mukherjee's criticism is not wholly unjustified. Some of the Calcutta disciples indeed have been inconsistent with their vow of secrecy. As early as 1977, Bijoy Nag, writing as Charan, declared in the *Jayasree* magazine that 'Today I have no hesitation in declaring that the person who was born in 1897 is the same as Mahakal.'[2] Anyone reading his column or *Oi Mahamanaba Ase* where these columns were compiled would have no doubt about the identity of Mahakal or the Mahamanaba referred to in the title of the book. In a most bizarre turn of events, Samar Guha along with Sunil Krishna Gupta and his elder brother released a morphed photograph of Subhas Chandra Bose in January 1979 at a press conference in Calcutta, announcing that Netaji had returned to India. Bhagwanji's other followers, including Pabitra Mohan Roy however, stayed away from the incident.

Caught in the dilemma between the urge to settle the mystery once and for all and the indecisiveness on how much to divulge on Bhagwanji, the expressions of the later generation of the followers have often been confusing and marked by extreme hero worship. Although their litigation led to the formation of the Justice Mukherjee Commission of Inquiry, Justice Prabha Shankar Mishra was compelled to point out the incoherent nature of their arguments at the opening of his judgement. He noted:

> It is difficult for us to pick up the threads to have any well-knit statement of facts from the contents of the instant petition, yet, after our several attempts and after hearing the petitioner in person and the learned Advocate representing the respondents Nos 1 to 4, we have been able to gather some bits from here and some bits from there to have some comprehension of the

---

2   Charanik, *Oi Mahamanaba Ase*, Jayasree Prakashan, 2010, p 227.

narration in the petition.[3]

This irrationality and incoherence continues to this day, as this band of followers, devotees to be more precise, for a long time refused to make a proper case before the Justice Sahai Commission on the grounds of the suspicion that the Commission was compromised. They shared with us Bhagwanji's letters and other notes considered less sensitive by them, in spite of knowing us for years, because after all, we are not 'believers' like them.

Justice Mukherjee's casual treatment of the matter of oath of secrecy, on the other hand, is baffling. It has been a well-established and widespread practice across the world through the ages. Among the Bengal revolutionaries, especially, it was a central theme: sacrificing life to safeguard information was not uncommon. Sharing of information too was strictly on a need to know basis. In fact, the success of revolutionary operations often depended on the fragmented dissemination of information where one person did not know who else were involved in the operation or how much they knew. If Gumnami Baba was Subhas Bose, such an approach wouldn't be out of place. It is worth recalling that even nearly three decades later, Dwijen Bose refused to divulge specific bits of information to the Justice G D Khosla Commission regarding Subhas Chandra Bose's escape from India, saying he could not do so as he was 'under an oath to Netaji'. He

---

3   Judgement of Justices P S Mishra and B Bhattacharya in Rudra Jyoti Bhattacharjee and others Vs Union of India and others, Calcutta High Court, 30 April 1998.

added, 'Unless I am asked by Netaji, I cannot do that.'

None of the extant followers of Bhagwanji mentioned anything about him to Justice Mukherjee in their initial submissions. It was only after their letters were discovered in Ram Bhawan that they started singing. It is unfortunate that one of the earliest persons to arrive at Neemsar—Samar Guha—didn't get a second chance to open his heart to Justice Mukherjee. He passed away in 2002 after remaining critically ill for a long time.

This brings us to the most critical lacuna in the retired judge's approach. Although he acknowledged the involvement of former revolutionaries with Bhagwanji, he ignored the crucial exercise of analysis of the documents that resulted from their interactions in the form of letters, notes and diaries. The other, and equally important lacuna in his approach was setting a temporal boundary to his investigation. This resulted in ignoring the evidence that could be extracted from the writings of Leela Roy, Pabitra Mohan Roy, Anil Das, Sunil Das, Ashutosh Kali, Samar Guha and Bishwanath Roy—all of whom belong to the category of people who knew both Subhas Bose and Bhagwanji. Apart from removing the most important evidence from the ambit of consideration, this approach led Justice Mukherjee to generalise the lapses of the other followers from Kolkata. These lapses did not evade the attention of the Lucknow Bench of the Allahabad High Court. In delivering the judgement on 31 January 2013, the court observed:

> Different articles of Gumnami Baba alias Bhagwanji were considered by Mukherjee Commission. The perusal of the report does not reveal that Mukherjee Commission has

considered the articles individually to arrive at a logical conclusion.

And again,

> From the aforesaid material discussed by Mukherjee Commission, there appears to be no room for doubt that there was substantial oral and documentary evidence which prima facie makes out a case for scientific investigation with regard to identity of late Gumnami Baba.

For this man, his associates, followers and devotees kept sending material to ensure at least the basic comforts of life. When the investigators started putting together the list of items that Bhagwanji left behind in Ram Bhawan, they were stunned. The thousands of items which were recovered of course did not belong to Subhas Chandra Bose, but stuffed in the small outhouse, they pointed to the personality of the man.

Remnants of a non-existence

For a man living in hiding and changing shelter often to have stored thousands of items would appear counter-intuitive. Remaining hidden and making quick moves demands minimising acquisitions. However, a closer look at the acquisitions of Bhagwanji tells us a story which is not visible on the surface.

The two largest components of his belongings were books, journals, newspapers and newspaper cuttings, correspondence (including receipts and counterfoils of registered letters and telegrams), photographs and miscellaneous pieces of paper. These account for about 4,331 of the more than 7,000 items discovered. Essential personal goods (which included medicines, spectacles, watches, clothes, walking sticks, study table, and chair), and luxury items (which included perfumes, smoking pipes, tobacco, cigarettes, record players and musical records) were fewer in number. There were a few odd items such as binoculars, spooling tapes, a recording system and some magnetic instruments. The most noticeable characteristic of these belongings is that none of these, except probably the letters, are incriminating in nature—at the most some of these could only raise a suspicion about his identity but never prove it decidedly. Hence, nothing except the letters, photographs and a few other essential items would matter even if he had to leave them behind in the eventuality of a hasty exit.

Of the many people from different parts of the country who came in touch with Bhagwanji and interacted with him through long hours of conversation or exchange of letters or both, none could be said to have grasped the full picture of the mystery man. They were all situated outside the man's inner world, which he protected zealously. On occasions, he shared his thoughts and plans with a select few, but on a strictly 'need to know' basis. In comparison, the inner world in the physical plane—his room with all that it could accommodate was completely out of bounds to everyone. No exceptions were allowed; even Saraswati Devi was only marginally wiser than the closest of his disciples in this regard. Essentially, therefore, each person's view of Bhagwanji was fragmented. Although the fragmented views—in certain instances by themselves but more often in conjunction with other fragments—are of great value in establishing the identity of Bhagwanji, they leave an important gap.

The opportunity to fill this gap emerged when the people of

Faizabad were able to step inside Bhagwanji's room for the first time in September 1985 and when subsequently each and every item in the room was meticulously catalogued by officials appointed by the Allahabad High Court. As hundreds of letters, newspapers, books and other documents were discovered, people watched in stunned silence. For the first time, people gathered around Ram Bhawan watched in awe the personal space of the man who had effectively created a world inside a room for decades. For the first time, it became possible to reconstruct the personality of Bhagwanji with the help of an inventory of his belongings. The list made it possible to imagine what kind of person Bhagwanji was. The investigative team of the *NIP* and Ashok Tandon (who assisted the Advocate Commissioner Satya Narain Singh) tried to integrate this new information into their narratives, but without a systematic scrutiny of the items, their efforts succeeded only to a limited extent.

It took over a year for the battery of officials aided by local followers of Bhagwanji to list all the items found in such a small room. Even then, the task proved so overwhelming that the team often took the approach of aggregating similar materials instead of listing them individually. For instance, letters, newspapers and paper cuttings were often listed as a 'collection' of letters, newspapers and cuttings. It is not possible to disaggregate all these collective items without going through them individually, but a methodical analysis of the list reveals the existence of over 7,000 items instead of 2,640 mentioned in the inventory (see graphic representation of the inventory on next page). The importance of the inventory of Bhagwanji's belongings lies in the fact that it demolishes all the alternative theories about his identity and then

Photographs [110]

Photos of parents and siblings of Netaji Subhas Chandra Bose; photos of Leela Roy & other followers from Bengal; pictures of Pandit Nehru, Rajendra Prasad and Mahatma Gandhi cut out from magazines; photos of functions held to commemorate birth anniversary of Netaji

Tobacco & related items [122]

11 pipes; 1 packet of Gold Flake & 3 packets of India Kings cigarettes; 4 ashtrays; 15 packets of cigarette papers; 1 cigarette roller; 11 bundles/packets of pipe cleaners; automatic cigarette case made in England; lighter refill & 63 spare lighter flints; pan chatni; chewing tobacco.

Puja-related items [126]

28 malas of Rudraksh, Tulsi, crystal; beads of Rudraksh (3-faced to 6-faced); Gangajal; agarbatti, with stand; frankincense; items for havan; achamani; Gomukhi Kamandal; statue and photographs of Kali; Shiv Ling; photographs of Shiva, Durga, Ramac and Maihar Devi; bundles of sandalwood; sindoor, alta, kajal; shankha (conch) from which one can hear sound when brought near the ears

Stationery [134]

Ball point pens & refills; carbon paper; 6 empty diaries; envelopes; 7 bottles of ink; glue; inch tape; stitching tape; 6 writing pads, 3 notebooks & 25 blank letter pads (18 of which are of foreign made paper); 4 bundles of blank white paper; 3 magnifying glasses; pencils; typewriter ribbons, stamp pads, scissors, carbon papers

Personal care items [175]

76 soaps (Yardley, Cuticura, Ponds, Pears, Neko, Lavender Dew); 27 bottles of perfume (Aguru, Ittar, Eau de Cologne); 21 packets of Gillette blades; Gillette razors & shaving machine;

Electrical, electronic & related items [178]

Spool tape recorder & tapes; 5 magnetic tapes; 2 transistor radios; 2 record players; 12 recording cassettes, room heater; ceiling fan; tape recorder; 61 batteries; gramophone needles; calling bell; different types of wires and leads.

Apparel, warm wear, footwear etc. [327]

13 shirts, 4 trousers; 31 vests, 31 underwears; 58 dhotis; 2 kurtas; 3 warmers; 3 gloves; 2 raincoats; 30 towels/gamchhas; 1 jacket; 2 pairs each of black shoes & slippers; 1 pair of red shoes; wooden khadam with a strap of deerskin; wooden chappal; 6 bottles of Cherry Blossom shoe polish & cream; woollen monkey caps; 7 mattresses; bedsheets; quilts (including one brown Rajasthani quilt with silkwork); pillows & pillow covers

Household goods [376]

Naphthalene, mosquito repellants & other insecticides & disinfectants, screws & screw drivers, stopcocks, washers, bundles of rope, forcep, pliers, mortar & pestle, window adjuster, sickles (hansua), tin cutter, stone for sharpening knives, balls of thread, brass flowerpots, stoves (made in England), iron locks, plastic pipe, big iron scissors, nut bolts, record cleaners, funnel, mouse traps, bottles of Shalimar paint, insecticide sprayer (made in USA), wrench, convex lens, weighing scale & weights, hammer, axe, safety pins, bunch of 46 keys, slingshot (gulel) umbrellas, glass & brass candlestands, candles, Petromax spare parts, torch & spares

Medicines & other health-related items [464]

10 bottles of balm; more than 200 bottles of medicine - mostly homeopathic; common medicines such as Pudin Hara, Iodex, Savlon, Vicks, Iodine, Aspirin (1,000 tablets), Suckcee (300 tablets), hand sanitizer, ear drops, eye lotion; medicinal herbs including Canabis; medicines for rheumatic arthritis, musculoskeletal pain - Multigesic, Systaflam, Nurofen, Robinax, Rumalaya, Algipan, Hadensa, Relaxyl, Ellimans Universal Embrocation; Anovate, Arsh Kuthar Ras (used for piles/hemorrhoids); Sarpagandha tablets; 2 bottles of Brandy.

Charles Dickens (51), Aleksandr Solzhenitsyn (11), Will Durant (11), Complete Works of Shakespeare, T Lobsang Rampa (10), Walter Scott (8), Alexandre Dumas (6), Erich von Daniken (4), PG Wodehouse (3), Kuldeep Nayar (3), Aldous Huxley, Homer, Andrei Sakharov, John Bunyan, Jonathan Swift, Lewis Caroll,

Walking stick, typewriter, Rolex & Omega wristwatches, chronometer, watch ornamentation (made in England), Favre Leuba timepiece; Hensoldt Wetzlar Nacht Dialyt binocular, Empire Corona typewriter, 8 round frame spectacles (one of them golden coloured); 40 maps; 83 gramophone records (songs of Nazrul Islam, Shyama Sangeet, Rabindra Sangeet, Mahishamardini Stotra; KL Saigal, Juthika Ray, Ustad Faiyaz Khan, Rajanikanta's songs, Ravi Shankar, Bismillah Khan and Vilayat Khan's recitals; Atul Prasad Sen's songs, Lalan Fakir, Krishna Chattopadhaya, Manju Gupta, Panna Lal Ghosh, Sabyasachi, Dilip Kumar Roy, Hemanta Kumar, Sumitra Sen, Debabrata Biswas, Suchitra Mukherjee, Subinoy Roy, Feroza Begum); an old umbrella which appears to be of Janaki Nath Bose

Miscellaneous items [467]

Pages on which mantras are written [39]
Catalogues [39]
Notes on various topics [52]
Receipts of telegrams, registered letters, cash memos etc. [69]
List of goods sent to Bhagwanji [76]
Telegrams [82]
Labels of airmail/express delivery letters [119]

Notebooks [28]
Accounts of expenditure [17]
Aerogramme [15]
Others [103]
Letters [614]
Stamps [248]
Envelopes [182]

Letters, telegrams & other documents [1,683]

Utensils [209]

Books [984]

Newspapers, magazines etc. [1,664]

Pages from newspapers & magazines [313]
Panchang [32]
Typed copy of news [5]
Newspapers [782]
Periodicals [532]

Hindi 180
Other 95
English 282
Bengali 427

Full set of Rabindra Rachanabali, Bankim Rachanabali, Vidyasagar Rachanabali, Madhusudan Rachanabali, Sarat Chandra Chattopadhyay (37), Gopinath Kaviraj (17), Subodh Kumar Chakraborty (13), Balai Chand Mukhopadhyay (13), Bibhuti Bhushan Bandopadhyay (12), Uma Prasad Mukhopadhyay (12), Bankim Chandra Chattopadhyay (9), Durga Das Lahiri (6), Tarasankar Bandhopadhyay (6), Dakshinaranjan Mitra Majumdar (4), Deena Bandhu Mitra (3), Rajani Kanta Sen, Sunil Gangopadhyay

The Pioneer (732), Aaj, Amrit Prabhat, Amrita Bazar Patrika, Ananda Bazar Patrika, Bartaman, Dainik Jagaran, Indian Express, Jan Morcha, Jugantar, Northern India Patrika, Sandesh, Swabhiman, Swatantra Bharat, The Statesman, The Telegraph, Times of India, Ujala.

Reader's Digest (87), Jayasree (86), Mirror (72), The Astrological Magazine (62), The Illustrated Weekly of India (35), The Plain Truth (27), Blitz (22), Arya Shastra (20), Organiser (15), Akhand Jyoti (11), Dharmayug (10), Kalyan, Rashtra Dharm, Betar Jagat, Paribartan, Desh, Jyotish Martand, Maya, Amrita, Christian Science Sentinnel, Manohar Kahaniyan, Shri Ram Janma Bhoomi, Time, Jugabani takes us for a guided tour towards his real identity.

In 2008, Sam Gosling, then an associate professor of psychology at the University of Texas at Austin published his first book *Snoop: What Your Stuff Says About You* that focussed on, in his words, 'décor decoding research'. In simpler words, his work explained 'how we can capture something about a person's character and personality, values and habits, hopes and dreams, just from looking closely at their rooms or offices.'[4] Items present in a room play a critical role in assessing the personality traits of a person by 'not just what they are, but the way they're arranged', Gosling told Neal Conan, the host of *Talk of the Nation* broadcast by the US-based National Public Radio.[5]

These principles, when applied to the belongings of Bhagwanji, piled up in a single room, provide fresh insights into the question of his identity.[6] To start making sense of the belongings, it is essential to categorise the items listed in the inventory. Although it isn't possible to place many individual items into a neat and exclusive category, it is possible to create broad indicative groups.

At first glance, the number of items seem too many for a man

---

4   Sam Gosling, Snoop: *What Your Stuff Says About You*, Basic Books (Kindle Edition).
5   Author Interview, What Your Stuff Says About You, 26 May 2008. https://www.npr. org/templates/transcript/transcript.php?storyId=90829875
6   Common sense-based and intuitive interpretations of the material recovered have of course been attempted previously by a few journalists and researchers, but the information generated by such approaches is quite different from a systematic study. As Gosling succinctly puts it, 'Our common sense can fool us into thinking that the results of studies merely confirm what we already know.' (*Snoop*, p 6). The other consideration that must be factored in is that apart from the authors, only a handful of people have had access to the complete official inventory of Bhagwanji's belongings.

who took extreme care not to make his presence conspicuous. It also appears unrealistic that he would be carrying around so many things while frequently moving from one place to another under strict secrecy. Bhagwanji always lived at places from where he could make quick exits. Yet he was forced to make such exits only about three or four times—from Lucknow in the late 1950s (he had to leave behind almost everything of whatever little he had that time), from Darshan Nagar and Lal Kothi in Ayodhya in the mid-1960s and lastly from Prahlad Dharamshala in 1974. All the other moves were well-planned and executed with great secrecy, with the help of his followers. His belongings couldn't have been a problem in moving out of Neemsar and then from Ayodhya a few years later since he had barely accumulated any material by that time. His move from Prahlad Dharamshala was also not a distress exit: his brief stay there was planned well in advance. Whether planned or unplanned, his followers arranged for transporting all his goods in trucks.

A scrutiny of the items and Bhagwanji's movement patterns, however, present a different picture. Firstly, since moving out of Basti towards the end of 1974, the different locations at which Bhagwanji stayed up to 1982 were all located within one town—Ayodhya. Thereafter, he moved to Faizabad just about seven kilometres away. Thus, during his last decade, the volume of his belongings wasn't much of a pressing factor from the point of view of shifting base. An assessment of the items to which a date can be ascribed also follows this pattern. For instance, among all the communication-related items (letters, telegrams, aerograms, acknowledgement cards, etc.) those belonging to the period

1975-1985 were nearly four times more than those belonging to the earlier years. More than half the letters, notes, etc. found in Ram Bhawan of course were without a date. It appears Bhagwanji had a keen interest in the British era stamps, 224 of which were found in his room.

The pattern is clearer in case of newspapers and periodicals which form a large chunk of what was found at Ram Bhawan; about three-quarters of newspapers were of the period from 1982 to 1985, and less than 1% were pre-1975 vintage. This makes it clear that the large volume of newspapers was just a pile up due to lack of disposal. This makes sense as instead of storing full newspapers, the keen reader in Bhagwanji would cut out the parts containing news of interest to him. It is not possible to estimate the total number of cuttings from newspapers and magazines among the belongings because out of the 166 cuttings-related items listed in the inventory, 120 were listed either as 'bundles' or 'collections'.

It was a little different in the case of periodicals, of which more than a quarter were pre-1975 vintage. Clearly, these were considered important enough by Bhagwanji to be carried around with him. Unfortunately, it is not possible to date the other categories of items such as books, medicines, stationery, household goods, clothing, utensils, etc. but it can be safely assumed that their numbers kept increasing—as did the number of trunks in which they were stored—as his followers kept bringing him more and more stuff over the years. A qualitative analysis of the belongings, however, yields more fascinating insights.

Letters, telegrams, etc.

The 136 letters and telegrams that Bhagwanji received from Pabitra Mohan Roy, accounting for a fifth of all letters and telegrams he received, and the nearly 150 letters that he wrote to his trusted lieutenant[7] (in addition to those written to his other followers in Calcutta) indicate that Bhagwanji was a frequent letter writer. The small number of pre-1975 letters, therefore, possibly validate Saraswati Devi's claim that bundles of letters were routinely destroyed by Bhagwanji. Bhagwanji's communications were, however, not restricted to his followers in Calcutta. Apart from the Calcutta group, the available correspondence can be categorised into two clear sets on the basis of the people with whom he corresponded.

One group included the ordinary folk outside Bengal who at some point came into contact with him or learnt about him from his followers. About 100 letters and telegrams Bhagwanji received since the late 1950s were from people outside Bengal. While a few of these were written by his local associates like Durga Prasad Pandey, Srikant Sharma and Rajkumar and other acquaintances through his followers, many were written by people whose names do not feature anywhere in the mass of narrative available from different sources. Most of them addressed Bhagwanji in highly adulating terms such as *'Pujaniya Bhagwanji'*, *'Mere Ishta Devata'*, *'Anant Vibhushit Param Pujaniya Shri Bhagwanji'*, etc. For example, one Chhote Lal Vaidya Shastri wrote to Bhagwanji in March 1957 asking him to continue with his efforts, assuring

---

7   Excluding the letters written during 1965 to mid-1970 which are not available.

him of success. Similarly, letters were written by Ram Narain Shukla, forest guard, Neemsar; one Phakkad Baba, Shiv Shankar Lal, Raj Shekhar and Shashank Shekhar, Jai Shankar Tripathi, Lal Vimalendra Pratap Singh, Ashtabhuja Pandey, Pramod (who wrote about rules for chanting mantras), J P Shukla (who wrote from Faizabad railway station with details of purchase of a magnetotherapy machine from Delhi and seeking permission to meet him) and many such. Practically no information is available on how these people came to know of Bhagwanji or continued to keep track of his new addresses.

Even a cursory look at Bhagwanji's correspondence with this group of people makes it abundantly clear that although the man of mystery was careful to cover his true identity, he wasn't living in fear. Only with extreme caution. The cover did not deter him from interacting with people outside, or allowing them to contact him through letters and telegrams. This, of course, does not prove that all of them were aware of his true identity, but they certainly knew that they were in touch with an extraordinary man of high spiritual calibre. And Bhagwanji didn't seem to have any problem with that. On the rare occasions when one of them confronted him with their 'knowledge' of him being Subhas Bose, Bhagwanji's response tended to be in line with the standard intelligence agency approach of 'neither confirm nor deny'. To a great extent, this confidence stemmed from his own security measures and to the people that he allowed in his inner circle.

[Bhagwanji's letter to Pabitra Mohan Roy, 19 January 1972: 'In the field of Matri Sadhana I have to write to many people. The letters that I write to people outside the "horizon" are personal.']

It is the third category of correspondence that introduces a fresh angle to the question of Bhagwanji's activities and mindset, more than the question of his identity. It throws up questions which cannot be answered on the basis of the available material evidence, and leads to fascinating and logically consistent possibilities that can help fill up some critical information gaps. In contrast to the common people in the second category described above, these were men of power and fame: not those in the top league, whose names featured frequently in Bhagwanji's discourse with his disciples, but nevertheless with significant clout. Yet another curious feature of this group of correspondence is that they are very few in number (five, including letters and telegrams). In fact, the long gaps in time between these few letters and telegrams impart a certain element of randomness which in turn seems to suggest that they are only a few surviving samples which escaped the routine destruction of sensitive papers undertaken by Bhagwanji.

We have already discussed the letter of Babu Banarasi Das which was the earliest letter that can be placed in this category. The only other available evidence of communication to a high-ranking politician was that of a letter Bhagwanji wrote to the then minister in Indira Gandhi's cabinet from Malda, West Bengal, ABA Ghani Khan Choudhury. No copy of the letter was found, so we won't know what Bhagwanji wrote. What survives is an acknowledgement receipt of Bhagwanji's letter dated 5 July 1980 delivered to Choudhury two days later.

The letter from M S Golwalkar written on 16 September 1972, however, offers much more clarity. It was written in response to Bhagwanji's letter asking for his help on finding his next address.

Bhagwanji was desperately trying to move out of Basti. Golwalkar was nearing the end of his life—he would be alive for only nine more months. Following his death, Bhagwanji lamented that, 'No one will ever know or understand what a loss this has been for me — a four in one loss...He was the supreme leader (key person) of those who work for Ma Kali's horizon from outside the horizon.'[8] The salutation used by Golwalkar for Bhagwanji was not that used for a politician or senior statesman, but one that shows almost devotional genuflection. We have no information when this contact was established and how it developed over the years, during and after the tenure of Golwalkar. Yet, the unambiguous public proclamations by K S Sudarshan, the fifth head of RSS, in April 2005, and again while releasing a book on Gumnami Baba at a function in Delhi in December 2008[9], show that the highest leadership of the organisation has been well aware of his existence. The only question that remains unanswered is just how much did they know and what was their role? Interestingly, as early as 1948, RSS was rumoured to be linked to Netaji, as recorded in a CIA information report. 'Some people believe that Bose is alive. According to their theory, Bose is at present active in the underground RSS movement,'[10] the report dated 10 January 1949 reads.

---

8   Noting made by Pabitra Mohan Roy on 29 August 1973. Bhagwanji's familiarity and positive impression of the RSS is evident from a letter of his to Pabitra asking why he didn't take the help of the RSS in finding a new place to shift to.

9   'Netaji was alive till 1985: RSS chief' (http://zeenews.india.com/home/netaji-was-alive-till-1985-rss-chief-the-hindustan-times_213308.html); 'Mystery of Netaji's death must be unveiled: KS Sudarshan' (http://organiser.org/archives/historic/dynamic/modulese928.html?name=Content&pa=showpage&pid=268&page=35).

10 Subhas Chandra Bose, 10 Jan 1949, 00-B-72-49 CIA(R), M.I.S. No. 521245. This record was released by the CIA in October 2009 following an FOIA appeal by Anuj Dhar.

There have been murmurs among those in the Bose family who are opposed to even exploring the phenomenon of Bhagwanji that he was a plant by the RSS as part of their conspiracy to overthrow the Congress governments led by Nehru and then by Indira Gandhi. Apart from the inherent absurdity of such a claim, the spread of Bhagwanji's contacts clearly establishes that it was not only the RSS, but the regional leadership of the Congress and those who broke away from the party who were no strangers to him. It would, of course, be absolutely relevant to recall Pandey's letter mentioning the presence of the country's top political and military leadership in the dark of the night at Basti to meet the man of mystery, and also the recollection of the children of Panda Ram Kishore to the same effect. These are people who have no motive to weave lies and there is no apparent reason to disbelieve them. If there is even a modicum of truth in their statements, it stands to reason that the highest authorities in the state machinery were aware of his presence after Pandit Nehru passed away.[11] Bhagwanji's use of a letter embossed with Indian government's official emblem only strengthens that line of conjecture.

Newspapers, magazines and books

There are too many famous book collectors and hoarders who built their personal libraries to be listed here, but the common thread that binds them together is the size of their apartments, mansions or estates being proportionate to the size of their

---

11 All such claims pertain to post-Nehru era. Bhagwanji himself indicated that the Nehru administration was under the impression that he was in the 'north of the Himalayas'.

collections. George Washington, who was considered to be a significant book collector of his time, for instance, had his Mount Vernon estate in Virginia to accommodate an estimated collection of 1,200 volumes.[12] Now compare that to nearly 1,000 books and over 500 periodicals, all cramped in a room not more than 300 square feet. Not to forget nearly 800 newspapers and hundreds of paper cuttings.

The man, without an iota of doubt, was a voracious reader. And a bit of a hoarder too. He built a veritable library, which on the face of it would appear counter-intuitive. Why would a man who needed to move frequently and quickly store so much reading material? A scenario like this makes sense only in a situation where books etc. mean the world to someone—someone who can't imagine being without books and other reading material under any circumstances, especially when living virtually in a state of imprisonment—imposed or adopted. Books kept arriving—a few bought by himself, but most sent across by his followers.

For those familiar with Subhas Bose's life, this would be reminiscent of his stints in the British jails, starting with Mandalay in 1924. Sarat, Dilip and the libraries were the sources of his book supply. In fact, when books that he had requisitioned from the Imperial Library in Calcutta while being imprisoned at the Madras Penitentiary in 1933 were censored and refused by the then Bengal government, it became the subject of a question in

12   Lonnae O'Neal Parker, 'Mount Vernon replicates George Washington's personal library,' *The Washington Post*, 25 May 2012. https://www.washingtonpost.com/entertainment/museums/mount-vernon-replicates-george-washingtons-personal-library/2012/05/24/gJQA1eY6pU_story.html?utm_term=.fe2bae5116c9.

the central legislative assembly.[13] 'Somehow find for me a World Atlas with large maps of all countries…the kind of book that was used for high school and colleges in 1910,' Bhagwanji wrote to Pabitra (see image). It is a moot question why anyone would want, in 1976, an Atlas published in 1910 unless there is a special emotional connect? There were many instances when they would send the books on their own.

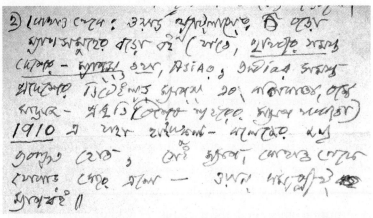

[*Bhagwanji's letter to Pabitra Mohan Roy, 15 January 1976*]

Old habits die hard. Subhas Bose often left such copious comments on the margins of the books he read, that two of them were published as part of his collected works by the Netaji Research Bureau.[14] When the motley crowd led by the local followers of Bhagwanji had a chance to glance through Bhagwanji's books for the first time, one of the characteristics that jumped out of the

---

13   Question by S C Mitra, 24 February 1933, File 22/73/33-Poll, Home Department, Political Section.

14   See Sisir K Bose (ed), *Collected Works of Netaji*, Vol 5, Netaji Research Bureau, 1985.

pages of the books was notes and remarks written by Bhagwanji on the margins of the pages (see images of *The Himalayan Blunder*).

While the language of preference was definitely Bengali, accounting for nearly half the books (leaving no doubt about the ethnicity of the holy man), English came a close second, followed by books written in Hindi and Sanskrit. If this demonstrated his multi-lingual proficiency, the range of topics of the books displayed a bewildering level of erudition. It was certainly not a lay person's reading list. Only someone with the highest level of intellect and intense curiosity to obtain knowledge would be a keen reader of books on classic literature, philosophy, unabridged scriptures in Sanskrit, homeopathy, ayurveda, occult and paranormal, cookery, physical exercise, India's freedom struggle, children's literature, history, politics, grammar, etc. Nothing seemed beyond the realm of his interest. And of course, the special interest was on the life and work of Subhas Bose and the contemporary research on him. A surprising omission in the trunkful of books discovered in Ram Bhavan was any serious literature on national or global politics or military studies, especially when Bhagwanji was incessantly obsessed with those topics. The only books found associated with military affairs were those related to the Indo-China war of 1962. Although the Vietnam and the Bangladesh wars occupied so much of Bhagwanji's correspondence with Pabitra and his discussions with visiting followers, no book discussing these was to be seen at Ram Bhawan.

Among the authors of English books, Charles Dickens was undoubtedly the favourite, comprising a fifth of all English books. In addition to having the several volumes of the authentic edition of Dickens's collected works published by Chapman and Hall in 1901, Bhagwanji, for some reason, collected the individual copies of Dickens's books too. His letters to Pabitra show that he was finicky about the editions and always wanted to read unabridged and original versions. 'Can you get me a copy of the old edition of *The Pilgrim's Progress* that we used to read as students?' he once wrote to Pabitra. Again, while asking for a copy of the *Sri Ramakrishna Kathamrita*, he wanted the old authentic version. The text of the later versions had been modified, he feared.

Among the other authors whose works he collected were Shakespeare, Walter Scott, Alexandre Dumas. If the volumes of Will Durant's *The Story of Civilization* held his attention, he was equally enamoured with the works of Aleksandr Solzhenitsyn. He read Aldous Huxley, Andrei Sakharov and Nietzsche. Among the Bengali literature, the complete works and single volume editions of Sarat Chandra Chattopadhyay, *Rabindra Rachanabali* (the collected works of Tagore), the novels of Bankim Chandra Chattopadhyay, works of Ishwar Chandra Vidyasagar, Tarashankar Bandhopadhyay and poet Rajani Kanta Sen featured most prominently. Multiple copies of the multi-volume translation of *Mahabharata* by Kaliprasanna Singha were present too. Among the other favourites were Balai Chand Mukhopadhyay, and Bibhuti Bhushan Bandopadhyay. These would be the staple of a well-read Bengali intellectual who lived in the first half of twentieth century Calcutta. Naturally, for someone travelling across the centres of pilgrimage in the country, Bhagwanji couldn't but have the classic travel series *Ramyani Beekshya* by Subodh Kumar Chakraborty and the books by Uma Prasad Mukhopadhyay in his collection.

He was equally fond of children's literature—the classics by Abanindra Nath Tagore (*Raj Kahini, Nalok, Buro Angla*) and Dakshinaranjan Mitra Majumdar (*Thakur Maar Jhuli, Thakur Dadar Jhuli, Dada Moshayer Tholey*) were among the books that he would ask his followers to send to him.

Books on religion and spiritual practices—numbering over 250—constituted the second largest chunk in Bhagwanji's collection. A simple glance through the collection is enough to reveal that this was a practitioner's collection where knowledge of scriptures is a sine qua non, not an enthusiast's. Thus it wasn't a surprise to find copies of the *Vedas*, the *Upanishads*, several *Puranas*, the *Chandi*, and of course the *Bhagavad Gita*. Along with these, a number of secondary texts adorned his collection including several volumes of *Japasutram* and *Stotra Ratnavali, Vaisheshika Darshanam* of Maharshi Kanad, *Ganga Lahari, Hanuman Chalisa, Kanakadhara Stotram, Yoga Vashistha Sar, Shaktanand Tarangini,* etc. Works of Swami Vivekananda, Anandamayi Ma, Swami Abhedananda, Lokenath Brahmachari, Sitaram Das Omkar Nath and unpublished typescript of a book by Baradacharan Majumdar. These were complemented by the scholarly work of Gopinath Kaviraj and the Bengali classics *Bharater Sadhika* and *Bharater Sadhak* by Shankar Nath Roy. Prominent authors of Hindi books on religion and spirituality that Bhagwanji read were Chaturbhuj Sahay, Hanuman Prasad Poddar and Jay Dayal Goyandka. The latter two were a trustee and a co-founder, respectively, of the Gita Press of Gorakhpur. Apart from the many books published by the Gita Press, Bhagwanji appears to have been a regular reader of their magazine *Kalyan*.

Not surprisingly, in view of tantric *sadhana* being a core theme of Bhagwanji's discourses and correspondence on spirituality, a number of texts were found among his collection. But more curious was Bhagwanji's fascination with the occult, alternative history, extraterrestrial intelligent life and conspiracy theories. Prominent among the authors of the paranormal, occult and conspiracy theory books were T Lobsang Rampa, Erich von Daniken, Charles Berlitz, Paul Brunton and the likes of P N Oak. These books assume greater significance as their contents and propositions found resonance in Bhagwanji's discourse with his followers. Comparing the claims of these authors and Bhagwanji's assertions, it would be fair to say that the resemblance was not accidental. In that case, it is also fair to deduce that either Bhagwanji was merely parroting what was written in these books, or he was reading them to compare notes with his own experience and thoughts. In view of the notes in the margins of many of these books, the latter seems more plausible.

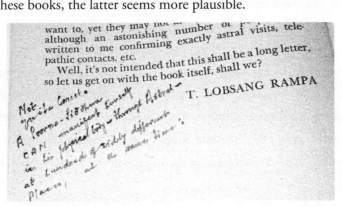

[A comment on Lobsang Rampa's Beyond the Tenth by Bhagwanji seems to be in line with what Subhas had told a friend in Berlin in the 1930s. 'A Poorna Siddha can manifest himself in his physical body—through Astral—at hundreds of widely different places, at the same time,' reads the comment. 'Yes indeed, Mrs Kurti, there are certain sanyasis or holy men who, though far away, are able to appear and talk to you,' Bose had told Kitty Kurti, who recounted it in her 1966 book Subhas Chandra Bose as I Knew Him.]

Items for personal use

Those who got to know Bhagwanji intimately (to the extent possible) noticed two key characteristics: (a) his obsession with cleanliness and (b) a pleasant fragrance. This could explain the finding of twenty-seven bottles of perfume (mainly attar) and a stock of seventy-five bathing soaps. Nail cutters, imported shaving equipment and talcum powder, all of the best brands—these tell the story of a person who had a fancy for the small luxuries of life, for whom at some point of time these were regular items of use. These might seem extravagant for a person living under the conditions that he did, yet the spartan life that he led during the days of destitution also speaks of his ability to do without these when required.

Watches were another category of item that reflected Bhagwanji's high taste. The two wrist watches recovered were Rolex and Omega, in addition to a Favre Leuba timepiece and a Swiss made Eberhard chronometer. As a columnist in *The Guardian* aptly put it, 'Watches are one of the few items that a man can wear that he believes display true character, and signal that he is a member of a particular club.'[15] That, however, can't explain why a man, scrupulously avoiding public contact, would wear what are also known as status or power watches. There has to be a different reason. And it could well be what another columnist in *The Wall Street Journal* explained: 'A man's desire for an expensive

---

15   Jeremy Langmead, 'Why are men obsessed with watches?' *The Guardian*, 14 December 2009. https://www.theguardian.com/lifeandstyle/2009/dec/14/men-wristwatches.

mechanical watch isn't about logic; it's about emotion.'[16] An Omega watch did form an important part of Subhas Bose's past.

But it wasn't entirely devoid of logic either. From laying down the specification of the chronometer that he wanted, to having Leela Roy run from pillar to post to ensure precision timing, Bhagwanji's obsession with accuracy seemed to border on the verge of mania. [*See image of his letter to Pabitra Mohan Roy*] That again does not square with a character said to be a fugitive and an ascetic. For that matter, neither does the possession of Second World War vintage high-powered binoculars.

[Bhagwanji's specifications of the chronometer required by him to Pabitra Mohan Roy, December 1962. We are not sure if this is his handwriting as we were given to understand it was copied from his original letter]

16   Kevin Gray, 'Do Men Still Crave Status Watches?' *The Wall Street Journal*, November 4, 2015. https://www.wsj.com/articles/do-men-still-crave-status-watches-1446666151.

[Bhagwanji's letter to Leela Roy regarding the problems related to precision timing of the chronometer. Undated letter. Courtesy Bijoy Nag]

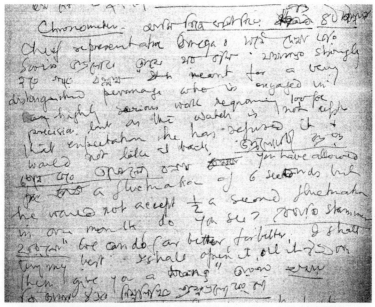

[Leela Roy's report to Bhagwanji recounting her efforts to ensure precision timing. Mukherjee Commission Exhibit 147. Obtained under Right to Information Act]

As far as clothes were concerned, Bhagwanji clearly preferred wearing a dhoti and a *banyan* (vest)—as evident from the presence of fifty-eight dhotis (many of them saffron coloured, the kind worn by ascetics) and over thirty *banyans*. This indicates that he spent most of the time indoors, but the presence of thirteen shirts (silk and terrycot), four trousers (denim, woollen and khaki), a woollen jacket, three pairs of leather gloves, two dozen pairs of socks, and three pairs of shoes point to his occasional slipping out to the world outside. Seven bottles of shoe polish and leather cream imply that he liked to keep his shoes polished and ready for use. Interestingly, in a letter to Pabitra soon after their meeting, Bhagwanji instructed him to arrange '6 pure Bengali Silk white shirts' for him. 'If I have not forgotten,' he wrote, 'you were— almost of my height. Get them made up to your measure.' At about 5' 9", Pabitra was nearly as tall as Netaji.

The secret world of Bhagwanji, behind the curtains, had more surprises in the form of electronic and electrical gadgets. It didn't take long for people to realise, when his room was no more a restricted zone, that this was no ordinary home of an obscure *sanyasi* of the type who frequent the holy centres of the country. There were tape recorders, record players, a significant collection of gramophone records and unfamiliar curiosities in the form of a Philips spool tape recorder (made in Holland) and spool tapes. The purpose of having record players and vinyl records was clear, but no one has been able to answer why Bhagwanji would need a spool tape recorder or later generation tape recorders (along with twelve Made in Japan Hitachi cassettes). A few among his regular visitors in Ayodhya and Faizabad have claimed that at times (especially at night) Bhagwanji could be heard talking softly for prolonged periods, often in a foreign tongue. Bhagwanji himself referred to taking copious notes from radio broadcasts and analysis information, in a letter to Pabitra. Was he recording too? Analysing the spool tapes and the cassettes might throw light on this, although given their small number, it is also possible that they were the unused ones.

It would be pertinent to refer to a secret British intelligence note on Subhas Bose's habits. The note by the CSDIC recorded on the basis of the eyewitness account of one of Bose's adjutants observed:

> A radio receiver was kept at Bose's residence, both while he was in Singapore and in Rangoon. Tara Chand used to come to Bose's house every night and listen to foreign broadcasts for three to four hours, making notes as required. He used to submit his report personally to Bose every day in Singapore.[17]

It is natural for those who cannot venture out to procure provisions on a regular basis to hoard them so that when the need arises the required items are at hand. And the extent of writing material and postal stationery stocked up by Bhagwanji helps us gauge the high frequency with which he interacted with people outside. He tried to make up with the written word what he couldn't do with the spoken word. Thirty-one writing/letter pads, four bundles of white papers, eleven pencils with lead refills, two ball point pens (many pens went missing as evident from empty pen boxes left behind), more than ten packets of plain envelopes, six bottles of writing ink, carbon paper, packet of acknowledgement forms, scores of envelopes for registered letters and airmail and labels for express delivery letters—these yet to

17   The personal staff, household and private affairs of SC Bose, Appendix "A" to CSDIC (I) 2 SEC Report No. 996. File 249 INA, National Archives of India.

used items speak of the mystery man's urge to communicate with the outside world while confining himself within the several layers of impenetrable walls.

Household items

The household items indicate a person with a do-it-yourself approach, someone who preferred to be self-sufficient and not dependent on others for small jobs. For obvious reasons. For a recluse who was barely interested in material affairs of a household, Bhagwanji appears to have been a remarkably meticulous person with an eye on the minutest details in his own household affairs. Variety of screwdrivers, scissors, pliers, thread and needles (which happened to be made in Germany), stopcocks, washers, forceps, pins, sickle, metal cleaning agents, flashlight, knife, hammer and axe indicate that Bhagwanji prepared himself (as he had to under the circumstances) for any contingency. Not only for himself, but for his visitors too, as is evident from his elaborate collection of kitchenware and tableware, as much as bedding-related items (seven mattresses, seven quilts and blankets, and a number of pillow covers and bedsheets).

Health

The medicines and medical accessories recovered from Ram Bhawan tell the story of an ageing man suffering from several physical ailments. The presence of knee caps, crepe bandage, hot water bags along with several ointments for musculoskeletal pain (systaflam, nurofen, relaxyl, etc.) confirms the narrative of his joint pains that we find in his letters. Bhagwanji struggled with the problem of haemorrhoids till the end (anovate and hadensa ointments were found among the medicines) and was also suffering from some ear problem as indicated by the presence of a number of ear drops. Five walking sticks point to his difficulty in movement, confirming his account in the letters, especially after his fall in the late 1970s in Ayodhya. Eight spectacles (all round-framed with one of them golden rimmed) are difficult to explain unless Bhagwanji was in the habit of not throwing away the old ones. There were actually more but a few were taken away once his Ram Bhawan room became accessible to public for a brief period. Rajkumar, for instance has a pair in his custody as a memento.

Maps

One can imagine a scholar, a cartographer, a planner, or a strategic affairs expert pouring over different kinds of detailed maps. But one can hardly expect a run-of-the-mill *baba* to obsess about maps. What then was Bhagwanji doing with sixteen large-sized detailed maps of various regions of India and its neighbourhood, and multiple copies of railways and roadways maps? It can't be said with certainity, but one can easily guess that he used the maps to plan his travel and possibly also to have a better grasp of (and have a ready reference of) the areas that were relevant to the 'great game' that he claimed to be a part of. These Survey of India maps, however, were not all. Fourteen more maps and architectural layouts of different buildings and their surrounding areas were also recovered. Some of these buildings were in Ayodhya; if he lived in the city he had to know the city well, so he needed a city map, of its localities and buildings. Five copies of a building in

Varanasi could have been of the house that was constructed for him to move in by some of his followers in Calcutta.

Among the heap of documents were found two huge hand-drawn maps that marked out prominent cities (along with their

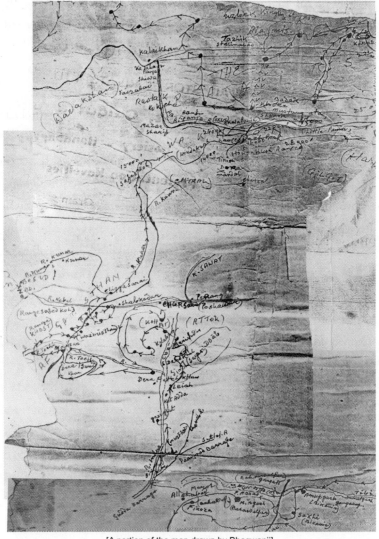

[A portion of the map drawn by Bhagwanji]

latitudes and longitudes), rivers, topographical features in the region from Russia, through Central Asia and extending up to Southeast Asia. The maps are criss-crossed with arrow-marked lines showing direction of travel in this wide area. The striking feature of the maps with their directional lines is that they tally with the narrative of his movements which Bhagwanji delivered to his Kolkata disciples.

Lottery tickets

Also found among his belongings were a number of lottery tickets as well as correspondence with the officials of the state lottery boards. These go on to re-affirm his state of penury and hence desperation for money. A total amount of Rs 3,491 (equivalent of approximately Rs 35,000 in today's currency value assuming a 7% average annual inflation), was all the cash that Bhagwanji had in September 1985. Going by his own estimate of his establishment costs, it wasn't adequate for even two months. Clearly what he was getting from his Calcutta followers wasn't enough to meet the establishment expenses, which primarily meant meeting the requirements of Saraswati Devi and her family too.

Eliminating doubts

A proper scrutiny of the documentary evidence would also have provided Justice Mukherjee a clear idea about how the old network of revolutionaries in Calcutta satisfied their residual scepticism about Bhagwanji's identity and not less important, in what manner Bhagwanji referred to his earlier days.

Prima facie it can be argued that if Leela Roy accepted

Bhagwanji to be Subhas Bose without ever seeing him, and having interacted with him only once, it points more towards her belief without proving the identity of the man. It can also be argued that it was possible to have such a belief induced by a skilled con man.

The weakness of such a line of argument, however, can be easily demonstrated. It can be counter-argued that such a line of argument can be forwarded only by those who are unaware of the personality and intellectual stature of Leela Roy, the rebel who refused to follow the beaten track and achieved what she did without allowing anyone to cloud her own judgement. It can be counter-argued also that one of the few firebrand revolutionaries and pioneering feminists whose portrait adorns the Parliament alongside the likes of Madame Bhikaji Cama, Sarat Chandra Bose, Kazi Nazrul Islam and Jawaharlal Nehru, was no gullible or sentimental fool. She wouldn't accept anything or anyone at face value; certainly not without satisfying her reasoning faculty.

Roy definitely missed the absence of Subhas sorely in independent India, but wasn't one of those who would 'sight' him here and there or put forth a vociferous claim that he would return on an unspecified date—'when the time is ripe'—to claim the mantle of the country's leadership. The multifarious reports springing up in Bengal's press, from time to time, irritated her. In fact, once she wrote to Bhagwanji, 'such rumours have been floating around in Calcutta for many years, and they will continue to do so, perhaps until Netaji himself appears'. There is no need, therefore, 'to pay too much importance to them'.

In contrast to her former revolutionary colleague Satya Gupta's insistence, Roy refused to accept the story of Bose living in Shaulmari. She didn't dismiss it out of hand, but reached her conclusion only after getting the reports of Sunil Das, Pabitra Mohan Roy and Kamalakanta Ghosh. It was the network of the old and trusted revolutionaries that Leela Roy utilised as the preliminary mode of scrutiny for both Saradananda and Bhagwanji.

With information from Atul Sen being confirmed by Pabitra, she proceeded with reasonable confidence that the news was not a hoax. Her notes reveal that she expected a revelation; that the mere thought of the possibility of meeting Bose produced an emotional surge in her. Her level of confidence at this stage was enough to make her procure the items which Bhagwanji had asked for. She did not wait to verify the identity of Bhagwanji first before arranging for those expensive things. Not being able to meet Bhagwanji, therefore, must have crash landed her frenzied imaginations. Samar Guha's letter to Shrikant Sharma describing her mental state on her way back from Neemsar to Calcutta after interacting with Bhagwanji leaves little doubt that she had been convinced about Bhagwanji's identity.

Roy honoured Bhagwanji's instruction of not visiting him ever again; henceforth, all her communications with him were through letters, which were long and frequent. There was much catching up to be done. At times they were intensely personal, where she opened up to Bhagwanji the depth of her feelings for Anil Roy and recounted how she coped with his death a decade ago. She sent him a detailed note on her journey from the days of Sri Sangha to her current position in free India. Mostly, however, her letters were in the form of local intelligence reports—how the former revolutionaries responded to her missives, the moves made by the state and the central governments, the utterances and attitude of political leaders, etc.

Through all her letters, however, two features stand out. Firstly, she wrote to Bhagwanji giving him all the respect due to someone she considered her leader, but never turning it into the obsequiousness noticeable in the letters of the later generation of followers. None of her available letters indicate that she ever treated him as a superman. Although she didn't press him to account for the missing years, she wrote in detail about her disillusionment with the revolutionary movement in Bengal and its leaders. 'I feel very bad writing about all this,' she wrote to him, 'Yet, probably because I have accepted you as my Guru in my mind I could make this confession.' Roy was extremely hesitant to bring the internal conflicts among the newly formed band of followers to Bhagwanji's notice. When, as a last resort she was compelled to, she also wrote, 'We should only try to reduce your worries. I consider increasing your burden of worries a crime.'

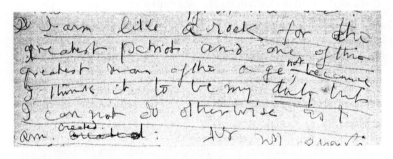

[Leela Roy's position in relation to Bhagwanji was never in doubt. 'I am like a rock for the greatest patriot and one of the greatest men of the age, not because I think it to be my duty but because I cannot do otherwise.' (Undated letter to Bhagwanji, Mukherjee Commission exhibit 147, obtained under Right to Information Act.)]

It should probably be construed as destiny's hand that just when her leader was back in her life, her worldview had started taking a different turn. Politically, things had not gone her way in independent India. The old Forward Bloc of Netaji had long broken up, with her faction—the Ruiker group—obliterated. Both she and Anil Roy lost the first elections to the Lok Sabha and to the state assembly. The Praja Socialist Party (PSP), which she subsequently joined was on a downward slope, with the party's vote share reducing by half between 1957 and 1962, and the number of seats in the state assembly going down from twenty-one to five. But over and above these setbacks in electoral politics, the overall direction of politics must have cast its shadow over her mind, frustrating her just as it deeply affected Bhagwanji. Compounding her despair must have been her physical condition. She suffered the first stroke in 1963.

It is only this state of mind that can explain her near indifferent response to the political discourse Bhagwanji subjected her to. Thus, in response to his letters outlining his plan that we have discussed in earlier chapters, she wrote back:

> Tell me what work can I accomplish for you? I won't do anymore what is known as 'work' because I don't find it appealing anymore. But as long as I live, I will continue to do what my inner self drives me to do. I won't serve any agenda set by anyone else. If that somehow serves the larger society or the country, well and good. Once you have read my letter, do let me know if my words have pained you. One thing that I don't want to do is to hurt you, demean you or to disrespect you.

The extent of detachment that pervaded her being becomes

clear from the melancholy question she posed to Bhagwanji at this time. 'You know what I want?' she asked, and went on to answer, 'I want to go to my mother. I loved her a lot.'

Bhagwanji was remarkably patient, playful and affectionate in his response to Roy's outbursts. The tone of his letters to Roy was completely different from those written to the others, including those written to Pabitra. While the latter too were affectionate, without exception they carried the mark of being written by someone elderly and with a superior personality. To Roy, Bhagwanji wrote as an equal. To Dulal Nandy, he rued: 'Only if I had a few more like her...'[18]

When Roy wrote to him that 'I don't have to follow everything you say, otherwise why do I carry a head on my shoulders?' Bhagwanji retorted in jest, 'You have made a mistake in your basic assumption. The truth is that the fairy head on those shoulders is not at all yours. It belongs to this pilgrim and you have no right on it.' If Roy wanted to ensure comfort for Bhagwanji, his letters in turn exhibit great concern about her health. 'Please believe me when I say unto thee, I am feeling tormented and miserable. If you love me even like a shadow, please, oh please, recover, and wire me your progressive recovery...' he pleaded with Roy. He strictly forbade her to send food and other items until she had fully recovered.

The affection and devotion of his old band of followers led by Leela Roy indeed brought succour to Bhagwanji, and he was grateful. Quoting the lines of Jalaluddin Rumi, he wrote to Leela

---

18 Diary of Dulal Nandy, May 1965. Mukherjee Commission Exhibit 190 (b). Obtained under Right to Information Act.

Roy: '*Shad bashay ishq khush soda-e-maa, Aye tabib-e-jumla illat haye maa*' (Hail love that brings happiness—[you] the physician of all our ills).

Roy wasn't one to always react kindly to Bhagwanji's treatment of her with kid gloves or with high emotions. 'I dislike hyperbolic language,' she would retort.

It was about four years later when Roy had gone into coma that Bhagwanji explained to a distressed Sunil Das the reason behind the show of his extreme affection for Roy. A natural respect due to which he genuinely held her in high esteem was of course one reason, but Bhagwanji told Das of a deeper reason. He knew since 1963, Bhagwanji wrote, that Roy was hurtling towards defeat in her 'struggle with time'. It was,

> to dam the inevitable that I tried my best to convey to her the seriousness of it with words wrapped in lightness, laughter and sweetness, all through limitless love and affection. I did this even with the possibility that I might be misunderstood and that my words will be interpreted wrongly because I don't care what the people of this world think or understand...I wanted to break her off from her obsession with politics, her surrounding developments and her routine work....[19]

In keeping with Roy's rational temperament, it was but natural that some of the behavioural streaks of Bhagwanji would strike her as odd—probably not in sync with the Bose she knew. For her, it wasn't easy to suddenly find him living in India without

19 Bhagwanji's response to Sunil Das's letter dated 24 December 1968. Source: Bijoy Kumar Nag.

having contacted any of his former comrades. Her letters and actions over the subsequent years leave us in no doubt that she was certain about Bhagwanji's identity, but it is equally clear that she was constantly evaluating him through his associates.

At times she expressed doubt whether it was Bhagwanji himself or his double who communicated with her. In one of her early letters, she brought the charge directly to the doorstep of Bhagwanji. 'It is only recently that I have become your disciple. Even then I do not have full faith on the guru. How can I? What will be the benefit of becoming the disciple of someone I have not been able to see or know, someone whose being a double of Netaji I cannot rule out?' Bhagwanji himself clarified to her that he had set up five doubles, who could function as him in his absence. He wrote to her that he himself was training them, filling them with all the details of his life which were known to none other or to a very few.

As a matter of practice, each one of her associates that she sent to Bhagwanji, from Kamalakanta Ghosh initially to Sunil Das and Anil Das later, doubled up as intelligence officers—reporting in minute details whatever they saw and heard when spending time with Bhagwanji. She insisted that he must allow Ghosh to examine him and Saraswati so that he could verify his identity on her behalf. Thus, if they too came to believe that Bhagwanji was Subhas Bose, the belief was a product of their own rational inquiry and not solely the result of Leela Roy's certification.

For instance, when Anil Das returned from Ayodhya in October 1964 after staying with Bhagwanji for over three months, he recounted incidents which couldn't have but strengthened his conviction:

Das reported to Leela Roy:

One day Amal Roy complained to Bhagwanji about Rajkumar that he was abusing Roy and his local helpers. Guruji became very excited (although it was possibly only a show) and started scolding Rajkumar very loudly. Later, he wanted to know our opinion about his voice. I told him that since he was talking from a closed room, his voice seemed a little distorted, but it was exactly as during the days of the INA. He told me that I should inform you that I have been able to recognise him.

Ranendra Mohan Roy, the youngest son of Pabitra had a similar experience. Just before he went with his father to Ayodhya, he had heard Netaji's speeches played over public broadcasting systems. After interacting with Bhagwanji for the first time, he told his father that it was the same voice, which Pabitra conveyed to Bhagwanji. Hearing it, Bhagwanji said that Ranendra must thank his father for bringing him to the right place. On another occasion, he asked a follower from Kolkata, 'Does my voice remind you of Shraddhananda Park?'

Anil Das, in his introductory letter to Bhagwanji that was submitted through Leela Roy had mentioned about the interview that Netaji had with him before leaving Bangkok in 1945, but omitted any mention of their first interaction at Singapore in 1943. While referring to the INA days, Bhagwanji reminded Das about their Singapore meeting. 'No one other than him [Netaji] is supposed to know about this interview,' Das wrote to Roy.

This practice of reporting continued till the time Roy went into coma. The reports did not always remain restricted to observations on Bhagwanji, but also on local developments. One such letter of

May 1967 from Sunil Das to Roy tells the other side of the story of how Durga Prasad Pandey came in contact with Bhagwanji. The situation in Basti during the past two years had become complicated due to Pandey's habit of discussing Bhagwanji everywhere in the small town, Das wrote to Roy. He would bring it up in the local bar library and even go to the house of the magistrate. As a result, a newspaper *Aaj* published a story on Bhagwanji. This led to an animated discussion in the city. Finally, the lawyer himself wrote to Bhagwanji with all the information that he had been able to collect about him. Realising the potential risk from Pandey, Bhagwanji responded to Pandey's letter but with a heavy emphasis on the religious aspects. At the same time, he asked Das to get close to Pandey in order to influence his views. Das succeeded in extracting a promise from Pandey that he would try to control the damage done. Thereafter, Pandey started speaking of Bhagwanji as a Mahatma with high levels of spiritual powers. Das then arranged Pandey's meeting with Bhagwanji.

The disturbances, however, were not over. In view of the talks going on in the town, the district magistrate and the DIG of police landed up one night in front of Bhagwanji's residence, remained in watch for some time in silence and left. A group of locals then turned up asking to meet the Mahatma in order to dispel their suspicion that he was Netaji. With great difficulty Das and Saraswati Devi managed to convince them to go back. Next was the turn of the local police who turned up for inspection. They left only after interrogating Das and Saraswati Devi for over an hour. Das reported that such incidences were now on the decline with the lawyer actively propagating the spiritual image of Bhagwanji.

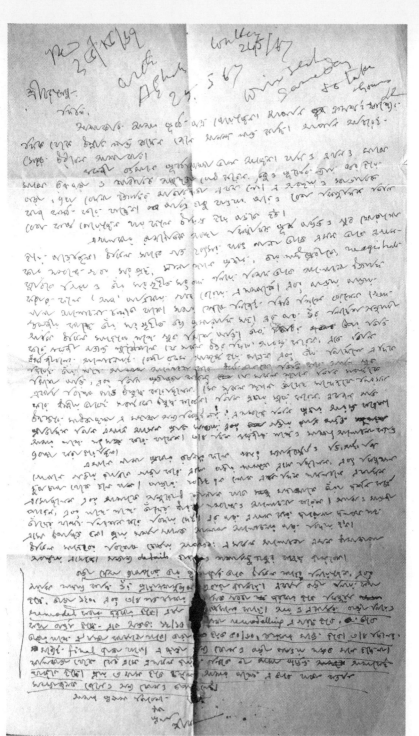

[Sunil Das's letter to Leela Roy, 24 May 1967 reporting to her how Bhagwanji, with his help, changed the attitude of Durga Prasad Pandey. Courtesy: Bijoy Nag]

We have already discussed how the others who visited Bhagwanji, such as Biswanath Roy and Apurba Chandra Ghosh came to be convinced about Bhagwanji's identity. All their letters were stored in the District Treasury along with other belongings of Bhagwanji.

Memories of a will–o'–the–wisp

The most apt description of the Netaji mystery came from Bhagwanji himself.

> I am nothing but a will-o'-the-wisp. That is the truth. But come to think of it, even a will-o'-the-wisp takes birth, has its life and work but no death. It appears, becomes visible, does its work, runs around, becomes still at some places and then vanishes only to reappear at another place. It manifests itself, but doesn't come in anyone's grip.[20]

With a wry smile on his face, he described himself as the *ignis fatuus* (foolish fire) a phenomenon that gained its fame for leading seekers astray and eventually came to signify an unattainable goal.

The will-o'-the-wisp who reappeared in India's Uttar Pradesh in the early 1950s didn't speak the words that people wanted to hear. He didn't proclaim to the people visiting him 'I am Subhas Chandra Bose.' Even to Pushpa Banerjee who identified him the moment she saw his face, he posed a mischievous counter-question: 'Look carefully, am I Subhas Chandra Bose?' Most people we met told us that he never referred to Subhas Bose in the first person. For him Bose was almost invariably 'Mr So and So',

---

20   Charanik, *Oi Mahamanaba Ase*, Jayasree Prakashan, 2010, pp 261-262

or 'your Netaji', or 'this body' or simply 'S'. That was the past. In the present, he was 'the dead ghost' or the *pathik faquir* or 'the wayfarer of the horizon'.

Yet, during the many sessions with his followers and in his many letters, the past would pop up sometimes in the form of an anecdote and at other times indirectly, in the context of a thread of discussion. We saw how Gandhi, Nehru, C R Das and officers of the INA and Azad Hind government featured in his talks and letters.

Once while talking of his hardships, especially the pangs of hunger that he had to withstand, he reminisced in front of Dulal Nandy about the days gone by. When hungry, 'I used to become restless and my eyes used to become big and red—then only *Ma Janani* [his mother] and *Mejo Boudi* [his sister-in -law] used to understand and say—"Subi[21] is hungry". *Ma Janani* used to tease, "Is this how you will stay in jail?"' Explaining his preference for bread, he would say, 'I love toast. Gandhiji used to arrange for toast and butter when I used to go and meet him.' Talking of food, he also told Bijoy Nag, '*Begun bhaja (*fried aubergine) was a favourite in my previous life. I like to eat *karela* (bitter gourd).'

Much consternation was created in the press recently when photos of Janakinath Bose and Prabhabati were found among the belongings of Bhagwanji. Pabitra Mohan Roy's diary of December 1968 shows that it was the mysterious monk who not only asked for the photographs but specified which ones to bring to him. 'There are photographs of mother and father in the *Dissentient Report*—frame them and send,' he told Pabitra.[22]

---

21 Subhas Bose was called 'Subi' by the elders in the family.
22 Diary of Pabitra Mohan Roy, November 1968.

At a particular candid moment, Bhagwanji reminisced about how he entered the revolutionary circles, and explained the true story behind the so-called 'Oaten incident' of Subhas Bose's life.[23] Bhagwanji more than once indicated that he did not assault Professor Oaten—'The incident was over in the time between my entering the library and coming out.' He said he was requested by the mother of one of his classmates who led the assault to protect him.

> On hearing it my first reaction was surprise. I was childish—call it good or bad, there was an ideal. Once I shut my mouth upon hearing the request, nobody could ever get a word out. The most respected Sir Ashutosh tried his best so that I give out something. But in my immature mind the line playing repeatedly was 'save my son.' Therefore, once silent, forever silent.[24]

'The seed of this side [secret revolutionary activities] was sowed because of my visits to Daulatpur...*Mastar Moshai*[25] took

---

23   In January 1916, while Subhas was studying in the library of the Presidency College, he came to know that some students of his batch were manhandled by Professor Oaten while walking along the corridor adjoining his classroom. After a temporary patch-up, Oaten had manhandled another student and as a consequence, some students decided to take action by themselves instead of depending on the college authorities, a process that they had found lacking in addressing their grievance. As Subhas described later in *An Indian Pilgrim*, Professor Oaten was therefore 'subjected to the argument of force and in the process was beaten black and blue'. Being the leader of the students' agitation, Subhas was naturally the primary suspect. The college was closed down by the Bengal Government, and an inquiry committee set up, headed by Ashutosh Mukherjee, former Vice chancellor of the Calcutta University. The Principal of the college summoned Subhas and 'said—or rather snarled—in unforgettable words, 'Bose, you are the most troublesome man in the College. I suspend you.' Subhas was eventually rusticated from the college. He took the responsibility of the assault as a leader of the students but maintained a studied silence on whether he himself had assaulted Oaten.

24   Charanik, *Oi Mahamanaba Ase*, Jayasree Prakashan, p 213.

25   Beni Madhab Das, the teacher of Subhas Bose.

me there.' This, he indicated happened while he was a student at the Presidency College.

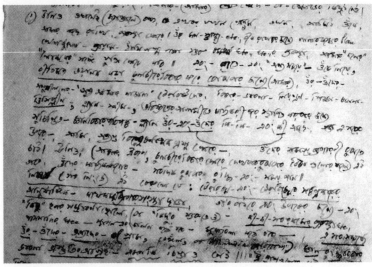

[*Bhagwanji's letter to Pabitra Mohan Roy, 3 August 1970*]

He had arranged '*shraddheya* Chakravarty *moshai*' (Trailokya Nath Chakravarty) to stay near him in Mandalay Jail for a specific purpose, Bhagwanji wrote to Pabitra on 3 August 1970, remembering 'Maharaj' Chakravarty who breathed his last a day before, while visiting India. He wanted to understand the plans and programmes of the terrorist revolutionary organisations like Anushilan Samiti and the thoughts of known and unknown revolutionaries who had taken the path of violence. After threadbare analysis of their politics, Bhagwanji wrote, it emerged that these organisations had not thought of dealing with post-revolutionary situations and thus had no preparation for such an eventuality. The prolonged discussions in Mandalay helped 'Maharaj' realise this lacuna.

At times his disappointment with the former freedom fighters would appear in his writing. 'Today almost 98% of those workers of the Swadeshi movement—whose minds were nurtured in the environment of great ideal of self-sacrifice—have changed. They are now busy exploiting old stories of their own heroics to serve their self-interest,' Bhagwanji lamented in a letter to Pabitra.

[*Bhagwanji's letter to Pabitra Mohan Roy, 8 May 1981*]

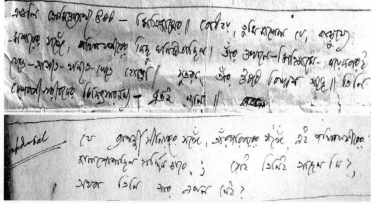

[*In his letter to Pabitra Mohan Roy (9 July 1973) Bhagwanji mentioned that he knew the Banerjis of Mihijam closely. In a subsequent letter (25 August 1973) he asked if the 'senior Dr Banerji' (Dr Pareshnath Banerji) was still alive*]

The floods of 1971 in Maldah brought back memories of bygone years. 'Bengal এর প্রলয়ঙ্করী-সর্বনাশী বন্যার বিবরণ তোমার পাঠানো আনন্দবাজারে পড়ে, মর্মব্যথায় বুকটা মুচড়ে উঠল (My heart wrung out in pain on reading the description of the devastating flood in Bengal in Anandabazar [Patrika] sent by you)' Bhagwanji wrote to Pabitra on 1 September.

I have worked with whatever little I had in a huge area in Bengal under extremely frightful flood. Therefore, I can say that I know something of it. I am pained by the plight of Maldah. I used to love that district. *Gombhira* songs were my favourite. (Translated from Bengali)

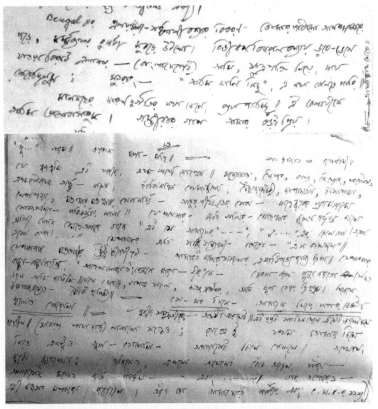

[Bhagwanji's letter to Pabitra Mohan Roy, 1 September 1971]

When during the discussion of his shifting from Basti to Odisha was going on, he ruled out Bhubaneshwar due to its climate but more importantly its proximity to Cuttack. Writing to Pabitra, he went into a reverie of his childhood days. People would easily identify him there, he wrote. Bhubaneshwar was the capital of the state and Bhagwanji was apprehensive of the risk of being identified by the person under whose chief ministership the city had become the capital (Cuttack being the earlier capital)—Harekrushna Mahatab. Mahtab was not only the CM of the state for multiple times, but was also a Congressman inducted into the party's Central Working Committee (CWC) by Subhas Chandra Bose in 1938.

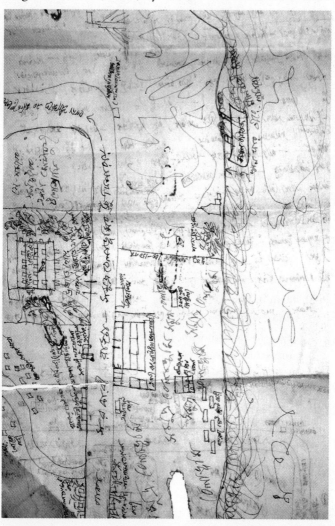

Hence, Bhagwanji preferred Puri over Bhubaneshwar. To help Pabitra navigate through the city, he drew by hand for him a map (see previous page) of the city near the sea beach as he remembered from his childhood.

Reconstructing the personality

This and the previous chapters have placed sufficient material with us that can help in recreating a character sketch of the person addressed differently by different people—Bhagwan, Bhagwanji, Guruji, Pardewala Baba, Sri Swami, Sat Gurudev, etc. Due to the fragmentary nature of information, this sketch will undoubtedly be incomplete, but there are enough pieces in the puzzle, when fitted together, to show us what we are looking at.

Thus, based on material evidence and witness accounts, we are reasonably certain that we are looking at a man, who:

- Repeatedly said that he was dead for the society at large
- Was living in the garb of a *yogi/sanyasi* but under that cover was highly political
- Had religious and classical literature at his fingertips
- Was highly proficient in Bengali and English and reasonably fluent in Hindi
- Didn't want his true identity to be revealed to the people at large. Interacted with people selected through a screening process and allowed only a handful of persons to see his face.
- In matters of being cautious that his correspondence wasn't intercepted or ensuring that it didn't give out his identity, went to the extent of being paranoid
- Had a personality that awed even the highly placed officials who had a chance to interact with him, let alone the ordinary followers
- Was intermittently in contact with high profile personalities

- Although in touch with a number of followers, didn't trust anyone exclusively with his safety and security, except probably Pabitra Mohan Roy
- Followed national and international political developments with keen interest and had extraordinary insights about the present and of the shape of things to come
- Was extremely well-versed in the discourse of military affairs
- Demonstrated insider's information of several events such as cabinet affairs, India's wars and activities of top politicians. Claimed personal involvement in the wars of 1962, 1965 and 1971 and occasionally seemed to have the uncanny knack of predicting developments.
- Was highly erudite in history, both ancient and modern, Indian and global
- Claimed to have travelled across continents. His hand-drawn maps show a very high degree of familiarity with Central, South and Southeast Asia. At the same time he could draw a more or less accurate map of Puri (part of the city that was close to the sea beach) from childhood memory.
- Was bitterly critical of Nehru and ambiguous towards Gandhi. Had high regard for Abul Kalam Azad and Khan Abdul Gaffar Khan.
- Was in the habit of collecting photographs, books, newspaper and periodical articles, and archival materials related to Subhas Chandra Bose.
- Referred to Sarat Chandra Bose as *Mejda* and Suresh Chandra Bose as *Parampujajiya Sejda*. Talked about other personal matters such as the reality behind the 'Oaten incident' or how 'Subi' would behave when hungry.
- Occasionally recounted stories of Subhas Chandra Bose's life in the first person but always referred to himself as the 'dead ghost', 'your S' or 'this body', 'so and so' and in letters simply as '——'
- In the considered view of old revolutionaries who were very close to Subhas Chandra Bose, he was none other than Bose.

Or, was he an impostor?

This composite depiction, in conjunction with the professional opinion of top handwriting experts, points quite forcefully towards the identity of the mysterious monk. Yet, before we reach the final conclusion, it is imperative that we assess the alternative possibilities that have been suggested by a divergent set of people. At the same time, we need to stress the fact that these alternative views have been formed without having access to even a minute fraction of the information presented here, and cannot be said to be anything more than uninformed belief.

The main thrust of most of these theories is that Bhagwanji was an impostor; 'someone' posturing as Subhas Chandra Bose. The divergence in these theories emerges in the identification of that 'someone', the most prominent among these number about five. These hypotheses propose that Bhagwanji, in reality, was:

- One Krishna Dutt Upadhyay, a murderer in hiding
- An Anand Margi
- A CIA agent
- A Subhas Bose impostor, set up by the Intelligence Bureau
- A diehard Subhas Bose follower

All these hypotheses are based on local rumours mixed with scraps of publicly available information and the fertile imagination of their proponents. At times, the political orientation of the proponent is also thrown in for good measure. None of these hypotheses, predictably, stands the most basic scrutiny in light of the information that we have presented in this book. Rather, they demonstrate how myths are created and propagated by mass media in the name of journalism and how statements of senior politicians made without any semblance of factual basis gain credence among his followers only to be amplified as *the* truth.

A murderer on the loose

The claim that Bhagwanji was actually one Krishna Dutt Upadhyay was floated by the Hindi newspaper *Janmorcha* on 3 November 1985. The story was reconstructed and expanded thirty years later in the online news portal *Scroll.in* by Dhirendra K Jha, a political journalist.

Janmorcha was founded by veteran journalist Sheetla Singh who continues to be in charge at age 85. Singh is a person of repute in the Faizabad area and one of the most well-known journalists from UP. [26] The newspaper's frontpage story ran with the headline 'Close associates of Netaji say that he was not Netaji.'

The framework created and conclusions drawn by Jha in four articles written in 2015 and 2016 actually serve better to expose the absurdity of this hypothesis, its ideological underpinning that forces the journalist to close his eyes to obvious loopholes in his theory and the shoddiness of what he calls an 'investigation'.

---

26 In 2012, following a complaint by Teesta Setalvad about a riot in Faizabad, Singh, then a member of the Press Council of India, was tasked by PCI chairman and former Supreme Court judge Markandey Katju to head an inquiry. Previously, Singh had come into prominence for his reporting and insights into the demolition of Babri mosque in Ayodhya in 1992 over which he was very critical of the role played by the Sangh Parivar. He is reported to have held 'Prime Minister Narasimha Rao a sinner of Masjid's demolition and building of make-shift temple', according to *The Milli Gazette*, which describes itself as the 'Indian Muslims' Leading Newspaper'. The way Singh 'has protected his pen for the past 50 years (from being sullied), even the soldiers posted at borders cannot defend our frontiers' opined the newspaper. Manzar Mehdi Faizabadi, Are we to be governed by Law or faith?: Sheetla, *The Milli Gazette*, 16-31 December 2009.

As narrated previously, in the wake of Bhagwanji's death on 16 September 1985, several local newspapers, especially *Naye Log* and *Janmorcha*, investigated the matter. *Naye Log*, then edited by Ashok Tandon, reported in October that the mostly unseen holy man could have been Subhas Bose.

Jha's allegation, however, is that Ashok Tandon ran a campaign 'based on either hearsay or unsubstantiated claims', as opposed to reporting, to establish that Gumnami Baba was Netaji. Then he moves on to paint the developments as a local newspaper rivalry. 'The heat generated by *Naye Log* forced its rival *Janmorcha* to investigate the case hyped up by its rival,' according to Jha. The journalist creates the narrative that a team led by Sheetla Singh visited Kolkata and interviewed Pabitra Mohan Roy. In his 'interview to *Janmorcha*' Roy stated categorically, 'I can say with certainty that he was not Netaji Subhash (sic) Chandra Bose.' Justice Mukherjee Commission's report was a validation of what Roy had told *Janmorcha*. Singh told Jha that 'the way this campaign was carried out gave the impression that financial benefits were motivating this newspaper's attempts to gain cheap popularity'.

Jha, thereafter, takes up the widespread use of a computer-generated image of Gumnami Baba which was first published by the investigation done by *Hindustantimes.com*, by other media houses and by Shakti Singh, without giving the proper source reference and the context. Jha alleges that the image and its modifications have been 'used as a proof that a mysterious sadhu was actually Netaji'. Subtly, Jha attempts to implicate the BJP and the RSS, through Shakti Singh (who has never concealed his association with BJP), for propagating a conspiracy theory. Soon, he drops all pretence and brings the accusation directly to the doorstep of the party. When the UP government under Akhilesh Yadav started acting on an order of the Allahabad High Court to preserve the belongings of Gumnami Baba, Jha cited the opinion of political observers (without naming any) claiming that the move was 'an attempt by the Samajwadi Party (sic) to score points over the Bharatiya Janata Party. So far, it is the BJP that has been at the forefront of the campaign to establish that the Faizabad sadhu was actually Bose'. His key concern was: 'Displaying Gumnami Baba's belongings in a museum would go a long way to establishing in the public imagination the still-dubious idea that he was actually Bose.' Thus, in Jha's analysis, if identification of Gumnami Baba with Netaji started as a move to gain cheap popularity by one newspaper, its propagation was taken up by the BJP and the RSS, and the Samajwadi Party government entered the fray to steal the wind from the Hindutva sail.

Jha's four-part series culminates with the presentation of 'facts' that 'hint at' Gumnami Baba being Krishna Dutta Upadhyay or Kaptan Baba. To summarise this storyline: The Lucknow edition of Hindi daily *Amrit Prabhat* reported on 8 November 1985 that the police were investigating whether the man of mystery was Upadhyay in hiding. Earlier, *Janmorcha* received an anonymous letter on 2 November claiming that it was indeed Upadhyay who had fled Ayodhya after committing a murder and after sometime started living in Basti. The newspaper published the contents of the letter the next day. According to Jha, the fact that Gumnami Baba also lived in Basti is a significant clue. Indu Kumar Pande, the then district magistrate of Faizabad told Jha that there were rumours that Gumnami Baba 'had killed somebody and was in hiding'. However, the investigation into Gumnami Baba's identity was closed after the Allahabad High Court ordered preservation of Baba's belongings, Pande told Jha. 'There is one more fact that hints at Gumnami Baba and Upadhyay being the same person,' wrote Jha while presenting the most significant finding of his investigation. In his autobiography, the brother of the murdered man claimed that one of the closest aides of Upadhyay was Seth Ishwardas Beni Prasad. Now Jha was told by Dr R P Mishra's wife that her husband used to meet Prasad often at Varanasi at the behest of Gumnami Baba.

In our assessment, Jha's 'investigation' is erected on arguments that are hopelessly full of loopholes, lack of information, an unwillingness to look at the available evidence and a desire to score a political point against the Sangh Parivar.

Apart from the anonymous letter claiming Gumnami Baba to be Upadhyay, *Janmorcha's* case against *Naye Log* rests completely on the statement of Pabitra Mohan Roy. It is pertinent to note that the final police report, whose copy we possess, reads different from what *Janmorcha* reported. The police report said that 'a police party was sent to Calcutta to talk to Dr Pabitra Mohan Roy and other associates of "Netaji" but *none of them were able to give any information about this matter and, in fact, they appeared to be reticent about providing any information to the police'*. (Emphasis by authors). What it means is that Roy dodged the cops and Sheetla Singh (as we have already shown in an earlier chapter, deliberately suppressed the truth).

Sheetla Singh's deduction that Bhagwanji was not Subhas Bose because Pabitra said so stands flipped on its head in view of the mass of evidence presented in this book. Pabitra's son Ranendra and his US-based granddaughter Indrani (who grew up hearing about Netaji from her *Dadai*) affirm that position to us. 'My father was Netaji's solider,' is how soft-spoken Ranendra introduced his father to us at his residence in Kolkata. Bhagwanji even wrote to Pabitra's wife Renu, who shared her husband's belief regarding him. Ranendra himself visited Bhagwanji along with his father and elder brother (now ailing, but obviously on the same page). 'Netaji' was the pivot around which Pabitra's world revolved, especially from 1962 when he met Bhagwanji. As Indrani told Anuj Dhar in Canton, Michigan, in the privacy of his home in Calcutta, her grandfather dropped all guards in his final years. He didn't even address Bhagwanji as 'Bhagwanji'. It was straight and simple 'Netaji'. Pabitra passed away in 1993, holding the same belief. Now that we know what Pabitra really thought, we wonder if Singh (and those who base their arguments on his piece) would now come forward to reverse his earlier conclusion.

As far as the reference to Krishna Dutt Upadhya is concerned, it was based solely on a letter from an unnamed *Janmorcha* reader. Incredibly, this claim was turned into a page one story by Sheetla Singh. *Janmorcha* provided no proper evidence in support of this narrative. It is surprising that Jha, who downplayed Ashok Tandon's meticulous investigation on the charge of hearsay and unsubstantiated claims would give so much importance to a cock and bull story told by an anonymous person. Or for that matter, what does it tell about a newspaper editor who chooses to place such a letter prominently on the front page of his newspaper?

It raises the justifiable doubt whether *Janmorcha* was desperate to discredit *Naye Log* by any means when its competitor broke a sensational story. Presenting the interrogation of Pabitra by a police investigator as an interview to the newspaper strengthens this possibility. It is important to remember, as a matter of journalistic ethics, that when on 18 January 1986, the *Northern India Patrika* published the transcript of the same interrogation, which was recorded, the reporters did not present it as an interview given to them.

According to this claim, Upadhyay had shot dead a rival priest Brahmadev Shastri in 1958 in Ayodhya. The motive for the murder was financial fraud and tussle for superiority. Upadhyay tried to mislead cops with a fake story of his suicide but was unable to do so. The police kept on his trail, due to which he turned into a fugitive. At first he escaped to Nepal and then returned and lived in many places, including Rishikesh. The paper further claimed that Upadhyay was variously known as Bengali Baba and Kaptan Baba. He was tall, well-built, had an impressive personality with the mannerisms of an army veteran, which, in the estimate of the paper matched with the accounts about Bhagwanji. Furthermore, Upadhyay was claimed to have been in contact with influential people of the areas he lived in. Since his sister lived in Calcutta, he would often receive visitors who brought him Bengali clothes, sweets, etc. According to *Janmorcha*, he also lived in Basti. And when he felt unsafe there, his lawyer brought him to Ayodhya. There is nothing but silence on what happened to Kaptan Baba or Upadhyay or whoever he was, in contrast to the detailed accounts available about Bhagwanji until 16 September 1985.

Bhagwanji indeed lived in Basti. He subsequently came to Ayodhya, using the services of a local disciple. A lawyer by profession, Durga Prasad Pandey never offered any legal services to Bhagwanji with regard to any murder case. Pandey was, unlike the unflattering depiction he received in *Janmorcha*, an honourable man who identified Bhagwanji as Subhas Bose, whom he had seen in 1939. He sincerely tendered evidence before the Mukherjee Commission of Inquiry and was rated a credible witness by Justice Mukherjee in his report. We leave it to the discretion of the readers to either rely on Durga Prasad's sworn statement before a commission of inquiry, or put their money on what was published in *Janmorcha*, and which has since then been rehashed and published in *Scroll.in* by Jha.

Three seemingly incriminating details in support of the Krishna Dutt Upadhya theory were supplied by Dhirendra K Jha in the course of his *Scroll.in* investigation. It is possible that Sheetla Singh furnished these bits either in part or full to Jha. Be that as it may, *Scroll.in* referred to a book written by Brahmadev Shastri's brother, Suryanarayan Mishra. The book provided a description of the murder by Krishna Dutt Upadhyay. Jha then picked up *Janmorcha*'s claim that 'Upadhyaya fled to Nepal following the killing incident. After some time, he started living in Basti.' Second, Indu Kumar Pandey, who was District Magistrate of Faizabad in 1985-86, told Jha that there was a rumour that he (Gumnami Baba) had killed somebody and was in hiding but the investigation was closed after the Allahabad High Court took over the matter following a plea by Netaji's niece (Lalita Bose) seeking preservation of Gumnami Baba's possessions. Third, according to Suryanarayan's book, Upadhyay had a wealthy friend—Seth Ishwardas Beni Prasad, who was a Calcutta-based businessman. 'Later, Prasad emerged as a prominent well-wisher of Gumnami Baba and was in constant touch with him, a fact confirmed by Laxmi Mishra, the wife of Dr R P Mishra,' wrote Jha.

How logical is Jha's attempt to link Bhagwanji with Upadhyay on the basis of a claimed connection with Seth Ishwardas Beni Prasad? Assuming that the Seth was a friend of Upadhyay and also had contact with Bhagwanji in no way proves that Bhagwanji and Upadhyay were one and the same. If 'A' is friends with 'B' and 'B' is friendly with 'C', it cannot be construed to mean that 'A' and 'C' are the same. Secondly, not one person who knew Bhagwanji ever identified him as Upadhyay. Thirdly, among the thousands of pages of records that we have seen, there is not a single mention of Prasad anywhere. Certainly, a prominent well-wisher would find a mention somewhere? Nor do the living followers of Bhagwanji in Kolkata, who shared his secrets, remember ever hearing this name. Fourthly, the source of information on Bhagwanji's alleged connection with Prasad is curious. Dr R P Mishra and his family, under whose care Bhagwanji spent the last few years in Faizabad have consistently maintained a stony silence in public about the identity of Bhagwanji. Dr Mishra went to the extent of telling the Mukherjee Commission in August 2001 that 'people confused themselves the identity of Gumnami Baba with Netaji'.

But is that the whole truth? Multiple interactions with the Mishra family have convinced us that what they say for public consumption and what they hold secret within their hearts are polar opposites. A little bit of true investigation would have informed Jha of this. It is significant that although Jha quoted Mrs Mishra, he remained silent on her take on the identity of Bhagwanji. Did she tell him nothing? Or did she tell him that Bhagwanji was Kaptan Baba? We wouldn't know. What we know is what she told us. Among many other things that she told us, citing two would suffice. First, that Bhagwanji told her about his visit to Teen Murti Bhawan when Nehru's dead body was laid for paying the last respects, because 'I always considered him as my elder brother.' Mrs Mishra never saw Bhagwanji's face, but her daughter accidentally did. Once, when she returned home after meeting Bhagwanji she exclaimed on seeing a photograph, 'This is the same man that I just met.' The photo was of Netaji, displayed on the occasion of 23 January. The daughter explained to her mother that the curtain between her and Bhagwanji had lifted due to strong wind for a few moments and she caught a glimpse of him before lowering her eyes. It is extremely difficult to bring down the wall of secrecy that the Mishras have built, but for once they willingly stepped out when we visited the family with Jayanti Rakshit and her sister—grandnieces of Netaji. There was no doubt about who they knew Bhagwanji to be. Till date, they have held on to Bhagwanji's promise that he would return. Devotion such as this for a Kaptan Baba? Hardly sounds like it.

Indu Kumar Pandey, who retired as the Chief Secretary of Uttarakhand, indeed handled the matter as the District Magistrate (DM) of Faizabad in 1985-86. However, the quote attributed to him by Jha that 'investigation was closed after the Allahabad High Court took over the matter' doesn't bear scrutiny. The files kept at the DM's office in Faizabad reveal that the local inquiry into the identity of Bhagwanji was already over when the Allahabad High Court issued an interim order on 10 February 1986 to secure Bhagwanji's belongings.

Nowhere in the bulky files, which also contain Indu Kumar Pandey's signed notes, etc. does one find any evidence to support the 'rumour that Gumnami Baba had killed somebody and was in hiding'. If Bhagwanji was suspected to be some fugitive murderer, the authorities would have splashed this everywhere given their intent to vociferously dismiss the claim that he was Netaji. But at no point in time did the DM's office offer any evidence to back this line. We don't even see a single reference to Upadhyay in the official papers accessed by us. No one uttered a word about him publicly. The state government never spoke along these lines either in the state assembly, where lengthy discussions took place in February 1986 and in March 2013, or before the Allahabad High Court as the case dragged on for years. The detailed counter-affidavit filed by the state government in 1999 in response to Lalita Bose's 1986 petition has no reference to Upadhyay at all. All it says is that the man couldn't have been Netaji because the police inquiry found no such evidence. Before the Allahabad High Court, all that the state government did was to merely deny that Gumnami Baba was Netaji. The state government counsel merely opposed the need for preserving Bhagwanji's belongings and carrying out a proper inquiry about his identity. At no point in time was a reference to Krishna Dutt Upadhyay or someone else made.

All papers on record in the DM office files, including those handled by Indu Kumar Pandey, discuss the claims and counterclaims whether or not Bhagwanji was Netaji. Summarising the outcome of the official inquiry, Pandey commented on 2 March 1986 that 'State Government has been informed of the inquiry conducted by the police in this matter and further instructions of the Govt are awaited.' The inquiry stopped because the state government did not give any further instructions. It had nothing to do with the court taking over the matter, as Jha's investigation suggests. The court never directed the administration to stop inquiring into the matter. In fact, Lalita Bose in her PIL before the Allahabad High Court charged Indu Kumar Pandey of 'sitting tight over the matter in a very callous manner'.

in fact, "Neta Ji". None of them claimed to have seen the fact of this person while he was alive. A police party was sent to Calcutta to talk to Dr. Pavitra Mohan Roy and other accociates of "Neta Ji" but none of them were able to given anyt information about this matter and, in fact, they appeared to be reticent about providing any information to the police.

State Govt. has been informed of the enquiry conducted by the police in this matter and further instructions of the Govt. are awaited. In the meantime the premises are sealed and under police guard.

District Magistrate
Faizabad.

[DM of Faizabad sums up the case on 2 March 1986]

Indu Kumar Pandey deserves more attention as he is a crucial character in the events of 1985-86. He can throw valuable light on the shoddy handling of the Gumnami Baba identity controversy by the UP government. In Chapter 1 of this book (A sleepy town shoots into fame) we have stated that in February 1986, the state Legislative Assembly discussed this matter. At the end, the UP government announced that an inquiry had revealed that Bhagwanji was not Subhas Bose, and that was all. The lawmakers wanted to see the inquiry report, but the government refused. Here's why. The inquiry of the state police was an eyewash, prompted as it was by a premeditated approach of the authorities. But much as they wanted to disprove the Netaji link, the cops could not do it fully. Nor could they tell, forget proving, who Bhagwanji really was, if not Bose. Sheetla Singh and Dhirendra K Jha would be dismayed to find that the final report had no mention of Upadhyay. It ran into just three pages, with another one carrying one concluding sentence, drawn by the then SSP of Faizabad. The report was based on the inputs of some junior cops who questioned a few Bhagwanji followers, seeking from them 'any solid evidence to suggest that this person was, in fact, Netaji'. Some of those questioned did not know much, others were afraid to say anything and some others were evasive—like Pabitra Mohan Roy. According to the report, when the cops scoured through Bhagwanji's room in September 1985,

> a large number of belongings and literature associated with the 'Indian National Army' in general and Sri Subhas Chandra Bose in particular came to light. There were a large number of family photographs, reports of enquiry commission related to the death of 'Neta Ji', etc. It also transpired that a special ceremony used to be held in the room of 'Bhagwanji' on every 23rd January, which incidentally is the birthday of Sri Subhas Chandra Bose and on this date no person from Faizabad was allowed to visit him. But some persons from Calcutta used to come and stay with him for that day.

Not intrigued by all this, the SSP concluded that 'on inquiry it could not be ascertained as to who was the deceased man', which in plain English means that the police found no clear clue about Bhagwanji's identity. On this basis, the state government falsely gave out that the police inquiry had proven that Bhagwanji was not Bose—when all it had done was to prove nothing.

If the police inquiry led to an inconclusive report, other top police officers of Uttar Pradesh have been more forthcoming. For instance, S K Dutta, the former Director of CBI who was posted in Lucknow in 1985, confided to Dhar that the rumours of 'Netaji being alive and in Uttar Pradesh' were there even before September 1985 and known to many officers. Dutta is no more today but he did write several articles attempting to link Netaji with Gumnami Baba in the Bangla daily *Dainik Statesman,* whose translated versions can be found in a declassified Central government file. Another IPS officer who has opened up on the issue is Dr Vikram Singh. A former DGP of UP police from 2007-09, Dr Singh is currently the Pro Chancellor of Noida University and a well-known current affairs commentator on top TV channels. According to *Limca Book of Records* (2014), Singh is the most decorated IPS officer in the country. In the course of his lecture at IIT Kanpur on 23 January 2014, Singh opined that he found sufficient evidence to link Bhagwanji to Subhas Bose. 'Gumnami Baba was Netaji, let me tell you as a police officer!' he said. 'What more circumstantial evidence do you require to show that Gumnami Baba was Subhas Chandra Bose?' he asked.[27]

---

27   Dr Vikram Singh on Netaji Subhas Chandra Bose at IIT Kanpur, https://www.youtube.com/watch?v=AwMk7RCwRBk.

What both Sheetla Singh and Jha missed out in their excitement of probably having cracked the mystery is the most crucial piece of evidence, which on its own is enough to demolish the Upadhyay story. Bhagwanji's known antecedents in India go back to the early 1950s with an unbroken narrative available up to 1985. Upadhyay became a fugitive in 1958.

Against this backdrop must be discussed the curious case of the Central government's near silence on the Bhagwanji matter. This is not understandable when we know that New Delhi lost no time in repudiating the Shaulmari sadhu-Netaji link soon after it came to the fore in the early 1960s. Some other similar claims were dismissed in internal papers. However, right from the start, the Government sidestepped the Bhagwanji matter, refraining from giving a clear answer. Questions raised about Bhagwanji in Parliament have not elicited straightforward answers. In fact, they have yielded nothing at all. The first time the matter was raised was on 22 March 1988. Ratnakar Pandey, described by *India Today* as a 'loudmouth MP and ostensible protector of the Nehru–Gandhi legacy'[28] asked the following questions in the Rajya Sabha about 'Gumnam Baba' (a variant of Gumnami Baba) from the Ministry of Home Affairs:

(A) Whether Gumnam Baba's identiy has been ascertained?
(B) If yes, how many belongings related to Netaji Subhas Chandra Bose have been located at his residence? (C) What

---

28   'For MP Ratnakar Pandey, drafting Sonia into Indian politics is no longer an issue,' *India Today*, 15 February 1992, https://www.indiatoday.in/magazine/indiascope/story/19920215-for-mp-ratnakar-pandey-drafting-sonia-into-indian-politics-is-no-longer-an-issue-765826-2013-06-20.

is the outcome of inquiries carried out? (D) What sort of inquiries have been carried out to probe the possibility that Gumnam Baba was a CIA agent? (E) What was the source of income of the baba?

In response, then Deputy Home Minister, the tough-talking, clear-headed, Harvard-educated P Chidambaram made this statement: 'The information is being collected and will be placed before the House.'

That no such information was subsequently tabled in the House is established by the fact that in March 1997, in response to a similar question in the Lok Sabha, the same response was repeated.

We have also not come across anything concerning these two questions in any of the files declassified by the Modi government. This is when there are several papers and even files among the declassified lot dealing with all sorts of Parliamentary questions raised at different points in time from the 1950s onwards concerning the Bose mystery issue. That some paperwork about the question raised by Ratnakar Pandey must have been created in New Delhi is evident from a perusal of the Faizabad DM's office file, where clear references to it appear. Interestingly, as early as 3 December 1985, the Home Department in Lucknow directed the DM to send 'a detailed report in the matter in triplicate at once for transmission to Government of India'. Indu Kumar Pandey is seen directing the SSP, Faizabad, to comply with the Home Department's order. There was no chance of the SSP not complying with the DM, and DM not responding to Lucknow, and Lucknow to New Delhi in turn. But this is where the paper trail surprisingly ends in this instance too.

As per a declassified file, following an appeal to Prime Minister I K Gujral by Shakti Singh, the Home Ministry, in 1997, asked the UP Home Department to have 'this matter investigated' and inform both MHA as well as the Prime Minister's Office. The Home Department was told to treat this as an 'urgent matter'. The UP government must have responded but there is nothing more in the declassified files. So, a clear pattern emerges.

The only deduction we can therefore make is that the relevant records are either being withheld or were destroyed at some point in time as happened to some other sensitive files related to the Bose mystery. It is not possible that with so much going for it, the Bhagwanji matter should not have been discussed in official papers.

In conclusion, the onus of proving that Gumnami Baba was Krishna Dutt Upadhya is on Sheetla Singh, and *Scroll.in*'s Jha. Failure to do so could open them, especially Singh, to a charge that they circulated a patently absurd theory possibly at the behest of those who did not want the Bhagwanji riddle to be disentangled.

The last piece of Jha's investigation that fails to stand up to scrutiny is his allegation that the people behind spreading the Bhagwanji-Netaji rumours were aligned to the BJP-RSS. He picked on Shakti Singh, a known BJP leader, but made no reference to the seminal *Northern India Patrika* inquiry by Sayed Kauser Hussain, Nirmal Nibedon (whose father was the bishop of Assam) and V N Arora (having no affiliation to any political party like Ashok Tandon); the PIL filed by Lalita Bose (then in Congress party), Mohammed Haleem (associated with Raj Narain) and Vishwa Bandhav Tewari. Neither was there any allusion to the fact that the 1986 order for securing Bhagwanji's belongings was given by Justice Saiyed Saghir Ahmad (a would-be Supreme Court judge) and Justice G B Singh. Anuj Dhar's 2002 inquiry under the aegis of *Hindustan Times*, which obviously has nothing to do with the Sangh Parivar, was ignored too. Probably even the BJP or the RSS are unaware of having so many secret activists posing as journalists and judges. When the Mukherjee Commission held its sitting in Faizabad that year, elderly Hussain and his colleague V N Arora, appeared to give evidence. Hussain, an affable unassuming old man, quietly made his submissions in an objective manner and left the venue. Unfortunately, he is no more now to see that the matter he prevented from being stifled in the 1980s in national interest has acquired international proportions.

Bhagwanji was an Anand Margi

The Anand Marg connection was invented by one Rakesh Kumar under the aegis of *Nav Bharat Times* which ran six 'investigative' articles on the Bhagwanji controversy in 1985-86. In the last instalment on 7 January 1986, Kumar, having rejected outright the view that Gumnami Baba was Netaji, somehow reached the conclusion that he was 'either some spy or some blind Anand Margi follower of Netaji'.

The arguments presented by Kumar in favour of his conclusion are preposterous. Any critical assessment would unnecessarily lengthen this chapter. After the Bhagwanji matter was stifled in 1986, Kumar has not been heard of again. He made no attempt to make his case which, if true, would have shot him into national spotlight, either before the Allahabad High Court or Mukherjee

Commission, and even local authorities. If only the Sahai Commission had located him, Kumar could have been asked to furnish proper details, such as the source of his information, the name of Anand Margi or spy he had in mind when he indulged in such absurdity in the name of journalism.

Most importantly, little did Kumar know that Bhagwanji's dislike for this religious organisation was recorded by his followers in their journals over a decade earlier.

Bhagwanji was a CIA agent

In a 'Secret' letter to Faizabad Superintendent of Police in February 1979, an Ayodhya-based journalist summed up rumours prevalent at that time that Gumnami Baba was either 'a CIA agent' or Subhas Chandra Bose. The importance of this letter lies in the fact that it was brought on record when court proceedings started in 1986. The letter was also sent to Indu Kumar Pandey and consequently appears in the District Magistrate's file concerning the controversy.

That journalist, Virendra Mishra, still lives in Ayodhya. In a meeting with the authors in 2014, Mishra (who in later years came around to backing the Netaji link) threw light on his letter and the reaction of the SP, Gyaneshwar Jha. Mishra said that after receiving the letter, Jha personally raided Gumnami Baba's residence. No one knows what transpired when he went inside. But when he emerged, someone or something seemed to have scared the living daylights out of him. On the verge of breaking down, Jha left in a huff. Within twenty-four hours he was transferred, it has been claimed.

The authors in their affidavit to the Justice Sahai Commission furnished relevant details, expecting that Jha (now retired and living in Noida) would be summoned before the commission to state on record what action he took after receiving Mishra's letter and what was the outcome. But the commission summoned neither Jha nor asked the state government to throw light on this claim. Justice Sahai would have done well to summon relevant records from police and Intelligence Bureau to verify the statements of Jha and Pandey. Counter intelligence falls in the remit of Intelligence Bureau and Jha must have informed at least the Subsidiary Intelligence Bureau. All he needed to do was to tell the Sahai Commission, and the people of India, what he saw when he entered Bhagwanji's room. Did he see a CIA agent or someone else? If yes, who was it and why did he panic after seeing him? What was this 'CIA agent' doing in a remote part of India sitting in a room when such agents are better off operating from big cities from where they can gather relevant intelligence? Why wasn't this 'CIA agent' charged and arrested at a time when hunting for the 'CIA agents', real or imaginary, was the favourite pastime in India?

Bhagwanji was an impostor, set up by the Intelligence Bureau

Several Subhas Bose family members, researchers and persons of repute such as Major General (Retd) G D Bakshi have asserted on numerous occasions that Subhas Chandra Bose was killed in Soviet Russia at the behest of India's first Prime Minister. Many have additionally claimed that Bhagwanji was an 'impostor' or 'dummy' planted by the Intelligence Bureau to cover-up the matter of Bose's killing in Russia by drawing a red herring that he was in India, alive. The most prominent figure among those who hold this view is former Minister, member of Parliament and senior BJP leader Subramanian Swamy. Addressing the media in Kolkata on 10 January 2015, Swamy repeated the killing charge. According to a report published in the online version of *The Times of India*, Swamy 'admitted that disclosing the secret files might jeopardise India's relations with Britain and Russia'. What really happened to Bose, according to Swamy is,

> Bose had faked his death and escaped to Manchuria in China which was under Russian occupation, hoping Russia would look after him. But Stalin put him in a jail in Siberia. Somewhere around 1953, he hanged or suffocated Bose to death.

Addressing a gathering of RSS workers in Gurgaon the next day, Swamy said that he'd make some important disclosure in Meerut on 23 January, Netaji's 118th birth anniversary. In Meerut, Swamy dropped what he considered a bombshell. Citing his own research in the matter, he said that 'Stalin wrote a letter to Nehru in December 1945 that Bose was in his custody and asked

Nehru what he should do with him. Nehru, after receiving the letter, immediately summoned his stenographer Sham Lal Jain [of Meerut] on December 26, 1945 and dictated a letter meant for the then British PM.' Swamy said that 'Jain had stated these facts before the Khosla Commission, set up in 1970 to investigate the mystery behind Bose's death'. *The Times of India* further reported:

> Swamy said as per Jain's version, Nehru had told the British PM that he had received information that Bose was in a jail in Soviet Union. 'In my opinion, soon after that British officials reached the Soviet Union and ensured Bose was put to death.'

As he asserted that Bose was put to death in Soviet Russia, Swamy rubbished the Bhagwanji angle out of hand. The following tweet of his came in response to a poser about the identity of Bhagwanji.

Subramanian Swamy ✔
@Swamy39

@nitz19arg : It was an IB trick to keep your hopes alive.

Prima facie, Swamy's charge about Stalin, a ruthless dictator, liquidating Subhas Bose would seem plausible. But plausibility cannot replace factuality. For all his genuine admiration for Subhas Bose and the long-standing desire to know the truth, Swamy got it all wrong. Just like many other Bose family members and scholars, who despite their protestations have not been able to produce a scrap of paper that supports Bose's presence in the erstwhile USSR—let alone evidence of his killing by Stalin, who had no particular liking for Nehru, described by him as a 'political prostitute', according to a claim by Asiatic Society researchers in 2000.[29]

The crux of Swamy's evidence, that is the charge made by Sham Lal Jain, has been widely known and believed by many for decades. Jain's story was that in 1946 he was serving as a steno to Asaf Ali, secretary of the INA Defence Committee fighting to secure the release of the INA prisoners. He claimed that in December that year, he was summoned to Ali's residence by Pandit Nehru. The rest of the account, as recorded in the proceedings of the Khosla Commission on 31 December 1970 is as follows:

```
Witness:   Then, Shri Jawaharlal Nehru began to dictate:

                "Clement Attlee, Esq.,
                 Prime Minister of Great Britain,
                 10, Downing Street,
                 London."

Chairman:  Yes.

Witness:   "Dear Mr. Attlee:

                    I understand from most reliable source that
                Subhas Chandra Bose, your War criminal, has been
                allowed by Stalin to enter the Russian territory
                which action of his is a clear treachery and
                betrayal of faith as, when Russia was an Ally of
                the British and the Americans, Stalin should not
                have done so. This is just for your information
                and to be taken notice of".

           Such was the letter. Now, your Lordship, the contents

       of this letter that was got typed by me by Shri Jawaharlal

       Nehru I am mentioning from my memory which is what I

       remember up to the present day. These were not the actual

       words. This is the purport of that letter. One thing more

       I would like to mention here is that after I finished the

       typing job, Jawaharlalji and Asaf Ali used to see that the

       carbon papers used by me in their works were got burnt in

       the 'angiti' and there was thus ...
```

Swamy changed Jain's words 'Bose...has been allowed to enter Russian territory by Stalin' to 'Bose was in a jail in Soviet Union'

---

29   'Slur on Nehru ensures Stalinian end to study,' *The Statesman*, 21 August 2000.

to suit his prejudice, because allowing Bose to enter Russia is very
different from having him imprisoned there.

Having gone through the nearly 100-page long testimony of
Sham Lal Jain as it appears in the record of the oral proceedings
of Khosla Commission, we do not think that on its own, this
testimony is worthy of any credence. But the reason why Jain's
account has become so well known is that Samar Guha, in his
1978 book *Netaji: Dead or Alive* carried a short-edited portion of
it with some additional notes backing it up. Guha himself believed
that Bhagwanji was Bose and all his efforts were motivated by a
desire to tell the people of India what he knew. That little detail
aside, Jain's version as it really was and as it has been amplified by
Swamy has a missing chunk. Not only did Jain not support the
theory that Bose was killed in Soviet Russia, he actually believed
that he was alive at the time he deposed before the Khosla
Commission. What was more sensational was that he claimed to
have met Netaji in Meerut in October 1967.

Witness: Yes, My Lord. At Jadugar ka Bagh we, that is myself
and my son, saw Netaji sitting on a wooden chowki on the
veranda smoking cigarettes.

Chairman: On the veranda ?

Witness: Yes. We went to him and he said to me: "How are you,
Sham Lal? Is it well with you and your family?" I replied,
"Yes, Babaji, we all are quite well". Thereafter he asked
me about his old associates of the time of Forward Bloc
such as, Pandit Jairam Sharma, Comrade Murari Lal, Pandit
Parmanand Sharma, Desh Bakhtji Avtar Singh, etc., and asked
me how they were doing. I replied that Jairam Sharma was

Likewise, Swamy's theory that Bhagwanji was planted by the Intelligence Bureau has nothing to stand on. The very question of IB keeping our hopes alive by planting Bhagwanji does not arise as the Faizabad holy man's case came to light only in late 1985 after he was reported dead. By that time, the Bose mystery had ceased to be of any consequence. At that time, the Congress party commanded the largest ever majority in Parliament in the history of India. So, for the IB to plant such a story at that time made no sense. Why would the Rajiv Gandhi government want to revive a long-dead issue at the peak of its popularity? Unknown to Swamy, in 1985 the Congress government in UP blamed the BJP and the Janata Party for 'trying to arouse public feelings regarding identity of one Gumnami Baba', as would be seen in this message from the state Home Department to Indu Kumar Pandey. Swamy was leading the Janata Party before he decided to merge it with the BJP.

Copy of No. BS-543/85-CX-2   Dated 3/12/85 U/C
From- Home UP Lucknow To- D.M.,Faizabad.
....   (24)

Janta Party B J P Leaders of Faizabad are reported to
have been trying to arouse public feelings regarding identity
of one Gumnami Babu who died on 16 th September 85(.)
Please furnish a detailed report in the matter in triplicate
atonce for transmission to Government of India(.)

....

                                          MOST URGENT

         OFFICE OF THE DISTRICT MAGISTRATE,FAIZABAD
              ....

NO. J.A./Gumnami Baba   Dated 4-12-85

All the same, the authors through their affidavit to the Justice Vishnu Sahai Commission outlined a sure shot way to verify Swamy's theory: that of summoning the Director, Intelligence Bureau, before the commission to clarify Swamy's charges. Under the law, Justice Sahai had all the powers to do so (just as Justice Khosla did when he summoned the then IB chief). If Bhagwanj was an IB plant, the agency would have the information about it and the same could be placed before the commission to end the controversy. Since the Sahai Commission steered clear of it, Swamy himself can prove his theory by doing the needful. Lest we forget, its Swamy's own party that is in power now. He can pull strings that we cannot even think of. We are left wondering what stopped Swamy from persuading the Modi government to produce IB records showing that Bhagwanji was their planted impostor? The government did not release even a single IB file, nor ever offered any explanation about snooping on Bose kin and others.

Swamy's theory has been taken to greater heights of ridiculousness by researcher Purabi Roy, a former member of the Indian Council of Historical Research (ICHR). Seen giving a talk at the Ahmedabad-based Indus University in a YouTube video, Roy claimed that she has seen files (whose details she didn't divulge) containing exchanges between Nehru and IB director B N Mullik over Netaji's fate. According to her, the files show that responding to the queries of Nehru 'perturbed' about the implications of Netaji's return from Russia, Mullik asked him to set up ten dummies of Netaji. Thereafter, Indira Gandhi used one of those dummies to 'create' Gumnami Baba. 'Baba was created in 1975 and he was there till January 1985,' claimed Roy. 'Baba had to leave this world' because it 'was very difficult for Baba to survive' as Indira Gandhi was assassinated in October 1984.[30]

As an extension of the 'Nehru-planted ten dummies' theory, Roy went on to allege that Bhagwanji's handwriting samples could have been faked by the government authorities. This claim has been forwarded by her in a discussion with Mission Netaji member Diptasya Jash. The authors possess a copy of the video recording of the talks. The problem with this hypothesis is that such a feat is not possible. It was beyond the capacity of the Intelligence Bureau or any authority in India to pull through a forensic fraud of that scale. Yes, documents can be fabricated, but only in a smaller number. A case in point pertains to the so-called five Black diaries of Irish revolutionary Roger Casement, purportedly containing accounts of his homosexual liaisons with young men. They came into the possession of Scotland Yard after Casement's capture in 1916. They were then used to publicise Casement's 'sexual degeneracy' before he was hanged. Since the 1930s, a controversy has raged about the authenticity of the diaries. It was repeatedly claimed that the British authorities had forged the diaries in order to discredit Casement. In 2002, tests carried out by Audrey Giles, an internationally respected figure in the field of document forensics, established that the handwriting appearing in the diaries was indeed that of Casement.[31]

---

30   Dr Purabi Roy, Subhash Chandra Bose: A Mystery Unraveled - Talk-40, Centre for Indic Studies, Indus University, https://www.youtube.com/watch?v=J-_k_D_d2yc.

31   Rachel Donnelly, 'Academics say Casement's Black Diaries genuine following forensic examination', The Irish Times, 13 March, 2002. https://www.irishtimes.com/news/academics-say-casement-s-black-diaries-genuine-following-forensic-examination-1.1053524.

Commenting on the issue in 2009 in *The Defence of the Realm: The Authorized History of MI5*, Christopher Andrew, the world's most well-known expert on the history of intelligence service, wrote that it was never possible for any British intelligence service to fake so many handwriting specimens. 'Even the KGB, whose disinformation department Service A made far more use of forgery than any Western intelligence agency, never fabricated a handwritten document of comparable length,' wrote Prof Andrew.

Hundreds of handwriting specimens, written by Bhagwanji across a span of three decades, couldn't have been fabricated even if the CIA were to attempt such a feat in 1985 or earlier. It is scientifically impossible for a man to write in someone else's handwriting in two different languages, English and Bangla, for decades. (We don't have Subhas Bose's handwriting samples in Sanskrit and Hindi to match the samples left behind by Bhagwanji.) In any case, B Lal, Curt Baggett and even the Government experts who gave negative reports did not detect any signs of forgery in Bhagwanji's handwriting samples.

The curious case of death in Russia

Before giving our considered view on the identity of Bhagwanji, we would like to deal with one last issue that merits a critical assessment: whether it can be established in any manner that Bose was liquidated in the former USSR. This theory sprouted from adventurer and former MEA official Satyanarayan Sinha, who first recounted it in his 1965 book *Netaji Mystery* and then repeated it before G D Khosla in 1970. Sinha sourced this information to the son of Abani Mukherji, a revolutionary and co-founder of the Communist Party of India. Sinha claimed that in Moscow in 1960, he met Abani's son 'Goga', from whom he gathered the following information:

> He was the first one to communicate to me the statement of the rehabilitated Comintern functionary Mazut, that he had seen Subhas Babu at Yakutsk in 1950-51. According to Mazut, Subhas Babu was locked up in Cell No 45 and Abani Babu in No 57 of the Central Prison of Yakutsk.

This claim that Netaji was a prisoner in the USSR again made headlines in the 31 August 2015 edition of *The Sunday Standard*. Backing this line, Subramanian Swamy added publicly that Nehru was aware about Bose being held captive in Yakutsk Prison in Siberia.

It is an established fact that Mukherji fell a victim to the Great Purge in the late 1930s. He was executed in October 1937. His soldier son Gora Guar Mukherji also died during the Second World War. Sinha's statement, and all those add-on claims thereafter are therefore erroneous. There was no chance of a long dead Abani Mukherji being locked up in a prison that also held

Bose as captive. For the record, in 1965, the Indian embassy officials informally took up his claim with the Soviet foreign ministry only to be told that it was a 'mischievous invention'. Later in November 1970, outraged by Sinha's allegations before the Khosla Commission that he was accosted by USSR Delhi embassy officials who threatened to execute his Russian contact, the Soviet embassy in Delhi issued a statement that they 'had absolutely nothing to do with the fate of Subhas Chandra Bose'.

After Sinha, the most persistent efforts to highlight Bose's Russia connection have come from Purabi Roy. She has also continued to harp on her belief that Subhas was killed in Russia—which she claims to have been told by Russian researchers. Roy's version sounds credible because of her credentials as a professor and her tendency to refer to important names—which in turn helps conjure up a believable scenario. Roy first flagged the issue before the nation in the 1990s when as a part of a research team from the Asiatic Society she came across some Russian documents mentioning Bose. She picked up a confrontation suggesting a government-sponsored cover-up of the Bose-Russia connection post-1945. To her credit, she fought when others lacked the courage to utter a single word. She came up with innumerable insights, inspired many, including the authors to an extent. But, nothing in her 2011 book *The Search for Netaji: New Findings* or any of the records furnished by her before the Mukherjee Commission, or the record of the cross-examination of Russian witnesses she helped bring before the Commission qualify as evidence for Bose's presence in Russia after 1945—forget the liquidation matter altogether.

Finally, in his well-argued book *Bose: An Indian Samurai* (KW Publishers, Delhi, 2016), G D Bakshi discusses the 'matrix of options regarding what happened to Bose', including the Bhagwanji angle. He writes that 'the evidence available so far and simple deductive reasoning, unfortunately seems to point towards' the hypothesis that Netaji met his end in Siberia as a prisoner. His arguments against the Bhagwanji-Netaji link are: Bose's health was not such as to survive Siachen-like conditions in Siberia; negative DNA report of CFSL Kolkata is empirical evidence against this theory; personality profile of Bose was such that he couldn't have lived incognito and silent for two decades plus.

The General wonders whether some intelligence agencies were not 'trying to plug into the universal hunger for news about Bose and soften the Russian death angle by creating an alternative hypothesis that Bose had survived the Siberian gulags and had come back to India to live as a mendicant'? Elsewhere in his book, he puts forward another hypothesis that since the British intelligence agencies had signed two agreements with the NKVD (forerunner of the KGB) during the war, it is possible that the British invoked them 'to seek to interrogate Bose in Soviet prisons and get him executed there, as it would avoid any repercussions or public outcry in India'.

Again, General Bakshi's case for Netaji's end in Russia takes off from Swami and Sinha's unsubstantiated claims. The Russians have stuck to their position still. After the matter was raised with them again by the Vajpayee government at the behest of the Mukherjee Commission, they stated in 2003, that following a search 'no information has been found about the fate of SC Bose' in the Central Archives of the Russian FSB (a KGB successor) and some other archives. On 14 October 2015, a delegation comprising the Bose family members, General Bakshi and the authors requested Prime Minister Narendra Modi and External Affairs Minister Sushma Swaraj to raise the issue with the Russians at the highest level. On 9 March 2017, Swaraj stated in Parliament that the Government of Russian Federation had informed that 'consequent upon receiving the fresh request of the Indian Government, a fresh search was conducted and no documents pertaining to Netaji Bose's death were found in the Russian Archives'. To break it down into comprehensible language—the Russians have consistently made it quite clear that they have no information about Netaji's death, which they would surely have if he had died in their territory.

Bakshi's reading too much in war-time pacts between the Soviet and British intelligence agencies is a bit of a stretch. In the absence of supporting evidence, it cannot be postulated that since such pacts existed, Russians could have compromised Bose's whereabouts to the British. It seems most unlikely that, pact or no pact, the Russians could have done anything not likely to serve their national interest. Handing over Bose to the British after he had sought shelter from them would have done them no good. Moreover, the relations between the Russians and British were not exactly cordial. They had simply been brought together for the sake of defeating a common enemy, the Nazi Germany. What to speak of them, even the relations between the cousins on either side of the Atlantic Ocean were not what they seemed. In *Intelligence and the War against Japan: Britain, America and the*

Politics of Secret Service—a most thorough and penetrating account of the interactions of both the British and American intelligence agencies—Dr Richard J Aldrich demonstrates that from 1942, the Allies increasingly spied on each other's future ambitions, rather than the common enemy. By 1944, Aldrich writes, 'this had translated into a barely disguised "Great Game" to achieve the upper hand in clandestine pre-occupational activities across South East Asia. At times, the war against Japan appeared relegated to a sideshow'. Come to think of it, even the CIA has been reported to be wary of sharing everything with the FBI, and this was one of the reasons the 9/11 attacks could not be averted. Here in India, (General Bakshi would know better), there has been much talk of rivalry between R&AW and IB.

On the issue of asking the Russians to lay bare any secret files they might have on Subhas Bose, the Indian government's attempts appear rather superfluous. A country can barely ask another one to release their secret files when it itself continues to hold similar files under lock and key. When the Indian government itself isn't making public its intelligence files, on or about Bose, and is cagey about whatever information it possesses about Bhagwanji, it is futile to expect Russians to divulge the truth, whose disclosure, for a start, isn't going to make everyone in India happy.

It would be apt to close this discussion with a rather sarcastic comment made by Bhagwanji on this issue. In an undated letter to Pabitra, written during the time when the G D Khosla Commission was running its inquiry, Bhagwanji wrote that it was beyond the 'fourteen generations' of the Indian government to extract the real truth from the Russians.

The non-forensic circumstantial and material evidence thus brings us to the same conclusion that the handwriting analysis yielded: Bhagwanji was none other than Subhas Chandra Bose. The impostor angle is neither impossible nor unthinkable, but falters on two grounds which make the proposition absurd. First, it is easy to imitate someone on specific characteristics. But as the composite character sketch makes it abundantly clear, maintaining consistency for nearly three decades on the looks, mannerisms, recollections, handwriting and knowledge of the world is practically impossible. The second factor working against the hoax or impostor theory is that what was not played for three decades cannot be a hoax. An impostor plays the hoax to gain something, not to sit and wait in the wings for three decades.

SIXTEEN

METAMORPHOSIS

IN THE END, one missing piece of the puzzle remains to be found to complete the picture: Why would a man who single-handed dared to challenge Mahatma Gandhi and the entire Congress top leadership, hopped across continents raising armies and setting up a government in exile, charmed the biggest of the world leaders (and dictators), generated the final push that expedited the end of the British Raj and sacrificed everything personal at the altar of the motherland hide away in his own country for such a long time? Why didn't he come out in the open and lead the country? Is it even conceivable that Netaji wouldn't contact his family on his return to his motherland? Could a man who was the living symbol of courage and defiance live in hiding, in fear of his political opponents?

The answers to these questions, which emanate from the warrior image of Netaji Subhas Chandra Bose etched on our minds, are so overwhelmingly in the negative that they have taken the form of the axiomatic truth. They have become assumptions, leading to wrong conclusions. Because, making these assumptions before establishing the identity of Bhagwanji is like putting the proverbial cart before the horse. It is only after establishing that Subhas Chandra Bose and Gumnami Baba were the same person that we need to re-examine these propositions and start peeling the layers of the seemingly impossible. It is only when we undertake this scrutiny that several probable causes come to the fore to explain why he did things which appear to be unbelievable. None of these causes appear to have been standalone or 'the only cause' coming in the way of his reappearance. Different reasons, interwoven with multiple strands of contemporary political—national and international—situations, seem to have been predominant at different times, reflecting changes in the contextual reality. Before arriving at a final conclusion, however, the narrative has to start from the beginning to follow the shifting contexts and consequently, the causes.

In view of Bhagwanji's sense of bitterness about the treatment he received at the hands of the Congress high command and those from whom he expected support, especially in Bengal, we will have to situate the starting point of the context in 1939 going on till January 1941. The events leading up to Subhas Bose's forming the Forward Bloc in May 1939 are too well known to be repeated. The alignment of the parties and their leaders was clear at the time the Pant resolution had come up for voting. Despite Jayaprakash Narayan's intention to support Bose, the Congress Socialist Party abstained from voting on the resolution with Minoo Masani,

Yusuf Meherally, Achyut Patwardhan, Ram Manohar Lohia and Asoka Mehta being more concerned about preserving unity in the Congress. Minoo Masani has given a pithy account in his memoirs of what went on inside the party at that time.

> The resolution of the Gandhians, placed before the session by Govind Ballabh Pant, put the Congress Socialist Party squarely on the spot. If the Congress Socialist party voted with Subhas Babu and the communists, it was likely that the Gandhian resolution would be defeated, in which case the Gandhians would be driven out of the Congress which would then, for all practical purposes, be controlled by Subhas Babu and the communists. So far as I was concerned, this was an unthinkable proposition and many of my colleagues shared my view. On the other hand, if we supported the Gandhians, Subhas Bose would be thrown out of the Presidentship. Jayaprakash was not prepared for this, nor did he want to antagonise Subhas Bose and the communists, because he believed in the concept of the 'Left Bloc of progressive forces'.[1]

By July 1939 Subhas was virtually thrown out of Congress after being suspended as president of the Bengal Provincial Congress Committee (BPCC) and was prevented from becoming

---

1   Minoo Masani, *Bliss was it in that Dawn...: A Political Memoir Upto Independence*, Arnold-Heinemann, pp 144-145. Minocher Rustom 'Minoo' Masani, a barrister, was one of the founding members of the Congress Socialist Party along with Jayaprakash Narayan. Masani became the Mayor of the Bombay Municipal Corporation and was a member of the Constituent Assembly. He formed the Swatantra Party along with C Rajagopalachari in 1960. He was elected to the Lok Sabha thrice from Rajkot in Gujarat.
Jayaprakash Narayan soon moved to quite a different attitude towards Bose. He 'strongly disapproves of Subhas Chandra Bose's country-wide propaganda against the Working Committee', reported the *Amrita Bazar Patrika* of 26 January 1940.

a member of any elective Congress body. Dr BC Roy, Kiran Sankar Roy, Surendra Mohan Ghose—all his backers earlier were now aligned against him, along with Prafulla Chandra Ghosh. So were GD Birla, Jamnalal Bajaj and Nalini Ranjan Sarker. A parallel ad hoc BPCC was set up with Maulana Abul Kalam Azad as its president against the BPCC controlled by Subhas and Sarat. Prominent newspapers in Bengal, the *Amrita Bazar Patrika* and *Jugantar* for example, gradually started getting more critical of the radical line taken by Subhas against Gandhi's politics.

Matters came to a head from February 1940 onwards over three incidents. On 21 February, the *Amrita Bazar Patrika* published a statement issued by the editors of *Amrita Bazar Patrika*, *Hindusthan Standard*, *Bharat*, *Advance*, *Matribhumi* and *Jugantar* that decried a warning issued by Subhas at a public meeting against 'so-called nationalist' newspapers for 'publishing half-truths and untruths'. Agitated public response in the meeting insisted for boycott of such newspapers. Calling it a fascist technique the statement asked him 'to desist from the crude and dangerous tactics'. Led by its editor Tushar Kanti Ghosh, *Amrita Bazar Patrika* went on an overdrive, soon to be joined by MN Roy, Jawaharlal Nehru and other Congress leaders. The conflict continued to intensify through March. On 9 March, in an editorial named 'Our Fascists' the *Patrika* charged that the Bengal Congress led by Subhas 'had been so intoxicated with consciousness of power that it had completely forgotten that the methods adopted by it were Fascist, only it had no "storm troopers" and organisation to give effect to its decision by force. It did not occur to it that Bengal or for that matter the rest of India would not fight British Imperialism to establish Fascism even of the Swadeshi brand.' Giving nomination for the upcoming Calcutta Corporation elections to Satish Chandra Bose, Subhas's eldest brother, was also questioned. 'The spectacle of power converging within a family is hardly edifying,' commented the *Amrita Bazar Patrika* editorial of 10 March. When a new BPCC was appointed in March, it rescinded the direction issued by the former committee controlled by Subhas of boycotting newspapers and the new members were 'entertained at a tea party' by the *Patrika* editor. 'The *Amrita Bazar Patrika* has long been lying in wait for an opportunity to catch him at a disadvantage: his attempt to start a boycott against this paper having failed, its tone is becoming more and more openly hostile to him,' the Governor of Bengal JA Herbert reported to the Viceroy in his report of 20 March.[2]

The second issue for which Subhas faced organised criticism was the Anti-Compromise Conference held alongside the official Congress annual session in March 1940 at Ramgarh in Bihar. Apart from the Congress high command, Jayaprakash Narayan issued stringent criticism against Subhas. The *Amrita Bazar Patrika*, leading the tirade against Subhas called the conference 'A Meaningless Show'. The criticism sharpened into ridicule as the Congress session commenced. 'Srijut Subhas Chandra Bose has discovered that the Congress delegates assembled at Ramgarh representing about forty lacs of Indian souls have become the allies of British Imperialism and "imperialist lackeys",' its editorial of 20 March commented, accusing Subhas of fomenting a civil war in the country. In comparison to the

---

2   E Rahim *et al*, *Bengal Politics: Documents of the Raj, Vol II 1940-43*, The University Press Ltd, p 16.

huge press coverage that the Congress session received in Calcutta papers, the presence of the Anti-Compromise Conference was barely felt. The Gandhian domination over Bengali intelligentsia and their media was near total.

Towards the end of February, the Subhas Bose-led Congress and the Hindu Mahasabha came to an agreement on seat sharing for the ensuing Calcutta Corporation elections. The arrangement, however, fell through within a few days with the parties unable to agree on candidates. The relations with the Mahasabha reached a low when on 15 March Subhas's supporters broke up a meeting of Syama Prasad Mookerjee and hurled stones that hit his head. 'The Plague of Fascism' asserted the lead editorial of the *Amrita Bazar Patrika* in its 17 March issue, and called the citizens of Calcutta to defeat 'the candidates of the Fascist Party' in the upcoming Corporation elections. Before long, the pages of the newspapers became the place of charges and counter-charges, with attacks on Subhas getting more prominence in the newspapers that had already turned against him.

It was clear that neither Bose Congress nor the Hindu Mahasabha would be able to garner majority seats on their own and that the Muslim League victory in the reserved Muslim seats would give it the decisive power. On the day of the election (28 March 1940), the *Patrika* warned the voters that Jinnah would prefer an alliance with Subhas's group not only because he wanted to wreck the Congress but also because both the Bose brothers and their followers were pandering to their interests. Efforts between Subhas and the Hindu Mahasabha to work out an understanding having failed, in mid-April he arrived at an agreement with the Muslim League for administering the Calcutta Corporation. 'Hindus Betrayed: Bose Group's Surrender Pact with Muslim League,' screamed the *Amrita Bazar Patrika* of 17 April, mincing no words to accuse that 'Hindus' Civic Rights Bartered for Getting Sj Subhas Bose Elected as Alderman'. It was a 'Great Betrayal', the paper's editorial declared the next day. The paper's 26 April editorial raised the level further:

> ...he is nothing more or less than a renegade Congressman who has betrayed the national cause and surrendered to rabid communalists for the sake of a trumpery honour. He may continue to deceive the public for some time more with words that so far as he is concerned have ceased to have any meaning; but future generations will remember him as the lost leader who sold himself for a mess of pottage.

For the Congress, Subhas wasn't any more a part of their programme or plans. Rather, a reorganised official provincial Congress would have its task cut out in reducing his mass influence. However, his supporters in Bengal were not going to take things lying down. Congress meetings were disrupted at various places and speakers beaten up on occasions. The clash had reached its pinnacle. The newly formed BPCC too carried on the attack on Subhas. 'The strength of an organisation is being sought to be replaced by the strength of a personality supposed to be imbued with wonderful powers,' read a statement issued by former revolutionaries Manoranjan Gupta, Bhupendra Kumar Datta (editor of *Forward* newspaper) and Suresh Chandra Das on 27 April. While Nalini Ranjan Sarker wasn't to be left behind, Comrades Muzaffar Ahmed and Somnath Lahiri of the

Communist Party too joined the party soon to call out Subhas's 'Bluff of a struggle'.

With only the *Anandabazar Patrika*[3] and the *Hindusthan Standard* among the newspapers, and his trusted band of Forward Bloc supporters standing firmly behind him, Subhas fought back the attacks, drawing large crowds at his meetings. The attacks on him continued to grow increasingly virulent. On 1 May, the *Amtrita Bazar Patrika* claimed that Subhas and Sarat secretly met the Bengal Premier AK Fazlul Huq with the aim of joining the provincial government. As the political atmosphere started getting hotter on this issue, the critics of Subhas got a boost in the form of Ramananda Chatterjee, editor of the two well-regarded magazines *The Modern Review* and *Prabasi*.

Governor Herbert of Bengal kept a keen eye on the developments. His fortnightly reports to the Viceroy apart from his own opinion on the developments, provide an inside view of the ongoing efforts to corner Subhas. He wasn't happy that the pact with Muslim League would help Subhas 'to keep his fingers on some of the resources of the Corporation'. He noted that some sections of the Muslims were happy to have Subhas as an asset who could be used to create divisions in the 'Hindu and Congress circles', but he wasn't convinced that they would succeed. Some of them also seemed to think that they would have a leverage in

---

3   The *Anandabazar Patrika* of those years, run by Suresh Chandra Majumdar and Prafulla Kumar Sarkar was a pillar of support to Subhas, a tradition that continued at the time of Prafulla's son Asoke Kumar Sarkar too. It is only in the recent past that there has been a visible change in the newspaper's attitude towards the legacy of Netaji.

Subhas as he would be devoid of friends if the Muslim League deserted him.

'I cannot help thinking, however, that they have taken a risk in trying to outwit so clever and slippery an opponent,' Herbert recorded in his report of 22 April. In his report of 7 May, he noted that 'He who sups with Subhas needs a long spoon, and even if the matter [Bose-League Pact] stopped at Municipal affairs only I would not be too confident of the Muslims getting the better of the deal.' The Governor's report of 7 June shows that Tushar Kanti Ghosh was conspiring on how to corner Subhas further. Ghosh 'in an interview I have just given him, confirmed the impression that so long as Subhas could be denied Press publicity he would weaken his position day by day,' the Governor wrote. Intrigues were on in the Muslim League too. Khwaja Nazimuddin, the home minister of Bengal, 'has hinted strongly that he himself is getting "fed up" with Subhas and that if he could secure a resolution of full support of war from the Moslem League he would then "pick up" Subhas and complete his political effacement,' Herbert noted.[4]

By the middle of the year, Subhas's position was somewhat like that of Abhimanyu, surrounded from all sides by the official Congress, the Hindu Mahasabha, the Socialists, the Royists, the Communists, the Muslim League and a hostile press. Subhas, however, was no Abhimanyu. Towards the end of June, he picked up the issue of removal of Holwell Monument as his next

---

4   E Rahim *et al*, *Bengal Politics: Documents of the Raj, Vol II 1940-43*, The University Press Ltd, pp 22-31.

campaign. As the movement started gathering momentum, a nervous government arrested him on 2 July under the Defence of India Act. As his biographer Leonard Gordon has noted, Subhas 'believed that he was to be detained for the duration of the war'.[5] That was the end of his political career within the country. The next five years saw Subhas reinvent himself and prove his mettle in a way probably no one could have imagined.[6] Subhas 'babu' transformed into 'Netaji'. As it happened, those who had tried to push him into submission formed the ruling and the opposition power blocs after Independence, and none had any qualms in exploiting the image of 'Netaji' and his INA for their political gains.

Two things must be highlighted before we proceed further. Firstly, despite his bitter confrontation with Subhas, Syama Prasad Mookerjee retained a tremendous amount of regard for Subhas. 'A national hero in exile to serve his country's cause' was how Mookerjee summed up his assessment of Subhas in his diary entry of 21 October 1944. In the same entry he also recalled the incidents of 1940.

---

5   Leonard Gordon, *Brothers Against the Raj*, Viking, 1990, p 412.
6   This transformation of Subhas and the attitude of a section of Bengal's intelligentsia towards him is captured in the memoirs of Sajanikanta Das, poet, staunch Gandhian and editor of the literary magazine *Shanibarer Chithi*. Das's antipathy towards Subhas was so strong that he refused to participate in the Calcutta Congress of 1928. Subhas was lampooned for his role of the GOC (General Officer Commanding) in military attire of the volunteer forces. He was nicknamed GOC (pronounced as 'gawk') Subhas. Das, however, had to admit in his memoirs: 'By becoming Netaji Subhas Chandra, GOC Subhas Chandra trashed our lampooning and turned the joke upon us. Today we are truly proud of him and our unmixed respect for him has covered our earlier embarrassment.' Sajanikanta Das, *Atma Smriti*, Subarnarekha, 1954, p 262.

We [Hindu Mahasabha], specially I, had no personal grudge against Subhas. Indeed I had for him admiration and affection, and genuinely believed that there was no other person who could come near him in the political field of India, specially Bengal…. He was so much exposed to public criticism and ridicule due to his unholy alliance with the [Muslim] League that he soon came down from the high pedestal on which his countrymen had placed him…. Today it must be admitted that taking him as he is, he is one of the foremost Indians of his time who regarded no means or method as bad if he felt he could thereby attain power to wrest the freedom of his country.

Mookerjee then noted something in his diary that holds some significance. He obviously still did not have the details of Subhas's campaigns and the story of the INA, but he was prescient to observe that 'If England wins—as she is likely to—and continues to hold her sway over India, it is doubtful if he will ever be permitted to return to India.'[7]

Secondly, it might be considered an irony of fate that the person who didn't hesitate to contrive with the British Governor of Bengal in 1940 to ensure ouster of Subhas from its political life, took great personal interest in overseeing the first methodical investigation into Bhagwanji's identity. It was the intervention of *Northern India Patrika*'s editor Tushar Kanti Ghosh that made the investigative series possible.[8] He died in 1994, at the age of 95, with the knowledge that Subhas had returned to India.

By 1950, among various hypothesised possibilities about

7 Syama Prasad Mookerjee, *Leaves from a Diary*, Oxford University Press, 2000, pp 35-36.
8 Various interactions with Vishwambar Nath Arora.

Subhas's fate, a few had taken firm hold on public perception. First was the government's insistence that Subhas had died in the air crash reported in August 1945. Opposed to it was the claim that he was somewhere in Siberia or China and that he was biding his time to return to India. With passage of time, new claims kept emerging. While in the mid-1950s, the most sensational claim was made by Muthuramalingam Thevar of his having met Subhas in China, the early 1960s saw the most elaborately attempted hoax surrounding Swami Saradananda, the sadhu of Shoulmari. Even as the theories and counter-theories made their play in the public domain, the Government stuck to its public stand that it believed in Subhas's death in 1945. People had no way of knowing that this was only its public posturing—the inner workings of the government and all documents related to Netaji and the INA were kept classified as secret for half a century and more.

Some of the intelligence records declassified in 2010 as a result of the sustained right to information campaign by the authors demonstrated that none of the 'evidence' highlighted by the advocates of the death-in-plane-crash theory had actually convinced the Government. All the people having any link to Subhas Chandra Bose, especially his kin, were placed under an elaborate state surveillance with the aim to trace his whereabouts. 'It was the kind of surveillance that would be conducted today on the family of a terror mastermind,' commented Aroon Purie, the editor-in-chief of *India Today*, looking back at the extensive spying carried on for more than two decades after independence.[9]

---

9 From the Editor-in-Chief, *India Today*, 20 April 2015.

Breaking the story for the magazine, deputy editor Sandeep Unnithan called it 'Independent India's dirty state secret.'[10] The sordid exercise blew a hole in the publicised official position regarding Subhas Bose's fate, to which our Government still continues to hang on, despite the spying scandal exposing the establishment's fear of Subhas Bose's return.

The hypothetical scenario of Subhas Bose's return to India in 1945, or thereafter, and its implications has been discussed by eminent thinkers. 'The implications of a defiant Netaji using the court to posit an uncompromising Indian nationalism would have been far-reaching,' wrote columnist and lawmaker Swapan Dasgupta in 2004, referring to the possible impact of Netaji's presence at the Red Fort trials. Acknowledging that 'the absence of Bose foreclosed a monumental challenge which would have reshaped post-Independence politics,' Dasgupta went on to postulate that Bose wouldn't have been able to stop the partition of the country. Being disallowed in the Congress party, he 'would have attracted the socialists, a few who had gravitated to the CPI and a section of the disaffected middle-classes', leading to a three-way political reorientation in the 1950s—the conservative Gandhians in Congress (led by Patel) teaming up with the Hindu Mahasabha, Nehru allying with the communists (who 'hated Bose passionately'), and 'the populist Bose'. In visualising the alternative reality, Dasgupta had no doubt that the 'primary casualty of Bose's re-emergence would have been the Congress and, particularly, Gandhi's anointed leader, Jawaharlal Nehru.' This, in

---

10 Sandeep Unnithan, 'When Nehru spied on Netaji,' *India Today*, 20 April 2015.

Dasgupta's view meant that 'Had he [Bose] played his cards well, displayed organisational rigour and ideological flexibility, he may well have become the prime minister of India's first non-Congress government.'[11]

Historian Ramachandra Guha too argued in his piece written five years later that the presence of Netaji wouldn't have stopped partition of the country. According to Guha, even if Netaji rejoined Congress as a result of a truce manoeuvred by Gandhi, he wouldn't stay in the party for long because he 'was too proud and independent-minded to have conceded the top spot to Jawaharlal Nehru'. Thereafter, he might have gone ahead with his own party or would have 'joined with other former Congressmen in nurturing a left-wing alternative to the ruling party', akin to the Praja Socialist Party experiment of Acharya Kripalani, Jayaprakash Narayan, and Ram Manohar Lohia, which in reality 'could not make a dent in the Congress hegemony'. Given Bose's countrywide appeal, however, a socialist party led by him would have 'mounted a serious challenge to Nehru and his colleagues' and 'might, by 1957, and definitely by 1962, have given the Congress a real run for its money'.[12]

Writing in *The Times of India*, a grandnephew of Abid Hassan, Bose's private secretary in Germany and his companion in the three months long submarine journey from Germany to Singapore, postulated three possible scenarios which could have

11   Swapan Dasgupta, 'What If Netaji Came Back?' *Outlook*, 23 August 2004, https://www.outlookindia.com/magazine/story/what-if-netaji-came-back/224857.
12   Ramachandra Guha, 'Netaji versus Panditji What if Subhas Chandra Bose had returned after the war?' *The Telegraph*, 10 October 2009.

materialised had Bose been present in independent India. First, Netaji would have split the Congress, leading a more leftist segment and thus squeezing out the CPI. Over time, Netaji's party would have squeezed out Nehru's Congress and joined the Soviet Bloc. The second scenario envisaged was that of India taken through the road of a 'quasi-fascist' regime of 'Ataturkism' by Netaji, driven by his 'strong streak of authoritarianism'. 'He would, as Ataturk did in Turkey, tower the nation like a colossus' becoming 'an architect of the nation in every detail, shaping it according to his own benevolent dictatorial vision'. In the third scenario visualised by the author, in a variant of the authoritarian scenario, Netaji could have become a Mao TseTung, a Kim Il Sung or a Fidel Castro, taking India 'down the battered leftist socialist road to ruination'.[13]

It is also pertinent to recall Ram Monahar Lohia's views on the impact of a possible return of Bose. Like many Indians of his time, Lohia too had accepted the story of Bose's death in 1945, but that didn't stop him from visualising a 'what if' scenario:

> [If] Netaji Subhas were ever to have returned home after his great and peerless adventure for freedom, he would have given six months of acute trouble to Mr Nehru but no more. If Mr Nehru had been able physically to survive the return of Mr Bose, he would have been on top again after six months, so that Subhas Bose would either have to go in Opposition or become the second-in-command. Mr Bose did not possess Mr Nehru's cunning and refinement. He might indeed have

---

13   Anvar Alikhan, 'What if Netaji had returned to India...,' *The Times of India*, 19 April 2015.

tried to be clever on certain occasions, and I believe that he did but he did not possess the sure touch of a master at such jobs and he made some big mistakes Whenever I remember my last exchanges with him, I am…sad that Mr Bose did not find some way to adjust in whatever loose manner with Gandhiji.

I wish often to give to Subhas Babu after his death what I withheld from him in his life. Netaji Subhas was the embodiment of the Haldighati spirit. His aim was clear; he accepted neither defeat nor the withdrawal of lassitude, and he tried to act in all situations. But one wishes that the Haldighati spirit was somewhat clever than it often is.[14]

The details may vary, but there's a broad agreement on two main points—that Bose would have taken centre stage leading to the marginalisation of Nehru and that India's development story would have looked very different. If such an eventuality can be grasped by historians and authors, there is no reason to believe that the ruling dispensation, especially the spooks in the Intelligence Bureau, did not consider the possibility. It may be an academic exercise now, but in the post-independence years when the spectre of Bose's return hung in the corridors of power, it must have been looked at with a sense of urgency. That sense of urgency or desperation alone makes sense of the elaborate surveillance mounted for decades. It is clear that the ruling establishment either wanted to prevent Bose's showing up or at least be prepared for it.

14   Ram Manohar Lohia, *Guilty Men of India's Partition*, BR Publishing Corporation, pp 88-89. 'Spirit of Haldighati' is a reference to the heroic battled waged by Maharana Pratap against the Mughal forces in the battle of Haldighati (in Rajasthan) on 18 June 1576.

A more sinister alternative that seems to have occupied the minds of the powers that be emerges from contemporary reportage and declassified documents. This line of inquiry, however, never got seriously picked up and hence the story never developed to its full shape. It started with a suggestion from the man who greatly contributed to the eruption of the controversy surrounding Bose's fate following the news of the air crash. Rather dramatically, Alfred Wagg, then a stringer for the *Chicago Tribune*, had interrupted a press meet of Jawaharlal Nehru on 29 August 1945 to claim that he had seen Bose near Saigon after his reported death. Wagg wasn't a rookie. As a war correspondent he covered the War in Southeast Asia, Middle East and North Africa from the ground, from 1941 to 1945, contributing to several newspapers across the world.[15]

In September 1946, more than a year after the alleged plane crash in Taiwan, Wagg explained in the Delhi-based newspaper *National Call*, which was reported by the Singapore-based *Indian Daily Mail*, why he believed Bose was alive and was 'about to launch a political campaign inside India with far reaching social and economic results which would most likely be inaugurated, I am told, with a huge rally "somewhere in Central India"'. The reason why Wagg disbelieved the crash theory was that in French Indo-China he learnt from his sources that 'ten days after the

---

15   Based on his experience Wagg wrote three non-fiction books— *A Million Died!*, *No Spaghetti for Breakfast*, and a collection of his stories published in newspapers and magazines, besides a novel called *No Bridge to Heaven*. Wagg also has to his credit recording one of the rare English speeches by Gandhi, which he donated to the US National Archives. 'Alfred Wagg is an excellent speaker with a charming personality, well versed in his subject with a vast resource of experience,' reported the *Daily Press*, Virginia, in March 1948 introducing him as a speaker at the Newport News Woman's Club. Newport News, *Daily Press*, 14 March 1948.

supposed crash in Taihoku, Formosa, Bose attended a meeting in Saigon'. Wagg saw and believed the photographs which were shown to him, purportedly of Bose in Saigon after the date of the crash. Wagg was also told by his sources that Bose was seen with a Chinese General (who was also known to Wagg) in the spring of 1946. When Wagg showed the photographs produced by Habibur Rahman to two officers who had been at the aerodrome in August 1945, they swore on oath that no plane crash had taken place and that the background in the photographs was not that of Taihoku. His final conclusion was:

> I do not claim that the evidence that has fallen into my hands during these journalistic investigations which I undertook purely through professional interests conclusively proves that Netaji Subhas Chandra Bose is alive, but it does show that all the facts hitherto put forward publicly to support the theory of his death are inconclusive, based on defective evidence and in several cases seem to be false.[16]

Two politicians who got to see probably the same photographs that Wagg had seen of Bose in Saigon were the then defence minister Baldev Singh and Congress leader Niranjan Singh Talib. Talib, a close comrade of Bose who had been thrown into jail for five years on the charge of abetting Bose's escape from India and who later became president of the Punjab Pradesh Congress Committee, recounted his story to GD Khosla twenty-five years later. At Baldev Singh's house in 1947 Wagg had showed him some pictures of Netaji and told him that Netaji had gone to

---

16 American Correspondent Says Netaji is Alive, *Indian Daily Mail*, 25 September, 1946.

Indo-China. Talib was too important a person for his story to be ridiculed, as many witnesses were in his final report, so Khosla took a different tack to reject it in his report. Since Wagg worked for American newspapers it was expected that his story would be published by them, Khosla argued—and since his story wasn't published, it couldn't have been true, the reasoning followed. No one presented to Khosla Wagg's stories published in the *New Republic*, *Chicago Tribune* or even the *Indian Daily Mail* where Wagg had provided the details of his claim.[17] Khosla also interpreted Talib's statement to have meant that Wagg met Bose personally after the story of his death was given out, whereas Talib had made no such claim.[18] Sardar Baldev Singh never let out what transpired between him and Wagg.

In his *New Republic* piece of April 1946, Alfred Wagg made a strange comment, which never featured in any of his other writings: that if Subhas failed to return, his diehard followers might go to the extent of setting up an impostor. He wrote,

> Dead or alive, Bose today represents the extremist elements in India—the elements which want to fight, not passively resist.... Most of them are convinced that their fighting leader will return to lead them. Some Indian observers have said that if Bose is dead, another leader will be found to take his place—to parade as Subhas Chandra Bose himself—and lead India's extremist

---

17   In hindsight, we very much doubt that presenting these news items to Khosla would have helped. His mind was made up in favour of the official narrative. Khosla claimed that he was not made aware of the statement of Sarat Bose that his brother was in China, whereas Samar Guha claimed that the judge was given copy of it, as published in *The Nation*.

18   *Report of the One-Man Commission of Inquiry into the Disappearance of Netaji Subhas Chandra Bose*, 30 June 1974, p 98.

factions in a fight against the British, the Moslems and the All-India Congress for the control of India's troubled destiny.[19]

Within the next few years, the Central Intelligence Agency (CIA) too picked up the rumour in the air about planting an impostor, but this time by a foreign power. In a ground report generated in Delhi in November 1950, the agency cited an unnamed, highly-placed source pointing out to the potential danger posed by Subhas's popularity in India:

I was impressed on many occasions by the fact that Subash Chandra Bose (sic)...is still a very popular hero in the eyes of the Indians. Recently his life story was told in the Indian movies and I attended several different native theatres to study native reaction. Every time that the actor representing Bose appeared on the screen, he was loudly applauded. This expression of great enthusiasm clearly indicated to me that Bose is a National hero, and, in the eyes of the man on the street, I think he ranks next to Ghandi (sic). The native Indian explanation for this is found in the fact that Bose took definite action against British rule. To the native Indians, it does not make any difference that he took the side of the Japs.

It is now currently rumored in the Delhi area that the 'Netaji', which is Bose's nickname, is alive and is in Siberia, where he is waiting for a chance to make a big comeback...Whether Bose is dead or alive is relatively unimportant but the possibility of an impostor should not be overlooked. *I have had several educated Indians tell me that the USSR would send an impostor for Bose into India and it would be easy to convince the people that he is Bose. If Bose or an impostor should return, it is probable*

19   Alfred Wagg, Subhas Chandra Bose, *The New Republic*, 15 April 1946, p 500.

that a great many of the people would accept his leadership.[20]
(Emphasis added).

What it leads to is this: If a foreign journalist, media and an intelligence agency, none of which had any particular interest in Bose, were alive to the possibility of an impostor being planted in the name of Subhas Bose, is it conceivable that the 'snooping' Indian government wasn't? The interaction between Sunil Das and Surendra Mohan Ghose on 20 January 1964, about which Das reported to Bhagwanji on the same day, shows that the top echelons in government, including Nehru, were not only aware but actively considering a plan of their own. Ghose had earlier been sent to Shoulmari ashram by Nehru to find out whether or not the sadhu was Subhas Bose. Documents accessed by us using RTI Act show that sending Ghose was a well-considered decision and, more importantly, there was a contingency plan to contact the British government in case the sadhu turned out to be Bose. Sunil Das met Ghose at Bengal Chief Minister Prafulla Chandra Sen's office along with Forward Bloc chief Hemanta Basu (who had made statements that Bose was still alive). From their conversation, Das was able to get an idea about the Central government's inner thinking. Subsequently, he conveyed to Bhagwanji that Ghose:

20   Document No 00-B 23798 CIA (C), MIS No 733556, Central Intelligence Agency, 22 November 1950. This report was released in response to a FOIA request by Anuj Dhar in 2009. Sarat Bose's granddaughter Madhuri Bose helped Dhar in this regard. This particular record was also part of documents released by CIA in 2014 in response to another FOIA request made by Maryland-based Abhishek Bose at our request. Reference No F-2014-00375. From Michele Meeks, Information and Privacy Coordinator, CIA, to Abhishek Bose, 28 January 2014.

went on to say the Allied Powers (this is Govt's opinion) have by common consent struck off the name of Netaji from the list of war criminals because they have officially concluded that Netaji was dead. Now, if Netaji reappeared he would immediately be declared an 'impostor' by the Allied Powers!

But there was more to it than given out by Ghose. Sunil Das continued:

Reading between the lines one could see that he was giving out the mind of the Government of India and not of the Allied Powers. Then, to undo this impression, he told us that before going to Shoulmari he had obtained Sri Jaharlal (sic) Nehru's authority to declare on the spot that Shoulmari's sadhu Saradanandaji was Netaji, if he (Suren Babu) was convinced of the identity. It was also arranged that in such an event, Rajen Babu [former President Rajendra Prasad] would have rushed to Shoulmari and Sri Morarji Desai who would have been in London by that time, would have been informed by cable who in his turn would have taken up the matter with the British Govt.[21]

But the Government's thoughts weren't in the public domain. They had to remain behind an iron curtain and for good reasons. The secrecy provided the Government with the flexibility to modify its course of action, which wouldn't be possible if all the information was out in the public domain. Declassified 1962-63 vintage documents[22] originating from the New Delhi embassy of The Netherlands offer an insight our own government won't let us have. On 13 October 1962, the foreign minister in The

---

21   Letter from Sunil Das to Bhagwanji, 20 January 1964.
22   Copies obtained by Seattle-based Dr Ananda Sankar Bandyopadhyay on our request.

Hague was informed that in view of the tensions with China, 'the security measures in India have been tightened up'. This makes interesting reading in the context of the impression B N Mullik gave in his memoirs, *My Years with Nehru, 1948-64*, that the Prime Minister was so devoted to the ideals of democracy that he was once reluctant to put even the suspected foreign diplomats in New Delhi under surveillance. Jhr G Beelaerts van Blokland, the Netherlands Ambassador, wrote:

> I had known for a long time that the Indian government was listening to telephone calls from embassies and keeping spies under the guise of servants. As I learned from a very reliable source, eavesdropping on telephone conversations was extended some time ago to many private foreigners. In the spring, officers of the armed forces were instructed to limit their contacts with foreigners. The telephone calls of officers are also tapped in order to make sure that the directive is followed.[23]

In his letter of 23 November 1962, Ambassador Blokland wrote that 'the Indian security service suspected that Subhas Chandra Bose... lives in an ashram'.

> I consider this story to be typical of the current state of search for an alternative to Nehru and for the reputation that Subhas Bose still enjoys, so that it might even be worthwhile to introduce a false Bose.[24]

---

23   To His Excellency the Minister of Foreign Affairs in The Hague from the Ambassador, 5163 GS - 213/1179, 13 October 1962, Nationaal Archief, The Hague. Translated from Dutch.

24   To His Excellency the Minister of Foreign Affairs in The Hague from the Ambassador, 5919/GS-277/1321, 23 November 1962, Nationaal Archief, The Hague. Translated from Dutch.

The ambassador's third dispatch was dated 9 January 1963. By this time, going by available records (including Surendra Mohan Ghose's report to Nehru and the assessment furnished by the IB chief), our Government had rejected the claim that Shoulmari sadhu was Bose.

```
5.       In his letter, Shri Malhotra has asked
the Prime Minister to officially recognise the
Shaulmari Sadhu as Netaji Subhas Chandra Bose.
This claim is quite false and the Shaulmari Sadhu
himself does not claim any connection with Netaji.
```

[Excerpt from a Top Secret letter B N Mullik wrote for the information of the PM. Obtained under Right to Information]

But, this determination was not reflected in the activities of the IB, as observed by G Beelaerts van Blokland in his letter to his foreign minister. He informed that the embassy spokesperson went to Shoulmari to 'investigate the case'. The spokesperson, who 'had met Bose more than twenty years ago...could not say with certainty whether the Sadhu, who was very little communicative, was Bose or not'. When the spokesperson returned to Delhi, he wanted to write articles about his experiences in the press, but 'he was requested to leave this to the Indian Intelligence Service'. Van Blokland concluded that

> the Indian Intelligence Service is watching the case and does not want the Sadhu to be extra cautious because of publications in the press, nor that the people in Bengal are made restless by false rumours before the government has enough material to intervene.[25]

---

25 To His Excellency the Minister of Foreign Affairs in The Hague from the Ambassador, 108/GS-7/41, 9 January 1963, Nationaal Archief, The Hague. Translated from Dutch.

5919/GS-277/1321   New Delhi, 23 november, 1962

G E H E I M .-

Is Subhas Chandra Bose nog in leven?

Naar ik verneem zou de Indische veiligheidsdienst
vermoeden dat Subhas Chandra Bose, de leider van de Indian
National Army, die heet in 1945 te zijn omgekomen bij een
vliegtuigongeluk in Assam, in een ashram (klooster) woont.
In Shaulmari (Assam) woont in een ashram een zekere
sadhu Shardanand. Het eigenaardige is dat deze Sadhu uit

[Nationaal Archief, The Hague]

That Bhagwanji was aware of the impostor trap that lay awaiting his 'return' is proven by his utterances and written comments. He articulated in a letter to Pabitra Mohan Roy on 5 February 1963:

In the back of their (Nehru and his associates) minds there's fear. They know extremely well what shall happen when 'the ghost who walks' appears. So, it is but natural that he should stake everything to set the stage before the ghost's possible appearance—with a fait accompli. But again I say, he is counting without his host.

In a comment made on the margins of Sunil Das's letter, he indicated that he was acutely alive to the possibility of the impostor angle.

নাছোড়বান্দা হাবাতে যে পেল্লাদের মতো বেঁচেই আছে এ কথা তিন পক্ষই পাক্কা-ই জানো। শুধু চার ফেলে বড়শিতে খেলিয়ে ড্যাঙ্গায় তুলতে পারছে না। SCB বেঁচে আছেন, এবং সাধুর বেশে আছেন। তিনি সকলের মধ্যে এলে 'আমরা খুশি হবো' (অর্থ সুস্পষ্ট ..
All's fair in love and war)

(All three sides [UK, USA and the Indian government] know for sure that the wretched and obstinate fellow is alive. They are just not able to reel the fish in. The meaning of 'SCB is alive in the garb of a sadhu and we will be happy if he appears' is clear. All's fair in love and war.)

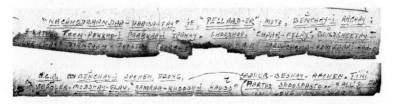

Significantly, Bhagwanji used the case of Kim Il-Sung as an illustration of his impostor theory. 'Have you ever heard the name of a certain "Netaji" named "Kim"?' he wrote to Leela Roy. According to his version, the real Kim Il-Sung was a 'great romantic figure' who as a 'real legend during the Korean independence struggle' was venerated and loved by the Koreans. However, he 'just disappeared' and was replaced by an impostor by the 'Communist Masters'. Those who once knew the real Kim Il-Sung and tried to talk about him were liquidated. As a result, Bhagwanji pointed out, the younger generation never learnt about the real Kim. The lessons Bhagwanji wanted to convey to his followers through this analogy are clear.[26]

26 It is a story that has been contested but remains in wide circulation to this day. In July 1950, *The Voice of America* announced that Kim Il-Sung was a 'phony' who 'took the name of a hero of the Korean independence movement who disappeared about 30 years ago'. *Detroit Free Press*, 12 July 1950, p 9. US Airforce planes were reported to have dropped 720,000 leaflets over cities in North Korea declaring Kim Il-Sung as 'an impostor masquerading under the name of a great Korean hero'. *Albuquerque Journal*, 25 October 1950, p 7. Newspapers in the US as well as in Britain continued to publicise the news of Kim being an impostor. A number of books by North Koreans who defected to the US have also repeated this story. For instance, in his memoir *A MiG-15 to Freedom: Memoir of the Wartime North Korean Defector Who First Delivered*

On the Shoulmari espisode, what Bhagwanji said was mind boggling. He gave his followers to understand that in the late 1950s, the Indian government came to know that he was either in China or in the vicinity of India. Bhagwanji claimed he either set up or utilised the Shoulmari tale as a 'parallel bluff' to make the Intelligence Bureau chase a mirage. 'If you go to Shoulmari, you will find letters in this faquir's handwriting,' he said on one occasion.[27] He indicated that he himself visited Shoulmari on certain occasions. He said he used to 'choke with laughter' over 'the game of Shoulmari' as it played out. Because he was not Netaji, Saradananda himself did not emerge to proclaim in front of a big crowd who he really was and end the controversy. If he had, Bhagwanji reasoned, the 'combine' (by which Bhagwanji meant Nehru, the British and the Americans) would have been 'free to concentrate' in one direction, in search of the 'real' person. He said he couldn't lower his guard because any 'carelessness' on his part would 'give the key of the puzzle' to the combine. 'তখন যে "ভয়ানক ভূত" কাঁধে চেপে আছে তাকে "ওঁরাদের" দ্বারা "সরিয়ে ফেলা" সম্ভব হয়ত হয়ে যাবে। (Then this "ghost" that is sitting on their shoulders could perhaps be eliminated by "ghostbusters".)'[28]

The Shoulmari episode, apart from gauging the reaction of the political establishment also helped Bhagwanji in assessing

---

the Secret Fighter Jet to the Americans in 1953, Senior Lieutenant No Kum-Sok wrote that after Kim Il-Sung showed up in North Korea in September 1945, it 'soon was clear that he was not the real Kim Il-Sung' (McFarland & Company, pp 32-33). According to another account published in 2016, 'The Russians brought in a fake Kim Il-Sung, an impostor of the original guerrilla leader…Although the Koreans recognised that the impostor was much too young (approximately thirty-two years old) to be the real Kim Il-Sung (who would have been forty-five to fifty years old), those who spoke out loudly were sent to the Siberian prison camps, where they lasted three to four years on average. (Hackchan Rhee and Marta L Tullis, *Under Five Flags*, Dorrance Publishing Co, p 84)

27 Notes of discussion with Bhagwanji taken by Dulal Nandy, January 1965.

28 Bhagwanji's letter to Pabitra Mohan Roy, 10 February 1963. Translated from Bengali.

the public reaction in the eventuality of his reappearance. When Pabitra Mohan Roy expressed his opinion that 'People might not understand everything but they will rise in anger if the Nehru government does something unwarranted. However, my earlier belief that there will be a political earthquake might not be true anymore,' Bhagwanji responded with a more realistic assessment of the situation:

> লোক ক্ষেপে উঠবে না পবিত্র! কোথায় তোমার 'ক্ষেপে ওঠার মত লোক'? সব মরে গ্যাছে। Earthquake-এর তো কথাই নেই। এ দুটো যদি হবার হতো তবে এ-তো-দিন-ধরে শোলমারী গড়াতো না। এটাও তোমার চোখ এড়িয়ে গেলো? যদি ক্ষেপে ওঠার এবং earthquake-এর মত বারুদ থাকতো তবে শোলমারীর প্রথম সূচনাতেই দপ করে আগুন লেগে যেতো (People won't be infuriated Pabitra! Where are your people who can be enraged? All of them are dead. There is no question of an earthquake. If these were to happen, Shoulmari would not have extended for so-o-o-o long. How could you miss this? If there was enough ammunition for being enraged and creating an earthquake, then the fire would have burst forth during the early days of Shoulmari.)[29]

It was the government's deliberate ploy to prolong the 'theatre' despite knowing that Saradananda was not Subhas Bose, he said, otherwise it doesn't take long to conclusively prove the identity of a person. However, for the Government too, 'It was important to project Saradanandaji for such an extended period and minutely analyse its impact on public mind.'[30] The Shoulmari incident served some purpose, but he knew that it couldn't continue for much longer. Thus, he wrote to Pabitra in the same letter:

---

29   Bhagwanji's letter to Pabitra Mohan Roy, 2 September 1963.
30   Bhagwanji's letter to Pabitra Mohan Roy, 12 February 1963.

The combine [Nehru, UK and the US] are no fools. They can well handle the situation from A to Z. Such a lovely theatre! The combine knows these international rules: (a) The public memory is proverbially short, (b) The public will come to believe in anything which will be constantly and repeatedly propagated to them over a long period, (c) Ordinarily, the public is incapable of remaining at a high pitch for a long time, (d) The overwhelming mass of the public are stupid and fools. They are mere rabble, they could be used in any way and for any purpose by any unscrupulous man or Party. (e) The public lose interest in anything which is long, and protracted. Pabitra! These are fundamental facts. JN (the Combine) is using these rules to his entire advantage.[31]

Bhagwanji described his reading of the situation in a letter written on 26 January 1965 to Sunil Krishna Gupta:

All the show that is being held in India (also elsewhere) is meant to lure 'the dead' out or to dragnet him, or to get him roused in hot wrath, thereby exposing himself, or if he doesn't care, then to palm off another as him and foist the same on the people. Because they know the awesome truth best that 'the dead' has not died...he anticipated their move and eluded.

In the final analysis, this whole affair helped him to test the public reaction to the news of his reappearance (which disappointed him), to watch how the government reacts and to spot if there was any loophole in his scheme of living under absolute secrecy. Even the appearance of an impostor wouldn't affect the plan which he was working on, Bhagwanji told Pabitra.

---

31 Bhagwanji's letter to Pabitra Mohan Roy, 2 September 1963.

'This "Netaji affair" is "important" only to a degree...not beyond that. We are interested only in watching which way the "wind" is blowing...even if 101 Netajis appears on the Indian scene—still, still—the Kali-dances shall occur.'[32]

Therefore, in contrast to Bhagwanji being an impostor as accused by the likes of Subramanian Swamy, Purabi Roy and certain Netaji kin, it was his apprehension about the consequences of reappearing and being accused of being an impostor that appears to have been one of the reasons why he decided to remain on the sidelines of the society which he once led. The ignominy of such a consequence would have been unbearable for such a proud man.

The common thread that thus runs through all the 'what if' scenarios is the assumption regarding the starting point. All such hypothetical scenarios start with the presumption that Netaji would return in 1946 or 1947. The scenario would vastly change if we advance the starting point to the early 1950s, the time when Bhagwanji crossed over into India through the porous Indo-Nepalese border.

The political situation of this time might have been another of the deterrents to Bose's return. Sardar Patel was dead, and Pandit Nehru was firmly ensconced at the helm without any serious challenge from within the Congress or any of the opposition parties. The Congress party led by Nehru captured almost the entire Lok Sabha, winning 419 of 489 seats. The principal opposition was the Communist Party, followed by the Socialist

32 Bhagwanji's letter to Pabitra Mohan Roy, 12 February 1963.

Party. While the Communist Party had nothing but bitter hatred towards Netaji, the Socialist Party's desertion when their support mattered in 1939 is something that he wouldn't forget. Although there was discussion of an armed uprising between Bose and Jayaprakash Narayan just before Bose left India in 1941, Narayan was more of a Gandhian now than ever. Moreover, in 1952, the Socialist Party merged with the Kisan Mazdoor Praja Party of JB Kripalani, the bête noire of Bose's Congress years. Syama Prasad Mookerjee (about whom Bhagwanji displayed favourable feelings) had set up the Bharatiya Jana Sangh, but he was dead by 1953. In the South, Chakravarti Rajagopalachari was on his way out of Congress, but the ideological differences with him were far too wide, and their history of confrontation since the time he joined the Congress was too deep to be forgotten. Bose's own party Forward Bloc had split into two and was on the cusp of further splits. In Bengal, Dr BC Roy, who had crossed over to the Gandhi-Nehru camp in the 1930s was the Chief Minister and the principal opposition, again, were the communists, a mere reference to whom Bhagwanji could not stand.

In short, except a few splinter groups, there was no large political party which would stand behind Bose if he returned. Even if they gave in to prevailing popular sentiment there was no common ground that could make such an alliance sustainable. Nor were there national political figures whom he could count on as loyal allies. He would have been his own man. This was partly the legacy of his own politics. As the wily Nirad C Chaudhuri correctly observed, despite his countrywide appeal and popularity, Bose had neglected building up his own power base.[33] Unfortunately, he was out of the country even before the Forward Bloc could be organised as a national party to reckon with. The former revolutionaries who had stood behind him in support didn't succeed in creating a formidable power base to challenge the Congress organisation. INA veterans and Bose's aides and supporters were not allowed to regroup in free India. In such a scenario, whether his individual popularity would have been enough to bring about a radical change in India's politics is debateable.

Although it never materialised, stepping out to proclaim himself was very much a part of Bhagwanji's plan, but only at the culmination of its execution. In other words, he planned to appear publicly only when he had achieved his goals. 'If during the coming thump, your Dead man finds the right time coming, an old man shall come over the horizon...An old man appearing,' Bhagwanji wrote to Pabitra in one of his earliest letters. This plan doesn't seem to have changed much. Bhagwanji instructed Shrikant Sharma to convey to Leela Roy during her Neemsar visit that he wouldn't emerge before his *sadhana* was accomplished. Till then, his coming out would do good neither to the country, nor to its people, nor himself. On Leela Roy's question regarding a timeframe, Bhagwanji hadn't given a specific date or year when he planned to come out in the open, but indicated two decades,

33 'Subhas Bose as a party leader failed to create a solid party behind himself...Bose had nothing behind him beyond unorganised popular support...In the end his enemies ousted him from the Bengal Congress, and his followers became the Jacobites of the province. On this score, his immense personal popularity gave him no strength.' Nirad C Chaudhuri, Subhas Chandra Bose, *The Illustrated Weekly of India*, 18 September 1955, pp 18-19.

same as in his letters to Pabitra. 'When I reappear, you will be the first one that I will meet,' Leela Roy noted Bhagwanji's assurance to her in her diary. As late as in 1980, asked by Panda Ram Kishore when he planned to appear, Bhagwanji indicated 1982, and '*Jab hum bahar ayenge to hum hi hum honge* (when I emerge in public, only I will prevail)'. When he arrives, he won't need anyone's permission or concurrence; he will arrive like a storm, Bhagwanji told his followers about himself.

Seen from the perspective of his hardcore followers, Bhagwanji had moved on to a different plane altogether. He just didn't want himself to be found so that he could work towards achieving his goals. There ought to be little surprise in this as it fits both the models of a secret revolutionary and an all-renouncing *sanyasi*. Yet, the fact remains that he was often in contact with those in positions of high power. From Sampurnanand to (if we believe the eyewitness account) Pranab Mukherjee, touching upon the military establishment, various stories float around among the people who came to know him. The man, however, clearly wanted to get away from any sort of special attention having no appetite to become a public phenomenon. An equally relevant question that often hides behind the questions directed towards Bhagwanji is why those in power, who knew, never uttered a word about him. Bhagwanji himself gave an explanation during the course of a conversation in July 1977, when he was queried by Sunil Das as to why couldn't the new Janata government ask him to 'come back and occupy his rightful place'. In his view, those who were in power wouldn't want that because their main worry would be 'if he takes his rightful place, then what will happen to us?' On a frightening note, he added, that if he emerged, 'lot of innocents will die', which means he feared a confrontation between his supporters and those of his opponents, leading to a serious law and order situation to say the least.

Bhagwanji repeatedly commented on his distaste for two key aspects of the political situation—the primacy of petty political self-interest trouncing the national interest, and the tug of war that would have ensued among parties to get him on board if he did appear on the scene. Subsequently, he observed with some amount of sadness that even if the current leaders made way for him, they would grudge the resultant suppression of their political ambitions and missed opportunities. The political structure and the spirit behind bringing the country out of its myriad problems, especially those related to poverty, health, education and communalism, were so different from what Bose had envisaged—and his views were very strong—it wouldn't be surprising if it led him to step aside and let the leaders of the free country chart its course of development. Clearly the politics of the new India was not something that he wanted to get involved with. 'The vagaries of wayward politicians have debased the very life and look of India,' he told his followers. His natural bend towards spiritual quest may have just strengthened his resolve.

In his own words

From the material available to us, the closest account explaining the reasons he remained in hiding appears in a letter Bhagwanji wrote to Sunil Krishna Gupta, the right-hand man of Suresh Bose, on 26 January 1965. Extracts from the letter, originally in

Bengali, with an English translation is as follows:

কল্যাণবর স্নেহাস্পদেষু
সুনীল
…

আমার দরকার হোলো, যে ধ্রুবতারা কে লক্ষ্য করে ঁমা কালীর নাম এবং ইশারায় এ জীবন এতকাল চলে এসেছে, সেই লক্ষ্য সেই সাধনার পূর্ণাহুতি দিয়ে ঁমা-এরই ইচ্ছাতে আরো কিছু পুরো করে সবার চোখের আড়ালে চলে যাওয়া।

সমস্ত জীবনে যে যে শিক্ষা পেয়েছি সে শিক্ষা ভুললে চলবে না আর।

ঁমা কালী যে যে বিভিন্ন ভূমিকার মধ্য দিয়ে নিয়ে গেছেন, সে সব ভূমিকায় পদে পদে চারিদিকে যা দেখেছি সে শিক্ষা ভুললে চলবে না। আমাকে শুধু ঁমা-এর কাজ পুরো করতে হবে এবং এ জন্য সব-সব-কিছুই দিতে হবে। এ কাজে নিজের কথা ভাবার যায়গা নেই।

কি দিয়েছি আমি! কিছুই তো দিতে পারিনি...সবচাইতে প্রিয়তম হোলো প্রাণ...সেই প্রাণটা তো এখনও রয়েচো। ওটাকে এখনও দিতে পারিনি...সুতরাং কিছুই দেওয়া হয়নি। আপনারা এবং সকলেই একটা মস্ত ভুল নিজেদের ভেতর পোষণ করছেন। সকলেই ধরে নিয়েচেন যে "আমাদের মৃত ঠিক আগের মতোই আছে। আমরা তাকে ঠিক আগের মতোই পাবো" etc. অথচ সকলেই এই "সর্বজনীন সামান্য সত্যটি একবারও মনে আনতে চান না যে মাতৃ গর্ভের ভ্রূণ শিশুরূপে বদলে প্রকট হয়, বীজ অঙ্কুরে বদলে যায়, অঙ্কুর চারাগাছে বদলে যায়, চারা মহীরুহ রূপে বদলে যায়। যে লোকটার সমস্ত জীবন এমনভাবে কাটলো, যে এমনভাবে গেলো, যে মরু-কান্তার-অধিত্যকা উপত্যকা-গুহা-পর্বত-সমুদ্র যবনের-কিরাতের-রাক্ষসের দেশে অতি দীর্ঘকাল কাটাতে বাধ্য হোলো, যে ঁমা কালীর-ই কৃপাতে এক এক কোরে যা কর্তব্য কোরে মরে গেল, যে মড়ার ভূতকে বাড়িতে হানা দেওয়া বন্ধ করবার জন্য, আত্মীয়-স্বজন-কুটুম্ব সবাই, হাজার হাজার ওঝা-রোজা মিলে মন্ত্র-তন্ত্র-সরষে পোড়ার অভেদ্য গণ্ডী দিয়ে, ভূত যাতে হানা দিতে না পারে তার জন্য সব রকমের উপায় করে রাখলো, যে সব ডাক্তারেরা মিলে মড়া থেকে এক বিকট ফ্র্যাঙ্কেনস্টাইন গড়ে তুলেছেন—সেই ডাক্তারেরাই জানছেন, তাঁদেরই গড়া ফ্র্যাঙ্কেনস্টাইন তাঁদেরই উপরে কি ভয়ঙ্কর পরিস্থিতি আনতে পারে। সুতরাং 'আত্মানং সততং রক্ষেৎ' এই শাস্ত্র নির্দেশ মেনে তাঁরা সেই ফ্র্যাঙ্কেনস্টাইনকে immobilise করবার জন্য এবং দরকার হোলে দফনাবারও জন্য সব রকমেরই ব্যবস্থা করেছেন (এতে আশ্চর্যের কিছুই নেই)। যার আপন বোলতে আর কেউ-ই নেই (রই-লো-না), কিছুই নেই, সেই লোকটাকেই যদি সকলে পূর্বের মতোই পেতে চায়: তবে বোলতেই হবে যে, তাঁরা সবাই সব নিজের মনে বুঝেও আত্ম এবং পরো বঞ্চনা কোরছেন কোনো বিশেষ কারণে (কি কারণ তা সহজেই বোঝা যায়)। যে কোন বুদ্ধিমান এটা বেশ বোঝেন যে যাঁর জীবনের

উপর দিয়ে এরূপ বিপুল প্রলয়কান্ড একটার পর একটা হোয়ে যায়, তাঁর জীবনের 100 per cent complete metamorphosis হোয়ে যাবেই—এ ধ্রুব সত্য।

হাসি আসে এই ভেবে যে,—যে লোকটা স্ব ইচ্ছাতেই, নিজের বোলতে সবকিছুর ওপর থুথু ফেলে লাথি মেরে অম্লান বদনে ত্যাগ কোরে (নীরব নিশীথে 'মা জননীকেও কিছু না জানিয়ে, প্রণাম তাঁর পায়ের উপর না কোরে) চলে গেলো: সে-ই কি না আসবে তার থুথু ফেলা চাটবার জন্য!!! এই ভয়েই তাকে রুখবার জন্য এতো বিরাট 'ঘরের লোক + বাইরের লোক + পার্টি + তিনটে গভর্নমেন্টের ব্যাপক হিংস্র ষড়যন্ত্র করতে হোচ্চে? না, না সুনীলবাবু! এ কখনও হোতে পারে না! সে মরে গেছে: মরে ভূত হোয়ে গেছে: শুধু আছে 'মৃতের ভূতাত্মা'!

সেই 'মৃতভূতাত্মা', সেই ডাক্তারদের দ্বারা raised Frankenstein আসচে—আসবেই: দুর্নিবার দুরন্ত নিয়তির মতো, কালবৈশাখীর তুফানের মতো unremitting nemesis-এরই মতন।

কিন্তু সে মৃতভূতাত্মা বাড়ি ঘরের ভাগ নিতে আসবে না; আত্মীয় স্বজনকে পুনরায় আপন বলে ডাকতে আসবে না (তারা তো নিজেরাই তার শ্রাদ্ধ করেছে!); পার্টি এবং দলাদলি করতেও আসবে না; কিছুই নিতে আসবে না।

সে আসচে-আসবে, 'মা কালীর হস্ত রূপে; সে আসবে এক অসম্ভবকে সম্ভব করে, রূপ দিতে (যা এখন সকলেই অসম্ভব বোলচেন, তা-ই কোরে, সকলের সামনে 'পরিবেশিত থালের' মতোই রাখতে)।...

...সহনশীলতা-cum-কোমলতা বশ যে 'ভুলগুলো' মৃত জেনে বুঝেই সহন করতো; যে অসংখ্য বিভিন্ন মতলবে লোভ-স্বার্থ-নীচতা-বিশ্বাসঘাতকতার লীলা চারিদিকে দেখতো; যে সব দিগন্তের পথে চলে শিক্ষা-দীক্ষা লাভ কোরেচে: সে সব ভুললে চলবে না মৃতের... তা-ই 'মা কালী-ই তাকে মৃত কোরে দিয়ে লক্ষ্যের দিকে এগিয়ে যাবার রাস্তা খুলে দিয়েছেন!

তা-ই এবার মৃতের কার্য ও ক্ষেত্র সুদূরপ্রসারী: 'সাধনপ্রণালী' দুর্গম, দুর্জেয়, foolproof-অমোঘ! সকলের বিস্মিত চোখের সামনে মাটীর ওপর astride চলবার পূর্ব মুহূর্ত পর্যন্ত 'মৃত এবং মৃতের কূটকৌশল চলন' ডেড থাকবে, সর্বসাধারণের জ্ঞান-বুদ্ধির অগম্য হয়ে: এই অপূর্ব কৌশলের মধ্যেই পূর্ণ সিদ্ধির চাবিকাঠি।

এবারের পূজাই মৃতের মহাপূজা। প্রায় দু যুগের (?) constant, unrelenting tests-trials-errors-campaigning-sifting -জীবনভোর সাধন অভিজ্ঞতার পর।

There's no power on earth which has or can have the capacity to halt or check, or stem the calculated terrible onrush of the

Dead—the Nemesis.

The Ghost needs no party: for when he is astride the land, he is the party.

The Dead needs no following, for when he is there, automatically the country as a whole becomes so.

The operation is that of a chessboard. That of blood and tears. That of total sacrifice…. There's no drawing back, no pulling of the punches. The Dead does not and shall never ask for quarters, nor shall he give quarters to any…The *Faquir* shall achieve his life's dream and *sadhana*—and to do this, if I cannot move the Gods, I will stir up hell itself.

This time, the *Faquir* is inscrutable! Even the devil himself shall not be able to fathom my thoughts; Yes, inscrutable I am!

এখনও 'আমার সকল দুখের
প্রদীপ জ্বেলে দিবস গেলে করব নিবেদন
আমার ব্যথার পূজা
হয় নি সমাপন…'

যে কোন সদবুদ্ধি সম্পন্ন মনুষ্য এ যুক্তি সহজেই বুঝতে পারে যে আমার এই ব্যথায় ভরা মাতৃপূজা ঠিকভাবে সমাপ্ত করতে হলে it is absolutely imperative (in fact, it is the sine qua non) that the Dead must remain dead.

কিন্তু
আমার ব্যথার পূজা হবে সমাপন
'যখন পূজার হোমানলে উঠবে জ্বলে একে একে তারা,
আকাশ-পানে ছুটবে বাঁধন-হারা,'
তখন আমার শেষ কথাটি করব নিবেদন
ফকিরের ব্যথার পূজা হবে সমাপন॥

…এই জন্যেই নিমসারে order দিয়েছিলুম: 'ভুলে যাবেন, এদিকে আসবেন না, কাউকে আসতে দেবেন না; কেউ জিজ্ঞাসু হলে সাফ উল্টো বুঝিয়ে সেইখানেই প্রশ্ন সমাপ্ত করে দেবেন'।…

Faquir

(Translation)
[Dear Sunil
…
All I need to do is to complete the *sadhana* that I have undertaken throughout my life in the name of Mother Kali, following a fixed goal, and then disappear.
I cannot afford to forget all the lessons that I have learnt in this life.

All the roles that Mother Kali has taken me through, everything that I have seen and learnt while playing those roles—I cannot forget. I have only to complete Mother's task and have to give up everything for that. In this mission there is no scope to think about my own self.

What have I given? I haven't been able to give anything…the dearest thing to a man is his life…but I am still alive. I haven't been able to give my life yet. Therefore, I haven't given anything. All of you are carrying a very big misconception in your mind. You have assumed that 'Our Dead is just as he was earlier and that we will have him in that form.' But no one is ready to understand the universal truth that an embryo transforms into a baby inside a mother's womb, a seed germinates into a sprout, a sprout transforms into a sapling and a sapling into a tree. The man who has lived his life in such a manner; who left home in such a manner; who had to spend such a long time in deserts, mountains, valleys and caves in the lands of Yavanas, Kiratas, Rakshasas; who died by the grace of Mother Kali after doing his duties; the man whose family has taken all measures to prevent his homecoming; a man who has been depicted as the Frankenstein's monster by the 'doctors'; a man who they are ready to bury to protect themselves; a man who no more has anyone to call his own—now if anyone wants to get back that man just as in his earlier days, then I must say that he is wilfully deceiving himself and others. Any intelligent person will surely understand that the life of a man who has gone through such upheavals will undergo 100% complete metamorphosis.

I find it amusing that people expect of a man, who spat on everything of his own and left home in the middle of the night (even without touching the feet of his mother) without any hesitation, to come back and lick clean that spit. And out of that fear they have set up such a huge conspiracy involving the family, outsiders, party, and three governments to stop him. No Sunilbabu, his return in the old form is not possible. He is dead. Now he is only a ghost of the dead.

What will come back is that ghost of the dead. He shall arrive like unstoppable destiny, like a summer storm, like an unremitting nemesis.

But that ghost of the dead will return neither to claim his share of property, nor to call his family his own (they have themselves done his *shraddha*), nor to get involved in party politics. He won't come to take anything. He will come as the hand of Mother Kali, to do something that is considered impossible by everyone and serve that in a platter....

...The Dead cannot afford to forget the lessons he learnt from the mistakes that he tolerated out of sympathy, from the greed, self-interest, meanness and treachery that he saw all around him. That is why Mother Kali has made him dead and facilitated his progress towards attaining the goal.

That is why the field and work of the dead is expansive; his method of *sadhana* is difficult, unknowable, foolproof and infallible. The dead and his strategy will remain non-existent— beyond the comprehension of the people—till moments before he walks astride on the soil of the country in front of all eyes. There lies the key to the success of the plan.

This worship is the Dead's great worship, after nearly two decades of constant, unrelenting tests-trials-errors-campaigning-sifting and a lifelong experience of *sadhana*.

There's no power on earth which has or can have the capacity to halt or check, or stem the calculated terrible onrush of the Dead—the Nemesis.

The Ghost needs no party: for when he is astride the land, he is the party.

The Dead needs no following, for when he is there, automatically the country as a whole becomes so.

The operation is that of a chessboard. That of blood and tears. That of total sacrifice...There's no drawing back, no pulling of the punches. The Dead does not and shall never ask for quarters, nor shall he give quarters to any...The *Faquir* shall achieve his life's dream and *sadhana*—and to do this, if I cannot move the Gods, I will stir up hell itself.

This time, the *Faquir* is inscrutable! Even the devil himself shall not be able to fathom my thoughts; Yes, inscrutable I am! Even now, 'I will light the lamp of all my sorrows and offer it at the end of the day. The tribute of all my agony is not yet complete.'

Any honest person will be able to comprehend it without difficulty that if I have to complete this agonising worship of the Mother, it is absolutely imperative (in fact it is the sine qua non) that the Dead must remain dead.

But, the tribute of all my pain will be complete 'When the stars rise from the sacred fire and travel unrestrained towards the sky'. I will then present my last words and this *Faquir*'s worship of pain will be complete....

...That is why I had issued the order in Neemsar: 'Forget me, don't come this side and don't let anyone come. If anyone is curious, end the discussion by saying completely opposite things.'...

—*Faquir*]

The call of renunciation

The arguments, seemingly axiomatic, that have been forwarded to contest even the possibility of Bhagwanji being Netaji are—(a) Subhas Bose could not have renounced the world for the life of an ascetic, and (b) Subhas Bose was too dynamic a person to have lived a life of exile instead of stepping forward to take charge of his motherland mired in a thousand problems. Along with other persons, a section of the 'Netaji kin' have vociferously argued along these lines. A granddaughter of Sarat Bose, Madhuri Bose, opined that 'If he [Subhas] could return to India, he is not a man who will sit behind curtains.' She quoted from one of Netaji's earliest collections of random writing penned in the Mandalay jail, titled *Pebbles on the Seashore*: 'Embracing *Sanyasa* when your country needs you is only a refined form of betrayal.' A person who enunciated this principle could not possibly have chosen 'to be in hiding or isolation from the trials and tribulations of his beloved motherland, as some have alleged'.[34]

Madhuri Bose and other 'Netaji kin' have further charged, in personal communications with the authors as well as on various social media platforms, that the authors have lowered Netaji's image by suggesting that the man known as 'Gumnami Baba' was Subhas Chandra Bose. The first outburst had however come from Madhuri's more famous first cousin, whose parents had joined the Congress ignoring the treatment meted out to Subhas and his legacy by the grand old party. 'Linking Netaji with some

---

34 'Netaji would never have lived in hiding, says grandniece.' *The Hindu*, 22 December 2015. http://www.thehindu.com/news/cities/kolkata/netaji-would-never-have-lived-in-hiding-says-grandniece/article8014798.ece.

Gumnami Baba is actually disrespect shown to a person who has devoted his entire life to the country,' Sugata Bose, MP, told PTI in January 2016.[35]

Needless to say, these are individual opinions and not arguments which can prove or disprove the identity of Bhagwanji. In fact, the loathing of these family members—whose primary identity in public life is that they are 'Netaji kin'—is so acute that it makes one wonder if there is more to their posturing than what meets the eye. Under the current state of inadequate information, it can neither be proved or disproved whether Bose actually took *sanyas,* and if he did, when. All we need to critically assess is whether the possibility was strong enough for Bose to have crossed over the line to have transformed it into reality. That would be corroboration enough for Bhagwanji's claim that he formally took *sanyas.*

It is only too well known that Subhas was spiritually inclined from his childhood and that the Ramakrishna-Vivekananda tradition had a tremendous impact on his adolescent mind. The goal of his life— *Atmano Mokshartham Jagaddhitaya cha* (for your own salvation and for the service of humanity) was settled early.[36] Even as his spiritual quest intensified with time, the two elements of personal salvation and service of humanity remained deeply intertwined. Meditation, study of scriptures, a vow of *brahmacharya* (celibacy) went hand in hand with intense service

35 'Netaji disrespected by linking him with Gumnami Baba: Sugata,' *India Today,* 8 January 2016, https://www.indiatoday.in/pti-feed/story/netaji-disrespected-by-linking-him-with-gumnami-baba-sugata-485526-2016-01-08.

36 Subhas Chandra Bose, *Netaji's Life and Writings, Part One: An Indian Pilgrim or Autobiography of Subhas Chandra Bose 1897-1920,* Thacker, Spink & Co, 1948, p 42

without care for personal welfare. His leaving home in search of
a guru is too well known to be repeated. These two ideals which
came to be formed by his systematic study of Western Philosophy
were the bedrock of his politics. Subhas stood at the intersection
of the individual, the collective, the esoteric and rationality.

As time went by, the synthesis of tradition and modernity and
the welfare of the collective became his public face, overshadowing
the esoteric and the individual which he began to guard under
an intense sheath of privacy. This perhaps was inevitable in a
sense as politics became his mainstay; a distance developed with
the groups with which he had become associated during this
student days in Calcutta. Even Hemanta Sarkar, his closest friend
from 1912 moved away for political differences. The continued
personal connect notwithstanding, ideological differences were
too wide to bridge. The one person who continued to have the
privilege of discussing with Subhas his deeper spiritual thoughts
was Dilip Kumar Roy, son of the famous poet, composer and
playwright Dwijendra Lal Roy, and his friend from college days at
Cambridge. Although Dilip might not have known every detail
of his friend's spiritual practice, he was perhaps the best informed
among friends as Subhas would reveal to him his deeper spiritual
self. He was also the most sensitive to Subhas's sustained inner
conflict between the mystic and the worldly.

Writing the preface to his reminiscences of Subhas in 1966,
Dilip summed up his impression: 'Netaji was a mystic par excellence
and not a politician'.[37] The mystic in Subhas had manifested

---

37   Dilip Kumar Roy, *Netaji—The Man: Reminiscences*, Bharatiya Vidya Bhavan,
     2nd Edition, p vii.

early in life and continued to evolve. Thrown into the turmoil of politics after his return from England, the incarceration from 1924 to 1927 gave him the opportunity to concentrate on doing what his busy public life of three years had severely curtailed. His broken health and persistent illness notwithstanding, he utilised the time in taking up some serious study on a variety of subjects, but more importantly turned to a deeper pursuit of the spiritual. Sarat sent him Swami Vivekananda's works containing *Raja Yoga*. In the jail, Subhas set up a *thakurghar* (a separate room or place for worship) for meditation. The incarceration—'the solitude and the distance from home'—benefitted him in terms of spiritual and philosophical advance, Subhas wrote to Dilip. He also shared his views on the secrets of meditation and overcoming lust:

> Meditation has two aims—(1) Destruction of the evil faculties, principally to overcome lust, fear and selfishness, and (2) Manifestation of love, devotion, sacrifice, intellect and such other noble attributes. The best means of conquering lust is to visualise the mother-image in all women, to invest women with that halo and to worship God in the mother-form, such as Durga and Kali. When man contemplates God or Guru in the form of the mother, he learns to see divinity in all women; when he reaches this state he has overcome lust. That is why our forefathers, in order to create an image of Divine Power, thought in terms of the form of woman. In practical life, man becomes pure and clean through the process of contemplating 'mother' in all women.... Devotion and love render a man selfless.... The way to conquer fear is to worship Power. The images of Durga, Kali, etc. are the expressions of Power....

Subhas sought to learn more about different spiritual practices (he asked Gopabandhu Das for books on Oriya saints and their methods of *sadhana*), but in the spiritual realm, what seems to have particularly grasped his attention during this time was Tantra. He had read Shivachandra Vidyarnava's *Tantra Tattva* earlier, but now took great interest in John Woodroffe's works (who translated many Sanskrit scriptures under the pseudonym Arthur Avalon) and asked Sarat whether Woodroffe had any disciple who could continue the work.[38]

Dilip was deeply influenced by Sri Aurobindo and therefore in his correspondence with Subhas the topic of Aurobindo's renunciation of political life to become a spiritual recluse naturally came up. Subhas thought that as a mystic Aurobindo had gone even deeper than Vivekananda. Spiritualism was in his nature, and he had chosen Aurobindo as his guru, but he was uneasy with the thought of renouncing everything in pursuit of the divine. He explained the reason to Dilip:

> I agree with you when you say that one may from time to time—and, on occasion, for a long spell—remain withdrawn in silent contemplation in perfect seclusion. But here there is a danger; the active side of a man might get atrophied if he

---

38   Among the other books that he requisitioned were *Tantrasar, Prantoshini, Brihat Tantrasar, Shaktananda Tarangini, Shyama Rahasya, Tara Rahasya,* Bengali translations of the *Sama Veda, Yajur Veda* and *Atharva Veda,* comparative study between the Vedas and the Avesta. A list of books which he requested a friend to send him also included *Haratatta Didhiti, Harivakti Bilas, Shuddhitattam, Shraddhatattam, Atri Samhita, Vishnu Samhita, Harit Samhita, Yajnyabalka Samhita, Usana Samhita, Ajnira Samhita, Yama Samhita, Upastamba Samhita, Sambarta Samhita, Kyattayan Samhita, Brihaspati Samhita, Parasar Samhita, Vyas Samhita, Sankhya Samhita, Likhita Samhita, Daksha Samhita, Goutam Samhita, Shatatap Samhita, Vashistha Samhita,* and *Baudhayan Samhita.* Clearly this was not an idle curiosity of an amateur exploring the spiritual possibilities, but point to a quest for attaining some progress based on knowledge and practice.

remained cut off for too long from the tides of life and society. This need not, indeed, apply to a handful of authentic seekers of uncommon genius, but the common run, the majority, ought, I think, to take to action in a spirit of service as the main plank of their *sadhana*. For a variety of reasons our nation has been sliding pauselessly down to the zero line in the sphere of action, so what we badly need today is a double dose of the activist serum, *rajas*.

There were also people outside the circle of his close friends who wished him success in his spiritual preparation. One of them, a former associate—an elderly Congressman who once belonged to the Gandhian 'no-changer' group, believing himself to be near the end of his life sent Subhas his blessings: 'Be immortal and as a *Yogasiddha* (one who has attained perfection in yogic practices) person gather strength to put an end to the sorrows of our motherland.'[39] Blessings, it is quite redundant to highlight, are not dispensed usually in that manner in our country.

Subhas's prison notebooks containing random notes written during his stay in the Mandalay jail show a lesser known side of his thinking on Hinduism. Since it was not directly relevant to his politics or his individual spiritual practice, it hasn't got much attention. The notes show that he was reflecting upon the expansion of the Hindu religion in other continents. Noting that only Christianity and Islam are preached in Africa, he asked, 'Why should Hinduism not be preached there?' He remembered the

39   Letter from Rajendra Dev, 9 November 1926, *Netaji Collected Works*, Volume 4, Netaji Research Bureau, p 94

efforts of Swami Vivekananda in taking Hinduism to the Western world. That was a good thing in so far as influencing the Western society and philosophy, but the Europeans and Americans were not going to adopt Hinduism, he argued. There was a better chance of Africans adopting Hinduism. The resultant benefits would be threefold, he wrote:

> Firstly, what is gained by preaching the truth is always there. Secondly, Africans not yet civilised or only half-civilised will be fully civilised in the light of Hinduism and civilisation. Thirdly, by being aggressive Hinduism will acquire further strength and, as a result of being preached in a different country, will be compelled to shed many of its prejudices and dogmatism.... If two hundred lakhs of Africans embrace Hinduism, then undoubtedly the influence of the Hindus and of India will be quite powerful in Africa. If India wants to be a world power then the preaching of Hinduism will facilitate the process.[40]

Subhas's outburst against Gandhi and Aurobindo during the Calcutta Youth Congress Conference in 1928 is often presented in defence of the contention that he could never take *sanyas*. The essence of his criticism was indeed in line with his outlook towards life, but presenting them without any reference to the context grossly distorts this incident. It was a time when Chittaranjan Das's death had left a huge vacuum in the political scape of Bengal and the Gandhian wing, led by Gandhi himself, dominated Bengal Congress. As Subhas worked towards regaining the lost

---

40 Sisir K Bose (ed), *Netaji Collected Works*, Vol 5, Netaji Research Bureau, 1985, pp 8-9.

space for Das's brand of politics and that of the radicals, he needed comrades who would take the struggle forward. But he found Dilip and Anil Baran—his old trusted friends—to have decided to move to Pondicherry. Barindra Nath Ghosh, Aurobindo's brother who on his return from the Cellular Jail was reinstituted by Das, fleeted between Calcutta and Pondicherry. Subhas tried to wean them back but without success. He was also extremely critical of the disciples who under the influence of spiritual leaders tended to withdraw from a life of action. The frustration and annoyance born out of this environment and its conflict with the dangling threat of the call of divinity within himself were most likely factors for his outburst.

Subhas's emphatic statements notwithstanding, Dilip didn't fail to notice the constant struggle between the two forms of spiritual quest—the private, where the *sadhana* aimed for personal realisation or *siddhi*, and the public, whose manifestation was the struggle for liberating the motherland. In this struggle Subhas appears to have placed more weight on the public side, at least for the time being, if only for fear that giving the other side a little more would take him away to a different plane. In 1932 Subhas wrote to Dilip from the Madras penitentiary, 'I do not know if I am sufficiently "open" to receive yogic-power—probably not.' Now why would a politician with an alleged antipathy towards the reclusive life even aspire for yogic power?

The fear of losing himself completely to the spiritual quest is apparent from a conversation which Dilip had with Subhas in 1938 but reported many years later:

I want you [Subhas] to fulfill your life following your *swadharma*, to wit, the deepest call of your nature. Why waste it? Come along with me to Pondicherry. One who has the capacity to become a nation-builder should not fritter away his precious energy in building a futile party which cannot achieve anything worthwhile even in the best of time. 'I know Dilip,' he retorted. 'But I can't turn to Yoga branded "defeated" by life.' His lips quivered and sparks flew from his eyes. 'Can't you at least come away with me for a few months, if only to see your way clearer?' 'But no, Dilip. Even that is impossible. Because if I go with you into even a temporary seclusion, I am afraid I may not be able to come out again into the open with the fire of the fighter in me.' He did not care to win peace not even a truer vision, because he loved the cause of his country too dearly.[41]

The conflict deeply influenced Dilip making him recall that 'the more I admired Subhash [sic] the more I prayed that he might be rescued from the perfidious tentacles of political adventurers. I reminded him again and again years later, when I saw him fighting with his back to the wall, that politics was not his native line, *swadharma*; but alas, he was born with an obstinate streak of rational madness.'[42]

The mystical streak in him not only drove Subhas to build his political life on the foundation of the spiritual, but he also attempted to pass it on to the next generation. In a letter written to nephew Amiya (Madhuri's father) in February 1934, Subhas

---

41   Dilip Kumar Roy, *Netaji The Man: Reminiscences*, Bharatiya Vidya Bhavan, 2nd Edition, p 51.
42   Ibid, p 55.

outlined the fundamentals of a moral life, prominently featuring *sanyas*, or renunciation.[43] *Sanyas*, wrote Subhas, manifests itself in different forms in different ages. The form required for the current age is *karma sanyas*, which implies completely dedicating one's life to a great ideal and in the process sacrificing narrow self-interest. In other words, it implies 'selfless work'.

It is remarkable that Subhas would feel it necessary to even broach the topic of *sanyas* in a general guidance to a young nephew in his early twenties. Understandably, he did not bring up the deeper aspects of *sadhana* leading to that *sanyas*, although he did touch upon the subject of *brahmacharya* (celibacy), for this was not a letter on spiritual guidance, but only a moral one. There is no known record of what exactly his spiritual practices were, but undoubtedly Subhas was going deeper with his *sadhana*. In a letter to Dilip written on 5 March 1933, he gave some insight: He was 'torn' between the symbols of divinity—Shiva, Kali and Krishna. He had to choose one of these according to his 'prevalent mood. Of these three again, the struggle is between Shiva and Shakti.' While Shiva, the ideal Yogi fascinated him, the appeal of Kali the Mother was no less. He had also moved on from the 'ordinary rationalistic view' that mantras were like symbols, being no more than aids to concentration. Now, he admitted that:

> my study of Tantra philosophy gradually convinced me that certain Mantras had an inherent Shakti—and that each mental constitution was fitted for a particular Mantra. Since then, I have tried my best to find out what my mental constitution

---

43   Letter to Amiya Nath Bose, 21 February 1934.

is like and which Mantra I would be suited for. But so far I have failed to find that out because my moods vary and I am sometimes a Shaiva, sometimes a Shakta and sometimes a Vaishnava. I think it is here that the Guru becomes useful—because the real Guru knows more about ourselves than we do—and he could at once tell us what Mantra we should take up and which method of worship we should follow.[44]

Subhas never spoke about it in public but that he was channelising his quest for spiritual realisation through an intense and systematic *sadhana* is indicated by the meetings he had in 1938 and 1939 with those who were considered to be spiritual adepts. He neither kept any record of these meetings nor did he ever share their details with anyone. Whatever fragmented information is available is from the disciples of these gurus. The three names that have emerged from these sources are Anandamayee Ma, Barada Charan Majumdar, and Tara Khepa of Tara Pith. Although what transpired at the meetings between them is not known, these were clearly not social calls. Each of these gurus was an expert in *tantra sadhana* and it wouldn't be a stretch to link Subhas's visits to that.

The worsening crisis over his re-election as the Congress president appeared to tilt the balance in the tussle between the spiritual and the political in favour of his 'first love of life—the eternal call of the Himalayas,' albeit for a limited time. The Tripuri experience compelled him to articulate the struggle in public and also his reluctant acceptance of the occult. It also showed glimpses of how he would react to the kind of politics he was subjected to.

---

44   Reminiscences, pp 67-68.

Owing to the morally sickening atmosphere of Tripuri, I left that place with such a loathing and disgust for Politics as I have never felt before during the last nineteen years. As I tossed in my bed at Jamadoba, by day and by night, I began to ask myself again and again what would become of our public life when there was so much of pettiness and vindictiveness even in the highest circles. My thoughts naturally turned towards what was my first love in life—the eternal call of the Himalayas. If such was the consummation of our Politics—I asked myself— why did I stray from what Aurobindo Ghose would describe as 'the life divine'. Had the time now come for me to tear the veil of Maya and go back to the fountain-head of all love? I spent days and nights of moral doubt and uncertainty. At times the call of the Himalayas became insistent.[45]

The realisation that a much larger section of the country beyond the small coterie of Congress schemers stood solidly behind him helped him sail through the bitterness, but only for the time being.

As amulets, *prasadi* flowers, leaves and ash (purportedly bestowed with special divine powers) piled up, being sent by numerous astrologers and sadhus, Subhas treated them with due respect but with an 'exceedingly rationalistic frame of mind'. Yet, when a professor of Calcutta University, 'an erudite scholar in Sanskrit Literature and a man of exemplary character' conveyed to him the conclusion of a 'number of Pundits and astrologers' who had met to discuss his illness that 'somebody in some part of the country had been practising what is known in the Tantra-Shastra as *Marana-Kriya*—that is, attempt to kill by tantric process or will

---

45   Subhas Chandra Bose, 'My Strange Illness,' *Modern Review*, 1939.

power,' he couldn't ignore it. Subhas took a middle ground on the phenomenon, expressing his unwillingness to believe yet difficulty in ignoring the source—leaving it open to the interpretation that it was a momentary weakness induced by the crisis. More so, as he claimed to have relieved himself of the amulets and rings which he had worn by suppressing his 'innate rationalism'.

His public attitude towards amulets and *prasadi* flowers notwithstanding, his private *sadhana* continued. As his jailmate from July 1940 till the time he was released for home internment in January 1941, and his close political follower Narendra Narayan Chakravarti observed, Subhas continued his Kali worship in a room in the Presidency jail. The effect of the Kali worship in the dark of the night when everyone else had gone to sleep startled Chakravarti, leaving him wondering which one of Subhas's identities was more representative of the man: revolutionary or that of a *sadhaka*?[46] In keeping with his strict privacy on the matter, the sessions of meditation and worship would typically take place in the middle of the night. Chakravarty also noticed that Subhas carried with him a pocket-sized version of *Chandi* and the *Gita*. Incidentally, 1940 was also the year when Subhas organised the *Durga puja* in the jail, not entirely with happy cooperation of the government.

His regular puja and *sadhana*, to the extent possible, continued during the War, as has been recorded by SA Ayer. This continued focus on the practice of spiritualism with personal realisation as the goal as opposed to mere theorising, even while running a

---

46   Narendra Narayan Chakravarti, *Netaji Sanga O Prasanga*, Volume 2, Granthaprakash, pp 77-78.

government in exile and leading an army, is an indicator of the intensifying call of the spiritual. Ayer recalled:

> Whenever he [Netaji] was not actually doing some work or talking to somebody, he would withdraw within himself in a trice and would be in communion with God…*Sanyasi* was writ large on his forehead even when the Supreme Commander's cap rested majestically on his head at an alluring angle over his right brow.
>
> Many a night, after dinner, while in Singapore, he used to send his car to the Ramakrishna Mission to fetch the Swami in charge or his fellow-missionary, Brahmachari Kailasam, and spend a good two hours or so in spiritual communion before retiring into his study sometime after midnight, to go through official papers. Or, late at night, he used to drive incognito to the Mission, there change into a priestly silk dhoti, shut himself up in the prayer room, rosary in hand, and spend a couple of hours in meditation…
>
> …The only external symbol of his godliness was the tiny little leather bag—the tiniest article of his personal luggage, holding the two-and-a-half by two-inches Gita, the small rosary of beads (*tulsi mala*) and his spare reading glasses.[47]

Based on what Subhas told Ba Maw, the then head of the Burmese government, his comment that 'the dream element in Bose…constituted the deepest part of him' assumes great significance in this context.

> 'I often have moments,' he once told me, 'when I would like to give up everything and spend my days in prayer and

---

47   SA Ayer, *Unto Him a Witness: The Story of Netaji Subhas Chandra Bose in East Asia*, Thacker & Co Ltd, pp 268-269.

contemplation. But I must wait till India is liberated.'[48]

What happened to Subhas between August 1945 and August 1947 is largely based on speculation, with only fragments of intelligence reports indicating his presence in French Indo-China, China and Russia. Even setting this matter aside, it can be easily seen that the India of 1947-48 was starkly different from what Subhas Bose had envisaged. The country was partitioned, religions divided, the link to the Commonwealth maintained, the armed forces led by Britishers, and the old men of Congress—those who he had presciently accused of compromising with the British—firmly entrenched in the seat of power. As Ba Maw put it succinctly, 'one man sowed and others reaped after him'.[49] Subhas may have tried his luck in raising a new front against the British Indian government after 1945, evidently without success, but once the scenario changed with India's independence, it is eminently plausible for him to have reverted to his first love, that is, spiritual realisation.

When his old associates from Calcutta started knowing Bhagwanji, they were faced with a very different person from the Subhas Bose they knew. From his preference for a free market, and a uniform legal code for all religious communities, to his antipathy for socialism and communism and a heightened sensitivity towards the threat of Islamic fundamentalism to India's socio-cultural fabric, and his immersion into the spiritual, he

48   Ba Maw, *Breakthrough in Burma: Memoirs of a Revolution*, p 349.
49   Ibid, p 348.

appeared to be an enigma to those who thought they knew him. 'I have undergone complete metamorphosis,' he said. On rare occasions, someone among his followers would muster courage to confront him with this change. 'Do you think people will spare you?' Sunil Das threw the question to Bhagwanji when he met him at Ayodhya during the Durga Puja in 1965. 'Your role in spreading the awareness about Socialism wasn't any less and you were a prominent spokesperson of Hindu-Muslim unity. In fact, the Muslims had more faith in you than in Gandhi,' Das continued.

'How dare you!' Bhagwanji flared up.

Tell me the name of the person who can corner me, I would like to know his name. Of course I have said that there will be socialism in India. I am not denying that. When have I said anything against Hindu-Muslim unity? The stance that we had taken in those years was a tactic. Do you think I wasn't aware of the reality? But they must pay the price for whatever has happened in the intervening period. Who gave them the right to slaughter by the lakhs? They must not forget that 95% of them used to be Hindus. The only identity must be the son of *Janani Janmabhoomi* and nothing else. Personal approach to God will be their personal affair. If being an Islamic country Turkey could completely reform its legal system why can't you? Why don't you have the courage to apply the laws equally to Muslims as on Hindus?[50] [Translated from Bengali]

He warned that trying to assess him through the lens of the

---

pre-August 1945 personality of Subhas Bose would lead to wrong conclusions. 'With all your erudition and discernment you simply cannot comprehend the state of metamorphosis of the Ghost of Mahakaal.' He explained:

[This] poor *Faquir* was saved by dying. Mother has saved him. He will no more be hag-ridden. No more will he have to carry with him what he has done or what he hasn't done in his old/earlier life. He won't have to answer. Old relations, old acquaintances will not pester him anymore. Or else he would have had to face questions every moment—'you said this 20 years ago and now you are saying this, you did that 20 years ago and now you are doing this.' A *Faquir* has nothing to be afraid of in that regard. Mother Kali has driven him through the correct path. His road is clear. What he propounded 20 years ago has become redundant due to special circumstances. Will you do the same things in winter as in summer? Will you do the same things at 20 years age as you did when you were 10 years old?[51]

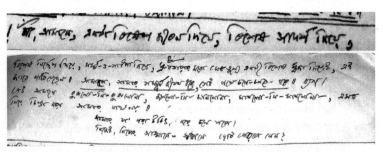

[Bhagwanji's letter to Pabitra Mohan Roy, 27 June 1977. *The Divine Mother has sent me to this world with a special purpose, a specific ideal, work and sadhana. I have to travel on that path throughout my life. That's it! It means nothing to me whether someone understands me or not, obeys me or not, knows me or not. I will leave after doing my duty. Why should I belittle my soul, myself?*]

---

51 Charanik, *Oi Mahamanaba Ase,* Jayasree Prakashan, 2010, p 129.

No family to call his own

For this man, his family had also lost all emotional connect, except one person—Suresh Chandra Bose, who had established contact through Sunil Krishna Gupta. All those who he could look up to were dead and gone. Among the innumerable documents that we have accessed, we have found fond and respectful reminiscences of only Janaki Nath, Prabhabati, Sarat and Bivabati Bose. Now only Suresh Bose was alive about whom Bhagwanji reminisced, 'He stood as the ever-vigilant guard for me, warning me about persons who were looking for me. He became the living form of Ma Janani and Baba [our mother and father].' [52] The only other person who was alive at that time about whom Bhagwanji professed affection was Dwijendra Nath Bose. In a letter to Pabitra, dated 27 June 1977, nearly five years after Suresh Bose's death, he described the emotional connect with his *Param Pujya Sejda* (my revered elder brother).

> I gave all my love and affection to Sukrit [Sunil Krishna Gupta] after *Sejda* sent him with his long letter. After that I continued corresponding with him (Suresh Chandra Bose) till one month before his demise. Fortunately, he was able to destroy all those letters in time. It was only one letter that he didn't want to destroy; his heart didn't permit. He returned it to me after Tripti (Santosh Bhattacharya) explained the risks to him.

Suresh Chandra Bose had sent a copy of his *Dissentient Report* to Bhagwanji by the hands of Kamalakanta Ghosh, but the person who often worked as the go-between for exchange of letters was

---

52   Bhagwanji's letter to Sunil Krishna Gupta, January 1965.

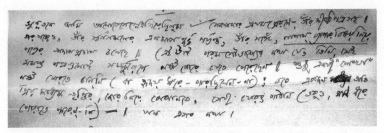

[*Bhagwanji's letter to Pabitra Mohan Roy, 27 June 1977*]

Santosh Bhattacharya. It was Bhattacharya who gave the news of Suresh Bose's demise to Bhagwanji and witnessed him break down and cry like a child.

On the face of it, it seems inconceivable that Bhagwanji wouldn't contact others in the family. The reason that Bhagwanji himself gave for not having anything to do with the rest of the family was astounding and deeply disturbing: To his mind, they had gone over to the Nehru-Gandhi camp, whom he detested.

In a letter written to Pabitra on 15 January 1973, Bhagwanji alleged that Aurobindo Bose (son of Suresh Bose) was secretly sent to Taiwan by 'Smt Gandhi' to figure out the real truth behind the story of the plane crash. It was only after knowing the truth from him that she tried her best to stop the Khosla Commission from visiting the island. According to him, when the Congress government failed to lure Suresh Chandra Bose with the offer of

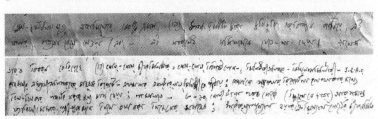

[Bhagwanji's letter to Pabitra Mohan Roy, 15 January 1973]

appointing him as a governor of a state, they spent a few crores to have the remaining family (except Dwijendra Nath Bose) brought over to their side under their control.

The most difficult to explain is Bhagwanji's attitude towards Emilie and Anita. When the matter came up for discussion once, he reacted sharply with revulsion, denying that he ever married or had a child. How could a man, he argued, who was about to take the most uncertain leap into the darkness marry a woman and beget a child? Would a person who has observed *brahmacharya* (celibacy) since his birth spoil his *sadhana* by being overtaken by momentary passion, he asked. He alleged that the letter written in Bengali by Subhas, addressed to Sarat was a forgery and that it surfaced only after the death of Sarat Bose. He warned them sternly not to bring up the issue ever again.

It is difficult to explain this confounding claim of Bhagwanji. That there was no marriage in the legal sense between Subhas Bose and Schenkl was admitted by Emilie herself. But contemporary records and accounts by people close to Subhas leave no doubt about their intimacy and birth of Anita. Moreover, the allegation of Subhas's letter to Sarat being a forgery doesn't stand scrutiny as it was seen by the people who informed Nehru and Patel of Emilie's presence, even before Sarat got to see the letter himself. Sarat too initially refused to believe that Subhas had left behind a wife and a daughter and never made a public statement acknowledging the marriage. However, his children who accompanied him on his first visit to Emilie have all endorsed the fact that he came around to accepting the marriage and was planning to have Emilie and Anita over to India when his death intervened.

The only logical explanation of his claims probably comes from the situation Bhagwanji was in. If he was living in constant danger, and if world powers against him were on the lookout, then the most natural position for him to take was to deny a relationship that might become a weakness for himself and a security threat for his own family located in the West. Happiness had to be sacrificed for safety.

Being hunted

When the game of shadows that Bhagwanji claimed to be playing was international in its scope, it is not surprising that he pointed out reasons for his lying low which were derived from international politics. To Atul Sen, he said that he was 'yet regarded as Enemy No 1 of the Allied Powers and that there is a secret protocol that binds the Government of India to deliver him to Allied "justice" if found alive'. The holy man was said to have been greatly angered in January 1971 when the news of India's accession to a UN treaty on the war criminals came. The 'convention on the non-applicability of statutory limitations to war crimes and crimes against humanity' ensured that persons responsible for war crimes during the World War II would 'not escape prosecution merely because no legal case is brought against them within a specified period after the commission of the crime'. The parties to the convention undertook 'to adopt domestic measures for the extradition of persons responsible for these crimes'. As discussed in Chapter 9: All in the Family, in 1973, when GD Khosla was hearing the final arguments of various parties, the Bose family, represented by legal luminary and former law minister of Bengal

Niharendu Dutt Majumdar took up the point Bhagwanji secretly discussed with his followers. Majumdar charged that the Government of India had suppressed/destroyed evidence which would have proved that Bose's name was included in the list of war criminals. Making the case for Netaji's escape in August 1945 to 'a place of safety where he could carry on his war', Majumdar insisted that he 'is living is an inference that we can draw unless it is rebutted'.[53]

Khosla's report went on to say that Bose's name was not included in the list of war criminals, and that has been the constant stand of the Government of India from day one. On numerous occasions, from the 1950s to the late 1990s, the matter was raised in Parliament, as well as in courts, and clarification sought from the Government. An appeal was even made in 1997 to UN Secretary General Kofi Annan for the same purpose. Replying to Air Vice Marshal Surenji Goyal (Retd) on Annan's behalf, his deputy Shashi Tharoor—former Minister of State for External Affairs—wrote that the Secretary General was 'powerless to undo any reference that may have been made in the past'.

The 'list of war criminals' in common parlance is actually the cumulative 80 lists of thousands of mostly German and Italian names. These were prepared by the United Nations War Crimes Commission (UNWCC) between December 1944 and March 1948. For example, the UNWCC list No 7 dated April 1945 had the names of Adolf Hitler and Martin Bormann. The

53 'Report of the one-man commission of inquiry into the disappearance of Netaji Subhas Chandra Bose,' Ministry of Home Affairs, 30 June 1974, New Delhi, p 59.

UNWCC was created prior to the present United Nation's birth and was assisted by a corpus called the Central Registry of War Criminals and Security Suspects (CROWCASS). The UNWCC also had a sub-commission at Chungking in China to investigate the war crimes allegedly committed by the Japanese. This sub-commission prepared 26 lists of its own. The records of the UNWCC, CROWCASS and Chungking sub-commission were in storage as classified material in different countries, especially the US, the UK and Australia, until fairly recently.

When the Mukherjee Commission tried to find out the facts, these lists were checked. On 11 April 2002, Deputy Permanent Representative of Permanent Mission of India to the United Nations in New York wrote to the Joint Secretary (Americas) in New Delhi that a First Secretary (Legal Adviser) from the mission 'had gone through the lists of war criminals in the records of the UN War Crimes Commission'.

'There is absolutely no indication whatsoever that Netaji's name was ever included in any list and was deleted subsequently. Therefore, it would be safe to conclude that the name of Netaji was not included in the lists at any time,' Deputy Permanent Representative A Gopinathan wrote, in what appeared to be the last word on the controversy. However, the Government's response to the commission's repeated query as to why India had ratified the UN treaty did not elicit any specific answer. It is quite strange that India ratified this treaty so readily, even though Indians had little interest in the world war and war crimes. On the other hand, the 'UN Convention against torture and other cruel, inhuman or degrading treatment or punishment', opened for signature, ratification and accession in 1984, was signed by India only in 1997. The land of *ahimsa* has not ratified it till date. Similarly, UN 'convention against corruption', which was entered in 2005 was ratified by India only in 2011. There is yet another suspicious circumstance that we can bring on record. In all these years, when the matter concerning the war criminal tag on Netaji was being discussed, the Government had innumerable chances to make all information public. They were specifically asked about the files and records destroyed. The Bose family clearly stated before the Khosla Commission that records concerning Subhas Bose war criminal controversy were destroyed. Khosla was not offered any information in this regard by the Government. When Justice Mukherjee pressed the issue of records related to his inquiry which were destroyed, he was told of destruction of certain files and records in 1969 and 1972. No other year was mentioned.

Now, we have come across a Ministry of External Affairs file, No 24 (5)-FEA/56 at the National Archive, which was created in response to notices of questions to be raised in the Lok Sabha in April 1956 by Sardar Iqbal Singh and in May 1956 by Amjad Ali. The questions were whether Netaji was still regarded a war criminal, and, whether the Government had taken any steps in this matter. These were inspired by a claim made on 1 April 1956 by Muthuramalingam Thevar, who, appearing as first witness before the Netaji Inquiry Committee said he wanted the Government to 'make it known categorically to the public whether Netaji's name is still in the list of war criminals, and if not, when it was removed and how?' Thevar's claim was that he had met Bose in China years after his death—and this claim came to be backed by Bhagwanji.

The first response noted in the file was that of Sarvepalli Gopal, the head of Historical Division of the Ministry of External Affairs. It read:

> I have consulted the Law and Defence Ministries. All records related to Subhas Bose were destroyed in 1947, but as far as we know Bose was not publicly designated a war criminal.

The fact that the Government should have all along concealed that 'all records relating to Subhas Bose were destroyed in 1947' and that this admission came in response to a query relating to the war criminal controversy demonstrates that there's more to this matter than meets the eye. Sarvepalli Gopal, son of President Sarvepalli Radhakrishnan, was far too intelligent to have made a mistake, for he was, as we all know, a celebrated historian and Nehru's biographer.

Suresh Bose reasoned in his *Dissentient report* that Subhas as 'a British Indian subject' had 'waged war against his king and emperor' and therefore invited this tag. In his view, Bose was 'a top-ranking "international war criminal", against which persons, after the last war, the maximum penalty was generally inflicted'. This seems reasonable when one takes into account that several INA men were branded 'war criminals' by the British Indian government, whose successor government (inheriting all legal and other obligations) was the free India government. Pre-1947 Ministry of Defence files available in the National Archives in New Delhi contain records providing details of alleged atrocities to which the loyal Indian Army soldiers were subjected after they refused to join the INA. File No INA 221 even contains a list of top INA men dubbed as 'war criminals'.

I.A. Rank.	Name.	Unit.	Category.	Witnesses.
	WAR CRIMINALS.			
	Those responsible for , condoned or took part in atrocities against Indian Ps.O.W.			
Captain	MOHAN SINGH	1/14 Punjab	I.N.A.	
Lieut.	MOHD ZAMAN KIANI	"	"	
(a) Major	AZIZ AHMED	Kapurthala S.F.	"	
Major	PRAKASH CHAND	R.I.A.S.C.	Ex-I.N.A.	Any loyal K.C.I.O. or I.C.O.
Lt-Col	A.C. CHATTERJEE	46 I.G.H., I.M.S.	I.N.A.	
	S.C. ALAGAPPAN	12 I.G.H., I.M.S.	"	
Capt.	B.M. PATTANAYAK	att 2/1 G.R., I.M.S.		
Naik	SURJA SINGH	I.A.O.C.	Changi Guard.	Capt H.C. BADHWAR (3 Cav)
Lieut	ABDUL RASHID	1/14 Punjab	I.N.A.	Any loyal K.C.I.O. or I.C.O.
(a) Sub	SHANGARA SINGH	5/14 Punjab	I.N.A.	Lt-Col P.C. DUTTA (40 Fd Amb, I.M.S.)
(a) Jem	FATEH KHAN	5/14 Punjab	I.N.A.	Hav Maj NUR KHAN (4/22 Mtn Regt)

[National Archives, New Delhi]

If that is true, why shouldn't we assume that Bose, as leader of these 'war criminals', was deemed to be as such? Our Government owes us some explanation, given that they have kept many secrets from us concerning the transfer of power—the instance of our IB reporting to British SLO stationed in New Delhi post-independence for example.

To Bhagwanji, what had happened to him was a consequence of 'three bloody brigands sworn to take revenge'.[54] He argued that while the UK and the US were after him for dealing the final blows to their imperial ambitions, Nehru joined them 'mortally and morally apprehensive of dire possibilities' should Subhas Bose appear on the scene. Although they know that he is alive, Bhagwanji said, they did not know his exact location, only being aware that he was somewhere on the northern side of the Himalayas. Any mistake on his part would bring him to their attention and possible capture. However, he assured Pabitra, 'Your Dead man carries "something" within him, which if activated, shall bring eternal sleep within six seconds.'[55] Cyanide?

---

54   Bhagwanji's letter to Pabitra Mohan Roy, 2 September 1963.
55   Bhagwanji's letter to Pabitra Mohan Roy, 10 February 1963.

A terrible secret?

The reasons explained thus far appear plausible, but to our mind they somehow do not add up to the final count. After years of minute reading of all materials available to us, we realised that there might be something more to the reasons for Bhagwanji's non-appearance. There is, and it is not a pleasant proposition. Yet, we have to make a clean breast of *everything* we know. We are doing so in a matter-of-fact manner without resorting to sensationalism in the least, hoping that exposing these loose ends might lead to developing fresh inputs to tie up the whole thing together. We see no reasons for holding anything back now, no matter how revolting or outlandish.

Hence it's time we delved into certain disturbing aspects of the Bhagwanji/Netaji mystery. What is going to be discussed henceforth is so horrendous that to even contemplate it would freeze one's spine out of shock. From what he told his followers, Bhagwanji did not slip back alone into India in the 1950s. He was accompanied by a few men. What Bhagwanji said about the identity of one of these men has been known to us for years, but it is only now that we are able to muster courage to go public with it. Even if a fraction of what Bhagwanji said, *or thought*, was true—then the very question of his surfacing did not arise.

We were not in a position to provide a presentable evaluation of this aspect earlier. If we had gone public earlier, we ran the risk of inviting ridicule, derision and charges of besmirching Netaji's image, the image of our country—by first suggesting that he was a certain Gumnami Baba in disguise and then brazenly linking the Baba to two of the most evil characters of the world history. But as we neared the end of writing this volume, we were compelled to revisit this aspect in view of the following reasons and developments:

The quest for the truth about Subhas Bose has reached its apogee largely due to the efforts made by the authors and their friends. We regard ourselves as the last in the line of all those who have endeavoured to get at the truth. We don't expect anyone to tread the same path as we have. We have spent years, sacrificed a lot in this quest, the sole focus of which has been to arrive at the truth—no matter what it is. The entire issue is of considerable importance to the public, **which overrides all other considerations.** The people want a closure, and given their track record, it doesn't seem likely our Government would ever offer it. 'The Bose family is prepared for the worst,' reported *India Today* on 16 April 2015. 'It is necessary for the people of India to know the truth,' Netaji's grandnephew Surya Kumar Bose told the magazine. 'Whether it is good or bad for Subhas, we don't know. But we are willing to face the revelations.'

Fiat justitia ruat caelum, so goes a Latin legal maxim. Let justice be done though the heavens fall. The same can be applied to truth, about which all us have been taught so much from our school days. In that spirit, we are putting all information on the table so that it can be dealt with in the proper context. There is an inherent risk of distorting the essence of any piece of extremely sensitive information, whether true or not, when it is stated in isolation. Particularly so, when that information generates widespread and deep emotions in people across the world. It makes sense and helps it in being measured up for the degree of truth it might contain only when placed in the context. Now that we have a largely complete narrative on Bhagwanji, we also have the context in which to place this piece of information.

The story goes thus: Going by his own words, Bhagwanji arrived in India with a group of people. There is no light on how, when, where and for what reasons these people came to be together. All we hear is that these people were together in the Manasarovar region as they travelled towards the Nepalese/Indian frontier. Two men were lost in the inhospitable terrain. Those who survived entered India and made their way into different directions. In the early 1960s Bhagwanji revealed the identity of these men to Shrikant Sharma in Naimisharanya's Shiva temple. In 2001, when he was 92 years old, Sharma appeared before the Mukherjee Commission. Just wanting to let everything out at the fag end of his life while his memories of those days were still vivid, Sharma narrated the following to the Commission on oath.

> One day, during the stay of Bhagawanji in Naimisharanya, out of curosity, I asked Bhagawanji as to how did he come to India. Bhagawanji stated that he along with other six persons including Hitlar came to India from China through Manas Sarovar with great difficulties, practically by crawling and gliding on the surface of snow region. He also stated that two his companions died on the way. He told the name of other persons but I do not remember now. After entering into India they were separated. Subsequently Bhagawanji came to know the news of death of Hitlar at Kankhal in Hardwar. One day Bhagawanji gave two thousand rupees to Amal Roy and asked him to see that the body of Hitlar was cremated in a dignified manner.

[Record of Shrikant Sharma's cross-examination before the Mukherjee Commission]

This isn't the only instance of Adolf Hitler making a shocking appearance in the context of the Bose mystery—though Shrikant's reference was direct and he commanded credence not enjoyed by others who made similar claims. S M Goswami, writer of 1954 booklet titled *Netaji mystery revealed,* made a claim before the Khosla Commission that 'Hitler ran away in a submarine to Japan'. According to him, Hitler and Bose fought the Americans during the Korean war. Bhagwanji was aware of Goswami's claims and seems to have approved of one or two—but not this.

A group of people from Sheopurkalan in Madhya Pradesh claimed before the Mukherjee Commission that a plane crash-landed in the village of Pandola and the three persons who survived the crash were a *sadhu*, Col Habibur Rahman and Hitler. According to them, this sadhu who came to be known as Jyotirdev was actually Subhas Bose—a claim summarily dismissed by Justice Mukherjee as 'wholly unfounded'. Unlike Shoulmari *sadhu*, we have found no link between Bhagwanji and this particular *sadhu*. Therefore, we do not know who was behind this fable.

Anuj Dhar met Shrikant in 2002 in the course of the *Hindustan Times* probe and the old man truthfully repeated the same account he had given to the Mukherjee Commission with some additional details thrown in. When told that Hitler had killed himself in 1945, Shrikant, who certainly had no axe to grind, retorted that Bhagwanji had told him that the Nazi dictator 'burnt his palace and fled'. Asked to recall other names, Shrikant strained his memory for a while and muttered what sounded like—'Himmler'. Another incomprehensible recollection was some 'mann'—a common surname in Germany.

The very thought is horrifyingly unbelievable. If it wasn't coming from Bhagwanji's followers, especially Shrikant who was rated as a credible witness by Justice Mukhejree, we would be paying no attention to it. Adolf Hitler and his deputy Heinrich Himmler, the names that bring to mind the horrors of Holocaust, were confirmed dead. The *Führer* had shot himself in his bunker in Berlin on 30 April 1945; *Reichsführer* Himmler took his turn on 23 May by chewing a cyanide capsule a day after he fell into the British hands.

Shrikant also provided a small detail which he had heard from Bhagwanji. That 'Chancellor Hitler' was fond of playing the violin in his private moments. How could someone like Shrikant, a poor man living in a remote part of India, have known about this? In April 1997, the Central Armed Forces' Museum in Moscow decided to exhibit its wartime booty that, as reported by the *Associated Press*, had 'remained hidden from the public eye for more than 50 years since they were taken from Hitler's bunker in Berlin by a Soviet unit responsible for collecting war trophies'. This included a violin. Newspapers across the US reported on the exhibition on 20 April 1997, mentioning that the violin had 'its scroll carved to represent Hitler's image'.[56]

In 2001, a British surgeon and forensic expert Hugh Thomas published his book *The Unlikely Death of Heinrich Himmler*. Thomas proffered circumstantial and forensic evidence that the man who consumed cyanide after rather easily falling into the

---

56   'Russia to display Hitler's violin among war relics,' *The Cincinnati Enquirer*, 20 April, 1997.

British hands was not Himmler but his double. Thomas theorised that Himmler was attempting to set up a Fourth Reich outside the boundaries of Hitler's Germany. Pictures produced in *The Unlikely Death of Heinrich Himmler* showed that one nostril of Himmler's corpse was larger than the other, whereas available pictures taken during his lifetime showed they were symmetrical. The corpse did not appear to show a duelling scar as Himmler had.

Bundesarchiv - Bild 101III-Alber-064-16A
Foto: Alber, Kurt | 1942

[On 15 July 1942, Himmler entertained Subhas Bose at his field headquarters in Hegewaldheim, East Prussia, in the presence of SS-Gruf Kurt Knobloch, SS-Staf Walther Wüst, Dr Adam von Trott and Dr Lösch. Picture: Bundesarchiv (German Federal Archives)]

Thomas added some suspicious details. Months after the suicide, Himmler's body was exhumed in a re-identification bid. While Himmler's death file was sealed by the British Ministry of Defence for 100 years (till 2045), something very strange happened in 2005. Certain documents showed up in the UK's National Archives in Kew, London, showing that Himmler had been murdered by the British secret service so that he couldn't talk to the Americans. Rivalries between different Allied intelligence agencies had surfaced during the war. Later in 2005 these documents were exposed as fake. The result of investigations by forensic document experts on behalf of *The Daily Telegraph* showed that bogus documents were somehow planted among genuine papers. But who could have planted such fakes in a National Archives file and for what purpose? How was this possible in a country like the UK?

In contrast to the death of Himmler, which was an accepted fact of history till Thomas's book questioned it to some extent, Hitler's fate became controversial from the start. The last days of Hitler were spent in *Führerbunker*, an air-raid shelter located 50 feet below the Chancellery buildings in Berlin. With the passing days, Hitler kept on receiving one bad news after another. He sank into depression and madness, according to the eyewitnesses, when he came to know that the British were announcing that Himmler had sought secret negotiations with the Allies and offered to surrender to the American General (future President) Dwight Eisenhower.

As the Red Army tightened its noose around Berlin on April 30, Hitler and Eva Braun went into Hitler's personal study in the bunker. There was a sound of a gunshot. After some time Hitler's aides entered the study and found that he had shot himself and Eva had taken cynide. 'Hitler was sitting at the table, slumped forward, and Eva Braun was lying next to him. I saw that with my own eyes,' Hitler's bodyguard Rochus Misch, the only eyewitness who lived till our times, told *AFP* in 2005.

Later in the day, the bodies were carried to the garden behind the Reich Chancellery and set afire. With the area having come under Russian shelling, the charred remains were hurriedly buried in a bomb crater.

On May 1, Hitler's successor Admiral Karl Dönitz made a radio announcement that Hitler was dead.

When they captured the Nazi capital, Russian soldiers discovered amid the ruins of Reich Chancellery a body which looked like Hitler's. They promptly released pictures and footage showing 'Hitler' lying on floor with a gunshot wound on his head. It turned out that this person was possibly a double. Hitler was known to have employed doubles. Bhagwanji also talked about that once. 'The US, the UK and the European Allies knew it to their cost that Hitler had two doubles. Stalin, also two. I personally know of Rasputin being alive 8 years back.' He further claimed that Hitler's and Lord Monty's (Field Marshal Montgomery) 'were 100 per cent ideal and scrutiny proof; but Stalin's were not'.[57]

On 5 May 1945, the badly burnt corpses of a man and woman were discovered by the Soviets in a ditch next to the emergency exit from the *Führerbunker*. These remains were then put in a wooden shell crate and transported to a makeshift Russian pathological lab in a Berlin suburb. A picture showing the purported remains in the wooden crate is now available. Evidently, the bodies were too disfigured and burnt to be identified physically. On 8 May, a four-man military medical team headed by Dr Faust Shkravaski examined these remains in a bid to identify them. It was noted that part of the skull from Hitler's supposed remains was missing.

---

57   In 2008, 88-year-old Felix Dadaev publicly declared, with the possible approval of the Russian government, that he used to be one of the four doubles for Stalin.

It was later found near the bunker. According to their report: 'The most important anatomical finding for identification of the person are the teeth, with much bridgework, artificial teeth, crowns and fillings.'[58]

The search for Hitler's dentist, Dr Johann Hugo Blaschke, led the Russian to his assistant Kaethe Heusemann and dental technician Fritz Echtmann. Heusemann was shown Hitler's jaw in a cigar box. Heusemann affirmed that the teeth were Hitler's. From her memory, she drew drawings of Hitler's teeth and jaw, which meshed well with Hitler's supposed jaw. Echtmann also confirmed this. Dr Blaschke, now in American custody, was also interrogated and he too said that the teeth were Hitler's and Eva Braun's.

Writing in the *Nexus Magazine* December 2007-January 2008 issue, independent Australian academic Giordan Smith, however, questioned whether the dentists were being forthright. According to Smith: 'In early 1948, while still in American captivity, Prof Blaschke gave an interview in which he stated that Heusemann "cannot give a positive identification because she knows only some X-rays of Hitler's teeth". ...But if Prof Blaschke's evidence corroborated Heusemann's identification, the proof itself has never been published. Although the Americans had Prof Blaschke in their hands from May 1945, when he was captured, until late 1948, they never made public any of the information he shared with them about Hitler's teeth.'

---

58   Quoted in 'Hitler, Adolf medical assessment (di file)', released by the Central Intelligence Agency in 2000. https://www.cia.gov/library/readingroom/docs/HITLER%2C%20 ADOLF%20%20MEDICAL%20ASSESSMENT%20%28DI%20FILE%29_0008.pdf.

Be that as it may, the controversy lingered on as Moscow handled the whole matter in a secretive, confusing way. The veil began to lift only in 1968. That year, Lev Bezymenski, a journalist, created a sensation worldwide by publishing a book. *The Death of Adolf Hitler: Unknown Documents from Soviet Archives* published documents from the Soviet investigations including the official autopsy report on the corpses of Hitler and Eva Braun concluding that he died from cyanide poisoning.

In 2000, the Russians put on display the part of Hitler's skull at the Russian State Archives in Moscow. The event prompted a fair overview of the entire controversy about Hitler's death in an essay in *Center for the Study of Intelligence Bulletin* (No 11, Summer 2000), an internal CIA journal. The essay, 'Hitler, Stalin, and "Operation Myth",' has been released to public since then. In it, writer Benjamin Fischer, former Chief Historian of the Central Intelligence Agency, quoted Russia's chief archivist saying that he was '99.9 per cent' certain the fragment was once part of Adolf Hitler's cranium.

Following a perusal of declassified Russian records, Fischer wrote that Stalin rejected Dr Faust Shkravaski's conclusions out of hand. To get at the 'truth', Stalin launched *Operatsiya Mif* (Operation Myth), an investigation into the possibility of Hitler still being alive. The aim of the inquiry was to (1) gather and review all records and forensic evidence collected during May-June 1945; (2) check and recheck interrogation reports from Hitler's bunker entourage; and (3) reconcile or explain inconsistencies and contradictions in the evidence.

According to Fischer, on 26 May, during a Kremlin meeting

with President Roosevelt's chief adviser Harry Hopkins, and diplomats Averell Harriman and Charles Bohlen, Stalin said that he believed Hitler had escaped from Berlin and was hiding in the West.

The next version of this myth appeared in the 28 May edition of *Time*, which featured Hitler's portrait on its cover with a large cross through it. According to a certain "Pvt Ivan Nikitin," a German SS officer had revealed under interrogation that he had heard Hitler ranting and raving about a coming conflict between the USSR and its western Allies once the war had concluded. (Hitler, in fact, anticipated the Cold War in a document known as "My Political Testament.") But, "Nikitin" claimed that, Hitler said that as long as he was still alive the wartime alliance would remain intact. The world would have to be convinced that he was dead. Once the former allies found themselves in conflict, he would reappear and lead the German people to their final victory over Bolshevism. The same "Nikitin" claimed that behind an armoire in the bunker was a moveable concrete wall with a man-size hole in it. On the other side of the wall was a passageway leading to a tunnel where an army troop train was waiting to take Hitler and his entourage to safety.[59]

At a major press conference in Soviet-controlled Berlin on 9 June 1945, Russian commander Marshal Georgy Zhukov, in the presence of Deputy Foreign Minister Andrey Vyshinsky, said that Hitler's 'present whereabouts are unknown'. 'Based on personal and official information, we can only say that Hitler had a chance to get away with his bride [Eva Braun, who married him hours

---

59   Fischer, Benjamin. 'Hitler, Stalin, and "Operation Myth",' Center for the Study of Intelligence Bulletin 11 (Summer 2000), p 4-8.

before they committed suicide]. Hitler could have flown out at the very last minute'. Zhukov added that his personal view was that Hitler had taken refuge in Spain.

With this press conference the myth of a living Hitler was born. In the years to come scores of wild rumours went into circulation. One placed Hitler disguised as a woman in Ireland; another said he had converted to Islam and was in Egypt. On a query by Chandrachur, the US National Archives sent this particular declassified report dated 21 July 1945 on the subject of 'Hitler's hideout'. It talked about his 'proposed flight to India'.

Hitler's hideout ~~it Germany~~ Δ Milan Italy
Voeringer Werner, agent of Thun, should know where is
Mickel or Mickels secretary of German General who has in
hands documents about Hitler's proposed flight to
India where he will be host of Marajaa

Thun refused these documents when offered to him.

In May 1950, a pro-German-Nazi magazine *Tempo Der Welt* made a ludicrous claim about Hitler's presence in a Tibetan Monastery. The magazine's chief editor, Karl Kaerner, claimed to have spoken with Martin Bormann, to whom Hitler had bequeathed the Nazi Party leadership. Bormann was at the bunker when Hitler shot himself. He was said to have died while fleeing Berlin but the absence of a body fuelled claims that he might have escaped. In 1998, a DNA test carried out on human remains discovered in 1972 established that they were of Bormann.

Anyhow, in 1950, 'Bormann' told Kaerner: 'Hitler is alive in a Tibetan monastery— and not alone. Many have succeeded in getting there. …Hitler and I are working for the same aim. We shall not give up the fight as long as we live. And if we die others will take our place. We are not alone; all over the world a revolution is building up. One day it will break out everywhere.'

The Nazi leadership's, especially Himmler and Hitler's, interest in Tibet and oriental occult, including some aspects of Hinduism, has been a subject matter of interest with some people. In the internet age, it has proliferated. Himmler was said to always carry a German translation of the *Bhagavad Gita*. Some people think that Nazi Germany's Tibet expedition of 1938–39 had some occult purpose, a search for some supernatural entities and even a mythical Shangri-La (Gyanganj). This expedition was said to have been inspired by the claims made in a 1936 book *Ratfelhaftes Tibet* by adventurer Theodore Illion about his journey to Tibet and the mysterious things he came across there. In 1937, the book was published in English as *In Secret Tibet*. It remains in circulation till date and has a sizeable number of admirers.

Illion, who was said to have been born in Canada and traced his ancestry to the British royal family, claimed (or imagined) that he entered an 'underground city in Tibet' where lived certain hermits who could 'read people's thoughts and possessed the strange power to maintain themselves young almost indefinitely'. Obviously, Illion offered no photographic or other evidence to substantiate his claims.

On his part, Bhagwanji talked a lot about Tibet. He told his followers that before he returned to India he spent considerable time practising tantric rituals in Tibetan caves. Those who lived there had the supernatural powers to wake up corpses and were themselves hundreds of years old.

Back in 1945, Vyshinsky and Zhukov travelled to Frankfurt to brief General Eisenhower about what Russia could make of Hitler's fate. In July 1945 Stalin himself told US Secretary of State James Byrnes that he believed Hitler was living in Spain or Argentina. He repeated this in the presence of Admiral William D Leahy, President Truman's military adviser.

Prompted by the Russian accusation that Hitler was possibly living in the West, the British carried out a proper inquiry into the Nazi leader's fate with whatever eyewitness accounts and records available to the Allies. In September 1945, Hugh Trevor-Roper, an academic historian turned intelligence officer, was entrusted the job. Roper worked at breakneck speed. On 1 November 1945, Trevor-Roper's finding that Hitler had committed suicide was made public through a press conference. Soon afterwards, Hitler's will was located. The will clearly said that he was ending his life. The signatures on this record were found genuine by an MI5 handwriting expert.

On 2 January 1946, several newspapers, including those controlled by the Russians, reported that Hitler's body had been identified by his dentist. But when the British sought information at an official level from the Russians, they were told there was 'no official information'. Benjamin Fischer believed that the Russian approach in the Hitler matter was prompted by Stalin's desire to launch a 'disinformation campaign that he had personally devised and directed'. His reading was that for the Russians, following the autopsy in 1945, Hitler was dead. Behind *Operatsiya Mif* lay Stalin's certain design.

> Why did Stalin go to such lengths to deceive the West while trying to convince himself that Hitler could still be alive? The short answer is: no one knows. Some historians believe that the Soviet dictator wanted to send Western intelligence services on a never-ending wild-goose chase. Whether that was his purpose or not, that, in fact, is what happened. For 30 years the FBI investigated every report it received regarding Hitler sightings or claims that the Führer was still alive. (A 734-page file of such reports is available on the Internet. The Bureau conducted its own 11-year probe into the possibility that Hitler had escaped and was still alive. Other historians maintain that Stalin manipulated the Hitler myth to put the onus on the West for 'hiding' the German dictator and protecting Nazi war criminals or because he wanted to use rumours that Hitler was in Spain to settle an old score with Franco and avenge the communist defeat in the Spanish Civil War.[60]

In conclusion, Fischer wrote that 'today, just as in 1945, the skull fragments may hold the final answer'.

'Genetic testing should be able to determine once and for all whether they are the missing pieces of Hitler's cranium.'

As it happened, on 27 September 2009, newspapers world over reported this finding:

---

60 Ibid.

The *Guardian* of London reported that 'American researchers claim to have demonstrated that the skull fragment, secretly preserved for decades by Soviet intelligence, belonged to a woman under 40, whose identity is unknown'.

Tests on skull fragment cast doubt on Adolf Hitler suicide story

Bone with bullet hole found by Russians in 1946 came from an unknown woman, not the German leader
Why Hitler's world may not be so far away

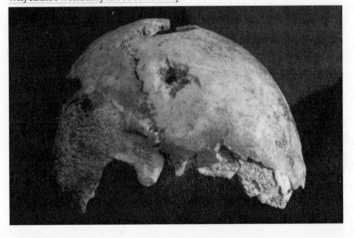

Commissioned by the *History* Channel, Connecticut State University archaeologist and bone specialist Nick Bellantoni studied the skull fragment and bloodstains from the bunker sofa on which Hitler and Braun were believed to have committed suicide. The Moscow state archives gave him unprecedented access, during which he applied cotton swabs and took DNA samples. The samples were then flown back to Connecticut. At the university's centre for applied genetics, Linda Strausbaugh closed her lab for three days to work exclusively on the Hitler project. According to *The Guardian*:

> The skull DNA was incontestably female. The only positive physical proof that Hitler had shot himself had suddenly been rendered worthless. The result is a mystery reopened and, for conspiracy theorists the tantalising possibility that Hitler did not die in the bunker.[61]

Now, assuming that Hitler somehow managed to escape from Berlin in 1945, where was he afterwards? Is there anything to connect with the line Bhagwanji gave to Shrikant?

Most theories are to the effect that he escaped to South America. On 3 June 2013, former Deputy Prime Minister LK Advani viewed a private screening of the movie *Vishwaroopam*. Two days later, actor director Kamal Haasan joined the veteran leader for lunch. In his blog on June 9, Advani recounted Haasan asking him if he had read the newly released Book *Grey Wolf: The Escape of Adolf Hitler*. As Haasan told Advani, the book 'is co-authored by Simon Dunstan, prominent author, film maker and photographer in the field of military history, and Gerard Williams, renowned television journalist for over thirty years with the *BBC, Sky News* and *Reuters*'.[62] In 2014, the book was turned into a movie.

After being presented with a copy of the book by Haasan, Advani commented in his blog that the book 'is extremely well

61   Uki Goñi, 'Tests on skull fragment cast doubt on Adolf Hitler suicide story,' *The Guardian*, 27 September 2009, https://www.theguardian.com/world/2009/sep/27/adolf-hitler-suicide-skull-fragment.

62   '*Vishwaroop*: A wonderful film,' http://www.bjp.org/en/media-resources/press-releases/shri-lk-advanijis-latest-blog-vishwaroop-a-wonderful-film.

researched'. 'Together, the two authors undertook seventeen research trips to Argentina where Hitler, according to them lived until 1962.'[63]

Grey Wolf: The Escape of Adolf Hitler tries to establish through 'deductive research' that Heinrich Müller and Martin Bormann orchestrated Hitler's escape from the embers of Berlin through a secret tunnel connected to the city's extensive underground railway system. Impersonators were left to die in the place of Hiter and Eva Braun, they claim. Müller, chief of the Gestapo, the political secret state police of Nazi Germany, disappeared at the end of the war. There are different, unproven claims about his fate—ranging from his death in 1945 to his secretly becoming a part of either Soviet or US intelligence.

The growing interest in Hitler's fate was further stoked in 2015. *History* channel ran a slick, full-fledged investigative TV series titled *Hunting Hitler* hosted by CIA veteran, author and *Time* columnist Bob Baer. Baer's books and experiences were the basis for the 2005 Oscar award-winning movie *Syriana*. For the TV series, Baer and war crimes investigator John Cencich used declassified FBI records and a host of experts, including a famous Nazi hunter, to look for the clues about Hitler's possible survival in Argentina. A second season of the *Hunting Hitler* series was aired in 2016. In October 2017, declassified JFK files yielded a CIA report showing that the agency was investigating whether Hitler escaped from Europe and was hiding in Colombia in 1954.

Lastly, in 2015 a claim was made in India. Retired bureaucrat,

---

63   Ibid.

former Congress leader and author Farooq Renzu Shah 'revived' what he claimed was a theory 'floated since 1945 that Maharaja of J&K secretly provided Hitler shelter'.[64] *Only Kashmir*, a news portal published from Srinagar, quoted him saying on 13 June 2015 that 'Hitler was buried in Khanyar known as Rozabal in Kashmir.' According to Shah, 'Those Maharajas of India who were close to Hitler through Azad Hind Fauj led by Subas Chandrar Bose [sic] had sympathy with Hitler against British imperialistic forces & J&K Maharaja was one prominent figure among them.

'Adolf Hitler died the same year according to various versions but the British Historian has now made all facts clear. He has been buried in an unknown grave in Rozabal in Kashmir.' [sic]

He further claimed that 'the grave of Hitler was titled in name of Yasuh in Rozabal and rumours were spread that the grave was of Jesus to keep it a highly guarded secret to conceal the fact about it actually being Hitler's grave.'

Shah's outrageous claim found virtually no space in Indian media, but British tabloid *Daily Star* picked it up in May 2016.

Bhagwanji mentioned no such thing—either the Maharaja of J&K or Hitler's grave in the Kashmir valley. According to what he said, Hitler's last rites were performed

Hitler was 'buried in BRITISH territory – in Jesus Christ's tomb'

ADOLF Hitler SURVIVED the end of World War 2 and fled to a British territory – and is now buried in Jesus Christ's tomb, explosive new claims suggest.

By Patrick Knox · Published 29th May 2016

226

CLAIMS: It is thought Hitler fled to India and is resting in a tomb with Jesus

---

64 Sameer Showkin, 'Could Hitler Be Buried In Kashmir? Another One For the Conspiracy Theorists!', https://www.scoopwhoop.com/news/hitler-buried-in-kashmir/#.1uhy15ibu.

by way of cremation in 1965 at Kankhal in Haridwar, a place swarming with Hindu mystics from the world over.

We cannot bring ourselves around to believing this could be true. In all fairness, we have narrated all that has come our way in the course of our research. There is no proof other than Bhagwanji's utterances. But assuming this horrifying scenario is true even in part, assuming that there were certain Nazis with Bhagwanji when he entered India—leave alone the two most notorious ones—then we have the answer to the question everyone has been asking us over the years.

As he thought back to the time Leela Roy first met Bhagwanji in 1963, Shrikant made more recollections in the course of his deposition before the Mukherjee Commission. In retrospect, they are spine-chilling. Bhagwanji told Roy not to visit him as it was neither in his interest, nor of the country. He reasoned that India would not be 'able to go against UNO and against the big powers'. Bhagwanji wanted his whereabouts kept top secret for if they were disclosed 'India will be the venue of third world war'.

Bolt from the blue

The complex web of reasons and scenarios discussed above provides an explanation why Bhagwanji preferred living in the shadows, but a scrutiny of all available material related to him has led us to another one. Like so many things about Bhagwanji, the details are sketchy and we have to follow a few stray leads from different places. None of his followers ever spoke about this particular possibility, and there is no direct hint of it in any of the material related to him. Yet, the signs are there. All we need to be sure of is whether we read the signs correctly.

Our thoughts started moving towards this tragic direction after we came across a letter Bhagwanji wrote (in English) in February 1963 to Pabitra Mohan Roy, who copied its text and either returned the original or destroyed it as ordered. 'Pabitra dear!' Bhagwanji began:

> You are an educated person. You possess quite fair intelligence. You have had a taste of politico-revolutionary activities. You also understand something about double talking and double crossing of puerile politics... You know that there are rules and rules; reports and reports; decisions and decisions; acts and acts; orders and orders; and laws and laws—don't you? ...again you also understand and know that there are types of rules, reports, decisions, acts, orders and laws which might be permitted to be tailored, fabricated, altered and or denied, if and as circumstances directed (for which the source shall not be punished). But you also know fully well that there are rules, reports, acts, orders and laws which cannot be permitted those privileges which are sacrosanct under national and international laws. You know these yourself very well because you have been on the verge of paying the highest price which a person can give for a cause (one's very life). My Divine mother Jagdamba Durga saved you, to save me. That's my belief.

Having drawn this backdrop, Bhagwanji started making startling claims—a series of incredible claims about the Second World War; about himself (he referred to himself as Subhas Chandra Bose); and, most importantly, about Douglas MacArthur—American Five-star General and Field Marshal of the Philippine Army, who commanded the Southwest Pacific Theatre in World War II and also administered post-war Japan during the Allied occupation. When the war in Korea erupted, MacArthur became head of United Nations forces but was after few months relieved of his commands by President Harry Truman in what became the topmost controversy of that time in the US.

'I hope you understand what a "Five star General" means?' Bhagwanji underscored. 'He is an autocrat—all powerful in his sphere and range of activities, with all the sanctions and power of his government behind him (to back him to the hilt). He is subject to none not even to the Defence Secretary! He gets his orders from the Head of the State. And only the Head of the State, in his capacity of the Head of the State and Supreme Commander-in-Chief can take him to task!'

Bhagwanji claimed that months before the surrender in August 1945, Japan was 'frantically trying to get and have some sort of peace and surrender terms to lay down her arms'. But these feelers sent through 'some high Generals and Ambassadors' that 'Japan is defeated for all practical purposes and it was time to dictate conditions' remained unanswered. 'Then, without any warning, without anyone knowing "why", or "what for", two successive "A" Bombs were dropped on Hiroshima and Nagasaki...The whole world (including the perpetrators of the ghoulish crime of all crimes against humanity) trembled....'

Using bombastic language, Bhagwanji then referred to MacArthur's ouster. 'Everyone asked everyone, why? What for? No one knew the real cause...A Five-Star General and such an ignoble end! He was not dismissed when he had to accept defeat and retreat from the Philippines war theatre. He was not dismissed for any lapses anywhere.' Instead, Bhagwanji incredibly claimed, the dismissal was the result of 'a final report' sent to the US President. A summary of this report was also sent to 'Prince Louis' (Mountbatten). The gist of the report, in Bhagwanji's words, was:

'Subhas Chandra Bose has escaped again.' Do you understand the weight and force of this report? The mighty Himalayas can be moved and proved false. But not that report of all reports of Five-star General Mac to his C-in-C. Such reports are inconvertible. They have to be because that's a report from a Supreme Authority to his superior. He is to see to it that all his reports be 100 per cent correct, on which depends his position, honour—and even his life.

But Mac, good strategist Mac—(with his vast ECA and British ally) pitted all his cunning with the brain of a mere *faquir*, a fanatic of his only God, his motherland…. Mac had to report 'Subhas has escaped again'. He was beaten at his own game.

Thus, what Bhagwanji claimed was that MacArthur had been fired because he reported about his inability to apprehend him (Subhas Bose). This was in the context of the war in Korea, where Bhagwanji claimed he had been sent by the Russians to settle old scores with the Americans for their help in the defeat of the INA by the Mountbatten-led South East Asia Command.

Even as one struggles to absorb this, Bhagwanji piled up another hyperbole:

There was absolutely no necessity of those two hellish A Bombs but they were dropped. You know whose strategy got Singapore, the much vaunted 'largest and biggest impregnable base in the world' as per official British quotation. Then came the three provinces of India proper, reconquered. The Allied high command (more pertinently the UK) became extremely jittery. The whole country was seething. They became panic-stricken with the certainty of 'the whole country including the forces rising in revolt the moment '__' come down to the plains. There was absolutely no time to lose. Every moment was precious and vital. Every day '__' was giving a clarion call—I am coming, I have come. We shall reach Delhi in no time once we get down to the plains. Oh, he had to be stopped—come what may. Because he shall not give any quarters to the Alien forces and nationalities. He must be stopped. It was UK which forced the hands of Truman. Nagasaki, Hiroshima were the only two ports of disembarkation; everything came to a shuddering stop....To get at one single man at all costs.

This bears no match with the history records. For the Americans, Subhas Bose was only of peripheral interest. They were interested in him only because their ally the British wanted him out of the picture. They came to be involved in the investigation relating to his reported death in 1945 because Japan and Taiwan were occupied by them at the end of the war. In May 1946, a representative of Military Intelligence met US Consul General in Bombay. Seeking information about Bose's fate, the representative told the Consul General that 'the hold which Bose had over the Indian imagination was tremendous, and that if he should return to this country, trouble would result which would be extremely difficult to quell'. The Consul General wrote to the State Department: 'Positive proof of some kind that Bose is dead would be most interesting.' The State Department conferred with the War Department (there was no Pentagon in those days) and reverted to the Consulate in June 1946: 'A search of our files in the Intelligence Division reveals that there is no direct evidence that Subhas Chandra Bose was killed in an airplane crash at Taihoko [sic], Formosa, despite the public statements of the Japanese to that effect. Nor is there any evidence available to Intelligence Division which would indicate that Bose is still alive.' That the Allied Powers continued to make further inquiries about Bose is proven by the deposition of Japanese officers (including those who survived the reported air crash) before the Khosla Commission. Lt Col Shiro Nonogaki, Tatsuo Hayashida, Lt Col Shibuya Masanori and Major Taro Kono told the commission that they were questioned towards the late 1940s. Shibuya was 'called by the British embassy once and also by the GHQ of the Occupation Forces once' some 'three or four years after' the air crash incident. Nonogaki said his statement, and that of Kono, was recorded at the British embassy around 1950. 'I was called through the Japanese foreign Office. I got a letter from the foreign office and I went.' Hayashida said that in 1948 some ten persons including him were 'examined by the Welfare Ministry authorities of the Japanese government'. Thereafter Hayashida was summoned by 'the prefectural police in Fukuoka city...on the request of the American and British intelligence services'.[65] No more information is available.

On the other hand, the issue of the dropping of the atomic bombs on Japan, given its significance in history, has been of considerable research for the last several decades. Reams have been written about it by numerous experts and even by those having

65   Record of proceedings of Khosla Commission obtained under RTI, Volume VI, p 2160, 2212-13, 2426.

direct or ringside information. Copious official documents and memoirs are available in the public domain for some time now. The Harry S Truman Library and Museum in particular has made public several formerly Top Secret records dealing with the decision of the US President. Here's how it unfolded: Beginning April 1945, a 'Target Committee' comprising top US military officers and scientists initiated the process of selecting the targets for final approval by Secretary of War (Defense Secretary) Henry Stimson. A note on the initial meeting of the Target Committee on 27 April discussed several potential target cities. Regarding Hiroshima, No 1 on the list, the note reads that it was 'the largest untouched target'. Not affected by Allied bombing raids, it was an ideal location to test and assess the deadly effectiveness of the new weapon. 'Tokyo is a possibility but it is now practically all bombed and burned out and is practically rubble with only the palace ground left standing,' the note further read.

The Target Committee meeting on 10 and 11 May listed 6 potential targets. Hiroshima was rated as AA because it was:

> an important army depot and port of embarkation in the middle of an urban industrial area. It is a good radar target and it is such a size that a large part of the city could be extensively damaged. There are adjacent hills which are likely to produce a focusing effect which would considerably increase the blast damage. Due to rivers it is not a good incendiary target. [66]

According to recently declassified minutes of a meeting of

---

66 US National Archives, Record Group 77, Records of the Office of the Chief of Engineers, Manhattan Engineer District, TS Manhattan Project File '42-'46, folder 5D Selection of Targets, 2 Notes on Target Committee Meetings.

the Combined Policy Committee in Washington on 4 July 1945, British Field Marshal Sir Henry Wilson told the meeting chaired by Stimson that the British government 'concurred in the use of the TA weapon against Japan'.[67] Under the Quebec Agreement of August 1943, the United States, Britain and Canada began coordinating on the development of atomic weapons. As early as September 1944 British Prime Minister Winston Churchill and US President Franklin Roosevelt had agreed that an atomic bomb would be used against Japan when it was developed. At the Potsdam conference, Churchill conveyed to President Truman the desire that Britain be represented when the atomic bomb was dropped.

This is what declassified documents reveal. No reference to Subhas Chandra Bose appears anywhere.

Similarly, the removal of MacArthur in April 1951 has been a much-discussed topic over the decades given its importance in American history. The most recent book about it, noted historian H W Brands's *The General vs. the President: MacArthur and Truman at the Brink of Nuclear War,* was released in October 2016. Truman's order to fire MacArthur and the papers related to it are available in the Truman Library now. MacArthur was relieved due to insubordination. He had made public statements contradicting Truman's policies. Since the decision did not go well with the American public in view of the popularity MacArthur enjoyed, the matter did not end with the dismissal. On his return, MacArthur,

---

67 'Hiroshima Day: Britain backed use of A-bomb against Japan,' says report, *India Today*, August 6, 2013, https://www.indiatoday.in/world/asia/story/britain-backed-use-of-a-bomb-against-japan-says-report-173026-2013-08-06.

hailed as a hero, addressed a joint session of the Congress and in May-June 1951, the Senate Armed Services Committee and the Senate Foreign Relations Committee held 'an inquiry into the military situation in the Far East and the facts surrounding the relieving of General of the Army, Douglas MacArthur'. All of this had a negative impact on Truman; his approval rating fell to the lowest possible level in US history for a sitting American President. *TIME* magazine in 1973 recalled these words said to have been spoken by Truman in the early 1960s: 'I fired him because he wouldn't respect the authority of the President. I didn't fire him because he was a dumb son of a bitch, although he was, but that's not against the law for generals.'[68]

Amid this slugfest all sort of things were said and discussed, but nowhere does anything appear which could even remotely be associated with Subhas Bose. As of now, nothing has come to light to show that either Truman Archives or MacArthur Archives have anything in their declassified holdings concerning Bose. The MacArthur Archives at Norfolk has only one record which deals with a Japanese associate of Bose. In India there is a clear reason for concealment and official silence. Let us assume that the British government is also not telling much because of the legacy of the Raj but the United States has no reasons to hide something of this sort if it really happened. In America, the levels of transparency and accountability are so high that even the highest level of security classified material routinely makes its way to the public

---

68 'Historical Notes: Giving Them More Hell,' *Time*, 3 December 1973.

domain, either lawfully or otherwise. A case in point for the latter is of the Pentagon Papers. This was a Department of Defense Top Secret study of United States' political and military involvement in Vietnam from 1945 to 1967. The entire volume was leaked to *The New York Times* in 1971.

From this we are led to another problem area in the Bhagwanji narrative. Going by Bhagwanji's claim, his involvement in the Vietnam war was known to the US government. In a letter to Pabitra, he referred to a public 'statement of the former US Defence Secretary Robert McNamara after he became president of the World Bank (in 1968)'. According to Bhagwanji, McNamara said that 'a team of expert Generals under the guidance of a "super mind" were overseeing the Vietminh's decision making on the Vietnam War. He, however, refused to name the "super mind" We have been able to locate no reference to any such statement even though there so many newspaper items, etc. available today, where McNamara, the most influential US defense secretary of the 20th century, can be seen discussing Vietnam in great detail. Throughout his long life, McNamara, who passed away in 2009 when he was 93, honestly articulated his views about the Vietnam war, and expressed remorse publicly. Twenty years after the end of the war, he wrote an authoritative #1 national bestseller *In Retrospect: The Tragedy and Lessons of Vietnam,* which detailed with unprecedented candour where he and his country went wrong.

All the same, to test the veracity of Bhagwanji's claim that he was involved in the Vietnam war, we rummaged through declassified US records about the Vietnam war—there are virtually lakhs of them—and found nothing in the records we could browse through. Not even a hint! Putting an official seal of approval on this finding was the Defense Intelligence Agency (DIA), the top US military spy agency, which informed us under the FOIA that it does not have any intelligence information reports pertaining to Bose's claimed involvement in the Vietnam war.

  DEFENSE INTELLIGENCE AGENCY

WASHINGTON, D.C. 20340-5100

U-12-3,827/DAN-1A (FOIA)

JAN 1 0 2012

Mr. Anuj Dhar

India

Dear Mr. Dhar:

This responds to your request under the Freedom of Information Act, dated September 24, 2007. Therein you requested information concerning copies of Intelligence Information Reports created in between 1962 and 1972 pertaining to Subhas Chandra Bose, specifically in the context of the war in Vietnam. I apologize for the delay in processing your request. DIA continues its efforts to eliminate the large backlog of pending FOIA requests.

Based on the information contained in your request, the Defense Intelligence Agency searched its systems of records for responsive documents. Despite a thorough search, no documents responsive to your request were found.

We even tried with the more well-known CIA, seeking from the agency relevant information from among the 'finished intelligence reports'—the high-end information used for national-level policy deliberations by the US policymakers. The Central Intelligence Agency processed the request under the provisions of the FOIA and the CIA Information Act and 'did not locate any records', that is finished intelligence reports, on Subhas Bose created between 1960 and 1970. If what Bhagwanji claimed about himself and Vietnam was true, there must have been several such reports—but it turns out there are none.

NOV 2 1 2007

Mr. Anuj Dhar

INDIA

Reference: F-2007-02063

Dear Mr. Dhar:

This is a final response to your 21 September 2007 Freedom of Information Act (FOIA) request for **"any finished intelligence reports between 1960 and 1970 on or relating to Subhas Chandra Bose."** We processed your request in accordance with the FOIA, 5 U.S.C. § 552, as amended, and the CIA Information Act, 50 U.S.C. § 431, as amended. Our processing included a search for records as described in our acceptance letter existing through the date of that letter, 3 October 2007.

We did not locate any records responsive to your request.

Although our searches were thorough and diligent, and it is highly unlikely that repeating those searches would change the result, you nevertheless have the legal right to appeal the finding of no records responsive to your request. Should you choose to do so,

Now that we are at it, it must be emphasised that there are several things that Bhagwanji talked about which aren't historically correct. This is not including his forays into the world of paranormal—out of body experience, UFOs, ghosts, and all that—because it can be argued that so many other great people across the world also believed in such things.

- Even though Bhagwanji was described by his disciples as having a photographic memory, he fumbled on basic facts concerning his own (Subhas Bose's) life. In a letter to Pabitra in September 1972, he cited a reported declaration of Jawaharlal Nehru that he'd fight Bose with a sword in his hand if he came to India before commenting, 'Where is the question of fighting someone who is already dead?' Nehru's purported statement was, however, made in 1942, that is 3 years before Bose was reported killed. How could Bhagwanji have mistaken the year when this was a matter of common knowledge?

- Even more suspicious was Bhagwanji's reference to Mahatma Gandhi sending a condolence message to his mother but thereafter on knowing the truth expressing his happiness, in the context of listing evidence against the Taihoku plane crash. The serious problem with this is that this account is from 1942, when fake news of Bose's death spread. Netaji was particularly attached to his mother. As noted by a Japanese general, he wept like a child when she passed away in 1943. We know of one instance of Bhagwanji breaking down remembering his mother, and so we cannot imagine how he could have made such an error.

- There are grammatical and other problems with several of Bhagwanji's letters and notes. Subhas Bose was a highly accomplished and refined writer in both Bengali and English. However, many of the words and idioms used by Bhagwanji, especially in Bengali, seem out of sync with a person of refined literary tradition. For a person who had taken up English composition while appearing for ICS exams in his youth, Bhagwanji, strangely, at times makes spelling and other errors. Could this all be the result of the torturous situation Bhagwanji was in?

- Based on a newspaper report (provided to him in a typed sheet by someone), Bhagwanji claimed that Chou-en Lai had given direct hints about the Asiatic Liberation Army and the mastermind behind it during a press conference in Paris. He claimed that this was reported in *The Times* of London. The only problem is that the real edition of the newspaper contains no such report.

- The gramophone records that Bhagwanji said he needed for his men in the unidentified headquarters of his 'horizon' were all found among his belongings in Ram Bhawan. Did he take them and bring them back all the way? Or does it raise questions about the factuality of such headquarters situated in a no-man's land, unclaimed by other countries?

At the same time, we cannot ignore the other side of the story. Bhagwanji did seem to be privy to information that couldn't have been known to a holy man living in isolation, without a phone or TV even. If his insights into the Vietnam war with regard to use of drugs was not intriguing enough, it is baffling that he should have made all those statements about the situation in East Pakistan and the eventual rise of Bangladesh. His comments about Jessore, in particular, are astonishing.

We are not qualified to authenticate this claim, nor back Bhagwanji's boast that it was his brain that was behind what happened in East Pakistan. But we are perplexed to note that invaluable records pertaining to the 1971 war were destroyed, as reported in *The Times of India* on 9 May 2010.

Bangladesh war files destroyed by Army

True Story Of 1971 Is Lost Forever

The story was filed by award-winning journalist Josy Joseph. The destroyed files include those on the creation of the Mukti Bahini, all appreciation and assessments made by the Army during the war period, the orders issued to fighting formations, and other sensitive operational details. On July 27, in response to the *TOI* story, Defence Minister AK Antony made a terse statement that 'no official records pertaining to the 1971 war that are available with the Defence Ministry have been destroyed'. Qualified as this statement was, it in a way did not clarify the *TOI* revelation sourced to 'authoritative Army sources' that 'all records of the period, held at the Eastern Command in Kolkata, were destroyed immediately after the 1971 war'. The Indira government had resorted to burying deep in the ground time capsules with a view to perpetuating myths favouring the Nehru-Gandhis, so we have good reasons to view this incidence of destruction of 1970 war records with suspicion.

We cannot also ignore that Bhagwanji did connect with Sitaram Omkarnath Thakur. A 1981 letter recovered from Ram Bhawan, in fact, conveyed a follower's word that Omkarnath had hinted that he was in contact with Subhas Bose. Omkarnath was a highly revered Bengali holy man who had known Subhas Bose prior to 1945, and many other leading personalities of that era too. What is quite interesting is that Omkarnath's leading disciples were B N Mullik, the czar of Indian intelligence, and Major General Sujan Singh Uban. A Military Cross holder and a legendary figure in the British India Army, Uban commanded the 22nd Mountain Regiment during World War II in Europe. In 1962, this regiment, after hectic lobbying by Intelligence Bureau, evolved into Establishment 22, or Special Frontier Force (SFF), a special force for carrying out covert operations behind enemy lines. Uban was its first head. The force operated under the operational command of IB, later on R&AW. In 1971, SFF carried out highly successful operations in East Pakistan that are the stuff of legends.

Now, here is the sensational bit. In 1977, Uban wrote in his book *The Gurus of India* (the foreword to which was written by The Dalai Lama) that in December 1970, when 'there were no signs of war anywhere', Omkarnath took him to a temple and standing before an idol of Durga said, 'Ma, this is Sujan. He will be going to war. Protect him and destroy his enemies. Make him a powerful instrument to bring victory to the country.'

> What actually happened in the war cannot be described here but it proved to me and my command that a force of immeasurable magnitude was working for us, destroying the enemy's will to fight and protecting us like an impenetrable shield.[69]

Moving further, we cannot comprehend how Bhagwanji was able to give a prescient description of the underground city in China or explosion of Chinese H bomb in 1964, or Arab-Israel talks—inside information on highest level diplomatic negotiations between Russia and Egypt or the cabinet proceeding where Prime Minister Jawaharlal Nehru scuffled with Syama Prasad Mookerjee, or predict the dissolution of the Soviet Union, unification of Germany, trouble flaring up in Baluchistan, etc. when these were either within the realm of state secrecy or far away in the future. Similarly inexplicable is Bhagwanji's knowledge of the story regarding Kim Il-Sung being an impostor. Although the US and British newspapers discussed it in the early 1950s, the story really became known on a wider scale after the fall of the Soviet Union. A man with his level of knowledge about geography and history wouldn't be easy to find among experts either.

Although Bhagwanji was a voracious reader, his astounding insights on global politics and developments in the Indian subcontinent are clearly not products of some idle general

69 Sujan Singh Uban, *The Gurus of India*, Sterling Publishers, 1977, p 117.

knowledge reading of a lay person. They are more in the format of intelligence summaries.

And then there's the hair-raising verbal account of late Surajit and Jagatjit Dasgupta's meeting (along with other senior followers) with Bhagwanji in early 1978. During the course of the conversation Bhagwanji bragged that he had his people in 15 different intelligence agencies around the world. Then somehow Louis Mountbatten's name figured in the talk. Jagatjit told us that due to the impatience of youth he blurted out that he would kill Mountbatten in case he ever saw him. Jagatjit's uncle Dinesh Gupta, along with Badal Gupta and Benoy Bose, had in 1930 killed Col NS Simpson, the Inspector General of Prisons, in a daring shootout inside the Writer's Building. Not accustomed to having his monologues interjected, especially by those much younger to him in age, the man behind the curtain flared up on hearing Jagatjit's words. 'This is my personal business!' he roared. Switching to Bengali, he went on to claim that when Mountbatten's body was lowered in its grave, it would not be in one piece. To Dasgupta brothers' horror, a few months after Bhagwanji had said this, the news broke that Irish terrorists had detonated a bomb in the yacht carrying Mountbatten. India's first governor general was blown to smithereens. 'By then he was an innocent old man doing no harm to anyone. Why on earth should IRA select him as a target?' Mountbatten's biographer Philip Ziegler rued in a documentary, *Mountbatten: Death of A Royal*, produced subsequently.

All these accounts and claims give rise to reasonable questions. Was Bhagwanji regaling his followers with fantastic accounts?

Was he intoxicated? Or was he hallucinating? The followers insist Bhagwanji never told lies. The only intoxicants recovered from Ram Bhawan were some Brandy and cannabis, both of which were used for medicinal purpose, as is clear from his letters to Pabitra. There is nothing to show that other than smoking cigarettes/cigars/pipes, Bhagwanji was into anything else. Then, how can one explain the coexistence of seemingly conflicting traits of memory lapses with great intelligence insights; of being deeply involved in the petty politics of some inconsequential followers with domination of diplomatic high tables? And most importantly, of a no-show of the grand scenario he had painted for sometime in the mid-1980s?

Since only the specialists in the field of psychiatry can offer an explanation for such traits in a person's personality, we approached two of them. To enable them to make a meaningful assessment, in our brief we outlined the two personas—Netaji (A) and Bhagwanji (B):

PERSON A—The man was a brilliant student. He studied in the UK and had a broad outlook, although very conservative in sexual matters. Fanatical nationalist. Deeply spiritual. Joined politics at a very young age and almost immediately rose to the heights of fame, inviting persecution by foreign rulers of the land. Suffered in terms of health, was imprisoned eleven times. Exiled from the country. Faced stiff opposition from the supreme leader of the national movement and his supporters, but emerged as an alternative leader with great mass following. Left the country secretly and created a big movement abroad.

PERSON B—Appeared in a north Indian state in the early 1960s. Lived in absolutely strict secrecy and often in extreme poverty as a hermit till the time he was found by his associates. There are strong indications of him having lived a traumatic and extremely difficult life. Claimed to be PERSON A, but showed the following traits:

1. Claimed that he was working in tandem with global powers in India's national interest but outside the knowledge of the Indian Government.

2. Told fantastic stories about him being considered a 'supermind', a genius and a 'superman' by the world powers and him influencing global developments at many levels.

3. Made quite a few accurate projections about future developments in global and national politics, based on experience and reasoning.

4. Sounded extremely pompous when talking about himself. Considered himself limitlessly superior to his ex-co-workers and supporters.

5. Claimed that he had his own kingdom somewhere in Central Asia, which no one knew about.

6. Made many factual errors while talking about the past life (that is, life of PERSON A). However, some of the claims and prophesies he made were correct.

7. Extremely spiritual and religious, claiming to have supernatural powers (some of which were corroborated by his disciples/followers/associates, some of whom were well-educated).

8. His writings clearly demonstrate a highly evolved mind, clarity of thought, suspicious nature and single-minded determination.

Based on these pointers, we drafted the following question:

Assuming PERSONS A and B were the same, what could induce such a transformation? He claimed that he had undergone complete metamorphosis compared to his previous life. Can this be scientifically or psychologically explained—with and without torture scenarios?

The first to apply his mind was Dr Arabinda Brahma, a Kolkata based psychiatrist and assistant general secretary of Indian Psychiatric Society. Dr Brahma responded that 'this transformation could be possible in a man of highest level of determination with strong spiritual underpinning'. He nonetheless agreed that the change of behaviour in Person B may be because of the torture scenario.

Some unpleasant experiences produce permanent changes in the brain and corresponding shifts in intelligence, emotional reactivity, happiness, sociability, and other traits that used to be thought of as set for life. These personality shifts are generally considered pathological, that is undoubtedly true of post-traumatic stress disorder, which ruins the lives of the sufferer. So an effect of post-traumatic stress disorders may be considered in his case, but the person had overcome a lot with his strong religious and spiritual power. As a matter of fact, effect of spirituality on an individual is very difficult to explain (eg Transformation of Aurobindo Ghose to Rishi Aurobindo).

This prompted us to make further pointed queries, to which Dr Brahma supplied his answers (in italics):

Question: About the trauma undergone—is there any threshold time period for such action to produce such a reaction? For instance, a few weeks or a few months, or at least a year?
No there is no such time limit documented ever, but the general rule is more time of exposure to trauma, more chance of changes in personality pattern.

Question: Is multiple personality disorder a possibility?
No chance of multiple personality disorder, as person A had a 'steel like' personality.

Question: Is it possible that the Post-traumatic stress disorder (PTSD) manifests only at times, with the person being 'normal' at other times?
That's possible as, post-traumatic stress disorder produces 'flashback' like episodes at times but not always.

Question: Is there any known case of spirituality or strong will power helping someone to overcome such disorder without proper medical treatment?
May be possible, 'Iron man' like Aurobindo Ghose transformed to Rishi Aurobindo—spirituality can do miracles, but difficult to prove scientifically (you probably heard of yogi Shyamacharan Lahiri and his spiritual activities).

Question: Can PTSD result in bouts of hallucinations, paranoia and delusions of grandeur?
Yes, post-traumatic stress disorder can produce hallucinations, paranoid delusions and grandiose delusions (not upto the manic level) in few cases.

Since Dr Brahma was aware that the matter referred to him was about the Gumnami Baba theory, we thought it better to consult a foreign expert as well. We reached out to one in an Australian university. This expert (who wishes to remain anonymous) had no clue at that time that the matter pertained to the Gumnami Baba/Subhas Bose controversy. All she received was the questionnaire from an Indian acquaintance residing in Australia—who kept us and the background of the case out of picture. Deprived of the background details, the expert at the outset of her response made it clear that it would be unethical for her 'to state whether he meets certain diagnostic labels or to say he has undergone these changes because of certain factors'. All the same, citing research undertaken by most credible names in the field and institutions such as American Psychiatric Association, she was good enough to reflect at length. The following appears at the end of her response:

> Without knowing their specific history (eg detailed account of life events including the personal, medical and psychosocial history), it is not possible for me to speculate whether such significant personality changes could occur in Person A, or what might have contributed to such changes. However, I also can't say such a change could not occur. It may be possible to construct a reasonable theory as to why individual aspects of their personality may have changed so drastically. For example, if Person A was a 'brilliant student' he may have always been surrounded by people to whom he was intellectually superior. Maybe there were certain events that reinforced this notion (eg he was able to find solutions to problems when no one else could). Furthermore, he may have received constant praise about his intellect and perhaps was consistently surrounded by people who only reinforced, but did not challenge his views. This could conceivably create the pomposity/sense of superiority described. Note that I am not saying that is how this change came about—I have no idea! But this theory may be quite plausible if there is evidence from his history like the events I suggest. Given what we know about how personality can change, I would investigate whether it is plausible/likely based on the person's history.
>
> There are also certain psychiatric issues that can affect personality. I cannot make any form of diagnosis based on the details above (even with a lot of detail it would be pretty dodgy ethically to make a diagnosis in the absence of a thorough assessment), but I can outline some of the disorders that can

affect personality, or may have some symptoms in common with the profile of Person B. I have taken the following information from the DSM 5, which is the standard for psychology/psychiatry in Aus/USA.

There are various disorders on the spectrum of schizophrenia and other psychotic disorders which can cause delusions. Delusions are 'fixed beliefs that are not amenable to change in light of conflicting evidence'. There are several types of delusions, one being delusions of grandeur where people believe they have exceptional skills, fame or connections. These could be the most potentially relevant to Person B. For the time being, I am assuming the points 1, 2, 5 & 7 are based on delusional beliefs, but this could easily be incorrect (?). Also, it is possible that these 'delusions' (esp number 7) are not actually delusions at all, but are deceptions that he has created for one reason or another (eg to receive gains/notoriety).

There is a disorder known as 'Delusional Disorder', which requires people to have held delusions for 1+ month (and not meet criteria for another psychotic disorder). As there is no obvious evidence in the profile of Person B of any other psychotic symptoms, I would be reluctant to extrapolate further re these kinds of disorders.

Delusions can also be a symptom of other disorders such as schizotypal personality disorder, or Bipolar disorder. Again, however, there are no other symptoms evident in the Person B profile provided that would suggest these were a factor.

Personality change is a consistent symptom of brain injury, especially damage to the frontal lobes. The degree/severity and type of changes that may occur are dependent on the specific location of the injury, extent of damage, and individual differences in people's ability to cope with brain damage. Damage to the brain can occur via traumatic head injuries (ie acceleration/deceleration injuries, close/penetrating), or other pathologies such as haemorrhages, clots, neurocognitive disorders or drug/alcohol abuse. Traumatic experiences would predispose a person to experiencing head injuries of various natures whether directly (eg getting beaten in prison) or indirectly (eg long-term malnutrition can lead to brain atrophy). Without knowing for certain whether Person A/B did sustain some form of brain injury it is impossible to say whether this may have been a factor in their personality change. However, given their experiences, it is reasonable to assume that Person A has a greater chance of having experienced some form of head injury than the average person.

With such disturbing indications having emerged, we are ready to discuss the final matrix of options as to why Bhagwanji did not or could not reveal himself to his country and continuously suffered inexplicable miseries brought about by his self-imposed virtual solitary confinement.

In picking the most logical of these options, we are going to be guided by 'Occam's razor' and the 'Sagan standard'. The first is a well-established philosophical principle (razor) of reasoning and investigation used to discard improbable options in a given situation. Occam's razor holds that a simpler explanation is better than a more complex one. Doctors know this by the adage, 'When you hear hoofbeats; think horses, not zebras.' One of the best-known quotes of Arthur Conan Doyle is what he put in the mouth of Sherlock Holmes in *The Sign of the Four* (1890): 'How often have I said to you that when you have eliminated the impossible, whatever remains, however improbable, must be the truth?' The 'Sagan standard' is an aphorism used quite often in scholarly publications. Made famous by celebrated astronomer Carl Sagan, it asserts that 'extraordinary claims require extraordinary evidence'.

For the purpose of illustration, let us apply these principles to the strange case of the reporting of the finding of the DNA test on the teeth presumed to be of Bhagwanji. As detailed in Chapter 5, in December 2003, the *Anandabazar Patrika* broke the news that the DNA test was negative. When this was contested by the Mukherjee Commission before the Press Council of India, the counsel for the paper claimed that their report was based on a genuine 'scoop' obtained by them. The paper also submitted that 'the information was substantiated by the official reports subsequently issued' in June 2004 when Justice Mukherjee made all handwriting and DNA reports public. However, it is a matter of record that the DNA test in question was completed six months after the paper reported its outcome. Therefore, the paper's claim that their report was based on a 'scoop' cannot be true. So how did *Anandabazar Patrika* come to know about something that was clearly in the realm of the future? There could be 3 possibilities:

Divine foreknowledge: Endowed with some supernatural power, the *ABP* journalist could see the future.

Time travel: As in the famous BBC sci-fi series *Doctor Who*, the *ABP* reporter time travelled to June 2004, noted the outcome of the DNA test, came back and filed the story in December 2003.

Forensic skullduggery: A fake news was planted in Bengal's most widely read paper with a view to discrediting the Gumnami Baba-Netaji link, opposed by the establishment.

Obviously only the last of these possibilities is reasonable. Likewise, among the matrix of options on why Bhagwanji did not emerge we need to pick the one that would be accepted universally as sensible. The first option that Bhagwanji became a *sadhak*/tantric in his quest for India's good is too fantastic to warrant any discussion. The claim that Bhagwanji was involved in covert operations and hence could not surface does not pass the 'Sagan standard'. In the absence of clear-cut evidence, such as official documentation or declaration, all these claims, though not wholly devoid of substance, can only be treated as interesting leads. Bhagwanji's followers have many more of his letters and notes that might contain information which could lead to turning these leads into evidence. But since they did not give us full access to their collection, we have no other option but to draw our conclusions on the basis of what is before us. Universally accepted narratives of historic events, such as the 1971 war, cannot be overturned with one or two startling disclosures. We did raise the issue of Netaji's possible involvement in the Bangladesh war with former intelligence and military officers. They scoffed at this suggestion. Therefore, unless some extraordinary evidence for Bhagwanji's extraordinary claims about his covert operations emerges in future, we cannot go with this construct. Bhagwanji's claim that the US and UK were desperately hunting for him also does not pass the test of scrutiny unless his role in global developments is established with proper evidence.

The idea of Bhagwanji returning to India along with Hitler defies imagination. Last year, a team of French pathologists inspected Hitler's teeth kept in Moscow—in what was the first ever proper examination of these remains allowed by the Russians. The researchers' conclusions, published in May 2018 in the *European Journal of Internal Medicine*, were unambiguous. 'The teeth are authentic—there is no possible doubt,' lead pathologist

Philippe Charlier told the AFP news agency. 'The teeth matched descriptions provided by Hitler's dentist and revealed no trace of meat—consistent with the fact that the Führer was vegetarian.'[70] Therefore, we classify Bhagwanji's claim about Hitler as a case of false memory, just as the claims about MacArthur are. False memory is an established area of psychological research with thousands of papers published on the subject. Apart from academic research institutions, organisations have been set up like the British False Memory Society and the False Memory Syndrome Foundation, which are focused on deeper research on the topic. When strong enough, research shows that the syndrome can affect the sense of identity and personality of an individual. In her remarkable book *The Memory Illusion*, criminal psychologist and memory expert Dr Julia Shaw offers this insight: 'Any event, no matter how important, emotional or traumatic it may seem, can be forgotten, misremembered, or even be entirely fictitious.'

From this, we are led to the last and the only credible option. Not only does this line of thinking provide a logical explanation as to why Bhagwanji chose not to, or could not, return to public life, it also fixes several of the anomalies in the entire Bhagwanji narrative. It is our conclusion that Bhagwanji was Subhas Chandra Bose and, on available details, his non-appearance can be attributed to an apparent Post-traumatic stress disorder (PTSD), which manifested in false memories, hallucinations, delusions

---

70   Jefferson Chase, 'Hitler teeth test dispels myths of Nazi leader's survival,' *Deutsche Welle*, 20 May 2018, https://www.dw.com/en/hitler-teeth-test-dispels-myths-of-nazi-leaders-survival/a-43861719.

(paranoid and grandiose) in him. Recent research suggests a link between schizophrenia and insomnia, and Bhagwanji clearly suffered the latter. These disturbing signs could not be detected by those around and close to Bhagwanji because they treated him like a God-like figure. They believed he could perform miracles, such as going out of his body, which science does not accept. Even in his decline, the man was so exalted intellectually, compared to the people around him, that the adverse signs remained invisible to them.

There isn't much in Bhagwanji's writings or in his discussions to show that this aspect was dwelt upon either by him or his followers, except on a couple of occasions, where he referred fleetingly to a problem with memory when he met with Mao in the late 1940s or early 1950s. The closest reference we get is from 1973, when, on reading the manuscript of *Oi Mahamanaba Ase* submitted to him for approval, he reacted rather strangely. 'Is this my writing? Did these words come out of my mouth? I am crying after reading what you have written.'[71] A few years earlier, his reaction to a column by Charanik in *Jayasree* magazine was similar. 'I started thinking. I understand that these words have been written by me only, but how could I write in such a manner? I find it difficult to believe that these are my words.'[72]

We are constrained to read in the light of these utterances, Bhagawanji's allegorical narrative of the tale of King Nala from the *Vana Parva* of the *Mahabharata*. Nala was the king of the

71   Charanik, *Oi Mahamanaba Ase*, Jayasree Prakashan, 2010, p 328.
72   Ibid, p 410.

Nishadha kingdom, known for his beauty, skill with horses and his righteousness. He was chosen by the princess of the Vidarbha kingdom Damayanti in her *swayamvara* (a practice described in ancient texts of choosing a husband by a princess from among a number of suitors). Unhappy with this development, Kali the destroyer of dharma (righteousness) who was desirous of marrying Damayanti entered the body of Nala and manipulated subsequent events to compel the king and the queen to leave their kingdom as paupers. With his influence on Nala's mind Kali thereafter made him leave Damayanti and go about on his own. While roaming around, Nala came across a forest fire and found the king of serpents Karkotaka crying out for help. Despite Nala saving his life, Karkotaka bit him and filled his body with poison, giving his body an ugly form. To a surprised Nala, Karkotaka said that the poison would save him from Kali who had possessed him, and from other dangers. Eventually, he assured, Nala would get back his earlier form, his kingdom, wife and children. Nala thereafter took shelter of another king and after going through many fortuitous circumstances received back everything. 'Think of it. Could anyone else survive even one per cent of what "this body" has endured?' Bhagwanji ended the story with his comment.

It is our considered view that our Government has been aware of the existence of Bhagwanji/Netaji. They figured out his location after Nehru was gone, and that not all was right with him. Since they knew he could not come out and even if he did, he was not in a position to threaten the position of powers that be, they let him stay the way he was. They kept an eye on him, and possibly sent representatives to him. Perhaps on some specific occasions, he was briefed about official matters and that might explain Bhagwanji's insights, including his vivid description of the state of affairs in the FATA region of Pakistan during the first Afghanistan Jihad of the late 1970s. Of course we cannot explain everything on account of paucity of information, as both the Government and Bhagwanji's followers prefer to keep things to themselves. As such, other than his identity, Bhagwanji's life remains a conundrum.

In our private discussions, people often questioned why Bose's detractors did not have him eliminated when they eventually came to be aware of his secret existence on Indian soil, and be through with 'the whole problem'? There can be two possible explanations. Firstly, there was always a chance that such an act might become known in public and that would create a problem of unmanageable proportions. The second possibility is that there was no threat perception from him. Certain followers of Bhagwanji and others in Faizabad have, however, spoken in hushed tones that Bhagwanji could have been silently eliminated on 16 September 1985 by one of his associates. We are not in a position to verify the extent of truth in such rumour mongering.

It is also very likely that our Government has kept the entire matter under wraps so as to conceal the original sin of Nehru and others in obfuscating the facts about Bose's fate. Now they have all reasons to be wary of the complications on both the home as well as foreign fronts. Their conspicuous silence on this matter evidences their culpability. Since Prime Ministers after Nehru decided not to go public with the truth about Netaji not dying in 1945, it became increasingly difficult for successive incumbents to state it as the complications compounded. Since telling the truth about Netaji's fate would have invariably led to spotlighting the pivotal role he played in making India free and the manner in which transfer of power deal was transacted, the establishment could not afford to let it out. The British-Congress party construct of *ahimsa* bringing India freedom was, and is, any day a better proposition for them than the idea of Bose doing it with the help of the Axis powers. That's because the Mahatma Gandhi myth has gone mainstream in the West, due to its joint boosting by Indian and British governments in their respective interests. The Indian elite, who form the establishment here no matter which party is in power, are by and large pro-West in their outlook, at least with regard to the WW II period, having their children settled there. No one is going to gain anything out of stating the truth.

The very fact that no political dividends could be reaped from stating the truth also went in favour of retaining the status quo. Subhas Chandra Bose's legacy, unlike that of some other national icons, does not translate into a vote-fetching proposition even in his home state of Bengal, what to speak of the rest of the country. Subhas Chandra Bose doesn't enjoy an iconic status in his home state comparable to, say, Sardar Patel in Gujarat. Most Bengali elites, the ruling class and the intellectuals in particular, are not bothered about him. Post-1947, Bengal was ruled by Congress and Communist parties, both of which were hostile towards him, and they have been successful in pushing his memories to the periphery. The annual ritual of paying lip service to Netaji in Bengal on his birth anniversary will vanish if the holiday to mark the occasion is withdrawn. We expect to be run down by Bengali intellectuals in particular following the publication of this book.

We also think that there are some (most likely intelligence) files on Bhagwanji hidden somewhere. If the Government claims that there are no such files, the only logical deduction which can be drawn is that such files were destroyed like other vital Bose related papers. It is not possible that Bhagwanji escaped the notice of the all-pervasive and very efficient intelligence sleuths of our country when they were going after anyone and everyone linked to Subhas Bose through the decades.

That something was terribly wrong with Bhagwanji is a finding also backed by Curt Baggett's report. With his main report that Bhagwanji and Subhas Chandra Bose were the same person, Curt appended a handwriting analysis whose significance can now be underlined. When he analyzed these handwritings in order to help determine the personality and character traits of what he thought was an 'anonymous person', Curt found out that he turned out to be 'an enigma of personality', with 'so many strong, tremendous outstanding positive traits sprinkled with a handful of traits which did not always serve him well'.

> The author's [Bhagwanji's] most outstanding personality traits were his need for perfection, his rare ability to focus and concentrate; tremendous diplomacy and loyalty; and his amazingly high IQ and super analytical ability.

Many of the motivational traits observed by Curt remind us of Netaji as he was: Initiative, Diplomacy, Fluidity of thought, Possessed artistic and/or writing ability, Dreamer, Quick wit and quick sarcasm, Trusted almost no one, Secretive, Stubborn,

Defiant, Physically Aggressive, Father Image Missing, Will Power Strong, Loved a Good Debate, Loyal, Good organisational ability, Blunt, Talkative, Generous.

And then there are these negative traits: Resentment and Anger, Sensitive to criticism of his ideas or person whether real or imagined, Fear of success, Good listener except when he did not want to hear something, had a Trauma at about age 15, Touch of paranoia.

We can only hazard a guess or two as to what might have brought this change in the personality of Bhagwanji/Subhas Bose. Going by his statements, he was greatly affected by the condition he was in, his inability to free India through INA's invasion because of lack of support, the treatment he was meted out as he was booted out of Congress in 1939. The subsequent partition of India, and the fate that befell Bengali women in particular in the wake of his motherland's division tormented him no end. As long as he lived, Bhagwanji would tell his followers from Bengal that had the people of his home state stood up like a rock behind him when the INA entered India, he would not have had to suffer like this. He used to bemoan that 'Bengal has killed Him'. He often gave heart wrenching accounts of tragedies in East Pakistan and cried for the women who had suffered. This might explain his extreme hatred for Jawaharlal Nehru whom he held responsible for Partition and what happened subsequently. This also explains the anger in him against Islamism, even though, most unusually for a Hindu holy man, he maintained secret contacts with some of them including sufis who, like him, believed in the paranormal.

Can we rule out that Bhagwanji suffered physical torture

at some point in time? Is there a possibility that the horrifying scenario thought of by Subramanian Swamy and Major General GD Bakshi (Retd) actually happened? Only Russia can tell the truth. To those he met, Bhagwanji talked about suffering he saw and possibly experienced in Siberia. At times, he made statements about the harshness of the Siberian winter or whatever he saw, or claimed to have been in gulags. 'This body has suffered torture in Siberia', he said once. The first volumes of *Oi Mahamanaba Ase*, written while he was still alive, quotes him describing horrible conditions there. 'Driven by hunger, people have gone to the extent of eating their own skin.' He says he personally witnessed hard forced labour. Even though he made claims of being treated like a VIP by the Russians, so much so that he claimed (or hallucinated) that he watched operas with Nikita Khrushchev, he made certain disturbing comments in his notes. He described scientific experiments on thought control and impact of music on living beings in Soviet Russia, and spoke at length about their methods of torture. In Bhagwanji's words, the Soviets were masters in making people vanish in complete secrecy, in a manner that no one ever would be able to trace them. He said he knew of over a hundred such people from Russia and other countries who had been vanished from the face of the earth without any trace. 'Even the Gods are in awe of the perfect finesse of their diabolical act.' Someone in Soviet Russia explained to him how to deal painless instantaneous death. 'I asked him how many times he had to do it to be able to understand.' With horror he told me how he saw the application of methods to make one forget his identity completely. 'If you ask him about the past he will keep staring blankly at your face,' said the man . 'Some even go mad while passing through this method. Completely mad.'

He wouldn't discuss in detail what he went through but would only give hints, as when he told Pabitra that in the beginning the Russians didn't treat him like a son-in-law (an idiomatic reference to the special affection shown to sons-in-law in Bengali households). We get a validation that he mentioned about his imprisonment and torture from a letter written by Shiva Prosad Nag. Nag could extract only part of the narrative from Kamalakanta Ghosh who had heard about Bhagwanji's travails directly from him:

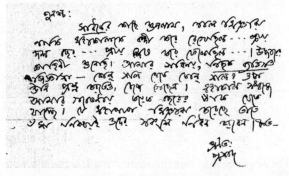

['I heard from sadhak (Kamalakanta Ghosh) that the Red forces had imprisoned Mahakal (Bhagwanji) for about ten years and nearly finished him. I heard the story of rescue from him. It is my humble personal request—kindly tell me from which year to which year? He (Kamalakanta) didn't answer my question.' Shiva Prosad Nag's undated letter to Bhagwanji. Exhibit 130 (a), Justice Mukherjee Commission of Inquiry.]

The horror of horrors is that Emilie was made aware of the fate that befell Subhas. In the words of Subhas's Germany-based grandnephew Surya Bose, sometime in the early 1950s, his grandaunt was told by Raimund Schnabel, a well-known German journalist who had settled down in East Berlin after the 2nd World War, 'that he had been informed that Netaji was in the Soviet Union after 1945'.[73] Consequently, Emilie never believed the air crash theory despite the Government's attempts to bring her around. In 1951, when the foreign correspondent of *Anandabazar Patrika* visited Emilie in Vienna, she scribbled a touching note behind a photograph: 'May God grant him many more years to live and fulfil his sacred oath.'

May God grant him many more years to live and fulfil his sacred oath.

17. 4. 51.

১৯৫১ সালে ১৭ই এপ্রিল ভিয়েনায় নেতাজীর পত্নী শ্রীমতী বসু উপরের কথাগুলি তাঁজীর একখানি চিত্রের পশ্চাৎভাগে লিখিয়া আনন্দবাজার পত্রিকার বৈদেশী প্রতিনিধি ডাঃ তারাপদ বসুকে স্মরণচিহ্ন হিসাবে প্রদান করেন।

[National Archives, New Delhi]

These are clearly not the words of a mourning widow. On the contrary, it almost gives a sense that she was aware where Subhas was. Speaking to Navina Sundaram (niece of Amrita Sher-Gil) for her early 1970s documentary *Portrait of a Patriot: Search for a Rebel*, however, she said in no unclear terms: 'I don't believe in the story of the plane crash. Why? He has disappeared so often and reappeared. But I am convinced that he is now no longer alive.'

---

73   Sworn affidavit filed by Surya Kumar Bose before the Justice Mukherjee Commission. Copy in our possession.

Surya Bose has in recent times added that Schnabel, citing his KGB sources, told Emilie that Subhas 'was being slowly poisoned and was losing his mind'.[74]

We are petrified as we are led to believe that despite his high capabilities Bhagwanji remained acutely aware of the problems stemming from the debility caused by the trauma of torture, even if the symptoms manifested only occasionally. This awareness and his apprehension about the possible consequences of the problem stopped him from coming out. It is possible that his intense spiritual practices helped him overcome the problem, but the web of other deterring factors too came in the way of his reappearing.

This is just about all the sense we can make of this conundrum—a heart-shattering epic tragedy of proportions we cannot bring ourselves around to even imagine. The one who sacrificed everything in his life at the altar of freedom for his country lived a life worse than death.

74   Ragini Bhuyan, Legacy wrapped in a mystery, *The Hindu Business Line*, 17 July 2015, https://www.thehindubusinessline.com/blink/meet/legacy-wrapped-in-a-mystery/article7429997.ece

ASSORTED UTTERANCES AND WRITINGS OF BHAGWANJI

Following are selections from various letters and notes of discussions Bhagwanji had with his followers. Most of the original text is a mix of English and Bengali. The Bengali parts of the text have been translated into English.

Politics, Geopolitics, History & Society

Whether war should be brutal, cathartic or a human business is beside the point. Everyone knows that no war can be conducted and fought with kid gloves. Modern war, especially, takes an appalling toll both in human life and property. No civilized nation risks it lightly but when it is forced on it, it has to be waged in a manner that makes the opponent wince. This is done not in any vindictive spirit but in a cold calculated manner to break the opponents' morale so that he is forced to sue for peace. Abstract principles have nothing to do with waging of war. *(Letter to Pabitra Mohan Roy, January 1963)*

Tell me why Dr Mukherjee was done away with?...Everyone knows it...It was only by his support that JN could get two very big things done entirely in his (JN's) favour. Then Dr M openly threatened to undo the wrongs, and he challenged JN dare stopping him. The price he paid. Why the so-called vocal saviours of Bengal gulped this murder down? Why these valiants of Bengal have not uprooted New Delhi and Allahabad and thrown them in the Ganges and gained the Valhalla? Why they have kept quiet? The fools! The d___d fools and —— of Mother Bengal!!...You tell me Pabitra, can any person believe, who is not USA-UK-JN's, that 'S____' can live scot free in this 'free world'?

(Letter to Pabitra Mohan Roy, 4 February 1963.)

In the modern world, the British are the most intelligent, cleverest, crafty, politicians and diplomats. They saw Bengal and the Bengalis and understood everything. Bengal was then cut up into pieces... only for one reason—Bengal must be weakened. If Bengal isn't made powerless, aimless, without responsibility, cultureless and inanimate in every way, it wouldn't be possible to rule over India. The biggest opportunity in thousand years to get back the lost glory came in front of the unfortunate Bengalis—an opportunity given by one of Bengal's all-sacrificing pilgrim *faquir*. Bengalis lost even that opportunity—only due to these pack of jackals, not for anyone else. *(Letter to Pabitra Mohan Roy, 5 February 1963.)*

Remember, Calcutta and Bombay—these two cities account for a full 80% of the country's national income. Don't forget that Calcutta 'was' the second city of the whole British Empire (first city was London). And Calcutta was the first city throughout the British Commonwealth. The port of Calcutta was the first and the best port and harbour. Calcutta University was the largest university in the world (even now it is). Remember that it is conceded in all quarters within and without India that Bengal has the best brains.

Remember, JN deeply humiliated Bengal's world-famous scientist.

Remember, there is no sympathy in his heart for the unfortunate refugees of Bengal. The condition in which mothers, daughters and sisters are spending their days has no impact on him.

Remember, there is not a single Bengalee in any key and vital position.

Remember, reason and arguments are being woven to fool the public while strangulating the port of Calcutta (this is terrible devilishness)—it is being allowed to be silted. Not only the port of Calcutta, but the harbour and Hugli too. Already port handling has declined to 60%. Shipping has reduced by 40% due to their diabolical conspiracy. As a result of this terrible unmanliness—Bengal will choke to death. It will become completely dependent on others, slave of others and a beggar.

Remember—the harbour, port Hoogly—up to the Padma is the lifeline of Bengal—the artery carrying its blood. Try to understand—who is this in the garb of a human being?

Remember, thousands of crores of Rupees are being invested to create major ports out of lesser, insignificant inland ports in the ruse of economy and importance. The sole objective is to degrade Calcutta port and harbour to make them insignificant.

Remember, foreign shippers have repeatedly attracted attention to this and have asked not only to take back the port to its pristine glory, but to take bold expansion steps. Yet, all this has been hushed up.

Remember, JN has said it himself 'Calcutta is a dead city.' When some people in Delhi complained, he has tried to hush it up by saying 'I did not mean in that sense.'

Remember, JN & company never wanted to set up key establishments or strategic establishments in Bengal (there are thousands of excuses)—why?—understand it yourself.

Remember, no Bengali has been placed in any vital position, crucial position or military position in Defence Service.

Remember, though Bengal has the greatest number of FRS and is far ahead of other scientists in the field of physics—none of them was entrusted with Atomic undertakings.

Remember—although it was promised and declared a number times in Parliament that encroachment of even one inch by Pak will be considered an act of war and shall be resisted by the entire force of the Govt, even then parts of Bengal are being given away (not inch, so excusable?). Let them try to give away any part of Punjab or Bikaner—they will then understand.

And more than all, remember that JN & company are mortally and morally afraid of a real Bengal and real Bengalee. At the back of their minds there's fear. They know extremely well what shall happen when 'the ghost-who-walks' appears! So it is but natural that he should stake everything to 'set the stage' before 'the ghost's' possible appearance—with a fait accompli. ...So you see, it is starkly plain even to a nincompoop that they are proceeding in a premeditated coordinated plan to stifle Bengal, for ever ....Oh! Pabitra! Pabitra! This is the stark, naked, factual truth—bare to its bones.

He [Nehru] has many skeletons in his cupboard and he knows that they might come out one day…Once a Mir Jafar had handed over India to the British. Once a Jaichand had handed over India to the Muslims. Now Mir Jafar and Jaichand are born in one body. This time Mir Jafar and Jaichand have come together. They are doing exactly what they had done in the past. *(Letter to Pabitra Mohan Roy, 6 February 1963.)*

You must understand once for all that JN is a confirmed communist-in-disguise…He knows very well the gullibility of the Indian masses who are mostly illiterate *kisans*, labourers, etc. It is on their cheated votes that he is in the chair. And he is a past master in guile. It is solely because of him that the communists are flourishing. In order to usher in communism he has been juggling with words and phrases all these years to whitewash communism with the brush of socialism and welfare. And he has tricked India into such a sinister-satanic web that, it might well require God's own intelligence to rescue Mother India from this diabolical plot…

…A little bit more than 60% of all foreign aid and loans have gone into the pockets of interested and connected sources…He is a Janus-faced man…He has nothing to lose and everything to gain. All his near and dear and other relatives have got huge fortunes…He has but a few years to live. So what does he care what happens to India or the world after his death? He is a Godless man. So why shall he feel the qualms of conscience? *(Letter to Pabitra Mohan Roy, March 1963)*

Noblesse Oblige is a French proverb which means that obtaining a post or a rank imposes obligations. If someone is delighted on acquiring/obtaining a post thinking that he has made a great personal gain, then he is a big idiot. He should know that obligations proportionate to that post have also been imposed upon him…If he fails to live up to his obligations then he shall prove himself (or herself) to be nothing more than a cad and a total failure. *(Letter to Pabitra Mohan Roy, 24 February 1963)*

12 annas (75%) of the house of cards which Stalin built has been destroyed. The remaining 4 annas will be destroyed in front of you. [Communism shall die at the place of its birth. It is God's truth. *(Notes of conversation taken by Pabitra Mohan Roy, 28 September 1971)*

Bengal was golden and it still is: the only requirement is to bring it out. There are plenty of resources in the 24 Parganas. If industrialists start developing these then there will be no unemployment problem. *(Notes of conversation taken by Dulal Nandy, 31 January 1965)*

This (VV) Giri—what he was and what he has become is due to self-seeking, greed and loss of intelligence. *(Notes of conversation taken by Bijoy Nag, 27 September 1971)*

After liberation of Bangladesh, Pakhtunistan and Baluchistan will start burning. *(Notes of conversation taken by Bijoy Nag, 28 September 1971)*

The rule of international diplomacy is that the diametrically opposite parties will shout at the top of their voice abusing each other to show the world. But later, they will sit in a room and share a smoke. *(Notes of conversation taken by Pabitra Mohan Roy, 25 January 1973)*

India cannot die, and it has not died; Bengal cannot die and it has not died. They are in *susupti* state. Bengal and India's current state are in line with the law of rising and setting, emergence and decline. Bengal and India will rise again by this very law of nature. *(Notes of conversation taken by Pabitra Mohan Roy, 4 May 1973)*

Top RSS Sanghchalaks have worked actively in the frontline during the Indo-Pak war of 1965—not in hundreds but in lakhs. In some sectors, in 12/14 hospitals where thousands of wounded soldiers were being treated, no blood was available from locals. When the local military commander informed the Zonal RSS leader, there was a long queue to donate blood within an hour. Just like soldiers were killed, RSS volunteers also gave their lives. The newspapers did not report this. Government knows, police knows and the army knows—they are silent workers. They have only one ideal—Mother India, religion Hindu. When you sacrifice for the motherland, don't ask for anything in return. Not a single RSS volunteer asked for even a penny.

Once I was travelling through a place where RSS was holding a large camp. I saw almost fifty thousand RSS volunteers carrying water to the camp from a distance of a mile. I stayed in the place for two-three days after the camping was over. After a few days I heard some of the Muslim villagers had come to apologise. They said two months ago the NCC had camped at the same place. They destroyed all vegetables within 4-5 miles. When villagers went to complain they were scolded. They wasted water, using 10 buckets instead of one. It was because of this bitter experience that we did not agree to provide water to the RSS camp. We were surprised to see that without any protest the RSS volunteers carried water from so far. Now understand the difference between the official NCC and the RSS which is a mass organisation. The main difference between the NCC and the RSS is that the former has no ideal to tie itself to; RSS on the contrary has an ideal and they are ready to sacrifice their lives for the ideal. That's the rub. The few who have tasted political power in the RSS might be fickle.

See the fun, everyone gives indiscipline the name of democracy; they call discipline dictatorial fascism. They have no idea what a hideous thing fascism is. They can function only in a disaffected population. Undisciplined democracy is nothing but mobocracy or factionalism. It is synonymous with demonocray. *(Notes of conversation taken by Bijoy Nag, 17 February 1975)*

This is also true that vanishing someone in complete secrecy— where no one will ever know—they [the Russians] are masters in that; no one like them. Even Gods praise the perfect finesse of their diabolical act. Once someone was explaining to me how to deal with painless instantaneous death. I asked him how many times he had to do it to be able to understand. There are methods to make one forget his identity completely. If you ask him about the past he will keep staring blankly at your face. Some however go mad passing through this method. Stark mad. But I will say that their purpose was served. The aristocracy and the middle class which they [Soviets] wanted to annihilate is now getting re-established for some reason. There are innumerable places where if I take you, where you will see that their lifestyle, culture are much more lavish than America, France, Spain, Great Britain, Old Prussians. There are lakhs of circles of so-called comrades where you will not be able to gain entry even if you do *tapasya* (penance) for many births. In those circles only their language and appearance is Russian. The women in those circles use fur worth 10,000 pounds, diamond tiara, gems. This is the kingdom of fairies. You will not get a single woman who has not done at least one abortion (which is prohibited by law). There are doctors to attend to them for 24 hours. Food and wine are flowing. Eat, drink and be merry. When they step out during the day they are stark Russian communists—that mask is intact. Black market? There is no circle where there is no black marketing.

When you go there from another country, you won't be able to see anything. You will not even realise that you are conducted—you will think that you are moving around freely. You will not be able to see the real truth. Unseen by you, unknown to you, you are conducted by them. You shudder to think of it, neither you nor your friends in that country will ever know that you are being watched. Those who were key persons once now have been put away at such places that they have become dunderheads. Countless number of scientists, authors, mathematicians, ministers, top executives. There are a few who despite severe oppression are straight as Sal trees. They obey all regulations but have not allowed their spirit to be taken away. They too shall die, but they say that death is inevitable—why should we give up our soul for that? The number of such people is very few.

China is dreaming of communism in the world. I say that this book of Karl Sahib that you have made your Gita was not written by him, but by his wife. And his wife was from the family of Lords. Karl neither had so much intellect nor did he have knowledge. He wasted his life drinking and borrowing money. If Karl would have been given a job with thousand pounds salary then he wouldn't have rebelled. China is dreaming that it has to re-establish the Central Celestial State that it once was. Communism is a fencing for the outer world. This is the key theme of Marx and Lenin's communism as interpreted by Mao. The second thing is that China is a huge race which was asleep or was under the spell of addiction for a very long time. It was under the domination of foreign races. A sleeping race like this cannot be reawakened to do something big by imposing a democratic framework. It is a physical impossibility. It cannot be done; it can never be done. There must be some material to guide. In one word, they need discipline. A race, a country cannot be disciplined. Only an individual can be disciplined.

If individuals are disciplined the whole race will be disciplined. At the initial stage everyone will complain of suppression and autocracy. When children in a house do not understand what food will cause harm to them, then it is ordered that the food will not be allowed—this is discipline. In the whole world this is the only country which has stood up from the ground on its own strength. Russia helped for the first one or two years, but withdrew when they saw that China was trying to appendix them. China has paid their last Rouble debt in one and a half years. They haven't taken a penny's worth of assistance from anyone. *(Notes of conversation taken by Bijoy Nag, 17 February 1975.)*

Of all the nations, China is the master in true diplomacy. I really liked China's diplomacy. All the Governments in the world can learn diplomacy from China. Their diplomacy is standing on Kautilya's principles. *(Notes of conversation taken by Surajit Dasgupta, 5 December 1982)*

The high calibre, the diplomatic ability of the Communists is right in front your eyes: JN and Ayyub Khan gave away 20,000-22,000 + 16,000-17,000 from the body of India on a plate to the Communists (let alone the matter of vast Tibet). They managed such huge dividend from Indo-Pak only through diplomacy. *(Letter to Pabitra Mohan Roy, March 1963)*

A sycophant like Siddhartha Shankar Ray cannot be found. *(Notes of conversation taken by Bijoy Nag, 30 September 1976)*

Non-alignment is a myth, a mere bluff. The real purpose of the Colombo meet [NAM Summit of August 1976] is that all of us will extract something from the powerful and the rich in the world by getting together and shouting. We won't do anything ourselves. But we will demand that 1% of the national income will have to be given away by the developed countries (Germany, America, France, Japan, etc). Let me tell you something straight. Double the wheat and rice have been wasted by rotting (and being eaten by mice) due to faulty storage than have been imported. If storage can be done properly then even if population doubles there will be surplus for export. Their socialism is like cutting down the tall trees to the heights of smaller plants. *(Notes of conversation taken by Bijoy Nag, 3 October 1976.)*

The way Indira is maintaining her own people with the help of ordinance, if the British government did it they could have ruled India for 100 more years. She had to impose MISA being afraid of the Opposition even when ruling over so-called free India—arrested 1.5 lakh people, censored and gagged the press—shut down the *Indian Express* which was being critical. *The Statesman* is still trying to stand straight. She has kept the Government under pressure with the help of injunction from the Calcutta High Court—common people are being punished if they talk against the Government. If the British government did all this they would have ruled for 100 more years. You would have submitted. You know to submit only, not how to fight. 75% (*baro ana*) of those who knew how to fight are dead. The remaining quarter are inactive. *(Notes of conversation taken by Bijoy Nag, 2 October 1976)*

This election wouldn't have taken place if not for the unrelenting criticism by BBC, European and American press. Nobody criticised this except the western countries. All the Arabian countries, SE Asia (Indo China), Africa, Latin America and all communist parties and countries rather praised it. The Western countries stuck like a leech, criticising her. BBC said it for the first time that 45 lakh are in jail. In recent times, BBC and European press are openly saying that India does not have democracy any more—it is a complete dictatorship and autocracy. ...Now that the change has come—Emergency has been lifted, MISA will not be applicable anymore, etc.—for this you should kneel down and thank the western press. BBC exerted the maximum pressure. 80% of its Hindi Dept is from UP. BBC's Hindi and Urdu broadcasting has a very sharp effect. *(Notes of conversation taken by Bijoy Nag, 24 January 1977)*

Sadhus don't understand anything of ethics and justice. They are pleased no end if you sit in front of them with folded hands. This is a tactic of Indira. Durga puja, Durga path, *Homa* and mantra are going on continuously. *Yagnas* were conducted at two places—at one place 50 lorries of goods were transported every day, at the other place water and *yagna* material have gone from the whole country. At one place a *Yagna* for her removal and at another place a *Yagna* to protect her safety were going on. Indira did *parikrama* of the Meenakshi Temple and the Tirupati Temple for 3-3.5 hours. Common people cannot do this. Anandamayi Ma gave her a garland. During Indira's meeting with Nandini Satpathy, Mother gave a small piece of wood. Out of 4 Jagadgurus, 3 Shankaracharyas are supporting her. *(Notes of conversation taken by Bijoy Nag, 24 January 1977)*

'I got this clue from Veer Savarkar.' *(Notes of conversation taken by Jagatjit Dasgupta, 16 December 1979. Bhagwanji said this while discussing his escape from home in 1941 and the plane crash. It has been claimed by some that Savarkar had recommended the option of raising armed forces outside India during their meeting in mid-1940.)*

Spiritualism & paranormal

Siddha Purushas are beyond the ambit of being judged by normal standards—it is not possible to judge them by normal intelligence. *(Notes of conversation taken by Pabitra Mohan Roy, 19 October 1972)*

When I learnt practically about coming down from Samadhi, I understood why they behave in such an odd manner during Samadhi. Samadhi is not liberation from physical needs. As soon as you emerge from Samadhi, you will need food. The yogi who has gone into Samadhi is not above the requirements of the upkeep of his physical body. There are too many troubles with this...There are many levels above Samadhi. This is the reason why Shri Shri Thakur used to behave like a half mad person after descending from Samadhi and waking up. *(Notes of conversation taken by Bijoy Nag, 19 February 1975)*

Your Dead man not only believes, but he has direct knowledge that Shri Shri Jagadamba Durga Kali herself resides inside him and is driving him. Whatever he has done from his childhood (*shaisab*) and whatever he does even now is actually being done by Shri Shri Jagadamba Durga Kali. He is only the machine. However foolproof the conspiracy of the devil himself, the Mother will definitely rescue her son and get her work accomplished. There are hundreds of proofs. The biggest proof is MacArthur's final report and to have been able to live like this even after that (the report and its resultant efforts). *(Letter to Pabitra Mohan Roy, 2 September 1963)*

Dharma is not an imaginary thing. Dharma has to be done by yourself. The path of Dharma is sharp like a razor's edge. The trajectory of Dharma and Adharma is subtle. *(Notes of conversation taken by Dulal Nandy, 31 January 1965)*

My garb of a *sanyasi* is no deception. Twenty years ago, after much debate and discussion, it was decided that this dress was the most suited for inside and outside India. I gave them an ultimatum: taking up the garb of a *sanyasi* without actually taking *sanyas* will not do…wherever a *sanyasi* goes, emperors and labourers alike fall at his feet…According to scriptures and according to civil laws I am dead. *(Notes of conversation taken by Bijoy Nag, 28 September 1971)*

The *sadhan* (procedure) that is given by Shri Sadguru is the best. The path to liberation that is ordained by Shri Sadguru should never be used for any other work; that is the rule. There must be no exception to this rule. It must not be applied for doing well or ill or for fulfilling any desire. Whether you want good or bad, the price for that must be paid. For instance, if you want to serve the country you will have to be ready to pay the price for that too—and that price is to be ready to sacrifice your life for the country. If you cannot do that then don't take that path; remain behind. The price must be paid to get the result of every action/work. *(Notes of conversation taken by Pabitra Mohan Roy, 13 October 1972)*

Even now a prayer to Jesus on the night before of X-mas is answered. One must not divulge the prayer. … 'I sat with fingers crossed'—the sign of a cross is made for ensuring good, hence this phrase. *(Notes of conversation taken by PM Roy and others, 28 August 1973)*

In every *Yuga* (age) a Maharishi is in charge of protecting all the books of knowledge. In this age there are two. I have been to them, have lived with them, have got their blessings. *(Notes of conversation taken by Pabitra Mohan Roy, 4 May 1973)*

Ved, Vedanga, Upanishad, Puranas—all these have three meanings—the gross (materialistic) meaning, subtle meaning (to be attained by *sadhana*) and *karanartha* (the knowable).

In the Dwapar yuga of every chatur-yuga, Vyasa appears to spread the teachings of *Vedas* and *Puranas*. Every chatur-yuga has a different

Vyasa. Vyas's name is Dwaipayan—the twenty eighth Vyasa's name was Apantartma. Dwaipayan and Apantartama mean the same thing. Apantartama means under water—one who lives inside water—island, *antareep* (cape, peninsula). Vyasa lives there. Satyavati is the ground—water is flowing on two sides the ground—Ganga and Yamuna. Saraswati is that ground—it can't be seen with bare eyes, but Yogis can see it with eyes after practising yoga.

Many Muslim *faquirs*, pirs and Sufis know me. One Bengali *faquir* told me about a climber (herb) which keeps ghosts 100 yards away—they can never do any harm. That *faquir* used to live in Bangladesh but came over before the turmoil of 1971. Now he lives in Ajmer Sharif for ten months in a year. The remaining two months he roams around at different places. *(Notes of conversation taken by Pabitra Mohan Roy, 29 August 1973)*

The soul can travel in two kinds of vehicles after one dies—*Devayan* and *Dhumrayan*. *Devayan* travels upward, goes towards light; *Dhumrayan* travels downwards, goes towards darkness.

You must know that no one in this world is alone. You might think that there is no one around me, but that is wrong. Probably 4-5 unembodied spirits are standing there. *(Notes of conversation taken by Surajit Dasgupta, 7 October 1982)*

Only the human body has been made in a way that if used properly, ghosts, gods and goddesses, *apsaras* and *gandharvas* become visible. Only the human body can break out free of this limiting web, with the help of *Siddha Purush* Shri Shri Sadgurudev. Gods can't attain liberation even if they want—for that they have to take birth in a human body, do *sadhana* and then attain liberation. *(Notes of conversation taken by Jagatjit Dasgupta, 14 December 1979)*

Gods and Goddesses, *Yaksha*, *Kinnar*—all of them are roaming around in the form of waves, each in a different frequency. The frequency that is created when you chant a mantra hits the relevant frequency—then that wavy form starts solidifying. *(Notes of conversation taken by Pabitra Mohan Roy, 5 May 1973)*

You do not know that a vibration emanates from each molecule, atom and dust particle of this creation. They have colours and tunes too. This world creation has a tune which is playing on for 24 hours, like a beautiful divine concert. At places of conflict it is a bit suppressed, but in peaceful places it increases. When this intensifies, I cannot hear others. When the intensity comes down then I ask, 'What were you saying?' *(Notes of conversation taken by Surajit Dasgupta, 7 October 1982)*

The whole creation is held in place by time, by motion…What is vibration? Vibration itself is the mother of all creation, everything. Vibration is life and death is also vibration. You are a collection of vibrations. The bed on which you are sitting is also made of vibrations. Your house is the solid form of vibrations. The sky, the air, are all different forms of vibration. The real name of vibration is *Prana* (life force). This is the alpha and omega of everything seen or unseen, comprehensible or incomprehensible. This *prana* is force…this vibration is encircling the entirety of unlimited creation. It is floating, it is being supported, it is being shaped and reshaped, altered by this *Prana* force. The vortex of this force is somewhat egg-shaped. Two spherical—initially there was only one sphere—due to tremendous vibration it split into two. You and I are in one sphere and the others in the other sphere. *(Notes of conversation taken by Bijoy Nag, 2 October 1976)*

Once your *sadhana* reaches a stage, the *pranasharir* can be taken out of this *sthulasharir*. After getting used to his, one can go anywhere in this *pranasharir*. *(Notes of conversation taken by Bijoy Nag, 29 September 1971)*

A British archaeologist dug the Egyptian desert and found fossils of huge ocean-going ships and ropes, which proved that there was an ocean and King Solomon's ship used to disembark from there. The books that were found from layer after layer of King David's palace proved that the story of the Old Testament is true to the word. *(Notes of conversation taken by PM Roy, 2 November 1972)*

The number of births you have taken before this, right from the first spark at the beginning of creation to the present day—everything is stored nicely at one place. When you attain mastery of all the centres of your body while doing yoga *sadhana*, if those centres are activated, then the whole truth commencing from your primordial journey will come up in front of your eyes. *(Notes of conversation taken by Bijoy Nag, 18 February 1975)*

What I am telling you is the unalterable truth. I am telling you in the name of my mother that religious and spiritual leadership will be re-established in India. This is bound to happen if my mother is true. *(Notes of conversation taken by Bijoy Nag, 1 October 1976)*

Kalpa is the measurement of our time. The four yugas make one *Kalpa*. A small *Pralay* happens after 10/15/30 Kalpas. After 100 Kalpas there is a bigger *pralay*, and after 1,000 Kalpa there is *Mahapralay*. Our civilisation and culture is based on this yardstick. Should we junk all this only to accept what the Westerners tell us? *(Notes of conversation taken by Bijoy Nag, 3 October 1976)*

How ancient your civilisation is! You have civilised so many countries and have now forgotten all about it hundreds of cities, races, clans have pure Hindu names which have changed over time. This is the reason why I roam around like a bewildered, mad man. *(Notes of conversation taken by Bijoy Nag, 26 January 1977)*

The current era is the 24th *Chatur-yuga* (four-eras).

Everyone from the edge of the Indian ocean to the Bosporus were Hindus. Thousands of idols that are available up to the Bosporus are in the form of Durga as described in Chandi. There is a huge area in Siberia, where fire used to burst forth from the ground. There is a bottomless ocean of fire beneath—dead bodies used to be thrown there. Kashyap made his ashram there with fifty thousand people. *(Notes of conversation taken by Surajit Dasgupta, 14 December 1979)*

An ideal is a must for improving life. An ideal is like a noose for hanging. One needs integrity like a mountain, honesty, total and unwavering dedication and sacrifice to improve life. Ideal demands your present, your future, everything that you have—if you cannot give then don't talk about ideal. *(Notes of conversation taken by Surajit Dasgupta, 29 September 1982)*

Reminiscences

Today I have no one in my life who can give me a call and say, 'Come back home dropping everything, you are so exhausted, come and lie down keeping your head on my lap, take some rest.' No one will call me in that way. Then? Then why am I? Why this life of mine? *(Letter to Pabitra Mohan Roy, 24 February 1963)*

Come and put the *Mohanbhog* in our mouth. We will savour it with our eyes closed. If Bengal hopes that he will return at our call, then that's a mistake. He is dead. Bengal has killed him. *(Notes of conversation taken by Dulal Nandy, January 1965)*

In our own times, the wars waged by the *Baro Bhuiyans*, Marathas, Rajputs are thousand times more glorious than Mazzini and Garibaldi. Guerrilla warfare is our own. We get overwhelmed when we read about Robin Hood, but can Robin Hood stand in comparison with Devi Chaudhurani and Bhavani Pathak? *(Notes of conversation taken by Pabitra Mohan Roy, 5 May 1973)*

I know [Satya] Sai Baba from the time he hadn't become Sai. At that time he was a fresh youth; used to wear jute-like khaddar and was a disciple of the original Sai. *(Notes of conversation taken by Bijoy Nag, 1 October 1976)*

I listen to the BBC and Australian radio routinely. When BBC news ends at 8.45 then I hear the Hindi news for 15 minutes. Sometimes I also tune in to Lahore and check if there is transmission of Bhutto's talk. I leave it if there is no news of Bhutto. The speaking style of Bhutto in both English and Urdu is excellent. Because of his bass voice his Urdu speeches are incomparable. No one in your country can speak like this on the radio. One can know by listening to BBC and Australia which news the GOI has suppressed. Keep on repeating the lies. This is Goebbels' lesson. They keep repeating the same lies. *(Notes of conversation taken by Bijoy Nag, 3 October 1976)*

I don't know compromise. You compromise on every value in your life. I am a man of strong likes and dislikes. I can never disown my principles. One who is not disciplined can never do anything in life. One who compromises has no discipline. Every step of life is based on a premise—that premise must be lived with truth. *(Notes of conversation taken by Surajit Dasgupta, 30 September 1982)*

Miscellaneous

Only a few people's photos are worth keeping in the Central Hall of Parliament: Mr Hume, [Shri Ramakrishna] Paramhansa Dev, Swami Vivekananda, Bal Gangadhar Tilak, Madan Mohan Malaviya, Gopal Krishna Gokhale, Sarvepalli Radhakrishnan and Mr M Viswesvarayya. No photo of political leaders should be kept there. *(Notes of conversation taken by Pabitra Mohan Roy, October 1972)*

I know the region that spreads from the Himalayas, through Pamir up to the point where the Alps meet the ocean like my palm. I have been to Mana Gaon near Badrinath, Vasudhara, Alakananda, Satopanth, Brahmakund, Rudrakund, Shivkund, the monastery at Thuri—this is the last renowned monastery of the Lamas towards India. This monastery was my favourite. There are hundreds of routes to travel to Tibet from India, one of them through Kulu valley. *(Notes of conversation taken by Bijoy Nag, 16 February 1975)*

The modern Ayodhya was rebuilt by Maharaj Vikramaditya. The original Ayodhya has gone under Sarayu. *(Notes of conversation taken by Bijoy Nag, 18 February 1975)*

Western classics should be read after you have completed reading Kalidas, Bhavabhuti—especially Dumas, Victor Hugo and Sir Walter Scott. *(Notes of conversation taken by Bijoy Nag, 30 September 1976)*

When respected Sisir babu [Bhaduri] was offered the Padma award he said, 'I am an actor, how can I take an award from the Government?' A Bengali can say this! My heart fills with pride. *(Notes of conversation taken by Bijoy Nag, 3 October 1976)*

At present the best songs in your country are those of Naushad Ali. He is a very polite man, and he has always stood respectfully by those who had helped him when he was poor. *(Notes of conversation taken by Surajit Dasgupta, 10 March 1982)*

The jewel among your announcers is Melville de Mello. Surajit Sen followed the style of Demello. *(Notes of conversation taken bySurajit Dasgupta, 4 October 1982)*

Caviar is the most preferred food for the Russian emperor. The best caviar is available from Lake Baikal. *(Notes of conversation taken bySurajit Dasgupta, 5 October 1982)*

PABITRA MOHAN ROY: PROFILE OF NETAJI'S INTELLIGENCE OFFICER

 Pabitra Mohan Roy was born on 2 July 1908. He completed his medical studies from Dhaka National Medical College in 1931. Roy got involved with revolutionary organisations, especially the Anushilan Samiti during his stay in Dhaka. It was at this time that he came in contact with Trailokya Nath Chakravarti (Maharaj).

Upon completion of his studies, when Roy learnt from his revolutionary comrades that his arrest was imminent, he migrated to Malaya. In the last week of 1932, he left Calcutta for Rangoon to stay with his uncle who was the senior deputy accountant general. From there he moved to Port Dickson near Kuala Lumpur. An arrest warrant was issued by the Bengal government in Roy's name after he left and the Malaya administration was informed about it. Luckily, however, the arrest did not materialise.

Roy returned home in 1940 for a couple of months to get married. During his visit he also attended the anti-compromise conference organised by Subhas Chandra Bose at Ramgarh.

After Malaya came under Japanese occupation, Rash Behari Bose visited the area to mobilise support for the Indian independence movement and to organise the Indian Independence League (IIL). Roy met with Rash Behari in early 1942 and joined the IIL movement along with his wife Renu. Leaving his family behind, Roy joined the IIL training camp at Port Dickson in July 1943. Within a few days, he was sent for further intelligence training to Penang.

Roy's first direct contact and extensive interaction at an individual level with Subhas Chandra Bose took place in September 1943, when Bose came for a three-day visit to the training camp.

Roy's training in guerrilla warfare made him an expert in the use of different types of guns, use of Morse code, repairing and setting up transmitter sets, and use of explosives.

In September 1972, while deposing before the GD Khosla Commission, Roy described the subsequent developments:

> In 1943, end of December or early January 1944, one day again Netaji called me and we had a long talk with him. He told me again that he had something to say. He wanted to send me to India for some intelligence work, to contact the revolutionary friends in India. This was in his mind. He wanted to select ne for that job.... It is in the middle of February 1944 one day he called me and told me 'I have a very big mission. I want to send somebody to India with some information and work to do. Will it be possible for you to do it? If so, you can give me a reply within 48 hours. I told him that we are taking the training for this. Why 48 hours? Anyway, he gave me the time of 48 hours to think about it.... Then of course Netaji had a long talk with me and he gave me so much of instructions that when I was sent these were the things that I had to do. Everything was explained to me. I had to tell him as to what was happening in various parts of the country and what the Govt was doing.... After that another week or so had passed. By Order of the Day we five were informed that we would have to proceed to India by a submarine. We were taken to a special camp cut off from everybody in our families and from all friends, and there special codes, etc. everything was given. When we completed that, I had the opportunity to meet Netaji—and that is the last time I met him....

…When I finished everything, I saluted him, and as I was about to move, he patted me on my back and said: Don't be afraid. Go ahead for the mother country. And I tell you one thing. In short time or in some time, if you hear miracle stories, if you hear any sort of stories, don't believe that or don't bother about that. Your duty is to go on with your work. (sic)

On 7 March 1944, Roy started his submarine journey for India along with Americk Singh Gill, Mohinder Singh and Tuhin Mukherjee. The team of four were offloaded near the beach close to the Konark Sun temple. While Mohinder Singh and Tuhin Mukherjee proceeded towards Bombay, Gill and Roy moved to Calcutta, where they established contact with Haridas Mitra, husband of Subhas's niece Bela.

Roy was arrested on 18 January 1945 in Puri, after Mukherjee handed himself over to the police and passed on all their secret operational details. In the meantime, twelve more INA secret agents who had landed near Baluchistan surrendered, divulging all the secret information about the INA's espionage infrastructure and agents to the police. It was used to intercept the active INA agents in India. According to Gill, Mohinder Singh was betrayed and captured in Phagwara and later was tortured to death in Lahore. Gill was soon arrested in Calcutta. So were Haridas Mitra and Jyotish Bose, the two people who provided pivotal support to this team of secret agents. All four—Roy, Gill, Mitra and Bose—were sentenced to death, while Mukherjee was pardoned for acting as the government's witness. As the war came to an end, the death sentences were however commuted.

Roy was released in December 1946 and settled in Dum Dum. He was elected to the South Dum Dum Municipality in 1952 and later became its vice chairperson. He worked tirelessly for rehabilitation of the refugees from East Pakistan and remained involved with a number of urban development initiatives. He joined the Praja Socialist Party (PSP) and was elected to the state Assembly in 1957, but lost in the 1962 elections.

Roy passed away on 14 March 1993.

Bhagwanji's eyes and ears

Pabitra Mohan Roy kept Bhagwanji informed about everything that was going on around him through detailed letters and notes. Eighty-five of those letters were selected by the Justice Mukherjee Commission for investigation and marked as 183 (a). Below is a sample of Roy's reportage from a letter he wrote to Bhagwanji on 2 December 1977, describing what he witnessed in the West Bengal Assembly during a debate on a motion to reinvestigate Netaji's disappearance.

-এই ৩৩০০.৩০- F/B এ.- ২২ন ....
Resolution mover 3 .... CPI (M) ...
....।

....
.... R.S.P. ....। ....
....। .... CPI (M) 3 ....
....
Ex-minister .... - ....
F/B ....
.... F/B ....
Minister ....
CPI (M) .... - .... 3 ....
[r communist ....। ....
.... - communist ....?

.... CPI (M) ....
....। .... F/B ..../

.... 3 ....। ....
.... - ....
.... - ....
....
.... - .... - ....
....। ....
....
.... CPI ....
....।

Assembly ....
....

Translation:

West Bengal Assembly

There was a discussion on 30 September 1977. The Forward Bloc (FB) moved a resolution that the government of India should reconsider the mystery surrounding Netaji's disappearance. The earlier inquiries were useless and done to serve specific purposes, etc.

I was requested on behalf of the FB to attend. Later they sent me a Pass for the Speaker Gallery and insisted that I should be present. That's why I went. Now I feel I did the right thing. I could see the true character of all.

All parties participated in the discussion and said nice things like 'come back', etc.

Only one or two things were out of tune.

Bhabani Mukherjee, the sole speaker from the CPI(M) (Communist Party of India (Marxist)) is from Chandernagore. He was the mayor there and currently the chief whip of the party in the Assembly. Apart from the good things he said, he also dwelt on the friendship with fascist Hitler, etc. The attitude was that despite knowing all this they were doing a favour by supporting the resolution. The funny thing is that of all people, the FB remained quiet and didn't register any protest. The speaker from the RSP (Revolutionary Socialist Party), however, protested in very strong language. After this, two ministers from FB and the mover of the resolution spoke, but didn't care to protest.

The speaker from the RSP protested in a very strong manner and spoke on other aspects too. The CPI(M) didn't dare to counterattack him.

A different kind of objection was raised by an ex-minister from the Congress, Zaimal Abedin. Addressing the FB members, he said that all was well, but it must be asked that those with whom they had allied now to become ministers had forgotten the past attitude of CPI(M) [towards Bose] or had they changed their views? Is it possible for those working for Netaji's ideals to be friends with the communists?

In response, the CPI(M) members created a ruckus trying to stop Abedin but even then, the FB kept quiet.

Another person spoke well—the sole representative of the Muslim League. He forcefully said that the Government of India must reveal the truth. 'We the Muslims of not only Bengal but of whole India think that he was the only leader who was truly concerned about us. His presence was like a protective amulet for us. No leader other than Netaji felt genuine concern about Indian Muslims.'

The Communist Party of India (CPI) did not participate in the discussion.

Even though he had been directed by Bhagwanji to keep his existence and identity top secret, Roy, mindful of historical significance of his reunion with his lost leader, must have desired to leave a clue for posterity. The authors found it in his memoirs *Netajir Secret Service* (in Bengali). The manuscript was read by Bhagwanji, who suggested a few modifications. The book was published on 15 August 1980 and reprinted in 1992. While it contained the details of Roy's early life and his activities as a secret agent of the Azad Hind government, it also had a very strange appendix titled 'Interview of the author with Netaji'. Spread over five pages were quotations which were completely incongruous with the theme of the book. No explanations were given either by the author or the publisher for including these pages.

No reader could have known that this was a compilation of some of Bhagwanji's letters to Roy.

Brave Soldier! I wish that from now on, you build up a fanatical-fire eating-band (secret) of everlasting patience-faith and - Stamina: who shall keep on practicing - practicing - practicing common tactical fighting amongst themselves (they shall live their ordinary day to day lives in home, attend to their respective avocations) they shall meet in a big body or in a group in any very specious math - maidan - Bagan, nadi-pookoover teer - Jungle. They shall prepare make - belive markings as of boundry, river, villages, houses, Army bunkers Ranks etc etc: [one or two things (of attachings and occupying and defending - repulsing at one meet) one side trying to tactically overwhelm and take over homes - village - boundries etc. otherside repulsing. using all possible and impossible types of intelligence, with the least bloodshed and harm to properties and absolutely no harm to inoffensive women + children. This force shall show them as village/Town/civil defence force. 100% Correct and innocuous to all eyes and Govt. They must maintain them (in cadre and O.R. just as the V./T.C. d[...] [...]) in finest top mettle and constant pratice. And they must be so fanatical (just like the Jesuits - famous throughout the world) that shall, with fanatical patience hold themselves ever ready in mettle for 5, 6, 8, 10, 12 years. They shall never sag. There number might be 4 to 10 thousands. Their discipline and obedience must be the envy to the Gods. They must be dedicated efface the stigmas "Doorbal - chira Doorbal Bangali" & "Kshanikar - Utsahi Bangali", "veeru-Biswasghati - Swarthapar Bangali", "Adhir - Bangali". I want to lead them (along with the forces) over to E.B. and be the only one Indian leading his men to retake and forever unite [...] mother of mothers Sonar Bangla.

[...] shall be one. one single country.
Every one, the Hindus, Muslims, Britishers & [...]: has tried to weaken, cut assunder, demoralise, debase Bengal and Bengrees.
But now the hour of Bengal is coming
Bengal's frontier is not the Himalayas. Yes brave son of mother Bengal! " Balo, Balo, Balo sabe
                Sata Bina Beni rabe.
                Banga Aaxar Jagat Savay
                Shreshtha Asana Labe.
                Dharme Mahan Habe.
                Karme Mahan Habe.
                Nata Dijamani Oodike rahar
                Pooratana a Poorabe."

Ah! mother, - mother, mine mother Bengal!, how far you are!
Banga amar, Janani Amar, Dhatri Amar, Amar Desh!!
        Mother! thou SHALL wear the CROWN!
            I swear! I swear!! I swear!!!
                Mother! hark! hear unto me,
                        your faqir-son

For heavens sake and for very life of me and mother Bengal's sake pause and understand what I want to you to understand, that I want to convey.
I was weeping today while dictating and spellingout the last lines. ─

[One of Bhagwanji's earliest letters to Pabitra Mohan Roy]

who are working only for self and ~~party parties~~ party or ~~own interest~~. choice your subject with care. Fill in your cards irrefutably. So that they could not refute when "confronted".

He has no rancour for Bapu. Though Bapu (because Bapu got twice defeated in his fight against him and was so rattled that he gave up his Cong: membership and also, started a whispering campaign against your Deadman) has no rancour because Bapu at last turned a volte-face and preached fighting for freedom and honour (which was your right creed); and, because, hearing and becoming stimulated and emboldened (he was a mere figurehead and marionette in the hands of ————) by the Radio exhortations of your Deadman, he stoutly opposed partition and during the last fateful meeting he wept like a child before them and sobbed out praying against Partition (this faquir has documentary evidence) but he was overridden roughshod. Also, It has been kept a secret that your Deadman went with Bapu's full blessings and concurrence of the inner committee. so your Deadman bore no rancour.

Ah, my child! Brave son of ^a Mother Bengal!, your last ~~letter~~ paragraph of 17th Dec'62 letter, appealing — and — crying out in the name of Divine Mother Gagadamba, praying to this old old ~~farquir~~, stating your hopes and utter darkness, — wrung my old heart to the core. My eyes became misty. It was, as if, I could hug you at that time. Despair not, fear not, Brave son! the future is yours. You don't know, you cannot comprehend, to what end your Dead Man is working and with what Powers. ~~your imaginations will be ~~ ~~ ~~ ~~ ~~ chance, you could come to know even a fractional part of his present activities. My child!, I can tell you with full affectionate honest gravity. your Deadman is now poised for all eventualities; he is now poised, cc with The Thunder of The in his hands. Ponder, think over and, try to fully fathom the real purport of the above phrase. If you can fathom, the real purport of the above ph If you can fathom it correctly, your breath will simply be taken away by the awfully - unfathomable magnitude of the constructive - Destructive Powers which he is now in a position to handle and press into action - if need arises.

Shocks after shock with mounting crescendo SHALL be coming for a ten ~~of~~ deep, deep malign: Cancer is sapping out the vital Sap of India. like devilish Octopus it has spread over and caught ~~it~~ in its tenta ~~in which today~~ in the whole body + outside. A serious disease req a serious diagnosis + treatment - your Dead man is not prepa that even after this thumps the Surgeon finds the malign: still ~~to~~ lingering then and only then that a Great War shall be unleashed. And it is only your dead man's sober hand? that rest reins. It is for not for nothing that an old man in the course of the last recent months went out of India twice, braving all the fatal hazards to his life and frail body. the result is before you. I can tell you a War is not an emotional business, it is a ~~so~~ ~~so~~ ste cold calculated business. A slight mistake might ~~some~~ spe doom + slavery.
          If during the coming thump, your Deadman finds right time comes, an old man shall come over the horizon. But if (I pray to Divine Mother to spare the necessity) He the situatio forces on him the imperative, decision of unleashing and deliver ~~it's broadside~~, oh! then watchout. An old man

no money, no help is wanted, this h— (?) for the execution of what is being executed and shall be effected to a successful end.

____

Your Dead man took nothing from "you" (meaning Bengal - India and home) He gave and left his everything & worldly wealth & worldly matters to you. He took away nothing. He kept nothing for himself. He did nothing for himself. He wanted nothing for himself or his personal aggrandisement and/or power. He gave himself to India. He gave something to India and effaced himself away. He again shall he giving Something to Bengal - India - S.E. Asia. And he shall again efface himself away. He is a Deadman, he is a Mystic. It was & only Dilip away from Desh Seva and Tutor a Mystic who always tried to tutor me

SUBHAS BOSE'S PLACE
IN INDIAN HISTORY

The official narrative on India's freedom struggle has usually accorded a side role to Subhas Chandra Bose and that too grudgingly. From government publications to text books to research by government-funded institutions, the focus has largely remained on Mohandas Karamchand Gandhi, Jawaharlal Nehru and, to some extent, the local movements led by the leftist organisations. The powerful State machinery supplemented by institutions it influences has done its best to drive in the myth of 'Sabarmati ke Sant' getting India her freedom through love and non-violence, to which the colonial British rulers of ours were presumably susceptible, and subsequently passing on the baton to his chosen successor. For this line of propaganda, Bose has been an inconvenience, remembered for his fierce opposition to the Gandhi-led Congress and thereafter for his association with the Axis bloc. Yet, his is too powerful a presence to be ignored altogether. Therefore, there have been occasional memorials, functions and postage stamps, but never anything compared to the mainstream adulation accorded to Gandhi and Nehru.

Bose's detractors and opponents, of whom there is no dearth in India (even in his own home state of Bengal), are not going to be pleased with the spotlight falling on him with the release of this volume and are expected to sharpen their most powerful arguments against him, harping on his association with the Axis bloc—especially Nazi Germany, and that he would have turned into a ruthless dictator. These arguments will be used to the hilt to besmirch his legacy and all that he did for India.

Here we take a look at the facts and put them in context to determine how much of the mainstream propaganda is based on truth and how valid are the arguments hurled against Bose.

Pact with the devil

There is no dispute that the dark shadow of the two dictators—Benito Mussolini and Adolf Hitler—continues to hang over Subhas Bose's legacy. While the Western sensibilities are perfectly understandable in view of the trail of destruction left behind, in particular by Adolf Hitler in that part of the world, the Indian attitude has been hypocritical, inspired as it is partly from the pro-Western outlook of the elite in India, and influenced partly by international communist movement which has determined the shape of the leftist movement within the country.

There have been insinuations that Bose harboured anti-Semitism. It is often pointed out that before he joined the Axis, Bose had opposed Jawaharlal Nehru's idea that the European Jews could be given sanctuary in India. The fact of the matter is that Nehru's resolution was turned down by the Working Committee of Congress on which occasion, Bose, by Nehru's own admission, 'didn't express himself definitely'. Bose wrote that he was 'astounded' that Nehru moved such a resolution and explained his attitude:

> Foreign policy is a realistic affair to be determined largely from the point of view of a nation's self-interest…. Frothy sentiments and pious platitudes do not make foreign policy. It is no use championing lost causes all the time and it is no use condemning countries like Germany and Italy on the one hand and on the other, giving a certificate of good conduct to British and French imperialism.[1]

Nehru's own thinking came to light from his correspondence with

---

1   *A Bunch of Old Letters: Written mostly to Jawaharlal Nehru and some written by him*, Oxford University Press, 1988, Letter from Subhas Chandra Bose to Jawaharlal Nehru, 28 March 1939, p 334.

Bose later in the aftermath of the Tripuri controversy. In his letter dated 3 April 1939, Nehru clarified that 'It was not from the point of view of helping Jews that I considered this question, though such help was desirable where possible without detriment to our country, but from the point of view of helping ourselves by getting first-rate men for our science, industry, etc. on very moderate payment.... Their coming here on low salaries would have helped us also to bring down other salaries.'[2]

On a personal level, Bose was as humane and enlightened as any other Cambridge alumni like him. Between 1933 and 1939, for example, he had for friends Kitty and Alex, a sensitive, newly married Jewish couple in Berlin. After being advised by Bose, the couple went to the US, and from her Massachusetts home in 1965 Kitty Kurti wrote her tribute for 'Netaji'—a book titled *Subhas Chandra Bose as I knew him*. In it she wrote that Bose 'did not attempt to hide' from her his deep contempt for the Nazis. In the same vein, he cited India's exploitation by British imperialism and explained why he had to do business with the Nazis. 'It is dreadful but it must be done. India must gain her independence, cost what it may,'[3] he told the couple after a meeting with Hermann Göring. Of Jews, Bose said, 'they are an old and fine race' gifted with 'depth and insight' and felt that they had been 'miserably persecuted'[4] across the centuries.

Leonard Gordon has aptly described Bose's position.

Bose gave priority to Indian nationalism and to the vanquishing of British imperialism in India that crowded out other concerns. Bose could see the connection of the plight of

---

2   Ibid., Letter from Jawaharlal Nehru to Subhas Chandra Bose, 3 April 1939, p 352.

3   Kitty Kurti, *Subhas Chandra Bose as I knew him*, Firma KL Mukhopadhyay, 1966, p 11.

4   Ibid, p 39. Bhagwanji held the Jews in high esteem and sympathised with their ordeal through the centuries, and lauded them for their 'unswerving faith in their destiny'. He lauded them for preserving their ancient culture. Nearly 2000 years of buffeting, he lamented, destroyed their everything. But their 'faith in their religion, faith in their destiny, faith in Old Testament is intact'. 'Could you achieve anything if you do not have this perspective?'

colonial people throughout Asia and Africa and even comment on it as he did when he was in Europe in 1936 and 1938. But he was an Indian-firster, more narrow and focused in his vision than Nehru.[5]

The stark truth is, that all nations and their leaders pursue nothing but their national interests. Explaining this in the summer of 1990 was Nelson Mandela. In the City College of New York Mandela was interacting for the first time with American people in a town meeting moderated by broadcast journalist Ted Koppel.[6] Mandela was bombarded with questions about his dealing with world leaders not approved by America. Diplomat and political writer Kenneth Adelman commented that 'those of us who share your struggle for human rights against apartheid have been somewhat disappointed by the models of human rights that you have held up since being released from jail'. Then he put this query:

> You've met over the past six months three times with Yasser Arafat, whom you have praised. You have told Gaddafi that you share his view and applaud him on his record of human rights in his drive for freedom and peace around the world; and you have praised Fidel Castro as a leader of human rights and said that Cuba was one of the countries that's head and shoulders above all other countries in human rights, in spite of the fact that documents of the United Nations and elsewhere show that Cuba is one of the worst. I was just wondering—are these your models of leaders of human rights, and if so, would you want a Gaddafi or an Arafat or a Castro to be a future president of South Africa?

5   Leonard A Gordon, *Brothers Against the Raj*, Viking, 1990, p 385.
6   The video recording of the full programme is available on YouTube at https://www.youtube.com/watch?v=q6eE9BIUfBg.

In response, Mandela asserted the following amid a standing ovation from the audience:

> One of the mistakes which some political analysts make is to think their enemies should be our enemies. Our attitude towards any country is determined by the attitude of that country to our struggle. Yasser Arafat, Colonel Gaddafi, Fidel Castro support our struggle to the hilt. There is no reason whatsoever why we should have any hesitation about hailing their commitment to human rights as they're being demanded in South Africa. They do not support [the anti-apartheid struggle] only in rhetoric; they are placing resources at our disposal for us to win the struggle. That is the position.

His response to Henry Siegman, executive director of the American Jewish Congress, was more pointed. 'Firstly, we are a liberation movement which is fully involved in a struggle to emancipate our people from one of the worst racial tyrannies the world has seen. We have no time to be looking into the internal affairs of other countries. It is unreasonable for anybody to think that this is our role.'[7]

In 2015, British Prime Minister David Cameron was constrained to accept during a TV interview that one's own country's interests are paramount to all other considerations. This was when Jon Snow of *Channel 4* News told him the following curtly during an interview.

> 'In November [we] did a deal with the Saudis that we would back them joining the Human Rights Council of the United Nations, providing they backed us. This sounds a bit squalid for one of the most human rights abusing regimes on earth.'
> 'Saudi Arabia is a member of the United Nations,' Cameron

7   Howard Kurtz, 'Mandela reiterates support for Arafat, Gadhafi, Castro,' *The Washington Post*, 22 June 1990, https://www.washingtonpost.com/archive/politics/1990/06/22/mandela-reiterates-support-for-arafat-gadhafi-castro/072b9d2a-ec38-4d6e-b680-b6afeebe5013.

replied evasively. His body language was clearly defensive.

'But why did you want them inside the Human Rights Council…?'

'We completely disagree with them about the punishment routines, about the death penalty, about those issues and we raise them.'

'Why did you do this deal then? They are not the right sort of people to be doing any sort of a deal with on human rights.'

'We totally oppose their record in that area.'

'Why did we do it?'

'Well, I said we totally oppose their record.'

'No, why did we do it?'

After failing to dodge the persistent TV presenter, Cameron admitted: 'We receive from them important intelligence and security information that keeps us safe. The reason we have the relationship is our own national security.'

Of course it would be easier for me to say, 'I'm not having anything to do with these people, it's all terribly difficult, et cetera, et cetera.' For me, Britain's national security and our people's security comes first. [8]

No country places her interests after those of the rest of mankind. In the pursuit of national interest, nations and their leaders would even shake hands with the devil. It is for the reason of larger national interests that the United States, the Land of the Free, is friends not only with regressive Saudi Arabia, but also Pakistan, which harboured their enemy No 1, Osama bin Laden. It was this very reason Subhas Chandra Bose shook hands with Adolf Hitler and, if you please, Indira Gandhi with Saddam Hussein.

---

8   David Cameron on Ali Mohammed al-Nimr and Saudi Arabia, *Channel 4 News*, https://www.youtube.com/watch?v=khGa49rM6iM.

While the Western nations regarded him as a monster in the league of Hitler, for India Saddam was an ally. Iraq did not denounce but supported India's right to possess nuclear bombs during the Vajpayee days. 'Oldest democracy supports maximum dictators,' charged former Prime Minister I K Gujral, an ex-diplomat, in an interview with the *Indian Express* on 14 April 2003. 'Saddam was a dictator but remember he was on our side when it came to Kashmir,' he fulminated. The world's greatest democracy, a long-standing ally of the country whose citizens cried publicly the day Bin Laden was killed, did not come around to appreciating India's position till the horrific 9/11 attacks.

While we would never ever contemplate placing the UK or the US in the same league as Nazi Germany, it is a plain fact of history that Great Britain, for all her goodness, was not willing to free India even as she and the United States waged war against Hitler in the name of liberty. It was not Hitler but the British Prime Minister during World War II, Winston Churchill, who hated Indians from the core of his heart. It was Churchill, not Hitler, who made the most offensive comments about Indians that made even his fellow Britons wince in disgust. Leo Amery, the Secretary of State for India and Burma noted that despite the full participation of the Indian troops in the Allied efforts against Nazi Germany, Churchill had a 'curious hatred of India', and was 'convinced that the Indian Army is only waiting to shoot us in the back'. Churchill's own private secretary recorded that 'the Hindus were a foul race' who were 'protected by their mere pullulation from the doom that is their due'. He wished that the head of British bomber command could 'send some of his surplus bombers to destroy them'.[9]

In recent years, considerable data has emerged to show Churchill was responsible for millions of deaths in the 1943 Bengal famine. Madhusree Mukerjee, physicist and former editor of *Scientific American*, after years of research wrote *Churchill's Secret War: The British Empire*

---

9   Richard J Aldrich, *Intelligence and war against Japan*, Cambridge University Press, 2000, p 159.

And The Ravaging Of India During World War II. In an interview with the *Outlook* magazine, Mukerjee summarised her findings, which were no surprise to Indians. She held Churchill responsible for 'deliberately deciding to let Indians starve'. 'Churchill contributed to the famine by removing the shipping from the Indian Ocean area in January 1943,'[10] as Japanese threatened the Empire.

Former Under-Secretary General at the UN and Minister of State for External Affairs Shashi Tharoor pulled no punches in telling the truth about Churchill from the Indian point of view.[11] 'Churchill is the man who the British insist on hailing as some apostle of freedom and democracy....when to my mind he is really one of the more evil rulers of the 20th century only fit to stand in company of the likes of Hitler, Mao and Stalin,' he said in London on 21 March 2017 at the launch of his book *Inglorious Empire*, which chronicles the atrocities of the British Empire.[12] *The Independent* of London further quoted Tharoor rubbing in that 'Churchill has as much blood on his hands as Hitler does'. 'Ships laden with wheat were coming in from Australia docking in Calcutta

---

10 Sheela Reddy, 'Churchill's Famine?' *Outlook*, 6 September 2010. In March 2019 was published the findings of IIT Gandhinagar scientists who, after analying 150 years of drought data, concluded that Bengal famine of 1943 was caused by British policy failure, not drought. Between 1935-45, the famine-affected region, which was Bengal, had no drought. 'Out of six major famines (1873-74, 1876, 1877, 1896-97, 1899, and 1943) that occurred during 1870-2016, five are linked to soil moisture drought, and one (1943) was not,' the researchers wrote in their study. See, 'Bengal famine of 1943 caused by British policy failure, not drought: Study,' 20 March, 2019, *The Economic Times*, https://economictimes.indiatimes.com/news/politics-and-nation/bengal-famine-of-1943-caused-by-british-policy-failure-not-drought-study/articleshow/68495710.cms.

11 Economist Utsa Patnaik, who has studied fiscal relations between colonial India and Britain put the figure siphoned off from India by the East India Company and the British Raj at GBP 9.2 trillion (USD 44.6 trillion). Ajai Sreevatsan, British Raj siphoned out $45 trillion from India: Utsa Patnaik, 21 November 2018, *Livemint*, https://www.livemint.com/Companies/HNZA71LNVNNVXQ1eaIKu6M/British-Raj-siphoned-out-45-trillion-from-India-Utsa-Patna.html.

12 Maya Oppenheim, 'Winston Churchill has as much blood on his hands as the worst genocidal dictators, claims Indian politician,' *Independent*, 8 September 2017, https://www.independent.co.uk/news/world/world-history/winston-churchill-genocide-dictator-shashi-tharoor-melbourne-writers-festival-a7936141.html.

and were instructed by Churchill not to disembark their cargo but sail on to Europe. And when conscience-stricken British officials wrote to the Prime Minister in London pointing out that his policies were causing needless loss of life all he could do was write peevishly in the margin of the report, "Why hasn't Gandhi died yet?"'

'I hate Indians. They are a beastly people with a beastly religion. The famine was their own fault for breeding like rabbits,' Tharoor recalled Churchill's words.

Tharoor's own party was in power in New Delhi in 1965 when Churchill died. Never mind what he had done to us, we mourned his passing away. The Tricolour was flown half-mast on government buildings in India and glowing tributes were paid on the All India Radio. There was no precedent for doing so over the passing away of a foreign private citizen. In a discussion in the Rajya Sabha on 31 August 1965, some Opposition members registered their protest. Bhupesh Gupta said: 'I have gone through the volume of Sir Winston Churchill and not a single word favourble to India occurs there. He has been known to be anti-Indian always. How is it that in that broadcast so much praise was showered on him, as if he were a liberator of the whole world, a great friend of India and the freedom movement and so on?'

No Indian leader or diplomat could ever summon courage to raise with Churchill the issue of his crimes against India. Jawaharlal Nehru merrily intermingled with the man who had the blood of Indians on his hands.

[Jawaharlal Nehru with Winston Churchill in 1948.
Source: Wikimedia Commons]

Subhas Chandra Bose's reaching out to Nazi Germany was in continuation of existing contacts between Germany and Indian patriots in the national interests of their respective countries. Girija Mookerjee, who was with Bose in Germany between 1941-43, explained in his 1975 biography of Netaji that 'even Imperial Germany during the World War I had taken up the cause of Indian independence and the German Foreign Office had, therefore, a precedent to go by'.

> Men who weighed this question at the German Foreign Office were men of career, who were neither National Socialists nor did they belong to the inner coteries of Hitler. They were German civil servants who performed their duties as good German citizens during the war. These men, guided by the desire to advance German national interests in India, thought it advisable for political reasons to support the movement sponsored by Netaji in Germany.[13]

In his first radio broadcast from Berlin on 1 May 1942, Bose stated that 'my concern is, however, with India, and if I may add further, with India alone'. According to the minutes of their meeting on 27 May 1942, he even raised with Hitler the issue of his disparaging comment about Indians in *Mein Kampf*. Hitler answered that his words were 'directed at certain tendencies among the suppressed peoples to form a united front against their oppressors'.[14] Churchill was never asked, so he never offered any explanation—satisfactory or otherwise.

Bose was naturally grateful to the Italians, Germans and the Japanese for all their help, but remained clear headed about the leaders, their power equations and their own political posturing. Focused on extracting the help required for India's liberation from a reluctant Hitler,

13   Dr Girija K Mookerjee, *Subhas Chandra Bose*, Publication Division, Ministry of Information and Broadcasting, Government of India, pp 75-76.
14   Rudolf Hartog, *The Sign of the Tiger: Subhas Chandra Bose and his Indian Legion in Germany, 1941-45*, Rupa, 2001, pp 27-28.

Bose had to play along the game of propaganda and do what was required to win a battle of perception. While it was imperative for him to portray the Axis bloc as a valuable and trusted ally, it was equally important for them to show the British that he was won over. He had made no secret about his liking for certain aspects of Fascism, National Socialism and Communism, whose positive aspects he wanted to synthesise into a new ideology but beneath the veneer of his bonhomie with the dictators was his dislike for Hitler and his rabid racism. Not insignificantly, two of his trusted aides—ACN Nambiar and Girija Mookerjee—were staunch anti-Nazi.

Yet, the reality was that he was there seeking help, not as an armchair critic. His purpose was to obtain as much help as possible without compromising on self-respect or India's interest. There is little doubt that he achieved whatever little was possible under those conditions admirably. 'He wanted to keep his own liberty of action and he did not want to be branded as pro-Nazi,' recalled Girija Mookerjee.[15] And when it was required, he didn't mince words. During his meeting with Hitler, for instance, irritated by the dictator's patronising attitude, he shot back, asking Adam von Trott zu Solz to 'Please tell His Excellency that I have been in politics all my life and that I do not need advice from anyone.'[16] Bose's personal assessment of Hitler was that he 'was a German version of the Fakir of Ipi'.[17]

It wouldn't be an exaggeration to state that Gandhi and Nehru were far closer to the British in mind and spirit (despite being on opposite sides) than Bose was ever with the Axis leaders despite being dependent on their help.

---

15 Giriji Mookerjee, *This Europe*, Saraswaty Library, 1950, p 132.

16 SK Bose, A Werth, SA Ayer, *A Beacon Across Asia: A Biography of Subhas Chandra Bose*, Orient Longman, 1996, p 117. Adam von Trott zu Solz was another anti-Nazi in the German Foreign Office, responsible for working closely with Bose. He was hanged to death on 26 August 1944 for playing a leading role in Colonel Claus von Stauffenberg's plot of 20 July 1944 to assassinate Hitler.

17 Rudolf Hartog, *The Sign of the Tiger: Subhas Chandra Bose and his Indian Legion in Germany, 1941-45*, Rupa, 2001, p 28.

Despite such a background, any Indian worth his name still wanting to raise an accusatory finger at Subhas Bose for his reaching out to Hitler would do well to apply their holier-than-thou outlook on free India's conduct and come up with a similar snap judgment.

- In 1980, Indira Gandhi said of Subhas Bose that while he was a patriot, 'because of our strong feelings against fascism and Nazism, we could not approve of any alliance with Hitler's Germany or Japan'.[18] But, since 1947, New Delhi has extended a friendly hand to all sorts of leaders reviled, especially in the Western world, as the worst dictators and tyrants of our times. The list includes Libyan leader Muammar Gaddafi, Nicolae Ceausescu of Romania and Robert Mugabe of Zimbabwe, the last ranked # 1 in the Forbes' list of world's ten worst dictators in 2011.[19] Mugabe was once compared to Adolf Hitler by Britain. He took it as a compliment, proclaiming 'Let me be Hitler tenfold'.[20] India continues to enjoy most friendly relations with Kim Jong-un's regime in North Korea. According to an official note put up on the website of the Indian embassy in Pyongyang, the relations between both the nations are 'generally characterised by friendship, cooperation and understanding'. It further tells us that India and North Korea have a 'commonality of views' on many issues such as disarmament. This is notwithstanding the fact that North Korea has been more supportive of Pakistan on the issue of J&K and is widely believed to have defence ties with India's

---

18 S K Dhawan, *Selected Thoughts of Indira Gandhi: A Book of Quotes*, Mittal Publications (Delhi), 1985, p 39.

19 Tim Ferguson, World's Worst Rulers: Scratch One Now?, *Forbes*, 22 August 2011, https://www.forbes.com/sites/timferguson/2011/08/22/worlds-worst-rulers-scratch-one-now/#46f727916190.

20 Andy Lines, 'Let me be Hitler tenfold: How lion-meat loving Robert Mugabe built £8million personal fortune as country lurched into financial chaos, *Mirror*, 16 November 2017, https://www.mirror.co.uk/news/world-news/let-hitler-tenfold-how-lion-11529464.

sworn enemy in the fields of ballistic missiles and nuclear technology. 'India reaches out, wants to upgrade ties with North Korea,' read a story in *The Hindu* on 16 September, 2015. The Americans were not very pleased about India-North Korea friendship, but then we had our national interest to think of first, not America's.

- It is not Aung San Suu Kyi, the winner of the Nobel Peace Prize and the Jawaharlal Nehru Award, but the Burmese junta which received most support from the land of Gandhi when they were in charge. Cut to our times—India has virtually turned a blind eye to the allegations that the Burmese under Suu Kyi's leadership engaged in 'ethnic cleansing' of the Rohingyas. All we are hearing from our Government is that we have our own security concerns first.

- Ignoring street protests of scores of average Indians and prominent leaders, India actively backed and even assisted militarily the Mahinda Rajapaksa regime as it was being accused of carrying out war crimes against the Tamils.

- Pervez Musharraf, directly responsible for the deaths of so many Indians, including the soldiers we lost during the Kargil war, was given a ceremonial Guard of Honour by the Indian armed forces upon his arrival in New Delhi in 2001 for a start. How many times did the Americans accord such an honour to Fidel Castro or the British to Russian heads of the governments? And, if this was a triumph of Indian diplomacy, how come Subhas Bose's reaching out to Hitler, who had not caused even a single Indian death, became a cause to beat one's chest in the name of morality and world peace?

In fact, it has been argued that 'Mahatma Gandhi was "accommodative" of violence of the Arab Palestinians, even as he advised the Jewish people to counter Germany's ruler Adolf Hitler through non-violence', in a 2017 book *Squaring the Circle: Mahatma Gandhi and the*

Jewish National Home by PR Kumaraswamy of the Jawaharlal Nehru University's School of International Studies. According to a report in *The Hindu*, Kumaraswamy contends that 'some of the writings of the Mahatma on Israel were not brought to the public by his secretary Pyarelal'. He further told the paper that Mahatma 'had imbibed Islam and Christianity's "anti-Jewish prejudices".'[21] This might be disputed, but there is no running away from the fact that so long as Nehru and his family ruled India, Israel was not allowed to open its embassy in New Delhi. Why? On 16 February 2005, *The Guardian* (London) carried an article by Israeli historian Benny Morris on recently discovered correspondence between Albert Einstein and Jawaharlal Nehru on the necessity of India's support for the birth of a Jewish state. Giving moral and historical arguments in his four-page letter of 13 June 1947, the great scientist appealed to Nehru as a 'consistent champion of the forces of political and economic enlightenment' to rule in favour of 'the rights of an ancient people whose roots are in the East'. Nehru's July 11 answer was that national leaders, 'unfortunately', had to pursue 'policies... [that were] essentially selfish policies'.

> Each country thinks of its own interest first... If it so happens that some international policy fits in with the national policy of the country, then that nation uses brave language about international betterment. But as soon as that international policy seems to run counter to national interests or selfishness, then a host of reasons are found not to follow that international policy.[22]

On 29 November India voted at the United Nations General Assembly with 12 Islamic countries against the partition of Palestine, and against the formation of a Jewish State. Noted activist Balraj Puri,

21   Kallol Bhattacherjee, 'Mahatma Gandhi was "accommodative" of Arab violence, claims book,' *The Hindu*, 19 October 2017, https://www.thehindu.com/news/national/gandhi-was-accommodative-of-arab-violence-claims-book/article19883767.ece.
22   Benny Morris, 'Einstein's other theory,' *The Guardian*, 16 February 2005, https://www.theguardian.com/world/2005/feb/16/israel.india.

who received honours such as Padma Bhushan and Indira Gandhi Award for National Integration, testified that Nehru too placed national interest above everything else. In his book *Kashmir: Towards Insurgency*, which came in for praise by former PM Dr Manmohan Singh, Puri recalled Nehru telling him in a private conversation in 1953 that India had 'gambled on the international stage on Kashmir' and consequently 'till things improve, democracy and morality can wait. National interest is more important than democracy...'.[23]

The standard Indian version of Bose's outreach to Nazi Germany, as articulated by most of our intellectuals and thinkers, doesn't take the idea of 'national interest first' into consideration. Senior journalist Sumit Mitra, writing in *The Telegraph* (Kolkata) of 17 April 2005 harangued that Bose was sitting 'in the lap of Hitler when the air of Auschwitz was acrid with the smell of the gas chamber'. The fact is that when Bose arrived in Berlin, the gas chambers had not gone into operation. The Holocaust began much later and there is nothing to show that Bose or anyone in his team had any clue about it. The world discovered the horrors of Holocaust only after the war ended, by which time Bose was in SE Asia, planning his future course of action looking at the endgame. After visiting Auschwitz (former Nazi death camp in Poland), Prime Minister Benjamin Netanyahu remarked the following on 13 June 2013 according to leading Israeli daily *Haaretz*: 'The Allied leaders knew about the Holocaust as it was happening. They understood perfectly what was taking place in the death camps. They were asked to act, they could have acted, and they did not.' Bearing him out was this revelation in *The Independent* (London) of 17 April 2017...

> Newly accessed material from the United Nations—not seen for around 70 years—shows that as early as December 1942, the US, UK and Soviet governments were aware that at least two million Jews had been murdered and a further five million

---

23   Balraj Puri, *Kashmir, Towards Insurgency, Tracts for the Times*, Sangam Books, 1993, p 55.

were at risk of being killed, and were preparing charges. Despite this, the Allied Powers did very little to try and rescue or provide sanctuary to those in mortal danger.[24]

His link to Hitler notwithstanding, one indisputable fact about Subhas Chandra Bose is that he was India's liberator. It is through this prism that we are going to assess his place in our history, and not how he is viewed in the West.

India shall be free

Bose's violent push for India's freedom during the Second World War with his quickly assembled, Japan-backed Indian National Army (INA) was an unprecedented step as Indians had lost the will to put up an armed resurrection after the 1857 revolt was crushed. His deep baritone on the radio sent Indian hopes soaring unbelievably high. And yet, his exhortation 'George Washington had an army when he won freedom, Garibaldi had an army when he liberated Italy' came to nothing, or so it seemed. The INA men were routed in battlefield, at the very hands of the Indian mercenaries enrolled in the British Indian Army. A dismissive Indian Army assessment of 1946 reads that 'the INA was 95% "ballyhoo" and 5% "serious business"'. It was 'still an embryo organisation' when it went to war; a 'purely guerilla force...with no aircraft, no artillery, no heavy mortars, no tanks or AFVs', a 'David against Goliath but a David without a sling'. 'It was never a cause of real trouble or annoyance to the Allies,'[25] the report, now available at the National Archives in New Delhi, concludes. Surely, it takes decades to build a formidable army. Bose got less than a year before the INA plunged into the Arakan, Imphal and Kohima campaigns.

---

24   Andrew Buncombe, 'Allied forces knew about Holocaust two years before discovery of concentration camps, secret documents reveal,' *Independent*, 18 April 2017, https://www.independent.co.uk/news/world/world-history/holocaust-allied-forces-knew-before-concentration-camp-discovery-us-uk-soviets-secret-documents-a7688036.html.

25   'Part played by the INA in active operations against Allied forces,' CSDIC (I), 12 May 1946, File No INA 402, National Archives, New Delhi.

The trouble was just starting. An Indian Army officer intermingled with the imprisoned INA men awaiting repatriation to India to get a sense of their outlook. He reported back that it was no use trying to belittle Bose: 'He is regarded by them as a Leader who is honest, utterly sincere and who has raised the status of the Indian community in the Far East far above that of the other minorities under Japanese occupation.'[26] These people were then brought to India and put on trial at the very place they had vowed to march into. But the idea to make the Red Fort trials the Indian version of Nuremberg and Tokyo trials backfired. Bose's war was justified. The humiliation of the INA soldiers—Hindu, Muslim, Sikh, Christian— galvanised the Indians like they hadn't been ever since India was brought under direct British government rule.

SECRET.

Survey of Press references to I.N.A. dated 7.2.46.
. . . . .

Publicity for the I.N.A.

1. "Mr. Frank Anthony, President of the All-India Anglo-Indian and Domiciled Europeans Association, on Tuesday, met Col. C.J. Stracey of the I.N.A. who is now in detention in the Red Fort, Delhi. Mr. Anthony spent several hours with him. Col. Stracey is a member of a distinguished Anglo-Indian family, one brother being in the Imperial Forest Service, another in the Indian Civil Service, a third in the Imperial Police Service and a sister an officer in the I.M.S. Col. Stracey himself received a permanent commission in the Indian Army, having passed through Dehra Dun after a competitive examination. His attitude is one of honest and deeply sincere conviction. He felt that he was serving India and the Anglo-Indian community by joining the I.N.A. He is popular with thousands of men of the I.N.A. Col. Stracey impressed Mr. Anthony by his deeply sincere and courageous conviction. Col. Stracey, not having participated in any acts of brutality, is not likely to be sent up for trial. If, however, the military authorities decide to try him, Mr. Anthony has indicated his willingness to defend him."
(Hindustan Times dated 7-2-46.)

[Courtesy National Archives, New Delhi]

INA's GS Dhillon openly engaged in fistfights with his captors and dared the jury, including future Indian Army chief KS Cariappa, to hang him. They would have done so without any delay, but in the

---

26 Operational Security Intelligence, File No INA 249, National Archives, New Delhi.

dead of night the city walls were plastered with handbills warning of bloody retribution. Similar reports were received from various parts of the country. The British were wise enough to see the writing on the wall. The swelling public opinion manifested in numerous meetings, felicitations of the INA soldiers, fund-raising to help their families and rallies in cities couldn't be brushed aside.

APPENDIX 'A'

EXTRACTS FROM THE PUNJAB POLICE ABSTRACT OF INTELLIGENCE DATED
19 JAN 46 (Para 2 of Summary)
- - - - - - - - - - - - - - -
REPORT ON THE THREE CASHIERED OFFICERS

"The three released INA Officers have remained very busy fulfilling their many social and other engagements. Their popularity shows no signs of waning and they remain most effective magnets wherever they appear at public meetings. An audience of 2000 at Chheharta (Amritsar) dwindled to 500 when they failed to arrive. Sehgal by himself addressed 25,000 persons at Sialkot. He acknowledged his private conviction that Subhas Chandra Bose is dead. Thirtyfive thousand people gathered to hear Shah Nawaz and Dhillon at Jallianwala Bagh, Amritsar, Shah Nawaz explained that the INA was a plant which had grown from the seed sown when the martyrs' blood wasspilt there. He thanked everyone, especially the students, for bringing about his release, not, he said, because he himself had been liberated but because the honour of Subhas Chandra Bose had been thoroughly vindicated by the way in which the British Government had been worsted. He claimed again that the INA had never been defeated in battle, but had been forced to surrender on account of the atom bomb. Dhillon recited his own poem which has now become a regular feature of his speeches. He admitted that Bhagat Singh and his companions had been executed for crimes which were far less serious than the ones he and his companions had committed.

[Extracts from the Punjab police abstracts of intelligence dated 19 January 1946: Thirty-five thousand people gathered to hear Shah Nawaz and Dhillon at Jallianwala Bagh, Amritsar. ...Dhillon admitted that Bhagat Singh and his companions had been executed for crimes which were far less serious than the ones he and his companions had committed. Courtesy National Archives, New Delhi]

There is no denying that Gandhiji did wonders for our freedom struggle and that he was one of our most towering leaders, but from all accounts available now it appears—borrowing a term from the cricket arena—that 'the man of the match' of the Indian freedom struggle was Subhas Chandra Bose. Ba Maw was spot on when he wrote that 'one man sowed and others reaped after him'.[27] 'Mass movements by the Congress between 1920 (when Gandhi arrived on the scene) and 1947 were niggardly, and hardly upset the British,' wrote former R&AW

---

27 Ba Maw, *Breakthrough in Burma: Memoirs of a Revolution*, p 348.

official Colonel RSN Singh.[28] In 1942, Gandhi launched the Quit India movement. The view from Bose's side was that it was his suggestion in 1939 to serve a six-month's ultimatum on the British government which was accepted by Gandhi in totality in his Quit India resolution of August 1942. Prior to this, Gandhi was, as Bose himself stated repeatedly, most reluctant to launch a movement. This is what he wrote in his book *Indian Struggle*.

> On 6 September (1939), Mahatma Gandhi, after meeting the Viceroy, Lord Linlithgow, issued a press statement saying that in spite of the differences between India and Britain on the question of Indian independence, India should cooperate with Britain in her hour of danger. This statement came as a bombshell to the Indian people, who since 1927 had been taught by the Congress leaders to regard the next war as a unique opportunity for winning freedom.

All the same, the Quit India movement was launched in good earnest. Bose praised Gandhi's stirring speech as he launched it. But, the movement 'failed to galvanise India', reasoned Colonel Singh.

> Immediately, the entire top leadership of Congress was taken into custody. Leaderless and rudderless, the movement died in a year's time, but the Congress leaders remained in prison till the rest of the war. This served the interest of the British as well as the reputation, prestige and political prestige of Congress leaders.

Putting it more bluntly was late author-journalist Khushwant Singh. He said the movement (contrary to the impression the people of India have been given since 1947 through officially-sanctioned propaganda)

---

28   R S N Singh, 'Why the Congress is jittery about the Subhash files,' *Sify*, 24 April 2015, http://www.sify.com/news/why-the-congress-is-jittery-about-the-subhash-files-news-columns-peypoWfecbfif.html.

was 'crushed within three weeks'.[29] Khushwant Singh was far from being an admirer of Bose.

'It was during this period, when the Congress leaders were ineffective, that Subhas Chandra Bose was exerting himself for India's independence,' Colonel Singh wrote.

'By the end of 1942, the British had definitely come out victorious in their immediate total confrontation with Indian nationalism, and the remaining two and a half years of the war passed without any serious political challenge from within the country,' summarised noted historian Sumit Sarkar.[30]

The failure of 1942 was such a shattering blow that the All Indian Congress Committee, which met in late September 1945 in Bombay saw little hope for independence at that time. Sardar Vallabhbhai Patel moved a resolution on September 23, reading: 'Neither the end of the War nor the change of Government in Britain appears to have resulted in any real change in British policy towards India, which seems to be based on delaying every advance and in attempting to create new problems and fresh complications. It is significant that there is no mention in these [British] broadcasts of the Independence of India.'[31]

This was the backdrop against which the Congress party geared up to go to the general elections in the winter of 1945-1946, as announced by the new Labour Government as a precursor to reaching an agreement about the question of India's freedom. The British were insisting on substantial agreement between the Congress and the Muslim League before considering giving independence. The war had affected the British capacity to rule India further. The Congress election manifesto

---

29 Khushwant Singh, 'History of one's own making,' *Hindustan Times*, 28 June 2003. 'The brutal and all-out repression succeeded within a period of six or seven weeks in bringing about a cessation of the mass phase of the struggle,' according to 'some of the most authoritative historians of modern India'. Bipan Chandra, et al., *India's Struggle for Independence*, Penguin Books, 1989, p 463.

30 Sumit Sarkar, *Modern India*, p 404.

31 NN Mitra (ed), The Indian Annual Register, July-December 1945, The Annual Register Office, p 93.

would go on to articulate that 'in these elections, petty issues do not count nor do individual or sectarian cries—only one thing counts: the freedom and independence of our motherland'.[32] The 'sectarian' jibe was aimed at the Muslim League, bent on partitioning India along religious lines. The Congress was all for secularism in contradiction of the League's claim that it alone had the right to represent the Muslims of India. At this crucial juncture, the Red Fort trials commenced against the INA soldiers.

[*Hindustan Times* on 6 November 1945]

It made all the sense for the Congress party to make the best of this opportunity. By September, the censorship had been lifted and the INA saga was becoming known to the people of India for the first time. The nationalist press had also dismissed the war time propaganda that an INA-Japanese win would have made India a colony of Japan.

At the September 1945 AICC meeting, the Congress paid a backhanded compliment to the INA soldiers. The INA resolution

---

32   Ibid, p 112

moved by Jawaharlal Nehru said, 'The AICC is, however, strongly of the opinion that…it would be a tragedy if these officers, men and women were punished for the offence of having laboured, however mistakenly, for the freedom of India. They can be of the greatest service in the heavy work of building up a new and free India.'[33] In other words, the Congress positioned itself as a magnanimous organisation which would support patriots who were 'mistaken' in not following the creed of non-violence. Come independence, the INA soldiers were however dropped like hot potatoes despite the exalted resolutions of the AICC.

Sardar Patel was more forthcoming in his assessment. Writing to Biswanath Das, later to be the chief minister of Orissa, in January 1946, he noted that benefits accruing to the Congress on account of the INA trials didn't mean that the party would yield ground to Subhas Bose or his men. All that was happening was tactical.

Naturally, our efforts have resulted in raising the strength of the Congress. The Forward Blocists may also try to derive strength and reorganise their forces in these circumstances. But their efforts are bound to fail if they do not see things in their proper perspective. The Congress recognises the sacrifice and bravery of the INA people. That does not mean that the stand their leader took or the policy that the Forward Bloc followed in this country was right. The Congress has never accepted that position nor is there any reason to do so in the future. **However, we must, for the time being, be a little more tolerant of their mistaken belief, if any, regarding the so-called justification of their attitude.**[34] (Emphasis added)

Thanks to records declassified by the UK Government, we now have a more granular insight into why Congress leaders came around

33   Ibid, p 92
34   PN Chopra (ed), Vallabhbhai Patel's letter to Biswanath Das, 5 January 1946, *Collected Works of Sardar Vallabhbhai Patel*, Vol X, Konark Publishers Pvt Ltd, pp 165-166.

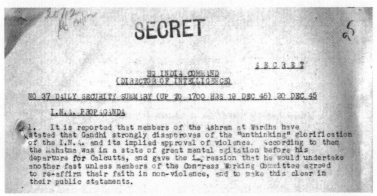

SUBJECT NATIONS' RIGHT TO OVERTHROW RULING POWER

H.T. 7-1

Sardar Patel's Praise For I.N.A. Men

BOMBAY, Jan. 6.—"If the I.N.A. trial had shown anything it was the recognition under International Law that any subject country had the right to organize its army and overthrow the ruling power," said Sardar Vallabhbhai Patel, presiding over a large public meeting here this evening.

The meeting was held under the auspices of the Bombay Provincial Congress Committee, to give a public reception to Mr Bhulabhai Desai, defence counsel in the first I.N.A. trial.

Sardar Patel expressed appreciation of the courage, capacity, determination, patriotism and sacrifice of the men of the Indian National Army. He said the country knew nothing about the I.N.A. men

160,000-DOLLAR AIR-RAID SHELTER

VIENNA, Jan. 6.—Von Schurach, former Vienna gauleiter, now on trial at Nuremberg, paid nearly 160,000 dollars of the city's funds to have a deep luxurious air-raid shelter built for himself, the Vienna Finance Office disclosed yesterday.—A.P.A.

[*Hindustan Times* on 7 January 1946: 'Sardar Patel's praise for INA men']

to backing Bose's INA, even though violence had no place in their worldview.[35]

SECRET

S E C R E T

HQ INDIA COMMAND
(DIRECTOR OF INTELLIGENCE)

NO 37 DAILY SECURITY SUMMARY (UP TO 1700 HRS 19 DEC 45) 20 DEC 45

I.N.A. PROPAGANDA

1. It is reported that members of the Ashram at Wardha have stated that Gandhi strongly disapproves of the "unthinking" glorification of the I.N.A. and its implied approval of violence. According to them the Mahatma was in a state of great mental agitation before his departure for Calcutta, and gave the impression that he would undertake another fast unless members of the Congress Working Committee agreed to re-affirm their faith in non-violence, and to make this clear in their public statements.

[**HQ India Command/Director of Intelligence, No 37 Daily Security Summary, 20 December 1945**: 'Gandhi strongly disapproves of the "unthinking" glorification of the INA and its implied approval of violence.' Courtesy National Archives, New Delhi]

---

35 The Congress Working Committee resolution of 11 December 1942, drafted by Mahatma Gandhi himself, emphasized 'the need for Congress strictly to adhere to the non-violent creed in their struggle for political freedom'. NN Mitra (ed), *The Indian Annual Register*, July-December 1945, The Annual Register Office, p 33.

On 23 October 1945, Brigadier TW Boyace of Military Intelligence sent a damning secret report to the Secretary of State for India in London. To understand the Congress gameplan, the MI had used a mole of theirs. Capt Hari Badhwar had first joined the INA, then switched sides and finally gave evidence against the INA men during the Red Fort trials. There were several other traitors like Badhwar.

Sourcing his information to Asaf Ali, a leading Congress Working Committee member, Capt Badhwar reported that before taking a stand on the INA issue, the Congress high command had sent Ali out on a recce mission to gauge public feeling. He travelled across India and discovered that people were overwhelmingly in support of the INA. 'This inflamed feeling forced Congress to take the line it did,' Badhwar told Boyace. In his free-wheeling talks with Badhwar, Asaf Ali, free India's first Ambassador to the United States, offered the information that 'Congress leaders had realised that those who joined the INA were far from innocent', and that's why Nehru always made it a point to refer to them as 'misguided men', even in his public speeches. Ali was positive that as and when Congress came to power, they 'would have no hesitation in removing all INA (men) from the Services and even in putting some of them on trial'. Badhwar, who led a comfortable life in free India and rose to be a general, asked Ali why couldn't the Congress 'repudiate their championship of the INA' when they knew 'the true facts?' Asaf Ali replied that 'they dare not take this line as they would lose much ground in the country'. Boyace's comment at the end of his note was: 'In other words, the present policy [to back the INA] is one of political expediency.'[36]

These facts belie the fantasy interpretation of history fed to us over the decades by loyal Congressmen and their cronies in historical and intellectual circles. PR Dasmunshi wrote in *The Pioneer* in January 2006 that 'Pandit Nehru, notwithstanding his political differences with Netaji, saluted the historical march of the INA and came forward

---

36   *Transfer of Power*, Volume VI, Her Majesty's Stationery Office, London, p 387-388.

SIKH PROPAGANDA ON BEHALF OF THE I.N.A.

3.   The birthday of Guru Nanak, the founder of Sikhism, was
celebrated in Calcutta on Nov 19. The congregation at the Gurdwara
and in the adjoining Park increased to about 30,000 in the afternoon,
when Sarat Bose was expected to arrive: of these some 2000 were
Sikh and non-Sikh officers and men of the Services. At about 1530
hrs a procession of about 500 Bengalis and others clad in Khadi,
shouting slogans and carrying tri-coloured flags, arrived in the
Park and placed a portrait of Subhas Bose alongside the Guru Granth
Sahib, the Holy Book of the Sikhs. Sarat Bose and other members of
the Bose family then arrived and were greeted with tremendous
enthusiasm. Sarat Bose, in a speech, praised the part of the Sikhs
in the I.N.A. and referred to the way in which the I.N.A. had broken
down communal barriers. Marching songs of the I.N.A. were also
sung, and released I.N.A. personnel were cleverly used for
propaganda purposes. The whole celebration appeared to have a most
moving effect on the audience, including the Service personnel.

It is noteworthy that political slogans, applause and the placing
of a portrait of Subhas Bose, a non-Sikh, on the stage near the
Holy Book, are unprecedented events at the Birthday celebrations of
Guru Nanak in Calcutta.

[HQ India Command/Director of Intelligence, No 16 Daily Security Summary,
26 November 1945. Courtesy National Archives, New Delhi]

to defend it...as a lawyer in the Red Fort trials'. In August that year, while defending his rejection of the Mukherjee Commission report, his Cabinet colleague Shivraj Patil proclaimed in Parliament that Nehru had 'donned the black coat and gown and gone to the Red Fort to defend' the INA men.

This line of argument isn't new. During his appearance before the Khosla Commission in August 1972, Subhas's nephew Dwijendra Nath Bose had given an angry retort. He accused Gandhi and other Congress leaders of 'rubbing their noses on the floor' before the British and washing their hands off the Quit India movement after it turned violent. 'This is not our movement. This is all violence going on. You have put us in jail before the movement was started,' Dwijendra taunted.[37] Noted historian Dr RC Majumdar seemed to agree with this line of thinking. 'Far from claiming any credit' for the 1942 movement, he wrote, 'both Gandhi and the Congress offered apology and explanation for the "madness" which seized the people participating in it.'[38] On 11 December 1945,

---

37   Excerpted from the record of Dwijendra Nath Bose's examination before the Khosla Commission on 9 August 1972.

38   Ramesh Chandra Majumdar, *History of the Freedom Movement in India, Volume 3*, Firma K L Mukhopadhyay, 1977, p 555.

deploring the violence during the Quit India movement. 'Non-violence
does not include burning of public property, cutting of telegraph
wires, derailing trains and intimidation,' the resolution specified.[39]
Jayaprakash Narayan went further when he said: 'To fasten the August
[1942] programme on Gandhiji is a piece of perjury of which only the
British ruling class is capable of.'[40]

Beginning late 1943, Gandhiji wrote several letters to Lord
Linlithgow, the Viceroy of India, explaining his position with regard
to the Quit India movement. These were compiled and published in
Gandhi's Correspondence with the Government 1942-44 by Navajivan
Publishing House (founded by Gandhiji himself). A reading of these
and other letters Gandhi wrote offers a view entirely different from
what the official publicity machinery routinely rolls out for public
consumption. The Government had blamed Gandhi for the turn of
events and obstructing the war efforts. Gandhi in his response to the
Viceroy, therefore, clarified:

1. It was not the 'Quit India' resolution but the action of the
   Government which led to the acts of violence. It was the
   Government which 'goaded the people to the point of madness'.[41]
2. The aim of 'Quit India' resolution was to bring about
   conditions under which India could effectively participate in
   the war efforts of the Allies.

---

39 NN Mitra (ed), *The Indian Annual Register*, July-December 1945, The Annual
   Register Office, p 100. The resolution further read: 'The Working Committee are
   further of opinion that the constructive activities of the Congress, beginning with the
   spinning wheel and Khadi at the centre, are emblematic of the policy of non-violence,
   and that every other Congress activity, including what is known be the Parliamentary
   programme, are subservient to and designed to promote the constructive activities
   as explained by Gandhiji.'
40 Madhu Dandavate, *Jayaprakash Narayan: Struggle with Values: a Centenary Tribute*,
   Allied Publishers, p 68.
41 *Gandhiji's correspondence with the government*, 1942-44, Navajivan Publishing House,
   Ahmedabad, 1957 (First edition 1945), p 43.

3.   The Congress had no plan for any big movement. The only person authorised to start civil disobedience (Gandhiji) was arrested before he could 'issue any instructions'.[42]

Further correspondence with the Government brought forth the following:

1.   Gandhiji had not asked for the physical withdrawal of the British from India. What he had asked for was the withdrawal of British power, not of individual Englishmen.

2.   He agreed to the use of India as a base of military operations against Japan.

3.   The injunction 'Do or die' was intended by Gandhiji to serve as a badge to distinguish every soldier of non-violence from other elements. They were to win freedom for India or die in the attempt to achieve it non-violently. The standing order of Gandhiji to Congressmen was to remain wholly non-violent.

Dwijendra, who had been tortured in jail during the freedom movement, was also not impressed with the argument that Nehru had set aside all past acrimony to defend the INA soldiers during the Red Fort trials. 'Do you understand the word *namavali*, which means the words "Hare Krishna Hare Rama" are printed on clothing worn by Brahmins? So, Panditji thought it proper to wear that *namavali* of INA to cross the river of election.'[43]

According to KK Ghosh, who was the first to write an authoritative and comprehensive account of the INA in 1960s, the Congress 'had no political programme ready at hand to rejuvenate' the dull political

42   Ibid, p XVII.
43   Excerpted from the record of Dwijendra Nath Bose's examination before the Khosla Commission on 9 August 1972.

atmosphere. As a 'ready-made issue' the cause of the INA officers offered the Congress 'an opportunity to organise an all-India nationalist front against the British'.[44] Several records in the Transfer of Power series released in the 1970s by the British government show that the Congress leadership's defence of the INA was motivated by a desire to excel in the elections of 1946. Commander-in-Chief of British Indian armed forces, General Claude Auchinleck wrote to Field Marshal Viscount Wavell on 24 November 1945 that 'the present INA trials are agitating all sections of Indian public opinion deeply and have also provided the Congress with an excellent election cry'.[45] Similarly, Wavell was informed by Sir M Hallett of the United Provinces on 19 Nov 1945 that 'the publicity on this subject (INA trials) has been a useful gift to political

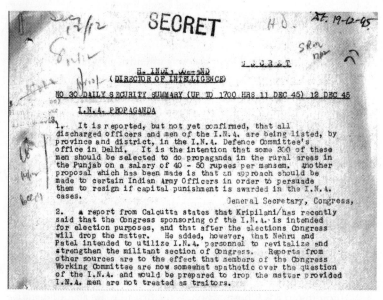

[HQ India Command/Director of Intelligence, No 30 Daily Security Summary, 12 Dec 1945: Congress general secretary Kripilani says the Congress sponsoring of the INA is intended for election purposes, and that after the elections Congress will drop the matter. National Archives, New Delhi]

---

44   KK Ghosh, *The Indian National Army*, Meenakshi Prakashan, 1969, p 208.
45   Transfer of Power, Volume VI, Her Majesty's Stationery Office, London, p 531.

parties, especially the Congress, in their electioneering campaign'.[46] The then Governor of UP wrote to the Viceroy the same month that those hitting the streets were actually suggesting that 'Bose is rapidly usurping the place held by Gandhi in popular esteem'.[47]

The perceptive politician that he was, Nehru was very much aware of the charges being levelled against the Congress. When he came across the issue initially, he wrote to Claude Auchinleck on 4 May 1946 that there was no thought of exploiting it for political purposes. The reactions in the country then surpassed his imagination and things started changing.

> It is sometimes said that we have exploited this INA situation for political purposes. Almost everything in India fits in somewhere into the political picture because the fact of India's subjection dominates life here. But I can say with some confidence that there was no desire or even thought of exploiting the INA issue for political purposes when this matter first came before the public…. The sole thought before me was that thousands of my countrymen, whom I believed to be patriotic, were in grave danger…. It did not strike me at all at the time that political advantage could be taken of this affair. Then a strange and surprising thing happened, not strange in itself but very surprising because of its depth and extent. Though I had sensed the mood of the Indian people, I had not fully realised how far it went in this direction. Within a few weeks, the story of the INA had percolated to the remotest villages in India and everywhere there was admiration for them and apprehension as to their possible fate. No political organisation, however strong and efficient, could have produced this enormous reaction in India. It was one of those rare things which just fit into the mood of the people, reflect, as it were, and provide an opportunity for the public to give expression to that mood….

---

46   Ibid, p 506.
47   Ibid, p 469.

The widespread popular enthusiasm was surprising enough, but even more surprising was a similar reaction of a very large number of regular Indian army officers and men. Something had touched them deeply. This kind of thing is not done and cannot be done by politicians or agitators or the like. It is this fundamental aspect of the INA question that has to be borne in mind. All other aspects, however important, are secondary.[48]

It was the 'failed' INA military onslaught and the Red Fort trials of 1945-46, and not the 'peaceful' Quit India movement which majorly impacted the British decision to quit India. The colonial British regarded Bose as their sworn enemy. No top Congressman of the 'peace loving' variant fell in that category. Documents spotted in 2005 by Prof Eunan O'Halpin of Dublin's Trinity College show that the British foreign office, which controls the MI-6, had ordered the assassination of Bose just after he left India in 1941. In 1946, Major General FS Tucker, GOC Eastern Command, thought Bose was a 'plump Bengali' of 'over-weening personal ambition' and like everyone else, demanded a 'condign punishment for the INA'.[49]

Confidential.

WAR DEPARTMENT.

I have spoken to Mr. Lal about the press cuttings below. Our definite view is that officers and men of the Indian Army who joined the so-called Indian National Army have not, in law, the status of combatants or belligerents and that they are traitors and rebels. We shall undoubtedly hear more of this in the Press and the competence of Courts-Martial to try these persons will probably be challenged. We should be most grateful for an exposition of the law on the subject.

Sd/- C.M. Trivedi.
1.9.45.

Legislative Deptt. (Mr. Lal).
W.D. U.O. 4628-S/WI dated 1.9.45.

[Officers and men of the INA were 'traitors and rebels' in the eyes of loyal servants of the Raj such as Sir Chandulal Madhavlal Trivedi. Awarded Padma Vibhushan in free India, he also became the Governor of Punjab and Andhra Pradesh. Document: National Archives, Delhi]

48   Jawaharlal Nehru's letter to Claude Auchinleck, 4 May 1946, *Selected Works of Jawaharlal Nehru*, Vol 15, Orient Longman, 1982, pp 90-91

49   Louis Allen, *The end of the war in Asia*, Hart-Davis, MacGibbon, London, 1976, p 146.

But in the face of public anger and much more in their own interest, the colonial rulers had to backtrack. India was sitting on a tinderbox. Viceroy Wavell received a letter from UP in November 1945. It read that 'handwritten leaflets are said to have been found in a hotel that if any INA soldiers were killed, Britishers would be murdered. These may be rather petty matters, but they do show which way the wind is blowing'.[50]

No one knew India's internal situation better in those days than the Director, Intelligence Bureau. Sir Norman Smith noted in a secret report of November 1945: 'The situation in respect of the Indian National Army is one which warrants disquiet. There has seldom been a matter which has attracted so much Indian public interest and, it is safe to say, sympathy… the threat to the security of the Indian Army is one which it would be unwise to ignore.'

SECRET.

INTELLIGENCE BUREAU,
(Home Department).
••••

The situation in respect of the Indian National Army is one which warrants disquiet. There has seldom been a matter which has attracted so much Indian public interest and, it is safe to say, sympathy. Public feeling is based on political, racial and sentimental considerations and has been influenced in a very great extent by

[Courtesy National Archives, New Delhi]

On 14 November 1945, William Christie, the Chief Commissioner of Delhi, wrote to the Home Secretary A E Porter:

I am very worried about the effect that all this propaganda by the Congress and in the nationalist press extolling the virtues of the INA, without any counter propaganda, is having on the people

---

50   *Transfer of Power*, Volume VI, Her Majesty's Stationery Office, London, p 507.

generally and on the Government servants and the loyal element of the army in particular. I am particularly worried about the effect it must be having on the police, especially the lower ranks, and it is on their loyalty that we shall have to depend in the event of trouble—and in my opinion there is certainly going to be trouble within the next few months if the present unbridled latitude to the Congress and the Press continues.[51]

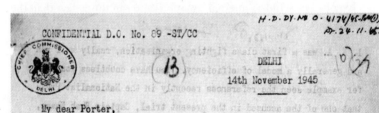

[Courtesy National Archives, New Delhi]

Between 21 and 24 Nov, serious rioting broke out in Calcutta, followed by riots in Bombay, Karachi, Patna, Allahabad, Banaras, Rawalpindi and other places.[52] By this time, Commander-in-Chief General Claude Auchinleck had received many disturbing reports. On 19 Nov 1945, he received a letter from Colonel K S Himatsinhji

---

51 Government of India, Home Department, File No. 21/6/45, Policy as to publicity in relation to the Japanese-sponsored 'Indian National Army'.

52 KK Ghosh, *The Indian National Army*, Meenakshi Prakashan, 1969, p 215.

(a scion of the Jamnagar royal family and later Major-General) apprising him of INA Defence Committee's Bhulabhai Desai's frank opinion that 'the INA trials have provided Indian nationalists with a most powerful weapon; that, if any of those who are being tried are subsequently executed, they will become India's greatest martyrs; that an armed revolution could ensue'.[53] On 29 December 1945, Sir Bertrand Glancy, the Governor of Punjab, wrote that 'enquiries made in the Punjab seem to suggest the existence of a very considerable degree of sympathy in the Indian Army for the INA'.[54] Himatsinhji (the first Lieutenant-Governor of Himachal Pradesh) again wrote to him on 17 February that 'the entire country is in a very hostile mood towards the British Government' and that 'the vast majority of Indians regarded the INA as, potentially, an army of liberation, and that this is the only issue upon which there is agreement between the Congress and the Muslim League'.[55] Consequently, Auchinleck was compelled to explain to his top military commanders on 12 February 1946 through a 'Strictly Personal and Secret' letter the reasons why the military had to let the INA 'war criminals' and 'traitors' get off the hook:

> Having considered all the evidence and appreciated to the best of my ability the general trend of Indian public opinion, and of the feeling in the Indian Army, I have no doubt at all that to have confirmed the sentence of imprisonment solely on the charge of 'waging war against the King' would have had disastrous results, in that it would have probably precipitated a violent outbreak throughout the country, and have created active and widespread disaffection in the Army, especially amongst the Indian officers and the more highly educated rank and file.[56]

---

53   Margaret M Wright, *The Military Papers, 1940-48, of Field-Marshal Sir Claude Auchinleck: A Calender and Index*, John Rylands University Library of Manchester, p 301.
54   Ibid, p 305.
55   Ibid, p 309.
56   *Transfer of Power*, Volume VI, Her Majesty's Stationery Office, London, p 944.

```
                    S E C R E T
                                    Annexure to Appx 'A'.

    Summary of Comments classified as "Pro-I.N.A. & Congress"
      in column 6 of the "Analysis of opinions on political
           matters in Security Intelligence Reports from
              Indian Army Units read during the period
                      26 Nov to 1 Dec 45".
                      -----------

1.         Indian Station Workshops Bangalore.
           Educated men are sympathetic to the I.N.A. and are willing
    to subscribe for their defence.

2.         464 Indian Field Coy. I.E.
           Politically minded I.O.Rs think the trial unjust because
    accused were forced to join the I.N.A.

3.         39 Indian General Hospital (Comb).
           All of 14 men questioned were in favour of lenient treat-
    ment for the I.N.A.

4.         3rd Bn Indian Grenadiers.
           Indian and Anglo Indian officers all consider Capt: SHAH
    NAWAZ, & co, acted in the best interests of India.

5.         Ordnance Depot, Whitefield.
           Records 6 individual opinions among which those of 2 K.C.I.Os
    and 1 havildar were, in effect, that the members of the I.N.A.
    were misguided patriots.
```

[Analysis of opinions on political matters in Security Intelligence Reports from Indian Array Units read during the period 26 November to 1 December 1945. Courtesy National Archives, New Delhi]

The nationalist fervour in the country had reached such levels by that time as to drown differences between the Hindus and the Muslims. Violence had broken out in many States. *The New York Times* reported on 17 February 1946: 'In spite of the uncompromising struggle between the two factions, last week for the first time since 1921, Moslems and Hindus together staged street protests and riot against the British in Calcutta, Bombay and New Delhi. The catalytic agent in this case was the Indian National Army, organised by a Japanese collaborator named Subhas Chandra Bose....'

An editorial in *The Times of India* further elaborated this on 26 February that as a result of the Red Fort trials in Delhi, 'there was released throughout India a flood of comment which had inevitable sequel in mutinies and alarming outbreaks of civil violence in Calcutta, Bombay, Delhi and elsewhere'. At the same time in London, a number of perceptive British MPs met Prime Minister Clement Attlee to give their frank reading of the situation. 'There are two alternative ways of meeting this common desire (a) that we should arrange to get out, (b) that we should wait to be driven out. In regard to (b), the loyalty of the Indian Army is open to question; the INA have become national heroes....'[57] KK Ghosh observed that 'the revolutionary condition in the country created by the INA trial contributed largely to the naval mutiny'.[58]

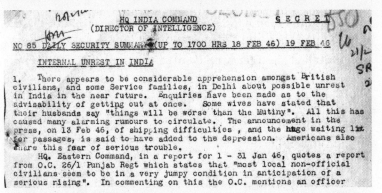

[HQ India Command/Director of Intelligence, No 85 Daily Security Summary, 19 February 1946: Apprehension amongst British civilians, and some Service families about possible unrest in India in the near future. Some wives have stated that their husbands say things will be worse than the Mutiny. Americans also share this fear of serious trouble. ... most local non-official civilians seem to be in a very jumpy condition in anticipation of a serious rising. National Archives, New Delhi]

Many luminaries who watched the events unfold agreed that the INA played a pivotal role in making India free. In a no-holds-barred interview in February 1955 with BBC's Francis Watson, Dr Bhimrao Ambedkar wondered, 'I don't know how Mr Attlee suddenly agreed to give India independence. That is a secret that he will disclose in his autobiography. None expected that he would do that.' In October 1956, two months before Ambedkar passed away, Clement Attlee himself disclosed in a confidential private talk that very secret. It would take two decades before Phani Bhusan Chakravartti, Chief Justice of Calcutta High Court and acting Governor of West Bengal, would muster courage to tell the public what the former British PM had told him in the Governor's mansion in Kolkata in 1956:

57   *Transfer of Power*, Volume VI, Her Majesty's Stationery Office, London, p 947.
58   KK Ghosh, *The Indian National Army*, Meenakshi Prakashan, 1969, p 234.

The INA activities of Subhas Chandra Bose, which weakened the very foundation of the British Empire in India, and the RIN mutiny which made the British realise that the Indian armed forces could no longer be trusted to prop up the British.

Justice Chakravartti, first Indian to become permanent Chief Justice of India's oldest court, also asked Attlee what was the extent of Gandhi's influence upon the British decision to quit India. In Chakravarty's words: 'Hearing this question, Attlee's lips became twisted in a sarcastic smile as he slowly chewed out the word, "m-i-n-i-m-a-l"!' [59]

In 1960, in Nuffield College, Oxford, Sir Attlee reiterated his position to historian Prof Barun De—a much respected name in the Leftist-Congress circles.[60] In 1967, at a New Delhi seminar to mark the 20th anniversary of Independence, then British High Commissioner and famous broadcaster John Freeman opined that 'independence became certain after the 1946 revolt of the Royal Indian Navy'. Among those who heard Freeman speak was would be columnist Swaminathan

[Copy of Justice Phani Bhushan Chakravartti's letter regarding Clement Attlee's disclosure to him. Source: RC Majumdar, *Jibaner Smritideepe*]

---

59 Justice Phani Bhusan Chakravartti described his interaction with Attlee in a letter on 30 March 1976, to Sureshchandra Das, publisher of historian Dr RC Majumdar. Subsequently in 1978, a facsimile copy of Chakravartti's letter was published by Dr Majumdar in his autobiographical book in Bengali, *Jibaner Smritideepe*.

60 Barun De, 'Experiments with truth in a fractured land,' *The Telegraph*, 30 January 2007.

Aiyar, brother of Congress leader Mani Shankar Aiyar. Swaminathan wrote in *The Economic Times* on 15 August 2007 that Freeman's admission 'astonished many youngsters in the audience, including me' for they 'had never been taught about the naval revolt'.

Rebellion on the waters

The Royal Indian Navy (RIN) revolt, which has begun to get some attention in recent times, was a watershed event in Indian freedom struggle. Its genesis, according to its leader BC Dutt, could be traced back to the impact of what Subhas Bose did in SE Asia. In 1970, Dutt stated during an interview with the University of Cambridge that the sailors (ratings) who caused the RIN mutiny 'were unaffected by the "Quit India" ultimatum of the Indian National Congress in 1942'. But 'there was a tremendous upsurge in the country when the men of Subhas Chandra Boes's Indian National Army were brought to India in 1945'. Dutt stated that the news of the impending trial of the Azad Hind soldiers made Naval ratings 'restless'. What stirred his conscience, he explained:

> One day a friend of mine, SM Shyam, returned from Malaya with strange tales of the Indian National Army. …
> He brought letters from some member of the former Azad Hind Government addressed to Jawaharlal Nehru and Sarat Chandra Bose, the elder brother of Subhas Chandra Bose. He also brought relevant literature and photographs. In the RIN this was considered high treason. In the course of clandestine efforts at getting those photos and literature to the destination, I got involved in the activities, which committed me to a cause officially illegal but, to a man in my state of mind, ennobling. In the ensuing weeks, my life changed. …I began to ask myself questions. What right had the British to rule over my country?[61]

61   Arun Gandhi, Interview with B C Dutt, 26 January 1970, https://www.s-asian.cam.ac.uk/archive/audio/collection/b-c-dutt/.

Dutt then found like-minded people on the signal training ship *HMIS Talwar* at Bombay's dockyards. 'We called ourselves *Azad Hindis* (free Indians).' On 18 February 1946, the sailors started their protest. Conditions inside the barracks had made the situation worse for them. Fired by nationalism, the sailors refused to put up with racism and unequal treatment. The uprising then spread to other locations in Bombay and other port cities like Calcutta. In Karachi, the ratings took over the ship *Hindustan* and the navy's offshore installations on Manora Island, south of Karachi.

While the British rulers were eventually able to put down the mutiny with active support of top Congress leaders—which partly explains why the RIN mutiny was not discussed in free India—a most astounding thing happened in Karachi. The most trusted soldiers of the Indian Army, the Gurkhas, and the troops from the Baloch regiment refused to fire at the striking ratings. It was the troops from Gurkha and Baloch regiments that had opened fire in Jallianwala Bagh. Later in February, 120 men of Indian Army's Signals Training Centre (STC), Jabalpur, rose in revolt. A young lieutenant on *HMIS Talwar* who did not take part in the mutiny watched the events unfold. Decades later, Sourendra Nath Kohli would go on to opine that the mutiny was 'largely instrumental in convincing the British that holding India was no longer feasible without the use of large-scale British force and was, inter alia, responsible for ushering in freedom'.[62] By this time, Kohli had retired from the Indian Navy after attaining the topmost rank of Admiral.

Dr Ambedkar would not have been surprised with any of these details, especially Attlee's admission that Bose's struggle had to do with his decision to free India. He told the *BBC* that from his 'own analysis' he had concluded what convinced the Labour party to take the decision to free India:

The national army that was raised by Subhas Chandra Bose. The British had been ruling the country in the firm belief

---

62   Baldeo Sahai, *Indian Navy, a perspective: from the earliest period to modern times*, Ministry of Information and Broadcasting Publications Division, p 75.

that whatever may happen in the country or whatever the politicians did, they would never be able to change the loyalty of soldiers. That was one prop on which they were carrying on the administration. And that was completely dashed to pieces.

Some thirty years after independence, Lt Gen SK Sinha came out with another inside account in an op-ed article titled 'The Army and Indian Independence' (*The Statesman*, 1 March 1976). The would-be Assam and J&K Governor, as a young captain along with fellow Lt Colonel Sam Manekshaw and Major Yahya Khan, were the only natives posted to the hitherto exclusively British Directorate of Military Operations in 1946. 'The real impact of the INA was felt more after the war than during the war,' Sinha agreed, adding: 'There was considerable sympathy for the INA within the Army. ...I am convinced that well over 90 per cent of officers at that time felt along those lines.'

SECRET

S E C R E T

HQ INDIA COMMAND
(DIRECTOR OF INTELLIGENCE)

Tel. No. 2043.

NO 43 DAILY SECURITY SUMMARY (UP TO 1700 HRS 28 DEC 45) 29 DEC 45

I.N.A.

1.   At the end of a meeting in Calcutta, on 21 Dec 45, which he had addressed for 90 minutes, Pandit Nehru re-appeared at the microphone and announced that an Indian Officer of the regular Army, who wished to remain anonymous, had contributed Rs. 701/-, on his own and his men's behalf, to the I.N.A. Defence Fund. The Pandit said that this act confirmed his earlier statement that the I.N.A. had the sympathy of officers and men of the Indian Army.

[HQ India Command/Director of Intelligence, No 43 Daily Security Summary, 28 December 1945: Nehru tells a gathering that an Indian officer of the regular Army, who wished to remain anonymous, contributed Rs 701 on his own and his men's behalf, to the INA Defence Fund. He adds that this act confirmed his earlier statement that the INA had the sympathy of officers and men of the Indian Army. Courtesy National Archives, New Delhi]

In 1946, I accidentally came across a very interesting document...prepared by the Director of Military Intelligence. It was a classified document marked 'Top Secret. Not for Indian Eyes.' ...The paper referred to the INA, the mutinies at Bombay and Jabalpur and also to the 'adverse' effect on the Indian officers and men of the humiliating defeats inflicted by the Japanese on the white nations in the early days of the war. The conclusion reached was that the Indian Army could no longer be relied upon to remain a loyal instrument for maintaining British rule over India.

Set against this fact sheet is an old hypothetical scenario, stemming from the war time propaganda against Japan during the war. It remains a powerful weapon in the armoury of those Indians who prefer the Gandhian path to Netaji's: If Bose and the Japanese had won the war, they argue, India would have been in for far worse times than British colonialism. Japanese would have overrun us far worse than the British did. We are reminded of Japan's war crimes, brutal treatment of Koreans, Chinese and even Indians.

Before we even discuss this, we Indians would do well to drop our holier-than-thou attitude. War crimes, excesses, torture, violation of human rights are reported in all wars and conflicts. Free India, whose Government and people incessantly preach the rest of the world to follow the path of Mahatma Gandhi, is no exception. Forget conflict zones, even in our cities and towns such aberrations happen all the time. This is in no way a defence of the perpetrators of all those horrendous war crimes during the world war, but just to remind us that we cannot delve into this narrative sanctimoniously. On 4 May 2017, *The Times of India* quoted Attorney General Mukul Rohatgi sermonising before UN Human Rights Council in Geneva that India believed in 'peace' and 'non-violence' and that 'the concept of torture is completely alien to our culture'. This was against the backdrop of India refusing to ratify, along with select nations such as Sudan, Brunei, Angola, and Gambia, the UN Convention Against Torture.[63]

---

63   For reasons not fully clear to us, India in 1971 took little time before acceding to a UN convention relating to the arrest of war criminals of World War II, which greatly displeased Bhagwanji.

In its 31 May 1977 edition, *India Today* ran a cover story by C Joshi on 'the diabolical dimensions of the types of torture currently being practised behind the innocuous facade of interrogation centres all over the country' which 'would make the Nazi interrogators lick their lips in approval'. Among the horrifying incidents reported included allegations that women prisoners at a particular police station in Kolkata 'were stripped naked, burned on all parts of the body and in some cases iron rulers were inserted into the vagina and rectum'.

> What has escaped public attention is the more sophisticated forms of psychological torture practised by the intelligence agencies including the Intelligence Bureau of the Central government, the RAW (Research and Analysis Wing) and the Special Branch of the state police. Apart from the sadistic physical tortures a wide range of modern torture techniques are used. RAW perfected the technique of the 'truth serum', imported through front organisations from West Germany and Japan, and the 'addict technique'.
> Highly prized political prisoners were handed over to RAW after they refused to divulge information after the normal 'physical torture' routine. In Calcutta's special interrogation room in Fort William and in Delhi's Red Fort and offices at RK Puram, arrangements had been made for the latest torture equipment. They included helmets which magnified the screams of the victim, psychedelic lights which tended to hypnotize a person and drugs that tended to lower resistance. The technique used by some of the foreign trained interrogators was to turn brilliant university students into heroin and opium addicts. They would then be released and continuously trailed and the only way they could get their 'fix' was from the police—in return for information.

Just to illustrate this point further, here two recent instances reported in the media: *The Telegraph* reported on 4 April 2018 that a retired Army officer after spending years in jail over the false charge of passing on sensitive information to an ISI agent returned home to recall his horror. Madan Mohan Pal told the paper that in jail he was sold 'as a slave' and tortured. 'It's a standard practice in the jail.' On 29 December 2018, the PTI flashed a horrific account of young girls being abused by staff at a Delhi shelter home. The members of the Delhi Commission for Women met hapless girls, who told them that the staff members 'put chilli powder in their private parts as punishment'.

Even in our enlightened times we saw what some among the world's most professional armed force did in Iraq. Remember those shocking images from Abu Ghraib? A 2014 report in *The Guardian* cited British Freedom of Information disclosures to report 'more than 200 allegations of rape and other sexual offences against their colleagues in the past three years'. In July that year, the British Ministry of Defence, as reported in *The Telegraph*, ran a powerful campaign warning service personnel that consent is always required before they have sex, using photographs of men and women who have been raped by soldiers. A 2015 Ministry of Defence study found that nearly four out of 10 women in the British Army had received unwanted comments or been exposed to material of a sexual nature. On the other side of the Atlantic, the statistics were worse. '26,000 unreported sexual assaults in the military—only 238 convictions', tweeted Donald Trump on 8 May 2013. But the conduct of some in no way meant that the entire force had carried out or backed those brutalities. Those were instances of deviations by a few with sick minds. Come to think of it, Indians do not blame the entire English race for what few colonial rulers did here. Subhas Chandra Bose did not. Bhagwanji did not.

Former SC judge Markendya Katju (grandson of Kailash Nath Katju, part of the Congress' defence team for the INA during the Red Fort trials) revived allegations against Japan in 2015 when he said: 'If the Japanese had been victorious against the British, do you seriously think they would have granted independence to India? No, they would have made India a Japanese colony, and ruthlessly exploited and looted it.'

Unknown to Katju and all those who share his outdated opinion, there is considerable data on record by way of statements of those who mattered, official records and sworn testimonies to prove that all such assumptions about Bose and his benefactor Japan are not correct. Here are the posers as they would put them, and the answers:

What was the nature of Japan-Bose relations?

In 1972, Bose's military secretary Colonel Mahboob Ahmed, then a senior Ministry of External Affairs official, in his deposition before the Khosla Commission stated:

> There was a great deal of respect for Netaji for his personality, for his person, amongst the Japanese that we came across, and his relation with the Japanese government was that of the two interests at that stage coinciding. That is to get the British out of India.

On his part, Bose was never a fair-weather friend. At the close of the war, a Japanese government communication to him referred to their 'spiritual' ties and said,

> Nippon Government pays deep respect with its whole heart to Your Excellency's cooperation with Nippon on the moral strength to the utmost in order to attain Indian independence without resorting in the least to opportunism.[64]

Was Bose a Japanese stooge?

The National Archive in Melbourne, Australia, has a file on Bose made up of formerly secret German-Japanese diplomatic communication intercepted by the Australian Navy. On 30 July 1943, Japanese Ambassador Hiroshi Oshima sent this account of his telling Adolf Hitler about Bose: 'The Japanese government too has absolute faith in him and

---

64   Reproduced in the Shah Nawaz Committee report.

is giving him carte blanche where India is concerned.'[65]

> Speaking of Bose, I said: 'It was good of you to think of sending Bose to East Asia. We thank you very much. As you have already read in the newspapers, after reaching Japan he went to Singapore where he is re-organising an Indian Army of Liberation. He is working hard on plans to bring India into line. The Japanese Government too, has absolute faith in him and is giving him carte blanche where India is concerned.'
>   Hitler answered: 'Yes, I am very satisfied with what Bose is doing.'
>   I told him that the submarine the Germans had given us had already reached one of our bases in the South Seas, and expressed great gratitude. I then went on to say: 'The Japanese Navy just wired my Naval Attache that those new bullets you ordered not long ago will reach you by the earliest convenience and plenty of them at that. As for the new warship you wanted, the Japanese Navy has informed Naval Attache Wenneker that it has been especially arranged to let you have it. We are not going to let the Italians or anybody else know about that. I just wanted you to know about it.'
>   Hitler answered: 'Thank you very much for that kindness. In this war we also want to co-operate in those technical matters. I do not mean to say that my army's equipment is inferior to your, we do not need to compare them, but if there is any service we can do for you in this respect, please let me know.'
>   I answered: 'Thank you very much.'"

T^P SECRET

[National Archive, Melbourne]

Carte blanche is a French word meaning 'complete freedom to do something'. And what it meant was explained in a report titled 'INA's role in Imphal battle' filed in *The Hindu* on 10 December 1945. During the Red Fort trials, General Tadasu Katakura, Chief of the Japanese staff of Burma Area Army, testified that 'though INA troops had come [to be under] overall Japanese command, they…had their own operational assignment'.

Was Japan interested in conquering India?

In a paper on Bose, eminent historian TR Sareen, who otherwise supports the air crash theory and is not on the same page as the authors, observed after studying the British records that it was just a myth propagated by the colonial British to enlist support of the Indian political parties

---

65   Item no 12, series B5555\O. Extract from communication intelligence, Top Secret 091927 August, 1943, Berlin (Oshima) to Tokyo 30th July, National Archive of Australia, Melbourne Office.

during the war. 'Interrogation of Japanese high officials confirmed that they had never contemplated the conquest of India.' At the Red Fort trial, the defence counsel called five Japanese witnesses who had been closely involved with the INA. Ota Saburo of the Japanese Foreign Ministry produced documentary evidence that Japan recognised the free and independent status of Netaji's government. Mastumoto Shun'ichi, Vice-Minister of Foreign Affairs and chief of the Treaty Bureau during the war, testified that the Japanese Government had helped Bose and the INA for two reasons: to promote Japan's own war aims and also to help India achieve independence, which was one of Japan's war aims. Lieutenant General Tadasu Katakura testified that that the Japanese Army never used the INA soldiers as labourers.

Lt General Iwaichi Fujiwara, co-founder of the INA, told the Khosla Commission on oath in 1972 that 'Netaji was highly respected by Japanese people'. In 1956 when Shah Nawaz committee went to Japan, it was noted that 'Netaji's name was still a household word in Japan, and a great deal of interest was taken about him both by the public and the Press'. Japan had a terrible record with the Koreans, the Chinese and others during the World War II, but not with the Indians—especially after Netaji's arrival in South East Asia. That's why many in Japanese establishment think of their wartime association with the INA as a bright spot. Even the Ministry of External Affairs in New Delhi came to hold the view that 'India as the country of origin of Buddhism and Netaji and INA's association with Japan during the war also invoke friendly feelings among a section of the Japanese society'. This factor is one of the reasons for the current bonding between India and Japan, which is still despised by her neighbours due to what happened during the war. In September 2014, Saichiro Misumi, a war veteran, Indologist and former executive director of Japan-India Association, became a symbol of that bonhomie. A picture of his with Prime Minister Narendra Modi kneeling down to listen to the old man became viral after it was tweeted by MEA spokesperson Syed Akbaruddin. On 30 March 2015, Misumi (99) was conferred the Padma Bhushan at the Rashtrapati Bhawan 'in recognition of his contribution to India-Japan relations for almost seven decades', according to a release from the Indian Embassy in Tokyo.

Specific claims of alleged Japanese excesses against 'Indian soldiers' during the war must be viewed from the Indian point of view. It should be first asked what were these 'Indian soldiers' doing in SE Asia in the mid-1940s fighting the Japanese? Were they part of some UN peace keeping force, or were they doing some work to make India free? And how were the Japanese supposed to deal with Indian belligerents fighting them, willing to kill them, for their colonial masters?

The very *raison d'être* of British Indian Army was to hold India in subjugation. Who put out the 1857 uprising? Never forget that General Dyer only gave an order—it was the men of the Indian Army, the mercenaries, now glorified as 'professionals', who fired upon their own people at Jallianwala Bagh and later during the Quit India movement. These mercenaries clashed with the Japanese not for their duty towards India but to protect the British Raj, for which they were handsomely rewarded. If the Japanese killed or even brutalised some of them, why should we shed tears? For that matter why should we care about the revelation made on the basis of declassified papers by *The Guardian* in August 2007 that British military scientists sent hundreds of loyal Indian soldiers into gas chambers and exposed them to mustard gas? At the initial stages, many suffered severe burns, including on their genitals. These tests were carried out across 10 years, before and during the Second World War in a military installation at Rawalpindi by scientists from the Porton Down chemical warfare establishment in order to develop poison gases to use against the Japanese. The paper added that the British military did not check up on the Indian soldiers after the experiments to see if they developed any illnesses. 'It is now recognised that mustard gas can cause cancer and other diseases,' the paper reported. That paper also reported the Porton officials explaining that these 'trials took place in a different era, during a conflict, and so their conduct should not be judged by today's standards'.[66]

---

66   Rob Evans, 'Military scientists tested mustard gas on Indians,' *The Guardian*, 1 September, https://www.theguardian.com/uk/2007/sep/01/india.military.

During the course of the war, the Japanese/INA suffered a humiliating setback as a party of spies from the INA Secret Service School in Penang surrendered to the British in India. The Japanese soon found out that one Captain Mahmood Khan Durrani, a former officer of the school had been on leave in Penang while his old pupils were under training there. Thus wrote former intelligence officer Hugh Toye in his biography of Bose *The Springing Tiger* (Jaico Publishing House, New Delhi): 'The Japanese strongly suspected a connection. The truth was that Durrani not only instructed the men to surrender, but gave them intelligence to pass on to the authorities in India.' Durrani was arrested and interrogated so that more could be extracted from him. By his own claim, in the dead of the night at a PoW camp he was confronted by Subhas Bose. Having suffered ten days of Japanese third degree, he was not in his full senses. 'You should be grateful to me that I have saved you from the Japanese firing squad, and that you will be shot by Indians,' he heard 'Bose' saying. There was another round of interrogation by the INA officers. 'Bose' returned to tell him a 'confession would be obtained before Durrani's execution, by one means or another'. Durrani was not executed after all, but actually given medical treatment. After the war, at a special investiture ceremony at the Red Fort, he was presented with George Cross, second highest award after Victoria Cross. He resumed his duties as an Indian Army officer, and in 1947 opted for Pakistan, joining its army. His autobiography was published in the UK in 1955. His George Cross is on display in the Imperial War Museum's Victoria & George Cross Gallery.

As Indians, we would rather be concerned about the instances of crimes perpetrated against the INA men who fought for our freedom. *The Journal of the United Service Institution* (Vol CXXXIV) in April-June 2004 carried an interview of Pratap Singh, an INA veteran, with Lieutenant Commander Neeraj Malhotra. In his 80s, penniless and frustrated, Singh recalled his harsh experiences—how in 1945 they were brought to Delhi and how those compatriots of his accused of serious charges were 'segregated'—'never heard or seen again'. He recalled that a 'team' was used to 'pull out such soldiers and take them to Red Fort—from where no one returned'. The INA men were incarcerated in the Salimgarh fortress, linked to the Red Fort by two arched bridges. Recalling his experience in his 1998 memoirs *From my bones,* INA veteran and Red Fort Trials hero Colonel Gurbaksh Singh Dhillon referred to the fate of Major Maghar Singh and Major Ajmer Singh of the INA secret service. 'When they felt that they might not be able to keep the secret under daily torture, they planned to snatch a guard's rifle one night and committed suicide.' It is commonly believed that the ghosts of forgotten INA martyrs continue to wander in the Salimgarh prison cells. Guards have in the past reported hearing groans and clanking of iron shackles at night.

Apart from the INA men, other supporters of Subhas Bose were made to suffer as well during the course of the war. Following the disappearance of Subhas Bose from India in 1941, people close to him were lodged in the notorious Lahore fort prison and subjected to torture by the officials, both British as well as Indians, who flourished in free India. Sardul Singh Caveeshar, the head of Forward Bloc after Bose's departure, was kept in an open room with no protection from the blazing summer sun. A broken commode was placed there for him to ease himself and was not cleared for days, making the cell, in his words, 'smell like a sewer'. Consequently, he developed hepatitis, piles and heart trouble. He lost about 40 lbs in two months. Caveeshar's secretary Ram Rup Sharma found himself in a windowless room full of insects. He was taken out only to be tortured for hours at stretch. He would be kept awake for nights and beaten up even if a 'little twinkle' was noticed in his eyes. Bose's newphew Dwijendra Nath was put in a cell unfit for animals with 'cobwebs, insects and marks of spit and cough everywhere'. In his words: 'In one corner there was even a chamber-pot containing dried up stool. There was a horrible stench in the cell.'[67] The beating he received there left him physically impaired for the rest of his life. On occasions, he would be deprived of food and water, chained

---

67 Sardul Singh Caveeshar, *The Lahore Fort: Torture camp*, Hero Publications, Lahore, 1946.

to the wall for the whole night and had coals burnt in his cell. During interrogations, he would be beaten up with fists and shoes and his tormentors would use abusive language against his uncle, brothers and sister. He was threatened that a bamboo stick would be shoved in his anus or be given the sort of torture meted out to Niranajn Singh Talib, one of the persons who had helped Subhas Bose escape.

LAHORE FORT–'HELL ON EARTH'

MORE REVELATION OF PUNJAB C.I.D. METHODS

Jaiprakash Narayan Not Allowed To Sleep For 21 Nights

(From Our Correspondent)
LAHORE, November 2.
How he was tied to a chair with hands handcuffed on the back and kept in that state without sleep or food for full three days that of Mr. Jai Prakash Narayan. "Within an hour of arrival in Lahore Fort, said the Professor, "I was produced before a horribly drunk Sikh police officer who showered filthy and foul abuse on

(Continued from page 1) every political prisoner and Prof. Anand had his share of them. From Lahore Fort Prof. Anand was taken to Calcutta police camp for interrogation. From Calcutta he was brought back to Lahore but as the Government had not specified as to where he was going to be detained, the police sent him to Lahore Fort. It was during these days a "habeas corpus" petition was filed for his release and Government fulfilled the formality of his detention by placing him under the custody of the D.I.G. (C.I.D.) Punjab in the Lahore Fort. During these days Prof. Anand was a companion to Mr. Jai Prakash Narayan in the Lahore Fort.

TWO MONTHS' DARKNESS
From the Lahore Fort he was

[*Bombay Chronicle* on 4 November 1945]

Since no one in free India bothered to carry out elaborate research into such charges, they were never documented the way Japanese excesses were by the Allies after the war. The National Archives in New Delhi have several war-era records wherein one sees trumped-up charges of 'war crimes' against top INA men, sought to be established by the testimonies of 'witnesses', such as Capt HC Badhwar—the treacherous Military Intelligence mole.

Surely these one-sided documents created by the victors do not record the other side of the story. In his memoirs, *In the Line of Duty: A Soldier Remembers* (Lancer, New Delhi, 2000) Lt Gen Harbakhsh Singh (Retd) recalled his encounter with Subhas Bose when he was a PoW. The Japanese escorted him to a house where Bose met him and his brother. He asked them why they hadn't joined the INA. The brothers gave three arguments: They had little faith in the previous INA leader; they were not patriotic enough otherwise 'why would we have joined the British Army in the first place'; and three, they were convinced that the Axis and Japanese were going to lose the war and so they were now 'even less willing to throw our lot with the Japanese backed INA'.

Singh then states that Bose 'appreciated our frankness' and said that 'no one would ever compel us to join [the INA] against our wish'. He asked them to partake of tea before leaving. 'And that was the last we saw of him. We returned to the camp and thereafter we were never worried by the "Azad Hind Fauj" again,' Singh underlines. After spending two and half years as a prisoner, he was repatriated to India—obviously unharmed. He went on to excel in free India and is remembered particularly for his heroic leadership in the 1965 war. Captain Amarinder Singh (now the Chief Minister of Punjab) served him as his ADC when he was heading the Western Command.

The official records also do not record the instances of war crimes against the INA men. The following, for instance, were published in (then pro-Congress) *Hindustan Times* in the late 1945. Even Nehru was constrained to say at a press meeting that if INA men were going to be tried as war criminals, in his own 'list there will be many high officials sitting in Delhi who will be war criminals'. But everything was forgotten once India began her tryst with destiny in 1947.

MYSTERY OF 1,900 I.N.A. MEN'S FATE

(From our Special Correspondent)

BANGKOK, Dec. 12.—Nineteen hundred and sixty-three independent officers and men of the I.N.A. being detained in Bangkok were transferred last month from the concentration camp on the premises of the Anglo-Siam Corporation to prisoner concentration camps where location has been kept a secret. Every attempt was made to camouflage their transfer and conceal their destinations.

All reports go to show that the morale of the I.N.A. men has been very high during the period of their detention. They have been raising considerable annoyance to their jailers by raising slogans and singing...

the I.N.A. being detained in Bong Khwa Jail are Col. Chopra, Col. P. R. Barloi, Col. Thakur Singh and Col. Mullick.

Bhonsle for surrender to the British forces.

At Chhaipuri Camp where the main I.N.A. forces in Siam were concentrated, the men were in the same mood and Nos. 1 and 2 "Janbaz" units swore that they would shoot down anyone who came to ask them to surrender.

MANY I.N.A. MEN ALREADY EXECUTED

LUCKNOW, Nov. 2.—Probably few people know that a large number of valiant soldiers of the I.N.A. have already been executed after some trials by court-martial," said Mr Annie Harvani, president, All-India Youth League and general secretary, U.P. Provincial Forward Bloc, while...

Dockers To Resume Work On Monday

LONDON, Nov. 2.—The National Strike Committee—an organisation...

Returning to the hypothetical scenario, here is one which no one in free India has the gumption to imagine: What would have become of India if we had religiously followed the path shown by Gandhiji?

Startled by our frank narration of facts, a lot many people would sense in this an attempt to 'trivialise' Gandhi's hallowed principles and philosophy. Some would even be revolted by what it would entail. They will protest: You are of no consequence; you cannot be irreverent towards the memory of the man revered by millions across the world; you cannot bring some polemical arguments to question the unquestionable legacy of the Father of the Nation, we would be warned. But how can being factual be irreverent? And doesn't Subhas Bose, revered by so many if not as many people as Gandhi, deserve the same consideration when hypothetical, utterly biased scenarios are conjured up to mar his legacy?

Being truthful, as Gandhi himself used to always emphsasise on, let us do this little exercise of imagining how history would have panned out if India had turned Gandhian in letter and spirit. India's Foreign Secretary asserted at the UN Headquarters on 2 October 2015 that Gandhian guiding principle of *ahimsa* continues 'to provide the world with approaches to address a range of complex challenges, many of which may not have even existed during his lifetime'. Really? How about applying all those guiding principles to India first?

For a start, India might have never emerged as a completely sovereign nation since Gandhi was contended to keep her a dominion of Great Britain. Our national flag, in deference to his views, would have carried the Union Jack.

Gandhi's Successor May Be Man Who'll Seek Full Independence From Britain

Chandra Bose Clinches His Hold on Indian Congress

By MILTON BRONNER
London—After Mahatma Gandhi
—who?

That is a question asked not only by the massed millions of India, but by the British government which must face the future desires of over 350,000,000 people in that great sub-continent.

Time was when it looked as if the man who would be the favorite leader of the masses would be Pandit Jawahar Lal Nehru. But now Gandhi's successor is expected to be Subhas Chandra Bose.

Pandit Nehru

The two last in past times have been Gandhi's bright young men. Both at times went far beyond his desires. Nehru broke away, but now stands more

Mahatma Gandhi

with Gandhi again. Bose has broken away entirely. Both have been president of the

Subhas Chandra Bose

Indian National Congress, that powerful political party which has 5,000,000 dues-paying members and which controls the government in nine out of the 11 provinces of British India

Officer of the big city of Calcutta and later, in 1930, was elected Mayor. In 14 years, he was arrested 10 times and jailed for a total of eight years, often without any trial. At one time, as Mayor, he conducted his office in jail. Several times the British had to release him lest he die of tuberculosis.

Last year he mocked Chamberlain, asking why, if he was so concerned about self-determination for the Sudeten Germans, he did not grant the same right to nationalists in the British Empire.

He scorns the constitution the British parliament voted to India. His objective is complete Indian independence, with the Indians making their own constitution.

"Then," he says, "we will determine our future relations with Britain through a voluntary treaty in which we will meet as equals."

N. BARNES, WIFE ARE GUESTS AT NORFOLK

Norfolk — Mr. and Mrs. Nelson Barnes of Brookdale spent Sunday

[*Ogdensburg Journal* on 11 May 1939]

Since industrialisation, according to Gandhi, was 'going to be a curse for mankind', there would have been no place for it in the India of our dreams. Wasn't Bose's push for it through the setting up of a planning committee (the forerunner of present-day Niti Ayog) a reason for his isolation and eventual ouster from Congress? 'God forbid that India should ever take to industrialism after the manner of the West. If an entire nation of 300 millions took to similar economic exploitation, it would strip the world bare like locusts,'[68] Gandhi said. His view was that industrialisation was not necessary for any country, 'much less so for India'. Instead, he opined that 'Independent India can only discharge her duty towards a groaning world by adopting a simple but ennobled life by developing her thousands of cottages and living at peace with the world. High thinking is inconsistent with complicated material life based on high speed imposed on us by Mammon worship. All the graces of life are possible only when we learn the art of living nobly'.[69] Are we game?

In this Gandhian utopia which would have thus emerged, people would live their life according to high ideals of *Satya* (truth), *Ahimsa* (non-violence) and *Brahmacharya* (celibacy). 'If the married couple can think of each other as brother and sister, they are freed for universal service,'[70] Gandhi said. He asserted that he and his wife 'tasted the real bliss of married life when we renounced sexual contact and that in the heyday of youth'.[71] This is discounting Gandhi's so-called outrageous 'experiments' with several young women, including those from his own family. When the scandal broke in 1946, Sardar Patel was pushed into a 'wildfire of agony', even as Nehru remained mum. 'Even if for the sake of taking pity on us you must leave it,' Patel beseeched Gandhi.

Your saying that others shouldn't follow you (on celibacy experiments) isn't going to make any difference. People always

---

68   *Harijan*, 20 December 1928, p 422.
69   *Harijan*, 1 September 1946.
70   M K Gandhi, *Non-Violent Resistance*, Dover Publications, New York, p 43.
71   Veena R Howard, *Gandhi's Ascetic Activism: Renunciation and Social Action*, Suny Press, p 151.

follow the elders. I can't understand why you are bent upon pushing the common people on the path of heterodoxy instead of religion. If only we could cut open our heart and show how deep are our wounds.[72]

And above all, free India, if she had followed the Gandhian path, would have been divested of her armed forces so that the new nation could wield the force of 'unadulterated non-violence'—the 'only force that can confound all the tricks put together of violence',[73] including nuclear weapons.

Believe it or not, Gandhians, led by Gandhiji himself, tried to form a Shanti Sena (Peace Army) to take on the challenges ranging from external aggression to internal disturbances. First reference to Shanti Sena was made by Gandhi during the time the British propaganda about Japanese 'aggression' during World War II was at its peak. Narayan Desai, son of Gandhi's chief secretary Mahadev Desai, overheard his parents discussing their prospects of joining a new force to oppose the Japanese/INA combine.

> Gandhi had said that if he had an army of non-violent soldiers, he would like to defend the country non-violently by standing before the advancing Japanese troops. And so these two members of Gandhi's ashram were trying to decide which of them should join this army.[74]

Narayan Desai added that in 1947 Gandhi again proposed the idea in view of the communal holocaust suffered by the new nation. He had called a meeting of his followers on this matter in February 1948 but he was assassinated at the end of January. The idea was later revived by

---

72   Uday Mahurkar, 'Sardar Patel's anger against Gandhiji over his celibacy experiments,' *India Today*, 6 June 2013, https://www.indiatoday.in/india/west/story/sardar-patel-gandhiji-celibacy-experiments-harijan-165848-2013-06-06.
73   'Outside his field,' *Harijan*, 16 November 1947.
74   Mark Shepard, *Gandhi Today: A Report on Mahatma Gandhi's Successors*, Seven Locks Press, Washington, DC, 1987, p 44.

Vinoba Bhave, the 'spiritual successor' of Gandhi. 'If it is not possible to dissolve the Army today, we must at least be agreed that we shall dissolve it tomorrow,'[75] Bhave felt.

In a hypothetical scenario of Bose getting rid of the British Empire but substituting it with a ruthless Japanese variant, there was a chance of India fighting back as Bose had openly said he would in case the Japanese betrayed him. But there would have been a zero chance of India surviving as a nation state if our armed forces were wiped out or decimated by the Gandhian brigade.

The Japanese army never overran India; Nazi Germany could never reach anywhere close, but the apostles of peace got the reigns of free India. It would send a shiver down the spine of most people to know that in 1955, a person no less than the President of India, actually advised the Prime Minister to implement the doomsday Gandhian plan. Through a letter,[76] the Supreme Commander of the Indian armed forces earnestly requested the '**Government to consider whether the time has not come when we should reduce, if not abolish, the armed forces**'. Rajendra Prasad asked Nehru, both true followers of Mahatma Gandhi, to consider 'to what extent it is necessary for us to continue the incongruity which is inevitable when we profess non-violence and at the same time maintain armed forces'. He reminded him that 'Mahatma Gandhi was in favour of disarmament. So are we suggesting disarmament to other nations when at the same time we are not prepared to practise it ourselves.' Underlining that he had had 'occasions to receive letters from foreign pacifists asking me to reconcile the maintenance of Armed Forces in Gandhi's India with non-violence', Prasad asked if it would be 'possible to work out some feasible plan' under which India could be moved 'not towards armament but towards disarmament'.

A turn like this, the President reminded the Prime Minister, 'will

75 Vinoba Bhave in *Vinoba on Gandhi*, compilation by Kanti Shah, https://earthlingopinion.wordpress.com/2014/07/03/a-peace-army-is-a-service-army/.
76 *Dr Rajendra Prasad, Correspondence and Select Documents (Volume 11)*, Allied Publishers, 1992, Document No 313, p 223-225.

furnish the beautiful *Kalash* to the temple of peace in the world' which was 'being built', so he claimed, under Nehru's 'great leadership'. Come to think of it, it is such a pity that even as leaders from that time to ours have continued their indefatigable efforts to build such a temple, none of them has been bestowed the Nobel prize for peace, which went to the likes of Yasser Arafat and Dr Henry Kissinger. Nehru's friend A C N Nambiar, according to a declassified MI6 record of 1955 vintage, believed the British saw to it that he did not get the Nobel, despite garnering nominations 11 times.

```
for this form of wishful thinking.   According to NAMBIAR it
is British influence that has prevented Pandit Jawarhalal
NEHRU's being awarded the Nobel Peace Prize.
      The Foreign Office is being informed.
                        Yours sincerely,


                        V. W. Smith.



M.I.6.
VWS/EC
```

[The National Archives, Kew]

Such noble ideas for the betterment of mankind (even as more than 99 per cent of Indians did not have an amenity as basic as a modern toilet) coming from the ruling class massively impacted the Indian strategic thinking. Post-Independence, the Gandhians went to the extent of castigating the Nehru government for making a marginal increase in India's defence expenditure. JB Kripalani, who like Prasad had helped Gandhi hound Bose from the country, protested in Parliament in 1958 that 'in a non-violent India, the last thing the Government should contemplate is an increase in the military budget, and I am sorry to say, I think it would disturb the soul of the Father of the Nation....' Writing in a journal brought out by the Centre for Land Warfare Studies (CLAWS) (a Delhi-based autonomous think tank) in 2005, Col Vikram Taneja expressed his outrage in these words:

Indeed, it must be conceded that Parliament as a whole generally shared Acharaya Kriplani's prejudice against expenditure on defence right from 1947 onwards and all along grudged funds for the modernisation of the armed forces. For quite a while, Parliament actually questioned the need for a strategic bomber air command for a Gandhian country on the ground that strategic bombers were offensive weapons which India did not need as it had no desire to go to war against any country. Similarly, for many years, the government had turned a deaf ear to the Navy's persistent plea for an aircraft carrier.[77]

Unknown to most Indians today, as with numerous other issues, Gandhiji did have a clear idea how independent India's national security doctrine should be. It was to be based on *ahimsa*, over which Gandhi would brook no argument whatsoever so long it was expected from Indians. Fortunately, one doesn't have to refer to the works of historians to understand this marvellous concept. There is simply no room for misinterpretation as Gandhiji's own words are available to us, thanks to the *Mahatma Gandhi Collected Works*—the most authoritative and exhaustive collection of his writings compiled and published at the behest of our Government. Since power was concentrated in the hands of Gandhi's followers, successive governments of ours have promoted Gandhi's memories to such lofty heights that he has become God, whose every commandment Indians are expected to follow. As Paul Johnson noted in *The New York Times* of 6 February 1977, 'there is now a sizeable Gandhi industry in the sub-continent, complete with innumerable foundations, museums, colleges and other hagiographical institutions'. Since innumerable highly-placed people—historians, bureaucrats, politicians, foreigners—have benefitted from this state-funded, gigantic exercise costing billions to the exchequer, no one

---

77 Vikram Taneja, 'The Guilty Men of 1962,' *Scholar warrior*, Spring 2015, http://www.claws.in/images/journals_doc/1571820146_VikramTaneja.pdf.

complains. The authors often banter with friends that if they had done this much research on Gandhi or Nehru instead of Subhas Bose, they would have probably received a Padma award by now. Decades ago, Ambedkar had voiced similar concerns as he told the *BBC* in 1956...

> His memory is kept up because the Congress party annually declares a holiday either on his birthday or any day connected with some event in his life. Celebrations every year go on for seven days a week to naturally revive people's memory. If these artificial respirations are not given, Gandhi would have long been forgotten.

So here is the gospel truth. Contrary to what the current dispensation led by Narendra Modi would like us to believe, it was not cleanliness but complete non-violence and truth that Gandhi stoutly stood for above everything else. Over *ahimsa*, Gandhi was willing to forsake Lord Krishna, what to speak of Subhas Chandra Bose or Bhagat Singh! If it was proved to me, he wrote in 1925, that 'Krishna of the *Mahabharata* actually did some of the acts attributed to him, even at the risk of being banished from the Hindu fold I should not hesitate to reject that Krishna as God incarnate'.[78]

On 16 November 2014, the Prime Minister unveiled Mahatma Gandhi's statue in Brisbane, Australia. According to a report carried in *The Economic Times*, 'exhorting the world to heed Mahatma Gandhi's advice to tackle terrorism', Modi said at the venue that 'Mahatma's teachings of non-violence and love are as relevant in our times as they were during his lifetime.' On 13 April 2015, after he unveiled a bust of Mahatma Gandhi at the city hall of Hannover in Germany, Modi again claimed that Gandhi's life provided answers to the challenge of terrorism. His ministerial colleague Venkaiah Naidu, now our Vice President, asserted in June 2017 that 'Gandhi's teachings and preachings

78 *Young India*, 1-10-1925, p 336.

are immortal and relevant to any problem, conflict, challenge, not only for India but humanity as a whole'.[79]

NON-VIOLENCE BEST DEFENCE

GANDHIJI'S REPLY TO MUSLIMS DEMANDING GUN LICENCES

(From Our Correspondent)

MASAURHI, March 18.—Far-reaching decisions were taken today at the Gandhi Camp, Masaurhi, when local Muslims representing the Jamait-ul-Ansar, Ahrars and others met and discussed their demands with Mahatma Gandhi.

[*Hindustan Times* on 21 March 1947]

Any follower of Gandhi worth his name must have complete faith in Gandhian sermons and tactics which, the official propaganda funded by public money tells us, defeated the greatest Empire in history. For starters, in 1932, Gandhiji said that 'India's defence lies in the cultivation of friendly relations with her neighbours and her ability to resist, through non-violent non-cooperation, her exploitation by any nation. The first act of a National Government should be to disband this menace [Indian Army]....' In November 1947, he said: 'Peace in Asia depends on India and China. These two countries are large. And if they build their edifices on the foundation of *ahimsa* they will become known among the great countries of the world.' The same month, his attention was drawn to the statement of Major General KM Cariappa: 'Non-violence is of no use under the present circumstances in India, and

79 'Gandhian teachings immortal and relevant to any problem, conflict: Venkaiah Naidu,' *DNA*, Jun 24, 2017, https://www.dnaindia.com/india/report-gandhi-s-teachings-immortal-relevant-at-any-time-says-naidu-2482671.

only a strong army can make India one of the greatest nations in the world.' Gandhiji's response to this was:

> I make bold to say that in this age of the atom bomb, unadulterated non-violence is the only force that can confound all the tricks put together of violence. ...Generals greater than General Cariappa have been wise and humble enough frankly to make the admission that they can have no right to speak of the possibilities of the force of *ahimsa*.[80]

In January 1949, Cariappa was appointed as the first Indian Commander-in-Chief of the Indian Army. It was General (later Field Marshal) Cariappa who had led the Indian forces during the Indo-Pakistan War of 1947. His statement in 1947 was made during that war and in its context. As it happened, on 3 December 1947, Cariappa met Gandhiji to seek his counsel. 'Pakistan will not heed my word, but if you, the Generals of the army of the Indian Union listen to me and help me, I shall believe we have truly gained freedom in a non-violent way,' he was told. Cariappa then made this pointed query: 'Pakistan has no use for non-violence. How then can we win their hearts and prove the efficacy of *ahimsa*?' Gandhiji replied:

> Violence can only be overcome through non-violence. This is as clear to me as the proposition that two and two make four. But for this one must have faith. **Even a weapon like atom bomb when used against non-violence will prove ineffective.** ...And if Pakistan does not stop violence, the violent killings can still be stopped if Hindus in the Union have faith in non-violence.[81] [Emphasis supplied]

Baffled, the General began to fumble. 'If we have to have an army

---

80 Outside his field, *Harijan*, 16-11-1947.
81 Talk with Lt Gen K M Cariappa, 3 December, 1947, *Mahatma Gandhi Collected Works*, VOL 97 (27 September, 1947 - 5 December, 1947), pp 453-455.

at all...it must be a good...Tell me, please, how I can put this over, i.e. the spirit of non-violence to the troops?'

'I am still groping in the dark for the answer,' Gandhiji said, claiming that 'even Lord Wavell and Lord Mountbatten, both veteran professional soldiers, had expressed their implicit faith in the value of non-violence' and 'hoped that our ideologies of non-violence and pacifism would be understood by the peoples of the world and practised by all in solving international disputes.' On 18 January 1948, before taking over charge of the Delhi and East Punjab Command executing operations in J&K, Cariappa again met Gandhiji. He was blessed with these words: 'I hope you will succeed in solving the Kashmir problem non-violently.'

On New Year's Eve in 1942, Gandhi wrote to Viceroy Lord Linlithgow that his mission in life was 'to spread truth and non-violence among mankind in the place of violence and falsehood in all walks of life' and that 'the law of *Satyagraha* knows no defeat'.[82] In his book *The Indian Struggle*, Bose discussed the reasons 'the Mahatma failed to liberate India'. One of which, according to him, was because Gandhi had a duality in his person—as a 'leader of an enslaved people' on one hand, and on the other as a 'world leader, who has a new doctrine to preach'.

'Congress leaders actually believed their own propaganda, that independence for India would inaugurate a period of high-mindedness in government and principled interactions between nations,' observed Jad Adams in *The Telegraph* of London on 28 August 2006. 'Even before full independence, the Indian delegation to the United Nations was exercising the moral scourge in attacking South Africa over apartheid, at a time when divisions at home were about to break out in bloody madness.' On 14 August 1947, in the Constituent Assembly, the members took a pledge to dedicate themselves 'to the service of India and her people', to make her great again so that she makes 'her full and willing contribution to the promotion of world peace and the welfare of mankind'.

---

82 *Gandhiji's correspondence with the government, 1942-44*, Navajivan Publishing House, Ahmedabad, 1957 (First edition 1945), p 24.

Wanting to rebuild free India on hallowed non-violent principles as a precursor to bringing peace to the entire world, Prime Minister Jawaharlal Nehru is well known to have harboured a pathological dislike for the armed forces from the day he took over as PM. An excerpt from the unpublished reminiscences of Major General AA Rudra has become quite well known of late. Rudra was Military Secretary at Army HQ after Partition and a close friend of General Rob Lockhart, first Commander-in-Chief of Indian Army after August 1947. The excerpt was first let out by Major General DK Palit in his 1992 book *War in High Himalaya: The Indian Army in Crisis, 1962* (Hurst Publishers, London). Palit published Lockhart's account (coming from Rudra) of his meeting the new PM with a Defence Paper, asking for a formal policy directive on the defence of India.

> Nehru glanced through Lockhart's paper but was not in the least amused. 'Rubbish! Total rubbish!' the Prime Minister exploded. 'We don't NEED a defence policy. Our policy is *ahimsa*. We foresee no military threats. As far as I am concerned, you can scrap the Army—the police are good enough to meet our security needs.'

It is not known who or what prevailed upon Nehru from fulfilling his desire, but left to the Gandhians, the Indian Army would have ceased to exist in free India. While, mercifully, they did not succeed, the anti-armed forces outlook of Indian leadership persisted right till the watershed year of 1962. In June that year, an 'Anti-Nuclear Arms Convention' was held under the aegis of public-funded Gandhi Peace Foundation (which operates till date on our money despite there being charges of financial wrongdoings levelled against it in the past). The convention was attended by the President, Vice President and Prime Minister of India with a large portrait of Gandhi in the background. The All India Radio ran several programmes on the convention. On the eve of the opening session, a panel discussion was aired. Panelists included eminent Gandhians such as K M Munshi, the conduit for supplying Intelligence Bureau reports concerning Bose to Gandhiji and other Congress leaders in the pre-1947 days.

Nehru in his opening remarks at the convention asserted that he was 'absolutely convinced that if any country adopted unilateral disarmament through strength, nobody would be able to injure it and it will win in the end'. In his keynote speech, Dr Rajendra Prasad, who had just stepped down as President, took a pot shot at the United States for 'spending 45 billion dollars per annum on military preparation' and publicly reiterated the advice he had earlier given to Nehru.

India has had the unique privilege of engaging in a successful non-violent struggle for independence under the leadership of Mahatma Gandhi. She should set the example if her appeal for unilateral disarmament is to carry any weight. I consider this to be a perfectly legitimate challenge. My appeal is addressed to India no less than to the other countries of the world.

In pursuance to deliberations in the convention, two delegations, backed by the Government, went to the US, UK and USSR in September-October 1962 to convince the world powers to stop all nuclear weapon tests. The delegation to the US was led by political heavyweight, first Indian Governor General of free India and another noted Bose baiter C Rajagopalachari.

This was just before the Chinese rattled our borders.

In 1942, at Calcutta's Shraddhanand Park, with his rhetorical flourish Nehru had taken a swipe at Subhas Bose: 'Let him not commit the error that they had fallen into in the past by thinking that they could ask for the aid of any power outside. Therein lay dangers; therein lay peril; and if any of them thought in those terms, it was not any kind of courage, it was a sign of cowardice.' And now, twenty years fast forward, Nehru—the father of Non-Alignment and an apostle of peace second only to Mahatma Gandhi—stared into the most devastating crisis since Independence. The impoverished Indian defences were collapsing like—we hate to use the phrase—a pack of cards. 'Gandhism will land free India in a ditch—if free India is sought to be rebuilt on Gandhian, non-violent principles. India will then be offering a standing invitation to all predatory powers,' Subhas Bose had prophesied in 1940. It unfortunately came to pass in 1962. All idealism and faith in the potency of *ahimsa* gone, Nehru was now compelled to beseech the US President for military assistance. The situation is really desperate, he wrote to Kennedy in November 1962. 'We have to have more comprehensive assistance if the Chinese are to be prevented from taking over the whole of eastern India. Any delay in this assistance reaching us will result in nothing short of a catastrophe for our country.'[83]

It was in this atmosphere of utter despondency and gloom that people began to wish Subhas Chandra Bose was there. An *Associated Press* story 'China invasion recalls fighting Indian leader' was published in many newspapers of the world in December 1962.

Unlike Mohandas Gandhi, Some Indians Like Fight

By HENRY S. BRADSHER

NEW DELHI —On the white-washed walls of many Indian homes is a picture of a man little known outside this country and representing a side of the Indian character that is also little known.

The picture is of Subhas Chandra Bose, who presumably died in a 1945 plane crash on Formosa. He was once a rival of Jawaharlal Nehru for leadership of the political movement that expelled the British from India. Bose led Indian soldiers who joined the Japanese in World War II to fight the British.

The man known to the world as the symbol of the independence movement was Mohandas K. Gandhi, an apostle of nonviolence.

Bose represented another tradition—of violent battle.

The second tradition is more deeply rooted in Indian culture and history than Gandhi's non-violence. This second tradition is now coming to the front as India faces China. It is in ready response to the bugle call for national defense sounded by Nehru, the man of peace turned war leader at age 72.

HUGE RESPONSE

The response of the Indian people overwhelmed army recruiting centers. This response contained a large element of the kind of pure idealism that motivates people of any nation whose boundaries are threatened.

Nehru has expressed the attitude that India must continue fighting aggression "whatever harm it may do to us."

The possible harm is great, not only in war destruction but also in diversion of resources from economic development.

Only a few voices have been heard questioning whether the impoverished, in some areas undernourished, masses of India should be asked to sustain a principle at the cost of their fu-

dia's five-year plans for economic development will continue, despite the diversion of some resources for defense efforts. But cuts in the current third plan are already being made. There

are bound to be unexpected drags on the economy.

The railway system is an example. India's railroads are loaded to move all the goods needed for an expanding economy.

NEEDS FOREIGN AID

In India, war industries have to be created almost from scratch. There are no massive automobile plants that can be converted to making tanks. India has only one big machine-tool factory that could readily make guns and more are needed to make machine tools.

What little industrialization there already is in India is primarily of the cotton textile and cement variety. It does not convert to war.

Therefore India is having to depend upon foreign countries for weapons that it must get quickly to build defenses.

Indian appreciation runs deep for the military aid already rushed here by the United States and Britain, with more coming from Canada, Australia, France and Germany. U.S. Ambassador John Kenneth Galbraith says he can hardly get his conspicuously tall self across a street without being stopped and thanked for the help.

India's president, philosopher Sarvepalli Radhakrishnan, left some visiting Americans the impression that there is no surprise here that the Western powers have come to India's help. It was taken for granted that the United States would help a democracy threatened by Communist aggression.

Indian Scientists To Launch Rocket

NEW DELHI—India is planning to launch her first space rocket for scientific purposes in 1963 from a site near the magnetic equator in Southern India. The aim is to further study of geo-

WAS ONCE NEHRU'S RIVAL—Subhas Chandra Bose, above, who presumably perished in a 1945 plane crash, was once a rival of Jawaharlal Nehru for leadership of movement that expelled

[*Lansing State Journal* on 2 December 1962]

Contrasting the enduring image of India as the land of non-violence, the story highlighted that there was another Indian tradition, of Bose in contrast to it. 'The second tradition is more deeply rooted in Indian culture and history than Gandhi's non-violence. This second tradition is now coming to the front as India faces China,' the story read.

---

83   Papers of John F Kennedy. Presidential Papers. National Security Files. India: Subjects: Nehru correspondence, 1962: 20 November-14 December. JFKNSF-111-017. John F. Kennedy Presidential Library and Museum.

Neville Maxwell in *India's China War* referred to the MPs' growing impatience at 'Nehru's harping on the special peaceableness of Indians, and the depth of the national commitment to non-violence'.

> This was partly because Nehru was transparently using evocations of his party's Gandhian past to ward off criticism of the Government's military unpreparedness; but more deeply, perhaps, it expressed the feeling that, now that war had come, the memory of Subhas Chandra Bose, who had taken up arms with the Japanese against Britain, was more meaningful to Indians than that of Gandhi and his non-violence.[84]

In a surrealistic fulfillment of this collective wishful thinking, Subhas Chandra Bose *was* in India in 1962. Sitting in his hideout in Neemsar, Bhagwanji was wracking his brains how to stop the Chinese in their tracks.

---

84 Neville Maxwell, *India's China War*, Jaico Publishing House, 1970, pp 386-387.